The Logical Basis
for
Computer Programming

Volume II
Deductive Systems

The Logical Basis for Computer Programming

Volume II
Deductive Systems

ZOHAR MANNA
Computer Science Department
Stanford University
and
Applied Mathematics Department
Weizmann Institute of Science

RICHARD WALDINGER
Artificial Intelligence Center
SRI International
and
Computer Science Department
Stanford University

ADDISON-WESLEY PUBLISHING COMPANY

Reading, Massachusetts • Menlo Park, California • New York • Don Mills, Ontario
Wokingham, England • Amsterdam • Bonn • Sydney • Singapore • Tokyo
Madrid • San Juan

This book is in the **Addison-Wesley Series in Computer Science**
Michael A. Harrison, Consulting Editor

Library of Congress Cataloging in Publication Data

Manna, Zohar.
  The logical basis for computer programming.
  (Addison-Wesley series in computer science)

  Includes bibliographies and indexes.
  Contents: v. 1. Deductive reasoning. v. 2. Deductive systems.
  1. Programming (Electronic digital computers)
  2. Logic, Symbolic and mathematical. I. Waldinger,
Richard. II. Title. III. Series.
QA76.6.M35595 1985   519.7   84-20346
ISBN 0-201-18260-2 (v. 1)
ISBN 0-201-18261-0 (v. 2)

ABCDEFGHIJ-HA-89

Preface

Welcome to Volume II of *The Logical Basis for Computer Programming*. In Volume I, we have given a general introduction to logic, emphasizing theories of importance to computer science, such as strings, trees, lists, and sets. Our presentation was rigorous but informal: we described the theories by giving axioms but used ordinary commonsense reasoning in deriving valid sentences from these axioms. In Volume II, we are more formal: in place of our common sense, we present a *deductive-tableau* system for proving the validity of sentences. The deductive system we provide is "machine-oriented": it is suitable for implementation in an automatic or interactive computer theorem-proving program.

INTENTIONS

Authors of conventional logic books often attempt to use very few, very simple deduction rules to make it easier to study their formal systems. The price they pay is that proofs expressed within such a system tend to be painfully detailed. Intuitively evident sentences may be quite difficult to prove. We choose instead to give several rather high-level rules, so that the proofs we construct within the system reflect the commonsense arguments we have presented informally.

In discussing a theorem-proving program, we can distinguish between the *logical* component, which tells us what inferences can legally be made in a given theory, and the *strategic* (or heuristic) component, which tells us what inferences are advantageous to make in searching for a proof of a given sentence. (The same distinction can be made between the rules for playing a game and the strategy for winning one.) The logical component of a theorem-proving program is provided by a deductive system. Designing the strategic component is still something of a black art, and our emphasis in this book is on the logical component.

Nevertheless, our system is intended to assist in the discovery of the proof, in the sense that it will forbid some inferences that are logically sound but that can never contribute to the proof. In restricting logical inference, the system allows us to consider fewer alternatives. In this way, the system is more amenable to implementation than a system that allows unlimited logical freedom.

We give only cursory treatment to some of the topics that occur in more philosophically oriented logic books, such as the completeness and undecidability results for predicate logic or the incompleteness of the theory of the nonnegative integers. While we believe that these topics are of great interest, to computer scientists as well as to mathematicians, we have focused this book on the use of logic as a practical tool.

APPLICATIONS

Automated theorem-proving systems have begun to be of interest to mathematicians because of their recent success in settling certain previously unsolved problems. Proving mathematical theorems is a demanding application, however, because the system must be capable of finding a proof that has somehow eluded the human mathematician. There are many uses for theorem-proving systems that do not require such superhuman logical abilities.

In software engineering, for instance, theorem provers have assisted in the construction, verification, and transformation of computer programs. Logic-programming languages (such as PROLOG) may be understood as special-purpose theorem-proving systems. Artificial-intelligence researchers have been applying theorem-proving systems for natural-language understanding, commonsense reasoning, and robotic planning. Expert systems may be regarded as rudimentary theorem provers, and application of better deductive techniques is expected to lead to more sophisticated expert systems. Theorem provers have been used to give some inferential abilities to database systems.

PREREQUISITES

Volume I is the prerequisite for Volume II. Readers who are familiar with other treatments of mathematical logic will still have to scan the first volume and to refer to it in reading the second, because we include many topics that are not ordinarily covered and use some original notation and terminology.

CONVENTIONS

Volume I was distinguished by the use of italicized words, such as *and, for all,* and *if-then,* in place of the customary mathematical symbols, such as $\land$, $\forall$, and $\supset$. We felt this to be less intimidating to readers who are not mathematically inclined, and also in keeping with the frequent use of words rather than symbols in programming languages. While we have retained most of the words in Volume

II, we have found the English versions of the quantifiers and the equivalence connective to be cumbersome. Therefore, in Volume II, we use

> $\forall$ for "*for all*"
>
> $\exists$ for "*for some*"
>
> $\equiv$ for "*if and only if.*"

We shall also apply quantifiers to more than one variable. Thus $(\forall\ x, y)$ will be an abbreviation for $(\forall\ x)(\forall\ y)$, and $(\exists\ integer\ u, v)$ will be an abbreviation for $(\exists\ integer\ u)(\exists\ integer\ v)$. We trust that the reader who has made it this far will not find these conventions frightening. All the other symbols are as in Volume I. In our classes, we have encouraged students submitting problem solutions to adopt whatever convention they find congenial.

As in Volume I, axioms and properties are given mnemonic names rather than numbers. Axioms are surrounded with a box in the text. The location of each axiom and property in this volume is given in the index. Each problem is associated with a particular location in the text, indicated by a boldface marker. In solving the problem, the reader may generally use the results of any axiom or property and also any problem cited in the text prior to the associated marker. Problems that are of unusual length or difficulty are marked with an asterisk (∗).

References to material in Volume I are prefixed by "[I]." For example, Section [I]3.5 indicates Section 3.5 of Volume I.

TOPICS

The book begins (Part I, Chapters 1–4) with a treatment of the *well-founded induction* principle, a single schema that can replace all the separate induction principles presented in Volume I. A preview at the beginning of Chapter 1 gives an informal summary of those aspects of the *well-founded induction* principle required for reading the rest of the book.

Chapter 1 introduces the induction principle and uses it to characterize the notion of a well-founded relation. Chapter 2 gives examples of the application of the principle. Chapter 3 shows that the earlier induction principles are instances of the *well-founded induction* principle. It then gives the equivalent conventional characterization of well-foundedness in terms of infinite sequences; a theory of sequences is introduced for this purpose. Chapter 4 shows how several well-founded relations can be combined to form a new well-founded lexicographic relation, and illustrates the application of this relation.

The basic structure we use for formal reasoning is called a *deductive tableau*. We first introduce a deductive-tableau system for propositional logic (Part II, Chapters 5 and 6). The system is based on simplification and a (nonclausal) *resolution* rule. A *rewriting* rule, some *splitting* rules, and an *equivalence* rule, which are not essential but which sometimes allow shorter and more natural proofs, are also included.

We then cover two topics necessary for adapting the deductive-tableau system from propositional logic to predicate logic: unification and skolemization.

Unification (Part III, Chapters 7–9) is the process of determining whether two expressions have a common instance. In theorem proving, it tells us how variables are to be replaced by terms during a proof. A preview at the beginning of Chapter 7 summarizes those aspects of unification that are used later. Chapters 7 and 8 introduce a theory of expressions and substitutions, respectively, that serve as the basis for the theory of unification. In Chapter 9, we introduce the notion of unifiers, present an algorithm for unification, and prove its correctness.

We then (Part IV, Chapters 10–13) apply the deductive-tableau system to predicate logic and special theories. In Chapter 10, we discuss the *skolemization* process for removing quantifiers from a sentence without altering its validity. In Chapter 11 we introduce the deductive-tableau system for predicate logic, incorporating the *unification* algorithm to control the replacement of variables by terms. A *skolemization* rule for quantifier removal is included. The deductive-tableau system is extended (in Chapter 12) to treat special theories. To handle theories with equality, an *equality* rule is introduced. In theories with mathematical induction, such as the nonnegative integers, trees, or tuples, the various induction principles are also represented as rules. In Chapter 13, we briefly discuss theoretical aspects, such as completeness and decidability issues, of the systems we have introduced.

An annotated list of selected references tells the reader where to look for further information.

CURRICULUM

For several years, the manuscripts for Volume I and this volume have been used as texts in a sequence of two courses taught at Stanford University, the Weizmann Institute of Science, and Hebrew University. Our classes have been attended by undergraduate and graduate students, as well as some computer professionals from industry. We believe that this material should be introduced quite early in the computer science curriculum. It does not require any familiarity with programming, but rather provides the intellectual foundation for the study of programming. The material in Volume II is particularly useful for software engineering, artificial intelligence, logic programming, and database studies.

A booklet of solutions to all the problems in this volume is available to instructors from Addison-Wesley.

THE FAST TRACK

The informal "previews" at the beginnings of Part I (Well-founded Induction) and Part III (Unification) give the highlights of their respective parts without going into details. The reader who is impatient to get to the deductive-tableau chapters may read these previews and skip the corresponding parts on first reading.

At times we have condensed material from both volumes into a single course. In teaching such a course, the only theories with induction we present are those of the nonnegative integers, trees, and tuples of Volume I. We also give only the previews of well-founded induction (Part I) and unification (Part III) from Volume II. Subsequent chapters are pruned accordingly.

THE TABLEAU DEDUCTIVE SYSTEM

Many of the students in our classes have used an interactive system, implemented on a personal computer, for proving theorems in the deductive-tableau framework. This system accepts direction to decide what inferences to attempt at each stage, but it will never allow the student to perform an erroneous step. For information about obtaining the system, write to

Tableau Deductive Systems
P.O. Box 9779
Stanford, California 94309.

ACKNOWLEDGMENTS

We have continually revised the manuscript for this book based on our teaching experience and the comments and suggestions of our students and colleagues. Particularly extensive suggestions have been made by Martín Abadi, Marianne Baudinet, Yoni Malachi, Andres Modet, Eric Muller, Jonathan Traugott, and Frank Yellin. We have benefited from discussions on skolemization with Sol Feferman, Dov Gabbai, and Dale Miller, and on unification with Larry Paulson.

Tomás Feder contributed to the treatment of permutation substitutions. Tom
Henzinger, Peter Ladkin, John Mitchell, and Benjamin Wells have taught courses
based upon our manuscript and have given us detailed comments and criticisms
that have been very helpful to us in our revision. Tom Henzinger has been of
special assistance in the preparation of problems for this volume and has written
the booklet of solutions. The implementers of the interactive Tableau Deductive
System, Ron Burback (project director), Hugh McGuire, Michael Winstandley,
and Jeff Smith, with assistance from Scott A. Fraser, have actively contributed to
the design of the formal system; we have benefited from their unique perspective
and their insights.

We would like to thank our colleagues at Stanford University, the Weizmann Institute, and SRI International for providing a supportive and encourag-
ing environment. For support of the research behind this book, we thank the
Air Force Office of Scientific Research, the Defense Advanced Research Projects
Agency, the National Science Foundation, and the Office of Naval Research. Eve-
lyn Eldridge-Diaz has done a magnificent job of typesetting the many versions of
the manuscripts for both volumes. Joe Weening's detailed technical knowledge
and expertise has been essential in using the TEX document-preparation system
of Donald Knuth.

Contents

PART II: PROPOSITIONAL LOGIC

PART III: UNIFICATION

PART IV: PREDICATE LOGIC

I

Well-founded

Induction

1

Well-founded Relations

1.1 PREVIEW OF WELL-FOUNDED INDUCTION

In Volume I, we presented a number of theories, each with a separate induction principle. In this part of Volume II, we introduce a single new principle, called "well-founded induction." All the induction principles we saw before, including the *stepwise* and *complete induction* principles, will turn out to be instances of the *well-founded induction* principle. Furthermore, for many proofs, it is easier to use well-founded induction than any of the earlier induction principles.

The *well-founded induction* principle will be introduced carefully in the rest of this part (Chapters 1–4). Here, in this "fast-track" section, we give a brisk and informal preview of the same material. Reading this section will give the reader an intuitive feel for the topics that are to be introduced more formally later.

WELL-FOUNDED RELATIONS

The *well-founded induction* principle resembles the *complete induction* principle for the nonnegative integers, except that we introduce an abstract class of "objects" in place of the nonnegative integers, and an abstract "well-founded" relation in place of the less-than relation $<$. Intuitively, a binary relation $\prec$ is *well-founded* over a class of objects if it satisfies the *no-decreasing* condition, that there are no infinite sequences of objects decreasing with respect to that relation. In other words, there are no sequences $\langle x_0, x_1, x_2, \ldots \rangle$ of objects x_i such that

$$x_0 \succ x_1 \succ x_2 \succ \ldots .$$

For example, the less-than relation $<$ itself is well-founded over the class of nonnegative integers because there are no infinite sequences of nonnegative integers decreasing with respect to $<$. In other words, there are no sequences $\langle x_0, x_1, x_2, \ldots \rangle$ of nonnegative integers x_i such that

$$x_0 > x_1 > x_2 > \ldots .$$

Similarly, the proper-substring relation $\prec_{string}$ is well-founded over the class of strings.

On the other hand, the less-than relation $<$ is not well-founded over the class of all the integers, including the negative integers, or over the class of nonnegative rational numbers. For example,

$$\langle 1, 0, -1, -2, \ldots \rangle$$

is an infinite sequence of integers decreasing with respect to $<$, and

$$\langle 1, 1/2, 1/4, 1/8, \ldots \rangle$$

is an infinite sequence of nonnegative rationals decreasing with respect to $<$. Thus we must be careful to specify the class of objects when we say that a relation is well-founded.

As a convention, we shall suppose that the class of objects is characterized (in a given theory) by a unary predicate symbol obj. In other words, $obj(x)$ holds precisely when x belongs to the class of objects. We shall say that $\prec$ is well-founded over obj. We use obj schematically to state general results in place of some particular unary predicate symbol of the theory, such as $integer$ or $string$. For example, we shall say that $<$ is well-founded over $integer$ and that $\prec_{string}$ is well-founded over $string$.

PROPERTIES OF WELL-FOUNDED RELATIONS

What properties follow from the well-foundedness of a relation?

Irreflexive

We can easily see that a relation that is well-founded over obj must also be irreflexive over obj; that is,

$$(\forall \ obj \ x)\big[not \ (x \prec x)\big]$$

must be valid (in the theory). For if there were an object x such that $x \prec x$, the "constant" infinite sequence $\langle x, x, x, \ldots \rangle$ would be decreasing with respect to $\prec$; that is,

$$x \succ x \succ x \succ \ldots .$$

Asymmetric

Furthermore, a relation that is well-founded over *obj* must also be asymmetric over *obj*; that is,

$$(\forall\ obj\ x,\ y) \begin{bmatrix} if\ \ x \prec y \\ then\ \ not\ (y \prec x) \end{bmatrix}$$

must be valid. For if there were two objects x and y such that $x \prec y$ and $y \prec x$, the "alternating" infinite sequence $\langle x, y, x, y, \ldots \rangle$ would be decreasing; that is,

$$x \succ y \succ x \succ y \succ \ldots .$$

Not necessarily transitive

A well-founded relation need not be transitive over the class of objects. In particular, consider the predecessor relation $\prec_{pred}$ over the nonnegative integers, defined by the axiom

$$(\forall\ integer\ x,\ y) \begin{bmatrix} x \prec_{pred} y \\ \equiv \\ x + 1 = y \end{bmatrix}.$$

This relation is well-founded over the nonnegative integers, but it is not transitive. For example,

$$1 \prec_{pred} 2 \quad \text{and} \quad 2 \prec_{pred} 3,$$

but not $1 \prec_{pred} 3$.

Remark (notational conventions)

Note that we have begun to adopt the conventions of Volume II. That is, we use $\forall$ instead of *for all*, we use $\equiv$ instead of *if and only if*, and we apply quantifiers to more than one variable (as we warned in the Preface). ⌙

WELL-FOUNDED INDUCTION PRINCIPLE

Well-founded relations are useful to us because of the role they play in well-founded induction. We shall establish that, in a given theory, a relation $\prec$ is well-founded over *obj* precisely when the following *well-founded induction* principle holds:

> For each sentence $\mathcal{F}[x]$ with no free occurrences of x',
> the universal closure of the sentence
>
> $$\textit{if } (\forall \textit{ obj } x) \begin{bmatrix} \textit{if } (\forall \textit{ obj } x') \begin{bmatrix} \textit{if } x' \prec x \\ \textit{then } \mathcal{F}[x'] \end{bmatrix} \\ \textit{then } \mathcal{F}[x] \end{bmatrix}$$
>
> $$\textit{then } (\forall \textit{ obj } x)\mathcal{F}[x]$$

is valid.

In the case in which *obj* is *integer* and $\prec$ is the less-than relation $<$, this reduces to the *complete induction* principle for the nonnegative integers (Section [I]6.8). Thus, in establishing the *complete induction* principle (Section [I]6.10), we have actually shown the well-foundedness of $<$ over the nonnegative integers.

In the case in which *obj* is *string* and $\prec_{string}$ is the substring relation, the *well-founded induction* principle reduces to the *complete induction* principle for the strings (Section [I]7.7).

THE MINIMAL-ELEMENT CONDITION

The well-foundedness of a relation is equivalent to a so-called "minimal element" condition. This condition sometimes provides a useful way of establishing the well-foundedness of a relation. With respect to a given relation $\prec$, an element x is said to be *minimal* in a given class (not necessarily finite) if there exists no element y of the class such that $y \prec x$. For instance, with respect to the substring relation $\prec_{string}$, the two strings A and C are both minimal elements of the class $\{A, C, AB\}$, but AB is not minimal because A $\prec_{string}$ AB.

A relation $\prec$ satisfies the *minimal-element* condition over a class of objects if every nonempty subclass of the class has a minimal element with respect to $\prec$. To express this condition in the language of predicate logic, we consider the subclass characterized by a sentence $\mathcal{G}[x]$; that is, the subclass of all objects x such that $\mathcal{G}[x]$ is true. The *minimal-element* condition, then, states

For each sentence $\mathcal{G}[x]$ with no free occurrences of x', the universal closure of the sentence

$$if \ \ (\exists \ obj \ x)\mathcal{G}[x]$$

$$then \ \ (\exists \ obj \ x) \left[\begin{array}{l} \mathcal{G}[x] \\ and \\ (\forall \ obj \ x') \left[\begin{array}{l} if \ \ x' \prec x \\ then \ \ not \ \mathcal{G}[x'] \end{array} \right] \end{array} \right]$$

is valid.

For instance, if we take *obj* to be *integer* and $\prec$ to be $<$, this is the *least-number* principle for the nonnegative integers (Section [I]6.12).

To show that the *minimal-element* condition implies the *well-founded induction* principle, we consider any sentence $\mathcal{F}[x]$, and take $\mathcal{G}[x]$ in the preceding schema to be its negation $(not \ \mathcal{F}[x])$. Applying equivalences of propositional and predicate logic, we obtain precisely the *well-founded induction* principle. Similarly, to show that the *well-founded induction* principle implies the *minimal-element* condition, we consider any sentence $\mathcal{G}[x]$, and take $\mathcal{F}[x]$ in the *well-founded induction* principle to be its negation $(not \ \mathcal{G}[x])$, obtaining by logical manipulations precisely the *minimal-element* condition. The details are given later in the chapter.

EQUIVALENCE OF THE CONDITIONS

In the detailed chapters on well-founded induction, we shall take the *well-founded induction* principle itself as the definition of well-foundedness, rather than the absence of decreasing infinite sequences, as we have done here. This is because to express the *no-decreasing* condition requires us to formulate a theory of infinite sequences, while to express the induction principle does not. Eventually, however, we do introduce a theory of (infinite) sequences and prove the equivalence of the *well-founded induction* principle and the *no-decreasing* condition. At this point, we prove the same result informally. The reader may find that proofs expressed in terms of the *no-decreasing* condition are actually more intuitive than the corresponding proofs expressed in terms of the induction principle.

We actually show the equivalence of the *no-decreasing* condition and the *minimal-element* condition.

Minimal-element condition $\Rightarrow$ *no-decreasing condition*

Suppose that $\prec$ satisfies the *minimal-element* condition over *obj*, but that, contrary to the *no-decreasing* condition, there exists an infinite sequence $\langle x_0, \ x_1,$

$x_2, \ldots\rangle$ decreasing with respect to $\prec$. We claim that then the class of elements $C : \{x_0, x_1, x_2, \ldots\}$ is a nonempty class with no minimal element, contradicting the *minimal-element* condition. No element x_j of C can be minimal for, since the sequence is decreasing with respect to $\prec$, $x_{j+1} \prec x_j$.

No-decreasing condition $\Rightarrow$ minimal-element condition

Suppose that $\prec$ satisfies the *no-decreasing* condition over *obj* but that, contrary to the *minimal-element* condition, there exists a nonempty class C with no minimal element. We construct an infinite sequence decreasing with respect to $\prec$, contradicting the *no-decreasing* condition.

Because C is nonempty, it has some element, call it x_0. Because C has no minimal elements, it must have some element, call it x_1, such that $x_1 \prec x_0$. Because x_1 cannot be minimal either, there must be some element of C, call it x_2, such that $x_2 \prec x_1$. Continuing in this way, we construct the infinite sequence $\langle x_0, x_1, x_2, \ldots\rangle$ of objects in C that is decreasing with respect to $\prec$.

USE OF WELL-FOUNDED INDUCTION

Typically, we define a theory using *stepwise-induction* principles, establish the well-foundedness of various relations in that theory, and then use well-founded induction with respect to those relations. For example, we defined in Chapter [I]6 the theory of the nonnegative integers using stepwise induction, established the well-foundedness of the less-than relation, and used the corresponding *well-founded induction* principle (the *complete induction* principle) for proofs that would have been awkward with stepwise induction.

The choice of a well-founded relation $\prec$ can influence the difficulty of a well-founded induction proof. A proof that is straightforward by induction with respect to one relation may be clumsy with respect to another.

ESTABLISHING WELL-FOUNDEDNESS

Once we have established the well-foundedness of one relation, we can use it to establish the well-foundedness of others.

One way of doing this is to "map" the relation into another known to be well-founded. More precisely, suppose a relation $\prec_2$ is known to be well-founded over obj_2 (characterizing the "object$_2$'s"), and we would like to show that another relation $\prec_1$ is well-founded over obj_1 (characterizing the "object$_1$'s"). For this purpose, we may find a function f that satisfies two conditions.

- *The sort condition*

  f maps the object$_1$'s into the object$_2$'s; that is,

  $$(\forall x) \begin{bmatrix} if & obj_1(x) \\ then & obj_2\big(f(x)\big) \end{bmatrix}.$$

- *The monotonicity condition*

  f maps $\prec_1$ into $\prec_2$; that is,

  $$(\forall\, obj_1\ x,\ y) \begin{bmatrix} if & x \prec_1 y \\ then & f(x) \prec_2 f(y) \end{bmatrix}.$$

If we can find such a function f, we know that $\prec_1$ is well-founded.

For example, we can show that the proper-subtuple relation $\subset$ is well-founded over the tuples by mapping it into the less-than relation $<$ over the nonnegative integers. For this purpose, we may take f to be the *length* function. We have the *sort* condition, that *length* maps tuples into nonnegative integers, that is,

$$(\forall\ x) \begin{bmatrix} if & tuple(x) \\ then & integer\big(length(x)\big) \end{bmatrix},$$

and the *monotonicity* condition, that *length* maps the subtuple relation $\subset$ into $<$, that is,

$$(\forall\ tuple\ x,\ y) \begin{bmatrix} if & x \subset y \\ then & length(x) < length(y) \end{bmatrix}.$$

An informal proof that, in general, if $\prec_2$ is well-founded over obj_2, then $\prec_1$ is well-founded over obj_1 is as follows. Suppose, to the contrary, that $\prec_2$ is well-founded over obj_2 but that $\prec_1$ is not well-founded over obj_1. Let $\langle x_0, x_1, x_2, \ldots \rangle$ be an infinite sequence of object$_1$'s decreasing with respect to $\prec_1$, that is,

$$x_0 \succ_1 x_1 \succ_1 x_2 \succ_1 \ \cdots \ .$$

Then (by the *sort* condition), $\langle f(x_0), f(x_1), f(x_2), \ldots \rangle$ is an infinite sequence of object$_2$'s, and (by the *monotonicity* condition)

$$f(x_0) \succ_2 f(x_1) \succ_2 f(x_2) \succ_2 \ \cdots \ ,$$

that is, the sequence is decreasing with respect to $\prec_2$, contradicting our supposition that $\prec_2$ is well-founded over obj_2.

LEXICOGRAPHIC RELATION

If we know that two relations $\prec_1$ and $\prec_2$ are well-founded over object$_1$'s and object$_2$'s, respectively, we can combine them to define a lexicographic relation

$\prec_{lex}$ that is well-founded over pairs of $object_1$'s and $object_2$'s. (These are pairs of form $\langle x_1, x_2 \rangle$, where $obj_1(x_1)$ and $obj_2(x_2)$. They are characterized by the predicate symbol *pair*.)

The lexicographic relation $\prec_{lex}$ is defined by the axiom

$$(\forall\ obj_1\ x_1,\ y_1) \atop (\forall\ obj_2\ x_2,\ y_2)\ \left[\begin{array}{l} \langle x_1,\ x_2 \rangle \prec_{lex} \langle y_1,\ y_2 \rangle \\ \equiv \\ \left[\begin{array}{l} x_1 \prec_1 y_1 \\ or \\ x_1 = y_1\ \ and\ \ x_2 \prec_2 y_2 \end{array} \right] \end{array} \right].$$

In using a single symbol $\prec_{lex}$, we are disguising the fact that the relation actually depends on our choice of component relations. Had we chosen a different $\prec_1$ or $\prec_2$, we would have obtained a different $\prec_{lex}$.

Justification

We can establish that, if $\prec$ and $\widetilde{\prec}$ are well-founded over *obj* and $\widetilde{obj}$, respectively, then the corresponding lexicographic relation $\prec_{lex}$ is well-founded over the appropriate class of pairs. For suppose, to the contrary, that

$$\langle x_0, \widetilde{x}_0 \rangle,\ \langle x_1, \widetilde{x}_1 \rangle,\ \ \ldots,\ \ \langle x_i, \widetilde{x}_i \rangle,\ \langle x_{i+1}, \widetilde{x}_{i+1} \rangle,\ \ \ldots$$

is an infinite sequence of pairs decreasing with respect to $\prec_{lex}$, that is,

$$\langle x_0, \widetilde{x}_0 \rangle\ \succ_{lex}\ \langle x_1, \widetilde{x}_1 \rangle\ \succ_{lex}\ \cdots\ \succ_{lex}\ \langle x_i, \widetilde{x}_i \rangle\ \succ_{lex}\ \langle x_{i+1}, \widetilde{x}_{i+1} \rangle\ \succ_{lex}\ \cdots .$$

By the definition of the lexicographic relation, we know that, for each nonnegative i,

$$x_i \succ x_{i+1}$$
$$or$$
$$x_i\ =\ x_{i+1}\ \ and\ \ \widetilde{x}_i\ \widetilde{\succ}\ \widetilde{x}_{i+1},$$

and hence

$$(*) \qquad x_i \succ x_{i+1}\ \ or\ \ x_i\ =\ x_{i+1}.$$

Let us consider the sequence of first components $\langle x_0, x_1, \ldots, x_i, x_{i+1}, \ldots \rangle$. By $(*)$ and the *no-decreasing* condition, we know that, after a certain point x_k, all the objects in the sequence must be equal; that is,

$$x_k\ =\ x_{k+1}\ =\ \cdots\ =\ x_{k+j}\ =\ x_{k+j+1}\ =\ \cdots .$$

Otherwise, for each object in the sequence we could find a subsequent object strictly less with respect to $\prec$. In this way, we could select an infinite subsequence of objects decreasing with respect to $\prec$, contradicting the well-foundedness of $\prec$ over obj.

We know that, for each nonnegative j,

$$\langle x_{k+j},\ \widetilde{x}_{k+j} \rangle \ \succ_{lex} \ \langle x_{k+j+1},\ \widetilde{x}_{k+j+1} \rangle.$$

Therefore, by the definition of the lexicographic relation,

$$x_{k+j} \succ x_{k+j+1}$$

or

$$x_{k+j} \ = \ x_{k+j+1} \ \ and \ \ \widetilde{x}_{k+j} \ \widetilde{\succ} \ \widetilde{x}_{k+j+1}.$$

But we also know (by the way x_k was chosen) that $x_{k+j} = x_{k+j+1}$. Hence (by the irreflexivity of $\prec$), we have *not* $(x_{k+j} \succ x_{k+j+1})$. Therefore

$$\widetilde{x}_{k+j} \ \widetilde{\succ} \ \widetilde{x}_{k+j+1}.$$

It follows that the subsequence $\langle \widetilde{x}_k, \widetilde{x}_{k+1}, \ \ldots, \widetilde{x}_{k+j}, \widetilde{x}_{k+j+1}, \ \ldots \rangle$ of second components is an infinite sequence of objects decreasing with respect to $\widetilde{\prec}$, contradicting the well-foundedness of $\widetilde{\prec}$ over $\widetilde{obj}$. ◢

The lexicographic relation plays a role in the following special *well-founded induction* principle with respect to $\prec_{lex}$:

For each sentence $\mathcal{F}[x_1, x_2]$ with no free occurrences of x'_1 or x'_2, the universal closure of the sentence

$$if \ \begin{matrix}(\forall \ obj_1 \ x_1)\\(\forall \ obj_2 \ x_2)\end{matrix} \left[if \ \begin{matrix}(\forall \ obj_1 \ x'_1)\\(\forall \ obj_2 \ x'_2)\end{matrix} \left[\begin{matrix}if \ \langle x'_1, x'_2 \rangle \prec_{lex} \langle x_1, x_2 \rangle\\ then \ \mathcal{F}[x'_1, x'_2]\end{matrix}\right] \\ then \ \mathcal{F}[x_1, x_2] \right]$$

$$then \ \begin{matrix}(\forall \ obj_1 \ x_1)\\(\forall \ obj_2 \ x_2)\end{matrix} \mathcal{F}[x_1, x_2]$$

is valid.

This induction principle can accomplish in a single application what would require two applications of the ordinary *well-founded induction* principle.

The lexicographic relation can be generalized to combine n well-founded relations $\prec_1, \prec_2, \ldots, \prec_n$ over $obj_1, obj_2, \ldots, obj_n$, respectively, into a single well-founded relation $\prec_{lex}$ over n-tuples of form $\langle x_1, x_2, \ldots, x_n \rangle$, where $obj_1(x_1)$, $obj_2(x_2), \ldots,$ and $obj_n(x_n)$.

WELL-FOUNDED INDUCTION IN DETAIL

In the remainder of Part I, we give a more precise and detailed version of what we have summarized here. In the rest of this chapter, we define well-founded relations (in terms of the induction principle), give their properties, and introduce methods for establishing well-foundedness. In Chapter 2, we present a few examples of the application of well-founded induction. In Chapter 3, an advanced chapter that may be skipped on first reading, we use a theory of sequences to characterize the well-foundedness of a relation in terms of the absence of infinite decreasing sequences. Finally, in Chapter 4, we introduce the lexicographic relation and establish its well-foundedness. We give several examples of the application of well-founded induction with respect to the lexicographic relation.

1.2   BASIC PROPERTIES

We begin with the *well-founded induction* principle, which serves as the definition of a well-founded relation.

WELL-FOUNDED INDUCTION PRINCIPLE

In the theory of the nonnegative integers, we introduced (Section [I]6.8) the *complete induction principle* proposition

> For each sentence $\mathcal{F}[x]$ with no free occurrences of x',
> the universal closure of the sentence
>
> $$if \ (\forall \ integer \ x) \ \left[if \ (\forall \ integer \ x') \ \left[\begin{array}{l} if \ x' < x \\ then \ \mathcal{F}[x'] \end{array} \right] \\ then \ \mathcal{F}[x] \right]$$
>
> then $(\forall \ integer \ x)\mathcal{F}[x]$

is valid.

The proposition was proved in Section [I]6.10.

Similarly, in the theory of the strings, we introduced (Section [I]7.7) the *complete induction principle* proposition

For each sentence $\mathcal{F}[x]$ with no free occurrences of x', the universal closure of the sentence

$$if \ (\forall \ string \ x) \ \begin{bmatrix} if \ (\forall \ string \ x') \ \begin{bmatrix} if \ x' \prec_{string} x \\ then \ \mathcal{F}[x'] \end{bmatrix} \\ then \ \mathcal{F}[x] \end{bmatrix}$$
$$then \ (\forall \ string \ x)\mathcal{F}[x]$$

is valid.

This proposition was not proved in Volume I; we promised to prove it in this volume.

The *well-founded induction* principle generalizes these two *complete induction* principles to an arbitrary theory.

In the following discussion, we take *obj* to stand for a unary predicate symbol, such as *integer* or *string*, and $\prec$ to stand for a binary predicate symbol, such as $<$ or $\prec_{string}$.

Definition (well-founded relation)

In a given theory, a binary relation $\prec$ is said to be *well-founded* over a unary predicate symbol *obj* if

For each sentence $\mathcal{F}[x]$ with no free occurrences of x', the universal closure of the sentence

$$if \ (\forall \ obj \ x) \ \begin{bmatrix} if \ (\forall \ obj \ x') \ \begin{bmatrix} if \ x' \prec x \\ then \ \mathcal{F}[x'] \end{bmatrix} \\ then \ \mathcal{F}[x] \end{bmatrix}$$
$$then \ (\forall \ obj \ x)\mathcal{F}[x]$$

$$(\textit{well-founded induction principle})$$

is valid (in the given theory). ⌐

Let us illustrate the application of this definition.

Example (less-than relation is well-founded)

Consider the theory of the nonnegative integers. If we take $\prec$ to be the less-than relation $<$, and *obj* to be the unary predicate symbol *integer*, then the *well-founded induction* principle is the universal closure of

$$\textit{if } (\forall \textit{ integer } x) \begin{bmatrix} \textit{if } (\forall \textit{ integer } x') \begin{bmatrix} \textit{if } x' < x \\ \textit{then } \mathcal{F}[x'] \end{bmatrix} \\ \textit{then } \mathcal{F}[x] \end{bmatrix}$$

$$\textit{then } (\forall \textit{ integer } x)\mathcal{F}[x],$$

where x' does not occur free in $\mathcal{F}[x]$, which is precisely the *complete induction* principle over the nonnegative integers. Because we have shown this sentence to be valid in the theory of nonnegative integers, it follows that

> the less-than relation $<$ is a well-founded relation (over *integer*) in the theory of nonnegative integers. ⌟

Example (proper-substring relation)

Similarly, consider the theory of the strings. If we take $\prec$ to be the proper-substring relation $\prec_{string}$, and *obj* to be the unary predicate symbol *string*, then the *well-founded induction* principle is the universal closure of

$$\textit{if } (\forall \textit{ string } x) \begin{bmatrix} \textit{if } (\forall \textit{ string } x') \begin{bmatrix} \textit{if } x' \prec_{string} x \\ \textit{then } \mathcal{F}[x'] \end{bmatrix} \\ \textit{then } \mathcal{F}[x] \end{bmatrix}$$

$$\textit{then } (\forall \textit{ string } x)\mathcal{F}[x],$$

where x' does not occur free in $\mathcal{F}[x]$, which is precisely the *complete induction* principle over the strings. In the following section, we shall show that the proper-substring relation $\prec_{string}$ is well-founded (over *string*) in the theory of strings, i.e., that the *complete induction* principle is valid over the strings, as we promised to show. ⌟

In the *well-founded induction* principle, the sentence $\mathcal{F}[x]$ is called the *inductive sentence* and the variable x is called the *inductive variable*. The antecedent of the principle,

$$(\forall \textit{ obj } x) \begin{bmatrix} \textit{if } (\forall \textit{ obj } x') \begin{bmatrix} \textit{if } x' \prec x \\ \textit{then } \mathcal{F}[x'] \end{bmatrix} \\ \textit{then } \mathcal{F}[x] \end{bmatrix},$$

is called the *inductive step*; the subsentences

$$(\forall \textit{ obj } x') \begin{bmatrix} \textit{if } x' \prec x \\ \textit{then } \mathcal{F}[x'] \end{bmatrix} \qquad \text{and} \qquad \mathcal{F}[x]$$

of the inductive step are called the *induction hypothesis* and the *desired conclusion*, respectively.

The *well-founded induction* principle may be paraphrased informally as follows:

> To prove that a sentence $\mathcal{F}[x]$ is true for every object x, it suffices to prove the inductive step
>
> > for an arbitrary object x,
> > if $\mathcal{F}[x']$ is true for every object x' such that $x' \prec x$,
> > then $\mathcal{F}[x]$ is also true.

Before we present some examples of well-founded relations, let us consider a relation that is not well-founded.

Example (greater-than relation not well-founded)

Consider again the theory of the nonnegative integers. If we take $\prec$ to be the greater-than relation $>$ and *obj* to be the unary predicate symbol *integer*, then the *well-founded induction* principle does not hold. In particular, take $\mathcal{F}[x]$ to be the sentence *false*; then the *well-founded induction* principle is the sentence

$$if \ (\forall \ integer \ x) \begin{bmatrix} if \ (\forall \ integer \ x') \begin{bmatrix} if \ x' > x \\ then \ false \end{bmatrix} \\ then \ false \end{bmatrix}$$

$$then \ (\forall \ integer \ x) false.$$

This reduces (by propositional and predicate logic) to

$$not \ (\forall \ integer \ x)\big[not \ (\forall \ integer \ x')\big[not \ (x' > x)\big]\big]$$

or, equivalently (by the duality between the quantifiers and properties of the nonnegative integers),

$$(\exists \ integer \ x)\,(\forall \ integer \ x')\,[x' \leq x].$$

This sentence is not valid in the theory of the nonnegative integers: it states the existence of a nonnegative integer x larger than all nonnegative integers x'. ⌐

In **Problem 1.1**, the reader is asked to show that two other relations are not well-founded.

WHY DO WE NEED THE CONSTRAINT?

The reader may have wondered why we include in the *well-founded induction* principle the constraint that x' does not occur free in $\mathcal{F}[x]$. In fact, if this constraint is violated, the sentence may not be valid.

Counterexample (constraint is essential)

In the theory of the nonnegative integers, take *obj* to be *integer*, $\prec$ to be the less-than relation $<$, and

$$\mathcal{F}[x]: \quad x < x'.$$

Note that, contrary to the constraint, x' occurs free in $\mathcal{F}[x]$.

The *well-founded induction* principle in this case is

$$(\forall\ integer\ x')\left[if\ (\forall\ integer\ x)\left[if\ (\forall\ integer\ x')\begin{bmatrix} if\ x' < x \\ then\ x' < x' \end{bmatrix} \\ then\ x < x' \right] \\ then\ (\forall\ integer\ x)[x < x'] \right].$$

(The outermost quantifier ($\forall\ integer\ x'$) was introduced in taking the universal closure.)

The subsentence

$$if\ x' < x$$
$$then\ x' < x'$$

is equivalent (by properties of the nonnegative integers and propositional logic) to

$$not\ (x' < x).$$

Let us make this replacement in the principle. The resulting subsentence

$$(\forall\ integer\ x')\big[not\ (x' < x)\big]$$

is equivalent (by properties of the nonnegative integers) to

$$x = 0.$$

Let us make this replacement. The resulting subsentence

$$(\forall\ integer\ x)\begin{bmatrix} if\ x = 0 \\ then\ x < x' \end{bmatrix}$$

is equivalent (by predicate logic) to

$$0 < x'.$$

Let us make this replacement. The resulting sentence is

$$(\forall \; integer \; x') \left[\begin{array}{l} if \;\; 0 < x' \\ then \;\; (\forall \; integer \; x)[x < x'] \end{array} \right].$$

If we take x' to be 1 and x to be 2, we have

$$if \;\; 0 < 1$$
$$then \;\; 2 < 1,$$

which is false. ⌙

Now let us consider some simple examples of well-founded relations.

THE EMPTY RELATION

For any theory and any unary predicate symbol *obj*, the *empty* relation

$$x \prec_{empty} y,$$

which is false for all objects x and y, is defined by the axiom

$$\boxed{(\forall \; obj \; x, y) \big[not \; (x \prec_{empty} y) \big] \qquad\qquad (empty)}$$

This relation may be seen to be well-founded (over *obj*).

Proposition (empty relation)

The empty relation $\prec_{empty}$ is well-founded over any unary predicate symbol *obj*. ⌙

Proof

We attempt to show the *well-founded induction* principle, that, for an arbitrary sentence $\mathcal{F}[x]$, where x' is not free in $\mathcal{F}[x]$, the universal closure of

$$if \;\; (\forall \; obj \; x) \left[\begin{array}{l} if \;\; (\forall \; obj \; x') \left[\begin{array}{l} if \;\; x' \prec_{empty} x \\ then \;\; \mathcal{F}[x'] \end{array} \right] \\ then \;\; \mathcal{F}[x] \end{array} \right]$$
$$then \;\; (\forall \; obj \; x) \mathcal{F}[x]$$

is valid.

By the definition of the empty relation, $x' \prec_{empty} x$ is false for any objects x and x'; therefore (by propositional logic) the induction hypothesis

$$(\forall \; obj \; x') \begin{bmatrix} if \;\; x' \prec_{empty} x \\ then \;\; \mathcal{F}[x'] \end{bmatrix}$$

is true for any object x, and (by propositional logic again) the inductive step

$$(\forall \; obj \; x) \begin{bmatrix} if \;\; (\forall \; obj \; x') \begin{bmatrix} if \;\; x' \prec_{empty} x \\ then \;\; \mathcal{F}[x'] \end{bmatrix} \\ then \;\; \mathcal{F}[x] \end{bmatrix}$$

reduces to

$$(\forall \; obj \; x)\mathcal{F}[x].$$

The entire sentence, therefore, reduces to

$$if \;\; (\forall \; obj \; x)\mathcal{F}[x]$$
$$then \;\; (\forall \; obj \; x)\mathcal{F}[x],$$

whose universal closure is valid (by propositional logic). ⌐

Note that we explain a step in a proof with the phrase "by propositional logic" if the principal justification for the step is based on propositional logic, even if some predicate logic is also involved.

In **Problem 1.2**, the reader is asked to show the well-foundedness of another relation.

1.3   MAPPINGS

It is important to be able to establish that a relation is well-founded so that we may apply the *well-founded induction* principle for that relation in proofs.

MAPPING FUNCTION

One of the most useful ways of establishing the well-foundedness of a given relation is to map it into another relation that is known to be well-founded, perhaps in a different theory. For example, in the combined theory of strings and non-negative integers, we shall establish that the proper-substring relation $\prec_{string}$ is well-founded (over *string*) by mapping it into the less-than relation $<$, which is known to be well-founded (over *integer*). A general method for doing this is the content of the *mapping* proposition of this section.

Definition (mapping function)

Suppose that obj_1 and obj_2 are unary predicate symbols and that $\prec_1$ and $\prec_2$ are binary relations.

A unary function f is said to *map* $\prec_1$ (over obj_1) *into* $\prec_2$ (over obj_2) if

- f maps the elements of obj_1 into the elements of obj_2, that is,

$$(\forall \ obj_1 \ x)\big[obj_2\big(f(x)\big)\big] \tag{sort}$$

and

- f maps pairs of object$_1$'s satisfying $\prec_1$ into pairs of object$_2$'s satisfying $\prec_2$, that is,

$$(\forall \ obj_1 \ x, y)\begin{bmatrix} if \ \ x \prec_1 y \\ then \ \ f(x) \prec_2 f(y) \end{bmatrix} \tag{monotonicity}$$

⌙

Recall that, by our relativized-quantifier notation (Section [I]5.6), a sentence such as

$$(\forall \ obj_1 \ x)\big[obj_2\big(f(x)\big)\big],$$

stands for the sentence

$$(\forall x)\begin{bmatrix} if \ \ obj_1(x) \\ then \ \ obj_2\big(f(x)\big) \end{bmatrix}.$$

Let us consider some mapping functions.

Example (length function)

In the combined theory of the nonnegative integers and strings, we defined (Section [I]7.8) the *length* function by the axioms

$$length(\Lambda) = 0 \qquad\qquad\qquad\qquad\qquad\qquad (empty)$$

$$\begin{matrix} (\forall \ char \ u) \\ (\forall \ string \ x) \end{matrix} \Big[length(u \bullet x) \ = \ length(x) + 1 \Big] \qquad\qquad (prefix)$$

The *length* function maps the proper-substring relation $\prec_{string}$ (over *string*) into the less-than relation $<$ (over *integer*), because the properties

$$(\forall \ string \ x) \big[integer \big(length(x) \big) \big] \qquad\qquad\qquad\qquad (sort)$$

and

$$(\forall \ string \ x, y) \begin{bmatrix} if \ \ x \prec_{string} y \\ then \ \ length(x) < length(y) \end{bmatrix} \qquad\qquad (monotonicity)$$

are both valid. (The latter is the *proper-substring* property of the *length* function.) ◢

Example (flattree function)

In the combined theory of strings and trees, we defined (Section [I]8.4) the *flattree* function by the axioms

$$(\forall \ atom \ x) \big[flattree(x) = x \big] \qquad\qquad\qquad\qquad (atom)$$

$$(\forall \ tree \ x, y) \big[flattree(x \bullet y) \ = \ flattree(x) * flattree(y) \big] \quad (construction)$$

The *flattree* function maps the proper-subtree relation $\prec_{tree}$ (over *tree*) into the proper-substring relation $\prec_{string}$ (over *string*), because the properties

$$(\forall \ tree \ x) \big[string \big(flattree(x) \big) \big] \qquad\qquad\qquad\qquad (sort)$$

and

$$(\forall \ tree \ x, y) \begin{bmatrix} if \ \ x \prec_{tree} y \\ then \ \ flattree(x) \prec_{string} flattree(y) \end{bmatrix} \qquad (monotonicity)$$

are both valid. ◢

THE MAPPING PROPOSITION

We are finally ready to state the main result.

Proposition (mapping)

In a theory with equality, suppose that

- obj_1 and obj_2 are unary predicate symbols,
- $\prec_1$ and $\prec_2$ are binary relations, and
- f is a unary function mapping $\prec_1$ (over obj_1) into $\prec_2$ (over obj_2).

If $\prec_2$ is well-founded (over obj_2),
then $\prec_1$ is well-founded (over obj_1). ⌟

We require a theory with equality because the equality relation is used in the proof. Once we have proved the proposition, we can easily establish the well-foundedness of several binary relations. In **Problem 1.3**, the reader is requested to show that this proposition does not hold in the other direction. In other words, the well-foundedness of $\prec_1$ does not imply the well-foundedness of $\prec_2$.

Example (proper-substring relation is well-founded)

We have indicated that the *length* function maps the proper-substring relation $\prec_{string}$ (over *string*) into the less-than relation $<$ (over *integer*) and that the less-than relation $<$ is well-founded (over *integer*). The *mapping* proposition then implies that

the proper-substring relation $\prec_{string}$ is well-founded (over *string*). ⌟

Example (proper-subtree relation is well-founded)

Because the *flattree* function maps the proper-subtree relation $\prec_{tree}$ (over *tree*) into the proper-substring relation $\prec_{string}$ (over *string*) and because the proper-substring relation $\prec_{string}$ is well-founded (over *string*), the *mapping* proposition tells us that

the proper-subtree relation $\prec_{tree}$ is well-founded (over *tree*). ⌟

Remark (combined theory)

Strictly speaking, in applying the preceding *mapping* proposition, we have established the well-foundedness of $\prec_{string}$ over *string* only in the combined theory of nonnegative integers and strings. To conclude that the result also holds in the pure theory of strings requires us to ensure that the two theories do not interact badly. In particular, we must guarantee that the combined theory is consistent. A similar remark pertains to the subtree relation $\prec_{tree}$. We do not deal with this problem here, but in both cases the combined theory behaves well. ◢

PROOF OF PROPOSITION

Now we are ready to prove the *mapping* proposition. This proof may be skipped on first reading.

Proof (mapping)

Suppose that f maps $\prec_1$ (over obj_1) into $\prec_2$ (over obj_2), that is, f satisfies the *sort* property

$$(\forall\ obj_1\ x)\big[obj_2\big(f(x)\big)\big]$$

and the *monotonicity* property

$$(\forall\ obj_1\ x,y)\begin{bmatrix} if\ x \prec_1 y \\ then\ f(x) \prec_2 f(y) \end{bmatrix}.$$

Also suppose that $\prec_2$ is well-founded (over obj_2). We would like to show that $\prec_1$ is then well-founded (over obj_1).

We establish the validity of the *well-founded induction* principle with respect to $\prec_1$ (over obj_1); that is, for an arbitrary sentence $\mathcal{F}[x]$, with no free occurrences of x', we show that the universal closure of

$$if\ (\forall\ obj_1\ x)\ \begin{bmatrix} if\ (\forall\ obj_1\ x')\begin{bmatrix} if\ x' \prec_1 x \\ then\ \mathcal{F}[x'] \end{bmatrix} \\ then\ \mathcal{F}[x] \end{bmatrix}$$
$$then\ (\forall\ obj_1\ x)\mathcal{F}[x]$$

is valid.

Suppose that the inductive step is true, that is,

$$(\dagger) \qquad (\forall\ obj_1\ x)\ \begin{bmatrix} if\ (\forall\ obj_1\ x')\begin{bmatrix} if\ x' \prec_1 x \\ then\ \mathcal{F}[x'] \end{bmatrix} \\ then\ \mathcal{F}[x] \end{bmatrix}.$$

We would like to show that the consequent then is true, that is,

(††) $(\forall \ obj_1 \ x)\mathcal{F}[x]$.

We actually show an alternative sentence,

(‡‡) $(\forall \ obj_2 \ y)(\forall \ obj_1 \ x)\begin{bmatrix} if & f(x) = y \\ then & \mathcal{F}[x] \end{bmatrix}$.

To show that this alternative sentence (‡‡) implies the desired consequent (††), consider an arbitrary object$_1$ x_0 (that is, an arbitrary element x_0 satisfying obj_1); we would like to show $\mathcal{F}[x_0]$. We know (by the *sort* property) that $f(x_0)$ is an object$_2$. Taking y to be the object$_2$ $f(x_0)$ and x to be the object$_1$ x_0 in (‡‡), we obtain

$$if \ \ f(x_0) = f(x_0)$$
$$then \ \ \mathcal{F}[x_0],$$

which implies the desired result $\mathcal{F}[x_0]$.

Proof of (‡‡)

To prove the alternative sentence (‡‡),

$$(\forall \ obj_2 \ y)\left[(\forall \ obj_1 \ x)\begin{bmatrix} if & f(x) = y \\ then & \mathcal{F}[x] \end{bmatrix}\right],$$

we apply the *well-founded induction* principle with respect to the relation $\prec_2$ (over obj_2); this is justified because we have supposed $\prec_2$ to be well-founded (over obj_2). The proof is by induction on y, taking the inductive sentence to be

$$\mathcal{G}[y]: \ \ (\forall \ obj_1 \ x)\begin{bmatrix} if & f(x) = y \\ then & \mathcal{F}[x] \end{bmatrix}.$$

To prove

$$(\forall \ obj_2 \ y)\mathcal{G}[y].$$

it suffices to establish the inductive step.

Inductive Step

We want to show

$$(\forall \ obj_2 \ y)\left[if \ (\forall \ obj_2 \ y')\begin{bmatrix} if & y' \prec_2 y \\ then & \mathcal{G}[y'] \end{bmatrix} \\ then \ \ \mathcal{G}[y] \right],$$

where y' does not occur free in $\mathcal{G}[y]$.

For an arbitrary object$_2$ y, assume the induction hypothesis

$$(*) \qquad (\forall\ obj_2\ y') \begin{bmatrix} if\ y' \prec_2 y \\ then\ \mathcal{G}[y'] \end{bmatrix}.$$

We would like to show that then $\mathcal{G}[y]$, that is,

$$(\forall\ obj_1\ x) \begin{bmatrix} if\ f(x) = y \\ then\ \mathcal{F}[x] \end{bmatrix}.$$

Consider an arbitrary object$_1$ x and suppose that

$$f(x) = y.$$

We would like to establish that then

$$\mathcal{F}[x].$$

By our earlier supposition (†), it suffices to show that

$$(\forall\ obj_1\ x') \begin{bmatrix} if\ x' \prec_1 x \\ then\ \mathcal{F}[x'] \end{bmatrix}.$$

Consider an arbitrary object$_1$ x' and suppose that

$$x' \prec_1 x.$$

We would like to establish that

$$(**) \qquad \mathcal{F}[x'].$$

Because $x' \prec_1 x$, we know (by the *monotonicity* property) that

$$f(x') \prec_2 f(x),$$

that is (because $f(x) = y$),

$$f(x') \prec_2 y.$$

Also, because x' is an object$_1$, we know (by the *sort* property) that $f(x')$ is an object$_2$.

Our induction hypothesis $(*)$ tells us (taking y' to be the object$_2$ $f(x')$) that

$$if\ f(x') \prec_2 y \\ then\ \mathcal{G}[f(x')].$$

Therefore we have $\mathcal{G}[f(x')]$, that is,

$$(\forall \ obj_1 \ x) \begin{bmatrix} if \ \ f(x) = f(x') \\ then \ \ \mathcal{F}[x] \end{bmatrix}.$$

In particular (taking x to be the object$_1$ x'), because $f(x') = f(x')$, we have

$$\mathcal{F}[x'],$$

which is the condition $(**)$ we wanted to establish. ⌐

MORE WELL-FOUNDED RELATIONS

Let us use the *mapping* proposition to establish the well-foundedness of several additional relations in various theories.

Example (member relation is well-founded)

In the theory of lists, we defined (Section [I]9.3) the member relation $u \in x$ by the axioms

$$(\forall \ atlist \ u)\big[nol \ (u \in [\ ])\big] \hspace{3cm} (empty)$$

$$(\forall \ atlist \ u,v) \\ (\forall \ list \ x) \begin{bmatrix} u \in v \circ x \\ \equiv \\ u = v \ \ or \ \ u \in x \end{bmatrix} \hspace{2cm} (insertion)$$

Intuitively, an atom or list u is a member of a list x (that is, $u \in x$) if u is one of the top-level elements of x. We establish that the member relation is well-founded (over *list*).

We consider the combined theory of lists and trees (over the same set of atoms), where the empty list [ ] is regarded also as an atom (Section [I]9.5). In this theory, we defined the *treelist* function, which maps a list into its tree representation (distinct lists are represented as distinct trees), by the axioms

$$treelist([\ ]) \ = \ [\ ] \hspace{4cm} (empty)$$

$$(\forall \ atom \ u) \\ (\forall \ list \ y)\big[treelist(u \circ y) \ = \ u \bullet treelist(y)\big] \hspace{1cm} (atom \ insertion)$$

$$(\forall \ list \ x,y)\big[treelist(x \circ y) \ = \ treelist(x) \bullet treelist(y)\big] \ (list \ insertion)$$

The *treelist* function maps the member relation $\in$ (over *list*) into the proper-subtree relation $\prec_{tree}$ (over *tree*) because the properties

$$(\forall\ list\ x)\left[tree\left(treelist(x)\right)\right] \hspace{4cm} (sort)$$

and (see Problem [I]9.7)

$$(\forall\ list\ x, y)\begin{bmatrix} if\ \ x \in y \\ then\ \ treelist(x)\ \prec_{tree}\ treelist(y)\end{bmatrix} \hspace{1.5cm} (monotonicity)$$

are both valid.

We have already established that the proper-subtree relation $\prec_{tree}$ is well-founded (over *tree*); therefore (by the *mapping* proposition)

the member relation $\in$ is well-founded (over *list*). ⌐

Note that the member relation $u \in x$ is not transitive since, for example, A $\in$ [A] and [A] $\in$ [[A]] but not A $\in$ [[A]]. This is another example of a well-founded relation that is not transitive.

Example (proper-subset relation is well-founded)

In the theory of sets, we defined (Section [I]10.6) the proper-subset relation $x \subset y$ by the axiom

$$(\forall\ set\ x, y)\begin{bmatrix} x \subset y \\ \equiv \\ x \subseteq y\ \ and\ \ not\ (x = y)\end{bmatrix} \hspace{1.5cm} (proper\ subset)$$

where the subset relation $x \subseteq y$ was defined by the axioms

$$(\forall\ set\ y)\left[\{\ \} \subseteq y\right] \hspace{4cm} (left\ empty)$$

$$\begin{array}{l}(\forall\ atom\ u) \\ (\forall\ set\ x, y)\end{array}\begin{bmatrix} (u \circ x) \subseteq y \\ \equiv \\ u \in y\ \ and\ \ x \subseteq y\end{bmatrix} \hspace{1.5cm} (left\ insertion)$$

We establish that the proper-subset relation $x \subset y$ is well-founded over the sets.

Consider the combined theory of sets and nonnegative integers. We defined (Section [I]10.8) the cardinality function $card(x)$, which denotes the number of distinct elements in the set x, by the axioms

$$card(\{\,\}) = 0 \qquad\qquad\qquad\qquad\qquad (empty)$$

$$(\forall\ atom\ u)\begin{bmatrix} if\ \ not\ (u \in x) \\ (\forall\ set\ x)\ \begin{bmatrix} then\ \ card(u \circ x) = card(x) + 1 \end{bmatrix}\end{bmatrix} \qquad (insertion)$$

This function maps the proper-subset relation $\subset$ (over *set*) into the less-than relation $<$ (over *integer*), because it satisfies the properties

$$(\forall\ set\ x)\,[integer\,(card(x))] \qquad\qquad\qquad (sort)$$

and

$$(\forall\ set\ x,y)\begin{bmatrix} if\ \ x \subset y \\ then\ \ card(x) < card(y) \end{bmatrix} \qquad\qquad (monotonicity)$$

(The latter is the *proper-subset* property of the cardinality function [I]10.8.)

Therefore (by the *mapping* proposition), because the less-than relation $<$ is well-founded (over *integer*),

the proper-subset relation $\subset$ is well-founded (over *set*). ⌐

Example (proper-subtuple relation is well-founded)

In the combined theory of nonnegative integers and tuples, we defined (Section [I]12.2) the function $length(x)$, which denotes the number of elements in the tuple x, by the axioms

$$length(\langle\ \rangle)\ =\ 0 \qquad\qquad\qquad\qquad (empty)$$

$$\begin{array}{l}(\forall\ atom\ u)\\ (\forall\ tuple\ x)\end{array}\begin{bmatrix} length(u \diamond x)\ =\ length(x) + 1 \end{bmatrix} \qquad (insertion)$$

This function maps the proper-subtuple relation $\subset$ (over *tuple*) into the less-than relation $<$ (over *integer*) because it satisfies the properties

$$(\forall\ tuple\ x)\,[integer\,(length(x))] \qquad\qquad\qquad (sort)$$

and

$$(\forall\ tuple\ x,y)\begin{bmatrix} if\ \ x \subset y \\ then\ \ length(x) < length(y) \end{bmatrix} \qquad\qquad (monotonicity)$$

Therefore (by the *mapping* proposition), because the less-than relation $<$ is well-founded (over *integer*),

the proper-subtuple relation $\subset$ is well-founded (over *tuple*). ⌟

We have used the *mapping* proposition to establish that particular relations are well-founded. In the following subsections we present three general consequences of the proposition.

INDUCED RELATION

The *mapping* proposition allows us to define a new well-founded relation over one class of objects (obj_1) in terms of a given well-founded relation $\prec_2$ over another class of objects (obj_2).

Definition (induced relation)

Suppose that

- obj_1 and obj_2 are unary predicate symbols,
- $\prec_2$ is a binary relation, and
- f is a unary function mapping obj_1 into obj_2, that is, satisfying the *sort* property
  $$(\forall\ obj_1\ x)\big[obj_2\big(f(x)\big)\big].$$

Then the binary relation *induced* (over obj_1) by $\prec_2$ *via* f, denoted by $\prec_f$, is defined by the axiom

$$
(\forall\ obj_1\ x, y)\left[\begin{array}{c} x \prec_f y \\ \equiv \\ f(x) \prec_2 f(y) \end{array}\right] \qquad (induced\ relation)
$$

⌟

Let us see first some induced relations.

Example (length relation)

In a combined theory of nonnegative integers and strings, let obj_1 be *string*, obj_2 be *integer*, $\prec_2$ be the less-than relation $<$, and f be the unary function *length* mapping the strings into the nonnegative integers. Then the relation $\prec_{length}$ induced (over *string*) by the less-than relation $<$ via the *length* function is defined by the axiom

$$(\forall \; string \; x, y) \begin{bmatrix} x \; \prec_{length} \; y \\ \equiv \\ length(x) < length(y) \end{bmatrix} \qquad\qquad (length \; relation)$$

Note that this relation over the strings is distinct from the proper-substring relation $\prec_{string}$; for instance,

$$\text{AB} \; \prec_{length} \; \text{CDE} \qquad \text{but not} \qquad \text{AB} \; \prec_{string} \; \text{CDE}. \qquad \lrcorner$$

We can now establish a corollary to the *mapping* proposition, that a relation induced by a well-founded relation is also well-founded.

Corollary (induced relation)

Suppose that

- obj_1 and obj_2 are unary predicate symbols,
- $\prec_2$ is a binary relation, and
- f is a unary function mapping obj_1 into obj_2, that is, satisfying the *sort* property
  $$(\forall \; obj_1 \; x) \big[obj_2 \big(f(x) \big) \big].$$

If the relation $\prec_2$ is well-founded (over obj_2),
then the induced relation $\prec_f$ is well-founded (over obj_1). $\qquad \lrcorner$

Let us illustrate the corollary before proving it.

Example (length relation is well-founded)

Let obj_1 be *string*, obj_2 be *integer*, $\prec_2$ be the less-than relation $<$, and f be the *length* function mapping *string* into *integer*. Then, because the less-than relation $<$ is well-founded (over *integer*), it follows by the preceding corollary that

the induced relation $\prec_{length}$ is well-founded (over *string*). $\qquad \lrcorner$

In **Problem 1.4** the reader is asked to show the well-foundedness of a new relation over the nonnegative integers.

We are now ready to prove the corollary.

Proof (induced relation)

We are given that f satisfies the *sort* property

$$(\forall \; obj_1 \; x)\left[obj_2\big(f(x)\big)\right].$$

Also, by definition of the induced relation, we have

$$(\forall \; obj_1 \; x, y)\left[\begin{array}{c} x \prec_f y \\ \equiv \\ f(x) \prec_2 f(y) \end{array}\right].$$

In particular, we have

$$(\forall \; obj_1 \; x, y)\left[\begin{array}{l} \textit{if } \; x \prec_f y \\ \textit{then } \; f(x) \prec_2 f(y) \end{array}\right],$$

which is exactly the *monotonicity* property.

Thus, because both the *sort* and the *monotonicity* properties are satisfied, f maps the induced relation $\prec_f$ (over obj_1) into the relation $\prec_2$ (over obj_2).

Therefore, by the *mapping* proposition, if $\prec_2$ is well-founded (over obj_2), then the induced relation $\prec_f$ is well-founded (over obj_1). $\quad\lrcorner$

SUBRELATION

The following corollary to the *mapping* proposition establishes that any "subrelation" of a well-founded relation is also well-founded. This is obtained by taking f to be the identity function, that is, $f(x) = x$, and both obj_1 and obj_2 to be a single unary predicate symbol obj.

Corollary (subrelation)

Suppose that

- obj is a unary predicate symbol, and
- $\prec_1$ and $\prec_2$ are two binary relations such that $\prec_1$ is a *subrelation* of $\prec_2$ (over obj), that is,

$$(\forall \; obj \; x, y)\left[\begin{array}{l} \textit{if } \; x \prec_1 y \\ \textit{then } \; x \prec_2 y \end{array}\right] \qquad\qquad (subrelation)$$

If $\prec_2$ is well-founded (over obj),
then $\prec_1$ is also well-founded (over obj). $\quad\lrcorner$

Proof

In the *mapping* proposition, take both obj_1 and obj_2 to be the predicate symbol obj, and let f be the identity function $f(x) = x$. Then, in this case, the *sort* property states that

$$(\forall\ obj\ x)\big[obj(x)\big],$$

which is true, and the *monotonicity* property states that

$$(\forall\ obj\ x, y)\ \begin{bmatrix} if\ \ x \prec_1 y \\ then\ \ x \prec_2 y \end{bmatrix},$$

which is precisely the assumed *subrelation* condition, that $\prec_1$ is a subrelation of $\prec_2$.

Therefore f maps $\prec_1$ (over obj) into $\prec_2$ (over obj). Hence (by the *mapping* proposition), if $\prec_2$ is well-founded (over obj), then its subrelation $\prec_1$ is also well-founded (over obj). ◢

Example (predecessor relation is well-founded)

In the theory of nonnegative integers, let the *predecessor* relation $\prec_{pred}$ be defined by the axiom

$$(\forall\ integer\ x, y)\ \begin{bmatrix} x \prec_{pred} y \\ \equiv \\ x + 1 = y \end{bmatrix} \qquad (predecessor\ relation)$$

That is, $x \prec_{pred} y$ is true precisely when x is the predecessor of y.

The predecessor relation $\prec_{pred}$ is a subrelation of the less-than relation $<$ (over *integer*), that is, the property

$$(\forall\ integer\ x, y)\ \begin{bmatrix} if\ \ x \prec_{pred} y \\ then\ \ x < y \end{bmatrix} \qquad (subrelation)$$

holds. Therefore the *subrelation* corollary implies that, because the less-than relation $<$ is well-founded (over *integer*),

the predecessor relation $\prec_{pred}$ is well-founded (over *integer*). ◢

SUBCLASS

The *mapping* proposition further implies that a relation that is well-founded over a given class of objects (obj_2) is also well-founded over any subclass (obj_1) of that class. This is obtained by taking f to be the identity function (that is, $f(x) = x$) and $\prec_1$ and $\prec_2$ to be a single binary relation $\prec$.

Corollary (subclass)

    Suppose that

- obj_1 and obj_2 are unary predicate symbols such that all the object$_1$'s are also object$_2$'s, that is,

$$(\forall\ obj_1\ x)\big[obj_2(x)\big] \qquad\qquad (subclass)$$

    and that

- $\prec$ is a binary relation.

If $\prec$ is well-founded over obj_2,
then it is also well-founded over the subclass obj_1. ⌟

Proof

    In the *mapping* proposition, let f be the identity function $f(x) = x$, and take both $\prec_1$ and $\prec_2$ to be $\prec$. Then, in this case, the *sort* property states that

$$(\forall\ obj_1\ x)\big[obj_2(x)\big],$$

which is precisely the given *subclass* property, and the *monotonicity* property states that

$$(\forall\ obj_1\ x, y) \begin{bmatrix} if\ \ x \prec y \\ then\ \ x \prec y \end{bmatrix},$$

which is true (by propositional logic). Therefore f maps $\prec$ over obj_1 into $\prec$ over obj_2.

    Hence (by the *mapping* proposition), if $\prec$ is well-founded over obj_2, then $\prec$ is also well-founded over the subclass obj_1. ⌟

    Let us consider an application of the *subclass* corollary.

Example (less-than relation over positive is well-founded)

In the theory of the nonnegative integers, the unary predicate symbol *positive*, which characterizes the positive integers, was defined (Section [I]6.4) by the axiom

$$
(\forall\ x) \left[\begin{array}{l} positive(x) \\ \equiv \\ integer(x) \ \ and \ \ not\ (x = 0) \end{array} \right] \hspace{3cm} (positive)
$$

Note that each positive integer is also a nonnegative integer, i.e., the property

$$
(\forall\ positive\ x)\big[integer(x)\big] \hspace{3cm} (subclass)
$$

is valid.

Therefore the *subclass* corollary implies that, because the less-than relation $<$ is well-founded over *integer*,

the less-than relation $<$ is well-founded over *positive*. ⌟

We now use the *subrelation* corollary together with the result of the previous example.

Example (proper-divides relation over positive is well-founded)

In the theory of the nonnegative integers, the divides relation $x \preceq_{div} y$, which holds when x divides y with no remainder, was defined (Section [I]6.11) by the axiom

$$
(\forall\ integer\ x, y) \left[\begin{array}{l} x \preceq_{div} y \\ \equiv \\ (\exists\ integer\ z)\big[x \cdot z = y\big] \end{array} \right] \hspace{2.5cm} (divides)
$$

The corresponding proper-divides relation $x \prec_{div} y$ was then defined by the axiom

$$
(\forall\ integer\ x, y) \left[\begin{array}{l} x \prec_{div} y \\ \equiv \\ x \preceq_{div} y \ \ and \ \ not\ (x = y) \end{array} \right] \hspace{1.5cm} (proper\ divides)
$$

Thus

$$
1 \prec_{div} 6, \quad 2 \prec_{div} 6, \quad 3 \prec_{div} 6, \quad \text{but not} \quad 6 \prec_{div} 6.
$$

Also

$$6 \prec_{div} 0, \quad \text{but not} \quad 0 \prec_{div} 6.$$

We can establish that, over the positive integers, the proper-divides relation $\prec_{div}$ is stronger than the less-than relation $<$, that is, the property

$$(\forall \ positive \ x, y) \begin{bmatrix} if \ x \prec_{div} y \\ then \ x < y \end{bmatrix} \qquad\qquad (subrelation)$$

is valid.

Therefore, because the less-than relation $<$ was shown to be well-founded (over *positive*), we may conclude (by the *subrelation* corollary) that

the proper-divides relation $\prec_{div}$ is well-founded (over *positive*). ∎

EVEN MORE WELL-FOUNDED RELATIONS

It is worthwhile to spend some time establishing that relations are well-founded, allowing us to use them as the basis for future proofs by well-founded induction.

Example (proper-end relation is well-founded)

In the theory of strings, we defined (Section [I]7.5) the end relation $x \preceq_{end} y$, which is true if the string x is at the end of the string y, that is, if x can be obtained from y by dropping some (perhaps none) of the initial characters of y.

The corresponding proper-end relation, $x \prec_{end} y$, is defined by the axioms

$$(\forall \ string \ x) \big[not \ (x \prec_{end} \Lambda) \big] \qquad\qquad (empty)$$

$$(\forall \ string \ x, y) \begin{bmatrix} if \ not \ (y = \Lambda) \\ then \begin{bmatrix} x \prec_{end} y \\ \equiv \\ x = tail(y) \ or \ x \prec_{end} tail(y) \end{bmatrix} \end{bmatrix} \qquad (tail)$$

The following properties can be proved from the axioms:

$$(\forall \ string \ x, y) \begin{bmatrix} x \prec_{end} y \\ \equiv \\ (\exists \ string \ z)[z * x = y \ \ and \ \ not \ (z = \Lambda)] \end{bmatrix}$$
$$(concatenation)$$

$$(\forall \ string \ x, y) \begin{bmatrix} if \ \ x \prec_{end} y \\ then \ \ x \prec_{string} y \end{bmatrix} \qquad (substring)$$

The reader is requested to prove (in **Problem 1.5(a)**) that the proper-end relation $\prec_{end}$ is well-founded (over *string*). ∎

Example (proper-intersperse relation is well-founded)

In the theory of strings, we introduced (Problem [I]7.14) the intersperse relation $x \preceq_{inter} y$, which holds if the elements of x occur in y in the same order but not necessarily consecutively. The following four axioms define the relation:

$$(\forall \ string \ y)[\Lambda \preceq_{inter} y] \qquad (left \ empty)$$

$$\begin{matrix} (\forall \ char \ u) \\ (\forall \ string \ x) \end{matrix} [not \ (u \bullet x \preceq_{inter} \Lambda)] \qquad (right \ empty)$$

$$\begin{matrix} (\forall \ char \ u) \\ (\forall \ string \ x, y) \end{matrix} \begin{bmatrix} u \bullet x \preceq_{inter} u \bullet y \\ \equiv \\ x \preceq_{inter} y \end{bmatrix} \qquad (equal \ prefix)$$

$$\begin{matrix} (\forall \ char \ u, v) \\ (\forall \ string \ x, y) \end{matrix} \begin{bmatrix} if \ u \neq v \\ then \ \begin{bmatrix} u \bullet x \preceq_{inter} v \bullet y \\ \equiv \\ u \bullet x \preceq_{inter} y \end{bmatrix} \end{bmatrix} \qquad (distinct \ prefix)$$

From the axioms, the following properties can be proved:

$$\begin{matrix} (\forall \ char \ u) \\ (\forall \ string \ x, y) \end{matrix} \begin{bmatrix} u \bullet x \preceq_{inter} y \\ \equiv \\ (\exists \ string \ y_1, y_2) \begin{bmatrix} y = y_1 * (u \bullet y_2) \\ and \\ x \preceq_{inter} y_2 \end{bmatrix} \end{bmatrix}$$
$$(concatenation)$$

$$(\forall \ string \ x, y) \begin{bmatrix} if \ x \preceq_{string} y \\ then \ \ x \preceq_{inter} y \end{bmatrix} \qquad (substring)$$

The reader is requested to prove (in **Problem 1.5(b)**) that the proper-intersperse relation $\prec_{inter}$, which is defined by the axiom

$$
(\forall\ string\ x,y) \left[\begin{array}{l} x \prec_{inter} y \\ \equiv \\ x \preceq_{inter} y \ \ and \ \ not \ (x = y) \end{array} \right] \qquad (proper\ intersperse)
$$

is well-founded (over *string*). ⌐

Example (**proper-subbag relation is well-founded**)

In the theory of bags, we defined (Section [I]11.5) the proper-subbag relation $\subset$ by the axiom

$$
(\forall\ bag\ x,y) \left[\begin{array}{l} x \subset y \\ \equiv \\ x \subseteq y \ \ and \ \ not \ (x \subset y) \end{array} \right] \qquad (proper\ subbag)
$$

where the subbag relation $\subseteq$ was defined by the axioms

$$
(\forall\ bag\ y) \left[\llbracket\ \rrbracket \subseteq y \right] \qquad\qquad\qquad (empty)
$$

$$
\begin{array}{l} (\forall\ atom\ u) \\ (\forall\ bag\ x,\ y) \end{array} \left[\begin{array}{l} (u \circ x) \subseteq (u \circ y) \\ \equiv \\ x \subseteq y \end{array} \right] \qquad (equal\ insertion)
$$

$$
\begin{array}{l} (\forall\ atom\ u) \\ (\forall\ bag\ x,\ y) \end{array} \left[\begin{array}{l} if\ \ (u \circ x) \subseteq y \\ then\ \ u \in y \end{array} \right] \qquad (member)
$$

The reader is requested to prove (in **Problem 1.5(c)**) that the proper-subbag relation $\subset$ is well-founded (over *bag*).

1.4   ASYMMETRY AND IRREFLEXIVITY

In this section, we establish properties that hold for all well-founded relations.

We have seen that well-founded relations need not be transitive; for example, the predecessor relation $\prec_{pred}$ is well-founded (over *integer*) but not transitive.

We can establish, however, that any well-founded relation is asymmetric and (therefore) irreflexive over the objects. We presented an informal proof of this in the preview, based on the absence of infinite decreasing sequences. Here we give a more precise proof based on the *well-founded induction* principle.

Proposition (asymmetry)

Suppose the relation $\prec$ is well-founded over the unary predicate symbol *obj*.

Then the sentence

$$(\forall\ obj\ x, y)\ \begin{bmatrix} if\ \ x \prec y \\ then\ \ not\ (y \prec x) \end{bmatrix} \qquad\qquad (asymmetry)$$

is valid. ⌟

Proof

Since $\prec$ is a well-founded relation (over *obj*), we may apply the *well-founded induction* principle with respect to $\prec$ (over *obj*). We prove

$$(\forall\ obj\ x)\ \left[(\forall\ obj\ y)\ \begin{bmatrix} if\ \ x \prec y \\ then\ \ not\ (y \prec x) \end{bmatrix} \right]$$

by induction on x, taking the inductive sentence to be

$$\mathcal{F}[x]:\quad (\forall\ obj\ y)\ \begin{bmatrix} if\ \ x \prec y \\ then\ \ not\ (y \prec x) \end{bmatrix}.$$

To prove $(\forall\ obj\ x)\mathcal{F}[x]$, it suffices to establish the inductive step.

Inductive Step

We would like to show

$$(\forall\ obj\ x)\ \begin{bmatrix} if\ (\forall\ obj\ x')\ \begin{bmatrix} if\ x' \prec x \\ then\ \ \mathcal{F}[x'] \end{bmatrix} \\ then\ \ \mathcal{F}[x] \end{bmatrix}.$$

Consider an arbitrary object x and assume the induction hypothesis,

$$(\dagger)\qquad (\forall\ obj\ x')\ \begin{bmatrix} if\ x' \prec x \\ then\ \ \mathcal{F}[x'] \end{bmatrix}.$$

We must show $\mathcal{F}[x]$, that is,

$$(\forall \ obj \ y) \begin{bmatrix} if & x \prec y \\ then & not \ (y \prec x) \end{bmatrix}.$$

Consider an arbitrary object y and suppose that

$$x \prec y.$$

It suffices to show that

$$not \ (y \prec x).$$

Suppose, to the contrary, that

$$y \prec x.$$

By our induction hypothesis (†), taking x' to be y, we have that

$$if \ \ y \prec x$$
$$then \ \ \mathcal{F}[y].$$

Therefore (by our supposition that $y \prec x$), we have $\mathcal{F}[y]$, that is,

$$(\forall \ obj \ y') \begin{bmatrix} if & y \prec y' \\ then & not \ (y' \prec y) \end{bmatrix}.$$

In particular, taking y' to be x, we have

$$if \ \ y \prec x$$
$$then \ \ not \ (x \prec y).$$

Because we have supposed that $y \prec x$, we establish that

$$not \ (x \prec y),$$

contradicting our earlier supposition that $x \prec y$. ∎

The irreflexivity of a well-founded relation $\prec$ follows directly, because any asymmetric relation is irreflexive (Section [I]4.4).

Corollary (irreflexivity)

Suppose the relation $\prec$ is well-founded over the unary predicate symbol *obj*.

Then the sentence

$$(\forall \; obj \; x)\big[not \; (x \prec x)\big] \hspace{4cm} (irreflexivity)$$

is valid. ◢

Although the original *irreflexivity* property was stated as $(\forall \; x)\big[not \, (x \; \prec \; x)\big]$, without a relative quantifier, the same proof applies to the relativized version.

1.5   MINIMAL-ELEMENT CONDITION

To prove that a binary relation $\prec$ is well-founded, it suffices to establish the validity of the corresponding *well-founded induction* principle. In this section, we discuss the *minimal-element* condition, which is equivalent to the *well-founded induction* principle and sometimes allows shorter, more intuitive proofs. This condition was introduced informally in the preview.

Proposition (minimal element)

In a given theory, a binary relation $\prec$ is well-founded over a unary predicate symbol *obj* precisely when

For each sentence $\mathcal{F}[x]$ with no free occurrences of x', the universal closure of

$$if \;\; (\exists \; obj \; x) \mathcal{F}[x]$$

$$then \;\; (\exists \; obj \; x) \begin{bmatrix} \mathcal{F}[x] \\ and \\ (\forall \; obj \; x') \begin{bmatrix} if \;\; x' \prec x \\ then \;\; not \; \mathcal{F}[x'] \end{bmatrix} \end{bmatrix}$$

$$(minimal\text{-}element \; condition)$$

is valid (in the given theory). ◢

The *minimal-element* condition states that, if a sentence $\mathcal{F}[x]$ is true for some object x, it must be true for some "minimal" object x, that is, one such that $\mathcal{F}[x]$ is true and $\mathcal{F}[x']$ is not true for any "smaller" object x'.

Before proving the proposition, we illustrate its application.

Example (least-number principle)

If, in the theory of the nonnegative integers, we take *obj* to be the unary predicate symbol *integer*, and $\prec$ to be the less-than relation $<$, then the *minimal-element* condition is the universal closure of

$$\textit{if } (\exists \textit{ integer } x)\mathcal{F}[x]$$

$$\textit{then } (\exists \textit{ integer } x)\begin{bmatrix} \mathcal{F}[x] \\ \textit{and} \\ (\forall \textit{ integer } x')\begin{bmatrix} \textit{if } x' < x \\ \textit{then } \textit{not } \mathcal{F}[x'] \end{bmatrix} \end{bmatrix},$$

where x' does not occur free in $\mathcal{F}[x]$. This is precisely the *least-number* principle over the nonnegative integers introduced in Section [I]6.12. The *minimal-element* proposition establishes that, in the theory of the nonnegative integers, the *complete induction* principle is equivalent to the *least-number* principle, as we mentioned without proof in Volume I. ⌙

Proof (minimal element)

We show that, for a given binary relation $\prec$, the *minimal-element* condition is equivalent to the *well-founded induction* principle.

For this purpose we first establish that, for any sentence $\mathcal{G}[x]$,

(†)
　　　　the *well-founded induction* principle is valid for a sentence $\mathcal{G}[x]$
　　　　precisely when
　　　　the *minimal-element* condition is valid for the sentence $(\textit{not } \mathcal{G}[x])$

Proof of (†)

We have that the sentence

$$\textit{if } (\forall \textit{ obj } x)\begin{bmatrix} \textit{if } (\forall \textit{ obj } x')\begin{bmatrix} \textit{if } x' \prec x \\ \textit{then } \mathcal{G}[x'] \end{bmatrix} \\ \textit{then } \mathcal{G}[x] \end{bmatrix}$$

$$\textit{then } (\forall \textit{ obj } x)\mathcal{G}[x],$$

whose universal closure is the *well-founded induction* principle, is true precisely when (by propositional logic, taking the contrapositive)

$$if \quad not \ (\forall \ obj \ x)\mathcal{G}[x]$$

$$then \quad not \ (\forall \ obj \ x) \left[\begin{array}{l} if \ (\forall \ obj \ x') \left[\begin{array}{l} if \ x' \prec x \\ then \ \mathcal{G}[x'] \end{array} \right] \\ then \ \mathcal{G}[x] \end{array} \right],$$

precisely when (by the duality between universal and existential quantifiers)

$$if \quad (\exists \ obj \ x)[not \ \mathcal{G}[x]]$$

$$then \quad (\exists \ obj \ x) \ not \left[\begin{array}{l} if \ (\forall \ obj \ x') \left[\begin{array}{l} if \ x' \prec x \\ then \ \mathcal{G}[x'] \end{array} \right] \\ then \ \mathcal{G}[x] \end{array} \right],$$

precisely when (by propositional logic)

$$if \quad (\exists \ obj \ x)[not \ \mathcal{G}[x]]$$

$$then \quad (\exists \ obj \ x) \left[\begin{array}{l} (\forall \ obj \ x') \left[\begin{array}{l} if \ x' \prec x \\ then \ \mathcal{G}[x'] \end{array} \right] \\ and \\ not \ \mathcal{G}[x] \end{array} \right],$$

precisely when (by propositional logic)

$$if \quad (\exists \ obj \ x)[not \ \mathcal{G}[x]]$$

$$then \quad (\exists \ obj \ x) \left[\begin{array}{l} not \ \mathcal{G}[x] \\ and \\ (\forall \ obj \ x') \left[\begin{array}{l} if \ x' \prec x \\ then \ not \ (not \ \mathcal{G}[x']) \end{array} \right] \end{array} \right].$$

But the universal closure of this sentence is precisely the *minimal-element* condition for the sentence *not* $\mathcal{G}[x]$. We thus have established (†).

We may now show the desired result that

(‡)   the *well-founded induction* principle is valid for any sentence $\mathcal{F}_1[x]$
            precisely when
       the *minimal-element* condition is valid for any sentence $\mathcal{F}_2[x]$.

Proof of (‡)

We show this in two directions.

Well-founded induction principle ⇒ minimal-element condition

Suppose that

the *well-founded induction* principle is valid for any sentence $\mathcal{F}_1[x]$.

Then, in particular, for an arbitrary sentence $\mathcal{F}_2[x]$,

the *well-founded induction* principle is valid for the sentence $\bigl(not\ \mathcal{F}_2[x]\bigr)$.

Therefore (by the preceding conclusion (†), taking $\mathcal{G}[x]$ to be $\bigl(not\ \mathcal{F}_2[x]\bigr)$)

the *minimal-element* condition is valid for $\bigl(not\ \bigl(not\ \mathcal{F}_2[x]\bigr)\bigr)$;

that is (by propositional logic),

the *minimal-element* condition is valid for $\mathcal{F}_2[x]$.

Because $\mathcal{F}_2[x]$ was taken to be an arbitrary sentence, it follows that

the *minimal-element* condition is valid for any sentence $\mathcal{F}_2[x]$,

as we wanted to show.

Minimal-element condition ⇒ well-founded induction principle

Suppose that

the *minimal-element* condition is valid for any sentence $\mathcal{F}_2[x]$.

Then, in particular, for an arbitrary sentence $\mathcal{F}_1[x]$,

the *minimal-element* condition is valid for $\bigl(not\ \mathcal{F}_1[x]\bigr)$.

Therefore (by the preceding conclusion (†), taking $\mathcal{G}[x]$ to be $\mathcal{F}_1[x]$),

the *well-founded induction* principle is valid for $\mathcal{F}_1[x]$.

Because $\mathcal{F}_1[x]$ was taken to be an arbitrary sentence, it follows that

the *well-founded induction* principle is valid for any sentence $\mathcal{F}_1[x]$,

as we wanted to show.

This establishes the equivalence between the *well-founded induction* principle and the *minimal-element* condition. ⏌

The *minimal-element* condition enables us to give another, more intuitive proof (requested in **Problem 1.6**) of the *asymmetry* proposition. This proposition states that any well-founded relation $\prec$ (over *obj*) is asymmetric (over *obj*). The original proof used the *well-founded induction* principle directly, rather than the *minimal-element* condition.

1.6   UNION RELATION

We have seen a few ways to establish that particular relations are well-founded, allowing us to use them in subsequent proofs by well-founded induction. Another way of establishing that a relation is well-founded is to show that it may be regarded as the "union" of two other relations, both of which are themselves well-founded. We make that method more precise in this section.

We begin with the definition.

Definition (union relation)

Suppose that obj_1 and obj_2 are unary predicate symbols, which characterize two classes of objects, and that $\prec_1$ and $\prec_2$ are binary relations.

Let the unary predicate symbol obj characterize the union of the two classes, that is,

$$(\forall\ x)\begin{bmatrix} obj(x) \\ \equiv \\ obj_1(x)\ \ or\ \ obj_2(x) \end{bmatrix}.$$

Then the *union* relation $\prec_{union}$ (over obj) of $\prec_1$ (over obj_1) and $\prec_2$ (over obj_2) is defined by the axiom

$$(\forall\ obj\ x, y)\begin{bmatrix} x \prec_{union} y \\ \equiv \\ \begin{bmatrix} obj_1(x)\ \ and\ \ obj_2(y) \\ or \\ obj_1(x)\ \ and\ \ obj_1(y)\ \ and\ \ x \prec_1 y \\ or \\ obj_2(x)\ \ and\ \ obj_2(y)\ \ and\ \ x \prec_2 y \end{bmatrix} \end{bmatrix} \qquad (union\ relation)$$

In other words, with respect to $\prec_{union}$, each of the $object_1$'s is regarded as less than any of the $object_2$'s; and $\prec_{union}$ agrees with $\prec_1$ on $object_1$'s and with $\prec_2$ on $object_2$'s. Note that the definition of $\prec_{union}$ depends on the choice of $\prec_1$, $\prec_2$, obj_1, and obj_2.

Example

Suppose $\prec_1$ is the proper-substring relation $\prec_{string}$ over the strings, and $\prec_2$ is the less-than relation $<$ over the nonnegative integers. Let obj characterize the union of the strings and the nonnegative integers, that is,

$$(\forall\ x)\begin{bmatrix} obj(x) \\ \equiv \\ string(x)\ \ or\ \ integer(x) \end{bmatrix}.$$

Then, for any two objects (strings or nonnegative integers) x and y, the union relation $\ x \prec_{union} y\ $ (of $\prec_{string}$ and $<$) is true if

- x is a string and y is a nonnegative integer, or
- x and y are both strings and $x \prec_{string} y$, or
- x and y are both nonnegative integers and $x < y$.

Thus

$$\text{ABC} \prec_{union} 2$$

$$\text{ABC} \prec_{union} \text{DAABCE}$$

$$2 \prec_{union} 3.$$

The principal result concerning the union relation is that the union of two well-founded relations (over disjoint classes of objects) is also well-founded.

Proposition (union relation)

Suppose that obj_1 and obj_2 are unary predicate symbols that characterize two disjoint classes of objects, that is,

$$(\forall\ x)\bigl[not\ \bigl(obj_1(x)\ \ and\ \ obj_2(x)\bigr)\bigr],$$

and that $\prec_1$ and $\prec_2$ are binary relations.

Let obj be a unary predicate symbol that characterizes the union of the two classes.

If $\prec_1$ and $\prec_2$ are well-founded over obj_1 and obj_2, respectively, then $\prec_{union}$ is well-founded over obj.

Remark (why disjoint classes?)

The proposition requires that obj_1 and obj_2 characterize disjoint classes. If this condition is not satisfied, the union relation $\prec_{union}$ is not well-founded. For suppose that the classes are not disjoint and that x is an element such that

$$obj_1(x) \quad and \quad obj_2(x).$$

Then (by the definition of $\prec_{union}$)

$$x \prec_{union} x.$$

Thus $\prec_{union}$ is not irreflexive. Therefore (by the *irreflexivity* corollary) $\prec_{union}$ is also not well-founded. ◢

The proof of the *union-relation* proposition is left as an exercise (**Problem 1.7**). Another exercise (**Problem 1.8**) pertains to other ways of combining well-founded relations.

Let us now apply the *union-relation* proposition to show that a particular relation is well-founded.

Example (proper-divides relation over integer is well-founded)

We have shown that the proper-divides relation $\prec_{div}$ is well-founded over the positive integers. We can actually establish that $\prec_{div}$ is well-founded over all the nonnegative integers.

The well-foundedness of $\prec_{div}$ over the positive integers was implied directly by the *subrelation* corollary because $\prec_{div}$ is stronger than the less-than relation $<$ over the positive integers; that is, the following *subrelation* property holds:

$$(\forall \ positive \ x, y) \begin{bmatrix} if \ x \prec_{div} y \\ then \ x < y \end{bmatrix}.$$

However, $\prec_{div}$ is not stronger than $<$ over all the nonnegative integers. For example, $2 \prec_{div} 0$ but not $2 < 0$. We therefore cannot again use the *subrelation* corollary for this extension. The *union* proposition provides a convenient way of proving the well-foundedness of $\prec_{div}$ over all the nonnegative integers.

The union relation $\prec_{union}$ (over *integer*) of

$$\prec_{div} \text{ over } positive \quad and \quad \prec_{empty} \text{ over } zero$$

(where the relation $zero(x)$ is true precisely when $x = 0$) is defined by

$$
(\forall \ integer \ x, y) \left[
\begin{array}{l}
x \prec_{union} y \\
\equiv \\
\left[
\begin{array}{l}
positive(x) \ \ and \ \ zero(y) \\
or \\
positive(x) \ \ and \ \ positive(y) \ \ and \ \ x \prec_{div} y \\
or \\
zero(x) \ \ and \ \ zero(y) \ \ and \ \ x \prec_{empty} y
\end{array}
\right]
\end{array}
\right] .
$$

Therefore (by the *union* proposition), because $\prec_{div}$ is well-founded over *positive*, because $\prec_{empty}$ is well-founded over *zero*, and because the positive integers and $\{0\}$ are disjoint classes, it follows that $\prec_{union}$ is well-founded over *integer*.

It can be proved that for every two nonnegative integers x and y, $x \prec_{div} y$ is equivalent to

$$
\begin{array}{l}
positive(x) \ \ and \ \ zero(y) \\
or \\
positive(x) \ \ and \ \ positive(y) \ \ and \ \ x \prec_{div} y,
\end{array}
$$

which is exactly the first two disjuncts in the preceding definition of $\prec_{union}$. Since the third disjunct is always false ($x \prec_{empty} y$ is false for any two elements), it follows that $\prec_{union}$ and $\prec_{div}$ are identical relations over the nonnegative integers, and therefore

the proper-divides relation $\prec_{div}$ is well-founded over *integer*. ◢

The reader is asked in **Problem 1.9** to establish the well-foundedness of an additional relation.

PROBLEMS

Problem 1.1 (non–well-founded relations)   page 15

In the theory of nonnegative integers, show that the following relations are not well-founded (over *integer*):

(a)   Less-than-or-equals relation $x \leq y$.

(b)   Nonequal relation $x \neq y$.

* **Problem 1.2 (cut relation)**   page 18

For any unary predicate symbols obj_1 and obj_2, suppose the *cut* relation $\prec_{cut}$ is defined by the axiom

$$(\forall\ obj_1\ x, y)\ \begin{bmatrix} x \prec_{cut} y \\ \equiv \\ obj_2(x)\ and\ not\ \big(obj_2(y)\big) \end{bmatrix}.$$

In other words, $x \prec_{cut} y$ for object$_1$'s x and y precisely when x is an object$_2$ but y is not.

Show that $\prec_{cut}$ is well-founded (over obj_1).

Problem 1.3 (backwards mapping)   page 21

Show that the converse of the *mapping* proposition is not valid. More precisely, present a theory with equality, unary predicate symbols obj_1 and obj_2, binary relations $\prec_1$ and $\prec_2$, and a unary function f mapping $\prec_1$ (over obj_1) into $\prec_2$ (over obj_2) such that

$$\prec_1 \text{ is well-founded (over } obj_1)$$

but

$$\prec_2 \text{ is not well-founded (over } obj_2).$$

Problem 1.4 (bounded-increase relation)   page 29

For each nonnegative integer n, consider the relation $\prec_{bd(n)}$, defined by the axiom

$$(\forall\ integer\ x, y)\ \begin{bmatrix} x \prec_{bd(n)} y \\ \equiv \\ x > y\ and\ y \leq n \end{bmatrix} \qquad (bounded\ increase)$$

Show that, for any nonnegative integer n, the relation $\prec_{bd(n)}$ is well-founded over *integer*.

Problem 1.5 (more well-founded relations)   pages 35, 36

In the appropriate theories, show that the following relations, which are defined in the text, are well-founded:

(a)   The proper-end relation, $x \prec_{end} y$, is well-founded (over *string*).

(b)   The proper-intersperse relation, $x \prec_{inter} y$, is well-founded (over *string*).

(c)   The proper-subbag relation, $x \subset y$, is well-founded (over *bag*).

State any basic properties of the theories of strings and bags you use; you need not prove them.

Problem 1.6 (asymmetry of well-founded relations)   page 42

Use the *minimal-element* condition to give an alternative proof of the *asymmetry* proposition, i.e., that any well-founded relation $\prec$ (over *obj*) is asymmetric (over *obj*).

Hint: Take $F[x]$ in the *minimal-element* condition to be

$$(\exists\ obj\ y)[x \prec y\ \ and\ \ y \prec x].$$

Problem 1.7 (union relation)   page 45

Prove the *union-relation* proposition, i.e., that if two binary relations $\prec_1$ and $\prec_2$ are well-founded over two disjoint classes of objects, characterized by obj_1 and obj_2, respectively, then the corresponding union relation $\prec_{union}$ is well-founded over the union of the two classes, characterized by obj.

Hint: Use the *minimal-element* condition for well-foundedness.

Problem 1.8 (combinations of well-founded relations)   page 45

Suppose that $\prec_1$ and $\prec_2$ are two binary relations that are well-founded over obj. Which of the following relations are also well-founded over obj? Justify your answers.

(a)   The conjunction relation $\prec_{and}$, defined by

$$(\forall\ obj\ x,\ y) \begin{bmatrix} x \prec_{and} y \\ \equiv \\ x \prec_1 y\ \ and\ \ x \prec_2 y \end{bmatrix}.$$

(b)   The disjunction relation $\prec_{or}$, defined by

$$(\forall\ obj\ x,\ y) \begin{bmatrix} x \prec_{or} y \\ \equiv \\ x \prec_1 y\ \ or\ \ x \prec_2 y \end{bmatrix}.$$

(c)   The composition relation $\prec_{comp}$, defined by

$$(\forall \; obj \; x, \; y) \begin{bmatrix} x \prec_{comp} y \\ \equiv \\ (\exists \; obj \; z)[x \prec_1 z \; and \; z \prec_2 y] \end{bmatrix}.$$

Problem 1.9 (log relation)   page 46

Show that the log relation $\prec_{log}$, defined by the axiom

$$(\forall \; integer \; x, y) \begin{bmatrix} x \prec_{log} y \\ \equiv \\ (\exists \; integer \; z)[x^z = y \; and \; not \, (x = y)] \end{bmatrix} \qquad (log)$$

is well-founded over $integer$.

Hint: Use the *union-relation* proposition.

2

Applications

Now that we have established that several relations are well-founded, we know that the *well-founded induction* principle holds for these relations. Let us see how to use the *well-founded induction* principle in proofs.

2.1 EXAMPLE: PRIME DECOMPOSITION

We shall use the *well-founded induction* principle to prove a property of the nonnegative integers, that

> every integer x greater than 1 can be expressed as a product
>
> $$x_1 \cdot x_2 \cdot \ \cdots \ \cdot x_n$$
>
> of (one or more) primes $x_1, x_2, \ldots, x_n$.

A prime is an integer greater than 1 that cannot be expressed as a product of positive integers other than itself and 1; thus 2, 3, 5, and 7 are primes, but 6 is not because $6 = 2 \cdot 3$. The primes are characterized by the predicate $prime(x)$, defined by the axiom

$$(\forall \, integer \ x) \left[\begin{array}{l} prime(x) \\ \equiv \\ x > 1 \ \ and \\ \\ not \ (\exists \, integer \ y, z) \left[\begin{array}{l} x = y \cdot z \\ and \ \ y > 1 \\ and \ \ z > 1 \end{array} \right] \end{array} \right] \qquad (prime)$$

To express the property we want, we first define the *decomposition* relation *decomp*(x), which is true if x can be decomposed into a product of (one or more) primes, by the axiom

$$(\forall\ integer\ x)\ \left[\begin{array}{c} decomp(x) \\ \equiv \\ \left[\begin{array}{c} prime(x) \\ or \\ (\exists\ integer\ y,\ z)\ \left[\begin{array}{l} decomp(y)\ and \\ decomp(z)\ and \\ x = y\cdot z \end{array}\right] \end{array}\right] \end{array}\right] \qquad (decomp)$$

This axiom immediately implies the two properties

$$(\forall\ integer\ x)\ \left[\begin{array}{l} if\ \ prime(x) \\ then\ \ decomp(x) \end{array}\right] \qquad\qquad (prime)$$

$$(\forall\ integer\ x,\ y)\ \left[\begin{array}{l} if\ \ decomp(x)\ and\ \ decomp(y) \\ then\ \ decomp(x\cdot y) \end{array}\right] \qquad (multiplication)$$

In other words, each prime is decomposable into a product of primes (namely, itself) and, if two nonnegative integers are decomposable, so is their product.

The property we would like to establish is then expressed as follows:

Proposition (prime decomposition)

The sentence

$$(\forall\ integer\ x)\ \left[\begin{array}{l} if\ \ x > 1 \\ then\ \ decomp(x) \end{array}\right] \qquad (prime\ decomposition)$$

is valid. ∎

Proof

It suffices (by the definition of *positive*) to establish the sentence

$$(\forall\ positive\ x)\ \left[\begin{array}{l} if\ \ x > 1 \\ then\ \ decomp(x) \end{array}\right].$$

The proof is by well-founded induction over *positive* with respect to the proper-divides relation $\prec_{div}$; this relation was shown to be well-founded over *positive*.

We shall use the following property of the proper-divides relation $\prec_{div}$:

$$(\forall\, positive\ x,\ y) \left[\begin{array}{c} x \prec_{div} y \\ \equiv \\ (\exists\, integer\ z) \left[\begin{array}{c} x \cdot z = y \\ and\ \ z > 1 \end{array} \right] \end{array} \right] \qquad (multiplication)$$

We take the inductive sentence to be

$$\mathcal{F}[x]: \quad \begin{array}{l} if\ \ x > 1 \\ then\ \ decomp(x) \end{array}$$

and prove

$$(\forall\, positive\ x)\,\mathcal{F}[x].$$

Inductive Step

We would like to show

$$(\forall\, positive\ x) \left[\begin{array}{l} if\ \ (\forall\, positive\ x') \left[\begin{array}{l} if\ \ x' \prec_{div} x \\ then\ \ \mathcal{F}[x'] \end{array} \right] \\ then\ \ \mathcal{F}[x] \end{array} \right].$$

Consider an arbitrary positive integer x, and assume the induction hypothesis

$$(\dagger) \qquad (\forall\, positive\ x') \left[\begin{array}{l} if\ \ x' \prec_{div} x \\ then\ \ \mathcal{F}[x'] \end{array} \right].$$

We would like to show that then the desired conclusion $\mathcal{F}[x]$ is true, that is,

$$\begin{array}{l} if\ \ x > 1 \\ then\ \ decomp(x). \end{array}$$

Suppose that

$$x > 1;$$

we must show that

$$(\dagger\dagger) \qquad decomp(x).$$

The proof distinguishes between two cases.

Case: $prime(x)$

Then (by the *prime* property of *decomp*)

$$decomp(x),$$

as we wanted to show.

Case: not $(prime(x))$

Then (by the *prime* axiom, because $x > 1$) there exist nonnegative integers y and z such that

$$x = y \cdot z \quad and \quad y > 1 \quad and \quad z > 1.$$

Since (by the *commutativity* property of multiplication)

$$y \cdot z = x \qquad \qquad z \cdot y = x$$
$$and \ z > 1 \quad and \quad and \ y > 1,$$

we have (by the preceding *multiplication* property of the proper-divides relation $\prec_{div}$) that

$$y \prec_{div} x \qquad and \qquad z \prec_{div} x.$$

By our induction hypothesis (†), taking x' to be y (because y is positive) and taking x' to be z (because z is positive), we have

$$if \ y \prec_{div} x \qquad\qquad if \ z \prec_{div} x$$
$$then \ \mathcal{F}[y] \quad and \quad then \ \mathcal{F}[z].$$

Therefore (because $y \prec_{div} x$ and $z \prec_{div} x$), we have $\mathcal{F}[y]$ and $\mathcal{F}[z]$, that is,

$$if \ y > 1 \qquad\qquad if \ z > 1$$
$$then \ decomp(y) \quad and \quad then \ decomp(z).$$

But we know that $y > 1$ and $z > 1$; therefore

$$decomp(y) \ and \ decomp(z).$$

It follows (by the *multiplication* property of *decomp*) that

$$decomp(y \cdot z).$$

That is (since $x = y \cdot z$),

$$decomp(x),$$

as we wanted to show (††). ⌐

Remark (why well-founded induction?)

The preceding proof is much more convenient to carry out by well-founded induction than by stepwise induction. If we attempted to use the decomposition version, say, of the *stepwise induction* principle, we would not have been able to use the induction hypothesis $\mathcal{F}[x-1]$ to establish that $\mathcal{F}[y]$ and $\mathcal{F}[z]$; we know that y and z are proper divisors of x, but not that $y = x - 1$ or that $z = x - 1$. To establish the same result by stepwise induction would require a more complex inductive sentence. ◢

2.2   EXAMPLE: ALTERNATIVE REVERSE

Recall that, in the theory of strings, we defined (Section [I]7.4) the function $reverse(x)$, which reverses the characters of the string x, by the following axioms:

$$reverse(\Lambda) = \Lambda \qquad\qquad (empty)$$

$$\begin{matrix}(\forall\ char\ u)\\(\forall\ string\ y)\end{matrix}\Big[reverse(u \bullet y) \;=\; reverse(y) * u\Big] \qquad (prefix)$$

Some properties of the *reverse* function that we established are

$$(\forall\ char\ u)\Big[reverse(u) \;=\; u\Big] \qquad\qquad (character)$$

$$(\forall\ string\ x)\Big[reverse\big(reverse(x)\big) \;=\; x\Big] \qquad\qquad (reverse)$$

We have already seen an alternative definition of the *reverse* function in terms of an auxiliary binary function symbol $rev2(x, y)$.

Now consider the unary function $rev1$, defined by the following axioms:

$$rev1(\Lambda) \;=\; \Lambda \qquad\qquad (empty)$$

$$(\forall\ char\ u)\Big[rev1(u) \;=\; u\Big] \qquad\qquad (character)$$

$$\begin{matrix}(\forall\ char\ u)\\(\forall\ string\ y)\end{matrix}\left[\begin{array}{l}if\ \ not\ (y = \Lambda)\\then\ \ rev1(u \bullet y)\ =\\\qquad \left\{\begin{array}{l}head\big(rev1(y)\big)\bullet\\rev1\big(u \bullet rev1\big(tail\big(rev1(y)\big)\big)\big)\end{array}\right\}\end{array}\right] \qquad (prefix)$$

This is intended to be another alternative definition for the *reverse* function. It was concocted (by E. Ashcroft) to show that *reverse* could be computed using only the simple functions $u \bullet y$, $head(y)$, and $tail(y)$ and without using an auxiliary function.

The explanation of the obscure *prefix* axiom is that, if *rev1* does reverse the characters of a string, $head\big(rev1(y)\big)$ is the last character of $u \bullet y$, and $u \bullet rev1\big(tail\big(rev1(y)\big)\big)$ is the result of deleting the last character of $u \bullet y$, where y is nonempty. For example, if u is A and y is BC, $head\big(rev1(y)\big)$ is C and $u \bullet rev1\big(tail\big(rev1(y)\big)\big)$ is AB.

We would like to show that *rev1* does indeed provide an alternative definition of the *reverse* function.

Proposition (alternative definition of reverse)

The sentence

$$(\forall \, string \; x)\big[reverse(x) \; = \; rev1(x)\big]$$

is valid. ⌟

In our proof we use the following axioms and properties:

The special *character* equality axiom for strings

$$(\forall \, char \; u)\big[u \bullet \Lambda \; = \; u\big] \qquad\qquad (character)$$

The *decomposition* property of strings

$$(\forall \, string \; x)\left[\begin{array}{l} if \;\; not \; (x \, = \, \Lambda) \\ then \quad \begin{array}{l}(\exists \, char \; u)\\ (\exists \, string \; y)\end{array} \big[x \; = \; u \bullet y\big]\end{array}\right] \qquad (decomposition)$$

The *left-prefix* axiom for concatenation

$$\begin{array}{l}(\forall \, char \; u)\\ (\forall \, string \; x, \, y)\end{array}\left[(u \bullet x) * y \; = \; u \bullet (x * y)\right] \qquad (left \; prefix)$$

The decomposition property of *head* and *tail*

$$(\forall \, string \; x)\left[\begin{array}{l} if \;\; not \; (x \, = \, \Lambda) \\ then \;\; x \; = \; head(x) \bullet tail(x)\end{array}\right] \qquad (decomposition)$$

We shall use several properties of the *length* function over strings (Section [I]7.8), including the axiom

$$\begin{array}{l}(\forall \, char \; u)\\ (\forall \, string \; x)\end{array}\left[length(u \bullet x) \; = \; length(x) + 1\right] \qquad (prefix)$$

and the properties

$$(\forall \, string \; x)\big[length\,(reverse(x)) \;=\; length(x)\big] \qquad\qquad (reverse)$$

$$(\forall \, string \; x) \begin{bmatrix} if & not \; (x = \Lambda) \\ then & length\,(tail(x)) < length(x) \end{bmatrix} \qquad\qquad (tail)$$

We also shall use other properties of the nonnegative integers without explicitly mentioning them.

Proof

We want to show that

$$(\forall \; string \; x)\big[reverse(x) \;=\; rev1(x)\big].$$

The proof is by well-founded induction with respect to the length relation $\prec_{length}$, which was defined by the axiom

$$(\forall \, string \; x, \; y) \begin{bmatrix} x \prec_{length} y \\ \equiv \\ length(x) < length(y) \end{bmatrix} \qquad\qquad (length \; relation)$$

We have established that this relation is well-founded over the strings.

We take the inductive sentence to be

$$\mathcal{F}[x] : \quad reverse(x) \;=\; rev1(x)$$

and prove

$$(\forall \, string \; x)\mathcal{F}[x].$$

Inductive Step

We would like to show

$$(\forall \, string \; x) \begin{bmatrix} if \; (\forall \, string \; x') \begin{bmatrix} if \; x' \prec_{length} x \\ then \; \mathcal{F}[x'] \end{bmatrix} \\ then \; \mathcal{F}[x] \end{bmatrix}.$$

Consider an arbitrary string x, and assume the induction hypothesis

$$(\dagger) \qquad (\forall \, string \; x') \begin{bmatrix} if \; x' \prec_{length} x \\ then \; \mathcal{F}[x'] \end{bmatrix}.$$

We show that then the desired conclusion $\mathcal{F}[x]$ is true, that is,

$$reverse(x) \ = \ rev1(x).$$

The proof distinguishes among three cases, corresponding to the three axioms for *rev1*.

Case: $x = \Lambda$

Then we would like to show $\mathcal{F}[\Lambda]$, that is,

$$reverse(\Lambda) \ = \ rev1(\Lambda).$$

But we have

$$reverse(\Lambda) \ = \ \Lambda$$
$$\text{(by the } empty \text{ axiom for } reverse\text{)}$$

$$= \ rev1(\Lambda)$$
$$\text{(by the } empty \text{ axiom for } rev1\text{)}.$$

Case: $char(x)$

We would like to show $\mathcal{F}[x]$, that is,

$$reverse(x) \ = \ rev1(x).$$

But (because x is a character) we have

$$reverse(x) \ = \ x$$
$$\text{(by the } character \text{ property of } reverse\text{)}$$

$$= \ rev1(x)$$
$$\text{(by the } character \text{ axiom for } rev1\text{)}.$$

Case: $not \ (x = \Lambda) \ \ and \ \ not \ \big(char(x)\big)$

Then (by the *decomposition* property of strings, because $not \ (x = \Lambda)$), there exist a character u and a string y such that

$$x \ = \ u \bullet y.$$

We know that

$$not \ (y = \Lambda)$$

because, otherwise (by the *character* equality axiom for strings), $x = u \bullet \Lambda = u$, and hence (because u is a character) $char(x)$, contrary to our case assumption.

Because $x = u \bullet y$, we must show $\mathcal{F}[u \bullet y]$, that is,

$$reverse(u \bullet y) \;=\; rev1(u \bullet y),$$

or, equivalently (by the *prefix* axioms for *reverse* and *rev1*, because *not* $(y = \Lambda)$),

$$(1) \qquad reverse(y) * u \;=\; \left\{ \begin{array}{l} head\,(rev1(y)) \bullet \\ rev1\,(u \bullet rev1\,(tail\,(rev1(y)))) \end{array} \right\}.$$

We use the induction hypothesis three times (steps 1 to 3) to replace *rev1* by *reverse* in (1) and then (step 4) prove the resulting equality.

Step 1: replacement of first rev1

By our induction hypothesis (†), taking x' to be y, we have

$$\text{if } y \prec_{length} x$$
$$\text{then } \mathcal{F}[y],$$

that is (because $x = u \bullet y$),

$$\text{if } y \prec_{length} u \bullet y$$
$$\text{then } reverse(y) \;=\; rev1(y).$$

But because (by the *prefix* axiom for the *length* function)

$$length(y) \;<\; length(u \bullet y),$$

it follows (by the definition of $\prec_{length}$) that

$$y \prec_{length} u \bullet y.$$

Therefore we can conclude that

$$reverse(y) \;=\; rev1(y).$$

Our desired result (1) can thus be transformed to

$$(2) \qquad reverse(y) * u \;=\; \left\{ \begin{array}{l} head\,(reverse(y)) \bullet \\ rev1\,(u \bullet rev1\,(tail\,(reverse(y)))) \end{array} \right\}.$$

Step 2: replacement of second rev1

By our induction hypothesis (†), taking x' to be $tail\,(reverse(y))$, we have

$$\text{if } tail\,(reverse(y)) \prec_{length} x$$
$$\text{then } \mathcal{F}\big[tail\,(reverse(y))\big];$$

that is (because $x = u \bullet y$),

$$\textit{if} \;\; tail(reverse(y)) \prec_{length} u \bullet y$$
$$\textit{then} \;\; \Big(reverse\big(tail(reverse(y))\big) \;=\; rev1\big(tail(reverse(y))\big)\Big).$$

But (by properties of the *length* function, because $not\,(y = \Lambda)$) we have

$$length\big(tail(reverse(y))\big)$$
$$< \;\; length\big(reverse(y)\big)$$
$$= \;\; length(y)$$
$$< \;\; length(u \bullet y),$$

and hence (by the definition of the $\prec_{length}$ relation)

$$tail\big(reverse(y)\big) \;\; \prec_{length} \;\; u \bullet y.$$

Therefore we may conclude that

$$reverse\big(tail(reverse(y))\big) \;\;=\;\; rev1\big(tail(reverse(y))\big).$$

Our desired result (2) can thus be transformed to

$$(3) \qquad reverse(y) * u \;\;=\;\; \left\{ \begin{array}{l} head\big(reverse(y)\big) \bullet \\ rev1\big(u \bullet reverse(tail(reverse(y)))\big) \end{array} \right\}.$$

Step 3: replacement of third rev1

By our induction hypothesis (†), this time taking x' to be the expression $u \bullet reverse\big(tail(reverse(y))\big)$, we have

$$\textit{if} \;\; u \bullet reverse\big(tail(reverse(y))\big) \prec_{length} x$$
$$\textit{then} \;\; \mathcal{F}\big[u \bullet reverse(tail(reverse(y)))\big];$$

that is (because $x = u \bullet y$),

$$\textit{if} \;\; u \bullet reverse\big(tail(reverse(y))\big) \prec_{length} \;\; u \bullet y$$
$$\textit{then} \;\; \left[\begin{array}{l} reverse\big(u \bullet reverse(tail(reverse(y)))\big) \\ = \\ rev1\big(u \bullet reverse(tail(reverse(y)))\big) \end{array} \right].$$

But (by properties of the *length* function, because $not\,(y = \Lambda)$ and therefore $not\,(reverse(y) = \Lambda)$), we have

$$length\big(u \bullet reverse(tail(reverse(y)))\big)$$
$$= \;\; length\big(reverse(tail(reverse(y)))\big) + 1$$

$$= \ length\big(tail\big(reverse(y)\big)\big) + 1$$

$$< \ length\big(reverse(y)\big) + 1$$

$$= \ length(y) + 1$$

$$= \ length(u \bullet y).$$

In short,

$$length\big(u \bullet reverse\big(tail\big(reverse(y)\big)\big)\big) \ < \ length(u \bullet y),$$

and hence (by the definition of the $\prec_{length}$ relation)

$$u \bullet reverse\big(tail\big(reverse(y)\big)\big) \ \prec_{length} \ u \bullet y.$$

Therefore we can conclude that

$$reverse\big(u \bullet reverse\big(tail\big(reverse(y)\big)\big)\big)$$
$$=$$
$$rev1\big(u \bullet reverse\big(tail\big(reverse(y)\big)\big)\big).$$

Our desired result (3) can thus be transformed to

$$(4) \qquad reverse(y) * u \ = \ \left\{ \begin{array}{l} head\big(reverse(y)\big) \bullet \\ reverse\big(u \bullet reverse\big(tail\big(reverse(y)\big)\big)\big) \end{array} \right\}$$

Step 4: proof of the equality

We have

$$\left\{ \begin{array}{l} head\big(reverse(y)\big) \bullet \\ reverse\big(u \bullet reverse\big(tail\big(reverse(y)\big)\big)\big) \end{array} \right\}$$

$$= \left\{ \begin{array}{l} head\big(reverse(y)\big) \bullet \\ \big(reverse\big(reverse\big(tail\big(reverse(y)\big)\big)\big) * u\big) \end{array} \right\}$$

(by the *prefix* axiom for *reverse*,
because u is a character)

$$= \ head\big(reverse(y)\big) \bullet \big(tail\big(reverse(y)\big) * u\big)$$

(by the *reverse* property of *reverse*)

$$= \ \big(head\big(reverse(y)\big) \bullet tail\big(reverse(y)\big)\big) * u$$

(by the *left-prefix* axiom for concatenation)

$$= \ reverse(y) * u$$

(by the *decomposition* property of *head* and *tail*,
because $not \ (reverse(y) = \Lambda)$).

In short,

$$
reverse(y) * u \;=\; \left\{ \begin{array}{l} head\big(reverse(y)\big) \bullet \\ reverse\big(u \bullet reverse\big(tail\big(reverse(y)\big)\big)\big) \end{array} \right\},
$$

which is our desired result (4). ⏌

Remark (why the length relation?)

The preceding proof uses well-founded induction with respect to the length relation $\prec_{length}$ over the strings. It could not be carried out by well-founded induction over the proper-substring relation $\prec_{string}$, that is, by complete induction over the strings. In particular, we have

$$
tail\big(reverse(y)\big) \prec_{length} u \bullet y,
$$

but we would not be able to show that

$$
tail\big(reverse(y)\big) \prec_{string} u \bullet y,
$$

which would be required to justify the use of the induction hypothesis in such a proof.

The choice of a well-founded relation for a particular proof is often suggested by the form of the axioms or other valid sentences of the theory. ⏌

Problem 2.1 requires the use of the *well-founded induction* principle.

2.3   EXAMPLE: QUICKSORT

The reasoning involved in the following example is typical of that found in many proofs of the correctness of programs.

THE SORT FUNCTION

Consider the theory of tuples of nonnegative integers. We introduced (Section [I]12.6) a unary function symbol $sort(x)$, which, for any tuple x, produces a tuple whose elements are the same as those of x but rearranged into (weakly) increasing order. It was defined by the axioms

$$sort(\langle\,\rangle) = \langle\,\rangle \qquad\qquad (empty)$$

$$\begin{aligned}&(\forall\ atom\ u)\\&(\forall\ tuple\ x)\end{aligned}\left[sort(u \diamond x)\ =\ insert\big(u,\ sort(x)\big)\right] \qquad (insertion)$$

where $insert\big(u,\ sort(x)\big)$ inserts a nonnegative integer u in its place in the sorted tuple x.

The $perm(x,\ y)$ relation, which indicates that a tuple x is a permutation (i.e., can be obtained by rearranging the elements) of another tuple y, was defined (Section [I]12.4) by the axioms

$$perm(\langle\,\rangle,\ \langle\,\rangle) \qquad\qquad (empty)$$

$$\begin{aligned}&(\forall\ atom\ u)\\&(\forall\ tuple\ x_1,\ x_2,\ y_1,\ y_2)\end{aligned}\left[\begin{array}{l}perm\big(x_1 \diamond \langle u\rangle \diamond x_2,\ y_1 \diamond \langle u\rangle \diamond y_2\big)\\ \equiv\\ perm(x_1 \diamond x_2,\ y_1 \diamond y_2)\end{array}\right]$$
$$(append\ singleton)$$

$$(\forall\ tuple\ x,\ y)\left[\begin{array}{l}if\ \ perm(x,\ y)\\ then\ \ (\forall\ atom\ u)\,[u \in x\ \equiv\ u \in y]\end{array}\right] \qquad (member)$$

In this definition we used the append function $x \diamond y$, which yields the tuple whose elements are the elements of the tuple x followed by the elements of the tuple y, and the member relation $u \in x$, which indicates that the atom u is one of the elements of the tuple x. (Both are defined in Section [I]12.1.)

The $ordered(x)$ relation, which indicates that the elements of the tuple x are (weakly) increasing, was defined (Section [I]12.5) by the axioms

$$ordered(\langle\,\rangle) \qquad\qquad (empty)$$

$$(\forall\ atom\ u)\left[ordered(\langle u\rangle)\right] \qquad\qquad (singleton)$$

$$\begin{aligned}&(\forall\ atom\ u,\ v)\\&\quad(\forall\ tuple\ x)\end{aligned}\left[\begin{array}{l}ordered\big(u \diamond (v \diamond x)\big)\\ \equiv\\ u \le v\ \ and\ \ ordered(v \diamond x)\end{array}\right] \qquad (double\ insertion)$$

In the *sort* proposition, we established that

$$(\forall\ tuple\ x)\big[ordered\big(sort(x)\big)\big] \qquad\qquad\qquad (ordered)$$

$$(\forall\ tuple\ x)\big[perm\big(x,\ sort(x)\big)\big] \qquad\qquad (permutation)$$

We indicated that *sort* is the only function that satisfies the *ordered* and *permutation* properties, that is,

$$(\forall\ tuple\ x,\ y)\ \begin{bmatrix} if\ \ ordered(y)\ \ and \\ perm(x,\ y) \\ then\ \ y = sort(x) \end{bmatrix} \qquad (uniqueness)$$

THE QUICKSORT FUNCTION

Here we provide an alternative definition of the *sort* function by introducing a unary function *quicksort*(x), which sorts the elements of x by a different method. This function is defined in terms of two auxiliary binary functions, *lesseq* and *greater*. If u is a nonnegative integer and y is a tuple, *lesseq*(u, y) is the subtuple of all elements of y less than or equal to u, and *greater*(u, y) is the subtuple of all elements of y strictly greater than u. For example,

$$lesseq\big(2,\ \langle 3,\ 2,\ 1,\ 5,\ 2,\ 4\rangle\big)\ =\ \langle 2,\ 1,\ 2\rangle$$

$$greater\big(2,\ \langle 3,\ 2,\ 1,\ 5,\ 2,\ 4\rangle\big)\ =\ \langle 3,\ 5,\ 4\rangle.$$

The function *quicksort* is defined by the axioms

$$\boxed{\begin{array}{ll} quicksort\big(\langle\ \rangle\big)\ =\ \langle\ \rangle & (empty) \\[2em] \begin{array}{l}(\forall\ atom\ u) \\ (\forall\ tuple\ y)\end{array}\ \begin{bmatrix} quicksort(u \diamond y) \\ = \\ \begin{bmatrix} quicksort\big(lesseq(u,\ y)\big)\diamond \\ \langle u\rangle\diamond \\ quicksort\big(greater(u,\ y)\big)\end{bmatrix}\end{bmatrix} & (insertion)\end{array}}$$

In other words, if the given tuple is the empty tuple $\langle\ \rangle$, the value of the function *quicksort* is also $\langle\ \rangle$. On the other hand, if the given tuple is of form $u \diamond y$, the value of the function is a tuple consisting of

- Those elements of y less than or equal to u (in increasing order),

- The element u itself, and

- Those elements of y strictly greater than u (in increasing order).

The auxiliary function $lesseq(u, y)$ is defined by the axioms

$$(\forall\ atom\ u)\big[lesseq(u, \langle\,\rangle) = \langle\,\rangle\big] \qquad\qquad\qquad (empty)$$

$$\begin{array}{c}(\forall\ atom\ u, v)\\ (\forall\ tuple\ x)\end{array}\left[lesseq(u, v \diamond x) = \left\{\begin{array}{l}if\ \ v \le u\\ then\ \ v \diamond lesseq(u, x)\\ else\ \ lesseq(u, x)\end{array}\right\}\right]$$

$$(insertion)$$

Similarly, the auxiliary function $greater(u, y)$ is defined by the axioms

$$(\forall\ atom\ u)\big[greater(u, \langle\,\rangle) = \langle\,\rangle\big] \qquad\qquad\qquad (empty)$$

$$\begin{array}{c}(\forall\ atom\ u, v)\\ (\forall\ tuple\ x)\end{array}\left[greater(u, v \diamond x) = \left\{\begin{array}{l}if\ \ not\ (v \le u)\\ then\ \ v \diamond greater(u, x)\\ else\ \ greater(u, x)\end{array}\right\}\right]$$

$$(insertion)$$

In the *insertion* axiom for *greater*, we have written **not** $(v \le u)$ rather than $v > u$ to simplify the discussion.

The axioms for the $quicksort(x)$ function suggest a **way to** sort a tuple x.

Example (computation of quicksort)

Suppose we want to "quicksort" the tuple $\langle 2,\ 2,\ 4,\ 1,\ 3\rangle$. Then we have

$$quicksort\big(\langle 2,\ 2,\ 4,\ 1,\ 3\rangle\big)$$

$$=\ quicksort\big(2 \diamond \langle 2,\ 4,\ 1,\ 3\rangle\big)$$

$$\begin{aligned}=\ &quicksort\big(lesseq(2,\ \langle 2,\ 4,\ 1,\ 3\rangle)\big)\diamond\\ &\langle 2\rangle\diamond\\ &quicksort\big(greater(2,\ \langle 2,\ 4,\ 1,\ 3\rangle)\big)\\ &\text{(by the *insertion* axiom for *quicksort*)}\end{aligned}$$

$$\begin{aligned}=\ &quicksort(\langle 2,\ 1\rangle) \diamond \langle 2\rangle \diamond quicksort(\langle 4,\ 3\rangle)\\ &\text{(by repeated application of the axioms}\\ &\text{for *lesseq* and *greater*)}\end{aligned}$$

$$\begin{aligned}=\ &\langle 1,\ 2\rangle \diamond \langle 2\rangle \diamond \langle 3,\ 4\rangle\\ &\text{(by repeated application of the axioms)}\end{aligned}$$

$$= \langle 1, 2, 2, 3, 4 \rangle.$$

In short,

$$quicksort(\langle 2, 2, 4, 1, 3 \rangle) = \langle 1, 2, 2, 3, 4 \rangle. \quad \blacksquare$$

We would like to show that the *quicksort* function provides an alternative definition of *sort*, that is, that

$$(\forall\ tuple\ x)\,[quicksort(x) = sort(x)] \qquad\qquad (sorting)$$

For this purpose, it suffices (by the *uniqueness* property of *sort*) to show that the tuple *quicksort*(*x*) is in increasing order, that is,

$$(\forall\ tuple\ x)\,[ordered\,(quicksort(x))] \qquad\qquad (ordered)$$

and that the elements of *quicksort*(*x*) are the same as those of *x*, that is,

$$(\forall\ tuple\ x)\,[perm\,(x,\ quicksort(x))] \qquad\qquad (permutation)$$

PROPERTIES USED

We shall use several properties of the auxiliary functions *lesseq* and *greater*.

From the axioms for *lesseq* we can prove the properties

$$\begin{matrix}(\forall\ atom\ u)\\(\forall\ tuple\ x)\end{matrix}\,[tuple\,(lesseq(u,\ x))] \qquad\qquad (sort)$$

$$\begin{matrix}(\forall\ atom\ u)\\(\forall\ tuple\ x)\end{matrix}\,[lesseq(u, x) \subseteq x] \qquad\qquad (subtuple)$$

$$\begin{matrix}(\forall\ atom\ u,\ v)\\(\forall\ tuple\ x)\end{matrix}\,\begin{bmatrix}if\ \ v \in lesseq(u,\ x)\\then\ \ v \le u\end{bmatrix} \qquad\qquad (bound)$$

From the axioms for *greater* we can prove the properties

$$\begin{matrix}(\forall\ atom\ u)\\(\forall\ tuple\ x)\end{matrix}\,[tuple\,(greater(u,\ x))] \qquad\qquad (sort)$$

$$\begin{matrix}(\forall\ atom\ u)\\(\forall\ tuple\ x)\end{matrix}\,[greater(u, x) \subseteq x] \qquad\qquad (subtuple)$$

$$\begin{array}{l}(\forall\,atom\ u,\ v) \\ (\forall\,tuple\ x)\end{array}\left[\begin{array}{l}if\ \ v\in greater(u,\ x) \\ then\ \ not\ (v\leq u)\end{array}\right] \qquad (bound)$$

We can then prove that the elements of x are the same as the elements of $lesseq(u,\ x)$ and $greater(u,\ x)$ together, that is,

$$\begin{array}{l}(\forall\,atom\ u) \\ (\forall\,tuple\ x)\end{array}\left[perm\big(x,\ lesseq(u,\ x)\diamond greater(u,\ x)\big)\right] \quad (permutation)$$

and that the *quicksort* function always yields a tuple, that is,

$$(\forall\,tuple\ x)\left[tuple\big(quicksort(x)\big)\right] \qquad (sort)$$

Furthermore, we shall use several properties that were proved or mentioned in Volume I, including

Properties of the weak less-than relation $\leq$

$$(\forall\,integer\ x,\ y)\left[x\leq y\ \ or\ \ y\leq x\right] \qquad (totality)$$

$$(\forall\,integer\ x,\ y,\ z)\left[\begin{array}{l}if\ \ x\leq y\ \ and\ \ y\leq z \\ then\ \ x\leq z\end{array}\right] \qquad (transitivity)$$

Property of the append function $\diamond$

$$\begin{array}{l}(\forall\,atom\ u) \\ (\forall\,tuple\ x)\end{array}\left[\langle u\rangle\diamond x\ =\ u\diamond x\right] \qquad (singleton)$$

Properties of the subtuple $\subseteq$ and proper-subtuple $\subset$ relations

$$\begin{array}{l}(\forall\,atom\ u) \\ (\forall\,tuple\ x)\end{array}\left[x\subset(u\diamond x)\right] \qquad (adjacent)$$

$$(\forall\,tuple\ x,\ y,\ z)\left[\begin{array}{l}if\ \ x\subseteq y\ \ and\ \ y\subset z \\ then\ \ x\subset z\end{array}\right] \qquad (left\ mixed\ transitivity)$$

Property of the permutation relation

$$(\forall\,tuple\ x_1,\ x_2,\ y_1,\ y_2)\left[\begin{array}{l}if\ \ perm(x_1,\ y_1)\ \ and \\ \qquad perm(x_2,\ y_2) \\ then\ \ perm(x_1\diamond x_2,\ y_1\diamond y_2)\end{array}\right] \quad (append)$$

Properties of the *ordered* relation

$$\begin{array}{l}(\forall\,atom\ u) \\ (\forall\,tuple\ x)\end{array}\left[\begin{array}{l}ordered(u\diamond x) \\ \equiv \\ \left[\begin{array}{l}ordered(x) \\ and \\ (\forall\,atom\ v)\left[\begin{array}{l}if\ \ v\in x \\ then\ \ u\leq v\end{array}\right]\end{array}\right]\end{array}\right] \qquad (insertion)$$

$$(\forall \ tuple \ x, \ y) \left[\begin{array}{l} ordered(x \diamond y) \\ \equiv \\ \left[\begin{array}{l} ordered(x) \quad and \quad ordered(y) \\ and \\ (\forall \ atom \ v, \ w) \left[\begin{array}{l} if \quad v \in x \quad and \quad w \in y \\ then \quad v \leq w \end{array} \right] \end{array} \right] \end{array} \right] \qquad (append)$$

We shall use other properties of the theory of tuples as well.

THE PROPOSITION

Let us establish the desired properties of *quicksort.*

Proposition (quicksort)

The sentences

$$(\forall \ tuple \ x)\left[perm(x, \ quicksort(x)) \right] \qquad\qquad (permutation)$$

$$(\forall \ tuple \ x)\left[ordered(quicksort(x)) \right] \qquad\qquad (ordered)$$

$$(\forall \ tuple \ x)\left[quicksort(x) \ = \ sort(x) \right] \qquad\qquad (sorting)$$

are valid. ⌋

We have already remarked that (by the *uniqueness* property of the *sort* function) the *ordered* and *permutation* properties imply the *sorting* property; thus we need prove only the first two properties. We prove the *permutation* property first, and then use it in the proof of the *ordered* property.

Proof (*permutation* of *quicksort*)

We show

$$(\forall \ tuple \ x)\left[perm(x, \ quicksort(x)) \right].$$

The proof is by well-founded induction with respect to the proper-subtuple relation $\subset$; we have indicated that this relation is well-founded over the tuples.

We take the inductive sentence to be

$$\mathcal{F}[x]: \quad perm(x, \ quicksort(x)).$$

Inductive Step

We would like to show

$$(\forall\ tuple\ x)\ \left[\begin{matrix} if\ (\forall\ tuple\ x')\ \left[\begin{matrix} if\ x' \subset x \\ then\ \mathcal{F}[x'] \end{matrix}\right] \\ then\ \mathcal{F}[x] \end{matrix}\right].$$

Consider an arbitrary tuple x, and assume the induction hypothesis

$$(\dagger) \qquad (\forall\ tuple\ x')\ \left[\begin{matrix} if\ x' \subset x \\ then\ \mathcal{F}[x'] \end{matrix}\right].$$

We would like to show that then the desired conclusion $\mathcal{F}[x]$ is true, that is,

$$perm\big(x,\ quicksort(x)\big).$$

The proof distinguishes between two cases.

Case: $x = \langle\ \rangle$

We then would like to show $\mathcal{F}[\langle\ \rangle]$, that is,

$$perm\big(\langle\ \rangle,\ quicksort(\langle\ \rangle)\big),$$

or, equivalently (by the *empty* axiom for *quicksort*),

$$perm\big(\langle\ \rangle,\ \langle\ \rangle\big).$$

But this is true (by the *empty* axiom for the permutation relation).

Case: $not\ (x = \langle\ \rangle)$

Then (by the *decomposition* property of tuples), for some atom u and tuple y,

$$x\ =\ u \diamond y.$$

We therefore would like to show $\mathcal{F}[u \diamond y]$, that is,

$$perm\big(u \diamond y,\ quicksort(u \diamond y)\big),$$

or, equivalently (by the *insertion* axiom for *quicksort*),

$$perm\left(u \diamond y,\ \left\{\begin{matrix} quicksort\,(lesseq(u,\ y)) \diamond \\ \langle u \rangle \diamond \\ quicksort\,(greater(u,\ y)) \end{matrix}\right\}\right)$$

or, equivalently (by the *singleton* property of the append function and the *left-empty* axiom for the append function),

$$
perm \left(\langle \, \rangle \diamond \langle u \rangle \diamond y, \;\; \left\{ \begin{array}{l} quicksort(lesseq(u,\,y))\diamond \\ \langle u \rangle \diamond \\ quicksort(greater(u,\,y)) \end{array} \right\} \right).
$$

This is equivalent (by the *append-singleton* axiom for the permutation relation) to

$$
perm \left(\langle \, \rangle \diamond y, \;\; \left\{ \begin{array}{l} quicksort(lesseq(u,\,y)) \\ \diamond \\ quicksort(greater(u,\,y)) \end{array} \right\} \right),
$$

which is equivalent (by the *left-empty* axiom for the append function) to

$$
(\dagger\dagger) \qquad perm \left(y, \;\; \left\{ \begin{array}{l} quicksort(lesseq(u,\,y)) \\ \diamond \\ quicksort(greater(u,\,y)) \end{array} \right\} \right).
$$

Proof of ($\dagger\dagger$)

To show ($\dagger\dagger$), we first want to use the induction hypothesis ($\dagger$) twice, taking x' to be $lesseq(u,\,y)$ and $greater(u,\,y)$, respectively. To justify this use of the induction hypothesis, we must show that $lesseq(u,\,y)$ and $greater(u,\,y)$ are proper subtuples of x, that is, because $x = u \diamond y$,

$$
lesseq(u,\,y) \subset (u \diamond y) \qquad \text{and} \qquad greater(u,\,y) \subset (u \diamond y).
$$

We know (by the *subtuple* properties of *lesseq* and *greater*) that

$$
lesseq(u,\,y) \subseteq y \qquad \text{and} \qquad greater(u,\,y) \subseteq y.
$$

Also (by the *adjacent* property of the proper-subtuple relation $\subset$) we have

$$
y \subset (u \diamond y).
$$

Therefore (by the *left mixed-transitivity* property of the subtuple relation $\subseteq$)

$$
lesseq(u,\,y) \subset (u \diamond y) \qquad \text{and} \qquad greater(u,\,y) \subset (u \diamond y).
$$

By our induction hypothesis ($\dagger$) (taking x' to be $lesseq(u,y)$ and $greater(u,y)$, respectively), we know, because $x = u \diamond y$,

$$
\begin{array}{ccc}
\text{if } \; lesseq(u,\,y) \subset (u \diamond y) & & \text{if } \; greater(u,\,y) \subset (u \diamond y) \\
\text{then } \; \mathcal{F}[lesseq(u,\,y)] & \text{and} & \text{then } \; \mathcal{F}[greater(u,\,y)].
\end{array}
$$

Therefore, we have $\mathcal{F}[lesseq(u,\ y)]$ and $\mathcal{F}[greater(u,\ y)]$, that is,

$$perm\Big(lesseq(u,\ y),\ quicksort(lesseq(u,\ y))\Big)$$

and

$$perm\Big(greater(u,\ y),\ quicksort(greater(u,\ y))\Big).$$

Therefore (by the *append* property of the permutation relation)

$$perm\left(\left\{\begin{matrix} lesseq(u,\ y) \\ \diamond \\ greater(u,\ y) \end{matrix}\right\},\ \left\{\begin{matrix} quicksort(lesseq(u,\ y)) \\ \diamond \\ quicksort(greater(u,\ y)) \end{matrix}\right\}\right).$$

We know (by the *permutation* property of *lesseq* and *greater*) that

$$perm\left(y,\ \left\{\begin{matrix} lesseq(u,\ y) \\ \diamond \\ greater(u,\ y) \end{matrix}\right\}\right).$$

Therefore (by the *transitivity* of the permutation relation)

$$perm\left(y,\ \left\{\begin{matrix} quicksort(lesseq(u,\ y)) \\ \diamond \\ quicksort(greater(u,\ y)) \end{matrix}\right\}\right).$$

But this is the condition (††) we wanted to show. ⌙

The proof of the *ordered* property depends on the *permutation* property of *quicksort*, which we have just proved.

Proof (*ordered* of *quicksort*)

We now want to show

$$(\forall\ tuple\ x)\big[ordered(quicksort(x))\big].$$

The proof is again by well-founded induction with respect to the proper-subtuple relation $\subset$, taking the inductive sentence to be

$$\mathcal{F}[x]:\quad ordered(quicksort(x)).$$

Inductive Step

We would like to show

$$(\forall \ tuple \ x) \ \begin{bmatrix} if \ (\forall \ tuple \ x') \begin{bmatrix} if \ x' \subset x \\ then \ \mathcal{F}[x'] \end{bmatrix} \\ then \ \mathcal{F}[x] \end{bmatrix}.$$

Consider an arbitrary tuple x, and assume the induction hypothesis

$$(\dagger) \qquad (\forall \ tuple \ x') \begin{bmatrix} if \ x' \subset x \\ then \ \mathcal{F}[x'] \end{bmatrix}.$$

We would like to show that then the desired conclusion $\mathcal{F}[x]$ is true, that is,

$$ordered \ (quicksort(x)).$$

The proof distinguishes between two cases.

Case: $x = \langle \ \rangle$

We therefore would like to show $\mathcal{F}[\langle \ \rangle]$, that is,

$$ordered \ (quicksort(\langle \ \rangle)),$$

or, equivalently (by the *empty* axiom for *quicksort*),

$$ordered(\langle \ \rangle).$$

But this is true (by the *empty* axiom for the *ordered* relation).

Case: $not \ (x = \langle \ \rangle)$

Then (by the *decomposition* property of tuples), for some atom u and tuple y,

$$x \ = \ u \diamond y.$$

We therefore would like to show $\mathcal{F}[u \diamond y]$, that is,

$$ordered \ (quicksort(u \diamond y)),$$

or, equivalently (by the *insertion* axiom for *quicksort*),

$$ordered \ \begin{pmatrix} quicksort \ (lesseq(u, \ y)) \diamond \\ \langle u \rangle \diamond \\ quicksort \ (greater(u, \ y)) \end{pmatrix},$$

that is (by the *singleton* property of the append function),

$$ordered \begin{pmatrix} quicksort\,(lesseq(u,y)) \\ \diamond \\ (u \diamond quicksort\,(greater(u,y))) \end{pmatrix}.$$

It suffices (by the *append* property of the *ordered* relation) to establish the conjunction of the three conditions

(1) $\qquad ordered\,(quicksort\,(lesseq(u,\ y)))$

(2) $\qquad ordered\,(u \diamond quicksort\,(greater(u,\ y)))$

(3) $\qquad (\forall\ atom\ v,\ w) \left[if \begin{bmatrix} v\ \in\ quicksort\,(lesseq(u,\ y)) \\ and \\ w\ \in\ u \diamond quicksort\,(greater(u,\ y)) \end{bmatrix} \\ then\ v \leq w \right].$

Condition (2) expands (by the *insertion* property of the *ordered* relation) to the conjunction of the two conditions

(2A) $\qquad ordered\,(quicksort\,(greater(u,\ y)))$

(2B) $\qquad (\forall\ atom\ v) \begin{bmatrix} if\ \ v\ \in\ quicksort\,(greater(u,\ y)) \\ then\ \ u \leq v \end{bmatrix}.$

We must show each of the conditions (1), (2A), (2B), and (3).

Proof of (1) *and* (2A)

As in the proof of the *permutation* part of this proposition, we can establish that

$$lesseq(u,\ y)\ \subset\ (u \diamond y) \qquad and \qquad greater(u,\ y)\ \subset\ (u \diamond y).$$

Therefore, by our induction hypothesis (†), taking x' to be $lesseq(u,y)$ and $greater(u,y)$, respectively, we can conclude $\mathcal{F}\,[lesseq(u,\ y)]$ and $\mathcal{F}\,[greater(u,\ y)]$, that is,

$$ordered\,(quicksort\,(lesseq(u,\ y)))$$

and

$$ordered\,(quicksort\,(greater(u,\ y))).$$

These are precisely the first two conditions (1) and (2A) we wanted to show.

Proof of (2B)

To show condition (2B), consider an arbitrary atom v such that

$$v \in quicksort\,(greater(u,\ y)).$$

We would like to show that then

(††) $u \leq v$.

We know (by the *permutation* property of *quicksort*, the first part of this proposition) that

$$perm\big(greater(u,\, y),\ quicksort(greater(u,\, y))\big).$$

Therefore (by the *member* axiom for the permutation relation, because v is an atom) we have

$$v \in greater(u,\, y)$$

$$\equiv$$

$$v \in quicksort(greater(u,\, y)).$$

Consequently, we can reduce our earlier supposition to

$$v \in greater(u,\, y).$$

We can therefore conclude (by the *bound* property of *greater*) that

$$not\ (v \leq u).$$

Then (by the *totality* of the less-than relation $\leq$) we obtain the desired condition (††), that is, $u \leq v$.

Proof of (3)

To show condition (3), consider arbitrary atoms v and w such that

$$v \in quicksort(lesseq(u,\, y))$$

and

$$w \in u \diamond quicksort(greater(u,\, y)),$$

and therefore (by the *insertion* axiom for the member relation)

$$w = u \quad or \quad w \in quicksort(greater(u,\, y)).$$

We would like to show that then

(‡‡) $v \leq w$.

We know (by the *permutation* property of *quicksort*, the first part of this proposition) that

$$perm\big(lesseq(u,\, y),\ quicksort(lesseq(u,\, y))\big)$$

and

$$perm\Big(greater(u,\ y),\ quicksort\big(greater(u,\ y)\big)\Big).$$

Therefore (by the *member* axiom for the permutation relation, because v and w are atoms) we have

$$v\ \in\ lesseq(u,\ y)$$
$$\equiv$$
$$v\ \in\ quicksort\big(lesseq(u,\ y)\big)$$

and

$$w\ \in\ greater(u,\ y)$$
$$\equiv$$
$$w\ \in\ quicksort\big(greater(u,\ y)\big).$$

Consequently, we can reduce our earlier suppositions to

$$v\ \in\ lesseq(u,\ y)$$

and

$$w = u\quad or\quad w\ \in\ greater(u,\ y).$$

We can therefore conclude (by the *bound* properties of *lesseq* and *greater*) that

$$v \le u$$

and

$$w = u\quad or\quad not\ (w \le u).$$

In the case in which $w = u$, the desired condition (‡‡), that is, $v \le w$, follows (because $v \le u$).

In the case in which $not\ (w \le u)$, we have (by the *totality* of the less-than relation $\le$) that $u \le w$. Therefore (by the *transitivity* of the less-than relation, because $v \le u$) we have the desired condition (‡‡), that is, $v \le w$. ∎

Remark (less-than relation is not essential)

In this section we have assumed that the atoms of our tuples are identified with the nonnegative integers. The only properties of the nonnegative integers we require for the proof of the *quicksort* proposition, however, are the transitivity and the totality of the weak less-than relation $\le$. Therefore we could establish the same results in an augmented theory of tuples in which $\leq$ is replaced by an arbitrary transitive total relation $\prec$ (over the atoms), without mentioning the nonnegative integers at all. ⌐

Remark (why well-founded induction?)

The preceding proofs could not have been carried out in the same way by stepwise induction over the tuples. In the well-founded induction proof, to prove $\mathcal{F}[u \diamond y]$, we used the induction hypothesis

$$(\forall \, tuple \, x') \begin{bmatrix} if \ x' \ \subset \ (u \diamond y) \\ then \ \ \mathcal{F}[x'] \end{bmatrix},$$

taking x' to be $lesseq(u, y)$ and $greater(u, y)$, respectively, to establish the two conditions $\mathcal{F}[lesseq(u, y)]$ and $\mathcal{F}[greater(u, y)]$, which then implied the desired conclusion $\mathcal{F}[u \diamond y]$. In a corresponding stepwise induction proof, the induction hypothesis $\mathcal{F}[y]$ is too weak to establish the conditions $\mathcal{F}[lesseq(u, y)]$ and $\mathcal{F}[greater(u, y)]$. A stepwise induction proof would require a more complex inductive sentence. ⌐

Well-founded induction can be used to prove the correctness of another sorting function.

YET ANOTHER SORTING FUNCTION

Consider again the theory of tuples of nonnegative integers. In this theory, the minimum function $mintuple(x)$, which produces the least element of a nonempty tuple x, was defined (Section [I]12.5) by the axioms

$$(\forall \, atom \, u)[mintuple(u \diamond \langle \, \rangle) = u] \qquad \qquad (singleton)$$

$$
\begin{array}{l}
(\forall \, atom \, u) \\
(\forall \, tuple \, x)
\end{array}
\begin{bmatrix}
if \ \ not \ (x = \langle \, \rangle) \\
then \begin{bmatrix} mintuple(u \diamond x) = \begin{cases} if \ \ u \leq mintuple(x) \\ then \ \ u \\ else \ \ mintuple(x) \end{cases} \end{bmatrix}
\end{bmatrix}
$$

$$(insertion)$$

One can then prove the property

$$(\forall \, tuple \; x) \left[\begin{array}{l} if \;\; not \; (x = \langle \, \rangle) \\ \\ then \; \left[\begin{array}{l} mintuple(x) \in x \\ \quad and \\ (\forall \, atom \; u) \left[\begin{array}{l} if \;\; u \in x \\ then \;\; mintuple(x) \le u \end{array} \right] \end{array} \right] \end{array} \right] \qquad (least)$$

Using the *mintuple* function, we can define the unary function $minsort(x)$ by the axioms

$$\begin{array}{l} minsort(\langle \, \rangle) = \langle \, \rangle \qquad\qquad\qquad\qquad\qquad\qquad\qquad (empty) \\ \\ \begin{array}{l} (\forall \, atom \; u) \\ (\forall \, tuple \; x, \; y) \end{array} \left[\begin{array}{l} if \;\; u = mintuple\left(x \diamond \langle u \rangle \diamond y\right) \\ then \left[\begin{array}{l} minsort\left(x \diamond \langle u \rangle \diamond y\right) \\ \quad = \\ u \diamond minsort(x \diamond y) \end{array} \right] \end{array} \right] \qquad (append) \end{array}$$

In **Problem 2.2** the reader is requested to prove that the *minsort* function provides an alternative definition of the *sort* function.

2.4   EXAMPLE: SQUARE ROOT

In the theory of the nonnegative integers, let the *integer square root* of a given nonnegative integer x be the largest nonnegative integer z such that $z^2 \le x$. For example, the integer square root of 5 is 2, the integer square root of 8 is also 2, but the integer square root of 9 is 3.

The unary function $binsqrt(x)$, which is intended to compute the integer square root of x using binary search, is defined by the axiom

$$(\forall \, integer \; x) \left[binsqrt(x) \;=\; binsqrt2(x, 1) \right] \qquad (binsqrt)$$

where the auxiliary function $binsqrt2(x, u)$ is defined by the axiom

$$\begin{array}{l} (\forall \, integer \; x) \\ (\forall \, positive \; u) \end{array} \left[\begin{array}{l} binsqrt2(x, u) = \\ \left\{ \begin{array}{l} if \;\; u \le x \\ then \;\; if \; \left[binsqrt2(x, 2 \cdot u) + u \right]^2 \le x \\ \qquad\quad then \;\; binsqrt2(x, 2 \cdot u) + u \\ \qquad\quad else \;\; binsqrt2(x, 2 \cdot u) \\ else \;\; 0 \end{array} \right. \end{array} \right] \qquad (binsqrt2)$$

Here the auxiliary function $binsqrt2(x, u)$ yields a nonnegative integer x that is within a positive tolerance u less than $\sqrt{x}$, the real square root of x. In other words, we can show that

$$binsqrt2(x,\ u)\ \leq\ \sqrt{x}\ <\ binsqrt2(x,\ u) + u$$

or, equivalently,

$$(\forall\ integer\ x) \quad \left[\begin{array}{l} \bigl(binsqrt2(x,u)\bigr)^2 \leq x \\ \quad and \\ not\ \bigl[\bigl(binsqrt2(x,u) + u\bigr)^2 \leq x\bigr] \end{array} \right] \qquad (tolerance)$$
$$(\forall\ positive\ u)$$

and therefore

$$(\forall\ integer\ x) \quad \left[\begin{array}{l} \bigl(binsqrt(x)\bigr)^2 \leq x \\ \quad and \\ not\ \bigl[\bigl(binsqrt(x) + 1\bigr)^2 \leq x\bigr] \end{array} \right] \qquad (range)$$

We may then conclude

$$(\forall\ integer\ x) \quad \left[\begin{array}{l} \bigl(binsqrt(x)\bigr)^2 \leq x \\ \quad and \\ (\forall\ integer\ y) \left[\begin{array}{l} if\ \ y^2 \leq x \\ then\ \ y \leq binsqrt(x) \end{array} \right] \end{array} \right] \qquad (square\ root)$$

In other words, the $binsqrt(x)$ function indeed computes the integer square root of x.

The intuitive rationale for the curious auxiliary program $binsqrt2(x,\ u)$ is as follows. If the error tolerance u is sufficiently large (i.e., greater than x), then 0 is a good enough approximation, that is, 0 is within u less than $\sqrt{x}$. Otherwise, the program finds a cruder approximation $b = binsqrt2(x,\ 2 \cdot u)$, which must be within $2 \cdot u$ less than $\sqrt{x}$. If $(b + u)^2 \leq x$, that is, if $b + u \leq \sqrt{x}$, then $b + u$ is a good enough approximation, that is, $b + u$ is within u less than $\sqrt{x}$. Otherwise, $\sqrt{x} < b + u$, and hence b itself is a good enough approximation, that is, b is within u less than $\sqrt{x}$.

The reader is requested to prove the preceding properties in **Problem 2.3**.

In **Problem 2.4** the reader is requested to devise an analogous set of axioms that define a binary function $binquot(x, y)$ that computes the quotient of dividing x by y.

PROBLEMS

Problem 2.1 (cumulative max and sum)   page 62

(a)   *Cumulative max*

In the theory of tuples of nonnegative integers, consider the function $maxc$ defined by the axioms

$$(\forall \; integer \; u)\big[maxc(\langle u \rangle) \; = \; u\big] \qquad\qquad (singleton)$$

$$\begin{matrix} (\forall \; integer \; u, v) \\ (\forall \; tuple \; x) \end{matrix} \left[maxc\big(u \diamond (v \diamond x)\big) \; = \; \begin{cases} if \; \; u \geq v \\ then \; \; maxc(u \diamond x) \\ else \; \; maxc(v \diamond x) \end{cases} \right] $$

$$(double \; insertion)$$

Show that the function $maxc(x)$ computes the maximum element of a given (nonempty) tuple x, in the sense that

$$(\forall \; tuple \; x) \begin{bmatrix} if \; \; not \; (x = \langle \; \rangle) \\ then \; \; maxc(x) \in x \end{bmatrix} \qquad\qquad (member)$$

$$\begin{matrix} (\forall \; tuple \; x) \\ (\forall \; integer \; u) \end{matrix} \begin{bmatrix} if \; \; u \in x \\ then \; \; maxc(x) \geq u \end{bmatrix} \qquad\qquad (greatest)$$

(b)   *Cumulative sum*

Consider also the function $sumc$, defined by the following axioms:

$$sumc(\langle \; \rangle) \; = \; 0 \qquad\qquad (empty)$$

$$(\forall \; integer \; u)\Big[sumc(\langle u \rangle) \; = \; u\Big] \qquad\qquad (singleton)$$

$$\begin{matrix} (\forall \; integer \; u, v) \\ (\forall \; tuple \; x) \end{matrix} \Big[sumc\big(u \diamond (v \diamond x)\big) \; = \; sumc\big((u + v) \diamond x\big)\Big]$$

$$(double \; insertion)$$

Show that these axioms provide an alternative method for computing the sum of the elements of a tuple. In other words,

$$(\forall \; tuple \; x)\big[sumc(x) \; = \; sum(x)\big] \qquad\qquad (alternative \; definition)$$

where the function $sum(x)$ is defined by the axioms

$$sum(\langle \; \rangle) \; = \; 0 \qquad\qquad (empty)$$

$$\begin{matrix} (\forall \; integer \; u) \\ (\forall \; tuple \; x) \end{matrix} \Big[sum(u \diamond x) \; = \; u + sum(x)\Big] \qquad\qquad (insertion)$$

Problem 2.2 (minsort)   page 77

Consider the theory of tuples of nonnegative integers. Show that the *minsort* function provides an alternative definition of the *sort* function by showing the following properties:

(a) *Permutation*

The tuple $minsort(x)$ is a permutation of the tuple x, that is,

$$(\forall\ tuple\ x)\big[perm\big(x,\ minsort(x)\big)\big].$$

(b) *Ordered*

The tuple $minsort(x)$ is in (weakly) increasing order, that is,

$$(\forall\ tuple\ x)\big[ordered\big(minsort(x)\big)\big].$$

(c) *Sorting*

The function *minsort* is identical to the function *sort*, that is,

$$(\forall\ tuple\ x)\big[minsort(x)\ =\ sort(x)\big].$$

Indicate clearly all the properties of tuples used in your proofs; you need not prove them.

Hint: You may want to use the *append-singleton* property of the member relation for tuples (Section [I]12.1),

$$(\forall\ atom\ u)\ \ \begin{bmatrix} u \in x \\ \equiv \\ (\exists\ tuple\ y_1,\ y_2)[x\ =\ y_1 \diamond \langle u \rangle \diamond y_2] \end{bmatrix},$$

and the *append-singleton* property of the subtuple relation,

$$\begin{matrix} (\forall\ atom\ u) \\ (\forall\ tuple\ x,\ y) \end{matrix} \big[x \diamond y\ \subset\ x \diamond \langle u \rangle \diamond y\big].$$

Problem 2.3 (binary-search square root)   page 78

We defined the $binsqrt(x)$ function by the axiom

$$(\forall\ integer\ x)\big[binsqrt(x)\ =\ binsqrt2(x, 1)\big] \qquad\qquad (binsqrt)$$

where the auxiliary function $binsqrt2(x)$ is defined by the axiom

$$
(\forall \, integer \; x) \atop (\forall \, positive \; u)
\left[
\begin{array}{l}
binsqrt2(x, u) = \\
\left\{
\begin{array}{l}
if \;\; u \leq x \\
then \;\; if \;\; \left[binsqrt2(x, 2 \cdot u) + u\right]^2 \leq x \\
\qquad then \;\; binsqrt2(x, 2 \cdot u) + u \\
\qquad else \;\; binsqrt2(x, 2 \cdot u) \\
else \;\; 0
\end{array}
\right.
\end{array}
\right]
$$

$$(binsqrt2)$$

Prove that $binsqrt(x)$ computes the integer square root of the nonnegative integer x in the following three steps:

(a)   *Tolerance*

$$
(\forall \, integer \; x) \atop (\forall \, positive \; u)
\left[
\begin{array}{l}
\left(binsqrt2(x, u)\right)^2 \leq x \\
and \\
not \;\left[\left(binsqrt2(x, u) + u\right)^2 \leq x\right]
\end{array}
\right].
$$

Hint: Use the bounded-increase relation (Problem 1.4).

(b)   *Range*

$$
(\forall \, integer \; x)
\left[
\begin{array}{l}
\left(binsqrt(x)\right)^2 \leq x \\
and \\
not \;\left[\left(binsqrt(x) + 1\right)^2 \leq x\right]
\end{array}
\right].
$$

(c)   *Square root*

$$
(\forall \, integer \; x)
\left[
\begin{array}{l}
\left(binsqrt(x)\right)^2 \leq x \\
and \\
(\forall \, integer \; y)
\left[
\begin{array}{l}
if \;\; y^2 \leq x \\
then \;\; y \leq binsqrt(x)
\end{array}
\right]
\end{array}
\right].
$$

Indicate clearly all the properties of the nonnegative integers used in your proofs; you need not prove them.

Problem 2.4 (binary-search quotient)   page 78

(a)   Devise a set of axioms, analogous to those of $binsqrt(x)$ in Problem 2.3, that define the binary function $binquot(x, y)$. This function computes the quotient of dividing a nonnegative integer x by a positive integer y, that is, the largest nonnegative integer z such that $y \cdot z \leq x$.

(b) Using your axioms, show that *binquot* satisfies the property

$$(\forall \, integer \; x) \atop (\forall \, positive \; y) \left[\begin{array}{l} y \cdot binquot(x, \, y) \leq x \\ \quad and \\ (\forall \, integer \; z) \left[\begin{array}{l} if \;\; y \cdot z \leq x \\ then \;\; z \leq binquot(x, \, y) \end{array} \right] \end{array} \right] \qquad (quotient)$$

3

Equivalent Conditions

In this chapter we relate the *well-founded induction* principle to other conditions. We first establish that the principle is sufficiently general to imply the *stepwise induction* principles for the various theories with induction we have introduced in Volume I. We then prove the equivalence between the principle and the formulation of well-foundedness in terms of infinite sequences.

This chapter covers advanced material and can be skipped on first reading without loss of continuity.

3.1   RELATION TO STEPWISE INDUCTION

We have remarked that the versions of the *stepwise induction* principle we have seen previously, for such theories as the nonnegative integers, strings, trees, and lists, may be regarded as instances of the *well-founded induction* principle. In other words, for each of these theories, if we take the binary relation $\prec$ to be a certain well-founded relation, the *well-founded induction* principle reduces to the *stepwise induction* principle. We illustrate this with the nonnegative integers and trees, leaving the strings and lists as an exercise. The reader should not be frightened of the large sentences in this section: the reasoning is actually quite straightforward.

THE NONNEGATIVE INTEGERS

Consider the theory of nonnegative integers.

We stated (Section [I]6.1) that, for each sentence $\mathcal{F}[x]$, the universal closure of the sentence

$$
if\ \begin{bmatrix} \mathcal{F}[0] \\ \quad and \\ (\forall\ integer\ x) \begin{bmatrix} if\ \ \mathcal{F}[x] \\ then\ \ \mathcal{F}[x+1] \end{bmatrix} \end{bmatrix} \qquad (stepwise\ induction)
$$
$$
then\ \ (\forall\ integer\ x)\mathcal{F}[x]
$$

is an axiom.

We established the *decomposition* property

$$
(\forall\ integer\ x) \begin{bmatrix} if\ \ not\ (x = 0) \\ then\ \ (\exists\ integer\ y)[x = y + 1] \end{bmatrix}
$$

or, equivalently (by propositional logic),

$$
(\forall\ integer\ x) \begin{bmatrix} x = 0 \\ \quad or \\ (\exists\ integer\ y)[x = y + 1] \end{bmatrix} \qquad (decomposition)
$$

We defined the predecessor relation $\prec_{pred}$ by the *predecessor* axiom

$$
(\forall\ integer\ x,\ y) \begin{bmatrix} x \prec_{pred} y \\ \equiv \\ x + 1 = y \end{bmatrix} \qquad (predecessor\ relation)
$$

Proposition (integer induction)

Consider the *predecessor-relation theory*, obtained from the theory of nonnegative integers by

- Omitting the *stepwise induction* principle and

- Introducing the *decomposition* property and the *predecessor-relation* definition as special axioms.

In this theory,

the *well-founded induction* principle over *integer* with respect to the predecessor relation $\prec_{pred}$

is equivalent to

the *stepwise induction* principle over *integer*. ⏌

This proposition suggests that, in the theory of nonnegative integers, we could replace the *stepwise induction* principle with the preceding instance of the *well-founded induction* principle, obtaining an equivalent theory, provided the *decomposition* property and the *predecessor* definition become additional axioms.

Our introduction of the *decomposition* property into the theory is essential: although this sentence is valid in the original theory of nonnegative integers, with stepwise induction, it is not valid in the version of the theory in which stepwise induction has been replaced by the preceding instance of the *well-founded induction* principle (**Problem 3.1**).

The proof relies on the following *universal-replacement* property of predicate logic with equality (Section [I]5.1), that, for any term t with no free occurrences of x, and for any sentence $\mathcal{F}[x]$,

$$(\forall x)\big[if \ \ x = t \ \ then \ \ \mathcal{F}[x]\big]$$

is equivalent to

$$\mathcal{F}[t].$$

Let us prove the *integer-induction* proposition.

Proof (integer induction)

We would like to show that in the predecessor-relation theory, for a given sentence $\mathcal{F}[x]$ with no free occurrences of x',

the *well-founded induction* principle (taking *obj* to be *integer* and $\prec$ to be $\prec_{pred}$), that is, the universal closure of

$$if \ (\forall \, integer \ x) \ \begin{bmatrix} if \ (\forall \, integer \ x') \begin{bmatrix} if \ x' \prec_{pred} x \\ then \ \mathcal{F}[x'] \end{bmatrix} \\ then \ \mathcal{F}[x] \end{bmatrix}$$
$$then \ (\forall \, integer \ x)\mathcal{F}[x]$$

is equivalent to

the *stepwise induction* principle over the nonnegative integers, that is, the universal closure of

$$\text{if } \begin{bmatrix} \mathcal{F}[0] \\ \text{and} \\ (\forall \text{ integer } x) \begin{bmatrix} \text{if } \mathcal{F}[x] \\ \text{then } \mathcal{F}[x+1] \end{bmatrix} \end{bmatrix}$$

then $(\forall \text{ integer } x)\mathcal{F}[x].$

We show that the antecedents of the two principles are equivalent.

The antecedent of the *well-founded induction* principle,

$$(\forall \text{ integer } x) \begin{bmatrix} \text{if } (\forall \text{ integer } x') \begin{bmatrix} \text{if } x' \prec_{pred} x \\ \text{then } \mathcal{F}[x'] \end{bmatrix} \\ \text{then } \mathcal{F}[x] \end{bmatrix},$$

is true precisely when (by the *predecessor-relation* definition)

$$(\forall \text{ integer } x) \begin{bmatrix} \text{if } (\forall \text{ integer } x') \begin{bmatrix} \text{if } x' + 1 = x \\ \text{then } \mathcal{F}[x'] \end{bmatrix} \\ \text{then } \mathcal{F}[x] \end{bmatrix}$$

precisely when (by the *decomposition* property and predicate logic)

$$(\forall \text{ integer } x) \begin{bmatrix} \text{if } x = 0 \\ \text{then } \text{if } (\forall \text{ integer } x') \begin{bmatrix} \text{if } x' + 1 = x \\ \text{then } \mathcal{F}[x'] \end{bmatrix} \\ \text{then } \mathcal{F}[x] \end{bmatrix}$$

and

$$(\forall \text{ integer } x) \begin{bmatrix} \text{if } (\exists \text{ integer } y)[x = y + 1] \\ \text{then } \text{if } (\forall \text{ integer } x') \begin{bmatrix} \text{if } x' + 1 = x \\ \text{then } \mathcal{F}[x'] \end{bmatrix} \\ \text{then } \mathcal{F}[x] \end{bmatrix}.$$

We choose a variable y that does not occur free in $\mathcal{F}[x]$.

We shall show that the first conjunct is equivalent to the base case of the *stepwise induction* principle and, similarly, that the second conjunct is equivalent to the inductive step of the *stepwise induction* principle.

The first conjunct is true precisely when (by the previously mentioned *universal-replacement* property of equality)

$$\text{if } (\forall \text{ integer } x') \begin{bmatrix} \text{if } x' + 1 = 0 \\ \text{then } \mathcal{F}[x'] \end{bmatrix}$$

then $\mathcal{F}[0],$

precisely when (by the *zero* uniqueness axiom for the nonnegative integers)

$$\textit{if} \ (\forall \ \textit{integer} \ x') \ \begin{bmatrix} \textit{if} \ \textit{false} \\ \textit{then} \ \ \mathcal{F}[x'] \end{bmatrix}$$
$$\textit{then} \ \ \mathcal{F}[0],$$

precisely when (by propositional logic)

$$\mathcal{F}[0],$$

which is the base case of the *stepwise induction* principle.

On the other hand, the second conjunct is true precisely when (by predicate logic, manipulating the quantifiers, because y does not occur free in $\mathcal{F}[x]$)

$$(\forall \ \textit{integer} \ x) \atop (\forall \ \textit{integer} \ y)} \begin{bmatrix} \textit{if} \ \ x = y + 1 \\ \textit{then} \ \ \textit{if} \ (\forall \ \textit{integer} \ x') \ \begin{bmatrix} \textit{if} \ \ x' + 1 = x \\ \textit{then} \ \ \mathcal{F}[x'] \end{bmatrix} \\ \textit{then} \ \ \mathcal{F}[x] \end{bmatrix}$$

precisely when (by the *universal-replacement* property of equality, again)

$$(\forall \ \textit{integer} \ y) \ \begin{bmatrix} \textit{if} \ \ (\forall \ \textit{integer} \ x') \ \begin{bmatrix} \textit{if} \ \ x' + 1 = y + 1 \\ \textit{then} \ \ \mathcal{F}[x'] \end{bmatrix} \\ \textit{then} \ \ \mathcal{F}[y + 1] \end{bmatrix}$$

precisely when (by properties of the nonnegative integers)

$$(\forall \ \textit{integer} \ y) \ \begin{bmatrix} \textit{if} \ \ (\forall \ \textit{integer} \ x') \ \begin{bmatrix} \textit{if} \ \ x' = y \\ \textit{then} \ \ \mathcal{F}[x'] \end{bmatrix} \\ \textit{then} \ \ \mathcal{F}[y + 1] \end{bmatrix}$$

precisely when (by the *universal-replacement* property of equality once again)

$$(\forall \ \textit{integer} \ y) \ \begin{bmatrix} \textit{if} \ \ \mathcal{F}[y] \\ \textit{then} \ \ \mathcal{F}[y + 1] \end{bmatrix}$$

precisely when (by *renaming of bound variables*, because y does not occur free in $\mathcal{F}[x]$)

$$(\forall \ \textit{integer} \ x) \ \begin{bmatrix} \textit{if} \ \ \mathcal{F}[x] \\ \textit{then} \ \ \mathcal{F}[x + 1] \end{bmatrix},$$

which is the inductive step of the *stepwise induction* principle over the nonnegative integers.   ⌟

THE STRINGS

We can similarly show that the *stepwise induction* principle of the theory of strings can be regarded as an instance of the *well-founded induction* principle.

We stated (Section [I]7.1) that, for each sentence $\mathcal{F}[x]$ with no free occurrences of u, the universal closure of the sentence

$$
if \begin{bmatrix} \mathcal{F}[\Lambda] \\ and \\ (\forall\, char\ u) \\ (\forall\, string\ x) \begin{bmatrix} if\ \ \mathcal{F}[x] \\ then\ \ \mathcal{F}[u \bullet x] \end{bmatrix} \end{bmatrix} \qquad (stepwise\ induction)
$$

$$
then\ \ (\forall\, string\ x)\mathcal{F}[x]
$$

is an axiom of the theory of strings.

We established the *decomposition* property

$$
(\forall\, string\ x) \begin{bmatrix} if\ \ not\ (x = \Lambda) \\ then\ \ \begin{matrix} (\exists\, char\ u) \\ (\exists\, string\ y) \end{matrix}[x = u \bullet y] \end{bmatrix} \qquad (decomposition)
$$

The tail relation $x \prec_{tail} y$ ("x is the tail of y") is defined by the axiom

$$
(\forall\, string\ x,\ y) \begin{bmatrix} x \prec_{tail} y \\ \equiv \\ (\exists\, char\ u)[u \bullet x = y] \end{bmatrix} \qquad (tail\ relation)
$$

In other words, $x \prec_{tail} y$ if y can be obtained by prefixing some character u to x.

From this axiom one can prove the property

$$
\begin{aligned} &if\ \ not\ (x = \Lambda) \\ &then\ \ tail(x) \prec_{tail} x \end{aligned} \qquad (tail)
$$

In **Problem 3.2** the reader is requested to prove the following proposition:

Proposition (string induction)

Consider the *tail-relation theory*, obtained from the theory of strings by

- Omitting the *stepwise induction* principle and

- Introducing the *decomposition* property and the *tail-relation* definition as special axioms.

In this theory,

> the *well-founded induction* principle over *string* with respect to the tail relation $\prec_{tail}$

> is equivalent to

> the *stepwise induction* principle over *string*. ⌐

This proposition suggests that, in the theory of strings, we could replace the *stepwise induction* principle with the preceding instance of the *well-founded induction* principle, obtaining an equivalent theory, provided we add the *decomposition* property and the *tail-relation* definition as axioms.

The proposition also establishes that

> the tail relation $\prec_{tail}$ is well-founded over *string*

in the full theory of strings (with the *tail-relation* axiom). For, in that theory, the *stepwise induction* principle and the *decomposition* property are valid, and therefore, by the preceding proposition, the *well-founded induction* principle (over *string*) with respect to $\prec_{tail}$ is also valid.

THE TREES

We now show that, in the theory of trees, the *stepwise induction* principle can be regarded as an instance of the *well-founded induction* principle.

We stated (Section [I]8.1) that for each sentence $\mathcal{F}[x]$ with no free occurrences of u, x_1, and x_2, the universal closure of the sentence

$$\textit{if}\ \begin{bmatrix} (\forall\ atom\ u)\mathcal{F}[u] \\ \quad and \\ (\forall\ tree\ x_1,\ x_2)\begin{bmatrix} if\ \mathcal{F}[x_1]\ \ and\ \ \mathcal{F}[x_2] \\ then\ \ \mathcal{F}[x_1 \bullet x_2] \end{bmatrix} \end{bmatrix} \qquad (\textit{stepwise induction})$$
$$\textit{then}\ \ (\forall\ tree\ x)\mathcal{F}[x]$$

is an axiom.

We established the *decomposition* property

$$(\forall\ tree\ x)\ \begin{bmatrix} if\ \ not\ (atom(x)) \\ then\ \ (\exists\ tree\ x_1,\ x_2)[x = x_1 \bullet x_2] \end{bmatrix}$$

or, equivalently (by propositional logic),

$$(\forall \ tree \ x) \begin{bmatrix} atom(x) \\ or \\ (\exists \ tree \ x_1, \ x_2)[x = x_1 \bullet x_2] \end{bmatrix} \qquad (decomposition)$$

Let us define the child relation $x \prec_{child} y$ ("x is a child of y") by the axiom

$$(\forall \ tree \ x, \ y) \begin{bmatrix} x \prec_{child} y \\ \equiv \\ \begin{bmatrix} (\exists \ tree \ z_2)[x \bullet z_2 = y] \\ or \\ (\exists \ tree \ z_1)[z_1 \bullet x = y] \end{bmatrix} \end{bmatrix} \qquad (child \ relation)$$

In other words, x is a child of a nonatomic tree y if it is either $left(y)$ or $right(y)$.

Proposition (tree induction)

Consider the *child-relation theory*, obtained from the theory of trees by

- Omitting the *stepwise induction* principle and

- Introducing the *decomposition* property and the *child-relation* definition as special axioms.

In this theory,

> the *well-founded induction* principle over *tree* with respect to the child relation $\prec_{child}$

> > is equivalent to

> the *stepwise induction* principle over *tree*. ◢

This proposition suggests that, in the theory of trees, we could replace the *stepwise induction* principle with the preceding instance of the *well-founded induction* principle, obtaining an equivalent theory, provided we add the *decomposition* property and the *child-relation* definition as axioms.

The proposition also establishes that

> the child relation $\prec_{child}$ is well-founded over *tree*

in the full theory of trees (with the *child-relation* axiom).

The proof of the proposition relies on the more general form of the *universal-replacement* property (Section [I]5.1), that, for any terms t_1 and t_2, with no free occurrences of x_1 and x_2,

$$(\forall x_1,\, x_2) \begin{bmatrix} if & x_1 = t_1 & and & x_2 = t_2 \\ then & \mathcal{F}[x_1,\, x_2] & & \end{bmatrix}$$

is equivalent to

$$\mathcal{F}[t_1,\, t_2].$$

In the case in which one of the variables, say x_1, does not occur in $\mathcal{F}[x_2]$, it suffices to show that

$$(\forall x_1,\, x_2) \begin{bmatrix} if & x_1 = t_1 & and & x_2 = t_2 \\ then & \mathcal{F}[x_2] & & \end{bmatrix}$$

is equivalent to

$$\mathcal{F}[t_2].$$

Let us prove the *tree-induction* proposition.

Proof (tree induction)

The proof resembles that for the *integer-induction* proposition, except that the child relation $\prec_{child}$ is defined in terms of a disjunction of two conditions, and the inductive step of the *stepwise induction* principle is expressed in terms of a conjunction of two induction hypotheses.

We would like to show that, in the child-relation theory, for an arbitrary sentence $\mathcal{F}[x]$, with no free occurrences of x', u, x_1, and x_2,

the *well-founded induction* principle (taking *obj* to be *tree* and $\prec$ to be $\prec_{child}$), that is, the universal closure of

$$if \ (\forall\, tree\ x) \begin{bmatrix} if \ (\forall\, tree\ x') \begin{bmatrix} if & x' \prec_{child} x \\ then & \mathcal{F}[x'] \end{bmatrix} \\ then \ \ \mathcal{F}[x] \end{bmatrix}$$
$$then \ (\forall\, tree\ x)\,\mathcal{F}[x],$$

is equivalent to

the *stepwise induction* principle over the trees, that is, the universal closure of

$$if \quad \begin{bmatrix} (\forall\ atom\ u)\,\mathcal{F}[u] \\ \quad and \\ (\forall\ tree\ x_1,\ x_2) \begin{bmatrix} if\ \ \mathcal{F}[x_1]\ \ and\ \ \mathcal{F}[x_2] \\ then\ \ \mathcal{F}[x_1 \bullet x_2] \end{bmatrix} \end{bmatrix}$$

$$then\ \ (\forall\ tree\ x)\,\mathcal{F}[x].$$

We show that the antecedents of the two principles are equivalent.

The antecedent of the *well-founded induction* principle,

$$(\forall\ tree\ x) \begin{bmatrix} if\ \ (\forall\ tree\ x') \begin{bmatrix} if\ \ x' \prec_{child} x \\ then\ \ \mathcal{F}[x'] \end{bmatrix} \\ then\ \ \mathcal{F}[x] \end{bmatrix},$$

is true precisely when (by the *child-relation* definition)

$$(\forall\ tree\ x) \begin{bmatrix} if\ \ (\forall\ tree\ x') \begin{bmatrix} if\ \begin{bmatrix} (\exists\ tree\ z_2)[x' \bullet z_2 = x] \\ or \\ (\exists\ tree\ z_1)[z_1 \bullet x' = x] \end{bmatrix} \\ then\ \ \mathcal{F}[x'] \end{bmatrix} \\ then\ \ \mathcal{F}[x] \end{bmatrix},$$

where we choose variables z_1 and z_2 that do not occur free in $\mathcal{F}[x]$.

This condition is true precisely when (by the *decomposition* property and predicate logic)

$$(\forall\ tree\ x) \begin{bmatrix} if\ \ atom(x) \\ then\ \ if\ \ (\forall\ tree\ x') \begin{bmatrix} if\ \begin{bmatrix} (\exists\ tree\ z_2)[x' \bullet z_2 = x] \\ or \\ (\exists\ tree\ z_1)[z_1 \bullet x' = x] \end{bmatrix} \\ then\ \ \mathcal{F}[x'] \end{bmatrix} \\ \qquad\qquad then\ \ \mathcal{F}[x] \end{bmatrix}$$

and

$$(\forall\ tree\ x) \begin{bmatrix} if\ \ (\exists\ tree\ x_1,\ x_2)\big[x = x_1 \bullet x_2\big] \\ then\ \ if\ \ (\forall\ tree\ x') \begin{bmatrix} if\ \begin{bmatrix} (\exists\ tree\ z_2)[x' \bullet z_2 = x] \\ or \\ (\exists\ tree\ z_1)[z_1 \bullet x' = x] \end{bmatrix} \\ then\ \ \mathcal{F}[x'] \end{bmatrix} \\ \qquad\qquad then\ \ \mathcal{F}[x] \end{bmatrix},$$

where we choose variables x_1 and x_2 that do not occur free in $\mathcal{F}[x]$.

We shall show that the first conjunct is equivalent to the base case of the *stepwise induction* principle and, similarly, that the second conjunct is equivalent to the inductive step of the *stepwise induction* principle.

The first conjunct is true precisely when (by predicate logic, manipulating the quantifiers, because z_1 and z_2 do not occur free in $\mathcal{F}[x]$ and hence in $\mathcal{F}[x']$)

$$(\forall\ tree\ x) \begin{bmatrix} if\ \ atom(x) \\ then\ \ if\ (\forall\ tree\ x',\ z_1,\ z_2)\begin{bmatrix} if\ \begin{bmatrix} x' \bullet z_2 = x \\ or \\ z_1 \bullet x' = x \end{bmatrix} \\ then\ \ \mathcal{F}[x'] \end{bmatrix} \\ then\ \ \mathcal{F}[x] \end{bmatrix}$$

precisely when (by the *atom* uniqueness axiom for trees)

$$(\forall\ tree\ x) \begin{bmatrix} if\ \ atom(x) \\ then\ \ if\ (\forall\ tree\ x',\ z_1,\ z_2)\begin{bmatrix} if\ false\ \ or\ \ false \\ then\ \ \mathcal{F}[x'] \end{bmatrix} \\ then\ \ \mathcal{F}[x] \end{bmatrix}$$

precisely when (by propositional logic)

$$(\forall\ tree\ x) \begin{bmatrix} if\ \ atom(x) \\ then\ \ \mathcal{F}[x] \end{bmatrix}$$

precisely when (by the *atom* generation axiom for trees and predicate logic, because u does not occur free in $\mathcal{F}[x]$)

$$(\forall\ atom\ u)\mathcal{F}[u],$$

which is the base case of the *stepwise induction* principle.

On the other hand, the second conjunct is true precisely when (by propositional logic)

$$(\forall\ tree\ x) \begin{bmatrix} if\ (\exists\ tree\ x_1,\ x_2)\big[x = x_1 \bullet x_2\big] \\ then\ \ if\ (\forall\ tree\ x')\begin{array}{l} \begin{bmatrix} if\ (\exists\ tree\ z_2)[x' \bullet z_2 = x] \\ then\ \ \mathcal{F}[x'] \end{bmatrix} \\ and \\ \begin{bmatrix} if\ (\exists\ tree\ z_1)[z_1 \bullet x' = x] \\ then\ \ \mathcal{F}[x'] \end{bmatrix} \end{array} \\ then\ \ \mathcal{F}[x] \end{bmatrix}$$

precisely when (by predicate logic, manipulating the quantifiers, because z_1, z_2, x_1, and x_2 do not occur free in $\mathcal{F}[x]$ and hence in $\mathcal{F}[x']$)

$$(\forall\ tree\ x,\ x_1,\ x_2) \begin{bmatrix} if\ \ x = x_1 \bullet x_2 \\[2ex] then\ \ if\ \ (\forall\ tree\ x',\ z_1,\ z_2)\ \begin{bmatrix} \begin{bmatrix} if\ \ x' \bullet z_2 = x \\ then\ \ \mathcal{F}[x'] \end{bmatrix} \\ and \\ \begin{bmatrix} if\ \ z_1 \bullet x' = x \\ then\ \ \mathcal{F}[x'] \end{bmatrix} \end{bmatrix} \\[2ex] then\ \ \mathcal{F}[x] \end{bmatrix}$$

precisely when (by the *universal-replacement* property of equality)

$$(\forall\ tree\ x_1,\ x_2) \begin{bmatrix} if\ \ (\forall\ tree\ x',\ z_1,\ z_2)\ \begin{bmatrix} \begin{bmatrix} if\ \ x' \bullet z_2 = x_1 \bullet x_2 \\ then\ \ \mathcal{F}[x'] \end{bmatrix} \\ and \\ \begin{bmatrix} if\ \ z_1 \bullet x' = x_1 \bullet x_2 \\ then\ \ \mathcal{F}[x'] \end{bmatrix} \end{bmatrix} \\[2ex] then\ \ \mathcal{F}[x_1 \bullet x_2] \end{bmatrix}$$

precisely when (by the *construction* uniqueness axiom for trees and by properties of equality)

$$(\forall\ tree\ x_1,\ x_2) \begin{bmatrix} if\ \ (\forall\ tree\ x',\ z_1,\ z_2)\ \begin{bmatrix} \begin{bmatrix} if\ \ x' = x_1\ \ and\ \ z_2 = x_2 \\ then\ \ \mathcal{F}[x'] \end{bmatrix} \\ and \\ \begin{bmatrix} if\ \ z_1 = x_1\ \ and\ \ x' = x_2 \\ then\ \ \mathcal{F}[x'] \end{bmatrix} \end{bmatrix} \\[2ex] then\ \ \mathcal{F}[x_1 \bullet x_2] \end{bmatrix}$$

precisely when (by the special *universal-replacement* property for equality mentioned earlier, because z_1 and z_2 do not occur free in $\mathcal{F}[x']$)

$$(\forall\ tree\ x_1,\ x_2) \begin{bmatrix} if\ \ \mathcal{F}[x_1]\ \ and\ \ \mathcal{F}[x_2] \\ then\ \ \mathcal{F}[x_1 \bullet x_2] \end{bmatrix},$$

where, by our assumption, x_1 and x_2 do not occur free in $\mathcal{F}[x]$. This is the inductive step of the *stepwise induction* principle. ◢

THE LISTS

An analogous result holds for the theory of lists.

We stated (Section [I]9.1) that for each sentence $\mathcal{F}[x]$ with no free occurrences of u and x', the universal closure of the sentence

$$
if \;
\begin{bmatrix}
\mathcal{F}[[\,]] \\
and \\
(\forall\, atom\; u) \begin{bmatrix} if & \mathcal{F}[x] \\ then & \mathcal{F}[u \circ x] \end{bmatrix} \quad (\forall\, list\; x) \\
and \\
(\forall\, list\; x',\, x) \begin{bmatrix} if & \mathcal{F}[x'] \;\; and \;\; \mathcal{F}[x] \\ then & \mathcal{F}[x' \circ x] \end{bmatrix}
\end{bmatrix}
\qquad (stepwise\; induction)
$$

$$then \;\; (\forall\, list\; x)\mathcal{F}[x]$$

is an axiom.

We established the *decomposition* property

$$
(\forall\, list\; x)
\begin{bmatrix}
if \;\; not\; (x = [\,]) \\
then \;\; \begin{matrix} (\exists\, atlist\; x_1) \\ (\exists\, list\; x_2) \end{matrix} [x = x_1 \circ x_2]
\end{bmatrix}
\qquad (decomposition)
$$

The component relation $x \prec_{comp} y$ ("x is a component of y"), which is true precisely when y is nonempty and $x = head(y)$ or $x = tail(y)$, is defined by the axiom

$$
(\forall\, list\; x,\, y)
\begin{bmatrix}
x \prec_{comp} y \\
\equiv \\
\begin{bmatrix} (\exists\, list\; z_2)[x \circ z_2 = y] \\ or \\ (\exists\, atlist\; z_1)[z_1 \circ x = y] \end{bmatrix}
\end{bmatrix}
\qquad (component\; relation)
$$

In **Problem 3.3** the reader is requested to prove the following proposition:

Proposition (list induction)

Consider the *component-relation theory*, obtained from the theory of lists by

- Omitting the *stepwise induction* principle and

- Introducing the *decomposition* property and the *component-relation* definition as special axioms.

In this theory

> the *well-founded induction* principle over *list* with respect to the component relation $\prec_{comp}$
>
> is equivalent to
>
> the *stepwise induction* principle over *list*. ⌐

Analogous results hold for the theories of sets, bags, and tuples.

3.2   THEORY OF SEQUENCES

In Section 1.2, we defined well-founded relations in terms of the *well-founded induction* principle. In Section 1.5, we used the *minimal-element* condition to characterize well-founded relations. In the rest of this chapter, we give an additional condition that characterizes well-founded relations; the condition is equivalent to the *well-founded induction* principle. This *no-decreasing* condition (which we previewed informally in Section 1.1) depends on the notion of an infinite sequence of elements $\langle x_0, x_1, x_2, \ldots \rangle$. To express this condition precisely, we digress to introduce a theory of sequences over a given class of objects. This theory resembles the theory of tuples, but, while tuples are finite, sequences are infinite.

THE VOCABULARY

The theory of (infinite) sequences (over *obj*) is an augmentation of the theory of nonnegative integers, whose vocabulary contains

- A unary predicate symbol $obj(w)$,

- A unary predicate symbol $seq(x)$, and

- A binary function symbol $[x]_u$, denoting the *u*th *element of* *x*.

Under the intended models for the theory, $obj(w)$ characterizes the objects that serve as elements of the sequences; $seq(x)$ characterizes the infinite sequences of objects; and, for a nonnegative integer u, the function $[x]_u$ is the *u*th element of the sequence x. (Do not be confused: $[x]_u$ is our personal notation for a

standard binary function symbol, such as $f_{17}(x, u)$.) The element function $[x]_u$
for sequences is analogous to the element function for tuples.

For example, if the class of objects is the nonnegative integers (i.e., *obj* is
integer), then

$$x = \langle 2,\ 4,\ 6,\ 8,\ \ldots \rangle$$

is an infinite sequence; that is, $seq(x)$ is true and

$$[x]_0 = 2, \quad [x]_1 = 4, \quad [x]_2 = 6, \quad [x]_3 = 8, \quad \ldots\ .$$

Beware: the ellipsis notation "..." is informal and may not be used in the theory.
Note also that we enumerate the elements of the sequence beginning with 0, not
1. This simplifies certain induction proofs.

THE AXIOMS

The theory of sequences (over *obj*) is a theory with equality whose axioms include
those of the theory of the nonnegative integers and the following axioms:

$$\begin{matrix} (\forall\ seq\ x) \\ (\forall\ integer\ u) \end{matrix} \left[obj\big([x]_u\big) \right] \qquad\qquad (sort)$$

$$(\forall\ seq\ x,\ y) \left[\begin{array}{l} if\ \ (\forall\ integer\ u)\Big[[x]_u = [y]_u\Big] \\ then\ \ x = y \end{array} \right] \qquad (equality)$$

and the axiom schema

For any term $t[u]$ in the theory with no free occurrences of x,
the universal closure of the sentence

$$if\ \ (\forall\ integer\ u)\big[obj\,(t[u])\big]$$

$$then\ \ (\exists\ seq\ x)(\forall\ integer\ u)\Big[[x]_u = t[u]\Big] \qquad (term)$$

is an axiom.

The *sort* axiom has the intuitive meaning that every element of a sequence
is an object.

The *equality* axiom says that two sequences are equal if each of their corresponding elements are equal. The converse,

$$(\forall\ seq\ x,\ y) \left[\begin{array}{l} if\ \ x = y \\ then\ \ (\forall\ integer\ u)\Big[[x]_u = [y]_u\Big] \end{array} \right],$$

is true by the *functional-substitutivity* axiom of equality.

The *term* axiom schema describes how sequences are constructed. It says that, for any term $t[u]$, there exists a sequence

$$x = \langle t[0], \ t[1], \ t[2], \ \ldots \rangle$$

whose uth element is the object $t[u]$, for each nonnegative integer u. For example, taking $t[u]$ to be the term

$$t[u] : \ 2 \cdot u + 1$$

in the theory of the nonnegative integers, the axiom guarantees that there is a sequence of nonnegative integers

$$\langle 2 \cdot 0 + 1, \ 2 \cdot 1 + 1, \ 2 \cdot 2 + 1, \ \ldots \rangle,$$

that is,

$$\langle 1, \ 3, \ 5, \ \ldots \rangle,$$

whose uth element is $2 \cdot u + 1$.

There is no induction principle in this theory. Of course, because the theory contains the theory of the nonnegative integers, we can use the induction principle from that theory.

We would like to augment the theory of sequences by defining additional functions and relations.

Remark (consistency)

In general, when we define a new function symbol by augmenting a given theory with a set of axioms, there is no guarantee that, in a model for the given theory, there actually exists a function over the domain that satisfies the new axioms. If there is no model in which such a function exists, the augmented theory will be inconsistent. There is no systematic way to detect whether a given set of axioms leads to an inconsistency.

In the theory of the nonnegative integers, we proved the *recursive-definition* proposition (Section [I]12.7), which guarantees the existence of a model for the augmented theory, if the axioms for the new functions are in a certain recursive form. In other words, there exists a function over the domain of the model that satisfies the axioms. In some of the other theories with induction, we could establish similar results. We could also establish an analogous proposition for the sequences, enabling us to define functions (and relations) by providing axioms in recursive form. We omit this proposition, which is technical, but we shall freely define functions and relations in the theory with axioms, without proving consistency. ◢

We first augment our theory by introducing three additional functions.

THE REPEAT FUNCTION

For any object w, the unary function symbol $repeat(w)$ denotes the sequence

$$\langle w, \ w, \ w, \ \ldots \rangle,$$

each of whose elements is w. It is defined by the following axioms:

$$(\forall \ obj \ w)\big[seq(repeat(w))\big] \qquad\qquad (sort)$$

$$\begin{array}{l}(\forall \ obj \ w)\\ (\forall \ integer \ u)\end{array}\Big[\big[repeat(w)\big]_u \ = \ w\Big] \qquad\qquad (element)$$

THE INSERTION FUNCTION

For any object w and sequence $x = \langle x_0, x_1, x_2, \ \ldots \rangle$, the binary *insertion* function symbol $w \diamond x$ denotes the sequence

$$\langle w, \ x_0, \ x_1, \ x_2, \ \ldots \rangle,$$

obtained by inserting w before the first element of x. Thus

$$0 \diamond \langle 1, \ 2, \ 3, \ 4, \ \ldots \rangle \ = \ \langle 0, \ 1, \ 2, \ 3, \ 4, \ \ldots \rangle$$

$$1 \diamond repeat(0) \ = \ \langle 1, \ 0, \ 0, \ 0, \ 0, \ \ldots \rangle.$$

The insertion function is defined by the following axioms:

$$\begin{array}{l}(\forall \ obj \ w)\\ (\forall \ seq \ x)\end{array}\Big[seq(w \diamond x)\Big] \qquad\qquad (sort)$$

$$\begin{array}{l}(\forall \ obj \ w)\\ (\forall \ seq \ x)\end{array}\Big[[w \diamond x]_0 \ = \ w\Big] \qquad\qquad (zero)$$

$$\begin{array}{l}(\forall \ obj \ w)\\ (\forall \ seq \ x)\\ (\forall \ integer \ u)\end{array}\Big[[w \diamond x]_{u+1} \ = \ [x]_u\Big] \qquad\qquad (successor)$$

From these axioms, we can establish the following property:

$$(\forall\ seq\ x)^{(\exists\ obj\ w)}_{(\exists\ seq\ y)}\Big[x\ =\ w \diamond y\Big] \qquad\qquad (decomposition)$$

The proof is left as an exercise (**Problem 3.4**).

THE ALTER FUNCTION

The *alter* function over sequences resembles very closely the *alter* function we used over tuples. For any sequence x, nonnegative integer u, and object w, the ternary function symbol $alter(x, u, w)$ denotes the sequence obtained by replacing the uth element of the sequence x with the object w. Thus, if

$$x\ =\ \langle 0,\ 0,\ 0,\ 0,\ \ldots\ \rangle,$$

then

$$alter(x,\ 2,\ 7)\ =\ \langle 0,\ 0,\ 7,\ 0,\ \ldots\ \rangle.$$

Here again, we begin our enumeration of the elements of the sequence with 0, not 1.

The *alter* function is defined by the following axioms:

$$\begin{array}{c}(\forall\ seq\ x)\\(\forall\ obj\ w_1, w_2)\end{array}\Big[alter(w_1 \diamond x,\ 0,\ w_2)\ =\ w_2 \diamond x\Big] \qquad (zero)$$

$$\begin{array}{c}(\forall\ seq\ x)\\(\forall\ integer\ u)\\(\forall\ obj\ w_1, w_2)\end{array}\left[\begin{array}{c}alter(w_1 \diamond x,\ u+1,\ w_2)\\=\\w_1 \diamond alter(x,\ u,\ w_2)\end{array}\right] \qquad (successor)$$

From these axioms we can establish the following properties:

$$\begin{array}{c}(\forall\ seq\ x)\\(\forall\ integer\ u)\\(\forall\ obj\ w)\end{array}\Big[seq\big(alter(x,\ u,\ w)\big)\Big] \qquad (sort)$$

$$\begin{array}{c}(\forall\ seq\ x)\\(\forall\ integer\ u)\\(\forall\ obj\ w)\end{array}\Big[\big[alter(x,\ u,\ w)\big]_u\ =\ w\Big] \qquad (equal)$$

$$\begin{array}{c}(\forall\ seq\ x)\\(\forall\ integer\ u, v)\\(\forall\ obj\ w)\end{array}\left[\begin{array}{l}if\ \ not\ (u = v)\\then\ \big[alter(x,\ u,\ w)\big]_v = [x]_v\end{array}\right] \qquad (nonequal)$$

$$\begin{array}{c}(\forall\ seq\ x)\\(\forall\ integer\ u)\end{array}\Big[alter\big(x,\ u,\ [x]_u\big)\ =\ x\Big] \qquad (nonalteration)$$

The proofs are left as an exercise (**Problem 3.5**).

SUMMATION AND MULTIPLICATION

We now use the theory of sequences over the nonnegative integers to establish some numerical identities.

In the theory of sequences over the nonnegative integers, the summation function $\Sigma(x,\, u)$ yields the sum

$$[x]_0 + [x]_1 + \ldots + [x]_u$$

of the first $u+1$ elements of the sequence x. The function is defined by the axioms

$$(\forall\, seq\ x)\Big[\Sigma(x,\, 0)\; =\; [x]_0\Big] \qquad\qquad (zero)$$

$$\begin{array}{l}(\forall\, seq\ x)\\ (\forall\, integer\ u)\end{array}\Big[\Sigma(x,\, u+1)\; =\; \Sigma(x,\, u) + [x]_{u+1}\Big] \qquad (successor)$$

Then, for example, the identity

$$2 \cdot (0 + 1 + 2 + \ldots + u)\; =\; u \cdot (u+1)$$

can be stated formally by the sentence

$$(\forall\, seq\ x)\left[\begin{array}{l} if\;\; (\forall\, integer\ v)\Big[[x]_v = v\Big] \\[2mm] then\;\; (\forall\, integer\ u)\Big[2 \cdot \Sigma(x,\, u)\; =\; u \cdot (u+1)\Big]\end{array}\right].$$

In **Problem 3.6** the reader is requested to state formally and establish the validity of several such "summation" identities.

In **Problem 3.7** the reader is requested to devise an analogous set of axioms for defining the multiplication function $\Pi(x,\, u)$, which yields the product

$$[x]_0 \cdot [x]_1 \cdot\; \ldots\; \cdot [x]_u$$

of the first $u+1$ elements of the sequence x. These axioms can then be used to establish the validity of "multiplication" identities.

3.3   NO-DECREASING CONDITION

We are now ready to present the condition that characterizes well-founded relations in terms of infinite sequences. We establish that a binary relation $\prec$ is well-founded precisely when it satisfies the *no-decreasing* condition, that there are no infinite decreasing sequences with respect to $\prec$. In other words, there are no infinite sequences $x = \langle x_0, x_1, x_2, \ldots \rangle$ such that

$$x_0 \succ x_1 \succ x_2 \succ \ldots .$$

This is the conventional definition of a well-founded relation and the one we used informally in the preview.

In the preview, we showed informally the equivalence of the *no-decreasing* condition and the *well-founded induction* principle (actually the *minimal-element* condition). We are about to produce a proof within the theory of sequences. For this purpose, we first augment the theory by defining a new relation.

For each given binary relation $\prec$, we would like to consider sequences that are increasing with respect to $\prec$, that is, sequences $\langle x_0, x_1, x_2, \ldots \rangle$ such that

$$[x]_0 \prec [x]_1 \prec [x]_2 \prec \ldots .$$

Note that, since we do not assume that $\prec$ is transitive, we do not mean to imply that $[x]_0 \prec [x]_2$, $[x]_1 \prec [x]_5$, and so forth. Let us make this more precise.

Definition ($\prec$-increasing relation)

For a given binary relation $\prec$, the unary predicate symbol $\prec\text{-}seq(x)$, indicating that the sequence x is *increasing* with respect to $\prec$, is defined by the axiom

$$(\forall \, seq \ x) \left[\begin{array}{l} \prec\text{-}seq(x) \\ \equiv \\ (\forall \, integer \ u) \left[[x]_u \prec [x]_{u+1} \right] \end{array} \right] \qquad (\prec\text{-}increasing)$$

The definition of the $\prec$-*increasing* relation depends on the choice of the relation $\prec$; thus, in the same theory, we may discuss different unary relations $\prec_1\text{-}seq$, $\prec_2\text{-}seq$, $\prec_3\text{-}seq$, and so forth.

Example

Consider the following sequences over the nonnegative integers:

$$x = \langle 0,\ 1,\ 2,\ 3,\ 4,\ \ldots \rangle$$

$$y = \langle 0,\ 0,\ 1,\ 2,\ 3,\ \ldots \rangle$$

$$z = \langle 5,\ 10,\ 0,\ 0,\ 0,\ \ldots \rangle.$$

With respect to the strict less-than relation $<$, we have

$$<\text{-}seq(x), \quad \text{not } <\text{-}seq(y), \quad \text{and} \quad \text{not } <\text{-}seq(z).$$

With respect to the weak less-than relation $\leq$, we have

$$\leq\text{-}seq(x), \quad \leq\text{-}seq(y), \quad \text{and} \quad \text{not } \leq\text{-}seq(z).$$

With respect to the divides relation $\preceq_{div}$, we have

$$\text{not } \preceq_{div}\text{-}seq(x), \quad \text{not } \preceq_{div}\text{-}seq(y), \quad \text{and} \quad \preceq_{div}\text{-}seq(z). \quad \lrcorner$$

For a given binary relation $\prec$, let us consider its inverse relation $\succ$. We shall say that a sequence x is *decreasing* with respect to $\prec$ if $\succ\text{-}seq(x)$, that is,

$$[x]_0 \succ [x]_1 \succ [x]_2 \succ \ldots .$$

Definition (no-decreasing condition)

In the theory of sequences (over *obj*), a binary relation $\prec$ is said to satisfy the *no-decreasing condition* (over *obj*) if there are no (infinite) decreasing sequences of objects with respect to $\prec$, that is,

$$not\ (\exists\ seq\ x)\big[\succ\text{-}seq(x)\big] \qquad\qquad (no\text{-}decreasing)$$

is valid. $\quad \lrcorner$

Proposition (no-decreasing)

A binary relation $\prec$ is well-founded (over *obj*)

precisely when

it satisfies the *no-decreasing* condition (over *obj*), that is, the sentence

$$not\ (\exists\ seq\ x)\big[\succ\text{-}seq(x)\big]$$

is valid. $\quad \lrcorner$

Thus this proposition states that the *no-decreasing* condition for sequences over *obj* is equivalent to the *well-founded induction* principle over *obj* with respect to $\prec$.

Proof

Let $\prec$ be a binary relation. It suffices to show (by the *minimal-element* proposition) that the *no-decreasing* condition is equivalent to the *minimal-element* condition. We prove each implication of this equivalence separately.

Minimal-element condition $\Rightarrow$ *no-decreasing condition*

We suppose that $\prec$ does not satisfy the *no-decreasing* condition, i.e., there exists some infinite sequence x such that

$$\succ\text{-}seq(x),$$

and show that then $\prec$ does not satisfy the *minimal-element* condition.

We supposed the existence of a sequence x such that $\succ\text{-}seq(x)$, that is,

$$(\dagger) \qquad (\forall \, integer \; u)\Big[[x]_u \succ [x]_{u+1}\Big].$$

Let $\mathcal{F}[w]$ be the sentence

$$\mathcal{F}[w]: \quad (\exists \, integer \; u)\Big[w = [x]_u\Big],$$

that is, w is an element of the sequence x. We shall show that $\mathcal{F}[w]$ violates the *minimal-element* condition with respect to $\prec$, that is, it is false that

$$(\ddagger) \qquad \begin{array}{l} if \;\; (\exists \, obj \; w)\mathcal{F}[w] \\[4pt] then \;\; (\exists \, obj \; w) \begin{bmatrix} \mathcal{F}[w] \\ and \\ (\forall \, obj \; w') \begin{bmatrix} if \;\; w' \prec w \\ then \;\; not \;\; \mathcal{F}[w'] \end{bmatrix} \end{bmatrix}, \end{array}$$

where w' does not occur free in $\mathcal{F}[w]$.

The proof relies on the observation that there cannot exist a minimal element $[x]_u$ of the sequence, because it is always the case that $[x]_{u+1} \prec [x]_u$. But let us be more precise.

The antecedent of the *minimal-element* condition ($\ddagger$),

$$(\exists \, obj \; w)\mathcal{F}[w],$$

that is,

$$(\exists \, obj \; w)(\exists \, integer \; u)\Big[w = [x]_u\Big],$$

is true, taking w to be $[x]_0$ and u to be 0, say, because $[x]_0 = [x]_0$. (We know, by the *sort* axiom for sequences, that $obj([x]_0)$.) In other words, there exists an element of the sequence x.

On the other hand, we now show that the consequent of the *minimal-element* condition ($\ddagger$),

$$(\exists\, obj\ w) \begin{bmatrix} \mathcal{F}[w] \\ and \\ (\forall\, obj\ w') \begin{bmatrix} if\ \ w' \prec w \\ then\ \ not\ \mathcal{F}[w'] \end{bmatrix} \end{bmatrix},$$

is false. In other words, there exists no minimal element of the sequence. For, suppose that w is any object satisfying the first conjunct,

$$\mathcal{F}[w].$$

We show that w cannot satisfy the second conjunct,

$$(\forall\, obj\ w') \begin{bmatrix} if\ \ w' \prec w \\ then\ \ not\ \mathcal{F}[w'] \end{bmatrix}.$$

We have supposed that w satisfies the first conjunct $\mathcal{F}[w]$, that is,

$$(\exists\, integer\ u) \Big[w = [x]_u \Big].$$

Let u be an integer such that

$$w = [x]_u.$$

We show that the second conjunct is false, taking w' to be $[x]_{u+1}$. We therefore show that (because $w = [x]_u$)

$$if\ \ [x]_{u+1} \prec [x]_u$$
$$then\ \ not\ \mathcal{F}\big[[x]_{u+1}\big]$$

is false.

The antecedent $[x]_{u+1} \prec [x]_u$ is true by our supposition ($\dagger$), but the consequent $not\ \mathcal{F}\big[[x]_{u+1}\big]$ is false, because $\mathcal{F}\big[[x]_{u+1}\big]$, that is,

$$(\exists\, integer\ u') \Big[[x]_{u+1} = [x]_{u'}\Big],$$

is true, taking u' to be $u + 1$.

No-decreasing condition ⇒ *minimal-element condition*

We give only a sketch of the proof. Suppose that $\prec$ satisfies the *no-decreasing* condition, that is,

(†) $not\ (\exists\, seq\ x)\,[\succ\text{-}seq(x)],$

but that, contrary to the proposition, there is some sentence $\mathcal{F}[w]$ with no free occurrences of w' that violates the *minimal-element* condition. Thus the antecedent of the *minimal-element* condition,

(‡) $(\exists\, obj\ w)\,\mathcal{F}[w],$

is true, but the consequent of the *minimal-element* condition,

(§) $(\exists\, obj\ w)\begin{bmatrix}\mathcal{F}[w] \\ and \\ (\forall\, obj\ w')\begin{bmatrix}if\ \ w' \prec w \\ then\ \ not\ \mathcal{F}[w']\end{bmatrix}\end{bmatrix},$

is false. We attempt to derive a contradiction.

The idea of the proof is as follows. We construct a sequence

$$x = \langle x_0,\ x_1,\ x_2,\ \dots\rangle$$

by first taking x_0 to be an object such that $\mathcal{F}[x_0]$; its existence is guaranteed by (‡). Since, by our supposition (§), x_0 cannot be a minimal element satisfying $\mathcal{F}[w]$, there must be a smaller such object, say x_1; that is, $x_1 \prec x_0$ and $\mathcal{F}[x_1]$. Because x_1 cannot be minimal either, we can find a smaller such object x_2, and so on; that is,

$$x_0 \succ x_1 \succ x_2 \succ \dots\ .$$

This contradicts the supposition (†) that $\prec$ satisfies the *no-decreasing* condition.

Let us be a little bit more precise. Because the consequent (§) is **false, we** know (by predicate logic) that

$$(\forall\, obj\ w)\begin{bmatrix}if\ \ \mathcal{F}[w] \\ then\ \ not\ (\forall\, obj\ w')\begin{bmatrix}if\ \ w' \prec w \\ then\ \ not\ \mathcal{F}[w']\end{bmatrix}\end{bmatrix}$$

is true, or, equivalently,

$$(\forall\, obj\ w)\begin{bmatrix}if\ \ \mathcal{F}[w] \\ then\ \ (\exists\, obj\ w')\begin{bmatrix}w' \prec w \\ and \\ \mathcal{F}[w']\end{bmatrix}\end{bmatrix},$$

or, equivalently (because w' does not occur free in $\mathcal{F}[w]$),

$$(*) \qquad (\forall\, obj\ w)(\exists\, obj\ w') \begin{bmatrix} if\ \ \mathcal{F}[w] \\ then\ \ \begin{bmatrix} w \succ w' \\ and \\ \mathcal{F}[w'] \end{bmatrix} \end{bmatrix}.$$

We now let x be a sequence satisfying the conditions

$$\mathcal{F}[[x]_0] \qquad\qquad\qquad (zero)$$

$$(\forall\, integer\ u) \begin{bmatrix} if\ \ \mathcal{F}[[x]_u] \\ then\ \ \begin{bmatrix} [x]_u \succ [x]_{u+1} \\ and \\ \mathcal{F}[[x]_{u+1}] \end{bmatrix} \end{bmatrix} \qquad (successor)$$

We indicated earlier the method by which x is constructed in giving the idea of the proof. Roughly, we construct such a sequence x as follows: we take $[x]_0$ to be any object w such that $\mathcal{F}[w]$; the existence of such an object follows from ($\ddagger$). Having selected $[x]_0$, $[x]_1$, $[x]_2$, $\ldots$, $[x]_u$, such that

$$[x]_0 \succ [x]_1 \succ [x]_2 \ldots \succ [x]_u$$

and

$$\mathcal{F}[[x]_0],\ \mathcal{F}[[x]_1],\ \ldots,\ \mathcal{F}[[x]_u],$$

we take $[x]_{u+1}$ to be any object w' such that

$$[x]_u \succ w'\ \ and\ \ \mathcal{F}[w'].$$

The existence of such an object w' follows from ($*$), taking w to be $[x]_u$. The formal proof of the existence of the sequence x satisfying the *zero* and *successor* conditions is omitted; it depends on the *function-introduction* proposition (Section [I]3.6).

From these conditions, we can establish (by stepwise induction over the non-negative integers — the straightforward proof is omitted) that

$$(\forall\, integer\ u) \Big[\mathcal{F}[[x]_u] \Big],$$

and hence (by the preceding *successor* condition)

$$(\forall\, integer\ u) \Big[[x]_u \succ [x]_{u+1} \Big],$$

that is, $\succ$-$seq(x)$, contrary to our initial supposition (†) that $\prec$ satisfies the *no-decreasing* condition. ∎

Remark (theory of sequences)

We have established the *no-decreasing* proposition in a theory of sequences of objects. If we establish that a relation $\prec$ satisfies the *no-decreasing* condition, we know that it is well-founded in this theory. For instance, if a relation $\prec$ satisfies the *no-decreasing* condition over *integer*, it is certainly well-founded over *integer* in the theory of sequences of nonnegative integers. But is it also well-founded over *integer* in the theory of nonnegative integers itself? Yes, but that is not immediately obvious.

It is conceivable that some sentence in the vocabulary of the theory of non-negative integers is actually valid in the corresponding theory of sequences but not in the theory of nonnegative integers itself. In particular, one may imagine that some instance of the *well-founded induction* principle with respect to $\prec$ is valid in the former theory but not in the latter. If this were true, $\prec$ would be well-founded in the theory of sequences but not in the theory of nonnegative integers. As it turns out, this can never happen, but the proof is technical and we omit it. ⌐

ASYMMETRY AND MAPPING

Now that we have established the equivalence between the *well-founded induction* principle and the *no-decreasing* condition, we can give alternative proofs of the *asymmetry* and *mapping* propositions for well-founded relations. These proofs are precise versions of the informal ones we saw in the preview.

The *asymmetry* proposition states that any well-founded relation $\prec$ over *obj* is asymmetric, that is,

$$(\forall \, obj \; x, \, y) \begin{bmatrix} if & x \prec y \\ then & not \; (y \prec x) \end{bmatrix}.$$

The original proof used the *well-founded induction* principle directly. In Problem 1.6 the reader was requested to give an alternative proof that used the *minimal-element* condition. The new alternative proof, using the *no-decreasing* condition, relies on the observation that if, contrary to the proposition, there exist objects x and y such that $x \prec y$ and $y \prec x$, then

$$\langle x, \; y, \; x, \; y, \; x, \; y, \; \ldots \rangle$$

is an infinite decreasing sequence, violating the *no-decreasing* condition. The precise proof of the *asymmetry* proposition is left as an exercise (**Problem 3.8**).

The *mapping* proposition states that if f is a unary function mapping the relation $\prec_1$ over obj_1 into the relation $\prec_2$ over obj_2, then

if $\prec_2$ is well-founded over obj_2,
then $\prec_1$ is well-founded over obj_1.

The alternative proof relies on the observation that, under the conditions of the proposition, if

$$\langle x_0,\ x_1,\ x_2,\ \ldots \rangle$$

is a sequence of object$_1$'s decreasing with respect to $\prec_1$, then

$$\langle f(x_0),\ f(x_1),\ f(x_2),\ \ldots \rangle$$

is a sequence of object$_2$'s decreasing with respect to $\prec_2$. Hence, if $\prec_2$ is well-founded, that is, if there are no sequences of object$_2$'s decreasing with respect to $\prec_2$, then there are also no sequences of object$_1$'s decreasing with respect to $\prec_1$, that is, $\prec_1$ is also well-founded. The precise proof of the *mapping* proposition is left as an exercise (**Problem 3.9**).

PROBLEMS

$*$ **Problem 3.1 (decomposition of the nonnegative integers)**   page 85

Show that the *decomposition* property is not valid in a new theory obtained by replacing the *stepwise induction* principle in the theory of the nonnegative integers with the *well-founded induction* principle with respect to the relation $\prec_{pred}$.

Hint: Consider an interpretation that includes in its domain two copies of the nonnegative integers, the ordinary nonnegative integers 0, 1, 2, ... and the special nonnegative integers $\overline{0}, \overline{1}, \overline{2}, \ldots$, where the special nonnegative integers are distinct from the ordinary nonnegative integers. Show that the interpretation is a model for this new theory, but that the *decomposition* property is not true under this model.

Problem 3.2 (string induction)   page 88

Prove the *string-induction* proposition, that is, in the tail-relation theory,

the *well-founded induction* principle over *string* with respect to the tail relation $\prec_{tail}$

is equivalent to

the *stepwise induction* principle over *string*.

Problem 3.3 (list induction)   page 95

Prove the *list-induction* proposition, that is, in the component-relation theory,

> the *well-founded induction* principle over *list* with respect to
> the component relation $\prec_{comp}$

> is equivalent to

> the *stepwise induction* principle over *list*.

Problem 3.4 (insertion)   page 100

Establish the validity of the following *decomposition* property of the insertion
function for sequences:

$$(\forall\ seq\ x)\,\genfrac{}{}{0pt}{}{(\exists\ obj\ w)}{(\exists\ seq\ y)}\Big[x\ =\ w \diamond y\Big].$$

Problem 3.5 (alter)   page 101

Establish the validity of the following properties of the *alter* function:

(a) *Sort*

$$\genfrac{}{}{0pt}{}{\genfrac{}{}{0pt}{}{(\forall\ seq\ x)}{(\forall\ integer\ u)}}{(\forall\ obj\ w)}\Big[seq\big(alter(x,\ u,\ w)\big)\Big]$$

(b) *Equal*

$$\genfrac{}{}{0pt}{}{\genfrac{}{}{0pt}{}{(\forall\ seq\ x)}{(\forall\ integer\ u)}}{(\forall\ obj\ w)}\Big[\big[alter(x,\ u,\ w)\big]_u\ =\ w\Big]$$

(c) *Nonequal*

$$\genfrac{}{}{0pt}{}{\genfrac{}{}{0pt}{}{(\forall\ seq\ x)}{(\forall\ integer\ u,v)}}{(\forall\ obj\ w)}\left[\begin{array}{l}if\ \ not\ (u=v)\\ then\ \big[alter(x,\ u,\ w)\big]_v = [x]_v\end{array}\right]$$

(d) *Nonalteration*

$$\genfrac{}{}{0pt}{}{(\forall\ seq\ x)}{(\forall\ integer\ u)}\Big[alter(x,\ u,\ [x]_u)\ =\ x\Big].$$

Problem 3.6 (summation)   page 101

In the theory of sequences over the nonnegative integers augmented with the summation function $\sum(x, u)$, state formally and then establish the validity of the following identities:

(a) *Successive integers*

$$2 \cdot (0 + 1 + 2 + \cdots + u) = u \cdot (u + 1)$$

(b) *Odd integers*

$$1 + 3 + 5 + \cdots + (2 \cdot u + 1) = (u + 1)^2$$

(c) *Powers of two*

$$1 + 2 + 2^2 + \cdots + 2^u = 2^{u+1} - 1$$

(d) *Cubes*

$$0^3 + 1^3 + 2^3 + \cdots + u^3 = (0 + 1 + 2 + \ldots + u)^2.$$

List the new properties of the nonnegative integers you use; you need not prove them.

Problem 3.7 (multiplication)   page 101

(a) Devise a set of axioms, analogous to those of the summation function $\sum(x, u)$ in Problem 3.6, that defines the multiplication function $\Pi(x, u)$, which yields the product $[x]_0 \cdot [x]_1 \cdot \ldots \cdot [x]_u$ of the first $u + 1$ elements of the sequence x.

In this augmented theory of sequences over the nonnegative integers, state formally and establish the validity of the following identities:

(b) *Exponential*

$$v \cdot v \cdot v \cdot \ldots \cdot v = v^{u+1}$$

(The term on the left-hand side contains $u + 1$ copies of v.)

(c) *Factorial*

$$1 \cdot 2 \cdot 3 \cdot \ldots \cdot u = u!$$

(The factorial function is defined in Problem [I]6.4.)

List the new properties of the nonnegative integers you use; you need not prove them.

Problem 3.8 (asymmetry)   page 108

Use the *no-decreasing* condition to establish the *asymmetry* proposition for well-founded relations:

For a well-founded relation $\prec$ over *obj*, the sentence

$$(\forall\, obj\ x,\ y)\begin{bmatrix} if\ \ x \prec y \\ then\ \ not\ (y \prec x) \end{bmatrix}$$

is valid.

Problem 3.9 (mapping)   page 109

Use the *no-decreasing* condition to establish the *mapping* proposition for well-founded relations:

For a unary function f that maps $\prec_1$ (over obj_1) into $\prec_2$ (over obj_2),
    if $\prec_2$ is well-founded (over obj_2),
    then $\prec_1$ is well-founded (over obj_1).

Hint: Let the unary predicate symbols seq_1 and seq_2 characterize the sequences over obj_1 and obj_2, respectively.

4

Lexicographic
Relations

In this chapter, we introduce a way of combining two well-founded relations, over two classes of objects, into a single well-founded relation over the class of pairs of these objects. In certain proofs, it is convenient to use such a composite relation as the basis for a well-founded induction argument. This material was summarized in the preview.

4.1   THEORY OF PAIRS

The theory of pairs was introduced in Section [I]5.5; here we use a slightly altered version. In the original theory, the elements of a pair are each from the same class of objects. In the altered theory, the first element is from one class and the second is from another, possibly different, class.

Suppose that, in a given theory, the unary predicate symbols obj_1 and obj_2 characterize two classes of elements, respectively. Then the vocabulary of the theory of pairs (over obj_1 and obj_2) consists of the following additional symbols:

- A unary predicate symbol $pair(x)$.

- A binary function symbol $\langle x_1, x_2 \rangle$, denoting the *pairing* function.

Under the intended model, $pair(x)$ characterizes the pairs $\langle x_1, x_2 \rangle$ of elements x_1 and x_2 satisfying obj_1 and obj_2, respectively. The value of the pairing function $\langle x_1, x_2 \rangle$ is the pair whose first element is the object$_1$ x_1 and whose second element is the object$_2$ x_2. As usual, we write the pairing function as $\langle x_1, x_2 \rangle$, using the familiar mathematical notation, rather than a standard predicate-logic binary function symbol, such as $f_{101}(x_1, x_2)$.

The theory of pairs (over obj_1 and obj_2) is a theory with equality and the following axioms:

$$(\forall x) \begin{bmatrix} pair(x) \\ \equiv \\ (\exists\, obj_1\ x_1) \\ (\exists\, obj_2\ x_2) \end{bmatrix} \left[x = \langle x_1, x_2 \rangle \right] \qquad (pair)$$

$$(\forall\, obj_1\ x_1,\ y_1) \begin{bmatrix} if\ \langle x_1, x_2 \rangle = \langle y_1, y_2 \rangle \\ then\ x_1 = y_1\ \ and\ \ x_2 = y_2 \end{bmatrix} \qquad (uniqueness)$$
$$(\forall\, obj_2\ x_2,\ y_2)$$

In other words, every pair is of form $\langle x_1, x_2 \rangle$, where x_1 is an object$_1$, x_2 is an object$_2$, and the pair can be constructed in only one way. We do not specify whether the object$_1$'s and object$_2$'s may themselves be pairs.

In this theory, we can define unary functions $first(x)$ and $second(x)$, the first and second elements, respectively, of the pair x, by the axioms

$$(\forall\, obj_1\ x_1) \left[first(\langle x_1, x_2 \rangle) = x_1 \right] \qquad (first)$$
$$(\forall\, obj_2\ x_2)$$

$$(\forall\, obj_1\ x_1) \left[second(\langle x_1, x_2 \rangle) = x_2 \right] \qquad (second)$$
$$(\forall\, obj_2\ x_2)$$

We can then establish the following property of the *first* and *second* functions:

$$(\forall\, pair\ x) \left[x = \langle first(x),\ second(x) \rangle \right] \qquad (decomposition)$$

THE INDUCTION PRINCIPLE

Up to now, we have been able to apply the *well-founded induction* principle to only a single inductive variable at a time. If a proof involves induction over more than one variable, we have been required to apply the rule several times in succession. The following proposition gives us a way to apply the induction principle to two variables at a time.

Proposition (well-founded induction over pairs)

In the theory of pairs over obj_1 and obj_2, suppose the binary relation $\prec$ is well-founded over *pair*.

Then, for each sentence $\mathcal{F}[x_1, x_2]$ with no free occurrences of x_1' and x_2', the universal closure of the sentence

$$if \ {(\forall \, obj_1 \ x_1) \atop (\forall \, obj_2 \ x_2)} \left[if \ {(\forall \, obj_1 \ x_1') \atop (\forall \, obj_2 \ x_2')} \left[{if \ \langle x_1', x_2' \rangle \prec \langle x_1, x_2 \rangle \atop then \ \ \mathcal{F}[x_1', x_2']} \right] \atop then \ \ \mathcal{F}[x_1, x_2] \right]$$

$$then \ {(\forall \, obj_1 \ x_1) \atop (\forall \, obj_2 \ x_2)} \mathcal{F}[x_1, x_2]$$

$$(\textit{well-founded induction over pairs})$$

is valid. ⌟

Proof

Note first that, because $\prec$ is a well-founded relation over *pair*, for each sentence $\mathcal{G}[x]$ with no free occurrences of x', the universal closure of the sentence

$$if \ (\forall \, pair \ x) \left[if \ (\forall \, pair \ x') \left[{if \ x' \prec x \atop then \ \ \mathcal{G}[x']} \right] \atop then \ \ \mathcal{G}[x] \right]$$

$$then \ (\forall \, pair \ x) \mathcal{G}[x]$$

is valid.

Suppose that the antecedent,

$$(\dagger) \qquad {(\forall \, obj_1 \ x_1) \atop (\forall \, obj_2 \ x_2)} \left[if \ {(\forall \, obj_1 \ x_1') \atop (\forall \, obj_2 \ x_2')} \left[{if \ \langle x_1', x_2' \rangle \prec \langle x_1, x_2 \rangle \atop then \ \ \mathcal{F}[x_1', x_2']} \right] \atop then \ \ \mathcal{F}[x_1, x_2] \right],$$

is true. We would like to show that then the consequent,

$$(\dagger\dagger) \qquad {(\forall \, obj_1 \ x_1) \atop (\forall \, obj_2 \ x_2)} \mathcal{F}[x_1, x_2],$$

is also true.

It suffices to establish the following sentence:

$$(\forall\,pair\ x)\genfrac{}{}{0pt}{}{(\forall\,obj_1\ x_1)}{(\forall\,obj_2\ x_2)}\left[\genfrac{}{}{0pt}{}{if\ \ x = \langle x_1,\ x_2\rangle}{then\ \ \mathcal{F}[x_1,\ x_2]}\right].$$

For an arbitrary object$_1$ x_1 and object$_2$ x_2, the sentence $\mathcal{F}[x_1, x_2]$ is obtained (by the *universal quantifier-instantiation* proposition and the reflexivity of equality) from this sentence by taking x to be $\langle x_1,\ x_2\rangle$.

The proof is by well-founded induction (over *pair*) with respect to the given well-founded relation $\prec$. We prove

$$(\forall\,pair\ x)\,\mathcal{G}[x],$$

where the inductive sentence is taken to be

$$\mathcal{G}[x]:\quad \genfrac{}{}{0pt}{}{(\forall\,obj_1\ x_1)}{(\forall\,obj_2\ x_2)}\left[\genfrac{}{}{0pt}{}{if\ \ x = \langle x_1,\ x_2\rangle}{then\ \ \mathcal{F}[x_1,\ x_2]}\right].$$

Inductive Step

For an arbitrary pair x, we assume the induction hypothesis

$$(\ddagger)\qquad (\forall\,pair\ x')\left[\genfrac{}{}{0pt}{}{if\ x' \prec x}{then\ \ \mathcal{G}[x']}\right],$$

where x' does not occur free in $\mathcal{G}[x]$, and attempt to show $\mathcal{G}[x]$, that is,

$$\genfrac{}{}{0pt}{}{(\forall\,obj_1\ x_1)}{(\forall\,obj_2\ x_2)}\left[\genfrac{}{}{0pt}{}{if\ \ x = \langle x_1,\ x_2\rangle}{then\ \ \mathcal{F}[x_1,\ x_2]}\right].$$

Consider an arbitrary object$_1$ x_1 and object$_2$ x_2, and suppose that

$$x = \langle x_1,\ x_2\rangle.$$

We would like to show that then

$$\mathcal{F}[x_1,\ x_2].$$

By the antecedent ($\dagger$), which we supposed to be true, it suffices to establish that

$$\genfrac{}{}{0pt}{}{(\forall\,obj_1\ x_1')}{(\forall\,obj_2\ x_2')}\left[\genfrac{}{}{0pt}{}{if\ \langle x_1',\ x_2'\rangle \prec \langle x_1,\ x_2\rangle}{then\ \ \mathcal{F}[x_1',\ x_2']}\right].$$

Consider an arbitrary object$_1$ x_1' and object$_2$ x_2', and suppose that

$$\langle x_1',\ x_2'\rangle \prec \langle x_1,\ x_2\rangle.$$

We would like to show that then

$$\mathcal{F}[x_1', \, x_2'].$$

We have assumed as our induction hypothesis (‡) that

$$(\forall \, pair \; x') \begin{bmatrix} if \;\; x' \prec x \\ then \;\; \mathcal{G}[x'] \end{bmatrix},$$

that is (since $x = \langle x_1, \, x_2 \rangle$),

$$(\forall \, pair \; x') \begin{bmatrix} if \;\; x' \prec \langle x_1, \, x_2 \rangle \\ then \;\; \begin{matrix} (\forall \, obj_1 \; y_1) \\ (\forall \, obj_2 \; y_2) \end{matrix} \begin{bmatrix} if \;\; x' = \langle y_1, \, y_2 \rangle \\ then \;\; \mathcal{F}[y_1, \, y_2] \end{bmatrix} \end{bmatrix},$$

where x' does not occur free in $\mathcal{F}[y_1, \, y_2]$. Therefore, taking x' to be $\langle x_1', \, x_2' \rangle$, we have (because by our supposition $\langle x_1', \, x_2' \rangle \prec \langle x_1, \, x_2 \rangle$)

$$\begin{matrix} (\forall \, obj_1 \; y_1) \\ (\forall \, obj_2 \; y_2) \end{matrix} \begin{bmatrix} if \;\; \langle x_1', \, x_2' \rangle = \langle y_1, \, y_2 \rangle \\ then \;\; \mathcal{F}[y_1, \, y_2] \end{bmatrix}.$$

Then, taking y_1 and y_2 to be x_1' and x_2', respectively, we have

$$\mathcal{F}[x_1', \, x_2'],$$

as we wanted to show.   ⌐

4.2   LEXICOGRAPHIC RELATION

We may now define the lexicographic relation in the altered theory of pairs. It was defined for the original theory of pairs in Section [I]5.7.

Definition (lexicographic relation)

Suppose that obj_1 and obj_2 are unary predicate symbols and that $\prec_1$ and $\prec_2$ are binary relations. Then, in the theory of pairs (over obj_1 and obj_2), the *lexicographic relation* $\prec_{lex}$ (*corresponding to* $\prec_1$ *and* $\prec_2$) is defined by the axiom

$$
\begin{array}{l}
(\forall\, obj_1\ x_1,\ y_1) \\
(\forall\, obj_2\ x_2,\ y_2)
\end{array}
\left[
\begin{array}{l}
\langle x_1,\ x_2 \rangle \prec_{lex} \langle y_1,\ y_2 \rangle \\
\qquad\equiv \\
\left[
\begin{array}{l}
x_1 \prec_1 y_1 \\
\quad or \\
x_1 = y_1\ \ and\ \ x_2 \prec_2 y_2
\end{array}
\right]
\end{array}
\right]
\qquad
\begin{array}{c}
(lexicographic \\
relation)
\end{array}
$$

In other words, the lexicographic relation $\prec_{lex}$ between two pairs initially compares the first components of the pairs; only if these are equal does it compare their second components. Thus the definition of $\prec_{lex}$ depends on the choice of $\prec_1$ and $\prec_2$.

Example

Take

$\prec_1$ to be the proper-substring relation $\prec_{string}$ over the strings

and

$\prec_2$ to be the less-than relation $<$ over the nonnegative integers.

Consider the theory of pairs over the strings and the nonnegative integers; that is, obj_1 is *string* and obj_2 is *integer*.

Then, for any strings x_1, y_1 and any nonnegative integers x_2, y_2, we have

$$
\langle x_1,\ x_2 \rangle \prec_{lex} \langle y_1,\ y_2 \rangle \quad if \quad
\left\{
\begin{array}{l}
x_1 \prec_{string} y_1 \\
\quad or \\
x_1 = y_1\ \ and\ \ x_2 < y_2
\end{array}
\right\}
$$

Thus

$\langle \text{ABC},\ 100 \rangle \ \prec_{lex}\ \langle \text{DABCE},\ 2 \rangle$ because ABC $\prec_{string}$ DABCE

$\langle \text{ABC},\ 2 \rangle \ \prec_{lex}\ \langle \text{ABC},\ 3 \rangle$ because ABC = ABC and $2 < 3$,

but

not $\langle \text{AB},\ 2 \rangle \ \prec_{lex}\ \langle \text{BCE},\ 3 \rangle$

not $\langle \text{ABC},\ 3 \rangle \ \prec_{lex}\ \langle \text{ABC},\ 2 \rangle.$

We now show that the lexicographic relation $\prec_{lex}$ is well-founded if its component relations $\prec_1$ and $\prec_2$ are well-founded.

Proposition (lexicographic relation)

In the theory of pairs over obj_1 and obj_2, let $\prec_1$ and $\prec_2$ be binary relations and $\prec_{lex}$ be the corresponding lexicographic relation.

If $\prec_1$ and $\prec_2$ are well-founded over obj_1 and obj_2, respectively, then $\prec_{lex}$ is well-founded over *pair*. ⌐

In the preview, we sketched an informal proof of this proposition using the *no-decreasing* condition. Here we use the equivalent *minimal-element* condition for well-foundedness.

Proof

Suppose that $\prec_1$ and $\prec_2$ satisfy the *minimal-element* condition over obj_1 and obj_2, respectively; we would like to show that then $\prec_{lex}$ satisfies the *minimal-element* condition over *pair*.

Consider an arbitrary sentence $\mathcal{F}[x]$, with no free occurrences of x', in the theory of pairs; we show the *minimal-element* condition over *pair*, that is,

$$
\begin{aligned}
&if \quad (\exists\, pair\ x)\mathcal{F}[x] \\
&then \quad (\exists\, pair\ x)
\begin{bmatrix}
\mathcal{F}[x] \\
and \\
(\forall\, pair\ x')
\begin{bmatrix}
if \quad x' \prec_{lex} x \\
then \quad not\ \mathcal{F}[x']
\end{bmatrix}
\end{bmatrix} .
\end{aligned}
$$

In other words, if there is some pair satisfying $\mathcal{F}[x]$, there is some minimal pair satisfying $\mathcal{F}[x]$.

Suppose that the antecedent,

(†) $(\exists\, pair\ x)\mathcal{F}[x],$

is true; we would like to show that the consequent,

$$
(\dagger\dagger) \qquad (\exists\, pair\ x)
\begin{bmatrix}
\mathcal{F}[x] \\
and \\
(\forall\, pair\ x')
\begin{bmatrix}
if \quad x' \prec_{lex} x \\
then \quad not\ \mathcal{F}[x']
\end{bmatrix}
\end{bmatrix} ,
$$

is also true.

In steps, we construct a minimal pair $\langle y_1, y_2 \rangle$ satisfying $\mathcal{F}[x]$. This will establish the desired consequent (††), taking x to be the pair $\langle y_1, y_2 \rangle$.

Take x to be an element such that

$$pair(x) \quad and \quad \mathcal{F}[x];$$

the existence of such a pair is guaranteed by the supposition (†). Then (by the *pair* axiom), there exists an object$_1$ x_1 and an object$_2$ x_2 such that $x = \langle x_1, x_2 \rangle$, and hence

$$obj_1(x_1) \quad and \quad obj_2(x_2) \quad and \quad \mathcal{F}[\langle x_1, x_2 \rangle].$$

Therefore we know

$$(\exists \, obj_1 \, x_1)(\exists \, obj_2 \, x_2)\mathcal{F}[\langle x_1, x_2 \rangle].$$

Take $\mathcal{F}_1[x_1]$ to be the sentence

$$\mathcal{F}_1[x_1]: \quad (\exists \, obj_2 \, x_2)\mathcal{F}[\langle x_1, x_2 \rangle].$$

Then we have

$$(\exists \, obj_1 \, x_1)\mathcal{F}_1[x_1].$$

Construction of y_1

We have supposed that $\prec_1$ satisfies the *minimal-element* condition over obj_1; therefore there is some minimal object$_1$ y_1 satisfying $\mathcal{F}_1[y_1]$, that is,

$$
\begin{aligned}
&obj_1(y_1) \\
&\quad and \\
&\mathcal{F}_1[y_1] \\
&\quad and \\
&(\forall \, obj_1 \, y_1') \begin{bmatrix} if \quad y_1' \prec_1 y_1 \\ then \quad not \ \mathcal{F}_1[y_1'] \end{bmatrix},
\end{aligned}
$$

where y_1' does not occur free in $\mathcal{F}_1[y_1]$. In other words (by the definition of $\mathcal{F}_1[x_1]$),

$$
(1) \quad
\begin{aligned}
&obj_1(y_1) \\
&\quad and \\
&(\exists \, obj_2 \, x_2)\mathcal{F}[\langle y_1, x_2 \rangle] \\
&\quad and \\
&(\forall \, obj_1 \, y_1') \begin{bmatrix} if \quad y_1' \prec_1 y_1 \\ then \quad not \ (\exists \, obj_2 \, x_2)\mathcal{F}[\langle y_1', x_2 \rangle] \end{bmatrix}.
\end{aligned}
$$

Construction of y_2

Take $\mathcal{F}_2[x_2]$ to be the sentence

$$\mathcal{F}_2[x_2]: \quad \mathcal{F}[\langle y_1, x_2 \rangle].$$

Then, by the second conjunct of (1), we know

$$(\exists\, obj_2\ x_2)\, \mathcal{F}_2[x_2].$$

We have supposed that $\prec_2$ satisfies the *minimal-element* condition over obj_2; therefore, there is some minimal object$_2$ y_2 satisfying $\mathcal{F}_2[y_2]$, that is,

$$obj_2(y_2)$$
$$\quad and$$
$$\mathcal{F}_2[y_2]$$
$$\quad and$$
$$(\forall\, obj_2\ y_2')\begin{bmatrix} if\ \ y_2' \prec_2 y_2 \\ then\ \ not\ \mathcal{F}_2[y_2'] \end{bmatrix},$$

where y_2' is not free in $\mathcal{F}_2[y_2]$. In other words (by the definition of $\mathcal{F}_2[x_2]$),

$$(2)\qquad \begin{array}{l} obj_2(y_2) \\ \quad and \\ \mathcal{F}\big[\langle y_1,\ y_2\rangle\big] \\ \quad and \\ (\forall\, obj_2\ y_2')\begin{bmatrix} if\ \ y_2' \prec_2 y_2 \\ then\ \ not\ \mathcal{F}\big[\langle y_1,\ y_2'\rangle\big] \end{bmatrix}. \end{array}$$

We claim that $\langle y_1,\ y_2\rangle$ is a minimal pair satisfying $\mathcal{F}[x]$, that is,

$$(3)\qquad \begin{array}{l} pair\big(\langle y_1,\ y_2\rangle\big) \\ \quad and \\ \mathcal{F}\big[\langle y_1,\ y_2\rangle\big] \\ \quad and \\ (\forall\, pair\ x')\begin{bmatrix} if\ \ x' \prec_{lex} \langle y_1,\ y_2\rangle \\ then\ \ not\ \mathcal{F}[x'] \end{bmatrix}. \end{array}$$

This will establish the desired consequent (††), taking x to be the pair $\langle y_1,\ y_2\rangle$.

Proof that $\langle y_1, y_2\rangle$ is the desired pair

The first conjunct of (3), $pair\big(\langle y_1,\ y_2\rangle\big)$, follows from the *pair* axiom, because (by (1) and (2), respectively) we know

$$obj_1(y_1)\ \ and\ \ obj_2(y_2).$$

The second conjunct of (3), $\mathcal{F}\big[\langle y_1,\ y_2\rangle\big]$, follows from (2).

To establish the third conjunct of (3), consider an arbitrary pair x' such that

$$x' \prec_{lex} \langle y_1,\ y_2\rangle.$$

We would like to show that

$$not \; \mathcal{F}[x'].$$

By the *pair* axiom, there exists an object$_1$ x'_1 and an object$_2$ x'_2 such that

$$x' = \langle x'_1, \, x'_2 \rangle.$$

Thus we know

$$\langle x'_1, \, x'_2 \rangle \prec_{lex} \langle y_1, \, y_2 \rangle,$$

and would like to show

(††) $not \; \mathcal{F}\big[\langle x'_1, \, x'_2 \rangle\big].$

By the definition of the lexicographic relation, we have

$$x'_1 \prec_1 y_1$$
$$or$$
$$x'_1 = y_1 \;\; and \;\; x'_2 \prec_2 y_2.$$

We treat each case separately.

Case: $x'_1 \prec_1 y_1$

Because by (1) we know that y_1 is minimal, that is,

$$(\forall \, obj_1 \; y'_1) \left[\begin{array}{l} if \;\; y'_1 \prec_1 y_1 \\ then \;\; not \; (\exists \, obj_2 \; x_2) \mathcal{F}\big[\langle y'_1, \, x_2 \rangle\big] \end{array} \right],$$

we have (taking y'_1 to be x'_1, because $x'_1 \prec_1 y_1$)

$$not \; (\exists \, obj_2 \; x_2) \mathcal{F}\big[\langle x'_1, \, x_2 \rangle\big],$$

that is (by the duality between the quantifiers),

$$(\forall \, obj_2 \; x_2) \; not \; \mathcal{F}\big[\langle x'_1, \, x_2 \rangle\big].$$

In particular (taking x_2 to be x'_2), we have

$$not \; \mathcal{F}\big[\langle x'_1, \, x'_2 \rangle\big],$$

which is our desired result (††).

Case: $x'_1 = y_1 \;\; and \;\; x'_2 \prec_2 y_2$

Because by (2) we know that y_2 is minimal, that is,

$$(\forall \, obj_2 \; y'_2) \left[\begin{array}{l} if \;\; y'_2 \prec_2 y_2 \\ then \;\; not \; \mathcal{F}\big[\langle y_1, \, y'_2 \rangle\big] \end{array} \right],$$

we have (taking y_2' to be x_2', because $x_2' \prec_2 y_2$)

$$not \ \mathcal{F}\big[\langle y_1, x_2' \rangle\big],$$

that is (because $y_1 = x_1'$),

$$not \ \mathcal{F}\big[\langle x_1', x_2' \rangle\big],$$

which is our desired result (††). ◢

Combining the results of the earlier *well-founded induction over pairs* proposition and the *lexicographic-relation* proposition, just proved, we obtain the following important result.

Corollary (lexicographic well-founded induction)

In the theory of pairs over obj_1 and obj_2, suppose the binary relations $\prec_1$ and $\prec_2$ are well-founded over obj_1 and obj_2, respectively.

Then, for each sentence $\mathcal{F}[x_1, x_2]$ with no free occurrences of x_1' and x_2', the universal closure of the sentence

$$if \ \genfrac{}{}{0pt}{}{(\forall \, obj_1 \ x_1)}{(\forall \, obj_2 \ x_2)} \left[if \ \genfrac{}{}{0pt}{}{(\forall \, obj_1 \ x_1')}{(\forall \, obj_2 \ x_2')} \left[\genfrac{}{}{0pt}{}{if \ \langle x_1', x_2' \rangle \prec_{lex} \langle x_1, x_2 \rangle}{then \ \mathcal{F}[x_1', x_2']} \right] \atop then \ \ \mathcal{F}[x_1, x_2] \right]$$

$$then \ \genfrac{}{}{0pt}{}{(\forall \, obj_1 \ x_1)}{(\forall \, obj_2 \ x_2)} \mathcal{F}[x_1, x_2]$$

(lexicographic well-founded induction)

is valid. ◢

In **Problem 4.1**, we use the well-foundedness of the lexicographic relation to establish the well-foundedness of the proper-divides relation.

Remark (lexicographic relation for triples)

The definition and results can be extended to apply to more than two binary relations. For instance, to extend the definition to three relations, we would use a theory of triples, analogous to the theory of pairs, over three unary predicate symbols obj_1, obj_2, and obj_3. In this theory, for three binary relations $\prec_1$, $\prec_2$, and $\prec_3$, we define the lexicographic relation $\prec_{lex}$ by the axiom

$$
\begin{matrix}
(\forall\, obj_1\ x_1,\ y_1) \\
(\forall\, obj_2\ x_2,\ y_2) \\
(\forall\, obj_3\ x_3,\ y_3)
\end{matrix}
\left[
\begin{matrix}
\langle x_1,\ x_2,\ x_3 \rangle \prec_{lex} \langle y_1,\ y_2,\ y_3 \rangle \\
\equiv \\
\left[
\begin{matrix}
x_1 \prec_1 y_1 \\
or \\
x_1 = y_1 \ \ and \ \ x_2 \prec_2 y_2 \\
or \\
x_1 = y_1 \ \ and \ \ x_2 = y_2 \ \ and \ \ x_3 \prec_3 y_3
\end{matrix}
\right]
\end{matrix}
\right].
$$

In the same way, we could define lexicographic relations over "quadruples," over "quintuples," and so on. For simplicity, however, we shall continue to deal with only two binary relations. ◢

In **Problem 4.2**, the reader is asked to show that the $\prec_{lex}$ relation is well-founded over triples if its three component relations are well-founded over their respective classes of objects, but that a plausible lexicographic relation over all tuples is actually not well-founded.

Now let us illustrate the use of lexicographic well-founded induction over pairs.

4.3 EXAMPLE: ACKERMANN FUNCTION

The binary Ackermann function $ack(x,\ y)$ is defined in the theory of the nonnegative integers by the following three axioms:

$$(\forall\, integer\ y)\big[ack(0,\ y)\ =\ y+1\big] \qquad\qquad (left\ zero)$$

$$(\forall\, integer\ x)\big[ack(x+1,\ 0)\ =\ ack(x,\ 1)\big] \qquad\qquad (right\ zero)$$

$$(\forall\, integer\ x,\ y)\big[ack(x+1,\ y+1)\ =\ ack\big(x,\ ack(x+1,\ y)\big)\big]$$
$$(double\ successor)$$

From these axioms, we can establish the following properties of the Ackermann function:

$$(\forall \, integer \; x, \, y)\big[integer\,(ack(x, \, y))\big] \qquad\qquad (sort)$$

$$(\forall \, integer \; x, \, y)\big[ack\,(x, \, y) \, > \, y\big] \qquad\qquad (greater \; than)$$

$$(\forall \, integer \; x, \, y, \, z) \begin{bmatrix} if & x < y \\ then & ack(z, \, x) < ack(z, \, y) \end{bmatrix}$$
$$(right \; monotonicity)$$

$$(\forall \, integer \; x, \, y, \, z) \begin{bmatrix} if & x < y \\ then & ack(x, \, z) < ack(y, \, z) \end{bmatrix}$$
$$(left \; monotonicity)$$

$$(\forall \, integer \; x)\big[ack\,(x, \, x) \, \geq \, 2^x\big] \qquad\qquad (exponent)$$

The function is interesting because its values grow extremely quickly, as suggested by the last property. For example,

$$ack(0, \, 0) = 1, \quad ack(1, \, 1) = 3, \quad ack(2, \, 2) = 7, \quad ack(3, \, 3) = 61,$$

and

$$ack(4, \, 4) \; = \; 2^{2^{2^{2^{16}}}} - 3.$$

We prove the *greater-than* property here. The proofs of the other properties are left as an exercise (**Problem 4.3**).

Proposition (greater than)

The sentence

$$(\forall \, integer \; x, \, y)\big[ack\,(x, \, y) \, > \, y\big]$$

is valid.   ⌙

Proof

The proof is by lexicographic well-founded induction, taking both $\prec_1$ and $\prec_2$ to be the less-than relation $<$, and both obj_1 and obj_2 to be *integer*.

We show (renaming x to x_1 and y to x_2)

$$(\forall \, integer \; x_1, \, x_2)\big[ack(x_1, \, x_2) \, > \, x_2\big],$$

taking the inductive sentence to be

$$\mathcal{F}[x_1, \, x_2]: \quad ack(x_1, \, x_2) \, > \, x_2.$$

Inductive Step

For arbitrary nonnegative integers x_1 and x_2, we assume as our induction hypothesis that

(†) $(\forall \ integer \ x'_1, \ x'_2) \begin{bmatrix} if \ \langle x'_1, \ x'_2 \rangle \ \prec_{lex} \ \langle x_1, \ x_2 \rangle \\ then \ \ \mathcal{F}[x'_1, \ x'_2] \end{bmatrix}$.

We would like to show that then $\mathcal{F}[x_1, x_2]$, that is,

(††) $ack(x_1, \ x_2) \ > \ x_2$.

The proof distinguishes among several cases, suggested by the axioms for *ack*.

Case: $x_1 = 0$

Since (by the *left-zero* axiom for *ack*)

$$ack(0, \ x_2) \ = \ x_2 + 1,$$

we have

$$ack(0, \ x_2) \ > \ x_2,$$

which is the desired result (††) in this case.

Case: *not* $(x_1 = 0)$

Then (by the *decomposition* property of the nonnegative integers), there exists some nonnegative integer y_1 such that

$$x_1 \ = \ y_1 + 1.$$

We distinguish between two subcases.

Subcase: $x_2 = 0$

We would like to establish (††), that is, in this subcase (since $x_1 = y_1 + 1$ and $x_2 = 0$), that

$$ack(y_1 + 1, \ 0) \ > \ 0$$

or, equivalently (by the *right-zero* axiom for *ack*),

$$ack(y_1, \ 1) \ > \ 0.$$

By our induction hypothesis (†), taking x'_1 to be y_1 and x'_2 to be 1, we have (because $x_1 = y_1 + 1$ and $x_2 = 0$)

$if \ \langle y_1, \ 1 \rangle \ \prec_{lex} \ \langle y_1 + 1, \ 0 \rangle$
$then \ \ \mathcal{F}[y_1, \ 1]$.

But, because $y_1 < y_1 + 1$, we have (by the definition of the lexicographic relation)

$$\langle y_1, 1 \rangle \prec_{lex} \langle y_1 + 1, 0 \rangle$$

and therefore $\mathcal{F}[y_1, 1]$, that is,

$$ack(y_1, 1) > 1.$$

Hence

$$ack(y_1, 1) > 0,$$

as we wanted to show in this subcase.

Subcase: not $(x_2 = 0)$

Then (by the *decomposition* property of the nonnegative integers), there exists some nonnegative integer y_2 such that

$$x_2 = y_2 + 1.$$

We would like to establish (††), that is, in this subcase (since $x_1 = y_1 + 1$ and $x_2 = y_2 + 1$), that

$$ack(y_1 + 1, y_2 + 1) > y_2 + 1$$

or, equivalently (by the *double-successor* axiom for ack),

(‡‡) $$ack\big(y_1, ack(y_1 + 1, y_2)\big) > y_2 + 1.$$

Taking x_1' to be y_1 and x_2' to be $ack(y_1 + 1, y_2)$ in our induction hypothesis (†), we have (because $x_1 = y_1 + 1$ and $x_2 = y_2 + 1$)

$$if \ \langle y_1, ack(y_1 + 1, y_2) \rangle \prec_{lex} \langle y_1 + 1, y_2 + 1 \rangle$$
$$then \ \mathcal{F}\big[y_1, ack(y_1 + 1, y_2)\big].$$

But, since $y_1 < y_1 + 1$, we have (by the definition of the lexicographic relation)

$$\langle y_1, ack(y_1 + 1, y_2) \rangle \prec_{lex} \langle y_1 + 1, y_2 + 1 \rangle$$

and therefore $\mathcal{F}\big[y_1, ack(y_1 + 1, y_2)\big]$, that is,

(1) $$ack\big(y_1, ack(y_1 + 1, y_2)\big) > ack(y_1 + 1, y_2).$$

By our induction hypothesis (†) again, taking x_1' to be $y_1 + 1$ and x_2' to be y_2, we have (because $x_1 = y_1 + 1$ and $x_2 = y_2 + 1$)

$$if \ \langle y_1 + 1, y_2 \rangle \prec_{lex} \langle y_1 + 1, y_2 + 1 \rangle$$
$$then \ \mathcal{F}[y_1 + 1, y_2].$$

But, since $y_1 + 1 = y_1 + 1$ and $y_2 < y_2 + 1$, we have (by the definition of the lexicographic relation)

$$\langle y_1 + 1, \, y_2 \rangle \prec_{lex} \langle y_1 + 1, \, y_2 + 1 \rangle$$

and therefore $\mathcal{F}[y_1 + 1, \, y_2]$, that is,

$$ack\left(y_1 + 1, \, y_2\right) \; > \; y_2.$$

Hence

(2) $ack(y_1 + 1, \, y_2) \; \geq \; y_2 + 1.$

From (1) and (2) (by the *mixed-transitivity* property of $\geq$) we have

$$ack\left(y_1, \, ack(y_1 + 1, \, y_2)\right) \; > \; y_2 + 1,$$

which is our desired result ($\ddagger\ddagger$).   ◢

Remark (why lexicographic relation?)

The definition of the Ackermann function suggests that the lexicographic relation will be the basis for the induction in the proofs of its properties. For, in each axiom in which a term $ack(s_1, \, s_2)$ constitutes the left-hand side of an equality and a term $ack(t_1, \, t_2)$ occurs in the corresponding right-hand side, we have

$$\langle s_1, \, s_2 \rangle \succ_{lex} \langle t_1, \, t_2 \rangle.$$

In particular, in the *right-zero* axiom we have

$$\langle x + 1, \, 0 \rangle \succ_{lex} \langle x, \, 1 \rangle$$

and in the *double-successor* axiom we have

$$\langle x + 1, \, y + 1 \rangle \succ_{lex} \langle x, \, ack(x + 1, \, y) \rangle$$

$$\langle x + 1, \, y + 1 \rangle \succ_{lex} \langle x + 1, \, y \rangle,$$

for all nonnegative integers x and y. These are the three properties of the lexicographic relation we required for the three applications of the induction hypothesis in the preceding proof.   ◢

4.4   EXAMPLE: GCDPLUS FUNCTION

Recall that, in the theory of the nonnegative integers, we defined a binary function $gcd(x, y)$ to be the greatest common divisor of x and y (Section [I]6.11). The gcd function was defined by the axioms

$$(\forall \, integer \; x)\big[gcd(x, \, 0) = x\big] \hspace{4cm} (zero)$$

$$\begin{matrix}(\forall \, integer \; x) \\ (\forall \, positive \; y)\end{matrix}\Big[gcd(x, \, y) \;=\; gcd\big(y, \; rem(x, \, y)\big)\Big] \hspace{1cm} (remainder)$$

We showed, by complete induction over the nonnegative integers, that $gcd(x, y)$ is indeed a common divisor of x and y, that is,

$$(\forall \, integer \; x, \; y) \begin{bmatrix} gcd(x, \; y) \preceq_{div} x \\ and \\ gcd(x, \; y) \preceq_{div} y \end{bmatrix} \hspace{1cm} (common \; divisor)$$

We indicated also that $gcd(x, y)$ is the greatest of the common divisors of x and y (with respect to the divides relation $\preceq_{div}$), that is,

$$(\forall \, integer \; x, \; y, \; z) \begin{bmatrix} if \;\; z \preceq_{div} x \;\; and \;\; z \preceq_{div} y \\ then \;\; z \preceq_{div} gcd(x, \; y) \end{bmatrix} \hspace{1cm} (greatest)$$

In this section, we present an alternative definition for the greatest-common-divisor function.

Let the binary function $gcdplus(x, y)$ be defined by the following axioms:

$$(\forall \, integer \; x)\big[gcdplus(0, \, x) \;=\; x\big] \hspace{3cm} (left \; zero)$$

$$(\forall \, integer \; x, \; y)\big[gcdplus(x, \, x + y) \;=\; gcdplus(x, \, y)\big] \hspace{1cm} (addition)$$

$$(\forall \, integer \; x, \; y)\big[gcdplus(x, \, y) \;=\; gcdplus(y, \, x)\big] \hspace{1cm} (symmetry)$$

We first illustrate the use of the axioms to compute the greatest common divisor of two particular nonnegative integers.

Example (computation of gcdplus)

Suppose we would like to determine the greatest common divisor of 6 and 3. Then

$$gcdplus(6,\ 3)\ =\ gcdplus(3,\ 6)$$
$$\text{(by the \emph{symmetry} axiom)}$$

$$=\ gcdplus(3,\ 3+3)$$

$$=\ gcdplus(3,\ 3)$$
$$\text{(by the \emph{addition} axiom)}$$

$$=\ gcdplus(3,\ 3+0)$$

$$=\ gcdplus(3,\ 0)$$
$$\text{(by the \emph{addition} axiom)}$$

$$=\ gcdplus(0,\ 3)$$
$$\text{(by the \emph{symmetry} axiom)}$$

$$=\ 3$$
$$\text{(by the \emph{left-zero} axiom).}$$

In short,

$$gcdplus(6,\ 3) = 3.$$ ⌐

Note that a judicious use of the axioms for *gcdplus* is required to avoid an infinite computation. Otherwise, we could repeatedly apply the *symmetry* axiom without ever reaching a final value.

We would like to show that *gcdplus* provides an alternative definition of the *gcd* function.

Proposition (gcdplus)

The sentences

$$(\forall\ integer\ x,\ y)\ \begin{bmatrix} gcdplus(x,\ y) \preceq_{div} x \\ and \\ gcdplus(x,\ y) \preceq_{div} y \end{bmatrix} \qquad (common\ divisor)$$

$$(\forall\ integer\ x,\ y,\ z)\ \begin{bmatrix} if\ \ z \preceq_{div} x\ \ and\ \ z \preceq_{div} y \\ then\ \ z \preceq_{div} gcdplus(x,\ y) \end{bmatrix} \qquad (greatest)$$

$$(\forall\ integer\ x)\big[gcdplus(x,\ y)\ =\ gcd(x,\ y)\big] \qquad (gcd)$$

are valid in the theory of nonnegative integers. ⌐

We first show that the *gcd* property is implied by the *common-divisor* and *greatest* properties; this proof does not require induction. We then show the *greatest* property, that $gcdplus(x, y)$ is the greatest of the common divisors of x and y (with respect to the divides relation $\preceq_{div}$). The proof of the *common-divisor* property, that $gcdplus(x, y)$ is a common divisor of x and y, is left as an exercise (**Problem 4.4**).

Proof (*gcd* property of *gcdplus*)

Assume that we have established the *common-divisor* and *greatest* properties of the *gcdplus* function. We would like to prove the *gcd* property.

Consider arbitrary nonnegative integers x and y. We know (by the *common-divisor* property of the *gcd* function) that

$$gcd(x, \ y) \preceq_{div} x$$
$$and$$
$$gcd(x, \ y) \preceq_{div} y.$$

Also (by the *greatest* property of the *gcdplus* function, taking z to be $gcd(x, \ y)$),

$$if \quad \begin{bmatrix} gcd(x, \ y) \preceq_{div} x \\ and \\ gcd(x, \ y) \preceq_{div} y \end{bmatrix}$$
$$then \quad gcd(x, \ y) \preceq_{div} gcdplus(x, \ y).$$

Therefore we have

$$(\dagger) \qquad gcd(x, \ y) \preceq_{div} gcdplus(x, \ y).$$

Similarly (by the *common-divisor* property of the *gcdplus* function), we know

$$gcdplus(x, \ y) \preceq_{div} x$$
$$and$$
$$gcdplus(x, \ y) \preceq_{div} y.$$

Also (by the *greatest* property of the *gcd* function, taking z to be $gcdplus(x, \ y)$),

$$if \quad \begin{bmatrix} gcdplus(x, \ y) \preceq_{div} x \\ and \\ gcdplus(x, \ y) \preceq_{div} y \end{bmatrix}$$
$$then \quad gcdplus(x, \ y) \preceq_{div} gcd(x, \ y).$$

Therefore

$$(\ddagger) \qquad gcdplus(x, \ y) \preceq_{div} gcd(x, \ y).$$

From (†) and (‡) (by the *antisymmetry* of the divides relation $\preceq_{div}$), we have

$$gcdplus(x, y) \;=\; gcd(x, y),$$

as we wanted to show.   ◢

Proof (*greatest* property of *gcdplus*)

We would like to show (renaming x to x_1 and y to x_2)

$$(\forall\ integer\ x_1,\ x_2,\ z) \begin{bmatrix} if\ \ z \preceq_{div} x_1\ \ and\ \ z \preceq_{div} x_2 \\ then\ \ z \preceq_{div} gcdplus(x_1,\ x_2) \end{bmatrix}.$$

Consider an arbitrary nonnegative integer z; we must show

$$(\forall\ integer\ x_1,\ x_2) \begin{bmatrix} if\ \ z \preceq_{div} x_1\ \ and\ \ z \preceq_{div} x_2 \\ then\ \ z \preceq_{div} gcdplus(x_1,\ x_2) \end{bmatrix}.$$

The proof is by lexicographic well-founded induction, taking both $\prec_1$ and $\prec_2$ to be the less-than relation $<$ and both obj_1 and obj_2 to be *integer*.

We prove

$$(\forall\ integer\ x_1, x_2)\,\mathcal{F}[x_1, x_2],$$

where the inductive sentence is

$$\mathcal{F}[x_1,\ x_2]: \quad \begin{array}{l} if\ \ z \preceq_{div} x_1\ \ and\ \ z \preceq_{div} x_2 \\ then\ \ z \preceq_{div} gcdplus(x_1,\ x_2) \end{array}.$$

Inductive Step

For arbitrary nonnegative integers x_1 and x_2, we assume as our induction hypothesis that

$$(†) \qquad (\forall\ integer\ x_1',\ x_2') \begin{bmatrix} if\ \ \langle x_1',\ x_2' \rangle \prec_{lex} \langle x_1,\ x_2 \rangle \\ then\ \ \mathcal{F}[x_1',\ x_2'] \end{bmatrix}.$$

We would like to show that then $\mathcal{F}[x_1,\ x_2]$, that is,

$$\begin{array}{l} if\ \ z \preceq_{div} x_1\ \ and\ \ z \preceq_{div} x_2 \\ then\ \ z \preceq_{div} gcdplus(x_1,\ x_2). \end{array}$$

Suppose that

$$(‡) \qquad z \preceq_{div} x_1\ \ and\ \ z \preceq_{div} x_2.$$

We show that then

$$(‡‡) \qquad z \preceq_{div} gcdplus(x_1,\ x_2).$$

The proof distinguishes among three cases.

Case: $x_1 = 0$

We would like to show (‡‡), that is (in this case),

$$z \preceq_{div} gcdplus(0, \; x_2)$$

or, equivalently (by the *left-zero* axiom for *gcdplus*),

$$z \preceq_{div} x_2.$$

But this follows from our initial supposition (‡).

Case: *not* $(x_1 = 0)$ *and* $x_2 < x_1$

We would like to show (‡‡), that is (by the *symmetry* axiom for *gcdplus*),

$$z \preceq_{div} gcdplus(x_2, \; x_1).$$

Because, in this case, $x_2 < x_1$, we have (by the definition of the lexicographic relation)

$$\langle x_2, \; x_1 \rangle \prec_{lex} \langle x_1, \; x_2 \rangle.$$

By our induction hypothesis (†), taking x_1' to be x_2 and x_2' to be x_1, we have

$$\textit{if} \; \langle x_2, \; x_1 \rangle \prec_{lex} \langle x_1, \; x_2 \rangle$$
$$\textit{then} \; \mathcal{F}[x_2, \; x_1].$$

Hence we have $\mathcal{F}[x_2, \; x_1]$, that is,

$$\textit{if} \; z \preceq_{div} x_2 \; \textit{and} \; z \preceq_{div} x_1$$
$$\textit{then} \; z \preceq_{div} gcdplus(x_2, \; x_1).$$

But by our initial supposition (‡)

$$z \preceq_{div} x_2 \; \textit{and} \; z \preceq_{div} x_1.$$

Therefore

$$z \preceq_{div} gcdplus(x_2, \; x_1),$$

as we wanted to show.

Case: *not* $(x_1 = 0)$ *and* *not* $(x_2 < x_1)$

Then (by the *total-asymmetry* property of the less-than relation)

$$x_1 \leq x_2.$$

Therefore (by the *left-addition* property of the weak less-than relation), there exists a nonnegative integer y such that

$$x_2 = x_1 + y.$$

We would like to show (‡‡), that $z \preceq_{div} gcdplus(x_1, x_2)$, that is (in this case),

$$z \preceq_{div} gcdplus(x_1, x_1 + y)$$

or, equivalently (by the *addition* axiom for *gcdplus*),

$$z \preceq_{div} gcdplus(x_1, y).$$

To apply our induction hypothesis, we first establish that

$$\langle x_1, y \rangle \prec_{lex} \langle x_1, x_2 \rangle,$$

that is,

$$\langle x_1, y \rangle \prec_{lex} \langle x_1, x_1 + y \rangle.$$

For this purpose, it suffices to show (by the definition of the lexicographic relation, because $x_1 = x_1$) that

$$y < x_1 + y.$$

But this follows (by the *left-addition* property of the strict less-than relation) because in this case *not* $(x_1 = 0)$.

By our induction hypothesis (†), taking x_1' to be x_1 and x_2' to be y, we have

$$if \ \ \langle x_1, y \rangle \prec_{lex} \langle x_1, x_2 \rangle$$
$$then \ \ \mathcal{F}[x_1, y].$$

Hence (because $\langle x_1, y \rangle \prec_{lex} \langle x_1, x_2 \rangle$) we have $\mathcal{F}[x_1, y]$, that is,

$$if \ \ z \preceq_{div} x_1 \ \ and \ \ z \preceq_{div} y$$
$$then \ \ z \preceq_{div} gcdplus(x_1, y).$$

We have supposed initially (‡) that $z \preceq_{div} x_1$ and $z \preceq_{div} x_2$. Therefore (because $x_2 = x_1 + y$)

$$z \preceq_{div} x_1 \ \ and \ \ z \preceq_{div} (x_1 + y).$$

Then (by the *addition* property of the divides relation $\preceq_{div}$)

$$z \preceq_{div} x_1 \ \ and \ \ z \preceq_{div} y.$$

It therefore follows that

$$z \preceq_{div} gcdplus(x_1, y),$$

as we wanted to show in this case. ⏌

Two other definitions of the *gcd* function are given as exercises (**Problems 4.5** and **4.6**).

4.5   EXAMPLE: MERGESORT

The example in this section illustrates the use of lexicographic well-founded induction over the theory of tuples.

THE MERGESORT FUNCTION

Consider the theory of tuples of nonnegative integers. In this theory, we provide an alternative definition of the *sort* function by introducing a unary function symbol $mergesort(z)$, which sorts the elements of z by a new method. We first split the given tuple z into two subtuples x and y, where $z = x \diamond y$; the division into a "left half" x and a "right half" y is arbitrary. We sort the elements of x and y separately and then we merge the elements of the resulting tuples, so that the final result is in (weakly) increasing order.

The axioms for the *mergesort* function are as follows:

$$
\begin{array}{ll}
mergesort(\langle\,\rangle) = \langle\,\rangle & (empty) \\[2ex]
(\forall\ atom\ u)\big[mergesort(\langle u\rangle)\ =\ \langle u\rangle\big] & (singleton) \\[2ex]
(\forall\ tuple\ x,\ y)\left[\begin{array}{l} mergesort(x \diamond y)\ = \\ merge\big(mergesort(x),\ mergesort(y)\big) \end{array}\right] & (append)
\end{array}
$$

Note that separate axioms treat the case in which the given tuple has only one element, or none at all. If we are computing the function according to these axioms, to ensure that the process terminates we should guarantee that neither half x nor y is actually the empty tuple, that is, that neither x nor y is the same as $x \diamond y$, although this is not required by the axioms.

The auxiliary function symbol $merge(x, y)$ intermixes the elements of the ordered tuples x and y so that the result remains in (weakly) increasing order. It is defined by the following axioms:

$$(\forall\, tuple\ y)\big[merge(\langle\ \rangle,\ y)\ =\ y\big] \qquad\qquad (left\ empty)$$

$$(\forall\, tuple\ x)\big[merge(x,\ \langle\ \rangle)\ =\ x\big] \qquad\qquad (right\ empty)$$

$$
\begin{aligned}
(\forall\, atom\ u,\ v) \\
(\forall\, tuple\ x,\ y)
\end{aligned}
\left[
\begin{array}{l}
merge(u \diamond x,\ v \diamond y) \\
\quad = \left\{
\begin{array}{l}
if\ \ u \le v \\
then\ \ u \diamond merge(x,\ v \diamond y) \\
else\ \ v \diamond merge(u \diamond x,\ y)
\end{array}
\right\}
\end{array}
\right]
\qquad (insertion)
$$

Thus

$$merge\big(\langle 1,\ 2,\ 5\rangle,\ \langle 2,\ 4,\ 4\rangle\big)\ =\ \langle 1,\ 2,\ 2,\ 4,\ 4,\ 5\rangle.$$

We would like to show that the *mergesort* axioms do indeed provide an alternative definition of *sort*, that is, that

$$(\forall\, tuple\ x)\big[mergesort(x)\ =\ sort(x)\big] \qquad\qquad (sorting)$$

As before, it suffices to establish (by the *uniqueness* property of *sort*) two properties of the *mergesort* function: that the tuple *mergesort(x)* is in increasing order, that is,

$$(\forall\, tuple\ x)\big[ordered\,(mergesort(x))\big] \qquad\qquad (ordered)$$

and that the elements of *mergesort(x)* are the same as those of *x*, that is,

$$(\forall\, tuple\ x)\big[perm\,(x,\ mergesort(x))\big] \qquad\qquad (permutation)$$

The *sort* function is the only function with these two properties. Recall that *ordered(x)* holds if the elements of the tuple *x* are in (weakly) increasing order and that *perm(x, y)* holds if the tuple *y* can be obtained from the tuple *x* by rearranging its elements (but preserving their multiplicity).

If we regard the axioms for *mergesort* as a program describing a computational sorting method, the proof of the *sorting* property can be regarded as part of the verification of the correctness of that program.

We shall require the following two properties of the auxiliary function *merge*. It is the proofs of these properties that require lexicographic well-founded induction.

Proposition (merge)

The sentences

$$(\forall \text{ tuple } x, \ y) \begin{bmatrix} if \ ordered(x) \ and \ ordered(y) \\ then \ ordered(merge(x, \ y)) \end{bmatrix} \qquad (ordered)$$

$$(\forall \text{ tuple } x, \ y) \Big[perm\big(x \diamond y, \ merge(x, \ y)\big) \Big] \qquad (permutation)$$

are valid. ⌟

That is, if x and y are in increasing order, so is $merge(x, y)$, and the elements of $merge(x, y)$ are the same as those of x and y together.

The proof of the *permutation* property of the *merge* proposition is left as an exercise (**Problem 4.7**). The proof of the *ordered* property, which follows, depends on the *permutation* property.

In the proof, we use the *insertion* property of the *ordered* relation:

$$(\forall \text{ atom } u) \\ (\forall \text{ tuple } x) \begin{bmatrix} ordered(u \diamond x) \\ \equiv \\ \begin{bmatrix} ordered(x) \\ and \\ (\forall \text{ atom } v) \begin{bmatrix} if \ v \in x \\ then \ u \le v \end{bmatrix} \end{bmatrix} \end{bmatrix} \qquad (insertion)$$

Proof (*ordered* property of *merge*)

We would like to show (renaming x to x_1 and y to x_2)

$$(\forall \text{ tuple } x_1, \ x_2) \begin{bmatrix} if \ ordered(x_1) \ and \ ordered(x_2) \\ then \ ordered(merge(x_1, \ x_2)) \end{bmatrix}.$$

The proof is by lexicographic well-founded induction, taking both obj_1 and obj_2 to be *tuple*, and both $\prec_1$ and $\prec_2$ to be the proper-subtuple relation $\subset$.

We prove

$$(\forall \text{ tuple } x_1, x_2) \mathcal{F}[x_1, x_2],$$

where we take the inductive sentence to be

$$\mathcal{F}[x_1, \ x_2]: \quad \begin{array}{l} if \ ordered(x_1) \ and \ ordered(x_2) \\ then \ ordered(merge(x_1, \ x_2)). \end{array}$$

Inductive Step

For arbitrary tuples x_1 and x_2, assume the induction hypothesis

(†) $(\forall \text{ tuple } x_1', x_2') \begin{bmatrix} if & \langle x_1', x_2' \rangle \prec_{lex} \langle x_1, x_2 \rangle \\ then & \mathcal{F}[x_1', x_2'] \end{bmatrix}$.

We would like to show the desired conclusion $\mathcal{F}[x_1, x_2]$, that is,

$$ if \ \ ordered(x_1) \ \ and \ \ ordered(x_2) $$
$$ then \ \ ordered\big(merge(x_1, x_2)\big). $$

We suppose that

(‡) $ordered(x_1) \ \ and \ \ ordered(x_2)$

and show that then

(‡‡) $ordered\big(merge(x_1, x_2)\big).$

The proof distinguishes among several cases, suggested by the axioms for *merge*.

Case: $x_1 = \langle \ \rangle$

We would like to show (‡‡), that is (in this case),

$$ ordered\big(merge(\langle \ \rangle, x_2)\big) $$

or, equivalently (by the *left-empty* axiom for the *merge* function),

$$ ordered(x_2). $$

But this is the second conjunct of our supposition (‡).

Case: $x_2 = \langle \ \rangle$

This case is similar to the preceding case (by the *right-empty* axiom for the *merge* function).

Case: $not \ (x_1 = \langle \ \rangle) \ \ and \ \ not \ (x_2 = \langle \ \rangle)$

Then (by the *decomposition* property of tuples), there exist atoms u_1 and u_2 and tuples y_1 and y_2 such that

(1) $x_1 = u_1 \diamond y_1 \ \ and \ \ x_2 = u_2 \diamond y_2.$

Because we have supposed (‡) that $ordered(x_1)$ and $ordered(x_2)$, that is (in this case),

$$ ordered(u_1 \diamond y_1) \ \ and \ \ ordered(u_2 \diamond y_2), $$

we have (by the *insertion* property of the *ordered* relation)

$$(2) \qquad ordered(y_1) \quad and \quad (\forall\, atom\ v_1) \begin{bmatrix} if & v_1 \in y_1 \\ then & u_1 \leq v_1 \end{bmatrix}$$

and

$$(3) \qquad ordered(y_2) \quad and \quad (\forall\, atom\ v_2) \begin{bmatrix} if & v_2 \in y_2 \\ then & u_2 \leq v_2 \end{bmatrix}.$$

We would like to show (‡‡), $ordered(merge(x_1,\ x_2))$, that is (in this case),

$$(\dagger\dagger) \qquad ordered(merge(u_1 \diamond y_1,\ u_2 \diamond y_2)).$$

We distinguish between two further subcases.

Subcase: $u_1 \leq u_2$

Then (by the *insertion* axiom for *merge*), to show (††), it suffices to show

$$ordered(u_1 \diamond merge(y_1,\ u_2 \diamond y_2))$$

or, equivalently (by the *insertion* property of the *ordered* relation),

$$(4) \qquad ordered(merge(y_1,\ u_2 \diamond y_2))$$

and

$$(5) \qquad (\forall\, atom\ w) \begin{bmatrix} if & w \in merge(y_1,\ u_2 \diamond y_2) \\ then & u_1 \leq w \end{bmatrix}.$$

Proof of (4)

We first prove (4). By our induction hypothesis (†), taking x_1' to be y_1 and x_2' to be $u_2 \diamond y_2$, we have (because, by (1), $x_1 = u_1 \diamond y_1$ and $x_2 = u_2 \diamond y_2$)

$$if\ \langle y_1,\ u_2 \diamond y_2 \rangle \prec_{lex} \langle u_1 \diamond y_1,\ u_2 \diamond y_2 \rangle$$
$$then\ \mathcal{F}[y_1,\ u_2 \diamond y_2].$$

But because (by the *adjacent* property of the subtuple relation)

$$y_1 \subset (u_1 \diamond y_1),$$

we have (by the definition of the lexicographic relation)

$$\langle y_1,\ u_2 \diamond y_2 \rangle \prec_{lex} \langle u_1 \diamond y_1,\ u_2 \diamond y_2 \rangle,$$

and hence $\mathcal{F}[y_1,\ u_2 \diamond y_2]$, that is,

$$if\ ordered(y_1)\ and\ ordered(u_2 \diamond y_2)$$
$$then\ ordered(merge(y_1,\ u_2 \diamond y_2)).$$

But from our earlier conclusion (2) and supposition (‡) (because, by (1), $x_2 = u_2 \diamond y_2$), it follows that

$$ordered(y_1) \quad and \quad ordered(u_2 \diamond y_2).$$

Therefore

$$ordered\bigl(merge(y_1, \ u_2 \diamond y_2)\bigr),$$

which is the desired result (4).

Proof of (5)

It remains to prove (5), that is,

$$(\forall \ atom \ w) \begin{bmatrix} if & w \in merge(y_1, \ u_2 \diamond y_2) \\ then & u_1 \leq w \end{bmatrix}.$$

Consider an arbitrary atom w and suppose that

(6) $w \ \in \ merge(y_1, \ u_2 \diamond y_2).$

We would like to show that

(7) $u_1 \leq w.$

We know (by the *permutation* property of *merge*, the other part of this proposition) that

$$perm\bigl(y_1 \diamond (u_2 \diamond y_2), \ merge(y_1, \ u_2 \diamond y_2)\bigr).$$

Therefore (by the *member* axiom for the permutation relation), because, by our supposition (6), $w \in merge(y_1, \ u_2 \diamond y_2)$, we have

$$w \ \in \ y_1 \diamond (u_2 \diamond y_2)$$

or, equivalently (by the *member* property of the append function $\diamond$),

$$w \in y_1 \quad or \quad w \in (u_2 \diamond y_2)$$

or, equivalently (by the *insertion* axiom for the member relation),

$$w \in y_1 \quad or \quad w = u_2 \quad or \quad w \in y_2.$$

We treat each of these three possibilities separately.

First possibility: $w \in y_1$

We have (by our earlier conclusion (2), taking v_1 to be w)

$$if \ \ w \in y_1$$
$$then \ \ u_1 \leq w.$$

Therefore, in this case, we have the desired result (7), that

$$u_1 \leq w.$$

Second possibility: $w = u_2$

We would like to show (7), $u_1 \leq w$, that is (in this case),

$$u_1 \leq u_2.$$

But this is our subcase assumption.

Third possibility: $w \in y_2$

We have (by our earlier conclusion (3), taking v_2 to be w)

$$if \ \ w \in y_2$$
$$then \ \ u_2 \leq w.$$

Therefore, in this case, we have

$$u_2 \leq w.$$

We also know (from our subcase assumption) that

$$u_1 \leq u_2.$$

Therefore (by the *transitivity* of $\leq$) we have the desired result (7), that

$$u_1 \leq w.$$

This concludes the proof of (5).

Subcase: $not \ (u_1 \leq u_2)$

Then (by the *insertion* axiom for *merge*) to show (††), it suffices to show that

$$ordered\big(u_2 \diamond merge(u_1 \diamond y_1, \ y_2)\big).$$

The proof is similar to the proof for the previous subcase, in which $u_1 \leq u_2$. In this subcase, to apply the induction hypothesis we use the *adjacent* property of the subtuple relation,

$$y_2 \subset (u_2 \diamond y_2),$$

to conclude (by the definition of the lexicographic relation, because $u_1 \diamond y_1 = u_1 \diamond y_1$) that

$$\langle u_1 \diamond y_1, \ y_2 \rangle \prec_{lex} \langle u_1 \diamond y_1, \ u_2 \diamond y_2 \rangle.$$

Hence (by (†), the induction hypothesis)

$$\mathcal{F}[u_1 \diamond y_1, \ y_2].$$

The other details of the proof are omitted. ⌐

Once the properties of the auxiliary function *merge* are established, we can prove the required properties of the *mergesort* function.

Proposition (mergesort)

The sentences

$$(\forall\ tuple\ x)\big[ordered\,(mergesort(x))\big] \qquad\qquad (ordered)$$

$$(\forall\ tuple\ x)\big[perm\,(x,\ mergesort(x))\big] \qquad\qquad (permutation)$$

$$(\forall\ tuple\ x)\big[mergesort(x)\ =\ sort(x)\big] \qquad\qquad (sorting)$$

are valid. ⌐

The proofs of the three parts of the proposition, which do not require lexicographic well-founded induction, are left as an exercise (**Problem 4.8**). An exercise in the theory of tuples that does require a lexicographic relation is given in **Problem 4.9**.

PROBLEMS

Problem 4.1 (proper divides)   page 123

We have shown (in Section 1.6) that the proper-divides relation $\prec_{div}$ is well-founded over all the nonnegative integers. That proof was based on the well-foundedness of the union relation $\prec_{union}$. Give another proof based on the well-foundedness of the lexicographic relation.

Hint: Map $\prec_{div}$ into the lexicographic relation over pairs of nonnegative integers corresponding to $<$ and $<$.

Problem 4.2 (triples and tuples)   page 124

(a)   *Triples*

Suppose that $\prec_1$, $\prec_2$, and $\prec_3$ are well-founded over obj_1, obj_2, and obj_3, respectively. Show (informally) that the corresponding lexicographic relation $\prec_{lex}$ is well-founded over *triple*, in a theory of triples analogous to our theory of pairs.

Hint: Use the result of the *lexicographic-relation* proposition for pairs.

(b) *Tuples*

In the theory of tuples, suppose that $\prec$ is well-founded over *atom*. Consider the relation $\prec_{lex}$ defined by the axioms

$$\begin{matrix} (\forall \; atom \; u) \\ (\forall \; tuple \; y) \end{matrix} \left[\langle \, \rangle \; \prec_{lex} u \diamond y \right] \qquad\qquad (left\ empty)$$

$$(\forall \; tuple \; x) \left[not \; \left(x \prec_{lex} \langle \, \rangle \right) \right] \qquad\qquad (right\ empty)$$

$$\begin{matrix} (\forall \; atom \; u, \; v) \\ (\forall \; tuple \; x, \; y) \end{matrix} \left[\begin{matrix} u \diamond x \prec_{lex} v \diamond y \\ \equiv \\ \left[\begin{matrix} u \prec v \;\; or \\ u = v \;\; and \;\; x \prec_{lex} y \end{matrix} \right] \end{matrix} \right] \qquad (insertion)$$

For example, in the theory of tuples of nonnegative integers, taking $\prec$ to be $<$, we have

$$\langle \, \rangle \prec_{lex} \langle 0 \rangle, \qquad \langle 1, \, 2, \, 3 \rangle \prec_{lex} \langle 1, \, 2, \, 4 \rangle, \qquad \langle 1, \, 2, \, 100 \rangle \prec_{lex} \langle 1, \, 3 \rangle.$$

Show, by exhibiting an infinite decreasing sequence, that $\prec_{lex}$ is not necessarily well-founded over *tuple*.

Problem 4.3 (Ackermann)   page 125

*: indicates problem of unusual difficulty or length.

Establish the validity of the following properties of the Ackermann function:

(a) *Sort*

$$(\forall \; integer \; x, \; y) \left[integer \left(ack(x, \; y) \right) \right]$$

(b) *Right monotonicity*

$$(\forall \; integer \; x, \; y, \; z) \left[\begin{matrix} if \;\; x < y \\ then \;\; ack(z, \; x) < ack(z, \; y) \end{matrix} \right]$$

(c) *Left monotonicity*

$$(\forall \; integer \; x, \; y, \; z) \left[\begin{matrix} if \;\; x < y \\ then \;\; ack(x, \; z) < ack(y, \; z) \end{matrix} \right]$$

* (d) *Exponent*

$$(\forall \; integer \; x) \left[ack(x, \; x) \geq 2^x \right].$$

Note: Not all of these require lexicographic well-founded induction.

Problem 4.4 (gcdplus)   page 131

Prove the *common-divisor* property of the *gcdplus* function, that is,

$$(\forall \ integer \ x, \ y) \begin{bmatrix} gcdplus(x, \ y) \preceq_{div} x \\ and \\ gcdplus(x, \ y) \preceq_{div} y \end{bmatrix}.$$

Problem 4.5 (gcdbinary)   page 135

Let the *gcdbinary* function be defined by the following axioms:

$$(\forall \ integer \ x) \big[gcdbinary(x, \ 0) \ = \ x \big] \qquad\qquad (right \ zero)$$

$$(\forall \ integer \ x, \ y) \big[gcdbinary(2 \cdot x, \ 2 \cdot y) \ = \ 2 \cdot gcdbinary(x, \ y) \big] \\ (even \ even)$$

$$(\forall \ integer \ x, \ y) \begin{bmatrix} if \ \ not \ (even(x)) \\ then \ \ gcdbinary(x, \ 2 \cdot y) \ = \ gcdbinary(x, \ y) \end{bmatrix} \\ (odd \ even)$$

$$(\forall \ integer \ x, \ y) \begin{bmatrix} if \ \ not \ (even(x)) \ \ and \\ \quad not \ (even(y)) \ \ and \ \ x \leq y \\ then \ \ gcdbinary(x, \ y) \ = \ gcdbinary(x, \ y - x) \end{bmatrix} \\ (odd \ odd)$$

$$(\forall \ integer \ x, \ y) \big[gcdbinary(x, \ y) \ = \ gcdbinary(y, \ x) \big] \quad (symmetry)$$

where the relation $even(x)$, which is true if x is even, is defined by the *two* axiom

$$(\forall \ integer \ x) \big[even(x) \ \equiv \ 2 \preceq_{div} x \big]. \qquad\qquad (two)$$

(a) *Common divisor*

Show that $gcdbinary(x, \ y)$ is a common divisor of x and y, that is,

$$(\forall \ integer \ x, \ y) \begin{bmatrix} gcdbinary(x, \ y) \preceq_{div} x \\ and \\ gcdbinary(x, \ y) \preceq_{div} y \end{bmatrix}.$$

(b) *Greatest*

Show that *gcdbinary*(*x*, *y*) is the greatest of the common divisors of *x* and *y*, that is,

$$(\forall \, integer \; x, \; y, \; z) \begin{bmatrix} if \;\; z \preceq_{div} x \;\; and \;\; z \preceq_{div} y \\ then \;\; z \preceq_{div} gcdbinary(x, \; y) \end{bmatrix}.$$

(c) *Gcd*

Show that *gcdbinary* provides an alternative definition for the *gcd* function, that is,

$$(\forall \, integer \; x, \; y) \Big[gcdbinary(x, \; y) \; = \; gcd(x, \; y) \Big].$$

State whatever properties of the nonnegative integers you use; you need not prove them, but use the simplest properties you can.

Problem 4.6 (**revised gcdbinary**)   page 135

Suppose that, in the definition of the *gcdbinary* function (defined in Problem 4.5), we replace the *odd-odd* axiom by the following two axioms:

$$(\forall \, integer \; x) \Big[gcdbinary(x, \; x) = x \Big] \hspace{3cm} (equal)$$

$$(\forall \, integer \; x, \; y) \begin{bmatrix} if \;\; not \; \big(even \; (x)\big) \;\; and \\ \quad not \; \big(even \; (y)\big) \;\; and \;\; x < y \\ then \;\; gcdbinary(x, \; y) = gcdbinary(x, \; x + y) \end{bmatrix}$$
$$(odd \; plus)$$

Show that *gcdbinary* still provides an alternative definition of the *gcd* function. (You need present only those parts of the proof that differ from the previous proof.)

Problem 4.7 (**merge**)   page 137

Prove the *permutation* property of the *merge* function, that is,

$$(\forall \, tuple \; x, \; y) \Big[perm \big(x \diamond y, \; merge(x, \; y) \big) \Big].$$

Problem 4.8 (**mergesort**)   page 142

Establish the following properties of the *mergesort* function:

(a)   *Permutation*

The tuple $mergesort(x)$ is a permutation of the tuple x, that is,

$$(\forall\ tuple\ x)\big[perm(x,\ mergesort(x))\big].$$

(b)   *Ordered*

The tuple $mergesort(x)$ is in (weakly) increasing order, that is,

$$(\forall\ tuple\ x)\big[ordered(mergesort(x))\big].$$

(c)   *Sorting*

The $mergesort$ function is identical to the $sort$ function, that is,

$$(\forall\ tuple\ x)\big[mergesort(x)\ =\ sort(x)\big].$$

These problems do not require lexicographic well-founded induction.

Problem 4.9 (ones)   page 142

In the theory of tuples of nonnegative integers, suppose that the unary *ones* function is defined by the following axioms:

$$ones(\langle\ \rangle)\ =\ \langle\ \rangle \qquad\qquad\qquad (empty)$$

$$(\forall\ tuple\ x)\big[ones(0 \diamond x)\ =\ ones(x)\big] \qquad\qquad (zero)$$

$$\begin{matrix}(\forall\ integer\ u)\\ (\forall\ tuple\ x)\end{matrix}\Big[ones\big((u+1)\diamond x\big)\ =\ 1\diamond ones(u\diamond x)\Big] \qquad (successor)$$

For each nonnegative integer n in the given tuple x, the function $ones(x)$ inserts n copies of the integer 1 into the resulting tuple. For example, $ones(\langle 2,\ 1\rangle) = \langle 1,\ 1,\ 1\rangle$ and $ones(\langle 2,\ 0,\ 3\rangle) = \langle 1,\ 1,\ 1,\ 1,\ 1\rangle$.

Suppose further that the unary *sum* function is defined by the axioms

$$sum(\langle\ \rangle)\ =\ 0 \qquad\qquad\qquad (empty)$$

$$\begin{matrix}(\forall\ integer\ u)\\ (\forall\ tuple\ x)\end{matrix}\Big[sum(u\diamond x)\ =\ u+sum(x)\Big] \qquad\qquad (insertion)$$

Thus $sum(x)$ is the sum of the nonnegative integers in the tuple x.

Finally, let $\prec_{\ell\text{-}s}$ be the binary relation defined by the axiom

$$(\forall\ tuple\ x,\ y)\left[\begin{array}{l} x \prec_{\ell\text{-}s} y \\ \equiv \\ \left[\begin{array}{l} length(x) < length(y)\ \ or \\ length(x)\ =\ length(y)\ \ and\ \ sum(x) < sum(y) \end{array}\right] \end{array}\right]$$
$$(length\text{-}sum)$$

(a)   Show that $\prec_{\ell\text{-}s}$ is well-founded over *tuple*.
      Hint: Map $\prec_{\ell\text{-}s}$ into a lexicographic relation.

(b)   Prove that

$$(\forall\ tuple\ x)\big[sum(x)\ =\ sum\big(ones(x)\big)\big].$$

You may use any properties of the nonnegative integers you wish without
proof.

Hint: Use well-founded induction with respect to $\prec_{\ell\text{-}s}$.

II

Propositional Logic

5

Logical
Apparatus

So far, we have given somewhat informal proofs of the validity of sentences, in that we relied on our common sense in going from one step to the next. In the rest of this book, we develop a deductive system for conducting the same proofs formally. In such a system, each step is developed by applying a precise deduction rule. Formal systems are valuable both to ensure the correctness of proofs and to serve as the basis for computer theorem-proving systems.

We shall present formal deductive systems for propositional logic, predicate logic, theories with equality, and special theories with mathematical induction. In this chapter, we present technical notions from propositional logic that are required for developing these formal systems.

5.1 POLARITY

Polarity is a syntactic indicator as to how the truth of a subsentence contributes to the truth of the sentence as a whole. We shall assign a polarity, positive $(+)$ or negative $(-)$, to each occurrence of a subsentence $\mathcal{E}$ of a given sentence $\mathcal{S}$. Roughly, an occurrence of $\mathcal{E}$ is positive [negative] in $\mathcal{S}$ if it is in the scope of an even [odd] number of *not*'s (negations).

POLARITY OF OCCURRENCES

We define the polarity of each individual occurrence of a subsentence of a given sentence.

Definition (polarity of occurrences)

> If S is a sentence, we assign a *polarity in S*,
>
> > positive $(+)$, or negative $(-)$, or both $(\pm)$,
>
> to every occurrence of a subsentence of S, according to the following *polarity-assignment rules*.
>
> In stating these rules, we say that two subsentences are of *opposite polarity* if one of them is positive and the other is negative, even if one or the other has both polarities. Also, π indicates a polarity $(+$ or $-$ or $\pm)$ and $-\pi$ indicates the opposite polarity $(-$ or $+$ or $\pm$, respectively).
>
> - *Top* rule
>
>   The sentence S itself is positive in S; that is,
>
> $$S^+.$$
>
> - *Not* rule
>
>   If a subsentence $\mathcal{E}$ of S is of form
>
>   > *not $\mathcal{F}$,*
>
>   then its component $\mathcal{F}$ has polarity in S opposite to that of $\mathcal{E}$; that is, we have the rule
>
> $$[not\ \mathcal{F}]^\pi \;\Rightarrow\; not\ \mathcal{F}^{-\pi}.$$
>
> - *And* and *or* rules
>
>   If a subsentence $\mathcal{E}$ of S is of form
>
>   > *$\mathcal{F}$ and $\mathcal{G}$*   or   *$\mathcal{F}$ or $\mathcal{G}$,*
>
>   then its components $\mathcal{F}$ and $\mathcal{G}$ have the same polarity as $\mathcal{E}$ in S; that is,
>
> $$[\mathcal{F}\ and\ \mathcal{G}]^\pi \;\Rightarrow\; \mathcal{F}^\pi\ and\ \mathcal{G}^\pi$$
> $$[\mathcal{F}\ or\ \mathcal{G}]^\pi \;\Rightarrow\; \mathcal{F}^\pi\ or\ \mathcal{G}^\pi.$$

- *If-then* rule

  If a subsentence $\mathcal{E}$ of S is of form

  $$if \ \mathcal{F} \ then \ \mathcal{G},$$

  then its consequent $\mathcal{G}$ has the same polarity as $\mathcal{E}$ in S, but its antecedent $\mathcal{F}$ has polarity in S opposite to that of $\mathcal{E}$; that is,

  $$[if \ \mathcal{F} \ then \ \mathcal{G}]^\pi \ \Rightarrow \ if \ \mathcal{F}^{-\pi} \ then \ \mathcal{G}^\pi.$$

- $\equiv$ rule

  If a subsentence $\mathcal{E}$ of S is of form

  $$\mathcal{F} \equiv \mathcal{G},$$

  then its components $\mathcal{F}$ and $\mathcal{G}$ have both positive and negative polarity in S (independent of the polarity of $\mathcal{E}$ in S); that is,

  $$[\mathcal{F} \equiv \mathcal{G}]^\pi \ \Rightarrow \ \mathcal{F}^\pm \equiv \mathcal{G}^\pm.$$

- *If-then-else* rule

  If a subsentence $\mathcal{E}$ of S is of form

  $$if \ \mathcal{F} \ then \ \mathcal{G} \ else \ \mathcal{H},$$

  then its *then*-clause $\mathcal{G}$ and its *else*-clause $\mathcal{H}$ have the same polarity as $\mathcal{E}$ in S, and its *if*-clause $\mathcal{F}$ has both positive and negative polarity in S; that is,

  $$\left[if \ \mathcal{F} \ then \ \mathcal{G} \ else \ \mathcal{H}\right]^\pi \ \Rightarrow \ if \ \mathcal{F}^\pm \ then \ \mathcal{G}^\pi \ else \ \mathcal{H}^\pi. \quad \lrcorner$$

Starting with S itself, we can assign a polarity to each of its components by applying one of the preceding rules. Thus, step by step, we can assign a polarity to each occurrence of each subsentence of S.

Example (polarity assignment)

Let us gradually annotate the sentence

$$if \ ((not \ P) \ or \ Q)$$
$$then \ \Big(Q \ and \ (P \equiv (not \ Q))\Big)$$

with the polarities of each of its subsentences. We use the preceding *polarity-assignment* rules to obtain each row from the preceding row (the boxes indicate the subsentences being considered at each stage).

By the *top* rule, the sentence itself has a positive polarity:

$$\left[\begin{array}{l} if \ ((not\ P)\ or\ Q) \\[2mm] then \quad \left[\begin{array}{c} Q \\ and \\ P\ \equiv\ (not\ Q) \end{array}\right] \end{array}\right]^{+}.$$

By the *if-then* rule, the consequent is positive and the antecedent is negative:

$$\left[\begin{array}{l} if \quad \boxed{(not\ P)\ or\ Q}^{\;-} \\[2mm] then \quad \boxed{\begin{array}{c} Q \\ and \\ P\ \equiv\ (not\ Q) \end{array}}^{\;+} \end{array}\right]^{+}.$$

By the *and* and *or* rules, the connectives *and* and *or* do not change polarity:

$$\left[\begin{array}{l} if \quad \left[\ \boxed{not\ P}^{\;-} \ \ or \ \ \boxed{Q}^{\;-}\ \right]^{-} \\[2mm] then \quad \left[\begin{array}{c} \boxed{Q}^{\;+} \\ and \\ \boxed{P\ \equiv\ (not\ Q)}^{\;+} \end{array}\right]^{+} \end{array}\right]^{+}.$$

Applying the *not* rule to the antecedent and the $\equiv$ rule to the consequent:

$$\left[\begin{array}{l} if \quad \left[\left[not\ \boxed{P}^{\;+}\right]^{-} \ \ or \ \ Q^{-}\right]^{-} \\[2mm] then \quad \left[\begin{array}{c} Q^{+} \\ and \\ \left[\boxed{P}^{\;\pm}\ \equiv\ \boxed{not\ Q}^{\;\pm}\right]^{+} \end{array}\right]^{+} \end{array}\right]^{+}.$$

Finally, by the *not* rule, if the subsentence *not Q* has both polarities, Q itself has both polarities:

$$\left[\begin{array}{l} if \quad \left[\left[not\ P^{+}\right]^{-} \ \ or \ \ Q^{-}\right]^{-} \\[2mm] then \quad \left[\begin{array}{c} Q^{+} \\ and \\ \left[P^{\pm}\ \equiv\ \left[not\ \boxed{Q}^{\;\pm}\right]^{\pm}\right]^{+} \end{array}\right]^{+} \end{array}\right]^{+}.$$

Thus, as a result of this annotation process, we obtain the full polarity annotation:

$$
\left[
\begin{array}{l}
\textit{if} \quad \Big[\big[\textit{not } P^{+}\big]^{-} \quad \textit{or} \quad Q^{-}\Big]^{-} \\[4pt]
\textit{then} \quad
\left[
\begin{array}{l}
Q^{+} \\
\textit{and} \\
\big[P^{\pm} \;\equiv\; [\textit{not } Q^{\pm}]^{\pm}\big]^{+}
\end{array}
\right]^{+}
\end{array}
\right]^{+}
$$

Note that different occurrences of the same subsentence may have different polarities. For instance, one occurrence of the subsentence Q is negative, one is positive, and one has both polarities. ⌐

The reader is requested to annotate the polarity of a sentence in the same way (**Problem 5.1**).

Remark (implicit negation)

Roughly, the polarity of a subsentence indicates whether it is enclosed in an even or odd number of negation connectives; here, we include "implicit" as well as "explicit" negations. The *polarity-assignment* rules for the *if-then*, $\equiv$, and *if-then-else* connectives take into consideration implicit negations.

If-then rule: $[\textit{if } \mathcal{F} \textit{ then } \mathcal{G}]^{\pi} \;\Rrightarrow\; \textit{if } \mathcal{F}^{-\pi} \textit{ then } \mathcal{G}^{\pi}$

The implication

$$\textit{if } \mathcal{F} \textit{ then } \mathcal{G}$$

can be regarded as an abbreviation for

$$(\textit{not } \mathcal{F}) \textit{ or } \mathcal{G}.$$

Thus the antecedent $\mathcal{F}$ is enclosed within an additional implicit negation connective, and therefore has polarity opposite to that of the implication.

$\equiv$ *rule:* $[\mathcal{F} \equiv \mathcal{G}]^{\pi} \;\Rrightarrow\; \mathcal{F}^{\pm} \equiv \mathcal{G}^{\pm}$

The equivalence

$$\mathcal{F} \equiv \mathcal{G}$$

can be regarded as an abbreviation for

$$
\begin{array}{ccc}
\begin{array}{c}
\mathcal{F} \textit{ and } \mathcal{G} \\
\textit{or} \\
(\textit{not } \mathcal{F}) \textit{ and } (\textit{not } \mathcal{G})
\end{array}
&
\textit{or}
&
\begin{array}{c}
\textit{if } \mathcal{F} \textit{ then } \mathcal{G} \\
\textit{and} \\
\textit{if } \mathcal{G} \textit{ then } \mathcal{F}.
\end{array}
\end{array}
$$

Thus, if the polarity of the equivalence is π, the polarity of the subsentences is

$$\mathcal{F}^\pi \ and \ \mathcal{G}^\pi \qquad\qquad\qquad if \ \mathcal{F}^{-\pi} \ then \ \mathcal{G}^\pi$$
$$or \qquad\qquad\qquad\qquad\qquad and$$
$$(not \ \mathcal{F}^{-\pi}) \ and \ (not \ \mathcal{G}^{-\pi}) \qquad if \ \mathcal{G}^{-\pi} \ then \ \mathcal{F}^\pi.$$

That is, there are actually two occurrences of $\mathcal{F}$ and of $\mathcal{G}$ buried in the $\equiv$ formula, one enclosed within an additional implicit negation connective. Therefore $\mathcal{F}$ and $\mathcal{G}$ in the equivalence are each considered to have both polarities.

If-then-else rule: $\ \left[if \ \mathcal{F} \ then \ \mathcal{G} \ else \ \mathcal{H}\right]^\pi \ \Rightarrow \ if \ \mathcal{F}^{\pm} \ then \ \mathcal{G}^\pi \ else \ \mathcal{H}^\pi$

The conditional

$$if \ \mathcal{F} \ then \ \mathcal{G} \ else \ \mathcal{H}$$

can be regarded as an abbreviation for

$$\mathcal{F} \ and \ \mathcal{G} \qquad\qquad\qquad if \ \mathcal{F} \ then \ \mathcal{G}$$
$$or \qquad\qquad or \qquad\qquad and$$
$$(not \ \mathcal{F}) \ and \ \mathcal{H} \qquad\qquad if \ (not \ \mathcal{F}) \ then \ \mathcal{H}.$$

Thus, if the polarity of the conditional is π, the polarity of the subsentences is

$$\mathcal{F}^\pi \ and \ \mathcal{G}^\pi \qquad\qquad\qquad if \ \mathcal{F}^{-\pi} \ then \ \mathcal{G}^\pi$$
$$or \qquad\qquad\qquad\qquad\qquad and$$
$$(not \ \mathcal{F}^{-\pi}) \ and \ \mathcal{H}^\pi \qquad\qquad if \ (not \ \mathcal{F}^\pi) \ then \ \mathcal{H}^\pi.$$

That is, $\mathcal{F}$ is considered to have both polarities, but $\mathcal{G}$ and $\mathcal{H}$ have the same polarity as the conditional.

Note that, by repeated application of the *polarity-assignment* rules, every proper subsentence of an equivalence, and every proper subsentence of the *if*-clause $\mathcal{F}$ of a conditional, has both polarities. ⌐

Definition (strict polarity of occurrences)

An occurrence of a subsentence $\mathcal{E}$ in a sentence $\mathcal{S}$ has *strictly positive polarity* in $\mathcal{S}$ if $\mathcal{E}$ has positive but not negative polarity in $\mathcal{S}$; that is,

$$\mathcal{E}^+ \quad but \ not \quad \mathcal{E}^{\pm}.$$

Similarly, $\mathcal{E}$ has *strictly negative polarity* in $\mathcal{S}$ if $\mathcal{E}$ has negative but not positive polarity in $\mathcal{S}$; that is,

$$\mathcal{E}^- \quad but \ not \quad \mathcal{E}^{\pm}. \quad ⌐$$

Thus each occurrence of a subsentence has strictly positive polarity, strictly negative polarity, or both polarities, in the enclosing sentence.

THE POLARITY LEMMA

Note that, if $\mathcal{E}$ is a subsentence of S' and S' is a subsentence of S, the polarity of an occurrence of $\mathcal{E}$ in S' may be different from the polarity of the same occurrence of $\mathcal{E}$ in S. For example, the subsentence

$$\mathcal{E}: \quad P \ \ and \ \ Q$$

has negative polarity in the sentence

$$S': \quad not \ \boxed{P \ \ and \ \ Q}^{\,-},$$

but positive polarity in the sentence

$$S: \quad if \ \left[not \ \boxed{P \ \ and \ \ Q}^{\,+} \right]^{\,-} \\ then \ \ R,$$

in which S' has negative polarity.

This example serves to illustrate the following fundamental *polarity* lemma. We use the notation $\mathcal{E} \trianglelefteq S$ to stand for "$\mathcal{E}$ is a subsentence of S."

Lemma (polarity)

Suppose that S is a sentence, S' is an occurrence of a subsentence in S, and $\mathcal{E}$ is an occurrence of a subsentence in S'; that is,

$$\mathcal{E} \trianglelefteq S' \trianglelefteq S.$$

Then

$\mathcal{E}$ is positive in S

    precisely when

$$\left[\begin{array}{l} \mathcal{E} \text{ is positive in } S' \text{ and } S' \text{ is positive in } S \\ \text{or} \\ \mathcal{E} \text{ is negative in } S' \text{ and } S' \text{ is negative in } S \end{array} \right] \qquad (\textit{positive})$$

and

$\mathcal{E}$ is negative in S

    precisely when

$$\left[\begin{array}{l}\mathcal{E} \text{ is positive in } S' \text{ and } S' \text{ is negative in } S \\ \text{or} \\ \mathcal{E} \text{ is negative in } S' \text{ and } S' \text{ is positive in } S\end{array}\right] \qquad (negative)$$

⌐

Note that, in speaking of the polarity of a subsentence in the lemma, we are referring to the polarity of the particular occurrence of that subsentence under consideration, even though the same subsentence may have other occurrences.

The proof of the lemma is left as an exercise (**Problem 5.2**).

Remark (both polarities)

The lemma applies even if the polarities are not strict. Thus the lemma implies that, in particular,

    if $\mathcal{E}$ has both polarities in S' and S' is negative in S,
    then $\mathcal{E}$ has both polarities in S.

For, if $\mathcal{E}$ has both polarities in S', then $\mathcal{E}$ is positive in S' and $\mathcal{E}$ is negative in S'. If S' is negative in S, then (by the *negative* part of the lemma) $\mathcal{E}$ is negative in S, but also (by the *positive* part of the lemma) $\mathcal{E}$ is positive in S. Thus $\mathcal{E}$ has both polarities in S. ⌐

From the lemma, we can conclude the following corollary.

Corollary (polarity)

Suppose that S is a sentence, S' is an occurrence of a subsentence in S, and $\mathcal{E}$ is an occurrence of a subsentence in S'; that is,

    $\mathcal{E} \trianglelefteq S' \trianglelefteq S$.

Then

    if $\mathcal{E}$ is strictly positive in S
      and S' is negative [positive] in S,
      then $\mathcal{E}$ is strictly negative [strictly positive] in S' (*positive*)

and

> if $\mathcal{E}$ is strictly negative in S
>   and S' is negative [positive] in S,
>   then $\mathcal{E}$ is strictly positive [strictly negative] in S'.   (*negative*) ⌐

As in the *polarity* lemma, we are referring to the polarities of the particular subsentence occurrences under consideration.

The proof is omitted.

PARTIAL SUBSTITUTION

We will need an extension of our concise partial-substitution notation (Section [I]1.9) to allow us to replace only strictly positive, or only strictly negative, occurrences of one subsentence with another.

Definition (partial substitution with polarity)

> Suppose that $\mathcal{E}$, $\mathcal{F}$, and $S\langle\mathcal{E}^+\rangle$ are sentences; then $S\langle\mathcal{F}^+\rangle$ denotes the result of replacing zero, one, or more strictly positive occurrences of $\mathcal{E}$ in $S\langle\mathcal{E}^+\rangle$ with $\mathcal{F}$.
>
> Similarly, suppose that $\mathcal{E}$, $\mathcal{F}$, and $S\langle\mathcal{E}^-\rangle$ are sentences; then $S\langle\mathcal{F}^-\rangle$ denotes the result of replacing zero, one, or more strictly negative occurrences of $\mathcal{E}$ in $S\langle\mathcal{E}^-\rangle$ with $\mathcal{F}$. ⌐

Here we write $S\langle\mathcal{E}\rangle$ as $S\langle\mathcal{E}^+\rangle$ so that later, when we refer to $S\langle\mathcal{F}^+\rangle$, it is clear that we are replacing only strictly positive occurrences of $\mathcal{E}$ with $\mathcal{F}$. (When we write $S\langle\mathcal{E}^+\rangle$, we may imagine that we have already selected zero, one, or more strictly positive occurrences of $\mathcal{E}$ to be replaced.) Similarly, we write $S\langle\mathcal{E}\rangle$ as $S\langle\mathcal{E}^-\rangle$ so that later, when we refer to $S\langle\mathcal{F}^-\rangle$, it is clear that we are replacing only strictly negative occurrences of $\mathcal{E}$ with $\mathcal{F}$.

Example

Consider the sentence

$$S\langle P^+\rangle: \quad \textit{if } P^\pm \textit{ then } P^+ \textit{ else } (\textit{not } P^-).$$

This sentence contains three occurrences of the propositional symbol P, with positive, negative, and both polarities.

Then $S\langle Q^+\rangle$ denotes either of the sentences

$$if \ \ P \ \ then \ \ P \ \ else \ \ (not \ P),$$

that is, S itself (zero replacements), or

$$if \ \ P \ \ then \ \ Q \ \ else \ \ (not \ P),$$

that is, the result of replacing the only strictly positive occurrence of P with Q. ⌐

A similar extension can be defined for the concise total-substitution notation, but we will not need it here.

THE POLARITY PROPOSITION

The relation of polarity to the truth of a sentence is elucidated by the following proposition.

Proposition (polarity)

Suppose that $\mathcal{E}$, $\mathcal{F}$, and $S\langle\mathcal{E}^+\rangle$ are sentences. Then the sentence

$$if \ (if \ \ \mathcal{E} \ \ then \ \ \mathcal{F})$$
$$then \ \left(if \ \ S\langle\mathcal{E}^+\rangle \ \ then \ \ S\langle\mathcal{F}^+\rangle\right) \tag{positive}$$

is valid.

Suppose that $\mathcal{E}$, $\mathcal{F}$, and $S\langle\mathcal{E}^-\rangle$ are sentences. Then the sentence

$$if \ (if \ \ \mathcal{E} \ \ then \ \ \mathcal{F})$$
$$then \ \left(if \ \ S\langle\mathcal{F}^-\rangle \ \ then \ \ S\langle\mathcal{E}^-\rangle\right) \tag{negative}$$

is valid. ⌐

If a subsentence of the form ($if \ \ \mathcal{E} \ \ then \ \ \mathcal{F}$) is true, we say informally that $\mathcal{F}$ is "truer" than $\mathcal{E}$, and that $\mathcal{E}$ is "falser" than $\mathcal{F}$. For, according to the semantic rule for implication, it is impossible for $\mathcal{E}$ to be true and $\mathcal{F}$ to be false in this case.

The proposition says, roughly, that the truth of a sentence is directly related to the truth of its strictly positive subsentences, but inversely related to the truth of its strictly negative subsentences. In other words, if we replace some strictly positive occurrences of a subsentence with a "truer" sentence (i.e., one that it implies), the entire sentence becomes "truer" (i.e., the resulting sentence is implied by the original). On the other hand, if we replace some strictly negative occurrences of a subsentence with a "truer" sentence, the entire sentence becomes "falser" (i.e., the resulting sentence implies the original).

Example

The occurrences of P are annotated with their polarities in the following sentences:

$$S_1: \quad P^+ \ and \ R$$

$$S_2: \quad not \ P^-$$

$$S_3: \quad if \ P^- \ then \ P^+$$

$$S_4: \quad if \ (not \ P^+) \ then \ P^+.$$

Therefore, by the *positive* part of the *polarity* proposition, taking

$$\mathcal{E}: P \quad and \quad \mathcal{F}: Q,$$

the following sentences are valid. (The boxes indicate the subsentences being replaced; the annotations indicate the polarity of the boxed subsentences in the corresponding sentence bracketed with [and].)

- For S_1:

  $$if \ (if \ P \ then \ Q)$$
  $$then \ if \ \left[\boxed{P}^+ \ and \ R \right]$$
  $$then \ (Q \ and \ R).$$

- For S_3:

  $$if \ (if \ P \ then \ Q)$$
  $$then \ if \ \left[if \ P \ then \ \boxed{P}^+ \right]$$
  $$then \ (if \ P \ then \ Q).$$

- For S_4:

  $$if \ (if \ P \ then \ Q)$$
  $$then \ if \ \left[if \ \left(not \ \boxed{P}^+ \right) \ then \ P \right]$$
  $$then \ (if \ (not \ Q) \ then \ P)$$

  $$if \ (if \ P \ then \ Q)$$
  $$then \ if \ \left[if \ (not \ P) \ then \ \boxed{P}^+ \right]$$
  $$then \ (if \ (not \ P) \ then \ Q)$$

$$if \ (if \ P \ then \ Q)$$
$$then \ if \ \left[if \ \left(not \ \boxed{P}^{+} \right) \ then \ \boxed{P}^{+} \right]$$
$$then \ (if \ (not \ Q) \ then \ Q).$$

The three sentences are obtained from S_4 by replacing, respectively, the first, the second, and both strictly positive occurrences of P with Q.

Similarly, by the *negative* part of the *polarity* proposition, the following sentences are valid:

- For S_2:

$$if \ (if \ P \ then \ Q)$$
$$then \ if \ (not \ Q)$$
$$then \ \left[not \ \boxed{P}^{-} \right].$$

- For S_3:

$$if \ (if \ P \ then \ Q)$$
$$then \ if \ (if \ Q \ then \ P)$$
$$then \ \left[if \ \boxed{P}^{-} \ then \ P \right]. \ \blacksquare$$

Remark (both polarities)

Note that the *polarity* proposition does not predict what will happen if we replace an occurrence of a subsentence of both polarities with a truer sentence. This is because the result of making such a replacement is unpredictable. For example, the occurrence of P has both polarities in the sentence

$$S: \quad P^{\pm} \equiv R.$$

In fact, neither

$$if \ (if \ P \ then \ Q)$$
$$then \ if \ \left[\boxed{P}^{\pm} \equiv R \right]$$
$$then \ (Q \equiv R)$$

nor

$$if \ (if \ P \ then \ Q)$$
$$then \ if \ (Q \equiv R)$$
$$then \ \left[\boxed{P}^{\pm} \equiv R \right]$$

is a valid sentence. (The first sentence is false when P and R are false but Q is true, while the second is false when Q and R are true but P is false.) ◢

Now let us prove the *polarity* proposition.

Proof (polarity)

We prove both the *positive* and the *negative* part at once, but we will not give all the details for both parts because the reasoning is repetitive.

The proof is by induction on the structure of the sentence $S\langle\mathcal{E}\rangle$. In other words, we consider an arbitrary sentence $S\langle\mathcal{E}\rangle$, assume inductively that the proposition holds for each proper subsentence $S'\langle\mathcal{E}\rangle$ of $S\langle\mathcal{E}\rangle$, and prove that the proposition then holds for $S\langle\mathcal{E}\rangle$ as well.

In the case in which $\mathcal{E}$ does not occur in $S\langle\mathcal{E}\rangle$ at all, $S\langle\mathcal{F}\rangle$ is identical to $S\langle\mathcal{E}\rangle$ and the proposition is evident. We henceforth assume that $\mathcal{E}$ does occur in $S\langle\mathcal{E}\rangle$ at least once.

We distinguish among several cases.

Case: $S\langle\mathcal{E}\rangle$ is identical to $\mathcal{E}$

Then $\mathcal{E}$ is strictly positive in $S\langle\mathcal{E}\rangle$ and $S\langle\mathcal{F}\rangle$ is $\mathcal{E}$ or $\mathcal{F}$ itself, depending on whether zero or one occurrence is replaced. The sentence of the *positive* part,

> *if* (*if* $\mathcal{E}$ *then* $\mathcal{F}$)
> *then* (*if* $S\langle\mathcal{E}^+\rangle$ *then* $S\langle\mathcal{F}^+\rangle$),

reduces to the valid sentence

> *if* (*if* $\mathcal{E}$ *then* $\mathcal{F}$)   or   *if* (*if* $\mathcal{E}$ *then* $\mathcal{F}$)
> *then* (*if* $\mathcal{E}$ *then* $\mathcal{E}$)   *then* (*if* $\mathcal{E}$ *then* $\mathcal{F}$).

The *negative* part holds vacuously because in this case there are no strictly negative occurrences of $\mathcal{E}$ in $S\langle\mathcal{E}\rangle$, and therefore $S\langle\mathcal{F}\rangle$ is identical to $S\langle\mathcal{E}\rangle$.

Note that this includes the case where $S\langle\mathcal{E}\rangle$ is a proposition; that is, $S\langle\mathcal{E}\rangle$ is *true*, *false*, or a propositional symbol.

Henceforth, we assume that $S\langle\mathcal{E}\rangle$ and $\mathcal{E}$ are not identical and that $S\langle\mathcal{E}\rangle$ is not a proposition.

Case: $S\langle\mathcal{E}\rangle$ is of form (*not* $S'\langle\mathcal{E}\rangle$)

Then, by our assumption that $\mathcal{E}$ and $S\langle\mathcal{E}\rangle$ are distinct, $\mathcal{E}$ is a subsentence of $S'\langle\mathcal{E}\rangle$. Because $S'\langle\mathcal{E}\rangle$ is a proper subsentence of $S\langle\mathcal{E}\rangle$, we may apply our induction hypothesis to $S'\langle\mathcal{E}\rangle$.

Let us first prove the *positive* part, in which the replaced occurrences of $\mathcal{E}$ in $S\langle\mathcal{E}\rangle$ are strictly positive in $S\langle\mathcal{E}\rangle$; we therefore write $S\langle\mathcal{E}\rangle$ as $S\langle\mathcal{E}^+\rangle$. Then, because $S'\langle\mathcal{E}\rangle$ is negative in $S\langle\mathcal{E}\rangle$, we know (by the *positive* part of the *polarity* corollary) that the replaced occurrences of $\mathcal{E}$ are strictly negative in $S'\langle\mathcal{E}\rangle$; we therefore write $S'\langle\mathcal{E}\rangle$ as $S'\langle\mathcal{E}^-\rangle$. The sentence resulting from the replacement is then

$$S\langle\mathcal{F}^+\rangle : \quad not\ S'\langle\mathcal{F}^-\rangle.$$

By the *negative* part of our induction hypothesis, the sentence

$$if\ (if\ \mathcal{E}\ then\ \mathcal{F})$$
$$then\ \left(if\ S'\langle\mathcal{F}^-\rangle\ then\ S'\langle\mathcal{E}^-\rangle\right)$$

is valid. But then (by propositional logic) the sentence

$$if\ (if\ \mathcal{E}\ then\ \mathcal{F})$$
$$then\ \left(if\ (not\ S'\langle\mathcal{E}^-\rangle)\ then\ (not\ S'\langle\mathcal{F}^-\rangle)\right),$$

that is,

$$if\ (if\ \mathcal{E}\ then\ \mathcal{F})$$
$$then\ \left(if\ S\langle\mathcal{E}^+\rangle\ then\ S\langle\mathcal{F}^+\rangle\right),$$

is also valid. But this is the sentence of the *positive* part.

The proof of the *negative* part in this case is similar. We use the *negative* part of the *polarity* corollary instead of the *positive* part, and the *positive* part of the induction hypothesis instead of the *negative* part.

Case: $S\langle\mathcal{E}\rangle$ is of form $(if\ S_1\ then\ S_2)$

Then, by our assumption that $\mathcal{E}$ and $S\langle\mathcal{E}\rangle$ are distinct, $\mathcal{E}$ must occur in S_1, in S_2, or in both. Let us consider only the worst case, in which $\mathcal{E}$ occurs in both S_1 and S_2.

We prove only the *positive* part, in which the replaced occurrences of $\mathcal{E}$ in $S\langle\mathcal{E}\rangle$ are strictly positive in $S\langle\mathcal{E}\rangle$; we therefore write $S\langle\mathcal{E}\rangle$ as $S\langle\mathcal{E}^+\rangle$. Then, because S_1 is negative and S_2 is positive in $S\langle\mathcal{E}^+\rangle$, we know (by the *positive* part of the *polarity* corollary) that the replaced occurrences of $\mathcal{E}$ are strictly negative in S_1 and strictly positive in S_2; we therefore write S_1 as $S_1\langle\mathcal{E}^-\rangle$ and S_2 as $S_2\langle\mathcal{E}^+\rangle$. That is, $S\langle\mathcal{E}^+\rangle$ may be written $\left(if\ S_1\langle\mathcal{E}^-\rangle\ then\ S_2\langle\mathcal{E}^+\rangle\right)$, and therefore the resulting sentence is

$$S\langle\mathcal{F}^+\rangle : \quad if\ S_1\langle\mathcal{F}^-\rangle\ then\ S_2\langle\mathcal{F}^+\rangle.$$

By the *negative* part of our induction hypothesis, the sentence

(†)
$$\begin{aligned}
&\textit{if } (\textit{if } \mathcal{E} \quad \textit{then} \quad \mathcal{F}) \\
&\textit{then } (\textit{if } S_1\langle \mathcal{F}^-\rangle \quad \textit{then} \quad S_1\langle \mathcal{E}^-\rangle)
\end{aligned}$$

is valid. By the *positive* part of our induction hypothesis, the sentence

(‡)
$$\begin{aligned}
&\textit{if } (\textit{if } \mathcal{E} \quad \textit{then} \quad \mathcal{F}) \\
&\textit{then } (\textit{if } S_2\langle \mathcal{E}^+\rangle \quad \textit{then} \quad S_2\langle \mathcal{F}^+\rangle)
\end{aligned}$$

is valid. Combining these sentences (by propositional logic), the sentence

$$\begin{aligned}
&\textit{if } (\textit{if } \mathcal{E} \quad \textit{then} \quad \mathcal{F}) \\
&\textit{then if } \big(\textit{if } S_1\langle \mathcal{E}^-\rangle \quad \textit{then} \quad S_2\langle \mathcal{E}^+\rangle\big) \\
&\qquad \textit{then } \big(\textit{if } S_1\langle \mathcal{F}^-\rangle \quad \textit{then} \quad S_2\langle \mathcal{F}^+\rangle\big)
\end{aligned}$$

is valid. (Intuitively, one can easily deduce from (†) and (‡) that the three antecedents *if $\mathcal{E}$ then $\mathcal{F}$, if $S_1\langle \mathcal{E}^-\rangle$ then $S_2\langle \mathcal{E}^+\rangle$,* and $S_1\langle \mathcal{F}^-\rangle$ imply the conclusion $S_2\langle \mathcal{F}^+\rangle$.) We therefore have that

$$\begin{aligned}
&\textit{if } (\textit{if } \mathcal{E} \quad \textit{then} \quad \mathcal{F}) \\
&\textit{then } (\textit{if } S\langle \mathcal{E}^+\rangle \quad \textit{then} \quad S\langle \mathcal{F}^+\rangle)
\end{aligned}$$

is valid; but this is the sentence of the *positive* part.

The proof of the *negative* part is similar.

Case: $S\langle \mathcal{E}\rangle$ is of form $(S_1 \equiv S_2)$

This case cannot occur because we have assumed that $\mathcal{E}$ is not identical to $S\langle \mathcal{E}\rangle$ but that $\mathcal{E}$ cannot occur in S_1 or in S_2, since then $\mathcal{E}$ would have both polarities, and could be neither strictly positive nor strictly negative in $S\langle \mathcal{E}\rangle$.

The proofs for the other cases, which are similar to the preceding proofs, are omitted. ⌐

5.2   SIMPLIFICATION

Simplification allows us to replace every occurrence of a subsentence $\mathcal{E}$ of a given sentence $S[\mathcal{E}]$ with an equivalent, simpler subsentence $\mathcal{E}'$, obtaining an equivalent, simpler sentence $S[\mathcal{E}']$.

For example, we know that any sentence of form

$\mathcal{E}$:   *not* (*not* $\mathcal{F}$)

is equivalent to the corresponding sentence of form

$\mathcal{E}'$: $\mathcal{F}$.

By the *substitutivity-of-equivalence* corollary (Section [I]1.11), this means that if $\mathcal{E}$ occurs as a subsentence of some sentence $S[\mathcal{E}]$, then the sentence $S[\mathcal{E}']$, obtained by replacing every occurrence of $\mathcal{E}$ with $\mathcal{E}'$, is equivalent to $S[\mathcal{E}]$. We will say that $S[\mathcal{E}']$ is obtained from $S[\mathcal{E}]$ by applying the *simplification*

not (*not* $\mathcal{F}$) $\Rightarrow$ $\mathcal{F}$.

In particular, applying the preceding simplification to the sentence

S : P *or* *not* (*not* Q),

we obtain the sentence

S' : P *or* Q

because S' is obtained from S by replacing the subsentence $\mathcal{E}$:   *not* (*not* Q), which is of form *not* (*not* $\mathcal{F}$), with the equivalent sentence $\mathcal{E}'$: Q, which is the corresponding sentence of form $\mathcal{F}$.

This motivates the following definition.

Definition (simplification)

Suppose that any sentence of form $\mathcal{E}$ is equivalent to the corresponding sentence of form $\mathcal{E}'$, and that

$\mathcal{E} \Rightarrow \mathcal{E}'$

is a *simplification* (see the catalogs following the example).

The result of *applying a simplification* to a sentence S is the sentence obtained by replacing every occurrence of a subsentence of form $\mathcal{E}$ in S with the corresponding sentence of form $\mathcal{E}'$.

The result of *simplifying* S is the sentence S' obtained by successively applying all possible simplifications to S until no more can be applied. We shall also say that S *reduces to* S' *under simplification.* ⌟

Each simplification in our catalog reduces the length of the sentence to which it is applied. Therefore we can be sure that we cannot apply simplifications to a given sentence indefinitely.

Example

Consider the sentence

$$S: \quad not\ not\ \begin{bmatrix} if & \boxed{not\ (not\ P)} & or & Q \\ then & \boxed{not\ (not\ P)} & \end{bmatrix}.$$

By a single application of the simplification

$$not\ (not\ \mathcal{F})\ \Rightarrow\ \mathcal{F},$$

replacing the two occurrences of the subsentence

$$not\ (not\ P)$$

(annotated with boxes) with the equivalent sentence

$$P,$$

we obtain the new sentence

$$S': \quad not\ not\ \begin{bmatrix} if & P & or & Q \\ then & P & \end{bmatrix},$$

which is equivalent to S.

We can now apply the same simplification to the new sentence

$$S': \quad \boxed{not\ not\ \begin{bmatrix} if & P & or & Q \\ then & P \end{bmatrix}}$$

(annotated with a box), obtaining the sentence

$$S'': \quad \begin{matrix} if & P & or & Q \\ then & P, \end{matrix}$$

which is also equivalent to S. Since no more simplifications can be applied, S'' is the result of simplifying S.

Note that, alternatively, we could first apply the simplification to the entire sentence, obtaining

$$\begin{matrix} if & \boxed{not\ (not\ P)} & or & Q \\ then & \boxed{not\ (not\ P)}, & \end{matrix}$$

and then apply the simplification to the two occurrences of $not\ (not\ P)$. The result would be the same. ∎

Simplification will be part of our deductive system for proving the validity of sentences. In this system, only simplifications from the catalog may be applied, and only in the specified ⇒ (left-to-right) direction.

CATALOG OF TRUE-FALSE SIMPLIFICATIONS

Certain of the simplifications contain occurrences of the truth symbols *true* and *false* on their left-hand sides; we will call them *true-false simplifications*. For example,

$$\mathcal{F} \ and \ true \quad \Rightarrow \quad \mathcal{F} \qquad and \qquad if \ false \ then \ \mathcal{G} \quad \Rightarrow \quad true$$

are both *true-false* simplifications.

Because of their importance, we list all the *true-false* simplifications here.

• Negation

$$not \ true \quad \Rightarrow \quad false \qquad\qquad (not \ true)$$
$$not \ false \quad \Rightarrow \quad true \qquad\qquad (not \ false)$$

• Conjunction

$$\mathcal{F} \ and \ true \quad \Rightarrow \quad \mathcal{F} \qquad\qquad (and \ true)$$
$$true \ and \ \mathcal{F} \quad \Rightarrow \quad \mathcal{F} \qquad\qquad (true \ and)$$
$$\mathcal{F} \ and \ false \quad \Rightarrow \quad false \qquad\qquad (and \ false)$$
$$false \ and \ \mathcal{F} \quad \Rightarrow \quad false \qquad\qquad (false \ and)$$

• Disjunction

$$\mathcal{F} \ or \ true \quad \Rightarrow \quad true \qquad\qquad (or \ true)$$
$$true \ or \ \mathcal{F} \quad \Rightarrow \quad true \qquad\qquad (true \ or)$$
$$\mathcal{F} \ or \ false \quad \Rightarrow \quad \mathcal{F} \qquad\qquad (or \ false)$$
$$false \ or \ \mathcal{F} \quad \Rightarrow \quad \mathcal{F} \qquad\qquad (false \ or)$$

• Implication

$$if \ true \ then \ \mathcal{G} \quad \Rightarrow \quad \mathcal{G} \qquad\qquad (if \ true)$$
$$if \ false \ then \ \mathcal{G} \quad \Rightarrow \quad true \qquad\qquad (if \ false)$$
$$if \ \mathcal{F} \ then \ true \quad \Rightarrow \quad true \qquad\qquad (then \ true)$$
$$if \ \mathcal{F} \ then \ false \quad \Rightarrow \quad not \ \mathcal{F} \qquad\qquad (then \ false)$$

- Equivalence

$$\mathcal{F} \equiv true \;\Rightarrow\; \mathcal{F} \qquad\qquad (\textit{iff true})$$
$$true \equiv \mathcal{F} \;\Rightarrow\; \mathcal{F} \qquad\qquad (\textit{true iff})$$
$$\mathcal{F} \equiv false \;\Rightarrow\; not\; \mathcal{F} \qquad\qquad (\textit{iff false})$$
$$false \equiv \mathcal{F} \;\Rightarrow\; not\; \mathcal{F} \qquad\qquad (\textit{false iff})$$

- Conditional

$$if\; true\; then\; \mathcal{G}\; else\; \mathcal{H} \;\Rightarrow\; \mathcal{G} \qquad\qquad (\textit{cond if true})$$
$$if\; false\; then\; \mathcal{G}\; else\; \mathcal{H} \;\Rightarrow\; \mathcal{H} \qquad\qquad (\textit{cond if false})$$
$$if\; \mathcal{F}\; then\; true\; else\; \mathcal{H} \;\Rightarrow\; \mathcal{F}\; or\; \mathcal{H} \qquad\qquad (\textit{cond then true})$$
$$if\; \mathcal{F}\; then\; false\; else\; \mathcal{H} \;\Rightarrow\; (not\; \mathcal{F})\; and\; \mathcal{H} \qquad\qquad (\textit{cond then false})$$
$$if\; \mathcal{F}\; then\; \mathcal{G}\; else\; true \;\Rightarrow\; if\; \mathcal{F}\; then\; \mathcal{G} \qquad\qquad (\textit{cond else true})$$
$$if\; \mathcal{F}\; then\; \mathcal{G}\; else\; false \;\Rightarrow\; \mathcal{F}\; and\; \mathcal{G} \qquad\qquad (\textit{cond else false})$$

CATALOG OF OTHER SIMPLIFICATIONS

We present some additional simplifications:

- Negation

$$not\; (not\; \mathcal{F}) \;\Rightarrow\; \mathcal{F} \qquad\qquad (\textit{not not})$$
$$not\; ((not\; \mathcal{F})\; and\; (not\; \mathcal{G})) \;\Rightarrow\; \mathcal{F}\; or\; \mathcal{G} \qquad\qquad (\textit{not and})$$
$$not\; ((not\; \mathcal{F})\; or\; (not\; \mathcal{G})) \;\Rightarrow\; \mathcal{F}\; and\; \mathcal{G} \qquad\qquad (\textit{not or})$$
$$not\; (if\; \mathcal{F}\; then\; (not\; \mathcal{G})) \;\Rightarrow\; \mathcal{F}\; and\; \mathcal{G} \qquad\qquad (\textit{not if})$$
$$not\; (\mathcal{F} \equiv (not\; \mathcal{G})) \;\Rightarrow\; \mathcal{F} \equiv \mathcal{G} \qquad\qquad (\textit{not iff})$$
$$not\; (if\; \mathcal{F}\; then\; (not\; \mathcal{G})\; else\; (not\; \mathcal{H})) \;\Rightarrow\; if\; \mathcal{F}\; then\; \mathcal{G}\; else\; \mathcal{H} \quad (\textit{not cond})$$

- Conjunction

$$\mathcal{F}\; and\; \mathcal{F} \;\Rightarrow\; \mathcal{F} \qquad\qquad (\textit{and two})$$
$$\mathcal{F}\; and\; (not\; \mathcal{F}) \;\Rightarrow\; false \qquad\qquad (\textit{and not})$$
$$(not\; \mathcal{F})\; and\; \mathcal{F} \;\Rightarrow\; false \qquad\qquad (\textit{not and})$$

- Disjunction

$$\mathcal{F}\; or\; \mathcal{F} \;\Rightarrow\; \mathcal{F} \qquad\qquad (\textit{or two})$$

$$\mathcal{F} \ or \ (not \ \mathcal{F}) \ \Rightarrow \ true \qquad\qquad (or \ not)$$

$$(not \ \mathcal{F}) \ or \ \mathcal{F} \ \Rightarrow \ true \qquad\qquad (not \ or)$$

- Implication

$$if \ \mathcal{F} \ then \ \mathcal{F} \ \Rightarrow \ true \qquad\qquad (if \ two)$$

$$if \ (not \ \mathcal{F}) \ then \ \mathcal{F} \ \Rightarrow \ \mathcal{F} \qquad\qquad (if \ not)$$

$$if \ \mathcal{F} \ then \ (not \ \mathcal{F}) \ \Rightarrow \ not \ \mathcal{F} \qquad\qquad (then \ not)$$

$$if \ (not \ \mathcal{G}) \ then \ (not \ \mathcal{F}) \ \Rightarrow \ if \ \mathcal{F} \ then \ \mathcal{G} \qquad\qquad (contrapositive)$$

- Equivalence

$$\mathcal{F} \equiv \mathcal{F} \ \Rightarrow \ true \qquad\qquad (iff \ two)$$

$$\mathcal{F} \equiv (not \ \mathcal{F}) \ \Rightarrow \ false \qquad\qquad (iff \ not)$$

$$(not \ \mathcal{F}) \equiv \mathcal{F} \ \Rightarrow \ false \qquad\qquad (not \ iff)$$

- Conditional

$$if \ \mathcal{F} \ then \ \mathcal{G} \ else \ \mathcal{G} \ \Rightarrow \ \mathcal{G} \qquad\qquad (cond \ two)$$

$$if \ (not \ \mathcal{F}) \ then \ \mathcal{G} \ else \ \mathcal{H} \ \Rightarrow \ if \ \mathcal{F} \ then \ \mathcal{H} \ else \ \mathcal{G} \qquad\qquad (cond \ not)$$

In **Problem 5.3**, the reader is requested to simplify several sentences.

REDUCTION

We introduce some additional terminology.

Definition (reduction under true-false simplification)

If a sentence S can be simplified to a sentence S' by applying only *true-false* simplifications, and if no further *true-false* simplifications can be applied to S', we shall say that S *reduces to* S' *under true-false simplification.* ◢

For any sentence S, we have

$$S \ reduces \ to \ true, \qquad S \ reduces \ to \ false, \qquad or \qquad S \ reduces \ to \ S',$$

under *true-false* simplification, where S' contains no occurrences of any truth symbols *true* or *false*.

This follows from the observation that, wherever a truth symbol occurs as a proper subsentence of a given sentence, we have some *true-false* simplification for removing it and shortening the sentence. Since we cannot reduce the length of a sentence indefinitely, we ultimately reach a point at which no truth symbol occurs as a proper subsentence; that is, either all truth symbols have been removed or the entire sentence is a truth symbol.

In particular, if S contains no propositional symbols (P, Q, R, etc.), but only truth symbols, we have

$$S \text{ reduces to } \textit{true} \qquad \text{or} \qquad S \text{ reduces to } \textit{false},$$

under *true-false* simplification.

This follows from the additional observation that none of the *true-false* simplifications may introduce a new propositional symbol into a sentence to which it is applied.

PROBLEMS

Problem 5.1 (polarity annotation)   page 155

Annotate all the subsentences of the following sentence according to their polarity:

$$(not\ P)\ \ and\ \ \left[if\ \begin{bmatrix} if\ \ Q\ \ then\ \ R\ \ else\ \ P \\ or \\ Q\ \equiv\ (P\ \ or\ \ R) \end{bmatrix} \\ then\ \ (not\ R) \right].$$

* Problem 5.2 (polarity lemma)   page 158

Prove the *polarity* lemma.

Problem 5.3 (simplification)   page 170

Simplify the following sentences as much as possible:

(a) $not\ (if\ \ true\ \ then\ \ (not\ P))$

(b) $P\ \ or\ \ (if\ \ true\ \ then\ \ (true\ \ or\ \ Q))$

(c)
$$\begin{bmatrix} if \ not \ (P \ or \ P) \\ then \ (not \ Q) \ or \ false \end{bmatrix}$$

(d)
$$\begin{bmatrix} P \ and \ P \\ and \\ not \ (not \ (Q \ or \ false)) \end{bmatrix} \quad or \ not \quad \begin{bmatrix} if \ true \ then \ P \\ and \\ if \ R \ then \ Q \ else \ Q \end{bmatrix}.$$

6

Deductive Tableaux

If our only concern were to develop a formal deductive system for proving the validity of propositional-logic sentences, we might be happy with one based on the semantic-tree (Section [I]1.6) or the proof-by-falsification (Section [I]1.7) techniques. Our main interest in propositional logic, however, is to introduce techniques we can later extend to predicate logic. In this chapter, we develop a deductive-tableau system for proving the validity of propositional-logic sentences, which will also serve as a foundation for the deductive systems of predicate logic and the more expressive predicate-logic theories.

6.1   TABLEAUX: NOTATION AND MEANING

The fundamental structure of our deductive system is the *tableau*, which consists of a collection of *rows* of two *columns* each. Each row contains a sentence, either an *assertion* $\mathcal{A}$ or a *goal* $\mathcal{G}$. The assertions appear in the first column and the goals in the second column. An assertion and a goal may not both appear in the same row.

For example, the tableau $\mathcal{T}_1$ has two assertions and two goals:

assertions	goals
	G1. Q
A2. P *or* Q	
A3. *if* P *then* R	
	G4. R

Tableau T_1

MEANING OF A TABLEAU

For a given interpretation of its propositional symbols, a tableau will be either true or false according to the following semantic rule for tableaux.

Definition (semantic rule for tableaux)

A tableau with assertions A_1, A_2, ..., A_m and goals G_1, G_2, ..., G_n is *true under* an interpretation I if the following condition holds:

> if all the assertions A_i are true under I,
> then at least one of the goals G_j is true under I.

On the other hand, the tableau is *false under* I if the following condition holds:

> all the assertions A_i are true under I and
> all the goals G_j are false under I. ⌟

Example

Consider the tableau T_2:

assertions	goals
	G1. *not P*
A2. Q *or* R	
	G3. *if* P *then* Q

Tableau T_2

This tableau is true under any interpretation in which

- Q and R are false, because then the assertion A2 is false, or

- Q is true, because then the goal G3 is true, or

- P is false, because then the goal G1 is true (and also the goal G3 is true).

On the other hand, the tableau $\mathcal{T}_2$ is false under the interpretation in which

- P is true, Q is false, and R is true, because then the assertion is true but both goals are false.

In fact, this is the only interpretation under which $\mathcal{T}_2$ is false. ⌐

Note that the order in which the rows occur in the tableau has no significance. In other words, under a given interpretation, we can reorder the rows without changing the truth of the tableau.

Remark (semantic rule)

By the semantic rule for tableaux and propositional logic, a tableau $\mathcal{T}$ is true under an interpretation $\mathcal{I}$ precisely when

> at least one of the assertions $\mathcal{A}_i$ is false under $\mathcal{I}$ or
> at least one of the goals $\mathcal{G}_j$ is true under $\mathcal{I}$.

We shall regard this as an alternative form of the rule. ⌐

THE ASSOCIATED SENTENCE

The meaning of a given tableau can be characterized in terms of a single propositional-logic sentence.

Definition (associated sentence)

If a tableau contains the assertions

$$\mathcal{A}_1, \mathcal{A}_2, \ldots, \mathcal{A}_m$$

and the goals

$$\mathcal{G}_1, \mathcal{G}_2, \ldots, \mathcal{G}_n,$$

its *associated sentence* is

> *if* $[A_1 \ and \ A_2 \ and \ \ldots \ and \ A_m]$
> *then* $[G_1 \ or \ G_2 \ or \ \ldots \ or \ G_n]$.   ⌐

Example

The associated sentence of the tableau T_2 is

$$if \ (Q \ or \ R) \ then \ \begin{bmatrix} not \ P \\ or \\ if \ P \ then \ Q \end{bmatrix}.$$

The associated sentence of the earlier tableau T_1 is

$$if \ \begin{bmatrix} P \ or \ Q \\ and \\ if \ P \ then \ R \end{bmatrix} \ then \ \begin{bmatrix} Q \\ or \\ R \end{bmatrix}. \quad ⌐$$

Remark (no assertions or no goals)

In the special case in which a tableau has no assertions (i.e., if $m = 0$), the conjunction

> $A_1 \ and \ A_2 \ and \ \ldots \ and \ A_m$

is taken to be the truth symbol *true*, and the associated sentence is

> *if true*
> *then* $[G_1 \ or \ G_2 \ or \ \ldots \ or \ G_n]$,

which is equivalent to

> $G_1 \ or \ G_2 \ or \ \ldots \ or \ G_n$.

If furthermore there is only one goal G_1 (i.e., if $m = 0$ and $n = 1$), the disjunction

> $G_1 \ or \ G_2 \ or \ \ldots \ or \ G_n$

is taken to be

> G_1

itself, and the associated sentence is simply G_1.

On the other hand, in the special case in which the tableau has no goals (i.e., if $n = 0$), the disjunction

$$\mathcal{G}_1 \;\; or \;\; \mathcal{G}_2 \;\; or \;\; \ldots \;\; or \;\; \mathcal{G}_n$$

is taken to be the truth symbol *false*, and the associated sentence is

$$if \; \left[\mathcal{A}_1 \; and \; \mathcal{A}_2 \; and \; \ldots \; and \; \mathcal{A}_m\right]$$
$$then \; false,$$

which is equivalent to

$$not \; \left[\mathcal{A}_1 \; and \; \mathcal{A}_2 \; and \; \ldots \; and \; \mathcal{A}_m\right]. \quad \lrcorner$$

The importance of the associated sentence follows from the following property.

Proposition (truth of a tableau)

A tableau is true under an interpretation $\mathcal{I}$
   precisely when
its associated sentence is true under $\mathcal{I}$.

Proof

For an arbitrary interpretation $\mathcal{I}$,

a tableau is true under $\mathcal{I}$

precisely when (by the semantic rule for tableaux)

if all the assertions $\mathcal{A}_i$ are true under $\mathcal{I}$
then at least one of the goals $\mathcal{G}_j$ is true under $\mathcal{I}$

precisely when (by the semantic rules for *and* and *or*)

if $[\mathcal{A}_1 \; and \; \mathcal{A}_2 \; and \; \ldots \; and \; \mathcal{A}_m]$ is true under $\mathcal{I}$
then $[\mathcal{G}_1 \; or \; \mathcal{G}_2 \; or \; \ldots \; or \; \mathcal{G}_n]$ is true under $\mathcal{I}$

precisely when (by the semantic rule for *if-then*)

the associated sentence is true under $\mathcal{I}$. $\quad \lrcorner$

VALIDITY

The notion of validity for a tableau is analogous to that for a sentence.

Definition (validity of a tableau)

A tableau is said to be *valid* if it is true under every interpretation.

Equivalently, a tableau is *valid* precisely when its associated sentence is valid. ⌟

Example

The tableau T_2 is not valid; we have already seen an interpretation (P is true, Q is false, and R is true) under which it is false.

On the other hand, the tableau T_1 is valid. We shall give later a formal method for proving the validity of tableaux; however, we can informally demonstrate the validity of T_1 by an extension of the proof-by-falsification method, as follows:

Suppose T_1 is false under some interpretation; then

- Each of its assertions is true and each of its goals is false.

- In particular, the goals Q and R are both false.

- Because the assertion (P *or* Q) is true and Q is false, we know that P must be true.

- Because the assertion (*if* P *then* R) is true and P is true, we know that R must be true. But this contradicts our previous conclusion that R is false.

Hence T_1 cannot be false under any interpretation; that is, T_1 is valid.

Alternatively, one can demonstrate the validity of the associated sentence

$$
\textit{if} \quad
\begin{bmatrix} P \ or \ Q \\ and \\ if \ P \ then \ R \end{bmatrix}
\quad \textit{then} \quad
\begin{bmatrix} Q \\ or \\ R \end{bmatrix}
$$

using one of the techniques presented in Chapter [I]1. ⌟

Remark (special cases)

A tableau is automatically valid if one of its assertions is the truth symbol *false* or if one of its goals is the truth symbol *true*, that is,

false	

or

	true

This is because the corresponding associated sentences of form

$$if \ [\dots \ and \ false \ and \ \dots] \qquad \text{and} \qquad \begin{array}{l} if \ \dots \\ then \ [\dots \ or \ true \ or \ \dots] \end{array}$$

$$\begin{array}{l} if \ [\dots \ and \ false \ and \ \dots] \\ then \ \dots \end{array}$$

are valid. These two special cases will be important to remember later. ⌐

EQUIVALENCE

The notion of equivalence for tableaux is again analogous to that for sentences.

Definition (equivalence of tableaux)

Two tableaux are said to be *equivalent* if, under each interpretation, they have the same truth-value.

Equivalently, two tableaux are equivalent precisely when their associated sentences are equivalent. ⌐

Example

The following tableau T_2' is equivalent to the preceding tableau T_2. For, this tableau is false only under the interpretation in which P is true, Q is false, and R is true. This is also the only interpretation under which T_2 is false.

assertions	goals
	G1'. Q
A2'. P	
	G3'. $not \ (if \ (not \ R) \ then \ Q)$

Tableau T_2'

⌐

IMPLIED-ROW PROPERTY

The *implied-row* property gives a simple condition under which we may add or
remove assertions or goals from a given tableau without changing its meaning.

Proposition (implied row)

Assertion part

Suppose a sentence A is implied by all the assertions $A_1, \ldots, A_m$ of a
tableau T, that is,

$$(\dagger) \quad \begin{array}{l} \textit{if } [A_1 \textit{ and} \ldots \textit{and } A_m] \\ \textit{then } A \end{array}$$

is valid. Then T is equivalent to the tableau T_A obtained from T by
introducing the new assertion

A	

Goal part

Similarly, suppose a sentence G implies some of the goals $G_1, \ldots, G_n$ of
the tableau T, that is,

$$(\ddagger) \quad \begin{array}{l} \textit{if } G \\ \textit{then } [G_1 \textit{ or } \ldots \textit{ or } G_n] \end{array}$$

is valid. Then T is equivalent to the tableau T_G obtained by introducing
the new goal

	G

Proof

The sentence associated with T, that is,

$$\begin{array}{l} \textit{if } [A_1 \textit{ and } \ldots \textit{ and } A_m] \\ \textit{then } [G_1 \textit{ or } \ldots \textit{ or } G_n] \end{array}$$

is equivalent, by $(\dagger)$, to the sentence associated with T_A,

$$\begin{array}{l} \textit{if } [A_1 \textit{ and } \ldots \textit{ and } A_m] \textit{ and } A \\ \textit{then } [G_1 \textit{ or } \ldots \textit{ or } G_n]. \end{array}$$

The sentence associated with $\mathcal{T}$ is also equivalent, by ($\ddagger$), to the sentence associated with $\mathcal{T}_{\mathcal{G}}$, that is,

> *if* $[\mathcal{A}_1$ *and* ... *and* $\mathcal{A}_m]$
> *then* $[\mathcal{G}_1$ *or* ... *or* $\mathcal{G}_n]$ *or* $\mathcal{G}$. ⌐

Remark (valid assertions and contradictory goals)

By the *implied-row* property, any valid sentence $\mathcal{A}$ may be added to a tableau as an assertion, preserving the equivalence of the tableau, because then the sentence (†) is automaticaly valid. In other words, the tableau before $\mathcal{A}$ is added is equivalent to the tableau after $\mathcal{A}$ is added.

Applying the property in reverse, for any valid sentence $\mathcal{A}$, the assertion

$\mathcal{A}$	

may be dropped from a tableau, preserving its equivalence. In particular, the assertion

true	

may always be dropped, because the truth symbol *true* is valid. We shall refer to this as the *trivial assertion*.

Similarly, if $\mathcal{G}$ is a contradictory sentence (i.e., one that is false under any interpretation), the goal

	$\mathcal{G}$

may be added to or dropped from any tableau, preserving equivalence, because then the sentence ($\ddagger$) of the *implied-row* property is automatically valid. In particular, the goal

	false

may be dropped from any tableau, because the truth symbol *false* is contradictory. We shall refer to this as the *trivial goal*. ⌐

Remark (initial tableau)

In our deductive system, presented in the next section, we use as our *initial tableau* a special tableau that consists of m assertions $\mathcal{A}_1, \ldots, \mathcal{A}_m$ and a single goal $\mathcal{G}$

assertions	goals
A_1	
$\vdots$	
A_m	
	$\mathcal{G}$

where each assertion A_i is a sentence known to be valid. (We admit the possibility that $m = 0$.)

This tableau is equivalent (by repeated application of the *implied-row* property) to the tableau

assertions	goals
	$\mathcal{G}$

in which $\mathcal{G}$ is the only goal. The sentence associated with this goal is simply $\mathcal{G}$. Hence the initial tableau is valid precisely when $\mathcal{G}$ is valid.   ◢

DUALITY PROPERTY

The *duality property* states that we can move sentences freely between the assertion and goal columns simply by negating them, obtaining an equivalent tableau.

Proposition (duality)

> A tableau containing an assertion A
>   is equivalent to
> the tableau containing instead the goal (*not* A).
> (assertion-to-goal)

> A tableau containing a goal $\mathcal{G}$
>   is equivalent to
> the tableau containing instead the assertion (*not* $\mathcal{G}$).
> (goal-to-assertion)   ◢

Proof

To prove the *assertion-to-goal* part, observe that, under a given interpretation,

> the original tableau (containing *A* as an assertion) is false

precisely when (by the semantic rule for tableaux)

> *A* is true, the other assertions are all true, and the goals are all false

precisely when

> the other assertions are all true, (*not A*) is false, and the goals are all false

precisely when (by the semantic rule for tableaux, again)

> the new tableau (containing (*not A*) as a goal) is false.

Thus the original tableau (containing *A* as an assertion) is false under a given interpretation *I* precisely when the new tableau (containing (*not A*) as a goal) is false under *I*; that is, the two tableaux are equivalent.

The *goal-to-assertion* part is proved similarly. ◾

By the *duality* property, assertions and goals may be moved freely from one column to the other simply by negating them. Thus the distinction between assertions and goals is artificial and does not increase the "logical power" of the system. In particular, any tableau is equivalent to a tableau with only assertions and no goals and to a tableau with only goals and no assertions. Nevertheless, distinguishing between assertions and goals makes proofs easier to understand.

Remark (replacing versus adding rows)

The *duality* property allows us to replace an assertion *A* with a goal (*not A*), maintaining the equivalence of the tableau. We could also add the new goal (*not A*) to the original tableau without replacing the assertion *A*, and still maintain the equivalence of the tableau. To see this, we first note that the original tableau is equivalent to one with two copies of the assertion *A*; we may then (by the *duality* property) replace only one of them with the goal (*not A*), obtaining an equivalent tableau.

In the same way, any property that allows us to replace one row with another also allows us to add the new row without removing the original one. ◾

SUBTABLEAUX

It will be useful for us to think of a tableau as a set of rows, and to apply to
tableaux some notions from the theory of sets.

Definition (subtableau)

A tableau $\mathcal{T}'$ is a *subtableau* of a tableau $\mathcal{T}$, written $\mathcal{T}' \subseteq \mathcal{T}$, if every
row of $\mathcal{T}'$ is also a row of $\mathcal{T}$. ⏌

Proposition (subtableau)

For any tableaux $\mathcal{T}$ and $\mathcal{T}'$,

> if $\mathcal{T}' \subseteq \mathcal{T}$
> then, for any interpretation $\mathcal{I}$,
> > if $\mathcal{T}'$ is true under $\mathcal{I}$
> > then $\mathcal{T}$ is true under $\mathcal{I}$. ⏌

Proof

Suppose $\mathcal{T}'$ is true under $\mathcal{I}$. Then (by the alternative form of the semantic
rule for tableaux) at least one assertion of $\mathcal{T}'$ is false under $\mathcal{I}$ or at least one goal
of $\mathcal{T}'$ is true under $\mathcal{I}$. But since (by the definition of a subtableau) every row of
$\mathcal{T}'$ is also a row of $\mathcal{T}$, this means that at least one assertion of $\mathcal{T}$ is false under
$\mathcal{I}$ or at least one goal of $\mathcal{T}$ is true under $\mathcal{I}$; that is (by the semantic rule, again),
$\mathcal{T}$ is true under $\mathcal{I}$. ⏌

Definition (union of tableaux)

The *union* $\mathcal{T}_1 \cup \mathcal{T}_2$ of two tableaux $\mathcal{T}_1$ and $\mathcal{T}_2$ is the tableau whose rows
are all the rows of $\mathcal{T}_1$ and all the rows of $\mathcal{T}_2$. ⏌

In other words, the assertions of $\mathcal{T}_1 \cup \mathcal{T}_2$ are the assertions of $\mathcal{T}_1$ and the assertions
of $\mathcal{T}_2$, and the goals of $\mathcal{T}_1 \cup \mathcal{T}_2$ are the goals of $\mathcal{T}_1$ and the goals of $\mathcal{T}_2$.

Proposition (union tableau)

For any tableau $\mathcal{T}_1$ and $\mathcal{T}_2$ and any interpretation $\mathcal{I}$,

> $\mathcal{T}_1 \cup \mathcal{T}_2$ is true under $\mathcal{I}$
> > precisely when
> $\mathcal{T}_1$ is true under $\mathcal{I}$ or
> $\mathcal{T}_2$ is true under $\mathcal{I}$. ⏌

The proof of this proposition is requested in an exercise (**Problem 6.1(a)**).

Proposition (intermediate tableau)

For any tableaux $\mathcal{T}_1$, $\mathcal{T}_2$, and $\mathcal{T}_3$,

> if $\mathcal{T}_1 \subseteq \mathcal{T}_2 \subseteq \mathcal{T}_3$
> then if $\mathcal{T}_1$ is equivalent to $\mathcal{T}_3$
> > then $\mathcal{T}_1$ is equivalent to $\mathcal{T}_2$ and $\mathcal{T}_2$ is equivalent to $\mathcal{T}_3$. ⌟

As a consequence of this *intermediate-tableau* property, we observe that if we can add a certain number of rows to a tableau while preserving its equivalence, we can add instead any portion of those rows and still preserve equivalence. The proof is requested in an exercise (**Problem 6.1(b)**).

6.2   THE DEDUCTIVE PROCESS

In the deductive system for propositional logic we are about to describe, we establish the validity of a tableau by applying *deduction rules* that add new rows to the tableau in such a way that equivalence is preserved; in other words, the new tableau (after applying the rule) is equivalent to the old tableau (before applying the rule). Hence at each stage the new tableau is equivalent to the initial tableau. The process continues until we obtain a tableau that is clearly valid; in this case, we know that the initial tableau is valid too.

Simplification is a fundamental part of the operation of the deductive system.

SIMPLIFICATION

We have already discussed simplification as applied to sentences (Section 5.2), in which a subsentence is replaced by an equivalent but simpler sentence. An assertion or goal introduced into a tableau is first automatically subjected to such a simplification process. This will include the rows of the initial tableau as well as rows introduced subsequently by deduction rules. In other words, the deductive system will never deal with a tableau with unsimplified rows.

Example

In the deductive system, we shall never derive a tableau containing the assertion

$$P \ \ or \ \ \boxed{not \ (not \ (Q \ \ and \ \ R))}$$

The boxed subsentence would automatically be replaced with $(Q \ and \ R)$, by application of the simplification

$$not \ (not \ \mathcal{F}) \ \Rightarrow \ \mathcal{F},$$

yielding the assertion

$P \ \ or \ \ (Q \ \ and \ \ R)$	

⌐

OUTLINE OF THE DEDUCTIVE SYSTEM

In the deductive system, to *prove* that a given sentence S is valid, we form an initial tableau and then apply deduction rules successively until we arrive at the final tableau.

Initial Tableau

We form the *initial tableau*, whose sole goal is the (simplified) sentence S. We may (by the *implied-row* property) include as assertions $\mathcal{A}_1, \ldots, \mathcal{A}_m$ any sentences that have previously been proved (by this deductive system) to be valid.

assertions	goals
$\mathcal{A}_1$	
$\vdots$	
$\mathcal{A}_m$	
	S

Therefore,

S is valid precisely when the initial tableau is valid.

Applying Deduction Rules

The tableau is developed by applying *deduction rules* successively; each rule adds one or more rows to the tableau, in such a way that equivalence is preserved, that is,

> the new tableau (after the rows are added)
>   is equivalent to
> the old tableau (before the rows are added).

(We shall say that a rule that preserves equivalence is *sound*.) Hence each tableau produced by applying another deduction rule is equivalent to the initial tableau.

Each new row contains either an assertion or a goal, which is simplified before being introduced into the tableau.

Final Tableau

The process continues until one of the new rows contains the goal *true*, that is,

	true

or the assertion *false*, that is,

false	

We know that

> the final tableau is valid.

Because the final tableau is valid and the deduction rules preserve equivalence, this means that the initial tableau, and hence the given sentence S, are also valid. We shall say that the final tableau is a *proof* of the sentence S. Any sentence that has a proof will be called a *theorem* of propositional logic.

Any theorem S may be added as an assertion in the initial tableaux of subsequent proofs. This is because S has been proved to be valid, and we may add a valid sentence as an assertion to any tableau, preserving the equivalence of the tableau.

THE DEDUCTION RULES

The deduction rules we will employ are divided into four groups:

- The *rewriting* rule, which replaces a subsentence with an equivalent sentence.

- The *splitting* rules, which break a row down into its logical components.

- The *resolution* rule, which performs a case analysis on the truth of a subsentence.

- The *equivalence* rule, which facilitates our handling of the equivalence connective $\equiv$.

Of these groups, only the *resolution* rule is essential.

Each deduction rule requires that certain rows (assertions and goals), called the *required rows*, already be present in the tableau, and generates certain new rows (assertions and goals), called the *generated rows*, to be introduced into the tableau. For simplicity, in applying a deduction rule, we always add rows, never delete rows.

In the tableau notation, we write a rule in the form

	assertions	goals
$\mathcal{T}_r$:		
$\mathcal{T}_g$:		

where the required rows are those that appear above the double line, and the generated rows are those that appear below the double line.

The required rows form the *required subtableau*, denoted by $\mathcal{T}_r$, and the generated rows form the *generated subtableau*, denoted by $\mathcal{T}_g$.

The deduction rule is applied only if the required subtableau $\mathcal{T}_r$ occurs as part of the old tableau. The new tableau is obtained by adding the generated subtableau $\mathcal{T}_g$ to the old tableau. That is, we require that $\mathcal{T}_r$ be a subtableau of the old tableau $\mathcal{T}$ (that is, $\mathcal{T}_r \subseteq \mathcal{T}$), and obtain the new tableau $\mathcal{T} \cup \mathcal{T}_g$.

We shall ensure that all of our deductive rules are *sound*, that is, that they preserve the equivalence of the tableau.

6.3   REWRITING RULE

Simplification is applied automatically because it always reduces the complexity of the tableau and never makes it more difficult to prove. There is another category of equivalent sentences that can be used to manipulate a tableau, such as *and-or distributivity*,

$$\mathcal{F} \ \textit{and} \ (\mathcal{G} \ \textit{or} \ \mathcal{H}) \ \Leftrightarrow \ (\mathcal{F} \ \textit{and} \ \mathcal{G}) \ \textit{or} \ (\mathcal{F} \ \textit{and} \ \mathcal{H}),$$

which are not regarded as simplifications. Replacing subsentences with equivalent sentences from this category does not necessarily make the tableau simpler, but it may sometimes make it easier to prove. We call this operation *rewriting*.

We do not apply rewriting automatically; we regard it as a deduction rule, to be applied only at our discretion. (In this regard, we differ from the usual use of the term "rewriting" in the literature.) Also, we do not replace the rewritten assertion or goal; both the original row and the rewritten row are included in the new tableau because we are not sure which will be used in the proof.

Rewritings may be applied in either direction; for this reason, they are written with a double-headed arrow ($\Leftrightarrow$). Only one occurrence of a subsentence can be replaced with each application of the rule. For example, *and associativity*,

$$\mathcal{F} \ \textit{and} \ (\mathcal{G} \ \textit{and} \ \mathcal{H}) \ \Leftrightarrow \ (\mathcal{F} \ \textit{and} \ \mathcal{G}) \ \textit{and} \ \mathcal{H},$$

can be used right-to-left to replace a single subsentence occurrence of the form $((\mathcal{F} \ \textit{and} \ \mathcal{G}) \ \textit{and} \ \mathcal{H})$ with the corresponding sentence of the form $(\mathcal{F} \ \textit{and} \ (\mathcal{G} \ \textit{and} \ \mathcal{H}))$, as well as in the other direction.

Justification of the *rewriting* rule, that is, showing that it is sound, is straightforward because we are always replacing a subsentence with an equivalent sentence. The new tableau contains an additional row equivalent to one of the given rows.

Rewriting is never an essential step; it is always possible to do without it. It can, however, give us simpler and more natural proofs.

Example

Let us apply left-to-right the *and-or* distributivity rewriting,

$$\mathcal{F} \ \textit{and} \ (\mathcal{G} \ \textit{or} \ \mathcal{H}) \ \Leftrightarrow \ (\mathcal{F} \ \textit{and} \ \mathcal{G}) \ \textit{or} \ (\mathcal{F} \ \textit{and} \ \mathcal{H}),$$

to a tableau containing the goal

	$P \ \textit{and} \ \boxed{Q \ \textit{and} \ (R \ \textit{or} \ S)}$

(As usual, we enclose the subsentence to be replaced in a box.) We obtain the new goal

	P *and* $((Q$ *and* $R)$ *or* $(Q$ *and* $S))$

which is added to the tableau without dropping the given goal. ⌐

CATALOG OF REWRITINGS

We present several rewritings, to be used at our discretion. Note that this catalog does not include simplifications, which are performed automatically. A catalog of simplifications is contained in Section 5.2.

- Negation

$$not\ (\mathcal{F}\ and\ \mathcal{G})\ \Leftrightarrow\ (not\ \mathcal{F})\ or\ (not\ \mathcal{G}) \qquad (not\ and)$$

$$not\ (\mathcal{F}\ or\ \mathcal{G})\ \Leftrightarrow\ (not\ \mathcal{F})\ and\ (not\ \mathcal{G}) \qquad (not\ or)$$

$$not\ (if\ \mathcal{F}\ then\ \mathcal{G})\ \Leftrightarrow\ \mathcal{F}\ and\ (not\ \mathcal{G}) \qquad (not\ if)$$

$$not\ (\mathcal{F}\equiv\mathcal{G})\ \Leftrightarrow\ \mathcal{F}\equiv(not\ \mathcal{G}) \qquad (not\ iff)$$

$$not\ (if\ \mathcal{F}\ then\ \mathcal{G}\ else\ \mathcal{H})\ \Leftrightarrow\ if\ \mathcal{F}\ then\ (not\ \mathcal{G})\ else\ (not\ \mathcal{H}) \quad (not\ cond)$$

- Elimination

$$if\ \mathcal{F}\ then\ \mathcal{G}\ \Leftrightarrow\ (not\ \mathcal{F})\ or\ \mathcal{G} \qquad (if\ or)$$

$$\mathcal{F}\equiv\mathcal{G}\ \Leftrightarrow\ (if\ \mathcal{F}\ then\ \mathcal{G})\ and\ (if\ \mathcal{G}\ then\ \mathcal{F}) \qquad (iff\ and)$$

$$\mathcal{F}\equiv\mathcal{G}\ \Leftrightarrow\ (\mathcal{F}\ and\ \mathcal{G})\ or\ ((not\ \mathcal{F})\ and\ (not\ \mathcal{G})) \qquad (iff\ or)$$

$$if\ \mathcal{F}\ then\ \mathcal{G}\ else\ \mathcal{H}\ \Leftrightarrow\ (if\ \mathcal{F}\ then\ \mathcal{G})\ and\ (if\ (not\ \mathcal{F})\ then\ \mathcal{H}) \quad (cond\ and)$$

$$if\ \mathcal{F}\ then\ \mathcal{G}\ else\ \mathcal{H}\ \Leftrightarrow\ (\mathcal{F}\ and\ \mathcal{G})\ or\ ((not\ \mathcal{F})\ and\ \mathcal{H}) \qquad (cond\ or)$$

- Commutativity

$$\mathcal{F}\ and\ \mathcal{G}\ \Leftrightarrow\ \mathcal{G}\ and\ \mathcal{F} \qquad (and)$$

$$\mathcal{F}\ or\ \mathcal{G}\ \Leftrightarrow\ \mathcal{G}\ or\ \mathcal{F} \qquad (or)$$

$$\mathcal{F}\equiv\mathcal{G}\ \Leftrightarrow\ \mathcal{G}\equiv\mathcal{F} \qquad (iff)$$

- Associativity

$$(\mathcal{F}\ and\ \mathcal{G})\ and\ \mathcal{H}\ \Leftrightarrow\ \mathcal{F}\ and\ (\mathcal{G}\ and\ \mathcal{H}) \qquad (and)$$

$$(\mathcal{F}\ or\ \mathcal{G})\ or\ \mathcal{H}\ \Leftrightarrow\ \mathcal{F}\ or\ (\mathcal{G}\ or\ \mathcal{H}) \qquad (or)$$

$$(\mathcal{F}\equiv\mathcal{G})\equiv\mathcal{H}\ \Leftrightarrow\ \mathcal{F}\equiv(\mathcal{G}\equiv\mathcal{H}) \qquad (iff)$$

- Distributivity

$$\mathcal{F} \text{ and } (\mathcal{G} \text{ or } \mathcal{H}) \;\Leftrightarrow\; (\mathcal{F} \text{ and } \mathcal{G}) \text{ or } (\mathcal{F} \text{ and } \mathcal{H}) \qquad (\text{and or})$$

$$\mathcal{F} \text{ or } (\mathcal{G} \text{ and } \mathcal{H}) \;\Leftrightarrow\; (\mathcal{F} \text{ or } \mathcal{G}) \text{ and } (\mathcal{F} \text{ or } \mathcal{H}) \qquad (\text{or and})$$

Remark (cond-and rewriting)

The *cond-and* rewriting

$$(\textit{if } \mathcal{F} \textit{ then } \mathcal{G} \textit{ else } \mathcal{H}) \;\Leftrightarrow\; (\textit{if } \mathcal{F} \textit{ then } \mathcal{G}) \textit{ and } (\textit{if } (\textit{not } \mathcal{F}) \textit{ then } \mathcal{H})$$

should really be written

$$(\textit{if } \mathcal{F} \textit{ then } \mathcal{G} \textit{ else } \mathcal{H}) \;\Leftrightarrow\; (\textit{if } \mathcal{F} \textit{ then } \mathcal{G}) \textit{ and } (\mathcal{F} \textit{ or } \mathcal{H})$$

because any subsentence of form

$$\textit{if } (\textit{not } \mathcal{F}) \textit{ then } \mathcal{H}$$

is immediately simplified to the corresponding sentence of form

$$\mathcal{F} \textit{ or } \mathcal{H},$$

by application of the *if-or* simplification. We have given the former version because it is more immediately understandable. ⌐

6.4   SPLITTING RULES

The splitting rules decompose a row (assertion or goal) into its logical components. We first describe the splitting rules and then show their soundness, i.e., that they preserve the equivalence of the tableaux to which they are applied.

There are three splitting rules.

AND-SPLIT RULE

If a tableau contains an assertion of form

$$\mathcal{A}_1 \text{ and } \mathcal{A}_2,$$

we may add the corresponding sentences of form $\mathcal{A}_1$ and $\mathcal{A}_2$ to the tableau as new assertions. We shall express our deduction rules in the following tableau notation:

assertions	goals
$\mathcal{A}_1$ and $\mathcal{A}_2$	
$\mathcal{A}_1$	
$\mathcal{A}_2$	

This notation means that, if an instance of row above the double line is present in the tableau (the required rows), then we may add the corresponding instance of the rows below the double line (the generated rows). Intuitively, if we know that the conjunction ($\mathcal{A}_1$ and $\mathcal{A}_2$) is true, we also know that each of the conjuncts $\mathcal{A}_1$, $\mathcal{A}_2$ is true.

In using the preceding notation, we do not restrict the location of the row containing the assertion

$$\mathcal{A}_1 \quad and \quad \mathcal{A}_2$$

in the given tableau. In particular, it need not be the first or the last row; the order of the rows is not significant. As usual, we do not delete the required assertion when we apply the deduction rule.

OR-SPLIT RULE

If the tableau contains a goal of form

$$\mathcal{G}_1 \quad or \quad \mathcal{G}_2,$$

we may add the corresponding sentences $\mathcal{G}_1$ and $\mathcal{G}_2$ as new goals; that is,

assertions	goals
	$\mathcal{G}_1$ or $\mathcal{G}_2$
	$\mathcal{G}_1$
	$\mathcal{G}_2$

Intuitively, if we want to prove the disjunction ($\mathcal{G}_1$ or $\mathcal{G}_2$), it suffices to establish any one of the disjuncts $\mathcal{G}_1$, $\mathcal{G}_2$.

Note that there is no *or-split* rule for assertions or *and-split* rule for goals.

IF-SPLIT RULE

If the tableau contains a goal of form

$$if \ \mathcal{A} \ then \ \mathcal{G},$$

then we may add the corresponding sentence $\mathcal{A}$ as a new assertion and $\mathcal{G}$ as a new goal; that is,

assertions	goals
	$if \ \mathcal{A} \ then \ \mathcal{G}$
$\mathcal{A}$	
	$\mathcal{G}$

Intuitively, if we want to prove the implication ($if \ \mathcal{A} \ then \ \mathcal{G}$), it suffices to assume that the antecedent $\mathcal{A}$ is true and to establish that then the consequent $\mathcal{G}$ is also true.

Let us consider a simple example of the use of all three splitting rules.

Example

Suppose we have the initial tableau

assertions	goals
	G1. $if \ (P \ and \ Q)$ $then \ (Q \ or \ R)$

Then we can apply the *if-split* rule to goal G1, obtaining the new assertion and the new goal

assertions	goals
A2. $P \ and \ Q$	
	G3. $Q \ or \ R$

We can then apply the *and-split* rule to assertion A2, yielding the new assertions

assertions	goals
A4. P	
A5. Q	

We can also apply the *or-split* rule to goal G3, yielding the new goals

	G6. Q
	G7. R

The tableau we obtain is then

assertions	goals
	G1. *if* $(P$ *and* $Q)$ *then* $(Q$ *or* $R)$
A2. P *and* Q	
	G3. Q *or* R
A4. P	
A5. Q	
	G6. Q
	G7. R

We have not yet proved the sentence because we have not derived the final goal
true or the final assertion *false*. ◢

Remark (multiple conjunction and disjunction)

The *and* and *or* connectives apply to two arguments. In Section [I]1.8, we
extended these connectives to apply to several arguments as well. We defined the
multiple conjunction

$$\mathcal{F}_1 \ and \ \mathcal{F}_2 \ and \ \mathcal{F}_3 \ and \ \ldots \ and \ \mathcal{F}_k$$

to be an abbreviation for

$$(\ldots((\mathcal{F}_1 \ and \ \mathcal{F}_2) \ and \ \mathcal{F}_3) \ldots) \ and \ \mathcal{F}_k,$$

and the multiple disjunction

$$\mathcal{F}_1 \ or \ \mathcal{F}_2 \ or \ \mathcal{F}_3 \ or \ \ldots \ or \ \mathcal{F}_k$$

to be an abbreviation for

$$(\ldots((\mathcal{F}_1 \ or \ \mathcal{F}_2) \ or \ \mathcal{F}_3) \ldots) \ or \ \mathcal{F}_k.$$

Therefore, from a multiple-conjunction assertion

assertions	goals
A_1 *and* A_2 *and* ... *and* A_k	

we can deduce, by $k-1$ applications of the *and-split* rule, the assertions

A_1	
A_2	
$\vdots$	
A_k	

Similarly, from a multiple-disjunction goal

	G_1 *or* G_2 *or* ... *or* G_k

we can deduce, by $k-1$ applications of the *or-split* rule, the goals

	G_1
	G_2
	$\vdots$
	G_k

When we introduce a new deduction rule we must show that it is sound, i.e., that it actually does preserve the equivalence of any tableau to which it is applied. We now introduce a *justification* proposition, which will facilitate such proofs.

6.5   JUSTIFICATION CONDITION

Recall that we called those rows (assertions and goals) that must be present in the tableau for a deduction rule to be applied the *required rows*, forming the *required subtableau* $\mathcal{T}_r$, and those that are added to the tableau by the rule the *generated rows*, forming the *generated subtableau* $\mathcal{T}_g$. Thus the required rows are those that appear above the double line in the tableau form of the rule, and the generated rows are those that appear below the double line.

Proposition (justification)

A deduction rule is sound (i.e., preserves equivalence) if the following *justification condition* holds:

For every interpretation $\mathcal{I}$,

if the required subtableau $\mathcal{T}_r$ is false under $\mathcal{I}$,
then the generated subtableau $\mathcal{T}_g$ is false under $\mathcal{I}$.   ⌐

In other words, the *justification* condition states that

if all the required assertions are true and
all the required goals are false under $\mathcal{I}$,
then all the generated assertions are true and
all the generated goals are false under $\mathcal{I}$.

Equivalently (taking the contrapositive), the *justification* condition says that

if the generated subtableau $\mathcal{T}_g$ is true under $\mathcal{I}$,
then the required subtableau $\mathcal{T}_r$ is also true under $\mathcal{I}$.

The *justification* proposition states that, if the *justification* condition holds, the new tableau (produced by adding the generated assertions and goals) is equivalent to the old tableau (before the generated assertions and goals are added). Hence, to justify a rule, we need not consider any of the assertions and goals of the tableau other than those required or generated by the rule.

Before we prove the proposition, let us apply it to justify one of our splitting rules.

Justification (*if-split* rule)

The *if-split* rule requires a goal

	if $\mathcal{A}$ then $\mathcal{G}$

and generates the assertion and goal

$\mathcal{A}$	
	$\mathcal{G}$

To justify this deduction rule, we need only consider an arbitrary interpretation under which the required goal (*if $\mathcal{A}$ then $\mathcal{G}$*) is false, and show that, under this interpretation, the generated assertion $\mathcal{A}$ is true and the generated goal $\mathcal{G}$ is false. But this follows from the semantic rule for the *if-then* connective. ⌐

The other splitting rules can be justified in the same way.

Remark (deleting rows)

Recall that in applying a deduction rule, we do not delete the required rows from the tableau. In fact, in the case of the splitting rules, we could have deleted the required assertion or goal and still preserved the equivalence of the tableau. For some rules, however, deleting a required row may cause us to lose validity. That is, the old tableau may be valid, but the new tableau may be nonvalid. ⌐

Let us now prove the *justification* proposition.

Proof (justification)

Suppose the deduction rule is applied to a tableau $\mathcal{T}$ and the *justification* condition holds. We want to show that the new tableau $\mathcal{T} \cup \mathcal{T}_g$ is equivalent to $\mathcal{T}$, the old tableau. We show that, if either tableau is true under some interpretation, then the other is true under the same interpretation. We treat each direction separately.

Old tableau is true $\Rightarrow$ new tableau is true

This direction does not depend on the *justification* condition. The old tableau $\mathcal{T}$ is a subtableau of the new tableau $\mathcal{T} \cup \mathcal{T}_g$. It follows, by the *subtableau* property, that if the old tableau is true for a given interpretation, the new tableau is also true under the same interpretation.

New tableau is true $\Rightarrow$ old tableau is true

Suppose, for a given interpretation, that the new tableau $\mathcal{T} \cup \mathcal{T}_g$ is true. Then, by the *union* property, $\mathcal{T}$ is true or $\mathcal{T}_g$ is true under the same interpretation. In the first case, the old tableau, $\mathcal{T}$ itself, is true. In the other case, if $\mathcal{T}_g$ is true then (by the *justification* condition) $\mathcal{T}_r$ is true. But $\mathcal{T}_r$ is a subtableau of $\mathcal{T}$; therefore (by the *subtableau* property) the old tableau, $\mathcal{T}$ itself, is true. ⌐

In **Problem 6.2** the reader is requested to formulate and prove a more ambitious *justification* proposition.

6.6   RESOLUTION RULE

The *resolution* rule allows us to perform a case analysis on the truth of an arbitrary sentence, where that sentence occurs as a common subsentence of two rows.

There are four different versions of the *resolution* rule: *AA-resolution* (applied to two assertions), *GG-resolution* (applied to two goals), *AG-resolution* (applied to an assertion and a goal), and *GA-resolution* (applied to a goal and an assertion). We present first the *AA-resolution* rule, which is considered to be the basic form.

THE BASIC FORM

The basic form of the *resolution* rule is expressed as follows.

Rule (AA-resolution)

assertions	goals
$\mathcal{A}_1[P]$	
$\mathcal{A}_2[P]$	
$\mathcal{A}_1[\textit{false}]$ *or* $\mathcal{A}_2[\textit{true}]$	

where P is a sentence that occurs as a subsentence of both $\mathcal{A}_1$ and $\mathcal{A}_2$. ⌐

In other words, to apply the rule to a tableau, we do the following:

- Choose any two assertions $\mathcal{A}_1[P]$ and $\mathcal{A}_2[P]$ with a common subsentence P.

- Replace every occurrence of P in $\mathcal{A}_1[P]$ with the truth symbol *false*, and every occurrence of P in $\mathcal{A}_2[P]$ with the truth symbol *true*, obtaining $\mathcal{A}_1[false]$ and $\mathcal{A}_2[true]$, respectively.

- Take the disjunction $(\mathcal{A}_1[false]$ *or* $\mathcal{A}_2[true])$ and apply to it all possible simplifications.

- Add the simplified disjunction to the tableau as a new assertion.

We will say that the new assertion is a *resolvent*, obtained by *applying* the *resolution* rule to the assertions $\mathcal{A}_1[P]$ and $\mathcal{A}_2[P]$, *matching* P.

Note that $\mathcal{A}_1[P]$ and $\mathcal{A}_2[P]$ may be chosen to be any two assertions in the tableau; their location in the tableau is completely irrelevant.

Normally, in describing a step in a proof, we mention the sentence $\mathcal{A}_1[P]$, whose subsentence is replaced by *false*, before the sentence $\mathcal{A}_2[P]$, whose subsentence is replaced by *true*. This is not necessarily the actual order of the assertions in the tableau. Nor need the assertions be adjacent in the tableau.

Example

Suppose our tableau contains the assertions

$\mathcal{A}_1[P]: \quad P \; or \; Q$

$\mathcal{A}_2[P]: \quad if \; (P \; or \; Q) \; then \; R.$

Let P be $(P \; or \; Q)$. Both of the assertions contain $(P \; or \; Q)$ as a subsentence.

The required rows are therefore

assertions	goals
$\mathcal{A}_1[P]: \quad \boxed{P \; or \; Q}$	
$\mathcal{A}_2[P]: \quad if \; \boxed{P \; or \; Q} \; then \; R$	

We use the boxes to indicate the subsentences about to be matched in applying the rule.

Replacing every occurrence of $(P \; or \; Q)$ in $\mathcal{A}_1[P]$ with the truth symbol *false*, we obtain

$\mathcal{A}_1[false]: \quad false.$

Replacing every occurrence of $(P\ or\ Q)$ in $\mathcal{A}_2[P]$ with the truth symbol *true*, we obtain

$\mathcal{A}_2[true]$:   *if   true   then   R.*

Therefore, matching $(P\ or\ Q)$, we can apply the *resolution* rule to $\mathcal{A}_1[P]$ and $\mathcal{A}_2[P]$, replacing $(P\ or\ Q)$ with *false* and *true*, respectively, and add to our tableau as a new assertion the resolvent

$\mathcal{A}_1[false]$ *or* $\mathcal{A}_2[true]$,

that is,

> *false*
> > *or*
>
> *if   true   then   R.*

This assertion can be reduced (by means of the *false-or* and *if-true* simplifications) to the assertion

R	

The *resolution* rule is asymmetric in the sense that, if we reverse the roles of $\mathcal{A}_1[P]$ and $\mathcal{A}_2[P]$ in applying the rule, we may get different results.

Example (reversing the order)

In the preceding example, suppose we reverse $\mathcal{A}_1[P]$ and $\mathcal{A}_2[P]$:

assertions	goals
$\mathcal{A}_1[P]$: *if* $\boxed{P\ or\ Q}$ *then R*	
$\mathcal{A}_2[P]$: $\boxed{P\ or\ Q}$	

Then, again matching the subsentence $(P\ or\ Q)$, we obtain the assertion

$\mathcal{A}_1[false]$ *or* $\mathcal{A}_2[true]$,

that is,

> *if   false   then   R*
> > *or*
>
> *true.*

This assertion can be reduced (by *or-true* simplification) to the trivial assertion

true	

By interchanging the two assertions in applying the *resolution* rule, we have obtained a different result. The results of both examples are legal consequences of applying the rule to the two given assertions. The second result is not useful, however, as we explain later.

Note that we do not exclude the possibility of applying the *resolution* rule to an assertion and itself, that is, taking both $\mathcal{A}_1[P]$ and $\mathcal{A}_2[P]$ to be the same assertion.

Example (assertion and itself)

Suppose we apply the *resolution* rule, taking both $\mathcal{A}_1[P]$ and $\mathcal{A}_2[P]$ to be the assertion

assertions	goals
if $\left(P \ or \ \boxed{Q} \right) \ then \ \left(\boxed{Q} \ and \ R \right)$	

that is,

$$\mathcal{A}_1[P]: \quad if \ \left(P \ or \ \boxed{Q} \right) \ then \ \left(\boxed{Q} \ and \ R \right)$$

$$\mathcal{A}_2[P]: \quad if \ \left(P \ or \ \boxed{Q} \right) \ then \ \left(\boxed{Q} \ and \ R \right),$$

taking P to be Q, that is, matching the subsentence Q. Our unsimplified resolvent is the assertion

$$\mathcal{A}_1[false] \ or \ \mathcal{A}_2[true],$$

that is,

$$if \ (P \ or \ false) \ then \ (false \ and \ R)$$
$$or$$
$$if \ (P \ or \ true) \ then \ (true \ and \ R),$$

which is reduced (by *or-false, false-and, then-false, or-true, true-and,* and *if-true* simplifications) to the assertion

$(not\ \ P)\ \ or\ \ R$	

Remark (at least one replacement)

Although our substitution notation admits the possibility that the subsentence P does not occur in the assertions A_1 or A_2, the wording of the rule requires that the subsentence occur at least once in each of the assertions. Otherwise, the assertion we derive would be weaker than the ones we were given.

Let us justify the basic *resolution* rule, showing that the old tableau, before applying the rule, is equivalent to the new tableau, obtained by adding the resolvent.

Justification (AA-resolution)

First we make an observation. Suppose a sentence $F[P]$ is true under some interpretation. Clearly, we do not alter the truth of a sentence by replacing one of its subsentences with another having the same truth-value under this interpretation. Thus, if P is false under the interpretation, then $F[false]$ is true under the same interpretation. And, if P is true under the interpretation, then $F[true]$ is true under the same interpretation.

Suppose the required assertions $A_1[P]$ and $A_2[P]$ both contain P as a subsentence. Consider an interpretation I under which the required subtableau T_r is false, that is, $A_1[P]$ and $A_2[P]$ are both true under I. By the *justification* proposition, it suffices to establish that the generated subtableau T_g is false under I, that is, the assertion generated by the rule, the simplified disjunction

$$A_1[false]\ \ or\ \ A_2[true],$$

is also true under I.

We distinguish between two subcases.

Case: P is false under I

Then, by our initial observation, because P and *false* have the same truth-values, and because $A_1[P]$ is true under I, we know that

$$A_1[false]$$

is also true under I. By the semantic rule for the *or* connective, the disjunction

$$A_1[false]\ \ or\ \ A_2[true]$$

is true under I. The simplified disjunction is true under I as well.

Case: P is true under I

Then, because P and *true* have the same truth-values, and because $A_2[P]$ is true under I, we know that

$$A_2[true]$$

is also true under I, and (by the semantic rule for *or*) the disjunction

$$A_1[false] \quad or \quad A_2[true]$$

is true under I. The simplified disjunction is true under I as well.

Because, in each case, the conclusion of the *AA-resolution* rule is true under I, the *justification* condition for the rule is established. ⌟

DUAL FORMS

The basic form of the *resolution* rule derives a conclusion from two assertions; we therefore called this form *AA-resolution*. Because of the duality between assertions and goals, there exist different forms of the rule applied to two goals (*GG-resolution*), an assertion and a goal (*AG-resolution*), and a goal and an assertion (*GA-resolution*). Because all these forms of the rule can be justified by duality, we call them *dual forms*.

The form that applies to two goals is as follows.

Rule (GG-resolution)

assertions	goals
	$G_1[P]$
	$G_2[P]$
	$G_1[false]$ *and* $G_2[true]$

where P is a sentence that occurs as a subsentence of both G_1 and G_2. ⌟

Note that the GG form of the rule introduces a conjunction rather than a disjunction.

Justification (GG-resolution)

This form, like *AA-resolution*, can be justified directly by establishing the appropriate *justification* condition. It is more instructive, however, to derive *GG-resolution* from *AA-resolution* by appeal to the *duality* property. The relationship between the two forms then becomes clear.

A tableau with the goals required by *GG-resolution*,

assertions	goals
	$\mathcal{G}_1[P]$
	$\mathcal{G}_2[P]$

is equivalent (by the *duality* property) to a tableau with the additional assertions

not $\mathcal{G}_1[P]$	
not $\mathcal{G}_2[P]$	

This tableau is equivalent (by the soundness of *AA-resolution*) to the tableau to which we add the simplified assertion

not $(\mathcal{G}_1[false])$ *or* *not* $(\mathcal{G}_2[true])$	

or, equivalently (by propositional logic),

not $\begin{bmatrix} \mathcal{G}_1[false] \\ and \\ \mathcal{G}_2[true] \end{bmatrix}$	

But (by the *duality* property, again) a tableau with this assertion is equivalent to a tableau with the additional goal

	$\mathcal{G}_1[false]$ *and* $\mathcal{G}_2[true]$

This is precisely the goal generated by *GG-resolution*.

We have shown that we can add to the tableau the preceding goal and the intermediate assertions, maintaining the equivalence of the tableau. Therefore, by the *intermediate-tableau* property, we may add only the goal and still maintain equivalence. ⌐

Remark (properties are not rules)

In justifying the *GG-resolution* rule, we used the *duality* property to justify introducing a new row into the tableau. The reader is not to get the impression that we may use duality as if it were a deduction rule, to add new rows to a tableau during a proof. The reason for not including duality as a deduction rule is that it never helps the proof; for, whatever deduction rule that can be applied to the added goal $\mathcal{A}$, there is a dual version that can be applied directly to the given assertion (*not* $\mathcal{A}$). The *duality* property is useful in justifying the dual versions but is not itself necessary in the proof. A similar remark applies to the *implied-row* property. ⌐

Let us illustrate the *GG-resolution* rule.

Example

Suppose we are given a tableau containing the two goals

assertions	goals
	$\mathcal{G}_1[P]:$ *if* $\boxed{P}$ *then* Q
	$\mathcal{G}_2[P]:$ $\boxed{P}$

Then, taking P to be the sentence P, which occurs as a subsentence of both goals, we can apply the *GG-resolution* rule to obtain the new goal

> *if false then* Q
>   *and*
> *true*,

which reduces (by the *if-false* and *and-true* simplifications) to

	true

⌐

The two other dual forms of the *resolution* rule apply to an assertion and a goal and to a goal and an assertion.

Rule (AG-resolution)

assertions	goals
$\mathcal{A}[P]$	
	$\mathcal{G}[P]$
	not $\mathcal{A}[false]$ *and* $\mathcal{G}[true]$

where P is a sentence that occurs as a subsentence of both $\mathcal{A}$ and $\mathcal{G}$. ⌟

Rule (GA-resolution)

assertions	goals
	$\mathcal{G}[P]$
$\mathcal{A}[P]$	
	$\mathcal{G}[false]$ *and* *not* $\mathcal{A}[true]$

where P is a sentence that occurs as a subsentence of both $\mathcal{A}$ and $\mathcal{G}$. ⌟

These *AG-* and *GA-resolution* rules are not identical because of the asymmetric role of the assertion and the goal in each case. In *AG-resolution*, a subsentence of the assertion is replaced by *false*; in *GA-resolution*, a subsentence of the goal is replaced by *false*. By the *duality* property, each of these forms is equivalent to *AA-resolution*. The justification of these two forms resembles the justification of *GG-resolution* and is omitted.

Example

Suppose we are given a tableau that contains the assertion $\mathcal{A}[P]$ and the goal $\mathcal{G}[P]$:

assertions	goals
$\mathcal{A}[P]$: if P then $\boxed{\text{if } Q_1 \text{ then } Q_2}$	
	$\mathcal{G}[P]$: $\boxed{\text{if } Q_1 \text{ then } Q_2}$ and R

Then, taking P to be the sentence

$$P: \quad \text{if } Q_1 \text{ then } Q_2,$$

which occurs as a subsentence of both $\mathcal{A}[P]$ and $\mathcal{G}[P]$, we can apply AG-*resolution* to obtain the new goal

$$not \begin{bmatrix} \text{if } P \\ \text{then } \text{false} \end{bmatrix}$$
$$and$$
$$true \ and \ R,$$

which reduces (by *then-false*, *not-not*, and *true-and* simplifications) to

	P and R

In **Problem 6.3** the reader is requested to justify the *hyper-resolution* rule, which is a variant of the *resolution* rule.

COMMON EXAMPLES

Certain special applications of the *resolution* rule occur frequently enough that it is worthwhile to recognize them. We illustrate these applications with a few examples.

The first three applications establish the final goal *true* or the final assertion *false*.

Identity

Suppose P is both an assertion and a goal:

assertions	goals
$\boxed{P}$	
	$\boxed{P}$

Then we can derive (by *AG-resolution*, matching P) the goal

> *not false*
>   *and*
> *true*,

which reduces (by *not-false* and *true-and* simplifications) to the final goal

	true

In other words, if we want to show P and P is known to be true, we are done.

Contradiction

Suppose we are given two assertions, contradicting each other:

assertions	goals
$\boxed{P}$	
not $\boxed{P}$	

Then we can derive (by *AA-resolution*) the assertion

> *false*
>   *or*
> *not true*,

which reduces (by *false-or* and *not-true* simplifications) to the final assertion

false	

In other words, from two contradictory assertions, every goal can be proved.

Excluded middle

Suppose our problem is to establish either of two complementary goals (*not P*) or *P*.

assertions	goals
	not $\boxed{P}$
	$\boxed{P}$

Then we can derive (by *GG-resolution*) the goal

> *not false*
>   *and*
> *true,*

which reduces (by *not-false* and *true-and* simplifications) to the final goal

	true

In other words, if it suffices to establish either *P* or its negation, the proof is complete.

Forward chaining (modus ponens)

Suppose we are given the two assertions *P* and (*if P then Q*).

assertions	goals
$\boxed{P}$	
if $\boxed{P}$ *then Q*	

Then, we can derive (by *AA-resolution*, matching *P*) the assertion

> *false*
>   *or*
> *if true then Q,*

which reduces (by *false-or* and *if-true* simplifications) to the assertion

Q	

In other words, from P and (if P $then$ Q) we can conclude Q.

Backward chaining

Suppose we know (if P $then$ Q) and want to show Q:

assertions	goals
if P $then$ $\boxed{Q}$	
	$\boxed{Q}$

Then (by AG-*resolution*, matching Q) we obtain the goal

> not (if P $then$ $false$)
> and
> $true$,

which reduces (by *then-false, not-not,* and *and-true* simplifications) to the goal

	P

In other words, if we know (if P $then$ Q) and want to show Q, then it suffices to show P.

Clausal resolution

Suppose we know both (P or Q) and ((not P) or R):

assertions	goals
$\boxed{P}$ or Q	
$\left(not \ \boxed{P}\right)$ or R	

Then (by AA-*resolution*, matching P) we obtain the goal

> $false$ or Q
> or
> (not $true$) or R,

which reduces (by *false-or* and *not-true* simplifications) to the assertion

Q *or* R	

In **Problem 6.4** the reader is asked to apply the *resolution* rule in several other common cases.

A SAMPLE PROOF

Although we will later present another rule, for dealing with equivalence (Section 6.8), we already have enough rules to prove any valid propositional sentence, as we remarked. (This will be shown in general in Chapter 13.) Let us now consider an example of a complete proof of the validity of a propositional-logic sentence.

We let S be the sentence

$$S: \quad \begin{array}{l} \textit{if } (P \textit{ and } Q) \\ \textit{then } (Q \textit{ or } R), \end{array}$$

which was discussed in an earlier example. We present three different proofs of the validity of S, depending on the extent to which the splitting rules are applied.

Proof 1:   full splitting

Consider the initial tableau in which S is the only goal:

assertions	goals
	G1. *if* $(P$ *and* $Q)$ *then* $(Q$ *or* $R)$

Applying the *if-split* rule to goal G1, we obtain the assertion and the goal

A2. P *and* Q	
	G3. Q *or* R

Applying the *and-split* rule to assertion A2, we obtain the assertions

A4. P	
A5. $\boxed{Q}$	

Applying the *or-split* rule to goal G3, we obtain the goals

	G6. $\boxed{Q}$
	G7. R

Now we can apply *AG-resolution* to assertion A5 and goal G6, matching Q, obtaining the goal

> *not false*
>   *and*
> *true,*

which reduces (by *not-false* and *true-and* simplifications) to the final goal

	G8. *true*

Because we have obtained the final goal *true*, it follows that the given sentence S is valid.

Proof 2:   partial splitting

    The preceding proof is not the only possible proof of S. For example, suppose we have developed the first three rows as before, that is,

assertions	goals
	G1. *if* (P *and* Q) *then* (Q *or* R)
A2. P *and* $\boxed{Q}$	
	G3. $\boxed{Q}$ *or* R

Then, if (instead of applying the splitting rules to rows A2 and G3) we apply *AG-resolution* to assertion A2 and goal G3, matching Q, we obtain the goal

> *not* (P *and* *false*)
>   *and*
> *true or R,*

which reduces (by *and-false, not-false, true-and,* and *true-or* simplifications) to the final goal

	G4. *true*

Proof 3:   no splitting

In fact, still another proof can be obtained. Suppose we begin with the same initial tableau:

assertions	goals
	G1. *if* $\left(P \;\; and \;\; \boxed{Q}\right)$ *then* $\left(\boxed{Q} \;\; or \;\; R\right)$

If (instead of applying the *if-split* rule) we apply *GG-resolution* to goal G1 and itself, matching Q, we obtain the goal

$$\begin{bmatrix} if \;\; (P \;\; and \;\; false) \\ then \;\; (false \;\; or \;\; R) \end{bmatrix}$$
$$and$$
$$\begin{bmatrix} if \;\; (P \;\; and \;\; true) \\ then \;\; (true \;\; or \;\; R) \end{bmatrix},$$

which reduces (by *and-false, if-false, true-and, true-or,* and *then-true* simplifications) to

	G2. *true*

In fact, as will be shown later, any valid propositional-logic sentence can always be proved by applying only *GG-resolution* and *true-false* simplifications. Proofs often become more readable, however, if we do use the splitting rules, the rewriting rule, the other simplifications, and the other forms of the *resolution* rule.

6.7   POLARITY STRATEGY

Between two rows of a tableau, there may be many ways to apply the *resolution* rule. Not all these ways, however, are equally useful. In this section, we introduce a method for avoiding certain unproductive applications of the *resolution* rule.

Example

Suppose our tableau contains the following assertion and goal:

assertions	goals
if P *then* $\boxed{Q}$	
	P *and* $\boxed{Q}$

Then there are four different ways to apply the *resolution* rule.

AG-resolution, matching Q

We can apply *AG-resolution*, matching the subsentence Q, obtaining the new goal

$$not \ (if \ \ P \ \ then \ \ false)$$
$$and$$
$$P \ \ and \ \ true,$$

which reduces (by *then-false*, *not-not*, *and-true*, and *and-two* simplifications) to the goal

	P

AG-resolution, matching P

From the same assertion and goal, however

assertions	goals
if $\boxed{P}$ *then* Q	
	$\boxed{P}$ *and* Q

we can apply *AG-resolution*, matching P instead of Q, to obtain the new goal

$$not \ (if \ \ false \ \ then \ \ Q)$$
$$and$$
$$true \ \ and \ \ Q,$$

which reduces (by *if-false*, *not-true*, and *false-and* simplifications) to the trivial goal

	false

GA-resolution, matching P

  If we consider the goal and the assertion

assertions	goals
	$\boxed{P}$ *and* Q
if $\boxed{P}$ *then* Q	

we can apply *GA-resolution*, matching P, to obtain the new goal

> *false and* Q
>   *and*
> *not* (*if true then* Q),

which reduces (by *false-and* simplification) to the trivial goal

	false

GA-resolution, matching Q

  If we consider again the goal and the assertion

assertions	goals
	P *and* $\boxed{Q}$
if P *then* $\boxed{Q}$	

we can apply *GA-resolution*, matching Q this time, to obtain the new goal

> P *and false*
>   *and*
> *not* (*if* P *then true*),

which reduces (by *and-false* and *false-and* simplifications) to the trivial goal

	false

  Thus, in the preceding example, there are four possible ways to apply the *resolution* rule to the given assertion and goal, only one of which (*AG-resolution,* matching Q) produces a nontrivial resolvent. In this section, we employ the notion of polarity to detect many fruitless applications of resolution before actually applying the rule. The three trivial applications of the rule in the example will be detected in advance.

POLARITY IN A TABLEAU

We have already defined (in Section 5.1) the notion of the polarity of a subsentence of a given sentence. We now extend that notion to tableaux.

Definition (polarity in a tableau)

If $\mathcal{T}$ is a tableau, we assign a *polarity*, positive $(+)$, negative $(-)$, or both $(\pm)$, to every occurrence of a subsentence of the assertions and goals of $\mathcal{T}$, according to the following *polarity-assignment rules*:

- Each goal has positive polarity in $\mathcal{T}$.

- Each assertion has negative polarity in $\mathcal{T}$.

- The polarity of a proper subsentence of an assertion or goal in $\mathcal{T}$ is determined by the *polarity-assignment* rules for a proper subsentence of a sentence.

An occurrence of a subsentence of a tableau is said to have *strict polarity* in the tableau if it does not have both polarities. ⌐

The polarity of a subsentence in a tableau is the same as the polarity of the corresponding subsentence in the associated sentence. Indeed, assertions $\mathcal{A}_i$ have negative polarity and goals $\mathcal{G}_j$ have positive polarity in the sentence

$$\textit{if } \left(\boxed{\mathcal{A}_1}^- \textit{ and } \boxed{\mathcal{A}_2}^- \textit{ and } \ldots \textit{ and } \boxed{\mathcal{A}_m}^- \right)$$
$$\textit{then } \left(\boxed{\mathcal{G}_1}^+ \textit{ or } \boxed{\mathcal{G}_2}^+ \textit{ or } \ldots \textit{ or } \boxed{\mathcal{G}_n}^+ \right).$$

Example

The subsentences of the goals and assertions of the following tableaux are annotated according to their polarities.

Annotated goals

assertions	goals
	$\left[\textit{if } P^- \ \textit{ then } \ Q^+ \right]^+$
	$\left[\textit{not } P^- \right]^+$
	$\left[\begin{array}{l} \left[\textit{not } [P^- \ \textit{ or } \ [\textit{not } Q^+]^-]^- \right]^+ \\ \textit{and} \\ P^+ \end{array} \right]^+$

Annotated assertions

$\left[\textit{not } P^+ \right]^-$	
$\left[\begin{array}{l} [P^- \ \textit{ or } \ Q^-]^- \\ \textit{and} \\ [\textit{not } [P^+ \ \textit{ or } \ Q^+]^+]^- \end{array} \right]^-$	
$\left[\begin{array}{l} \textit{if } [\textit{not } P^-]^+ \\ \textit{then } \ Q^- \end{array} \right]^-$	

Here, for instance, the last assertion is negative in the tableau because all assertions are negative in a tableau; therefore (by a *polarity-assignment* rule), the antecedent $[\textit{not } P]$ is positive and the consequent Q is negative in the tableau; therefore P is negative in the tableau.

Occurrences of both polarities

	$\left[\textit{not } [P^\pm \equiv [\textit{not } Q^\pm]^\pm]^- \right]^+$
$\left[\begin{array}{l} \textit{if } [\textit{not } P^\pm]^\pm \\ \textit{then } \ Q^- \\ \textit{else } [\textit{not } R^+]^- \end{array} \right]^-$	

Remark (polarity and duality)

Note that if a sentence is pushed (by the *duality* property) from one column to the other and negated, its polarity does not change. For example, a tableau with the goal

is by duality equivalent to the tableau containing instead the assertion

The polarity of the occurrence of P in the goal is positive in the tableau; the polarity of the occurrence of P in the assertion is also positive in the tableau because it is within the scope of both an implicit and an explicit negation. ⌟

The polarity of an occurrence of a subsentence of an assertion or goal in a tableau, as in a sentence, indicates whether the occurrence has a positive or a negative impact on the truth of the tableau; that is, the truth of a tableau is directly related to the truth of its strictly positive subsentences, but inversely related to the truth of its strictly negative subsentences. For instance, replacing a strictly negative subsentence of the tableau with a "truer" sentence (i.e., one that it implies) can only make the entire tableau "falser."

POLARITY STRATEGY

Now let us use the notion of polarity to restrict the application of the *resolution* rule; this restriction will avoid many fruitless applications of the rule.

Strategy (polarity)

Suppose that $\mathcal{F}_1[P]$ and $\mathcal{F}_2[P]$ are two assertions or goals in a tableau with a matching subsentence P.

Assume that the *resolution* rule has been applied to $\mathcal{F}_1[P]$ and $\mathcal{F}_2[P]$, replacing every occurrence of P in $\mathcal{F}_1[P]$ with *false* and replacing every occurrence of P in $\mathcal{F}_2[P]$ with *true*.

Then we will say that the rule has been applied in accordance with the
polarity strategy if

at least one occurrence of P in $\mathcal{F}_1[P]$ is negative in the tableau

and

at least one occurrence of P in $\mathcal{F}_2[P]$ is positive in the tableau. ⌐

In other words, according to the *polarity* strategy, we may apply the *resolution*
rule to a tableau only if at least one of the occurrences of the subsentence that are
replaced by *false* is negative, and at least one of the occurrences that are replaced
by *true* is positive, in the tableau. These polarities need not be strict.

Let us see how the *polarity* strategy applies to the example we considered at
the beginning of this section.

Example

Assume a tableau has the assertion and the goal

assertions	goals
$\left[\textit{if } P^+ \textit{ then } \boxed{Q}^{-}\right]^{-}$	
	$\left[P^+ \textit{ and } \boxed{Q}^{+}\right]^{+}$

We have annotated each subsentence of this assertion and goal with its polarity in the tableau. Note that the only subsentence that has both a positive
occurrence and a negative occurrence is Q. Therefore, if resolution is to be applied to these rows according to the *polarity* strategy, the matching subsentence
must be Q.

Thus the only application of resolution to these rows that obeys the *polarity*
strategy is *AG-resolution*, replacing the occurrence of Q in the assertion, which
is negative in the tableau, with *false*, and the occurrence of Q in the goal, which
is positive in the tableau, with *true*.

This application yields the new goal

not (if P then false)
    and
P and true,

which reduce (by *then-false, not-not, and-true,* and *and-two* simplifications) to the nontrivial goal

	P

Each of the three other applications of the rule, which yield trivial goals, is forbidden by the *polarity* strategy. ⌟

Remark (rationale for the polarity strategy)

Any valid sentence can be proved using only applications of the *resolution* rule that are in accordance with the *polarity* strategy. As it turns out, if we apply the rule in violation of the strategy, we always derive a row we can do without. For instance, if the derived row is an assertion (obtained by *AA-resolution*), it will always be implied by one of the two given assertions. We could use that given assertion in place of the derived one in any proof. ⌟

COMPLETE EXAMPLE

Let us give another complete example: the proof of the validity of the sentence

$$S: \quad if \; \begin{bmatrix} if \;\; P \;\; then \;\; R \\ and \\ if \;\; Q \;\; then \;\; R \end{bmatrix} \quad then \quad \begin{bmatrix} if \;\; (P \;\; or \;\; Q) \\ then \;\; R \end{bmatrix}.$$

We begin with the tableau

assertions	goals
	G1. $if \; \begin{bmatrix} if \;\; P \;\; then \;\; R \\ and \\ if \;\; Q \;\; then \;\; R \end{bmatrix} \quad then \quad \begin{bmatrix} if \;\; (P \;\; or \;\; Q) \\ then \;\; R \end{bmatrix}$

We first apply the splitting rules in succession.

Applying the *if-split* rule yields

A2.   *if P then R*
        and
     if Q then R	

	G3. *if (P or Q)* *then R*

We now present two alternative ways to complete the proof.

Proof 1

Applying the *and-split* rule to assertion A2 yields

A4. *if P then* $\boxed{R}^{-}$	
A5. *if Q then* $\boxed{R}^{-}$	

Applying the *if-split* rule to goal G3 produces

A6. $\boxed{P}^{-}$ *or Q*	
	G7. $\boxed{R}^{+}$

Applying the *AG-resolution* rule twice, to assertion A4 and goal G7, and to assertion A5 and goal G7, matching R, yields the goals

$$
\begin{array}{ccc}
\textit{not (if P then false)} & & \textit{not (if Q then false)} \\
\textit{and} & \textit{and} & \textit{and} \\
\textit{true} & & \textit{true,}
\end{array}
$$

which reduce (by the *then-false*, *not-not*, and *and-true* simplifications) to

	G8. $\boxed{P}^{+}$
	G9. $\boxed{Q}^{+}$

respectively.

Applying *AG-resolution* to assertion A6 and goal G8, matching P, yields the goal

$$
\begin{array}{l}
\textit{not (false or Q)} \\
\quad \textit{and} \\
\textit{true,}
\end{array}
$$

which reduces (by the *false-or* and *and-true* simplifications) to

	G10. *not* $\boxed{Q}^{-}$

Finally, we can apply *GG-resolution* to goals G9 and G10, matching Q, to yield the goal

> *not false*
> *and*
> *true,*

which reduces (by *not-false* and *true-and* simplifications) to the final goal

	G11. *true*

Thus the given sentence S is valid.

Note that each application of the *resolution* rule has been in accordance with the *polarity* strategy.

Proof 2

Let us again apply splitting rules to assertion A2 and goal G3, obtaining

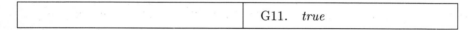

A4. *if* $\boxed{P}^{+}$ *then* R	
A5. *if* $\boxed{Q}^{+}$ *then* R	
A6. $\boxed{P}^{-}$ *or* Q	
	G7. $\boxed{R}^{+}$

The rows are the same as before, but the polarity annotations reflect the application of the *resolution* rule in Proof 2.

Applying *AA-resolution* to assertions A6 and A4, matching P, we obtain the assertion

> *false or Q*
> *or*
> *if true then R,*

which reduces (by the *false-or* and *if-true* simplifications) to

A8′. Q *or* $\boxed{R}^{\,-}$	

Applying *AG-resolution* to assertion A8′ and goal G7, matching R, yields the goal

     not (Q *or*   *false*)
         and
     true,

which reduces (by *or-false* and *and-true* simplifications) to

	G9′. *not* $\boxed{Q}^{\,-}$

Applying *GA-resolution* to goal G9′ and assertion A5, matching Q, we obtain

     not false
         and
     not (*if*   *true*   *then* R),

which reduces (by *not-false*, *true-and*, and *if-true* simplifications) to

	G10′. *not* $\boxed{R}^{\,-}$

By *GG-resolution*, applied to goal G10′ and goal G7, matching R, we obtain the goal

     not false
         and
     true,

which reduces (by *not-false* and *true-and* simplifications) to the final goal

	G11′. *true*

          ⌐

We have thus proved in two different ways the validity of the sentence

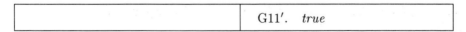

$$\textit{if} \begin{bmatrix} \textit{if} \ \ P \ \ \textit{then} \ \ R \\ \textit{and} \\ \textit{if} \ \ Q \ \ \textit{then} \ \ R \end{bmatrix} \ \textit{then} \ \begin{bmatrix} \textit{if} \ (P \ \ \textit{or} \ \ Q) \\ \textit{then} \ \ R \end{bmatrix}.$$

We can also prove the converse of this sentence, that is,

$$
if \ \begin{bmatrix} if \ (P \ or \ Q) \\ then \ R \end{bmatrix} \ then \ \begin{bmatrix} if \ P \ then \ R \\ and \\ if \ Q \ then \ R \end{bmatrix}.
$$

The proof is requested as an exercise (**Problem 6.5(a)**).

Remark (implicit simplification)

In deriving a new row we always simplify the result before adding it to the tableau. Up to now, we have been scrupulous in mentioning that simplification has occurred, and we have specified exactly which simplifications have occurred. Henceforth we shall usually apply simplification automatically as part of each deduction rule, not mentioning exactly which simplifications have been used. ⌐

In **Problem 6.5(b)–(f)** the reader is requested to prove the validity of several sentences.

USE OF VALID SENTENCES

Once we have proved the validity of a sentence, we may add it as an initial assertion in proofs of subsequent theorems. Let us illustrate this.

Example

Suppose we would like to show the validity of the equivalence

$$
\begin{bmatrix} if \ P \ then \ R \\ and \\ if \ Q \ then \ R \end{bmatrix} \ \equiv \ \begin{bmatrix} if \ (P \ or \ Q) \\ then \ R \end{bmatrix}.
$$

We begin with the initial tableau

assertions	goals
	G1. $\begin{bmatrix} if \ P \ then \ R \\ and \\ if \ Q \ then \ R \end{bmatrix} \ \equiv \ \begin{bmatrix} if \ (P \ or \ Q) \\ then \ R \end{bmatrix}$

Because we proved the validity of the sentence

$$
if \quad \begin{bmatrix} if \;\; P \;\; then \;\; R \\ and \\ if \;\; Q \;\; then \;\; R \end{bmatrix} \quad then \quad \begin{bmatrix} if \;\; (P \;\; or \;\; Q) \\ then \;\; R \end{bmatrix}
$$

in an earlier example, and requested as an exercise to prove its converse,

$$
if \quad \begin{bmatrix} if \;\; (P \;\; or \;\; Q) \\ then \;\; R \end{bmatrix} \quad then \quad \begin{bmatrix} if \;\; P \;\; then \;\; R \\ and \\ if \;\; Q \;\; then \;\; R \end{bmatrix},
$$

we may add these sentences as new assertions in our initial tableau:

A2.	$if \quad \begin{bmatrix} if \;\; P \;\; then \;\; R \\ and \\ if \;\; Q \;\; then \;\; R \end{bmatrix} \quad then \quad \begin{bmatrix} if \;\; (P \;\; or \;\; Q) \\ then \;\; R \end{bmatrix}$ $^{-}$	
A3.	$if \quad \begin{bmatrix} if \;\; (P \;\; or \;\; Q) \\ then \;\; R \end{bmatrix} \quad then \quad \begin{bmatrix} if \;\; P \;\; then \;\; R \\ and \\ if \;\; Q \;\; then \;\; R \end{bmatrix}$ $^{-}$	

By the *iff-and* elimination rewriting (left-to-right)

$$
\mathcal{F} \equiv \mathcal{G} \quad \Leftrightarrow \quad \begin{bmatrix} if \;\; \mathcal{F} \;\; then \;\; \mathcal{G} \\ and \\ if \;\; \mathcal{G} \;\; then \;\; \mathcal{F} \end{bmatrix},
$$

we decompose the equivalence in goal G1 into a conjunction of implications, that is,

	G4.	$if \quad \begin{bmatrix} if \;\; P \;\; then \;\; R \\ and \\ if \;\; Q \;\; then \;\; R \end{bmatrix} \quad then \quad \begin{bmatrix} if \;\; (P \;\; or \;\; Q) \\ then \;\; R \end{bmatrix}$ $^{+}$ *and* $\begin{bmatrix} if \;\; \begin{bmatrix} if \;\; (P \;\; or \;\; Q) \\ then \;\; R \end{bmatrix} \quad then \quad \begin{bmatrix} if \;\; P \;\; then \;\; R \\ and \\ if \;\; Q \;\; then \;\; R \end{bmatrix} \end{bmatrix}$	

The two conjuncts of goal G4 are identical to the assertions A2 and A3. We may drop the first conjunct of goal G4 by *AG-resolution* applied to assertion A2 and goal G4, leaving the second conjunct:

By *AG-resolution* applied to assertion A3 and goal G5, we obtain the final goal,

	G6. *true*

We could have proved the equivalence of the preceding example even if we had not previously proved the two implications, but the proof would have been more cumbersome.

In general, if we are given an equivalence of form

$$\mathcal{F} \equiv \mathcal{G}$$

to prove, we may find it convenient first to prove separately the corresponding two implications

$$if\ \mathcal{F}\ then\ \mathcal{G} \qquad and \qquad if\ \mathcal{G}\ then\ \mathcal{F},$$

and then to add these implications as assertions in the proof of the equivalence.

In **Problem 6.5(g)** the reader is requested to prove the validity of such an equivalence.

PROOFS MAY RUN ON FOREVER

As we have mentioned, many different sequences of deduction rules can be applied to a given sentence. Even if the tableau is valid and the *polarity* strategy is observed, not all of these possible paths will lead to a proof. Special care must be taken with the *rewriting* rule, as illustrated in the following example.

Example

Consider the valid sentence

$$S:\quad \begin{array}{l} (not\ P)\ \ or\ \ (not\ Q) \\ \quad or \\ P\ \ and\ \ Q. \end{array}$$

First, let us give a successful proof of this sentence.

Successful proof

We begin with the tableau

assertions	goals
	G1. (*not P*) *or* (*not Q*) *or* *P* *and* *Q*

Applying the *or-split* rule (twice), we decompose goal G1 into

	G2. *not* $\boxed{P}^{-}$
	G3. *not* $\boxed{Q}^{-}$
	G4. $\boxed{P}^{+}$ *and* *Q*

By *GG-resolution* applied to goals G2 and G4, matching P, we obtain

	G5. $\boxed{Q}^{+}$

Then, by the *GG-resolution* rule applied to goals G3 and G5, we obtain the final goal,

	G6. *true*

This shows that there is a sequence of deduction rules that does lead to a proof.

Failed attempt

Now let us exhibit a sequence of deduction rules that continues endlessly but fails to lead to a proof of S.

We begin with the same initial tableau:

assertions	goals
	G1. $\begin{array}{l}(not\ P)\ \ or\ \ (not\ Q)\\ or\\ P\ \ and\ \ Q\end{array}$

By the *or-and* distributivity rewriting (left-to-right),

$$\mathcal{F}\ \ or\ \ (\mathcal{G}\ \ and\ \ \mathcal{H})\quad\Leftrightarrow\quad(\mathcal{F}\ \ or\ \ \mathcal{G})\ \ and\ \ (\mathcal{F}\ \ or\ \ \mathcal{H}),$$

we obtain the goal

assertions	goals
	G2. $\begin{array}{l}((not\ P)\ \ or\ \ (not\ Q))\ \ or\ \ P\\ and\\ ((not\ P)\ \ or\ \ (not\ Q))\ \ or\ \ Q\end{array}$

By the *and-or* distributivity rewriting (left-to-right),

$$\mathcal{F}\ \ and\ \ (\mathcal{G}\ \ or\ \ \mathcal{H})\quad\Leftrightarrow\quad(\mathcal{F}\ \ and\ \ \mathcal{G})\ \ or\ \ (\mathcal{F}\ \ and\ \ \mathcal{H}),$$

we obtain the goal

assertions	goals
	G3. $\begin{bmatrix}((not\ P)\ \ or\ \ (not\ Q))\ \ or\ \ P\\ and\\ (not\ P)\ \ or\ \ (not\ Q)\end{bmatrix}$ or $\begin{bmatrix}((not\ P)\ \ or\ \ (not\ Q))\ \ or\ \ P\\ and\\ Q\end{bmatrix}$

The form of this goal enables us to apply *or-and* distributivity rewriting again. Afterwards, we will be able to apply the *and-or* distributivity rewriting again, and so on, indefinitely. In other words, even though the original sentence was valid, it is possible to apply the infinite sequence *or-and, and-or, or-and, and-or,* ... distributivity rewritings without ever discovering a proof. ⌟

6.8 EQUIVALENCE RULE

If some of the assertions and goals of our tableau contain the equivalence connective ≡, we can treat it like any other connective. Such deductions can be made shorter, easier to find, and more readable, however, if we use a special *equivalence* rule, which we introduce in this section. The *equivalence* rule enables us to replace subsentences of the tableau with equivalent sentences. This rule does not increase the logical power of the system, in the sense that it does not allow us to prove the validity of any new sentences that cannot be proved by the *resolution* rule alone; it does, however, make the system easier to use.

THE BASIC FORM

The basic form of the *equivalence* rule is expressed as follows.

Rule (AA-equivalence, left-to-right)

assertions	goals
$\mathcal{A}_1[P \equiv Q]$	
$\mathcal{A}_2\langle P\rangle$	
$\mathcal{A}_1[\mathit{false}]$ *or* $\mathcal{A}_2\langle Q\rangle$	

where $\mathcal{A}_1$ contains at least one occurrence of a subsentence $(P \equiv Q)$ and $\mathcal{A}_2$ contains at least one occurrence of the subsentence P. ⌐

In other words, to apply the rule to a tableau, we do the following:

- Choose an assertion $\mathcal{A}_1[P \equiv Q]$ with a subsentence of the form $(P \equiv Q)$, where P and Q are distinct.

- Choose an assertion $\mathcal{A}_2\langle P\rangle$ with a subsentence P.

- Replace every occurrence of $(P \equiv Q)$ in $\mathcal{A}_1[P \equiv Q]$ with the truth symbol *false*, obtaining $\mathcal{A}_1[\mathit{false}]$.

- Replace some (one or more) of the occurrences of P in $\mathcal{A}_2\langle P\rangle$ with Q, obtaining $\mathcal{A}_2\langle Q\rangle$.

- Take the disjunction $\big(\mathcal{A}_1[\mathit{false}] \ or \ \mathcal{A}_2\langle Q\rangle\big)$ and apply to it all possible simplifications.

- Add the simplified disjunction to the tableau as a new assertion.

We will say that we have applied the *AA-equivalence* rule to $A_1[P \equiv Q]$ and $A_2\langle P \rangle$, *replacing* P with Q.

Note that, because the replacement of $(P \equiv Q)$ with *false* simplifies the sentence, the rule is defined to replace every occurrence of $(P \equiv Q)$ in $A_1[P \equiv Q]$ with *false*. On the other hand, because in some proofs we want to replace certain occurrences of P with Q, but leave others intact, the rule is defined to replace some (at least one) but not necessarily all occurrences of P in $A_2\langle P \rangle$ with Q. Also, even though we use the partial-substitution notation, we deliberately exclude the possibility of zero replacements.

The preceding left-to-right version of the *AA-equivalence* rule replaces occurrences of the left-hand side P of the equivalence with the right-hand side Q. By the symmetry of the $\equiv$ connective, i.e., because $(P \equiv Q)$ and $(Q \equiv P)$ are themselves equivalent, we can apply the rule right-to-left to replace occurrences of the right-hand side Q with the left-hand side P instead.

Rule (AA-equivalence, right-to-left)

assertions	goals
$A_1\big[P \equiv Q\big]$	
$A_2\langle Q \rangle$	
$A_1\big[false\big]$ *or* $A_2\langle P \rangle$	

where A_1 contains at least one occurrence of a subsentence $(P \equiv Q)$ and A_2 contains at least one occurrence of the subsentence Q. ⌟

EXAMPLES

Before we justify the rule, let us illustrate it with two examples.

Example

Suppose that our tableau contains the assertions

assertions	goals
$\mathcal{A}_1:\quad \big[\,\boxed{P}\ \equiv\ Q\,\big]\ \text{or}\ R$	
$\mathcal{A}_2:\quad if\ \Big(\,\boxed{P}\ and\ S\,\Big)\ then\ P$	

Here, taking $\mathcal{P}$ to be P and $\mathcal{Q}$ to be Q, $\mathcal{A}_1[\mathcal{P} \equiv \mathcal{Q}]$ contains a subsentence $(P \equiv Q)$, and $\mathcal{A}_2\langle \mathcal{P}\rangle$ contains a subsentence P.

We annotate with brackets the equivalence and with boxes the subsentences that are matched in applying the rule. Replacing every occurrence of $(P \equiv Q)$ in $\mathcal{A}_1[\mathcal{P} \equiv \mathcal{Q}]$ with the truth symbol *false*, we obtain

$$\mathcal{A}_1[\mathit{false}]:\quad \mathit{false}\ \ or\ \ R.$$

Replacing the first occurrence of P in $\mathcal{A}_2\langle \mathcal{P}\rangle$ with Q, we obtain

$$\mathcal{A}_2\langle \mathcal{Q}\rangle:\quad if\ \ (Q\ \ and\ \ S)\ \ then\ \ P.$$

By the *AA-equivalence* rule (left-to-right version), we may add the disjunction

$$\mathcal{A}_1[\mathit{false}]\ \ or\ \ \mathcal{A}_2\langle \mathcal{Q}\rangle:\quad \begin{array}{c} \mathit{false}\ \cdot\ or\ \ R \\ or \\ if\ \ (Q\ \ and\ \ S)\ \ then\ \ P \end{array}$$

as a new assertion, which reduces (by *false-or* simplification) to

$R\ \ or$ $if\ \ (Q\ \ and\ \ S)\ \ then\ \ P$	

In the preceding example, we replaced only the first occurrence of P in $\mathcal{A}_2$ with Q. We could have replaced only the second occurrence of P, however, ultimately obtaining the assertion

$R\ \ or$ $if\ \ (P\ \ and\ \ S)\ \ then\ \ Q$	

Alternatively, we could have replaced both occurrences of P in $\mathcal{A}_2$ with Q, ultimately obtaining the assertion

$R\ \ or$ $if\ \ (Q\ \ and\ \ S)\ \ then\ \ Q$	

Each of the three assertions was obtained by different applications of the *equivalence* rule to the same two assertions A_1 and A_2. ◢

Example

Suppose our tableau contains the assertions

assertions	goals
$A_1:$ if S then $\left[(Q \ or \ R) \ \equiv \ \boxed{not \ P}\right]$	
$A_2:$ $\boxed{not \ P}$ *and* Q	

Then we can apply the right-to-left version of the *AA-equivalence* rule to the assertions replacing $Q:(not \ P)$ in assertion A_2 with $P:(Q \ or \ R)$, to obtain the new assertion

   if S then false
     or
   $(Q \ or \ R) \ and \ Q,$

which reduces (by *then-false* simplification) to

not S *or* $(Q \ or \ R) \ and \ Q$	

Note that in this example we replaced the subsentence $(not \ P)$, not just a single propositional symbol. ◢

Remark (at least one replacement)

Although our substitution notation admits the possibility that the subsentence $P \equiv Q$ not occur in the assertion A_1, the wording of the rule requires that it occur at least once. Otherwise, the assertion we derive would be weaker than A_1. Similarly, we require in words that at least one occurrence of P in A_2 be replaced by Q; otherwise, there would be little point in applying the rule. For the same reason, we insist that P and Q be distinct. ◢

JUSTIFICATION

Now let us justify the *AA-equivalence* rule.

Justification (AA-equivalence)

The justification for the *AA-equivalence* rule is analogous to that for the *AA-resolution* rule. We consider the left-to-right version; the proof of the right-to-left version is similar.

Consider an interpretation I under which the required subtableau $\mathcal{T}_r$ is false, i.e., the required assertions $\mathcal{A}_1[P \equiv Q]$ and $\mathcal{A}_2\langle P \rangle$ are both true under I. By the *justification* proposition, it suffices to establish that the generated subtableau $\mathcal{T}_g$ is false under I, that is, that the assertion generated by the rule, the simplified disjunction

$$\mathcal{A}_1[\textit{false}] \quad or \quad \mathcal{A}_2\langle Q \rangle,$$

is also true under I.

We distinguish between two subcases.

Case: P and Q have different truth-values under I

Then (by the semantic rule for $\equiv$), the equivalence $(P \equiv Q)$ is false under I, that is, $(P \equiv Q)$ and the truth symbol *false* have the same truth-values under I. Thus, because $\mathcal{A}_1[P \equiv Q]$ is true under I, $\mathcal{A}_1[\textit{false}]$ is also true under I. By the semantic rule for the *or* connective, the disjunction

$$\mathcal{A}_1[\textit{false}] \quad or \quad \mathcal{A}_2\langle Q \rangle$$

is true under I. The simplified disjunction is true under I as well.

Case: P and Q have the same truth-values under I

Then, because $\mathcal{A}_2\langle P \rangle$ is true, $\mathcal{A}_2\langle Q \rangle$ is also true under I, and (by the semantic rule for the *or* connective) the disjunction

$$\mathcal{A}_1[\textit{false}] \quad or \quad \mathcal{A}_2\langle Q \rangle$$

is true under I. The simplified disjunction is true under I as well.

Because, in each case, the conclusion of the *AA-equivalence* rule is true under I, the *justification* condition for the rule is established. ◣

DUAL FORMS

The form of the *AA-equivalence* rule we have just introduced applies to two assertions. By the duality between assertions and goals, we can establish the following alternative forms.

Rule (GG-equivalence, left-to-right)

assertions	goals
	$\mathcal{G}_1[P \equiv Q]$
	$\mathcal{G}_2\langle P \rangle$
	$\mathcal{G}_1[false]$ *and* $\mathcal{G}_2\langle Q \rangle$

where $\mathcal{G}_1$ and $\mathcal{G}_2$ satisfy the same requirements as $\mathcal{A}_1$ and $\mathcal{A}_2$, respectively, in the *AA-equivalence* rule. ◢

Rule (AG-equivalence, left-to-right)

assertions	goals
$\mathcal{A}[P \equiv Q]$	
	$\mathcal{G}\langle P \rangle$
	not $(\mathcal{A}[false])$ *and* $\mathcal{G}\langle Q \rangle$

where $\mathcal{A}$ and $\mathcal{G}$ satisfy the same requirements as $\mathcal{A}_1$ and $\mathcal{A}_2$, respectively, in the *AA-equivalence* rule. ◢

Rule (GA-equivalence, left-to-right)

assertions	goals
	$\mathcal{G}[P \equiv Q]$
$\mathcal{A}\langle P \rangle$	
	$\mathcal{G}[false]$ *and* *not* $(\mathcal{A}\langle Q \rangle)$

where $\mathcal{G}$ and $\mathcal{A}$ satisfy the same requirements as $\mathcal{A}_1$ and $\mathcal{A}_2$, respectively, in the *AA-equivalence* rule. ⌐

The right-to-left versions of these rules are analogous. The reader is requested to justify related rules in **Problems 6.6** and **6.7**.

We have remarked that the *equivalence* rule gives no additional power to our propositional-logic system, in the sense that no sentences can be proved with the rule that cannot be proved without it. The rule does, however, make some deductions shorter, easier to find, and more readable.

Example

Suppose we would like to prove the validity of the sentence

$$if \begin{bmatrix} P \equiv Q \\ and \\ (P \ and \ R) \ or \ S \end{bmatrix}$$
$$then \ (Q \ and \ R) \ or \ S.$$

We first give a proof that uses the *equivalence* rule. Later, we prove the same sentence without using the rule.

Proof (*with equivalence rule*):

We begin with the initial tableau

assertions	goals
	G1. $if \begin{bmatrix} P \equiv Q \\ and \\ (P \ and \ R) \ or \ S \end{bmatrix}$ $then \ (Q \ and \ R) \ or \ S$

Applying the *if-split* and *and-split* rules, we decompose goal G1 to obtain the rows

A2. $\begin{bmatrix} P \equiv \boxed{Q} \end{bmatrix}$	
A3. $\overline{\boxed{(P \ and \ R) \ or \ S}}$	

	G4. $\left(\boxed{Q}\ \textit{and}\ R\right)\ \textit{or}\ S$

Applying the *AG-equivalence* rule (right-to-left) with assertion A2, we may replace Q with P in goal G4, to obtain

> *not false*
>   *and*
> $(P\ \textit{and}\ R)\ \textit{or}\ S,$

which reduces (by *not-false* and *true-and* simplifications) to

	G5. $\boxed{(P\ \textit{and}\ R)\ \textit{or}\ S}^{+}$

Then, by *AG-resolution* applied to assertion A3 and goal G5, we obtain the final goal

	G6. *true*

We now prove the same sentence without using the *equivalence* rule.

Proof (without equivalence rule):

We begin with the initial tableau

assertions	goals
	G1. *if* $\begin{bmatrix} P \equiv Q \\ \textit{and} \\ (P\ \textit{and}\ R)\ \textit{or}\ S \end{bmatrix}$ *then* $(Q\ \textit{and}\ R)\ \textit{or}\ S$

Applying the *if-split* and *and-split* rules, we decompose goal G1 to obtain

A2. $P \equiv \boxed{Q}^{\pm}$	
A3. $(P\ \textit{and}\ R)\ \textit{or}\ \boxed{S}^{-}$	
	G4. $(Q\ \textit{and}\ R)\ \textit{or}\ S$

Applying the *or-split* rule, we may decompose goal G4 into

	G5. Q *and* $\boxed{R}^+$
	G6. $\boxed{S}^+$

By *AG-resolution*, applied to assertion A3 and goal G6, matching S, we obtain the goal

	G7. $not\left(P \ and \ \boxed{R}^-\right)$

(Intuitively, G7 is equivalent to an assertion (P *and* R).)

By *GG-resolution*, applied to goals G7 and G5, matching R, we obtain the goal

	G8. $\boxed{Q}^+$

By *AG-resolution*, applied to assertion A2 and goal G8, matching Q, we obtain the goal

	G9. $\boxed{P}^+$

(Note that the preceding application of the *resolution* rule is in accordance with the polarity strategy, because the occurrence of Q in A2 has both polarities, while the occurrence of Q in G8 is positive, in the tableau.)

By *GG-resolution*, applied to our earlier goal G7,

	$not\left(\boxed{P}^- \ and \ R\right)$

and goal G9, we obtain the goal

	G10. *true*

The reader may confirm that the proof without the *equivalence* rule is some-what longer. ◢

POLARITY STRATEGY

We can be guided in applying the *equivalence* rule by a strategy that is analogous
to the *polarity* strategy for the *resolution* rule and allows us to avoid many fruitless
applications of the *equivalence* rule.

Strategy (polarity)

Consider an application of the *equivalence* rule in which every occurrence
of a subsentence $(P \equiv Q)$ in the assertion or goal $\mathcal{F}[P \equiv Q]$ is replaced
by the truth symbol *false*.

Then we will say that the rule has been applied in accordance with the
polarity strategy if

at least one occurrence of $(P \equiv Q)$ in $\mathcal{F}[P \equiv Q]$ is negative in
the tableau. ⌟

Note again that the negative polarity of $(P \equiv Q)$ need not be strict. The polarity
of the occurrences of P in $\mathcal{G}\langle P \rangle$ is not restricted by the strategy at all.

All the examples of the application of the *equivalence* rule in this section
have been in accordance with the *polarity* strategy. For instance, in one of the
examples we applied the rule to the assertions

$\mathcal{A}_1:$ *if S* *then* $\Big[(Q \ or \ R) \ \equiv \ \boxed{not \ P}\Big]^{-}$	
$\mathcal{A}_2:$ $\boxed{not \ P}$ *and Q*	

This application was in accordance with the *polarity* strategy because one occurrence (the only occurrence) of

$$(Q \ or \ R) \ \equiv \ \boxed{not \ P}$$

in assertion $\mathcal{A}_1$ is negative in the tableau.

Now let us see how a violation of the strategy can lead in a fruitless direction.

Example (violating the strategy)

Suppose our tableau contains the assertion and goal

assertions	goals
$not \; \left[\boxed{P} \; \equiv \; Q\right]^{+}$	
	$\boxed{P} \;\; and \;\; S$

Note that the assertion contains no negative occurrences of the equivalence ($P \equiv Q$). If we apply the *AG-equivalence* rule (left-to-right) to replace P with Q in the goal, in violation of the *polarity* strategy, we obtain the new goal

> *not* (*not false*)
>   *and*
> Q *and* S,

which reduces (by simplifications) to the trivial goal

	false

This goal cannot help us in any proof. ◢

   In **Problem 6.8**, the reader is requested to prove the transitivity of equivalence, that is,

$$if \; \begin{bmatrix} P & \equiv & Q \\ & and & \\ Q & \equiv & R \end{bmatrix} \; then \; (P \; \equiv \; R),$$

in two different ways: with and without the *equivalence* rule.

PROBLEMS

Problem 6.1 (tableaux as sets)   page 185

(a) *Union of tableaux*

   Prove the *union-tableau* proposition:

> For any tableaux T_1 and T_2 and interpretation I,
>
> > $T_1 \cup T_2$ is true under I
> >   precisely when
> > T_1 is true under I or T_2 is true under I.

(b) *Intermediate tableau*

Prove the *intermediate-tableau* proposition:

For any tableaux T_1, T_2, and T_3,

if $T_1 \subseteq T_2 \subseteq T_3$,
then if T_1 is equivalent to T_3,
    then T_1 is equivalent to T_2 and T_2 is equivalent to T_3.

Problem 6.2 (extended justification proposition)   page 198

(a) The *justification* proposition allows us to establish the soundness of rules
that add new rows to a tableau without deleting any old rows. Suppose
we want to justify rules that may both add new rows and delete old
ones. Formulate a *justification* condition, analogous to the one given
in the proposition, for this extended class of rules. Show that, if this
condition holds, the rule is sound, i.e., it preserves the equivalence of the
tableau.

(b) Suppose the extended *and-split* rule deletes the assertion $(A_1 \; and \; A_2)$ as
well as adding the two new assertions A_1 and A_2. Use your extended
justification proposition to establish the soundness of this rule.

Problem 6.3 (hyper-resolution rule)   page 207

Justify the following extension of the *resolution* rule:

assertions	goals
$A_1[P]$	
$A_2[Q]$	
$A_3[P, Q]$	
$A_1[true]$ $\;$ or $\;$ $A_2[false]$ $\;$ or $\;$ $A_3[false, true]$	

Here P has at least one occurrence in $A_1[P]$, Q has at least one occurrence in
$A_2[Q]$, and P and Q each have at least one occurrence in $A_3[P, Q]$.

Problem 6.4 (common examples of the resolution rule)   page 211

Apply the *resolution* rule to the following rows:

(a)   *Transitivity of implication*

assertions	goals
if P then Q	
if Q then R	

(b)   *Double backward chaining*

assertions	goals
if P_1 then (if P_2 then Q)	
	Q

Problem 6.5 (tableau proofs of valid sentences)   pages 224, 226

Use the deductive-tableau system to prove the validity of the following sentences:

(a)   if $\begin{bmatrix} if \ (P \ or \ Q) \\ then \ R \end{bmatrix}$ then $\begin{bmatrix} if \ P \ then \ R \\ and \\ if \ Q \ then \ R \end{bmatrix}$

(b)   if (if (not P) then Q)
      then (if (not Q) then P)

(c)   if $\begin{bmatrix} if \ (if \ P \ then \ Q) \\ then \ P \end{bmatrix}$ then P

(d)   if P
      then $(P \ and \ (P \ or \ Q))$

(e)   if $\begin{bmatrix} if \ (not \ P) \ then \ (not \ Q) \\ and \\ if \ (not \ P) \ then \ Q \end{bmatrix}$ then P

(f)   if $\begin{bmatrix} (P \ or \ Q) \ and \\ (if \ P \ then \ R) \ and \\ if \ Q \ then \ R \end{bmatrix}$ then R .

(g)   if P then $(Q \ or \ R)$

      $\equiv$

      if $\big(P \ and \ (not \ Q)\big)$ then R.

Problem 6.6 (equivalence matching rule)   page 235

Consider the following *AA-equivalence matching* rule:

assertions	goals
$A_1[P]$	
$A_2[Q]$	
$\begin{aligned}&\text{if } (P \equiv Q)\\ &\text{then } (A_1[\textit{false}] \text{ or } A_2[\textit{true}])\end{aligned}$	

where A_1 and A_2 contain at least one occurrence of P and Q, respectively.

(a) Justify the rule.

(b) Give the *GG-equivalence matching* rule and its justification.

Problem 6.7 (implication rule)   page 235

Justify the following two special rules for the implication connective *if-then*:

(a) *Left-to-right version*

assertions	goals
$A_1[\textit{if } P \textit{ then } Q]$	
$A_2\langle P^-\rangle$	
$A_1[\textit{false}] \text{ or } A_2\langle Q^-\rangle$	

where A_1 has at least one occurrence of the subsentence (*if P then Q*), and A_2 has at least one occurrence of the subsentence P that is strictly negative in the tableau. Here $A_2\langle Q^-\rangle$ indicates the result of replacing with Q one or more occurrences of P in $A_2\langle P^-\rangle$ that are strictly negative in the tableau.

(b) *Right-to-left version*

assertions	goals
$A_1[if\ P\ then\ Q]$	
$A_2\langle Q^+\rangle$	
$A_1[false]$ or $A_2\langle P^+\rangle$	

where A_1 has at least one occurrence of the subsentence (*if P then Q*), and A_2 has at least one occurrence of the subsentence Q that is strictly positive in the tableau. As before, $A_2\langle P^+\rangle$ indicates the result of replacing with P one or more occurrences of Q in $A_2\langle Q^+\rangle$ that are strictly positive in the tableau.

Problem 6.8 (transitivity of equivalence)   page 239

Use the deductive-tableau system to prove the validity of the sentence

$$
if\ \begin{bmatrix} P\ \equiv\ Q \\ and \\ Q\ \equiv\ R \end{bmatrix}\ then\ (P\ \equiv\ R)
$$

in two different ways:

(a) Using the *equivalence* rule.

(b) Without using the *equivalence* rule.

III

Unification

7

Expressions

In proving the validity of predicate-logic sentences, we shall carry over all of our propositional-logic deductive-tableau methods. Many of the rules, however, will require adaptation. The propositional resolution rule, for instance, applies to two rows, assertions or goals $\mathcal{F}[P]$ and $\mathcal{G}[P]$, with identical subsentences P. The corresponding rule for predicate logic also applies to two rows, but requires subsentences that are not necessarily identical but that instead are "unifiable": they can be made identical by replacing some of their variables with terms. The purpose of the following chapters is to make precise this notion of unification. We introduce a computational method, called the *unification algorithm*, for determining whether given subsentences are unifiable and, if so, for finding a "unifier," a substitution that makes them identical. Both the *resolution* and *equivalence* rules for predicate logic will require this *unification* algorithm; it will also be used in a new *equality* rule for theories with equality.

7.1 PREVIEW OF UNIFICATION

In this section, we give a brief preview of the theory of expressions and substitutions leading up to an informal *unification* algorithm. Many properties will be stated without proof. It is our intention that the first-time reader of the book should be able to read this section, skip the formal unification part (the balance of Chapter 7, and Chapters 8 and 9), and still make sense of the rest of the book. The notions we discuss informally in this section are presented systematically and in more detail in subsequent sections.

EXPRESSIONS

There is a pervasive confusion in any careful discussion of expressions, a confusion more severe than for other sorts of objects. In the theory of families or nonnegative integers, for example, we were careful not to confuse the objects of our intended domain, people or numbers, with the terms we used to denote them (under some interpretation). We must be especially careful in the theory of expressions because here the objects of the intended domain are themselves terms.

In an attempt to avoid this confusion, we use small capitals (such as A, X, F(X,Y)) in examples of object terms, and ordinary lower-case letters (such as a, x, $f(x, y)$) in the predicate-logic terms that denote them. Thus we may speak about unifying the predicate-logic terms d and e, where (under some interpretation) d denotes an object variable X and e denotes an object term F(X).

In the theory of nonnegative integers, for two constants d and e to be equal (under some interpretation) they must denote the same nonnegative integer. If d denotes 0 and e denotes 1, they cannot be equal. In the same way, in the theory of expressions, for d and e to be equal, they must denote the same object term, say F(X). If d denotes A and e denotes B, they cannot be equal. When we say that d equals e, we are not claiming that the symbols d and e are identical; they are of course distinct.

In our theory of expressions, the objects of the intended domains are terms (called "expressions"), not sentences. We also exclude the conditional-term construct. Later, we see that the same methods also apply to sentences and to terms with conditional-term constructors.

There are two additional differences between the terms of our intended domain and the terms of predicate logic. Because constants and function symbols are treated similarly, we shall introduce into the domain 0-ary function symbols (with no arguments) instead of constants. Informally, we shall still use letters near the beginning of the alphabet (such as A, B, C) as constants, but when we write A we shall really mean A( ).

Also, rather than associating a fixed arity with each function symbol in the domain, we shall allow the number of arguments to vary. Thus F(A), F(A, X), and F( ) can all occur in the same expression.

We shall write $d \Subset e$ to mean d occurs in e; thus X $\Subset$ F(X) because X occurs in F(X). If d occurs properly in e (that is, if d occurs in e and d and e are distinct), then we shall write $d \in e$; thus we also have X$\in$ F(X).

SUBSTITUTIONS

We introduce the notion of a *substitution*, a (finite) set

$$\{x_1 \leftarrow e_1, \; x_2 \leftarrow e_2, \; \ldots, \; x_n \leftarrow e_n\}$$

of *replacement pairs* $x_i \leftarrow e_i$, where the x_i are variables, the e_i are expressions, and each x_i is distinct from the corresponding expression e_i and from all the other variables x_j. The *domain* of the substitution is the set $\{x_1, x_2, \ldots, x_n\}$ of variables. For example,

$$\{\text{x} \leftarrow \text{F(y)}, \; \text{y} \leftarrow \text{A}\}$$

is a substitution (with domain $\{\text{x}, \text{y}\}$), but $\{\text{A} \leftarrow \text{x}\}$, $\{\text{x} \leftarrow \text{x}\}$, and $\{\text{x} \leftarrow \text{A}, \text{x} \leftarrow \text{B}\}$ are not.

The order of the replacement pairs in a substitution is not significant; two substitutions are regarded as the same if they have the same replacement pairs, regardless of the order in which they are written. The *empty substitution* { } has no replacement pairs at all.

For any expression e and substitution $\theta : \{x_1 \leftarrow e_1, x_2 \leftarrow e_2, \ldots, x_n \leftarrow e_n\}$, the result $e \blacktriangleleft \theta$ of *applying* θ to e is obtained by simultaneously replacing every occurrence of a variable x_i in e with the corresponding expression e_i. For example,

$$\text{G(x, y)} \blacktriangleleft \{\text{x} \leftarrow \text{F(y)}, \; \text{y} \leftarrow \text{A}\} \; = \; \text{G}\big(\text{F(y)}, \text{A}\big).$$

Note that we do not replace the newly introduced occurrence of y with A, even though the substitution contains a replacement pair y $\leftarrow$ A. That is, substitutions are applied in a single stage.

Applying the empty substitution { } to any expression e has no effect; that is,

$$e \blacktriangleleft \{\,\} \; = \; e.$$

This notion of a substitution application $\blacktriangleleft$ is similar to the total substitution operator $\blacktriangleleft$ of predicate logic, except that here we allow replacements only for variables, not constants or other expressions, and we allow replacement only by terms, not sentences. We do not introduce an analog to the partial substitution operator $\triangleleft$ of predicate logic.

Substitution application has an important *monotonicity* property, namely,

$$\text{if} \;\; d \Subset e$$
$$\text{then} \;\; d \blacktriangleleft \theta \Subset e \blacktriangleleft \theta.$$

In other words, if one expression occurs properly in another before application of a substitution, it also does so afterwards.

COMPOSITION

Applying the *composition* $\theta \square \lambda$ of two substitutions θ and λ has the same effect as applying first θ and then λ; that is,

$$e \blacktriangleleft (\theta \square \lambda) \;=\; (e \blacktriangleleft \theta) \blacktriangleleft \lambda.$$

We can compute the composition of two given substitutions by considering their combined effect on all the variables in their domains. For example,

$$\{X \leftarrow F(Z),\, Y \leftarrow Z\} \square \{X \leftarrow A,\, Z \leftarrow Y\} \;=\; \{X \leftarrow F(Y),\, Z \leftarrow Y\}.$$

Since the first substitution replaces X with $F(Z)$ and the second replaces Z with Y, their composition replaces X with $F(Y)$. Since the first substitution replaces Y with Z and the second replaces Z with Y again, their composition makes no replacement for Y. Since the first substitution makes no replacement for Z and the second replaces Z with Y, their composition replaces Z with Y too.

The empty substitution $\{\,\}$ is both a left- and right-identity under composition, that is,

$$\{\,\} \square \theta \;=\; \theta \square \{\,\} \;=\; \theta,$$

and composition is associative, that is,

$$\theta \square (\phi \square \psi) \;=\; (\theta \square \phi) \square \psi.$$

Composition is not commutative. For example,

$$\{X \leftarrow Y\} \square \{Y \leftarrow X\} \;=\; \{Y \leftarrow X\},$$

but

$$\{Y \leftarrow X\} \square \{X \leftarrow Y\} \;=\; \{X \leftarrow Y\}.$$

A *permutation* substitution is one that rearranges the variables in its domain. For example, the substitution

$$\pi_0 : \;\; \{X \leftarrow Y,\, Y \leftarrow Z,\, Z \leftarrow X\}$$

is a permutation because it replaces its domain elements X, Y, and Z with Y, Z, and X, respectively. On the other hand, $\{X \leftarrow Y\}$ is not a permutation, because it replaces its domain element X with a new variable Y.

Formally, we define a permutation to be a substitution π that has an inverse under composition, that is, a substitution π^{-1} such that

$$\pi \square \pi^{-1} \;=\; \{\,\}.$$

If π is a permutation, so is its inverse, and

$$\pi^{-1} \square \pi = \{\,\}.$$

For example, if π_0 is the preceding permutation, we have

$$\pi_0^{-1} = \{X \leftarrow Z, \; Y \leftarrow X, \; Z \leftarrow Y\}$$

because

$$\pi_0 \square \pi_0^{-1} = \{X \leftarrow Y, \; Y \leftarrow Z, \; Z \leftarrow X\} \square \{X \leftarrow Z, \; Y \leftarrow X, \; Z \leftarrow Y\}$$

$$= \{\,\}.$$

Also,

$$\pi_0^{-1} \square \pi_0 = \{X \leftarrow Z, \; Y \leftarrow X, \; Z \leftarrow Y\} \square \{X \leftarrow Y, \; Y \leftarrow Z, \; Z \leftarrow X\}$$

$$= \{\,\}.$$

In fact, permutation substitutions can be regarded as a group, with the composition function and the empty substitution playing the roles of the group operation and the identity element, respectively (see Section [I]5.4). In other words, permutation substitutions constitute a model for the theory of groups.

GENERALITY

A substitution θ is said to be *more general* than another substitution ϕ, written $\theta \succeq_{gen} \phi$, if ϕ can be obtained from θ by composition with some other substitution λ, that is, if

$$\theta \square \lambda = \phi.$$

Roughly, more general substitutions make fewer changes to an expression. For example,

$$\{X \leftarrow Y\} \succeq_{gen} \{X \leftarrow A, \; Y \leftarrow A\}$$

because

$$\{X \leftarrow Y\} \square \{Y \leftarrow A\} = \{X \leftarrow A, \; Y \leftarrow A\}.$$

Any substitution θ is more general than itself, that is,

$$\theta \succeq_{gen} \theta,$$

because $\theta \,\square\, \{\,\} = \theta$. (It would therefore be more accurate to use the phrase "at least as general as" for $\succeq_{gen}$.) Also, the empty substitution is more general than any substitution θ, that is,

$$\{\,\} \succeq_{gen} \theta,$$

because $\{\,\} \,\square\, \theta = \theta$. The generality relation $\succeq_{gen}$ is transitive but clearly not symmetric.

It is possible for two distinct substitutions each to be more general than the other. For example,

$$\{x \leftarrow y\} \succeq_{gen} \{y \leftarrow x\} \qquad \text{and} \qquad \{y \leftarrow x\} \succeq_{gen} \{x \leftarrow y\}$$

because

$$\{x \leftarrow y\} \,\square\, \{y \leftarrow x\} \;=\; \{y \leftarrow x\} \qquad \text{and} \qquad \{y \leftarrow x\} \,\square\, \{x \leftarrow y\} \;=\; \{x \leftarrow y\}.$$

That is, the generality relation is not antisymmetric.

If two substitutions θ and ϕ are more general than each other, we shall say that they are *equally general*, written $\theta \approx_{gen} \phi$. Thus, because $\{x \leftarrow y\}$ and $\{y \leftarrow x\}$ are each more general than the other, we have that

$$\{x \leftarrow y\} \approx_{gen} \{y \leftarrow x\}.$$

The equal-generality relation is an equivalence relation; that is, it is transitive, symmetric, and reflexive.

If $\theta \approx_{gen} \phi$, the two substitutions are related by composition with a permutation; in other words, there is a permutation π such that

$$\theta \,\square\, \pi \;=\; \phi \qquad \text{and (hence)} \qquad \phi \,\square\, \pi^{-1} = \theta.$$

For example,

$$\{x \leftarrow y\} \approx_{gen} \{y \leftarrow x\},$$

and hence we would expect them to be related by composition with a permutation. In fact, $\{x \leftarrow y, y \leftarrow x\}$ is a permutation that is its own inverse, and

$$\{x \leftarrow y\} \,\square\, \{x \leftarrow y, y \leftarrow x\} \;=\; \{y \leftarrow x\}$$

and

$$\{y \leftarrow x\} \,\square\, \{x \leftarrow y, y \leftarrow x\} \;=\; \{x \leftarrow y\}.$$

UNIFIERS

The expressions d and e are said to be *unifiable* if they can be made identical by application of some substitution θ. We shall say that θ is a *unifier* of d and e. For example, the expressions

$$F(X, B) \quad \text{and} \quad F(A, Y)$$

are unifiable, and

$$\{X \leftarrow A, Y \leftarrow B\}$$

is a unifier. On the other hand, the expressions

$$F(X, X) \quad \text{and} \quad F(A, B)$$

are not unifiable.

If d is a proper subexpression of e, then d and e are not unifiable; for example,

$$X \quad \text{and} \quad F(X)$$

are not unifiable. This is so because, if d is a proper subexpression of e, then by monotonicity, for any substitution θ, $d \blacktriangleleft \theta$ is a proper subexpression of $e \blacktriangleleft \theta$; therefore $d \blacktriangleleft \theta$ and $e \blacktriangleleft \theta$ cannot be equal.

Unifiers are not unique; for example,

$$\{X \leftarrow A\}, \qquad \{X \leftarrow A, Y \leftarrow A\}, \quad \text{and} \quad \{X \leftarrow A, Y \leftarrow B, Z \leftarrow C\}$$

are all unifiers of the expressions

$$F(X, Y) \quad \text{and} \quad F(A, Y).$$

If d and e are equal, then any substitution θ is a unifier of d and e.

MOST-GENERAL UNIFIERS

A unifier is said to be *most-general* if it is more general than any other unifier. For example, $\{X \leftarrow A\}$ is a most-general unifier of $F(X,Y)$ and $F(A,Y)$. The unifier $\{X \leftarrow A, Y \leftarrow A\}$ is not most-general. In fact,

$$\{X \leftarrow A\} \succeq_{gen} \{X \leftarrow A, Y \leftarrow A\}$$

because

$$\{X \leftarrow A\} \,\square\, \{Y \leftarrow A\} \;=\; \{X \leftarrow A, Y \leftarrow A\},$$

but there is no substitution λ such that

$$\{X \leftarrow A, Y \leftarrow A\} \square \lambda \;=\; \{X \leftarrow A\}.$$

Roughly, a most-general unifier makes the two expressions identical without doing any unnecessary work.

If d and e are equal, then the empty substitution $\{\ \}$ is a most-general unifier of d and e. If the variable x does not occur in the expression e, then $\{x \leftarrow e\}$ is a most-general unifier of x and e.

Most-general unifiers are not unique. For example,

$$\{X \leftarrow Y\} \quad \text{and} \quad \{Y \leftarrow X\}$$

are both most-general unifiers of X and Y. If two substitutions θ and ϕ are both most-general unifiers of the same two expressions, then each must be more general than the other. In other words, they must be equally general, that is, $\theta \approx_{gen} \phi$, and either may be obtained from the other by composition with a substitution. Thus the two most-general unifiers $\{X \leftarrow Y\}$ and $\{Y \leftarrow X\}$ for X and Y are equally general.

On the other hand, if θ is a most-general unifier for two expressions, and ϕ and θ are equally general, that is, $\theta \approx_{gen} \phi$, then ϕ is also a most-general unifier of the two expressions. In short, if θ is a single most-general unifier, the set of all most-general unifiers is precisely the set of substitutions equally general to θ, which are the substitutions $\theta \square \pi$, where π is a permutation substitution.

For example, we know that $\{X \leftarrow F(Y)\}$ is a most-general unifier of X and $F(Y)$, and that $\{X \leftarrow Y, Y \leftarrow X\}$ is a permutation substitution. Since

$$\{X \leftarrow F(Y)\} \square \{X \leftarrow Y, Y \leftarrow X\} \;=\; \{X \leftarrow F(X), Y \leftarrow X\},$$

it follows that $\{X \leftarrow F(X), Y \leftarrow X\}$ is also a most-general unifier of X and $F(Y)$.

Perhaps surprisingly,

$$\phi: \ \{X \leftarrow Z, Y \leftarrow Z\}$$

is not a most-general unifier of X and Y. In particular, ϕ is not more general than the unifier $\{X \leftarrow Y\}$. Intuitively, ϕ has done some unnecessary work by making X and Y identical to Z.

In adapting our propositional-logic deductive-tableau rules to predicate logic, we shall always want to find a most-general unifier. Finding a less general unifier will cause our rules to derive a conclusion less general than possible. This may cause the procedure to fail to find a proof of a valid predicate-logic sentence.

UNIFICATION

The aim of this part of the book is to produce an informal *unification algorithm*, a systematic method for testing whether two expressions are unifiable and, if so, producing a most-general unifier. If the two expressions are not unifiable, the algorithm is to indicate failure. The method may be described roughly as follows:

- Given two expressions d and e, attempt to find a *difference pair* σ, a singleton substitution $\{x \leftarrow s\}$ where the variable x and the term s occupy corresponding positions in d and e (or vice versa), and where x does not occur in s.

For example, a difference pair for F(X,B) and F(A,Y) could be either $\{\text{X} \leftarrow \text{A}\}$ or $\{\text{Y} \leftarrow \text{B}\}$. Our algorithm searches from left to right, so it would find $\{\text{X} \leftarrow \text{A}\}$.

- If we discover that the two expressions are actually identical, we yield the most-general unifier $\theta = \{\ \}$.

- If we discover two corresponding subexpressions $f(d_1, \ldots, d_m)$ and $g(e_1, \ldots, e_n)$, where f and g are distinct function symbols, we indicate failure: the given expressions are not unifiable. This includes the case in which f, g, or both are actually constants (0-ary function symbols).

For example, in searching for a difference pair for F(A,C) and F(B,C), we would discover the corresponding subexpressions A and B, that is, A( ) and B( ), whose function symbols A and B are distinct. Therefore we would fail.

- If we discover two corresponding subexpressions x and s, where x occurs properly in s, we also fail.

For example, we would fail in attempting to find a difference pair for G(X) and $\text{G}\big(\text{F}(\text{X})\big)$ because X occurs properly in the corresponding subexpression F(X).

- If we succeed in finding a nonempty difference pair σ, we apply σ to our expressions, and recursively attempt to unify the resulting expressions $d \blacktriangleleft \sigma$ and $e \blacktriangleleft \sigma$. If we fail, then we also fail to unify d and e.

- If, on the other hand, we succeed in unifying $d \blacktriangleleft \sigma$ and $e \blacktriangleleft \sigma$, obtaining a most-general unifier θ, we yield the composition $\sigma \square \theta$ as a most-general unifier for the given expressions d and e.

Example

Suppose we want to unify the following expressions:

$$d_1 : \text{F}(\text{X, B}) \quad \text{and} \quad e_1 : \text{F}(\text{A, Y}).$$

We discover the difference pair $\sigma_1 : \{\text{X} \leftarrow \text{A}\}$. We apply σ_1 to d_1 and to e_1 and attempt (recursively) to unify the resulting expressions $d_1 \blacktriangleleft \sigma_1 = d_2$ and $e_1 \blacktriangleleft \sigma_1 = e_2$.

We now must unify the expressions

$$d_2 : \text{F}(\text{A, B}) \quad \text{and} \quad e_2 : \text{F}(\text{A, Y}).$$

We discover the difference pair $\sigma_2 : \{\text{Y} \leftarrow \text{B}\}$. We apply σ_2 to d_2 and e_2 and attempt to unify the resulting expressions $d_2 \blacktriangleleft \sigma_2 = d_3$ and $e_2 \blacktriangleleft \sigma_2 = e_3$.

We now must unify the expressions

$$d_3 : \text{F}(\text{A, B}) \quad \text{and} \quad e_3 : \text{F}(\text{A, B}).$$

We discover no difference between d_3 and e_3. Therefore we yield as a most-general unifier for d_3 and e_3 the substitution

$$\theta_3 : \{\ \}.$$

We yield as a most-general unifier for d_2 and e_2 the substitution

$$\theta_2 = \sigma_2 \,\square\, \theta_3 : \quad \{\text{Y} \leftarrow \text{B}\} \,\square\, \{\ \} = \{\text{Y} \leftarrow \text{B}\}.$$

We yield as a most-general unifier for d_1 and e_1 the substitution

$$\theta_1 = \sigma_1 \,\square\, \theta_2 : \quad \{\text{X} \leftarrow \text{A}\} \,\square\, \{\text{Y} \leftarrow \text{B}\} = \{\text{X} \leftarrow \text{A, Y} \leftarrow \text{B}\}. \quad \lrcorner$$

Example

Suppose we want to unify the following expressions:

$$d_1 : \text{F}\big(\text{X, G(X)}\big) \quad \text{and} \quad e_1 : \text{F}(\text{Y, Y}).$$

We discover the difference pair $\sigma_1 : \{\text{X} \leftarrow \text{Y}\}$. We apply σ_1 to d_1 and to e_1 and attempt to unify the resulting expressions $d_1 \blacktriangleleft \sigma_1 = d_2$ and $e_1 \blacktriangleleft \sigma_1 = e_2$.

We now must unify the expressions

$$d_2 : \text{F}\big(\text{Y, G(Y)}\big) \quad \text{and} \quad e_2 : \text{F}(\text{Y, Y}).$$

We discover corresponding subexpressions Y and G(Y) where Y ∈ G(Y). Therefore we fail to unify d_2 and e_2.

Because we fail to unify d_2 and e_2, we also fail to unify d_1 and e_1. ⌐

UNIFYING TUPLES

The preceding algorithm applies to two expressions. In formulating the *resolution* rule and other rules for predicate logic, we must often unify more than two expressions. Once we can unify pairs of expressions, however, we can easily extend the algorithm to unify an arbitrary tuple of expressions.

We define a *unifier* for a tuple of expressions $\langle e_1, e_2, \ldots, e_n \rangle$ as a substitution θ that makes all the elements of the tuple identical, that is,

$$e_1 \triangleleft \theta \ = \ e_2 \triangleleft \theta \ = \ \ldots \ = \ e_n \triangleleft \theta.$$

(We regard any substitution as a unifier for the empty tuple or a tuple of one expression.) A *most-general unifier* for a tuple of expressions must be more general than any other unifier. The *tuple-unification algorithm* is stated informally as follows:

- To unify an empty tuple or a singleton tuple, we simply yield the empty substitution { }.

- To unify a tuple t of two or more expressions, we first attempt to unify the first two elements, d and e, of the tuple, using the preceding algorithm.

- If we fail to unify d and e, we also fail to unify the tuple t.

- Otherwise, we obtain a most-general unifier ϕ for d and e. We then apply ϕ to $tail(t)$, the tuple of expressions other than d. We attempt (recursively) to unify the resulting tuple $tail(t) \triangleleft \phi$. If we fail to unify $tail(t) \triangleleft \phi$, we also fail to unify the given tuple t.

- Otherwise, we obtain a most-general unifier θ for $tail(t) \triangleleft \phi$, and we yield the composition $\phi \square \theta$ as a most-general unifier of t.

Example

Suppose we want to unify the tuple

$$t_1 : \ \langle \text{F}(\text{A}, \text{Y}, \text{Z}), \ \text{F}(\text{X}, \text{B}, \text{Z}), \ \text{F}(\text{X}, \text{Y}, \text{C}) \rangle.$$

To unify t_1, we first unify $d_1 : \text{F}(\text{A}, \text{Y}, \text{Z})$ and $e_1 : \text{F}(\text{X}, \text{B}, \text{Z})$. We obtain the most-general unifier $\phi_1 : \{\text{X} \leftarrow \text{A}, \text{Y} \leftarrow \text{B}\}$. We attempt (recursively) to unify $t_2 = tail(t_1) \blacktriangleleft \phi_1 : \langle \text{F}(\text{X}, \text{B}, \text{Z}), \text{F}(\text{X}, \text{Y}, \text{C}) \rangle \blacktriangleleft \phi_1$.

We now must unify the tuple

$$t_2 : \langle \text{F}(\text{A}, \text{B}, \text{Z}), \text{F}(\text{A}, \text{B}, \text{C}) \rangle.$$

To unify t_2, we first unify $d_2 : \text{F}(\text{A}, \text{B}, \text{Z})$ and $e_2 : \text{F}(\text{A}, \text{B}, \text{C})$. We obtain the most-general unifier $\phi_2 : \{\text{Z} \leftarrow \text{C}\}$. We attempt to unify $t_3 = tail(t_2) \blacktriangleleft \phi_2 : \langle \text{F}(\text{A}, \text{B}, \text{C}) \rangle \blacktriangleleft \phi_2$

We now must unify the tuple

$$t_3 : \langle \text{F}(\text{A}, \text{B}, \text{C}) \rangle.$$

Because t_3 is a singleton tuple, we immediately yield the empty substitution

$$\theta_3 : \{\ \}.$$

We yield as a most-general unifier for t_2 the substitution

$$\theta_2 = \phi_2 \square \theta_3 : \{\text{Z} \leftarrow \text{C}\} \square \{\ \} = \{\text{Z} \leftarrow \text{C}\}.$$

We yield as a most-general unifier for t_1 the substitution

$$\theta_1 = \phi_1 \square \theta_2 : \quad \{\text{X} \leftarrow \text{A}, \text{Y} \leftarrow \text{B}\} \square \{\text{Z} \leftarrow \text{C}\}$$

$$= \{\text{X} \leftarrow \text{A}, \text{Y} \leftarrow \text{B}, \text{Z} \leftarrow \text{C}\}. \quad \blacksquare$$

This has been a brisk and informal preview of the theory of unification. In the succeeding sections, we shall make the theory precise and establish the correctness of our results.

7.2   THEORY OF EXPRESSIONS

The formal theory of expressions is similar to the formal theories we have seen earlier, except that the elements of its intended domain are expressions (more precisely, terms) rather than nonnegative integers, tuples, or trees. We shall also include tuples of expressions in our intended domain.

THE INTENDED DOMAIN

The elements of our intended domain include the following categories:

- *Variables*: The symbols U, V, W, X, Y, Z, U$_1$, V$_1$, ...

- *Function symbols*: The symbols F, G, H, F$_1$, G$_1$, ...

- *Applications*: Terms composed of the function symbols and variables, such as G(Y) and F$\big($X, G(Y)$\big)$.

- *Expressions*: The variables and the applications.

- *Tuples of expressions*: Such as $\langle$G(X, Y), F(X)$\rangle$.

As noted earlier, we do not associate an arity with each function symbol in this domain. Thus we have expressions F(X) and F(X, Y) in the same domain. Also, we include no constants in our domain. On the other hand, we shall include applications such as A( ) and B( ), in which the function symbol is applied to no arguments; such applications may play the role of constants.

VOCABULARY

In previous theories, we have adhered to the convention that variables (of the language) are symbols from the end of the alphabet, such as u, v, w, x, y, z (with optional subscripts). In this theory, we have several classes of objects in our intended domain, and we usually use different sets of variables to denote elements of each class. Therefore we change our convention and declare that all symbols consisting of single letters of the alphabet (with optional subscripts) are variables, such as e, f, ℓ, and t. Again, do not be confused: in this paragraph, we have been talking about variables in the language of the theory, not variables in the intended domain.

The theory of expressions is a theory with equality whose basic vocabulary contains the following symbols:

- Special predicate symbols:

  - A unary predicate symbol $var(x)$, characterizing the variables (of the intended domain).

  - A unary predicate symbol $fun(x)$, characterizing the function symbols (of the intended domain).

  - A unary predicate symbol $appl(x)$, characterizing the applications (of the intended domain).

  - A unary predicate symbol $exp(x)$, characterizing the expressions (of the intended domain).

- Special function symbol:

    - A binary function symbol $f \bullet t$, denoting the *application* function.

- Symbols from the theory of tuples:

    - The constant symbol $\langle \ \rangle$, denoting the empty tuple.

    - The unary predicate symbol *tuple*(x), characterizing the tuples of expressions (of the intended domain).

    - The binary function symbol $e \diamond t$, denoting the *insertion* function.

    - The additional binary predicate symbol $e \in t$, denoting the *member* relation.

We do not include the symbol *atom* from the theory of tuples. The symbol *exp* will play its role.

Under the intended models, for a given function symbol f and a tuple of expressions t, the application function $f \bullet t$ yields the application whose function symbol is f and whose arguments are the elements of t. Thus, under a given model, if f is F and t is $\langle$U, G(X)$\rangle$, then $f \bullet t$ is F$($U, G(X)$)$. If f is G and t is $\langle \ \rangle$, then $f \bullet t$ is G( ). Again, do not be confused: here f is a variable in our theory, while F is an element in our intended domain.

Because the theory of expressions is a theory with equality, it contains the predicate symbol $=$ in its vocabulary.

AXIOMS

The special axioms for the theory of expressions are as follows.

The generation axioms

$$
\begin{array}{l}
(\forall \textit{fun } f) \\
(\forall \textit{tuple } t)
\end{array}
\Big[\textit{appl}(f \bullet t) \Big]
\hspace{3cm} (\textit{application})
$$

In other words, the result of applying a function symbol to a tuple of expressions is an application.

$$(\forall\, var\ x)\big[exp(x)\big] \qquad\qquad (variable\text{-}expression)$$

$$(\forall\, appl\ e)\big[exp(e)\big] \qquad\qquad (application\text{-}expression)$$

In other words, variables and applications are expressions.

The tuple axioms

We include the axioms for tuples in our theory of expressions. To express the fact that the tuples are tuples of expressions, we identify the atoms of the tuples with the expressions in the theory by replacing the predicate symbol *atom* in each tuple axiom with *exp*. For example, the *insertion* generation axiom for tuples in the theory of expressions is

$$\begin{array}{l}(\forall\, exp\ u)\\ (\forall\, tuple\ x)\end{array}\big[tuple(u \diamond x)\big] \qquad\qquad (insertion)$$

rather than

$$\begin{array}{l}(\forall\, atom\ u)\\ (\forall\, tuple\ x)\end{array}\big[tuple(u \diamond x)\big]$$

We also have the *empty* generation axiom, the *empty* and *insertion* uniqueness axioms, and the *tuple induction* principle, altered as appropriate. In addition, we have the *empty* and *insertion* axioms for the member relation $\in$.

The uniqueness axioms

$$(\forall x)\big[not\ \big(var(x)\ \ and\ \ appl(x)\big)\big] \qquad (variable\text{-}application)$$

In other words, the variables and the applications are disjoint.

$$(\forall x)\big[not\ \big(exp(x)\ \ and\ \ tuple(x)\big)\big] \qquad (expression\text{-}tuple)$$

In other words, the expressions and the tuples are disjoint.

$$\begin{array}{l}(\forall\, fun\ f,\ g)\\ (\forall\, tuple\ s,\ t)\end{array}\left[\begin{array}{l}if\ \ f \bullet s = g \bullet t\\ then\ \ f = g\ \ and\ \ s = t\end{array}\right] \qquad (application)$$

In other words, every application may be constructed in no more than one way from a function symbol and a tuple of expressions.

The expression induction principle

The *expression induction principle* allows us to show that a property holds for all expressions.

> For each sentence $\mathcal{F}[e]$ in the theory, where x, f, and t do not occur free in $\mathcal{F}[e]$,
> the universal closure of the sentence
>
> $$if \begin{bmatrix} (\forall\, var\ x)\mathcal{F}[x] \\ and \\ (\forall\, fun\ f) \begin{bmatrix} if\ (\forall\, exp\ e) \begin{bmatrix} if\ \ e \in t \\ then\ \ \mathcal{F}[e] \end{bmatrix} \\ then\ \ \mathcal{F}[f \bullet t] \end{bmatrix} \end{bmatrix}$$
>
> $$then\ \ (\forall\, exp\ e)\mathcal{F}[e] \qquad\qquad (expression\ induction)$$
>
> is an axiom.

According to the *expression induction* principle, to establish that

$$(\forall\, exp\ e)\mathcal{F}[e],$$

it suffices to show the *base case*,

$$(\forall\, var\ x)\mathcal{F}[x],$$

and the *inductive step*,

$$\begin{matrix}(\forall\, fun\ f) \\ (\forall\, tuple\ t)\end{matrix} \begin{bmatrix} if\ (\forall\, exp\ e) \begin{bmatrix} if\ \ e \in t \\ then\ \ \mathcal{F}[e] \end{bmatrix} \\ then\ \ \mathcal{F}[f \bullet t] \end{bmatrix}.$$

The inductive step states that, for an arbitrary application $f \bullet t$, if the *induction hypothesis*,

$$(\forall\, exp\ e) \begin{bmatrix} if\ \ e \in t \\ then\ \ \mathcal{F}[e] \end{bmatrix},$$

is true, that is, if $\mathcal{F}[e]$ holds for every argument e in t, then the *desired conclusion*,

$$\mathcal{F}[f \bullet t],$$

is also true. We call $\mathcal{F}[e]$ the *inductive sentence*.

This concludes the axioms for the theory of expressions. From these axioms, we can establish the following property of expressions:

$$(\forall\ exp\ e)\begin{bmatrix} var(e) \\ or \\ (\exists\ fun\ f) \\ (\exists\ tuple\ t) \end{bmatrix}\begin{bmatrix} e = f \bullet t \end{bmatrix}\qquad (decomposition)$$

We may augment our theory by adding the axioms for the auxiliary functions and relations of the theory of tuples, such as the append function $\diamond$ and the subtuple relation $\subseteq$, with the same modification as for the basic axioms for tuples, i.e., replacing *atom* by *exp*.

We now augment our theory by introducing additional functions and relations.

THE FUNCT AND ARGS FUNCTIONS

For any application $e = f \bullet \langle e_1,\ e_2,\ \ldots,\ e_n \rangle$, the functions $funct(e)$ and $args(e)$, called the *function symbol* of e and the *arguments* of e, yield the function symbol f and the tuple of arguments $\langle e_1, e_2, \ldots, e_n \rangle$ of e, respectively. They are defined by the following axioms:

$$(\forall\ fun\ f) \atop (\forall\ tuple\ t) \begin{bmatrix} funct(f \bullet t) = f \end{bmatrix}\qquad (funct)$$

$$(\forall\ fun\ f) \atop (\forall\ tuple\ t) \begin{bmatrix} args(f \bullet t) = t \end{bmatrix}\qquad (args)$$

From these axioms we can establish the following properties of the *funct* and *args* functions:

$$(\forall\ appl\ e)\begin{bmatrix} fun\,(funct(e)) \end{bmatrix}\qquad (sort\ of\ funct)$$

$$(\forall\ appl\ e)\begin{bmatrix} tuple\,(args(e)) \end{bmatrix}\qquad (sort\ of\ args)$$

$$(\forall\ appl\ e)\begin{bmatrix} e = funct(e) \bullet args(e) \end{bmatrix}\qquad (decomposition)$$

In other words, any application is the result of applying its function symbol to its arguments. Furthermore, its function symbol is indeed a function symbol, and its arguments form a tuple.

Let us prove a simple property of the theory. We show that no application is identical to one of its own arguments. For example, in the intended domain, G(... , X, ...) is distinct from X itself.

Proposition (nonidentity)

The sentence

$$\begin{matrix} (\forall\ fun\ g) \\ (\forall\ tuple\ s) \end{matrix} \Bigl[not\ (g \bullet s \in s) \Bigr]$$ (*nonidentity*)

is valid. ⌟

Proof

We show instead the validity of the sentence

$$\begin{matrix} (\forall\ exp\ e) \\ (\forall\ fun\ g) \\ (\forall\ tuple\ s) \end{matrix} \begin{bmatrix} if & e \in s \\ then & not\ (g \bullet s = e) \end{bmatrix}.$$

This implies the desired result, taking e to be $g \bullet s$.

For arbitrary function symbol g and tuple s, we would like to show

$$(\forall\ exp\ e) \begin{bmatrix} if & e \in s \\ then & not\ (g \bullet s = e) \end{bmatrix}.$$

The proof is by expression induction on e, taking the inductive sentence to be

$$\mathcal{F}[e]: \quad \begin{matrix} if & e \in s \\ then & not\ (g \bullet s = e). \end{matrix}$$

According to the induction principle, it suffices to establish a base case and an inductive step.

Base Case

We would like to show $(\forall\ var\ x)\mathcal{F}[x]$, that is,

$$(\forall\ var\ x) \begin{bmatrix} if & x \in s \\ then & not\ (g \bullet s = x) \end{bmatrix}.$$

Suppose that x is a variable, that is,

$$var(x).$$

We know (by the *application* generation and *variable-application* uniqueness axioms) that

$$not\ \bigl(var(g \bullet s) \bigr),$$

and hence

$$not\ (g \bullet s = x).$$

In other words, the consequent of the desired implication is true, regardless of whether or not the antecedent $x \in s$ holds.

Inductive Step

We would like to show

$$(\forall\ fun\ f) \atop (\forall\ tuple\ t) \left[if\ (\forall\ exp\ e') \begin{bmatrix} if\ \ e' \in t \\ then\ \ \mathcal{F}[e'] \end{bmatrix} \atop then\ \ \mathcal{F}[f \bullet t] \right].$$

(To avoid confusion, we have renamed the bound variable e of the inductive step as e'.)

For an arbitrary function symbol f and tuple t, we suppose as our induction hypothesis that

$$(\dagger) \qquad (\forall\ exp\ e') \begin{bmatrix} if\ \ e' \in t \\ then\ \ \mathcal{F}[e'] \end{bmatrix}.$$

We would like to show the desired conclusion,

$$\mathcal{F}[f \bullet t],$$

that is,

$$if\ \ f \bullet t \in s \\ then\ \ not\ (g \bullet s = f \bullet t).$$

Suppose, to the contrary, that

$$(\dagger\dagger) \qquad not\ \mathcal{F}[f \bullet t].$$

Then

$$f \bullet t \in s \quad and \quad g \bullet s = f \bullet t.$$

We would like to derive a contradiction.

We have (by the *application* uniqueness axiom, because $g \bullet s = f \bullet t$) that

$$g = f \quad and \quad s = t$$

and hence (because $f \bullet t \in s$)

$$f \bullet t \in t.$$

Therefore (by our induction hypothesis (†), taking e' to be $f \bullet t$), we have

$$\mathcal{F}[f \bullet t],$$

which contradicts (††). ⌐

In the preceding *nonidentity* proposition, we have established that an application cannot be identical to one of its own arguments. We can also establish that no two applications can be each other's arguments, that is,

$$\begin{pmatrix} \forall \, fun \ f, \ g) \\ (\forall \, tuple \ s, \ t) \end{pmatrix} \Big[not \ \big(f \bullet s \in t \quad and \quad g \bullet t \in s \big) \Big] \quad (mutual \ nonidentity)$$

The proof is left as an exercise (**Problem 7.1**).

7.3   T-EXPRESSIONS

The *t-expressions* are expressions or tuples of expressions. We would like to augment our theory by adding a unary predicate symbol $t\text{-}exp(x)$, characterizing the t-expressions of the intended domain. It is defined by the axiom

$$(\forall \ell) \begin{bmatrix} t\text{-}exp(\ell) \\ \equiv \\ exp(\ell) \quad or \quad tuple(\ell) \end{bmatrix} \qquad\qquad (t\text{-}expression)$$

INDUCTION

Using the induction principle for the expressions and the induction principle for the tuples (of expressions), we can establish an induction principle for showing that a property holds for all t-expressions, i.e., all expressions and tuples of expressions.

Proposition (t-expression induction principle)

For each sentence $\mathcal{F}[\ell]$ in the augmented theory, where x, f, e, and t do not occur free in $\mathcal{F}[\ell]$, the universal closure of the sentence

$$
if \quad
\begin{bmatrix}
(\forall\, var\ x)\mathcal{F}[x] \\
\quad and \\
\mathcal{F}[\langle\ \rangle] \\
\quad and \\
\begin{array}{l}
(\forall\, fun\ f) \\
(\forall\, tuple\ t)
\end{array}
\begin{bmatrix}
if & \mathcal{F}[t] \\
then & \mathcal{F}[f \bullet t]
\end{bmatrix} \\
\quad and \\
\begin{array}{l}
(\forall\, exp\ e) \\
(\forall\, tuple\ t)
\end{array}
\begin{bmatrix}
if & \mathcal{F}[e]\ and\ \mathcal{F}[t] \\
then & \mathcal{F}[e \diamond t]
\end{bmatrix}
\end{bmatrix}
$$

$$then \quad (\forall\, t\text{-}exp\ \ell)\mathcal{F}[\ell] \qquad\qquad (t\text{-}expression\ induction)$$

is valid. ∎

This *t-expression induction* principle combines the *tuple* and *expression induction* principles. According to this induction principle, to establish that

$$(\forall\, t\text{-}exp\ \ell)\mathcal{F}[\ell],$$

it suffices to show the *variable base case*,

$$(\forall\, var\ x)\mathcal{F}[x];$$

the *empty base case*,

$$\mathcal{F}[\langle\ \rangle];$$

the *application inductive step*,

$$
\begin{array}{l}
(\forall\, fun\ f) \\
(\forall\, tuple\ t)
\end{array}
\begin{bmatrix}
if & \mathcal{F}[t] \\
then & \mathcal{F}[f \bullet t]
\end{bmatrix};
$$

and the *insertion inductive step*,

$$
\begin{array}{l}
(\forall\, exp\ e) \\
(\forall\, tuple\ t)
\end{array}
\begin{bmatrix}
if & \mathcal{F}[e]\ and\ \mathcal{F}[t] \\
then & \mathcal{F}[e \diamond t]
\end{bmatrix}.
$$

As usual, we call $\mathcal{F}[\ell]$ the *inductive sentence*.

We postpone establishing the validity of this induction principle until we have seen some examples of its application.

DECOMPOSITION PROPERTY

From the *t-expression induction* principle, we can easily establish the validity of the following property of t-expressions:

$$(\forall\, t\text{-}exp\ \ell)\ \begin{bmatrix} var(\ell) \\ or \\ \ell = \langle\ \rangle \\ or \\ \begin{matrix} (\exists\, fun\ f) \\ (\exists\, tuple\ t) \end{matrix}[\ell = f \bullet t] \\ or \\ \begin{matrix} (\exists\, exp\ e) \\ (\exists\, tuple\ t) \end{matrix}[\ell = e \diamond t] \end{bmatrix} \qquad (decomposition)$$

In other words, every t-expression is either a variable, the empty tuple, an application, or the result of an insertion.

A substantial example of the application of the *t-expression induction* principle is given in the next section.

7.4   OCCURRENCE RELATION

The *occurrence* relation is the analog for t-expressions of the subterm relation for terms in predicate logic. For example, the expression F(X) occurs in the expressions $G\big(F(X),\ Y\big)$ and $H\big(X,\ G(F(X),\ Y)\big)$. The relation applies not only to expressions, but also to tuples of expressions.

AXIOMS

We define two relations, ℓ *occurs properly in* m, denoted by $\ell \in m$, and its reflexive closure, ℓ *occurs in* m, denoted by $\ell \Subset m$, by the following axioms:

$$(\forall\, t\text{-}exp\ \ell,\ m)\ \begin{bmatrix} \ell \Subset m \\ \equiv \\ \ell \in m\ \ or\ \ \ell = m \end{bmatrix} \qquad (reflexive\ closure)$$

In other words, $\Subset$ is the reflexive closure of $\in$.

$$\begin{matrix}(\forall\,t\text{-}exp\ \ell)\\ (\forall\,var\ x)\end{matrix}\big[not\ (\ell \in x)\big] \qquad\qquad (variable)$$

$$(\forall\,t\text{-}exp\ \ell)\big[not\ (\ell \in \langle\ \rangle)\big] \qquad\qquad (empty)$$

$$\begin{matrix}(\forall\,t\text{-}exp\ \ell)\\ (\forall\,fun\ f)\\ (\forall\,tuple\ t)\end{matrix}\left[\begin{matrix}\ell \in f \bullet t\\ \equiv\\ \ell \Subset t\end{matrix}\right] \qquad\qquad (application)$$

$$\begin{matrix}(\forall\,t\text{-}exp\ \ell)\\ (\forall\,exp\ e)\\ (\forall\,tuple\ t)\end{matrix}\left[\begin{matrix}\ell \in e \diamond t\\ \equiv\\ \ell \Subset e\ \ or\ \ \ell \Subset t\end{matrix}\right] \qquad\qquad (insertion)$$

If a t-expression ℓ occurs [properly] in a t-expression m, we also say that ℓ is a [*proper*] *t-subexpression* of m.

PROPERTIES

The definition immediately implies the reflexivity of the occurrence relation $\in$,

$$(\forall\,t\text{-}exp\ \ell)\big[\ell \Subset \ell\big] \qquad\qquad (reflexivity)$$

We may also establish the irreflexivity of the proper-occurrence relation $\in$,

$$(\forall\,t\text{-}exp\ \ell)\big[not\ (\ell \in \ell)\big] \qquad\qquad (irreflexivity)$$

and the following *component* properties of the proper-occurrence relation $\in$:

$$\begin{matrix}(\forall\,fun\ f)\\ (\forall\,tuple\ t)\end{matrix}\big[t \in f \bullet t\big] \qquad\qquad (argument)$$

$$\begin{matrix}(\forall\,exp\ e)\\ (\forall\,tuple\ t)\end{matrix}\big[e \in e \diamond t\big] \qquad\qquad (head)$$

$$\begin{matrix}(\forall\,exp\ e)\\ (\forall\,tuple\ t)\end{matrix}\big[t \in e \diamond t\big] \qquad\qquad (tail)$$

Examples

We have, by *reflexivity* of $\Subset$,

$$\langle Y,\ X\rangle \Subset \langle Y,\ X\rangle.$$

Therefore, by the *tail* component property of $\in$ (because $\langle Z, Y, X \rangle$ is $Z \diamond \langle Y, X \rangle$),

$$\langle Y, X \rangle \in \langle Z, Y, X \rangle$$

and, by the *argument* component property of $\in$ (because $G(Y, X)$ is $G \bullet \langle Y, X \rangle$),

$$\langle Y, X \rangle \in G(Y, X).$$

Also, by the *head* component property of $\in$ (because $\langle Y, X \rangle$ is $Y \diamond \langle X \rangle$),

$$Y \in \langle Y, X \rangle.$$

Therefore, because $\sqsubseteq$ is the reflexive closure of $\in$,

$$Y \sqsubseteq \langle Y, X \rangle$$

and, by the *application* axiom for $\in$ (because $G(Y, X)$ is $G \bullet \langle Y, X \rangle$),

$$Y \in G(Y, X).$$

We can also show that

$$X \in G(Y, X), \quad \langle X \rangle \in G(Y, X), \quad \text{but} \quad \text{not} \quad \langle Y \rangle \in G(Y, X). \quad \lrcorner$$

The axioms easily imply the following properties of the occurrence relation $\in$:

$$(\forall\, t\text{-}exp\ \ell)\atop(\forall\, var\ x)\Big[(\ell \sqsubseteq x) \equiv (\ell = x)\Big] \qquad\qquad (variable)$$

$$(\forall\, t\text{-}exp\ \ell)\Big[(\ell \sqsubseteq \langle\ \rangle) \equiv (\ell = \langle\ \rangle)\Big] \qquad\qquad (empty)$$

TRANSITIVITY

We can show that the two occurrence relations are both transitive.

Proposition (transitivity of occurrence)

The sentences

$$(\forall\, t\text{-}exp\ k,\ \ell,\ m)\left[\begin{matrix}if\ \ k \in \ell\ \ and\ \ \ell \in m \\ then\ \ k \in m\end{matrix}\right] \qquad (transitivity\ of \in)$$

$$(\forall\, t\text{-}exp\ k,\ \ell,\ m)\left[\begin{matrix}if\ \ k \sqsubseteq \ell\ \ and\ \ \ell \sqsubseteq m \\ then\ \ k \sqsubseteq m\end{matrix}\right] \qquad (transitivity\ of \sqsubseteq)$$

are valid. $\lrcorner$

Proof

We show only the transitivity of the proper-occurrence relation $\in$. Because $\subseteq$ is the reflexive closure of $\in$, the transitivity of $\subseteq$ follows (see Section [I]5.3).

We actually establish the equivalent (by predicate logic) sentence

$$(\forall \text{ } t\text{-}exp \text{ } k, \text{ } \ell) \left[\begin{matrix} if \text{ } k \in \ell \\ then \text{ } (\forall t\text{-}exp \text{ } m) \left[\begin{matrix} if \text{ } \ell \in m \\ then \text{ } k \in m \end{matrix} \right] \end{matrix} \right].$$

Consider arbitrary t-expressions k and ℓ and suppose that

(†) $k \in \ell.$

We would like to show that then

$$(\forall \text{ } t\text{-}exp \text{ } m) \left[\begin{matrix} if \text{ } \ell \in m \\ then \text{ } k \in m \end{matrix} \right].$$

Our proof is by t-expression induction on m, taking the inductive sentence to be

$$\mathcal{F}[m]: \quad \begin{matrix} if \text{ } \ell \in m \\ then \text{ } k \in m. \end{matrix}$$

Variable Base Case

We would like to show that

$$(\forall \text{ } var \text{ } x) \left[\begin{matrix} if \text{ } \ell \in x \\ then \text{ } k \in x \end{matrix} \right].$$

Consider an arbitrary variable x; then (by the *variable* axiom for $\in$)

$$not \text{ } (\ell \in x),$$

and therefore the implication

$$\begin{matrix} if \text{ } \ell \in x \\ then \text{ } k \in x \end{matrix}$$

is true.

Empty Base Case

This case is analogous to the *variable base case*, using the *empty* axiom for $\in$.

Application Inductive Step

We would like to show that

$$\begin{matrix} (\forall \text{ } fun \text{ } f) \\ (\forall \text{ } tuple \text{ } t) \end{matrix} \left[\begin{matrix} if \text{ } \mathcal{F}[t] \\ then \text{ } \mathcal{F}[f \bullet t] \end{matrix} \right].$$

Consider an arbitrary function symbol f and tuple t and assume as our induction hypothesis that

$$\mathcal{F}[t] : \quad \begin{aligned} &if\ \ \ell \in t \\ &then\ \ k \in t. \end{aligned}$$

We would like to show the desired conclusion, that

$$\mathcal{F}[f \bullet t] : \quad \begin{aligned} &if\ \ \ell \in f \bullet t \\ &then\ \ k \in f \bullet t. \end{aligned}$$

It suffices (by the *application* axiom for $\in$) to show that

$$\begin{aligned} &if\ \ \ell \trianglelefteq t \\ &then\ \ k \trianglelefteq t \end{aligned}$$

or, equivalently (because $\trianglelefteq$ is the reflexive closure of $\in$),

$$\begin{aligned} &if\ \ (\ell \in t\ \ or\ \ \ell = t) \\ &then\ \ (k \in t\ \ or\ \ k = t). \end{aligned}$$

We suppose that

$$\ell \in t\ \ or\ \ \ell = t$$

and show that then

$$k \in t\ \ or\ \ k = t.$$

We actually show that

$$k \in t.$$

We distinguish between the two possible cases, $\ell \in t$ and $\ell = t$.

Case: $\ell \in t$

Then, by our induction hypothesis $\mathcal{F}[t]$, we have

$$k \in t,$$

as we wanted to show.

Case: $\ell = t$

Then it suffices to show

$$k \in \ell.$$

But this is our initial supposition (†).

Insertion Inductive Step

We would like to show that

$$(\forall\ exp\ e) \left[\begin{array}{l} if\ \ \mathcal{F}[e]\ \ and\ \ \mathcal{F}[t] \\ then\ \ \mathcal{F}[e \diamond t] \end{array} \right].$$
$$(\forall\ tuple\ t)$$

Consider an arbitrary expression e and tuple t and assume as our two induction hypotheses that

$$\mathcal{F}[e]: \quad \begin{array}{l} if\ \ \ell \in e \\ then\ \ k \in e \end{array}$$

and

$$\mathcal{F}[t]: \quad \begin{array}{l} if\ \ \ell \in t \\ then\ \ k \in t. \end{array}$$

We would like to show the desired conclusion that

$$\mathcal{F}[e \diamond t]: \quad \begin{array}{l} if\ \ \ell \in e \diamond t \\ then\ \ k \in e \diamond t. \end{array}$$

It suffices (by the *insertion* axiom for $\in$) to show that

$$\begin{array}{l} if\ \ (\ell \Subset e\ \ or\ \ \ell \Subset t) \\ then\ \ (k \Subset e\ \ or\ \ k \Subset t). \end{array}$$

We suppose that

$$\ell \Subset e\ \ or\ \ \ell \Subset t$$

and attempt to show that

$$k \Subset e\ \ or\ \ k \Subset t.$$

We distinguish between the two possible cases, $\ell \Subset e$ and $\ell \Subset t$. We show that $k \in e$ in the first case and $k \in t$ in the second; therefore (because $\Subset$ is the reflexive closure of $\in$) we have $(k \Subset e\ or\ k \Subset t)$.

Case: $\ell \Subset e$

Then (because $\Subset$ is the reflexive closure of $\in$)

$$\ell = e\ \ or\ \ \ell \in e.$$

In the subcase in which $\ell = e$, we know (by our earlier supposition (†), $k \in \ell$) that

$$k \in e,$$

as we wanted to show.

In the subcase in which $\ell \in e$, we know (by our first induction hypothesis $\mathcal{F}[e]$) that

$$k \in e,$$

as we wanted to show.

Case: $\ell \sqsubseteq t$

This case is analogous to the previous case; we show that $k \in t$ using the second induction hypothesis $\mathcal{F}[t]$ rather than the first. ∎

Now that we have seen an application of the *t-expression induction* principle, let us establish its validity.

7.5   THE T-EXPRESSION INDUCTION PRINCIPLE

The proof of the validity of the *t-expression induction* principle relies on both the *expression induction* principle and on the *tuple induction* principle from the theory of tuples.

Proof (t-expression induction principle)

We would like to establish the validity of the principle for every sentence $\mathcal{F}[\ell]$ in the theory, where x, f, e, and t do not occur free in $\mathcal{F}[\ell]$. For such a given sentence $\mathcal{F}[\ell]$, suppose that the two base cases and two inductive steps of the *t-expression induction* principle are true. These are as follows:

$$(\forall\, var\ x)\mathcal{F}[x] \qquad\qquad\qquad (variable\ base\ case)$$

$$\mathcal{F}[\langle\ \rangle] \qquad\qquad\qquad\qquad (empty\ base\ case)$$

$$\begin{matrix}(\forall\, fun\ f) \\ (\forall\, tuple\ t)\end{matrix} \left[\begin{matrix} if\ \ \mathcal{F}[t] \\ then\ \ \mathcal{F}[f \bullet t] \end{matrix}\right] \qquad (application\ inductive\ step)$$

$$\begin{matrix}(\forall\, exp\ e) \\ (\forall\, tuple\ t)\end{matrix} \left[\begin{matrix} if\ \ \mathcal{F}[e]\ \ and\ \ \mathcal{F}[t] \\ then\ \ \mathcal{F}[e \diamond t] \end{matrix}\right] \qquad (insertion\ inductive\ step)$$

We would like to show that then

$$(\forall\, t\text{-}exp\ \ell)\mathcal{F}[\ell]$$

is also true.

Because (by the *t-expression* axiom) every t-expression is either an expression or a tuple of expressions, it suffices to establish (by predicate logic) that

$$(\forall\ exp\ e)\mathcal{F}[e] \quad \text{and} \quad (\forall\ tuple\ t)\mathcal{F}[t].$$

We prove each of these conditions separately.

Proof of $(\forall\ exp\ e)\mathcal{F}[e]$

The proof is by expression induction on e, taking the inductive sentence to be $\mathcal{F}[e]$ itself.

Base Case

We would like to show

$$(\forall\ var\ x)\mathcal{F}[x],$$

but this is the *variable base* case of the *t-expression induction* principle, which we have supposed to be true.

Inductive Step

We would like to show

$$(\forall\ fun\ f)\ \left[if\ (\forall\ exp\ e)\ \begin{bmatrix} if\ e \in t \\ then\ \mathcal{F}[e] \end{bmatrix} \right] \\ (\forall\ tuple\ t)\ \left[then\ \mathcal{F}[f \bullet t] \right].$$

Consider an arbitrary function symbol f and tuple t and suppose as our induction hypothesis that

$$(\dagger) \qquad (\forall\ exp\ e)\ \begin{bmatrix} if\ e \in t \\ then\ \ \mathcal{F}[e] \end{bmatrix}.$$

We would like to show that then

$$\mathcal{F}[f \bullet t].$$

It suffices, by the assumed *application inductive* step of the *t-expression induction* principle, to show that

$$\mathcal{F}[t].$$

In fact, we show the more general property

$$(\dagger\dagger) \qquad (\forall\ tuple\ s)\ \begin{bmatrix} if\ s \subseteq t \\ then\ \ \mathcal{F}[s] \end{bmatrix},$$

where $s \subseteq t$ is the subtuple relation, which means that the elements of s occur in t in the same order (though not necessarily consecutively). The condition $(\dagger\dagger)$ implies the desired conclusion $\mathcal{F}[t]$ by taking s to be t itself, because $t \subseteq t$.

Proof of (††)

The proof of (††) is itself by tuple induction on s, taking the inductive sentence to be

$$if \ \ s \subseteq t$$
$$then \ \ \mathcal{F}[s].$$

Base Case

We would like to show that

$$if \ \ \langle \ \rangle \subseteq t$$
$$then \ \ \mathcal{F}[\langle \ \rangle].$$

But this is true, because its consequent $\mathcal{F}[\langle \ \rangle]$ is precisely the *empty base* case of the *t-expression induction* principle, which we have supposed to be true.

Inductive Step

Consider an arbitrary tuple s and suppose as our induction hypothesis that

(‡)
$$if \ \ s \subseteq t$$
$$then \ \ \mathcal{F}[s].$$

We would like to show that, for an arbitrary expression d,

$$if \ \ d \diamond s \subseteq t$$
$$then \ \ \mathcal{F}[d \diamond s]$$

is true.

We suppose that

$$d \diamond s \subseteq t$$

and attempt to show that then

$$\mathcal{F}[d \diamond s].$$

By the *insertion inductive* step of the *t-expression induction* principle, which we have supposed to be true, it suffices to establish that

(‡‡) $\mathcal{F}[d] \ \ and \ \ \mathcal{F}[s].$

We have (by our supposition $d \diamond s \subseteq t$ and by properties of the subtuple relation)

$$d \in t \ \ and \ \ s \subseteq t.$$

By our original expression induction hypothesis (†), it follows (taking e to be d, because $d \in t$) that

$$\mathcal{F}[d].$$

By our current tuple induction hypothesis (‡), it follows (because $s \subseteq t$) that

$$\mathcal{F}[s].$$

We have therefore established both conjuncts $\mathcal{F}[d]$ and $\mathcal{F}[s]$ of our desired result (‡‡).

This completes the inductive step in the proof of (††). It remains to show the second of our two conditions.

Proof of $(\forall\ tuple\ t)\mathcal{F}[t]$

The proof is by tuple induction on t, taking the inductive sentence to be $\mathcal{F}[t]$.

Base Case

We would like to show

$$\mathcal{F}[\langle\ \rangle],$$

but this is the *empty base* case of the *t-expression induction* principle, which we have supposed to be true.

Inductive Step

Consider an arbitrary expression e and tuple t. Assume as our induction hypothesis that

$$\mathcal{F}[t].$$

We would like to establish that then

$$\mathcal{F}[e \diamond t].$$

By the *insertion inductive* step of the *t-expression induction* principle, which we have supposed to be true, it suffices to show that

$$\mathcal{F}[e]\quad and\quad \mathcal{F}[t].$$

We know that $\mathcal{F}[e]$ is true because we have already established the first condition that $\mathcal{F}[e]$ is true for every expression e. Also, we have assumed as our induction hypothesis that $\mathcal{F}[t]$ is true. ◢

This concludes the proof of the validity of the *t-expression induction* principle.

7.6   WELL-FOUNDED INDUCTION

We established earlier that the proper-occurrence relation $\in$ is transitive and irreflexive. We would like to show that it is also well-founded. For this purpose, we will map the relation into the nonnegative integers via a function that measures the size of a given t-expression.

THE SIZE FUNCTION

Let us consider a combined theory of t-expressions and nonnegative integers. For a t-expression ℓ, the unary function $size(\ell)$ yields the number of symbols, parentheses, and angular brackets in the informal representation of ℓ (we do not count commas); for example,

$$size\big(\text{G}(\text{X}) \big) \ = \ 4$$

$$size\big(\text{F}\big(\text{X, G}(\text{Y})\big) \big) \ = \ 8$$

$$size\Big(\big\langle \text{F}\big(\text{X, G}(\text{Y})\big), \ \text{G}(\text{X}) \big\rangle \Big) \ = \ 14.$$

The last t-expression $\langle \text{F}(\text{X}, \text{G}(\text{Y})), \ \text{G}(\text{X}) \rangle$ consists of a pair of angular brackets (2), three pairs of parentheses (6), and the occurrences of the symbols F, X, G, Y, G, X (6): a total of 14.

The *size* function is defined by the following axioms:

$$(\forall\, var\ x)\big[size(x) = 1 \big] \qquad\qquad\qquad\qquad\qquad (variable)$$

$$size(\langle\, \rangle) = 2 \qquad\qquad\qquad\qquad\qquad\qquad\qquad (empty)$$

$$\begin{matrix} (\forall\, fun\ f) \\ (\forall\, tuple\ t) \end{matrix} \Big[size(f \bullet t) = 1 + size(t) \Big] \qquad\qquad (application)$$

$$\begin{matrix} (\forall\, exp\ e) \\ (\forall\, tuple\ t) \end{matrix} \Big[size(e \diamond t) = size(e) + size(t) \Big] \qquad\quad (insertion)$$

Note that, according to the *application* axiom, the size of an application $f(e_1, e_2, \ldots, e_n)$ is one more than the size of the tuple $\langle e_1, e_2, \ldots, e_n \rangle$. The angular brackets in the informal representation of the tuple are replaced by the parentheses in the informal representation of the application.

Example

We have

$$size(\langle \text{X} \rangle) \;=\; size(\text{X} \diamond \langle\,\rangle)$$

$$=\; size(\text{X}) + size(\langle\,\rangle)$$
$$(\text{by the } \textit{insertion} \text{ axiom})$$

$$=\; 1 + 2$$
$$(\text{by the } \textit{variable} \text{ and } \textit{empty} \text{ axioms})$$

$$=\; 3$$

$$size(\text{G}(\text{X})) \;=\; size(\text{G} \bullet \langle \text{X} \rangle)$$

$$=\; 1 + size(\langle \text{X} \rangle)$$
$$(\text{by the } \textit{application} \text{ axiom})$$

$$=\; 1 + 3 \;=\; 4. \quad \lrcorner$$

We can establish that the size of a t-expression is always a positive integer, that is,

$$(\forall\, t\text{-}exp\ \ell)\,[positive(size(\ell))] \hspace{3cm} (sort)$$

In **Problem 7.2**, the reader is asked to define another version of the *size* function that counts all the symbols in the informal representation of t-expressions, including the commas.

The main property that we need, that the size of a proper t-subexpression is always less than the size of a given t-expression, is expressed in the following result.

Proposition (monotonicity)

The sentence

$$(\forall\, t\text{-}exp\ \ell,\ m) \begin{bmatrix} if\ \ \ell \Subset m \\ then\ \ size(\ell) < size(m) \end{bmatrix} \hspace{2cm} (monotonicity)$$

is valid. $\lrcorner$

The proof is requested in an exercise (**Problem 7.3**).

PROPER OCCURRENCE IS WELL-FOUNDED

Once we have established the *monotonicity* property of the *size* function, we can show that the proper-occurrence relation $\in$ is well-founded over the t-expressions.

Proposition (well-foundedness of proper occurrence)

The proper-occurrence relation $\in$ is well-founded over *t-exp*. ⏌

The proof depends on the *mapping* proposition (Section 1.3), which states that a relation is well-founded if it can be mapped into another well-founded relation.

Proof

The *size* function maps the proper-occurrence relation $\in$ over the t-expressions into the less-than relation $<$ over the positive integers because it satisfies the *sort* property

$$(\forall \, t\text{-}exp \; \ell)\big[positive\big(size(\ell)\big)\big]$$

and the *monotonicity* property

$$(\forall \, t\text{-}exp \; \ell, \; m) \begin{bmatrix} if & \ell \in m \\ then & size(\ell) < size(m) \end{bmatrix}$$

Therefore, by the *mapping* proposition for well-founded relations, because the less-than relation $<$ is well-founded over the positive integers, it follows that the proper-occurrence relation $\in$ is well-founded over the t-expressions. ⏌

By the *subclass* corollary to the *mapping* proposition, it follows that the proper-occurrence relation is also well-founded over the expressions, which constitute a subclass of the t-expressions. These results are valuable because they allow us to establish properties of the t-expressions, or of the expressions, by well-founded induction over the proper-occurrence relation. Over the t-expressions, the appropriate instance of the *well-founded induction* principle is as follows.

Corollary (well-founded induction principle with respect to $\in$)

For each sentence $\mathcal{F}[\ell]$, where ℓ' does not occur free in $\mathcal{F}[\ell]$, the universal closure of the sentence

$$if \ (\forall\, t\text{-}exp \ \ell) \begin{bmatrix} if \ (\forall\, t\text{-}exp \ \ell') \begin{bmatrix} if \ \ell' \in \ell \\ then \ \ \mathcal{F}[\ell'] \end{bmatrix} \\ then \ \ \mathcal{F}[\ell] \end{bmatrix}$$
$$then \ (\forall\, t\text{-}exp \ \ell)\mathcal{F}[\ell]$$

$$(well\text{-}founded \ induction)$$

is valid. ⌐

In the next section, we define a new function and illustrate the use of the well-founded induction principle over t-expressions with respect to the proper-occurrence relation $\in$.

7.7   VARSET FUNCTION

The function $varset(\ell)$ yields the set of variables of a given t-expression ℓ. For example,

$$varset\Big(\langle\text{X}, \ \text{G}\big(\text{Z}, \ \text{F}(\text{X}, \ \text{Y})\big)\rangle\Big) \ = \ \{\text{X}, \text{Y}, \text{Z}\}.$$

COMBINED THEORY

To define the function formally, we augment the theory of t-expressions with the theory of sets of variables. This is a version of the theory of sets whose atoms are identified with the variables of our theory of t-expressions. To express this identification, we replace the predicate symbol *atom* with *var* in each of our original set axioms (Section [I]10.1).

For instance, the *empty* and *insertion* member axioms for sets

$$(\forall\, atom \ u)\big[not \ (u \in \{ \ \})\big]$$

$$\begin{matrix} (\forall\, atom \ u, \ v) \\ (\forall\, set \ x) \end{matrix} \begin{bmatrix} u \in (v \circ x) \\ \equiv \\ u = v \ \ or \ \ u \in x \end{bmatrix}$$

are written in the combined theory as

$$(\forall \, var \; u)\big[not \; (u \in \{ \; \})\big] \hspace{4cm} (empty)$$

$$(\forall \, var \; u, v) \quad \begin{bmatrix} u \in (v \circ x) \\ \equiv \\ u = v \;\; or \;\; u \in x \end{bmatrix} \hspace{2cm} (insertion)$$
$$(\forall \, set \; x)$$

We also add the generation axioms, the special *equality* axioms, and the *set induction* principle, altered by replacing the predicate symbol *atom* with *var*.

In the augmented theory, we define the unary *singleton* function $\{x\}$ by the axiom

$$(\forall \, var \; x)\big[\{x\} = x \circ \{ \; \}\big] \hspace{3cm} (singleton)$$

AXIOMS

The *varset* function is then defined by the following axioms:

$$(\forall \, var \; x)\big[varset(x) \; = \; \{x\}\big] \hspace{3cm} (variable)$$

$$varset(\langle \; \rangle) = \{ \; \} \hspace{4cm} (empty)$$

$$(\forall \, fun \; f) \atop (\forall \, tuple \; t) \Big[varset(f \bullet t) \; = \; varset(t)\Big] \hspace{1.5cm} (application)$$

$$(\forall \, exp \; e) \atop (\forall \, tuple \; t) \Big[varset(e \diamond t) \; = \; varset(e) \cup varset(t)\Big] \hspace{1cm} (insertion)$$

We can establish that the *varset* function always yields a set of variables, that is,

$$(\forall \, t\text{-}exp \; \ell)\big[set\big(varset(\ell)\big)\big] \hspace{3cm} (sort)$$

$$(\forall \, x) \atop (\forall \, t\text{-}exp \; \ell) \begin{bmatrix} if \;\; x \in varset(\ell) \\ then \;\; var(x) \end{bmatrix} \hspace{2cm} (variable)$$

OCCUR PROPERTY

The main property of the function $varset(\ell)$ we need, that is, that it yields the set of exactly those variables that occur in the given t-expression ℓ, is expressed in the following result.

Proposition (occur)

The sentence

$$(\forall\, var\ x) \atop (\forall\, t\text{-}exp\ \ell) \left[\begin{matrix} x \in varset(\ell) \\ \equiv \\ x \underline{\in} \ell \end{matrix} \right] \qquad\qquad (occur)$$

is valid. ◢

We illustrate the *well-founded induction* principle in the proof of this proposition. We freely use properties from the theory of sets.

Proof

Consider an arbitrary variable x; we would like to show that

$$(\forall\, t\text{-}exp\ \ell) \left[x \in varset(\ell)\ \equiv\ x \underline{\in} \ell \right].$$

The proof is by well-founded induction on ℓ with respect to the proper-occurrence relation $\in$. We take the inductive sentence to be

$$\mathcal{F}[\ell]:\quad x \in varset(\ell)\ \equiv\ x \underline{\in} \ell.$$

Then, according to the *well-founded induction* principle, to show that

$$(\forall\, t\text{-}exp\ \ell)\mathcal{F}[\ell],$$

it suffices to establish a single inductive step.

Inductive Step

We would like to show that

$$(\forall\, t\text{-}exp\ \ell) \left[\begin{matrix} if\ (\forall\, t\text{-}exp\ \ell') \left[\begin{matrix} if\ \ell' \in \ell \\ then\ \ \mathcal{F}[\ell'] \end{matrix} \right] \\ then\ \ \mathcal{F}[\ell] \end{matrix} \right].$$

We consider an arbitrary t-expression ℓ and assume as our induction hypothesis that

$$(\dagger) \qquad (\forall\, t\text{-}exp\ \ell') \left[\begin{matrix} if\ \ell' \in \ell \\ then\ \ \mathcal{F}[\ell'] \end{matrix} \right].$$

We would like to establish that then

$$(\ddagger) \qquad \mathcal{F}[\ell]: \quad x \in \mathit{varset}(\ell) \quad \equiv \quad x \sqsubseteq \ell.$$

By the *decomposition* property of t-expressions, we know ℓ is a variable, the empty tuple, an application, or the result of an insertion. We treat each possibility separately.

Case: $\mathit{var}(\ell)$

Then the left-hand side of ($\ddagger$),

$$x \in \mathit{varset}(\ell),$$

holds precisely when (by the *variable* axiom for *varset*, because $\mathit{var}(\ell)$)

$$x \in \{\ell\}$$

precisely when (by the *singleton* axiom and the *insertion* axiom for the member relation $\in$)

$$x = \ell \;\; or \;\; x \in \{\,\}$$

precisely when (by the *empty* axiom for the member relation $\in$)

$$x = \ell.$$

On the other hand, the right-hand side of ($\ddagger$),

$$x \sqsubseteq \ell,$$

holds precisely when (because $\sqsubseteq$ is the reflexive closure of $\in$)

$$x \in \ell \;\; or \;\; x = \ell$$

precisely when (by the *variable* axiom for $\in$, because $\mathit{var}(\ell)$)

$$x = \ell.$$

Because both sides hold precisely when $x = \ell$, the entire equivalence ($\ddagger$),

$$x \in \mathit{varset}(\ell) \quad \equiv \quad x \sqsubseteq \ell,$$

is true in this case.

Case: $\ell = \langle\,\rangle$

Then the left-hand side of ($\ddagger$),

$$x \in \mathit{varset}(\ell),$$

holds precisely when (by the *empty* axiom for *varset*, because $\ell = \langle\,\rangle$)

$$x \in \{\,\},$$

which is false (by the *empty* axiom for the member relation $\in$).

On the other hand, the right-hand side of (‡),

$$x \sqsubseteq \ell,$$

holds precisely when (because $\sqsubseteq$ is the reflexive closure of $\in$)

$$x \in \ell \ \ or \ \ x = \ell$$

precisely when (by the *empty* axiom for $\in$, because $\ell = \langle\,\rangle$)

$$x = \ell,$$

which is also false (by the *variable-expression* generation and the *expression-tuple* uniqueness axioms for expressions).

Because both sides are false, the entire equivalence (‡) is true in this case.

Note that, in the first two cases, the proof did not require the induction hypothesis; in the final two cases, however, the induction hypothesis will be required.

Case: $\ell = f \bullet t$ for some $fun(f)$ and $tuple(t)$

Then the left-hand side of (‡),

$$x \in varset(\ell),$$

holds precisely when

$$x \in varset(f \bullet t)$$

precisely when (by the *application* axiom for *varset*)

$$x \in varset(t).$$

On the other hand, the right-hand side of (‡),

$$x \sqsubseteq \ell,$$

holds precisely when

$$x \sqsubseteq f \bullet t$$

precisely when (because $\sqsubseteq$ is the reflexive closure of $\in$)

$$x \in f \bullet t \ \ or \ \ x = f \bullet t$$

precisely when (by the *application* generation and the *variable-application* uniqueness axioms for expressions)

$$x \Subset f \bullet t$$

precisely when (by the *application* axiom for $\Subset$)

$$x \Subset t.$$

Therefore, to show the equivalence ($\ddagger$),

$$x \in varset(\ell) \quad \equiv \quad x \Subset \ell,$$

it suffices to show (in this case) that

$$x \in varset(t) \quad \equiv \quad x \Subset t.$$

We know (by the *argument* component property of the proper-occurrence relation $\Subset$) that

$$t \Subset f \bullet t.$$

Therefore (by our induction hypothesis ($\dagger$), taking ℓ' to be t, because $\ell = f \bullet t$), we have $\mathcal{F}[t]$, that is,

$$x \in varset(t) \quad \equiv \quad x \Subset t,$$

as we wanted to show.

Case: $\ell = e \diamond t$ for some $exp(e)$ and $tuple(t)$

Then the left-hand side of ($\ddagger$),

$$x \in varset(\ell),$$

holds precisely when

$$x \in varset(e \diamond t)$$

precisely when (by the *insertion* axiom for *varset*)

$$x \in varset(e) \cup varset(t)$$

precisely when (by the *member* property of the union function $\cup$)

$$x \in varset(e) \quad or \quad x \in varset(t).$$

On the other hand, the right-hand side of ($\ddagger$),

$$x \Subset \ell,$$

holds precisely when

$$x \Subset e \diamond t$$

precisely when (because $\Subset$ is the reflexive closure of $\in$)

$$x \in e \diamond t \quad or \quad x = e \diamond t$$

precisely when (by the *variable-expression* generation and the *expression-tuple* uniqueness axioms for expressions)

$$x \in e \diamond t$$

precisely when (by the *insertion* axiom for $\in$)

$$x \Subset e \quad or \quad x \Subset t.$$

Therefore, to establish the equivalence (‡),

$$x \in varset(\ell) \quad \equiv \quad x \Subset \ell,$$

it suffices to establish (in this case) that

$$x \in varset(e) \quad or \quad x \in varset(t)$$
$$\equiv$$
$$x \Subset e \quad or \quad x \Subset t.$$

We know (by the *head* and *tail* component properties of the proper-occurrence relation $\in$) that

$$e \in e \diamond t \quad and \quad t \in e \diamond t.$$

Therefore (by two applications of our induction hypothesis (†), taking ℓ' to be e and t, respectively, because $\ell = e \diamond t$), we have $\mathcal{F}[e]$ and $\mathcal{F}[t]$, that is,

$$x \in varset(e) \qquad\qquad x \in varset(t)$$
$$\equiv \qquad and \qquad \equiv$$
$$x \Subset e \qquad\qquad x \Subset t,$$

and, consequently,

$$x \in varset(e) \quad or \quad x \in varset(t)$$
$$\equiv$$
$$x \Subset e \quad or \quad x \Subset t,$$

as we wanted to show.

Because we have established the desired conclusion in all four cases, this concludes the proof. ⌐

The preceding *occur* property and the transitivity of the occurrence relation immediately imply the *monotonicity* property of the *varset* function, that is,

$$(\forall\, t\text{-}exp\ \ell,\ m)\begin{bmatrix} if\ \ \ell \sqsubseteq m \\ then\ \ varset(\ell) \subseteq varset(m) \end{bmatrix} \qquad (monotonicity)$$

In other words, a t-expression that occurs in another t-expression cannot have any additional variables.

THE SUBEXPRESSIONS FUNCTION

Suppose we introduce a theory of sets of t-expressions, obtained by identifying the atoms of the sets with the t-expressions themselves. This identification is expressed by replacing the predicate symbol *atom* with *t-exp* in each of our original set axioms.

In this theory, let us define the unary *subexpressions* function $subexps(\ell)$ to be the set of t-expressions that occur in a given t-expression ℓ. The function is defined by the following axioms:

$(\forall\, var\ x)\big[subexps(x) = \{x\} \big]$ *(variable)*

$subexps(\langle\,\rangle) = \{\langle\,\rangle\}$ *(empty)*

$\begin{matrix}(\forall\, fun\ f)\\(\forall\, tuple\ t)\end{matrix}\big[subexps(f \bullet t) = (f \bullet t) \circ subexps(t) \big]$ *(application)*

$\begin{matrix}(\forall\, exp\ e)\\(\forall\, tuple\ t)\end{matrix}\begin{bmatrix} subexps(e \diamond t) = \\ (e \diamond t) \circ \big(subexps(e) \cup subexps(t) \big) \end{bmatrix}$ *(insertion)*

In **Problem 7.4** the reader is requested to prove the basic property of this function,

$$(\forall\, t\text{-}exp\ \ell,\ m)\begin{bmatrix} \ell \in exps(m) \\ \equiv \\ \ell \sqsubseteq m \end{bmatrix}.$$

This concludes our introduction to the theory of t-expressions. Building on this theory, we shall develop a theory of substitutions in the next chapter.

PROBLEMS

* **Problem 7.1 (mutual nonidentity)**   page 266

Show the *mutual-nonidentity* property that no two applications can be each other's arguments, that is,

$$(\forall\, fun\ f,\ g) \atop (\forall\, tuple\ s,\ t) \left[not\ (f \bullet s \in t\ \ and\ \ g \bullet t \in s) \right].$$

Hint: Prove the property

$$(\forall\, exp\ e) \atop (\forall\, fun\ f,\ g) \atop (\forall\, tuple\ s,\ t) \left[\begin{array}{l} if\ \ e = f \bullet s \\ then\ \ not\ (e \in t\ \ and\ \ g \bullet t \in s) \end{array} \right].$$

Problem 7.2 (size with commas)   page 279

Give axioms defining a function *size*1, which is like the *size* function but counts the commas in the informal representation of a t-expression as well as the symbols, parentheses, and angular brackets. For example,

$$size1\big(\mathrm{F}(\mathrm{Z},\ \mathrm{X},\ \mathrm{G}(\mathrm{Y})) \big)\ =\ 11.$$

Problem 7.3 (monotonicity of size)   page 279

Prove the *monotonicity* property of the *size* function, that is,

$$(\forall\, t\text{-}exp\ \ell,\ m) \left[\begin{array}{l} if\ \ \ell \unlhd m \\ then\ \ size(\ell) < size(m) \end{array} \right].$$

You may use without proof whatever properties of the nonnegative integers you require.

Problem 7.4 (subexpressions)   page 288

Show that the subexpressions function *subexps*(ℓ) is indeed the set of t-expressions that occur in ℓ, that is,

$$(\forall\, t\text{-}exp\ \ell,\ m)\big[\ell \in subexps(m)\ \equiv\ \ell \unlhd m\big].$$

8

Substitutions

We are about to augment our theory of t-expressions to include the notion of substitution. We have already used substitutions in propositional logic (Section [I]1.9) and predicate logic (Section [I]3.3). The difference in this chapter is that substitutions will become the object of discussion, i.e., domain elements of the intended model, just as nonnegative integers, trees, and tuples have been earlier. We shall be able to establish properties of substitutions that will play a crucial role in our construction of a deductive system for predicate logic.

8.1   THEORY OF SUBSTITUTIONS

In our preview (Section 7.1), we described the intended domain of the theory of substitutions. A substitution is a finite set of replacement pairs, in which variables are replaced by terms. Now let us present the theory formally.

THE VOCABULARY

The *theory of substitutions* augments the theory of t-expressions; the domain elements of its intended model include t-expressions as well as substitutions. We shall use Greek as well as italic symbols as variables; Greek letters will generally denote substitutions.

The vocabulary for this theory also includes the following:

- A unary predicate symbol $sub(\theta)$, characterizing the substitutions.

- A constant symbol $\{\ \}$, denoting the *empty substitution*, the substitution that makes no replacements at all.

- A binary function symbol $\ell \blacktriangleleft \theta$, denoting the *apply* function, which yields the t-expression obtained by applying the substitution θ to the t-expression ℓ.

- A ternary function symbol $(x \leftarrow e) \mathbin{\square} \theta$, denoting the *extension* function.

Under the intended model, $(x \leftarrow e) \mathbin{\square} \theta$ is the substitution that replaces the variable x with the expression e, and replaces any other variable y with $y \blacktriangleleft \theta$. Thus $(x \leftarrow e) \mathbin{\square} \theta$ agrees with the substitution θ on all variables other than x.

In the case in which θ already contains a replacement pair $x \leftarrow e'$, the new replacement $x \leftarrow e$ supersedes the original replacement $x \leftarrow e'$, which will be dropped.

In the case in which e is x itself, the replacement pair $x \leftarrow x$ is not included in the resulting substitution; furthermore, if a replacement pair $x \leftarrow e'$ is already contained in θ, it will be dropped from the resulting substitution in this case.

Note again that $(x \leftarrow e) \mathbin{\square} \theta$ is just an informal notation for a standard ternary function symbol such as $g_{17}(x,\ e,\ \theta)$.

Examples

Intuitively, in the intended model,

$$(Y \leftarrow B) \mathbin{\square} \{\ \} \quad \text{is} \quad \{Y \leftarrow B\}$$

$$(X \leftarrow F(Y)) \mathbin{\square} \{Y \leftarrow B\} \quad \text{is} \quad \{X \leftarrow F(Y),\ Y \leftarrow B\}$$

$$(X \leftarrow F(Y)) \mathbin{\square} \{X \leftarrow B\} \quad \text{is} \quad \{X \leftarrow F(Y)\}$$

$$(X \leftarrow X) \mathbin{\square} \{Y \leftarrow B\} \quad \text{is} \quad \{Y \leftarrow B\}$$

$$(X \leftarrow X) \mathbin{\square} \{X \leftarrow B\} \quad \text{is} \quad \{\ \}.\ \ \blacksquare$$

BASIC AXIOMS

The theory of substitutions is a theory with equality that includes the axioms for the theory of t-expressions as well as the following generation axioms and axioms for the apply function. It includes, in addition, special equality axioms and an induction principle, which will be presented later.

The generation axioms

$$sub(\{\,\}) \qquad\qquad\qquad\qquad\qquad\qquad (empty)$$

$$\begin{array}{l}(\forall\,var\,x)\\(\forall\,exp\,e)\\(\forall\,sub\,\theta)\end{array}\Big[sub\big((x \leftarrow e)\,{\scriptstyle\square}\,\theta\big)\Big] \qquad\qquad\qquad (extension)$$

The apply function axioms

The *apply* function $\ell \blacktriangleleft \theta$ is defined by the following axioms. There are separate axioms according to the sort of t-expression we consider.

For a variable, we have

$$(\forall\,var\,x)\big[x \blacktriangleleft \{\,\} = x\big] \qquad\qquad\qquad\qquad (variable\ empty)$$

$$\begin{array}{l}(\forall\,var\,x,\,y)\\\quad(\forall\,exp\,e)\\\quad(\forall\,sub\,\theta)\end{array}\left[y \blacktriangleleft \big((x \leftarrow e)\,{\scriptstyle\square}\,\theta\big) = \left\{\begin{array}{l}if\ \ x = y\\then\ \ e\\else\ \ y \blacktriangleleft \theta\end{array}\right\}\right] \quad (variable\ nonempty)$$

For an application, we have

$$\begin{array}{l}(\forall\,fun\,f)\\(\forall\,tuple\,t)\\(\forall\,sub\,\theta)\end{array}\Big[(f \bullet t) \blacktriangleleft \theta = f \bullet (t \blacktriangleleft \theta)\Big] \qquad\qquad (application)$$

For a tuple, we have

$$(\forall\,sub\,\theta)\big[\langle\,\rangle \blacktriangleleft \theta = \langle\,\rangle\big] \qquad\qquad\qquad (empty\ tuple)$$

$$\begin{array}{l}(\forall\,exp\,e)\\(\forall\,tuple\,t)\\(\forall\,sub\,\theta)\end{array}\Big[(e \diamond t) \blacktriangleleft \theta = (e \blacktriangleleft \theta) \diamond (t \blacktriangleleft \theta)\Big] \qquad (insertion)$$

Remark (supersedes)

According to the definition of the apply function, the replacement $x \leftarrow e$ in the substitution $(x \leftarrow e)\,{\scriptstyle\square}\,\theta$ supersedes any other replacement for x in θ, as mentioned earlier. For example, by the *variable-nonempty* axiom, if

$$\theta: \quad (x \leftarrow A)\,{\scriptstyle\square}\,\big((x \leftarrow G(Y))\,{\scriptstyle\square}\,\{\,\}\big),$$

then

$$X \triangleleft \theta : \quad A. \quad \lrcorner$$

The following example illustrates how we may use the axioms for the apply function $\triangleleft$ to compute the result of applying a particular substitution to a particular t-expression.

Example (computation of apply)

Consider the substitution

$$\theta : \quad \{X \leftarrow F(Y), \quad Y \leftarrow G(Z)\},$$

that is,

$$\theta : \quad \big(X \leftarrow F(Y)\big) \,\square\, \big(\big(Y \leftarrow G(Z)\big) \,\square\, \{\,\}\big).$$

Let us evaluate $H(X, U) \triangleleft \theta$ in steps.

By the axioms for the apply function $\triangleleft$, we have

$$X \triangleleft \theta \;=\; X \triangleleft \Big(\big(X \leftarrow F(Y)\big) \,\square\, \big(\big(Y \leftarrow G(Z)\big) \,\square\, \{\,\}\big)\Big)$$

$$=\; F(Y)$$
$$\text{(by the } \textit{variable-nonempty} \text{ axiom)}.$$

Also,

$$U \triangleleft \theta \;=\; U \triangleleft \Big(\big(X \leftarrow F(Y)\big) \,\square\, \big(\big(Y \leftarrow G(Z)\big) \,\square\, \{\,\}\big)\Big)$$

$$=\; U \triangleleft \big(\big(Y \leftarrow G(Z)\big) \,\square\, \{\,\}\big)$$
$$\text{(by the } \textit{variable-nonempty} \text{ axiom)}$$

$$=\; U \triangleleft \{\,\}$$
$$\text{(by the } \textit{variable-nonempty} \text{ axiom, again)}$$

$$=\; U$$
$$\text{(by the } \textit{variable-empty} \text{ axiom)}.$$

Also,

$$\langle\,\rangle \triangleleft \theta \;=\; \langle\,\rangle$$
$$\text{(by the } \textit{empty-tuple} \text{ axiom)}.$$

Therefore,

$$\langle X, U \rangle \triangleleft \theta \;=\; \big(X \diamond (U \diamond \langle\,\rangle)\big) \triangleleft \theta$$

$$= (\textsc{x} \triangleleft \theta) \diamond \big((\textsc{u} \diamond \langle\,\rangle) \triangleleft \theta\big)$$
$$\text{(by the \textit{insertion} axiom)}$$

$$= (\textsc{x} \triangleleft \theta) \diamond \big((\textsc{u} \triangleleft \theta) \diamond (\langle\,\rangle \triangleleft \theta)\big)$$
$$\text{(by the \textit{insertion} axiom, again)}$$

$$= \textsc{f}(\textsc{y}) \diamond (\textsc{u} \diamond \langle\,\rangle)$$
$$\text{(by the previous results of this example)}$$

$$= \langle \textsc{f}(\textsc{y}),\ \textsc{u} \rangle.$$

Finally,

$$\textsc{h}(\textsc{x},\ \textsc{u}) \triangleleft \theta = \big(\textsc{h} \bullet \langle \textsc{x},\ \textsc{u} \rangle\big) \triangleleft \theta$$

$$= \textsc{h} \bullet \big(\langle \textsc{x},\ \textsc{u}\rangle \triangleleft \theta\big)$$
$$\text{(by the \textit{application} axiom)}$$

$$= \textsc{h} \bullet \langle \textsc{f}(\textsc{y}),\ \textsc{u}\rangle$$
$$\text{(by the previous result of this example)}$$

$$= \textsc{h}\big(\textsc{f}(\textsc{y}),\ \textsc{u}\big).$$

In short,

$$\textsc{h}(\textsc{x},\ \textsc{u}) \triangleleft \theta = \textsc{h}\big(\textsc{f}(\textsc{y}),\ \textsc{u}\big). \quad \lrcorner$$

We are now ready to present the special equality axioms for substitutions.

EQUALITY AXIOMS

Informally we have said that two substitutions are equal if they have the same replacement pairs, regardless of their order. The equality axioms resemble the corresponding axioms for sets.

The equality axioms

$$(\forall var\ x,\ y) \atop (\forall exp\ d,\ e) \atop (\forall sub\ \theta) \left[{(x \leftarrow d) \circ ((y \leftarrow e) \circ \theta)} \atop {= \begin{cases} if\ x = y \\ then\ (x \leftarrow d) \circ \theta \\ else\ (y \leftarrow e) \circ ((x \leftarrow d) \circ \theta) \end{cases}} \right]$$

$$(double\ replacement)$$

$$(\forall var\ x)\Big[(x \leftarrow x) \circ \{\,\} = \{\,\}\Big] \qquad\qquad (identity)$$

The *double-replacement* axiom states, in the *then*-part, that a new replacement pair supersedes all existing replacement pairs in a substitution; the *else*-part states that the order of applying replacement pairs with distinct variables is irrelevant. The *identity* axiom expresses that the substitution with the single replacement pair $(x \leftarrow x)$ is identical to the empty substitution.

Substitutions, like sets, have no uniqueness property, and we therefore have no uniqueness axioms. Substitutions may be equal even though they have been constructed in different ways according to the generation axioms.

Example

We have

$$(Y \leftarrow Z) \circ \big((X \leftarrow V) \circ \big((U \leftarrow U) \circ \{\,\}\big)\big)$$

$$= (Y \leftarrow Z) \circ \big((X \leftarrow V) \circ \{\,\}\big)$$

$$= (X \leftarrow V) \circ \big((Y \leftarrow Z) \circ \{\,\}\big).$$

Also

$$(X \leftarrow Y) \circ \big((X \leftarrow Z) \circ \{\,\}\big)$$

$$= (X \leftarrow Y) \circ \{\,\}.$$

Furthermore,

$$(X \leftarrow X) \circ \big((X \leftarrow Y) \circ \{\,\}\big)$$

$$= (X \leftarrow X) \circ \{\,\}$$

$$= \{\,\}. \quad \lrcorner$$

Remark (not equal)

Note that it is not always the case that

$$(x \leftarrow x) \circ \theta \;=\; \theta,$$

where x is a variable and θ a substitution. For example,

$$(X \leftarrow X) \circ \big((X \leftarrow Y) \circ \{\,\}\big) \;\neq\; (X \leftarrow Y) \circ \{\,\}$$

because

$$X \blacktriangleleft \Big((X \leftarrow X) \circ \big((X \leftarrow Y) \circ \{\,\}\big)\Big) \;=\; X$$

$$X \blacktriangleleft \big((X \leftarrow Y) \circ \{\,\}\big) \;=\; Y.$$

Had the substitutions been equal, applying them to x would yield the same t-expression. ⌟

INDUCTION PRINCIPLE

The substitution induction principle

For each sentence $\mathcal{F}[\theta]$ in the theory, where x and e do not occur free in $\mathcal{F}[\theta]$,

the universal closure of the sentence

$$
if\quad
\begin{bmatrix}
\mathcal{F}[\{\,\}] \\
and \\
(\forall\,var\ x) \\
(\forall\,exp\ e) \\
(\forall\,sub\ \theta)
\end{bmatrix}
\begin{bmatrix}
if\ \ x \blacktriangleleft \theta = x\ \ and\ \ not\ (x = e) \\
then\ \ if\ \ \mathcal{F}[\theta] \\
then\ \ \mathcal{F}\big[(x \leftarrow e) \square\, \theta\big]
\end{bmatrix}
$$

$$
then\ \ (\forall\,sub\ \theta)\mathcal{F}[\theta] \qquad\qquad (substitution\ induction)
$$

is an axiom.

According to the *substitution induction* principle, to establish that

$$(\forall\,sub\ \theta)\mathcal{F}[\theta],$$

it suffices to show the *base case*,

$$\mathcal{F}[\{\,\}],$$

and the *inductive step*,

$$
\begin{matrix}
(\forall\,var\ x) \\
(\forall\,exp\ e) \\
(\forall\,sub\ \theta)
\end{matrix}
\begin{bmatrix}
if\ \ x \blacktriangleleft \theta = x\ \ and\ \ not\ (x = e) \\
then\ \ if\ \ \mathcal{F}[\theta] \\
then\ \ \mathcal{F}\big[(x \leftarrow e) \square\, \theta\big]
\end{bmatrix}.
$$

The inductive step states that, for an arbitrary extension $(x \leftarrow e) \square\, \theta$, if the *induction hypothesis*

$$\mathcal{F}[\theta]$$

is true, then the *desired conclusion*,

$$\mathcal{F}\big[(x \leftarrow e) \square\, \theta\big],$$

is also true. The *initial suppositions* of the inductive step,

$$x \blacktriangleleft \theta = x \quad and \quad not\ (x = e),$$

allow us to assume that the substitution θ makes no replacement for the variable x, but that the extension $(x \leftarrow e) \mathbin{\square} \theta$ does. We call $\mathcal{F}[\theta]$ the *inductive sentence*.

This concludes the axioms for the theory of substitutions.

PROPERTIES

From these axioms we can establish the basic property of the empty substitution,

$$(\forall\, t\text{-}exp\ \ell)\big[\ell \triangleleft \{\,\} = \ell\big] \qquad\qquad (empty\ substitution)$$

and the following sort properties of the apply function:

$$\begin{array}{l}(\forall\ var\ x)\\(\forall\ sub\ \theta)\end{array}\big[exp(x \triangleleft \theta)\big] \qquad\qquad (variable\ sort)$$

$$\begin{array}{l}(\forall\ appl\ e)\\(\forall\ sub\ \theta)\end{array}\big[appl(e \triangleleft \theta)\big] \qquad\qquad (application\ sort)$$

$$\begin{array}{l}(\forall\ exp\ e)\\(\forall\ sub\ \theta)\end{array}\big[exp(e \triangleleft \theta)\big] \qquad\qquad (expression\ sort)$$

$$\begin{array}{l}(\forall\ tuple\ t)\\(\forall\ sub\ \theta)\end{array}\big[tuple(t \triangleleft \theta)\big] \qquad\qquad (tuple\ sort)$$

$$\begin{array}{l}(\forall\ t\text{-}exp\ \ell)\\(\forall\ sub\ \theta)\end{array}\big[t\text{-}exp(\ell \triangleleft \theta)\big] \qquad\qquad (t\text{-}expression\ sort)$$

In other words, the result of applying a substitution to an expression or a tuple, for instance, is itself an expression or a tuple, respectively. The proofs are requested as an exercise (**Problem 8.1**).

MONOTONICITY

Let us introduce a simple property relating t-expressions and substitutions.

Proposition (monotonicity)

The sentences

$$\begin{array}{l}(\forall\, t\text{-}exp\ \ell,\ m)\\(\forall\ sub\ \theta)\end{array}\left[\begin{array}{l}if\ \ell \in m\\then\ \ell \triangleleft \theta \in m \triangleleft \theta\end{array}\right] \qquad (strict\ monotonicity)$$

$$(\forall\, t\text{-}exp\ \ell,\ m)\ \begin{bmatrix} if\ \ \ell \sqsubseteq m \\ (\forall\ sub\ \theta)\ \ then\ \ \ell \triangleleft \theta \sqsubseteq m \triangleleft \theta \end{bmatrix} \qquad\qquad (weak\ monotonicity)$$

are valid. ⌐

In other words, the occurrence and proper-occurrence relations are maintained after the application of a substitution. The proof is left as an exercise (**Problem 8.2**).

Let us now define two new functions.

THE SUBTRACTION FUNCTION

The *subtraction* function $\theta - x$ yields the substitution that agrees with the substitution θ on all variables other than the variable x, but that makes no replacement for x at all. For example,

$$\{\text{X} \leftarrow \text{A},\ \text{Y} \leftarrow \text{G}(\text{X})\}\ -\ \text{X}\ =\ \{\text{Y} \leftarrow \text{G}(\text{X})\}$$

$$\{\text{Y} \leftarrow \text{G}(\text{X})\}\ -\ \text{X}\ =\ \{\text{Y} \leftarrow \text{G}(\text{X})\}.$$

The subtraction function is defined by the axiom

$$\begin{array}{|l}
\hline
(\forall\ var\ x) \\
(\forall\ sub\ \theta)\ \Big[\theta - x\ =\ (x \leftarrow x) \circ \theta\Big] \qquad\qquad\qquad (subtraction) \\
\hline
\end{array}$$

From this axiom, we can establish the following properties:

$$\begin{array}{l}(\forall\ var\ x) \\ (\forall\ sub\ \theta)\end{array}\Big[sub(\theta - x)\Big] \qquad\qquad\qquad\qquad (sort)$$

$$\begin{array}{l}(\forall\ var\ x,\ y) \\ \quad\ (\forall\ sub\ \theta)\end{array}\left[y \triangleleft (\theta - x)\ =\ \left\{\begin{array}{l} if\ \ y = x \\ then\ \ y \\ else\ \ y \triangleleft \theta \end{array}\right\}\right] \qquad (variable)$$

THE REPLACEMENT FUNCTION

For any variable x and expression e, we define a binary function symbol, the *replacement* function $\{x \leftarrow e\}$, to yield the substitution that contains the single replacement pair $x \leftarrow e$. It is defined by the axiom

$$\begin{array}{l} (\forall \ var \ x) \\ (\forall \ exp \ e) \end{array} \Big[\{x \leftarrow e\} \ = \ (x \leftarrow e) \circ \{\ \} \Big] \qquad (replacement)$$

Somewhat inaccurately, we shall sometimes refer to the substitution $\{x \leftarrow e\}$ itself as a replacement pair.

We immediately obtain the following properties of the replacement function:

$$\begin{array}{l} (\forall \ var \ x) \\ (\forall \ exp \ e) \end{array} \Big[sub\big(\{x \leftarrow e\}\big) \Big] \qquad (sort)$$

$$(\forall \ var \ x) \Big[\{x \leftarrow x\} \ = \ \{\ \} \Big] \qquad (identity)$$

$$\begin{array}{l} (\forall \ var \ x, \ y) \\ (\forall \ exp \ e) \end{array} \left[y \blacktriangleleft \{x \leftarrow e\} \ = \ \left\{ \begin{array}{l} if \ \ x = y \\ then \ \ e \\ else \ \ y \end{array} \right\} \right] \qquad (variable)$$

The following properties summarize the effect of applying a replacement pair to a t-expression, in terms of the variables that occur in the t-expression:

$$\begin{array}{l} (\forall \ var \ x) \\ (\forall \ exp \ e) \\ (\forall \ t\text{-}exp \ \ell) \end{array} \Big[varset\big(\ell \blacktriangleleft \{x \leftarrow e\}\big) \ \subseteq \ varset(\ell) \cup varset(e) \Big]$$

$$(variable \ introduction)$$

In other words, if a variable occurs in a t-expression after application of a replacement pair $\{x \leftarrow e\}$, then either it was in the t-expression originally or it is in the right-hand side e of the replacement pair.

$$\begin{array}{l} (\forall \ var \ x) \\ (\forall \ exp \ e) \end{array} \left[\begin{array}{l} if \ \ not \ (x \Subset e) \\ then \ \ (\forall \ t\text{-}exp \ \ell) \Big[not \ \big(x \in varset\big(\ell \blacktriangleleft \{x \leftarrow e\}\big)\big) \Big] \end{array} \right]$$

$$(variable \ elimination)$$

In other words, if the replaced variable x of a replacement pair $\{x \leftarrow e\}$ does not occur in the right-hand side e, then applying the pair to a t-expression ℓ removes it from the t-expression.

The reader is requested to prove these properties in **Problem 8.3**.

8.2 EQUALITY RELATION

In this section, we establish the basic equality property that, if two substitutions have the same effect on all variables, they are equal. But now we must prove some preliminary results.

We first show that if a substitution has no effect on any variable, it is equal to the empty substitution.

Proposition (identity empty)

The sentence

$$(\forall \, sub \,\, \theta) \begin{bmatrix} if \,\, (\forall \, var \,\, x)[x \blacktriangleleft \theta = x] \\ then \,\, \theta = \{\,\} \end{bmatrix} \qquad (identity \,\, empty)$$

is valid. ◢

Proof

The proof is by substitution induction on θ, taking our inductive sentence to be

$$\mathcal{F}[\theta] : \quad \begin{matrix} if \,\, (\forall \, var \,\, x)[x \blacktriangleleft \theta = x] \\ then \,\, \theta = \{\,\} \end{matrix}$$

Base Case

We would like to show

$$\mathcal{F}[\{\,\}] : \quad \begin{matrix} if \,\, (\forall \, var \,\, x)\big[x \blacktriangleleft \{\,\} = x\big] \\ then \,\, \{\,\} = \{\,\}. \end{matrix}$$

But this is true because the consequent $\{\,\} = \{\,\}$ is true.

Inductive Step

For an arbitrary substitution θ, variable y, and expression e, we suppose initially

$$(\dagger) \qquad y \blacktriangleleft \theta = y \quad and \quad not \,(y = e),$$

assume the induction hypothesis

$$\mathcal{F}[\theta] : \quad \begin{matrix} if \,\, (\forall \, var \,\, x)[x \blacktriangleleft \theta = x] \\ then \,\, \theta = \{\,\}, \end{matrix}$$

and show the desired conclusion

$$\mathcal{F}[(y \leftarrow e) \square \theta] : \quad \begin{matrix} if \,\, (\forall \, var \,\, x)\Big[x \blacktriangleleft \big((y \leftarrow e) \square \theta\big) = x\Big] \\ then \,\, (y \leftarrow e) \square \theta = \{\,\}. \end{matrix}$$

We show that the antecedent must be false. For suppose that

$$(\forall\, var\ x)\big[x \blacktriangleleft ((y \leftarrow e) \mathbin{\square} \theta)\ =\ x\big].$$

Then we have (taking x to be y)

$$y \blacktriangleleft ((y \leftarrow e) \mathbin{\square} \theta)\ =\ y$$

and hence (by the *variable-nonempty* axiom for $\blacktriangleleft$)

$$e = y.$$

But this contradicts *not* $(y = e)$, an initial supposition (†) of our inductive step. ⌟

We can also establish the following property of substitutions:

$$\genfrac{}{}{0pt}{}{(\forall\, var\ x)}{(\forall\, sub\ \theta)}\big[\theta\ =\ (x \leftarrow x \blacktriangleleft \theta) \mathbin{\square} \theta\big] \qquad\qquad (representation)$$

As an immediate consequence of the *representation* property, we have the *decomposition* property that, for each variable x, any substitution θ may be decomposed into two parts: a replacement pair $(x \leftarrow (x \blacktriangleleft \theta))$ and the substitution $\theta - x$, which has no effect on x:

$$\genfrac{}{}{0pt}{}{(\forall\, var\ x)}{(\forall\, sub\ \theta)}\big[\theta\ =\ (x \leftarrow x \blacktriangleleft \theta) \mathbin{\square} (\theta - x)\big] \qquad\qquad (decomposition)$$

The reader is requested to prove both properties in **Problem 8.4**.

Finally, we are ready to establish the fundamental result of this section, that if two substitutions agree (i.e., have the same effect) on all variables, they are equal.

Proposition (variable equality)

The sentence

$$(\forall\, sub\ \theta,\ \phi)\ \begin{bmatrix} \theta = \phi \\ \equiv \\ (\forall\, var\ x)[x \blacktriangleleft \theta = x \blacktriangleleft \phi] \end{bmatrix} \qquad\qquad (variable\ equality)$$

is valid. ⌟

Proof

The proof in the forward direction is immediate, by the substitutivity of equality. We must show the other direction, that is,

$$(\forall\, sub\ \theta,\ \phi)\ \begin{bmatrix} if\ (\forall\, var\ x)[x \blacktriangleleft \theta = x \blacktriangleleft \phi] \\ then\ \theta = \phi \end{bmatrix}.$$

The proof is by substitution induction on ϕ, taking the inductive sentence to be

$$\mathcal{F}[\phi]: \quad (\forall \, sub \,\, \theta) \begin{bmatrix} if & (\forall \, var \,\, x)[x \blacktriangleleft \theta = x \blacktriangleleft \phi] \\ then & \theta = \phi \end{bmatrix}.$$

Base Case

We would like to show

$$\mathcal{F}[\{\,\}]: \quad (\forall \, sub \,\, \theta) \begin{bmatrix} if & (\forall \, var \,\, x)[x \blacktriangleleft \theta = x \blacktriangleleft \{\,\}] \\ then & \theta = \{\,\} \end{bmatrix},$$

that is (by the *variable-empty* axiom for $\blacktriangleleft$),

$$(\forall \, sub \,\, \theta) \begin{bmatrix} if & (\forall \, var \,\, x)[x \blacktriangleleft \theta = x] \\ then & \theta = \{\,\} \end{bmatrix}.$$

But this holds by the preceding *identity-empty* proposition.

Inductive Step

Consider an arbitrary substitution ϕ, variable y, and expression e. We assume the induction hypothesis

$$\mathcal{F}[\phi]: \quad (\forall \, sub \,\, \theta) \begin{bmatrix} if & (\forall \, var \,\, x)[x \blacktriangleleft \theta = x \blacktriangleleft \phi] \\ then & \theta = \phi \end{bmatrix}$$

and show the desired conclusion

$$\mathcal{F}[(y \leftarrow e) \,\square\, \phi]: \quad (\forall \, sub \,\, \theta') \begin{bmatrix} if & (\forall \, var \,\, x)[x \blacktriangleleft \theta' = x \blacktriangleleft ((y \leftarrow e) \,\square\, \phi)] \\ then & \theta' = (y \leftarrow e) \,\square\, \phi \end{bmatrix}.$$

(Note that, according to the induction principle, we could also make the initial supposition that $y \blacktriangleleft \phi = y$ and *not* $(y = e)$, but we shall not do so because we do not need these conditions for the proof.)

We consider an arbitrary substitution θ'. We suppose that

(†) $\qquad (\forall \, var \,\, x)\big[x \blacktriangleleft \theta' = x \blacktriangleleft ((y \leftarrow e) \,\square\, \phi)\big]$

and show that

(††) $\qquad \theta' = (y \leftarrow e) \,\square\, \phi.$

By our supposition (†), we have (taking x to be y)

$$y \blacktriangleleft \theta' = y \blacktriangleleft \big((y \leftarrow e) \,\square\, \phi\big)$$

$$= e$$

$$\text{(by the } \textit{variable-nonempty} \text{ axiom for } \blacktriangleleft).$$

Since (by the *representation* property of substitutions)

$$\theta' = (y \leftarrow y \blacktriangleleft \theta') \,\square\, \theta',$$

we therefore have (because $y \blacktriangleleft \theta' = e$)

(‡) $\quad \theta' = (y \leftarrow e) \,\square\, \theta'.$

Consider the substitution

(§) $\quad \phi' = (y \leftarrow y \blacktriangleleft \phi) \,\square\, \theta'.$

We claim that

(‡‡) $\quad (\forall\, var\ x)\big[x \blacktriangleleft \phi' = x \blacktriangleleft \phi\big].$

Let us first show that proving (‡‡) enables us to establish the desired result (††); then we shall prove (‡‡).

Proof (‡‡) $\Rightarrow$ (††)

If (‡‡) is true, we can apply our induction hypothesis $\mathcal{F}[\phi]$ (taking θ to be ϕ'), to conclude that

$$\phi' = \phi$$

and therefore that

$$(y \leftarrow e) \,\square\, \phi' = (y \leftarrow e) \,\square\, \phi,$$

that is (by (§)),

$$(y \leftarrow e) \,\square\, \big((y \leftarrow y \blacktriangleleft \phi) \,\square\, \theta'\big) = (y \leftarrow e) \,\square\, \phi.$$

Hence (by the *double-replacement* equality axiom for substitutions)

$$(y \leftarrow e) \,\square\, \theta' = (y \leftarrow e) \,\square\, \phi$$

and (by (‡))

$$\theta' = (y \leftarrow e) \,\square\, \phi,$$

which is our desired result (††).

Proof of (‡‡)

We would like to show that

$$(\forall\, var\ x)\big[x \blacktriangleleft \phi' = x \blacktriangleleft \phi\big].$$

We consider an arbitrary variable x and show that

$$x \blacktriangleleft \phi' = x \blacktriangleleft \phi.$$

We distinguish between two cases, depending on whether or not x is distinct from y.

Case: $x = y$

> Then
>
> $$x \blacktriangleleft \phi' \;=\; y \blacktriangleleft \phi'$$
>
> $$= \; y \blacktriangleleft \big((y \leftarrow y \blacktriangleleft \phi) \circ \theta'\big)$$
> (by (§))
>
> $$= \; y \blacktriangleleft \phi$$
> (by the *variable-nonempty* axiom for $\blacktriangleleft$)
>
> $$= \; x \blacktriangleleft \phi.$$

Case: $not\ (x = y)$

> Then
>
> $$x \blacktriangleleft \phi' \;=\; x \blacktriangleleft \big((y \leftarrow y \blacktriangleleft \phi) \circ \theta'\big)$$
> (by (§))
>
> $$= \; x \blacktriangleleft \theta'$$
> (by the *variable-nonempty* axiom for $\blacktriangleleft$,
> because $not\ (x = y)$)
>
> $$= \; x \blacktriangleleft \big((y \leftarrow e) \circ \phi\big)$$
> (by our supposition (†))
>
> $$= \; x \blacktriangleleft \phi$$
> (by the *variable-nonempty* axiom for $\blacktriangleleft$, once again). ◣

We have shown that two substitutions are equal if they agree on all variables. It follows that they are equal if they agree on all t-expressions.

Corollary (t-expression equality)

> The sentence
>
> $$(\forall\ sub\ \theta,\ \phi) \begin{bmatrix} \theta = \phi \\[2pt] \equiv \\[2pt] (\forall\ t\text{-}exp\ \ell)\big[\ell \blacktriangleleft \theta = \ell \blacktriangleleft \phi\big] \end{bmatrix} \qquad (\textit{t-expression equality})$$
>
> is valid. ◣

The proof in the left-to-right direction follows from the substitutivity of equality. The proof in the other direction follows from the preceding *variable-equality* proposition, because if two substitutions agree on all t-expressions, they certainly agree on all variables.

AGREEMENT

Two substitutions agree on a t-expression if they have the same effect on that t-expression. In this section, we establish several useful properties of this notion.

We first show that two substitutions agree on a t-expression precisely when they agree on all the variables of the t-expression.

Proposition (agreement)

The sentence

$$
(\forall\, t\text{-}exp\ \ell)\atop(\forall\, sub\ \theta,\ \phi)
\begin{bmatrix}
\ell \blacktriangleleft \theta = \ell \blacktriangleleft \phi \\
\equiv \\
(\forall\, var\ x)
\begin{bmatrix}
if\ \ x \in \ell \\
then\ \ x \blacktriangleleft \theta = x \blacktriangleleft \phi
\end{bmatrix}
\end{bmatrix}
\qquad (agreement)
$$

is valid. ⌟

As an immediate consequence of the *agreement* proposition, we can establish the following property of the subtraction function:

$$
(\forall\, var\ x)\atop{(\forall\, t\text{-}exp\ \ell)\atop(\forall\, sub\ \theta)}
\begin{bmatrix}
if\ \ not\ (x \in \ell) \\
then\ \ \ell \blacktriangleleft \theta\ =\ \ell \blacktriangleleft (\theta - x)
\end{bmatrix}
\qquad (agreement)
$$

In other words, if a variable x does not occur in a t-expression ℓ, then θ and $\theta - x$ agree on ℓ.

The reader is requested to prove these properties in **Problem 8.5**.

8.3   DOMAIN AND RANGE FUNCTIONS

We augmented the theory of t-expressions by introducing a theory of sets of variables. Augmenting the theory of substitutions in the same way, we define a unary function $dom(\theta)$ to yield the set of variables affected by the substitution θ. Under the intended model, if

$$\theta \;=\; \{x_1 \leftarrow e_1,\; x_2 \leftarrow e_2,\; \ldots,\; x_n \leftarrow e_n\},$$

then $dom(\theta)$ is the set of variables $\{x_1, x_2, \ldots, x_n\}$.

For example,

$$dom(\{\text{x} \leftarrow \text{y},\; \text{z} \leftarrow \text{u}\}) \;=\; \{\text{x, z}\}.$$

The *domain* function is defined formally by the following axioms:

$$dom(\{\,\}) \;=\; \{\,\} \qquad\qquad\qquad (empty)$$

$$(\forall\; var\; x) \atop {(\forall\; exp\; e) \atop (\forall\; sub\; \theta)} \left[dom((x \leftarrow e)\,\square\,\theta) = \left\{ \begin{array}{l} if\ \ x = e \\ then\ \ dom\,(\theta) \sim \{x\} \\ else\ \ x \circ dom(\theta) \end{array} \right\} \right] \quad (extension)$$

We must distinguish between the empty substitution (as on the left-hand side of the *empty* axiom) and the empty set (as on the right-hand side).

From the axioms, we can establish the following properties:

$$(\forall\; sub\; \theta)\big[set\big(dom(\theta)\big)\big] \qquad\qquad\qquad (sort)$$

$$(\forall\; var\; x) \atop (\forall\; exp\; e) \left[dom(\{x \leftarrow e\}) \;=\; \left\{ \begin{array}{l} if\ \ x = e \\ then\ \ \{\,\} \\ else\ \ \{x\} \end{array} \right\} \right] \qquad (replacement)$$

$$(\forall\; sub\; \theta) \left[\begin{array}{l} if\ \ dom(\theta) = \{\,\} \\ then\ \ \theta = \{\,\} \end{array} \right] \qquad\qquad (empty)$$

$$(\forall\; var\; x) \atop (\forall\; sub\; \theta) \left[dom(\theta - x) \;=\; dom(\theta) \sim \{x\} \right] \qquad (subtraction)$$

The proof of the *empty* property is requested as an exercise (**Problem 8.6(a)**).

CHARACTERIZATION OF DOMAIN

Let us now establish a proposition that characterizes the domain of a substitution.

Proposition (domain)

The sentence

$$(\forall\ var\ x) \atop (\forall\ sub\ \theta) \left[{x \in dom(\theta) \atop \equiv \atop not\ (x \blacktriangleleft \theta = x)} \right] \qquad\qquad (domain)$$

is valid. ⌟

In other words, the domain of a substitution is precisely the set of variables that are affected by the application of that substitution.

Proof

Consider an arbitrary variable x; we would like to show that

$$(\forall\ sub\ \theta) \left[{x \in dom(\theta) \atop \equiv \atop not\ (x \blacktriangleleft \theta = x)} \right].$$

The proof is by substitution induction on θ, taking the inductive sentence to be

$$\mathcal{F}[\theta]: \quad {x \in dom(\theta) \atop \equiv \atop not\ (x \blacktriangleleft \theta = x).}$$

Base Case

We would like to show

$$\mathcal{F}[\{\,\}]: \quad {x \in dom(\{\,\}) \atop \equiv \atop not\ (x \blacktriangleleft \{\,\} = x).}$$

We know that the left-hand side,

$$x \in dom(\{\,\}),$$

reduces (by the *empty* axiom for *dom*) to

$$x \in \{\,\},$$

which is false (by the *empty* axiom for $\in$).

On the other hand, the right-hand side,

$$not\ (x \blacktriangleleft \{\,\} = x),$$

is also false (by the *variable-empty* axiom for ◄).

Since both sides of the equivalence are false, the entire base case is true.

Inductive Step

We would like to show that

$$(\forall \, var \, y) \begin{bmatrix} if \ \ y \blacktriangleleft \theta = y \ \ and \ \ not \, (y = e) \\ then \ \ if \ \ \mathcal{F}[\theta] \\ then \ \ \mathcal{F}\big[(y \leftarrow e) \, \square \, \theta\big] \end{bmatrix}$$
$$(\forall \, exp \, e)$$
$$(\forall \, sub \, \theta)$$

For an arbitrary variable y, expression e, and substitution θ, we suppose initially

$$y \blacktriangleleft \theta = y \qquad and \qquad not \, (y = e),$$

assume the induction hypothesis

$$\mathcal{F}[\theta]: \quad \begin{array}{c} x \in dom(\theta) \\ \equiv \\ not \, (x \blacktriangleleft \theta = x), \end{array}$$

and show the desired conclusion

$$\mathcal{F}\big[(y \leftarrow e) \, \square \, \theta\big]: \quad \begin{array}{c} x \in dom\big((y \leftarrow e) \, \square \, \theta\big) \\ \equiv \\ not \, \big(x \blacktriangleleft \big((y \leftarrow e) \, \square \, \theta\big) = x\big). \end{array}$$

The proof distinguishes between two cases, depending on whether or not x and y are distinct.

Case: $x = y$

Then we have supposed that

$$x \blacktriangleleft \theta = x \qquad and \qquad not \, (x = e).$$

The left-hand side of $\mathcal{F}\big[(y \leftarrow e) \, \square \, \theta\big]$, which is in this case

$$x \in dom\big((x \leftarrow e) \, \square \, \theta\big),$$

holds precisely when (by the *extension* axiom for *dom*, because *not* $(x = e)$)

$$x \in x \circ dom(\theta)$$

precisely when (by the *insertion* axiom for $\in$)

$$x = x \ \ or \ \ x \in dom(\theta),$$

which is true.

But the right-hand side of $\mathcal{F}\big[(y \leftarrow e) \mathbin{\scriptstyle\square} \theta\big]$, which is in this case

$$not\ (x \blacktriangleleft ((x \leftarrow e) \mathbin{\scriptstyle\square} \theta)\ =\ x),$$

holds precisely when (by the *variable-nonempty* axiom for $\blacktriangleleft$)

$$not\ (e = x),$$

which is also true, by our supposition.

Since both sides of the equivalence are true, this establishes the desired conclusion in this case.

Case: $not\ (x = y)$

The left-hand side of $\mathcal{F}\big[(y \leftarrow e) \mathbin{\scriptstyle\square} \theta\big]$,

$$x\ \in\ dom((y \leftarrow e) \mathbin{\scriptstyle\square} \theta),$$

holds precisely when (by the *extension* axiom for *dom*, because by our supposition $not\ (y = e)$)

$$x\ \in\ y \circ dom(\theta)$$

precisely when (by the *insertion* axiom for $\in$)

$$x = y\ \ or\ \ x \in dom(\theta)$$

precisely when (by our case assumption that $not\ (x = y)$)

$$x \in dom(\theta)$$

precisely when (by our induction hypothesis $\mathcal{F}[\theta]$)

$$not\ (x \blacktriangleleft \theta = x).$$

But the right-hand side of $\mathcal{F}\big[(y \leftarrow e) \mathbin{\scriptstyle\square} \theta\big]$,

$$not\ (x \blacktriangleleft ((y \leftarrow e) \mathbin{\scriptstyle\square} \theta)\ =\ x),$$

holds precisely when (by the *variable-nonempty* axiom for $\blacktriangleleft$, because $not\ (x = y)$)

$$not\ (x \blacktriangleleft \theta = x).$$

Since both sides of the equivalence hold precisely when $not\ (x \blacktriangleleft \theta = x)$, this establishes the desired conclusion in this case.

We have thus established the inductive step in both cases. ∎

MODIFIED INDUCTION PRINCIPLE

We can now rephrase the *substitution induction* principle as follows:

For each sentence $\mathcal{F}[\theta]$, where x and e do not occur free in $\mathcal{F}[\theta]$, the universal closure of the sentence

$$
if\quad
\begin{bmatrix}
\mathcal{F}[\{\,\}] \\
and \\
(\forall\,var\ x) \\
(\forall\,exp\ e) \\
(\forall\,sub\ \theta)
\end{bmatrix}
\begin{bmatrix}
if\ \ not\ (x \in dom(\theta))\ \ and\ \ not\ (x = e) \\
then\ \ if\ \ \mathcal{F}[\theta] \\
\qquad then\ \ \mathcal{F}\big[(x \leftarrow e) \diamond \theta\big]
\end{bmatrix}
$$

$$then\ \ (\forall\,sub\ \theta)\mathcal{F}[\theta]\qquad\qquad (modified\ substitution\ induction)$$

is valid.

Here we have used the *domain* property to replace the condition $x \triangleleft \theta = x$ in the original induction principle with $not\ (x \in dom(\theta))$.

MODIFIED VARIABLE-EQUALITY PROPERTY

Using the domain function, we can now modify the *variable-equality* property to state that two substitutions are equal if they agree on all variables of their domains:

$$
(\forall\,sub\ \theta,\ \phi)
\begin{bmatrix}
\theta = \phi \\
\equiv \\
(\forall\,var\ x)
\begin{bmatrix}
if\ \ x \in \big(dom(\theta) \cup dom(\phi)\big) \\
then\ \ x \triangleleft \theta = x \triangleleft \phi
\end{bmatrix}
\end{bmatrix}
$$

$$(domain\ equality)$$

The reader is requested to prove this and another domain property in **Problem 8.6(b)(c)**.

THE RANGE FUNCTION

In our combined theory of t-expressions, substitutions, and sets of variables, we can define further a unary function symbol $range(\theta)$. Under the intended model, if θ is the substitution

$$\{x_1 \leftarrow e_1,\ x_2 \leftarrow e_2,\ \ldots,\ x_n \leftarrow e_n\},$$

then $range(\theta)$ is the set of variables that occur in any of the e_i's. For example,

$$range(\{X \leftarrow F(Y, Z), \; Y \leftarrow G(Z)\}) \;=\; \{Y, \; Z\}.$$

The *range* function is defined by the following axioms:

$$range(\{\,\}) \;=\; \{\,\} \qquad\qquad\qquad\qquad\qquad\qquad (empty)$$

$$(\forall\, var\ x) \atop (\forall\, exp\ e) \atop (\forall\, sub\ \theta)\ \left[\, range\left((x \leftarrow e) \circ \theta\right) \;=\; \begin{cases} if\ \ x = e \\ then\ \ range(\theta - x) \\ else\ \ varset(e) \cup range(\theta - x) \end{cases} \right]$$

$$(extension)$$

From the axioms we can establish the following properties:

$$(\forall\, sub\ \theta)\left[set\left(range(\theta)\right)\right] \qquad\qquad\qquad\qquad\qquad (sort)$$

$$(\forall\, var\ x) \atop (\forall\, exp\ e)\ \left[\begin{array}{l} range(\{x \leftarrow e\}) \\ = \; \begin{cases} if\ \ x = e \\ then\ \ \{\,\} \\ else\ \ varset(e) \end{cases} \end{array}\right] \qquad (replacement)$$

$$(\forall\, var\ y) \atop (\forall\, sub\ \theta)\ \left[\begin{array}{l} y \in range(\theta) \\ \equiv \\ (\exists\, var\ x)\left[\begin{array}{c} x \in dom(\theta) \\ and \\ y \sqsubseteq x \blacktriangleleft \theta \end{array}\right] \end{array}\right] \qquad (range)$$

That is, the range of a substitution θ is the set of all variables that occur on the right-hand side of a replacement pair of θ.

The *range* property characterizes the range of a substitution; the reader is requested to prove this property in **Problem 8.7**.

INVARIANCE PROPERTIES

An immediate consequence of the *agreement* proposition tells what happens if all the variables of a t-expression are unaffected by a substitution:

$$(\forall\, t\text{-}exp\ \ell) \atop (\forall\, sub\ \theta)\ \left[\begin{array}{l} \ell \blacktriangleleft \theta = \ell \\ \equiv \\ varset(\ell) \cap dom(\theta) \;=\; \{\,\} \end{array}\right] \qquad (invariance)$$

In other words, a substitution has no effect on a t-expression precisely when it has no effect on any of its variables.

A special instance of the property is obtained by taking θ to be a replacement $\{x \leftarrow e\}$:

$$
\begin{array}{l} (\forall \, var \; x) \\ (\forall \, exp \; e) \\ (\forall \, t\text{-}exp \; \ell) \end{array} \left[\begin{array}{l} if \;\; not \; (x \trianglelefteq \ell) \\ then \;\; \ell \triangleleft \{x \leftarrow e\} = \ell \end{array} \right] \qquad (replacement \; invariance)
$$

In other words, applying a replacement $\{x \leftarrow e\}$ to a t-expression ℓ has no effect on the t-expression if the variable x does not occur in ℓ.

The reader is requested to prove the two invariance properties in **Problem 8.8**.

8.4 COMPOSITION OF SUBSTITUTIONS

The composition $\theta \square \lambda$ of two substitutions θ and λ is a substitution that, when applied to a t-expression, will have the same effect as applying first θ and then λ. In other words, the composition function will have the *composition* property, that

$$
\ell \triangleleft (\theta \square \lambda) \;=\; (\ell \triangleleft \theta) \triangleleft \lambda,
$$

for every t-expression ℓ.

We do not take the preceding property as the definition, however, because it is not clear that any substitution $\theta \square \lambda$ satisfying the *composition* property actually exists, that is, can be expressed as a set of replacement pairs. Instead, we define the composition function by the following axioms:

$$
\boxed{\begin{array}{l}
(\forall \, sub \; \lambda) \big[\{ \, \} \square \lambda \;=\; \lambda \big] \qquad\qquad\qquad\qquad\qquad (left \; empty) \\[2em]
\begin{array}{l} (\forall \, var \; x) \\ (\forall \, exp \; e) \\ (\forall \, sub \; \theta, \; \lambda) \end{array} \Big[\big((x \leftarrow e) \square \theta\big) \square \lambda \;=\; (x \leftarrow e \triangleleft \lambda) \square (\theta \square \lambda) \Big] \\[1em]
\qquad\qquad\qquad\qquad\qquad\qquad\qquad\qquad\qquad (extension)
\end{array}}
$$

The *left-empty* axiom defines the composition function when the left-hand argument is the empty substitution $\{ \, \}$, while the *extension* axiom defines the function when the left-hand argument is a substitution of form $(x \leftarrow e) \square \theta$. The value of the composition $\big((x \leftarrow e) \square \theta\big) \square \lambda$ is defined, in the latter axiom, in terms of the simpler composition $\theta \square \lambda$.

From these axioms, we can immediately establish the familiar property

$$(\forall\, sub\ \theta,\ \lambda)\big[sub(\theta\,\square\,\lambda)\big] \qquad\qquad (sort)$$

An immediate consequence of the *extension* axiom for the composition function is obtained by taking θ to be the empty substitution $\{\ \}$:

$$\begin{array}{c}(\forall\, var\ x)\\(\forall\, exp\ e)\\(\forall\, sub\ \lambda)\end{array}\Big[\{x \leftarrow e\}\,\square\,\lambda \;=\; (x \leftarrow e\,\blacktriangleleft\,\lambda)\,\square\,\lambda\Big] \qquad (replacement)$$

The axioms for composition suggest a method for computing the set of replacement pairs. This is illustrated by the following example.

Example (computation of composition)

Suppose

$$\theta \;=\; \{x \leftarrow F(Y)\}$$

and

$$\lambda \;=\; \{x \leftarrow B,\ Y \leftarrow G(A,\ X),\ Z \leftarrow H(Y)\}.$$

Then

$$\theta\,\square\,\lambda \;=\; \big((x \leftarrow F(Y))\,\square\,\{\ \}\big)\,\square\,\lambda$$

$$\;=\; \big(x \leftarrow F(Y)\,\blacktriangleleft\,\lambda\big)\,\square\,\big(\{\ \}\,\square\,\lambda\big)$$
$$\qquad\text{(by the \emph{extension} axiom for the composition function $\square$)}$$

$$\;=\; \big(x \leftarrow F(Y)\,\blacktriangleleft\,\lambda\big)\,\square\,\lambda$$
$$\qquad\text{(by the \emph{left-empty} axiom for the composition function $\square$)}$$

$$\;=\; \big(x \leftarrow F(G(A,\ X))\big)\,\square\,\lambda$$
$$\qquad\text{(applying λ to $F(Y)$)}$$

$$\;=\; \big(x \leftarrow F(G(A,\ X))\big)\,\square\,\{x \leftarrow B,\ Y \leftarrow G(A,\ X),\ Z \leftarrow H(Y)\}$$
$$\qquad\text{(by the definition of λ)}$$

$$\;=\; \{x \leftarrow F(G(A,\ X)),\ Y \leftarrow G(A,\ X),\ Z \leftarrow H(Y)\}$$
$$\qquad\text{(by the definition of the extension function $\square$).}$$

Thus

$$\theta\,\square\,\lambda \;=\; \{x \leftarrow F(G(A,\ X)),\ Y \leftarrow G(A,\ X),\ Z \leftarrow H(Y)\}. \quad\lrcorner$$

The reader is asked to compute the composition of substitutions in **Problem 8.9**.

COMPOSITION PROPERTY

Let us now see why the substitution defined by the preceding axioms has the desired composition property,

$$\begin{matrix} (\forall\, t\text{-}exp\ \ell) \\ (\forall\, sub\ \theta,\ \lambda) \end{matrix} \Big[\ell \blacktriangleleft (\theta \,\square\, \lambda) \ =\ (\ell \blacktriangleleft \theta) \blacktriangleleft \lambda \Big] \qquad (composition)$$

The proof of the *composition* property depends on the following proposition, which establishes the property in the case in which ℓ is a variable.

Proposition (variable composition)

The sentence

$$\begin{matrix} (\forall\, var\ x) \\ (\forall\, sub\ \theta,\ \lambda) \end{matrix} \Big[x \blacktriangleleft (\theta \,\square\, \lambda) \ =\ (x \blacktriangleleft \theta) \blacktriangleleft \lambda \Big] \qquad (variable\ composition)$$

is valid. ⌐

We first prove the proposition.

Proof

Consider an arbitrary variable x and substitution λ; we would like to show

$$(\forall\, sub\ \theta) \big[x \blacktriangleleft (\theta \,\square\, \lambda) \ =\ (x \blacktriangleleft \theta) \blacktriangleleft \lambda \big].$$

The proof is by substitution induction on θ, taking the inductive sentence to be

$$\mathcal{F}[\theta]: \quad x \blacktriangleleft (\theta \,\square\, \lambda) \ =\ (x \blacktriangleleft \theta) \blacktriangleleft \lambda.$$

Base Case

We would like to show

$$\mathcal{F}[\{\,\}]: \quad x \blacktriangleleft (\{\,\} \,\square\, \lambda) \ =\ (x \blacktriangleleft \{\,\}) \blacktriangleleft \lambda.$$

But we have

$$x \blacktriangleleft (\{\,\} \,\square\, \lambda) \ =\ x \blacktriangleleft \lambda$$
$$\text{(by the } left\text{-}empty \text{ axiom for } \square\text{)}$$
$$=\ (x \blacktriangleleft \{\,\}) \blacktriangleleft \lambda$$
$$\text{(by the } variable\text{-}empty \text{ axiom for } \blacktriangleleft\text{)}.$$

In short,

$$x \blacktriangleleft (\{\,\} \,\square\, \lambda) \ =\ (x \blacktriangleleft \{\,\}) \blacktriangleleft \lambda,$$

as we wanted to show.

Inductive Step

Consider an arbitrary variable y, expression e, and substitution θ. We assume as our induction hypothesis that

$$\mathcal{F}[\theta]: \quad x \triangleleft (\theta \,\square\, \lambda) = (x \triangleleft \theta) \triangleleft \lambda$$

and would like to establish the desired conclusion that

$$\mathcal{F}\big[(y \leftarrow e) \circ \theta\big]: \quad x \triangleleft \big(((y \leftarrow e) \circ \theta) \,\square\, \lambda\big) = \big(x \triangleleft ((y \leftarrow e) \circ \theta)\big) \triangleleft \lambda.$$

It suffices (by the *extension* axiom for $\square$) to establish that

$$(\dagger\dagger) \qquad x \triangleleft \big((y \leftarrow e \triangleleft \lambda) \circ (\theta \,\square\, \lambda)\big) = \big(x \triangleleft ((y \leftarrow e) \circ \theta)\big) \triangleleft \lambda.$$

The proof distinguishes between two cases, depending on whether or not x and y are distinct.

Case: $x = y$

We must show ($\dagger\dagger$), that is (in this case),

$$x \triangleleft \big((x \leftarrow e \triangleleft \lambda) \circ (\theta \,\square\, \lambda)\big) = \big(x \triangleleft ((x \leftarrow e) \circ \theta)\big) \triangleleft \lambda.$$

But we have (by two applications of the *variable-nonempty* axiom for $\triangleleft$)

$$x \triangleleft \big((x \leftarrow e \triangleleft \lambda) \circ (\theta \,\square\, \lambda)\big) = e \triangleleft \lambda = \big(x \triangleleft ((x \leftarrow e) \circ \theta)\big) \triangleleft \lambda.$$

Case: $not\ (x = y)$

Then we have

$$x \triangleleft \big((y \leftarrow e \triangleleft \lambda) \circ (\theta \,\square\, \lambda)\big)$$

$$= x \triangleleft (\theta \,\square\, \lambda)$$
$$\text{(by the } \textit{variable-nonempty} \text{ axiom for } \triangleleft,$$
$$\text{because } not\ (x = y))$$

$$= (x \triangleleft \theta) \triangleleft \lambda$$
$$\text{(by our induction hypothesis } \mathcal{F}[\theta])$$

$$= \big(x \triangleleft ((y \leftarrow e) \circ \theta)\big) \triangleleft \lambda$$
$$\text{(by the } \textit{variable-nonempty} \text{ axiom for } \triangleleft \text{ again,}$$
$$\text{because } not\ (x = y)).$$

In short, we have our desired result ($\dagger\dagger$). ∎

Now that we have established the proposition, the proof of the *composition* property is by a straightforward t-expression induction, and is left as an exercise (**Problem 8.10(a)**).

PROPERTIES OF COMPOSITION

From the *composition* property, we can easily show the following properties of composition.

Proposition (right-empty and associativity)

The sentences

$$(\forall\, sub\ \theta)\big[\theta \,\square\, \{\ \} \ = \ \theta\big] \qquad\qquad (right\ empty)$$

$$(\forall\, sub\ \theta,\ \lambda,\ \phi)\big[(\theta \,\square\, \lambda) \,\square\, \phi \ = \ \theta \,\square\, (\lambda \,\square\, \phi)\big] \qquad (associativity)$$

are valid. ⌟

We prove only the *right-empty* property.

Proof (right empty)

It suffices (by the *t-expression equality* corollary) to show that, for an arbitrary substitution θ,

$$(\forall\, t\text{-}exp\ \ell)\big[\ell \blacktriangleleft (\theta \,\square\, \{\ \}) \ = \ \ell \blacktriangleleft \theta\big].$$

But, for an arbitrary t-expression ℓ, we have

$$\ell \blacktriangleleft (\theta \,\square\, \{\ \}) \ = \ (\ell \blacktriangleleft \theta) \blacktriangleleft \{\ \}$$
$$\text{(by the } composition \text{ property)}$$

$$= \ \ell \blacktriangleleft \theta$$
$$\text{(by the } empty\text{-}substitution \text{ property of } \blacktriangleleft),$$

as we wanted to show. ⌟

The proof of the *associativity* property is similar and is left as an exercise (**Problem 8.10(b)**). Because composition is associative, we may write both $(\theta \,\square\, \lambda) \,\square\, \phi$ and $\theta \,\square\, (\lambda \,\square\, \phi)$ as $\theta \,\square\, \lambda \,\square\, \phi$ without fear of ambiguity.

As mentioned in the preview, composition is not commutative. For example,

$$\{x \leftarrow y\} \square \{y \leftarrow x\} \;=\; \{y \leftarrow x\}$$

but

$$\{y \leftarrow x\} \square \{x \leftarrow y\} \;=\; \{x \leftarrow y\}.$$

8.5   GENERALITY

In this section, we introduce a *generality* relation between substitutions.

DEFINITION

The notion of generality is defined in terms of the composition function.

Definition (generality)

A substitution θ is said to be *more general than* a substitution ϕ, denoted by

$$\theta \succeq_{gen} \phi,$$

if ϕ can be obtained from θ by composition with some substitution. If $\theta \succeq_{gen} \phi$, we shall also say that ϕ is an *instance* of θ.

The *generality* relation $\succeq_{gen}$ between substitutions is defined by the following axiom:

$$(\forall \, sub \; \theta, \, \phi) \left[\begin{array}{c} \theta \succeq_{gen} \phi \\ \equiv \\ (\exists \, sub \; \lambda)[\theta \square \lambda = \phi] \end{array} \right] \qquad (substitution \; generality)$$

Example

The substitution

$$\theta \;=\; \{x \leftarrow F(y), \; y \leftarrow z\}$$

is more general than the substitution

$$\phi \;=\; \{x \leftarrow F\big(G(z)\big), \; y \leftarrow B, \; z \leftarrow B\},$$

that is,

$$\theta \succeq_{gen} \phi,$$

because

$$\theta \,\square\, \{Y \leftarrow G(Z),\ Z \leftarrow B\}$$
$$= \ \{X \leftarrow F(Y),\ Y \leftarrow Z\} \,\square\, \{Y \leftarrow G(Z),\ Z \leftarrow B\}$$
$$= \ \{X \leftarrow F\big(G(Z)\big),\ Y \leftarrow B,\ Z \leftarrow B\} \ = \ \phi,$$

and therefore (taking λ to be $\{Y \leftarrow G(Z),\ Z \leftarrow B\}$)

$$(\exists\, sub\ \lambda)[\theta \,\square\, \lambda = \phi].\quad\blacksquare$$

We can prove the following properties:

$$(\forall\, sub\ \theta)[\theta \succeq_{gen} \theta] \hspace{4cm} (reflexivity)$$

$$(\forall\, sub\ \theta,\ \phi,\ \psi) \begin{bmatrix} if\ \ \theta \succeq_{gen} \phi\ \ and\ \ \phi \succeq_{gen} \psi \\ then\ \ \theta \succeq_{gen} \psi \end{bmatrix} \hspace{1cm} (transitivity)$$

$$(\forall\, sub\ \theta)\big[\{\ \} \succeq_{gen} \theta\big] \hspace{4cm} (empty)$$

All the proofs are straightforward and are left as an exercise (**Problem 8.11**).

In **Problem 8.12** we introduce a generality relation between t-expressions and establish a connection between that and the generality relation between substitutions.

EQUAL GENERALITY

We can now define the notion of *equal generality* between substitutions.

Definition (equal generality between substitutions)

Two substitutions θ and ϕ are said to be *equally general*, denoted by $\theta \approx_{gen} \phi$, if $\theta \succeq_{gen} \phi$ and $\phi \succeq_{gen} \theta$.

The *equal-generality* relation $\approx_{gen}$ is defined by the axiom

$$(\forall \, sub \; \theta, \, \phi) \begin{bmatrix} \theta \approx_{gen} \phi \\ \equiv \\ \theta \succeq_{gen} \phi \;\; and \;\; \phi \succeq_{gen} \theta \end{bmatrix} \qquad (equal \; generality)$$

Example

Let

$$\theta \; = \; \{X \leftarrow F(Y)\} \qquad and \qquad \phi \; = \; \{X \leftarrow F(X), \; Y \leftarrow X\}.$$

Then θ is more general than ϕ, that is,

$$\theta \succeq_{gen} \phi,$$

because

$$\begin{aligned} \theta \, \square \, \{Y \leftarrow X\} \; &= \; \{X \leftarrow F(Y)\} \, \square \, \{Y \leftarrow X\} \\ &= \; \{X \leftarrow F(X), \; Y \leftarrow X\} \\ &= \; \phi. \end{aligned}$$

Also, ϕ is more general than θ, that is,

$$\phi \succeq_{gen} \theta,$$

because

$$\begin{aligned} \phi \, \square \, \{X \leftarrow Y\} \; &= \; \{X \leftarrow F(X), \; Y \leftarrow X\} \, \square \, \{X \leftarrow Y\} \\ &= \; \{X \leftarrow F(Y)\} \\ &= \; \theta. \end{aligned}$$

Therefore, by the definition of equal generality, θ and ϕ are equally general, that is,

$$\theta \approx_{gen} \phi.$$

Note that, although θ and ϕ are equally general, they are not equal, that is,

$$not \; (\theta = \phi).$$

For example, θ and ϕ do not agree on the variable X, for

$$X \blacktriangleleft \theta \; = \; F(Y) \quad and \quad X \blacktriangleleft \phi \; = \; F(X).$$

Also, θ and ϕ do not agree on the variable Y, for

$$Y \blacktriangleleft \theta \; = \; Y \quad and \quad Y \blacktriangleleft \phi \; = \; X.$$

PERMUTATIONS

We have said in the preview that a substitution is a *permutation* if it merely interchanges the variables of its domain. For example,

$$\{x \leftarrow y, \; y \leftarrow x, \; u \leftarrow v, \; v \leftarrow w, \; w \leftarrow u\}$$

is a permutation. On the other hand,

$$\{x \leftarrow y\}$$

is not a permutation, because it replaces its domain element x with a new variable y.

Formally, the unary *permutation* relation $permut(\pi)$, characterizing the permutation substitutions, is defined by the following axiom:

$$(\forall\,\pi) \; \left[\begin{array}{l} permut(\pi) \\ \equiv \\ \left[\begin{array}{l} sub(\pi) \\ and \\ (\exists\, sub\,\lambda)\,[\pi\,\square\,\lambda \; = \; \{\,\}] \end{array} \right] \end{array} \right] \qquad (permutation)$$

That is, a permutation substitution is one that has a (right) inverse under composition.

We can then establish the following two properties of permutation substitutions.

Applying a permutation to a variable yields a variable, that is,

$$\begin{array}{l} (\forall\; permut\; \pi) \\ (\forall\; var\; x) \end{array} \left[var(x \blacktriangleleft \pi) \right] \qquad (variable\; sort)$$

Applying a permutation to two distinct variables always yields distinct variables, that is,

$$\begin{array}{l} (\forall\; permut\; \pi) \\ (\forall\; var\; x, y) \end{array} \left[\begin{array}{l} if \;\; x \blacktriangleleft \pi \; = \; y \blacktriangleleft \pi \\ then \;\; x = y \end{array} \right] \qquad (one\text{-}to\text{-}one)$$

In fact, the preceding two properties constitute an alternative definition of the permutations (**Problem 8.13**). This and some of the other properties of permutations are surprisingly difficult to prove.

The equal-generality relation can be characterized in terms of permutation substitutions as follows:

$$(\forall\, sub\ \theta,\ \lambda) \begin{bmatrix} \theta \approx_{gen} \lambda \\ \equiv \\ (\exists\, permut\ \pi)[\theta = \lambda \square \pi] \end{bmatrix} \qquad (equally\ general)$$

We can then establish that

$$(\forall\, permut\ \pi)(\exists\, permut\ \phi)[\pi \square \phi = \{\,\}] \qquad\qquad (invertible)$$

That is, each permutation has an inverse that is itself a permutation. The proofs of these properties are requested in **Problem 8.14**.

We introduce a new function symbol π^{-1} to denote the inverse of a permutation π, defined by the axioms

$$\boxed{\begin{aligned} &(\forall\ permut\ \pi)\big[\pi \square \pi^{-1} = \{\,\}\big] && (inverse) \\[2mm] &(\forall\ permut\ \pi)\big[permut(\pi^{-1})\big] && (sort) \end{aligned}}$$

In fact, the permutation substitutions may be regarded as a group under composition (Section [I]5.4).

The permutation substitutions have the property that they "cover" every variable, that is,

$$\begin{array}{c}(\forall\, permut\ \pi)\\(\forall\, var\ x)\end{array}(\exists\, var\ y)\Big[x = y \blacktriangleleft \pi\Big] \qquad\qquad (onto)$$

In fact, the preceding property can be taken as another alternative definition of the permutation substitutions (**Problem 8.15**).

IDEMPOTENT SUBSTITUTIONS

Informally, a substitution $\{x_1 \leftarrow e_1,\ \ldots,\ x_n \leftarrow e_n\}$ is said to be idempotent if no variable x_i in its domain occurs in any of the terms e_j. Thus

$$\phi:\ \{x \leftarrow y,\ z \leftarrow F(x)\}$$

is not idempotent because the domain element x occurs in the term F(x).

Formally, the idempotent substitutions are defined as follows.

Definition (idempotence)

A substitution θ is *idempotent* if

$$\theta \,\square\, \theta = \theta.$$ ⌟

The preceding substitution ϕ is not idempotent under the definition, because

$$\phi \,\square\, \phi = \{X \leftarrow Y,\ Z \leftarrow F(X)\} \,\square\, \{X \leftarrow Y,\ Z \leftarrow F(X)\}$$

$$= \{X \leftarrow Y,\ Z \leftarrow F(Y)\}$$

$$\neq \phi.$$

The idempotent substitutions are characterized by the property that their domains and ranges are disjoint:

$$(\forall\ sub\ \theta) \begin{bmatrix} \theta \,\square\, \theta = \theta \\ \equiv \\ dom(\theta) \cap range(\theta) = \{\ \} \end{bmatrix} \qquad (idempotence)$$

The reader is requested to prove this property in **Problem 8.16**.

The *idempotence* property suggests an easy and practical way to decide whether a substitution is idempotent.

Example (idempotence property)

For the substitution

$$\theta : \ \{X \leftarrow F(Y)\}$$

we have

$$dom(\theta) = \{X\} \quad \text{and} \quad range(\theta) = \{Y\},$$

and hence the domain and range are disjoint, that is,

$$dom(\theta) \cap range(\theta) = \{\ \}.$$

Therefore the proposition implies that θ is idempotent, that is,

$$\theta \,\square\, \theta = \theta,$$

and indeed that is the case.

For the substitution

$$\phi : \ \{X \leftarrow Y,\ Z \leftarrow F(X)\},$$

on the other hand, we have

$$dom(\phi) = \{\text{x, z}\} \quad \text{and} \quad range(\phi) = \{\text{x, y}\}$$

and hence

$$dom(\phi) \cap range(\phi) = \{\text{x}\},$$

that is, the domain and range are not disjoint. Therefore the proposition implies that ϕ is not idempotent, that is,

$$\phi \square \phi \neq \phi,$$

and indeed that is the case, as we have just seen. ◢

The empty substitution is the only idempotent permutation; the proof is requested as an exercise (**Problem 8.17**).

PROBLEMS

Problem 8.1 (apply function)   page 298

Show the following properties of the apply function:

(a) *Empty substitution*

$$(\forall\, t\text{-}exp\; \ell)\big[\ell \blacktriangleleft \{\;\} = \ell\big]$$

(b) *Variable sort*

$$\genfrac{}{}{0pt}{}{(\forall\; var\; x)}{(\forall\; sub\; \theta)}\big[exp(x \blacktriangleleft \theta)\big]$$

(c) *Application sort*

$$\genfrac{}{}{0pt}{}{(\forall\; appl\; e)}{(\forall\; sub\; \theta)}\big[appl(e \blacktriangleleft \theta)\big]$$

(d) *Expression sort*

$$\genfrac{}{}{0pt}{}{(\forall\; exp\; e)}{(\forall\; sub\; \theta)}\big[exp(e \blacktriangleleft \theta)\big]$$

(e) *Tuple sort*

$$\genfrac{}{}{0pt}{}{(\forall\; tuple\; t)}{(\forall\; sub\; \theta)}\big[tuple(t \blacktriangleleft \theta)\big]$$

(f) *T-expression sort*

$$\genfrac{}{}{0pt}{}{(\forall\, t\text{-}exp\; \ell)}{(\forall\; sub\; \theta)}\big[t\text{-}exp(\ell \blacktriangleleft \theta)\big]$$

Hint: Prove parts (c) through (e) together.

Problem 8.2 (monotonicity)   page 299

Establish the following monotonicity properties:

(a) *Strict monotonicity*

$$(\forall\, t\text{-}exp\ \ell,\ m)\ \begin{bmatrix} if\ \ \ell \equiv m \\ then\ \ \ell \blacktriangleleft \theta \equiv m \blacktriangleleft \theta \end{bmatrix}$$
$$(\forall\, sub\ \theta)$$

(b) *Weak monotonicity*

$$(\forall\, t\text{-}exp\ \ell,\ m)\ \begin{bmatrix} if\ \ \ell \sqsubseteq m \\ then\ \ \ell \blacktriangleleft \theta \sqsubseteq m \blacktriangleleft \theta \end{bmatrix}.$$
$$(\forall\, sub\ \theta)$$

Problem 8.3 (replacement function)   page 300

Establish the following properties of the replacement function:

(a) *Variable introduction*

$$(\forall\, var\ x) \atop (\forall\, exp\ e) \Big[varset\big(\ell \blacktriangleleft \{x \leftarrow e\}\big)\ \subseteq\ varset(\ell) \cup varset(e) \Big]$$
$$(\forall\, t\text{-}exp\ \ell)$$

(b) *Variable elimination*

$$(\forall\, var\ x) \atop (\forall\, exp\ e) \begin{bmatrix} if\ \ not\ (x \sqsubseteq e) \\ then\ \ (\forall\, t\text{-}exp\ \ell)\Big[not\ \big(x \in varset(\ell \blacktriangleleft \{x \leftarrow e\})\big) \Big] \end{bmatrix}.$$

Problem 8.4 (representation and decomposition)   page 302

Establish the following properties:

(a) *Representation*

$$(\forall\, var\ x) \atop (\forall\, sub\ \theta) \Big[\theta\ =\ (x \leftarrow x \blacktriangleleft \theta) \square \theta \Big]$$

(b) *Decomposition*

$$(\forall\, var\ x) \atop (\forall\, sub\ \theta) \Big[\theta\ =\ (x \leftarrow x \blacktriangleleft \theta) \square (\theta - x) \Big].$$

Problem 8.5 (agreement)   page 306

(a) Establish the following *agreement* proposition:

$$(\forall\, t\text{-}exp\ \ell) \atop (\forall\, sub\ \theta,\ \phi) \begin{bmatrix} \ell \blacktriangleleft \theta = \ell \blacktriangleleft \phi \\ \equiv \\ (\forall\, var\ x)\begin{bmatrix} if\ \ x \sqsubseteq \ell \\ then\ \ x \blacktriangleleft \theta = x \blacktriangleleft \phi \end{bmatrix} \end{bmatrix}.$$

(b) Establish the following *agreement* property of the subtraction function:

$$(\forall\ var\ x)\ \begin{bmatrix} if\ \ not\ (x \equiv \ell) \\ then\ \ \ell \blacktriangleleft \theta\ =\ \ell \blacktriangleleft (\theta - x) \end{bmatrix}.$$
$$(\forall\ t\text{-}exp\ \ell)$$
$$(\forall\ sub\ \theta)$$

Problem 8.6 (domain function)   pages 307, 311

Establish the following properties of the domain function:

(a) *Empty*

$$(\forall\ sub\ \theta)\ \begin{bmatrix} if\ \ dom(\theta) = \{\ \} \\ then\ \ \theta = \{\ \} \end{bmatrix}$$

(b) *Subtraction*

$$(\forall\ var\ x)\ \begin{bmatrix} if\ \ not\ (x \in dom(\theta)) \\ then\ \ \theta = \theta - x \end{bmatrix}$$
$$(\forall\ sub\ \theta)$$

(c) *Equality*

$$(\forall\ sub\ \theta, \phi)\ \begin{bmatrix} \theta = \phi \\ \equiv \\ (\forall\ var\ x)\ \begin{bmatrix} if\ \ x \in (dom(\theta) \cup dom(\phi)) \\ then\ \ x \blacktriangleleft \theta = x \blacktriangleleft \phi \end{bmatrix} \end{bmatrix}.$$

Problem 8.7 (range function)   page 312

Prove the validity of the following *range* property, which characterizes the range of a substitution:

$$(\forall\ var\ y)\ \begin{bmatrix} y \in range(\theta) \\ \equiv \\ (\exists\ var\ x)\ \begin{bmatrix} x \in dom(\theta) \\ and \\ y \equiv x \blacktriangleleft \theta \end{bmatrix} \end{bmatrix}.$$
$$(\forall\ sub\ \theta)$$

Problem 8.8 (invariance)   page 313

Establish the following properties:

(a) *Invariance*

$$(\forall\ t\text{-}exp\ \ell)\ \begin{bmatrix} \ell \blacktriangleleft \theta = \ell \\ \equiv \\ varset(\ell) \cap dom(\theta)\ =\ \{\ \} \end{bmatrix}$$
$$(\forall\ sub\ \theta)$$

(b) *Replacement invariance*

$$\begin{matrix} (\forall \ var \ x) \\ (\forall \ exp \ e) \\ (\forall \ t\text{-}exp \ \ell) \end{matrix} \left[\begin{matrix} if \ \ not \ (x \trianglelefteq \ell) \\ then \ \ \ell \triangleleft \{x \leftarrow e\} \ = \ \ell \end{matrix} \right].$$

Problem 8.9 (computing composition)   page 314

Compute the composition $\theta \square \lambda$ of the following substitutions:

(a) θ: $\{X \leftarrow Y\}$

   λ: $\{Y \leftarrow A\}$

(b) θ: $\{X \leftarrow Y, \ Y \leftarrow Z\}$

   λ: $\{Y \leftarrow X\}$

(c) θ: $\{X \leftarrow F(Z), \ Y \leftarrow F(Z), \ Z \leftarrow X\}$

   λ: $\{Z \leftarrow F(Z)\}$.

Problem 8.10 (properties of composition)   page 317

Establish the following properties of the composition of substitutions:

(a) *Composition*

$$\begin{matrix} (\forall \ t\text{-}exp \ \ell) \\ (\forall \ sub \ \theta, \ \lambda) \end{matrix} \left[\ell \triangleleft (\theta \square \lambda) \ = \ (\ell \triangleleft \theta) \triangleleft \lambda \right]$$

(b) *Associativity*

$$(\forall \ sub \ \theta, \ \lambda, \ \phi) \left[(\theta \square \lambda) \square \phi \ = \ \theta \square (\lambda \square \phi) \right].$$

Problem 8.11 (generality between substitutions)   page 319

Establish the following properties of the generality relation $\succeq_{gen}$:

(a) *Reflexivity*

$$(\forall \ sub \ \theta)[\theta \succeq_{gen} \theta]$$

(b) *Transitivity*

$$(\forall \ sub \ \theta, \ \phi, \ \psi) \left[\begin{matrix} if \ \ \theta \succeq_{gen} \phi \ \ and \ \ \phi \succeq_{gen} \psi \\ then \ \ \theta \succeq_{gen} \psi \end{matrix} \right]$$

(c) *Empty*

$$(\forall \, sub \, \theta)\big[\{\,\} \succeq_{gen} \theta\big].$$

* **Problem 8.12 (generality between t-expressions)**   page 319

Suppose a *generality* relation $\succeq_{gen}$ between t-expressions is defined by the following axiom:

$$(\forall \, t\text{-}exp \, \ell, \, m) \begin{bmatrix} \ell \succeq_{gen} m \\ \equiv \\ (\exists \, sub \, \lambda)[\ell \blacktriangleleft \lambda = m] \end{bmatrix} \qquad (t\text{-}expression \ generality)$$

Prove the validity of the following sentence:

$$(\forall \, sub \, \theta, \, \phi) \begin{bmatrix} \theta \succeq_{gen} \phi \\ \equiv \\ (\forall \, t\text{-}exp \, \ell)[\ell \blacktriangleleft \theta \succeq_{gen} \ell \blacktriangleleft \phi] \end{bmatrix}.$$

In other words, a substitution θ is more general than a substitution ϕ precisely when, for any t-expression ℓ, the result of applying θ to ℓ is more general than the result of applying ϕ to ℓ.

Hint: First prove the following properties:

$$(\forall \, set \, s)(\exists \, tuple \, t)\big[varset(t) = s\big]$$

$$\begin{matrix}(\forall \, t\text{-}exp \, \ell)\\(\forall \, sub \, \theta)\end{matrix}(\exists \, sub \, \lambda)\Big[\ell \blacktriangleleft \lambda = \ell \blacktriangleleft \theta \quad and \quad dom(\lambda) \subseteq varset(\ell)\Big]$$

$$(\forall \, sub \, \theta, \, \phi)\big[dom(\theta \,\square\, \phi) \subseteq dom(\theta) \cup dom(\phi)\big]$$

$$\begin{matrix}(\forall \, t\text{-}exp \, \ell)\\(\forall \, sub \, \theta)\end{matrix}\Big[varset(\ell \blacktriangleleft \theta) \subseteq varset(\ell) \cup range(\theta)\Big].$$

Problem 8.13 (one-to-one permutations)   page 321

Establish the following properties of the permutation substitutions:

(a) *Variable sort*

$$\begin{matrix}(\forall \, permut \, \pi)\\(\forall \, var \, x)\end{matrix}\Big[var(x \blacktriangleleft \pi)\Big]$$

(b) *One-to-one*

$$\begin{matrix}(\forall \, permut \, \pi)\\(\forall \, var \, x, y)\end{matrix}\begin{bmatrix} if \quad x \blacktriangleleft \pi = y \blacktriangleleft \pi \\ then \quad x = y \end{bmatrix}$$

*(c) *Alternative definition*

Show that the *variable-sort* and *one-to-one* properties can be regarded as an alternative definition of the permutation substitutions, in the following sense.

Define a new unary relation $permut1(\pi)$ by the axiom

$$(\forall\,\pi)\left[\begin{array}{l} permut1(\pi) \\ \equiv \\ \left[\begin{array}{l} sub(\pi) \\ and \\ (\forall\,var\ x)\,[var(x\blacktriangleleft\pi)] \\ and \\ (\forall\,var\ x,\ y)\left[\begin{array}{l} if\ \ x\blacktriangleleft\pi\ =\ y\blacktriangleleft\pi \\ then\ \ x=y \end{array}\right] \end{array}\right] \end{array}\right] \qquad (permut1)$$

Then show

$$(\forall\,sub\ \pi)\left[\begin{array}{l} permut1(\pi) \\ \equiv \\ permut(\pi) \end{array}\right] \qquad (one\text{-}to\text{-}one\ definition)$$

Hint: First show (by induction over sets) the property

$$(\forall\,permut1\ \pi)(\forall\,set\ s)(\exists\,sub\ \lambda)(\forall\,var\ x)$$
$$\left[\begin{array}{l} if\ \ x\in s\ \ or\ \ not\ (x\in dom(\pi)) \\ then\ \ x\blacktriangleleft(\pi\,\square\,\lambda)\ =\ x \end{array}\right].$$

Problem 8.14 (equal generality)   page 322

(a) Show that any two permutations are equally general, that is,

$$(\forall\,permut\ \pi,\ \phi)[\pi\approx_{gen}\phi].$$

** (b) Establish the *equally general* property of permutations, that is,

$$(\forall\,sub\ \theta,\ \lambda)\left[\begin{array}{l} \theta\approx_{gen}\lambda \\ \equiv \\ (\exists\,permut\ \pi)[\theta\ =\ \lambda\,\square\,\pi] \end{array}\right] \qquad (equally\ general)$$

Hint: First show

$$(\forall\,sub\ \theta,\ \lambda_1,\ \lambda_2)\left[\begin{array}{l} \theta\,\square\,\lambda_1 = \theta\,\square\,\lambda_2 \\ \equiv \\ (\forall\,var\ x)\left[\begin{array}{l} if\ \ x\notin(dom(\theta)\sim range(\theta)) \\ then\ \ x\blacktriangleleft\lambda_1\ =\ x\blacktriangleleft\lambda_2 \end{array}\right] \end{array}\right]$$

and (by induction over sets)

$$(\forall\, sub\ \theta)\begin{bmatrix} if\ \ (\exists\, sub\ \lambda)(\forall\, var\ x)\big[if\ \ x \notin s\ \ then\ \ x \blacktriangleleft (\theta \,\square\, \lambda) = x\big] \\ (\forall\, set\ s)\ \ then\ \ (\exists\, permut\ \pi)(\forall\, var\ x)\big[if\ \ x \notin s\ \ then\ \ x \blacktriangleleft \theta = x \blacktriangleleft \pi\big] \end{bmatrix}.$$

(c) Establish the *invertible* property of permutations, that is,

$$(\forall\, permut\ \pi)(\exists\, permut\ \phi)\big[\pi \,\square\, \phi = \{\,\}\big] \qquad\qquad (invertible)$$

Problem 8.15 (onto permutations)   page 322

(a) *Unique inverse*

Establish the following property of substitutions:

$$(\forall\, sub\ \pi,\ \theta,\ \lambda)\begin{bmatrix} if\ \ \pi \,\square\, \theta\ =\ \{\,\}\ \ and\ \ \pi \,\square\, \lambda\ =\ \{\,\} \\ then\ \ \theta\ =\ \lambda \end{bmatrix}$$

$$(unique\ inverse)$$

(b) *Onto*

Establish the *onto* property of permutations:

$$\genfrac{}{}{0pt}{}{(\forall\, permut\ \pi)}{(\forall\, var\ x)}(\exists\, var\ y)\big[x\ =\ y \blacktriangleleft \pi\big] \qquad\qquad (onto)$$

*(c) *Alternative definition*

Show that the *onto* property can be regarded as an alternative definition of
the permutation substitutions, in the following sense.

Define a new unary relation $permut2(\pi)$ by the axiom

$$(\forall\, \pi)\begin{bmatrix} permut2(\pi) \\ \equiv \\ \begin{bmatrix} sub(\pi) \\ and \\ (\forall\, var\ x)(\exists\, var\ y)[x = y \blacktriangleleft \pi] \end{bmatrix} \end{bmatrix} \qquad\qquad (permut2)$$

Then show

$$(\forall\, sub\ \pi)\begin{bmatrix} permut2(\pi) \\ \equiv \\ permut(\pi) \end{bmatrix} \qquad\qquad (onto\ definition)$$

Hint: First show (by induction over sets) the property

$$(\forall\, permut2\ \pi)(\forall\, set\ s)(\exists\, sub\ \lambda)(\forall\, var\ x)$$
$$\begin{bmatrix} if\ \ x \in s\ \ or\ \ not\ (x \in dom(\pi)) \\ then\ \ x \blacktriangleleft (\lambda \,\square\, \pi)\ =\ x \end{bmatrix}.$$

Problem 8.16 (characterization of idempotence)   page 323

Prove the validity of the *idempotence* property:

$$(\forall\ sub\ \theta) \begin{bmatrix} \theta \square \theta\ =\ \theta \\ \equiv \\ dom(\theta)\ \cap\ range(\theta)\ =\ \{\ \} \end{bmatrix}.$$

Hint: Use the characterization (*range* property) of the *range* function.

Problem 8.17 (idempotent permutation)   page 324

Show that the empty substitution is the only idempotent permutation, that is,

$$(\forall\ permut\ \pi) \begin{bmatrix} if\ \pi \square \pi\ =\ \pi \\ then\ \pi\ =\ \{\ \} \end{bmatrix}.$$

9

Unification Algorithm

We have introduced a theory of t-expressions and substitutions. We are now ready to formalize our treatment of unification. That is, we express within the theory concepts that were introduced informally in the preview (Section 7.1).

9.1   UNIFIERS

A *unifier* of two t-expressions is a substitution that makes the two t-expressions identical. We first give the basic definitions.

DEFINITIONS

Definition (unifier)

> A substitution θ is said to be a *unifier* of two t-expressions ℓ and m if
>
> $$\ell \blacktriangleleft \theta \ = \ m \blacktriangleleft \theta.$$
>
> In this case, we also say that θ *unifies* ℓ and m. ⏌

For example, $\{X \leftarrow A, \ Y \leftarrow B\}$ is a unifier of $F(X, B)$ and $F(A, Y)$. We have seen in the preview that not every pair of t-expressions has a unifier.

In **Problem 9.1**, the reader is requested to identify unifiers for given pairs of t-expressions.

Definition (unifiable)

Two t-expressions ℓ and m are said to be *unifiable*, denoted by $unifiable(\ell,\, m)$, if they have a unifier. This is expressed by the axiom

$$(\forall\, t\text{-}exp\ \ell,\, m) \begin{bmatrix} unifiable(\ell,\, m) \\ \equiv \\ (\exists\, sub\ \theta)[\ell \triangleleft \theta = m \triangleleft \theta] \end{bmatrix} \qquad (unifiable)$$

Thus two t-expressions are not unifiable if they have no unifier.

BASIC PROPERTIES

We now establish some elementary properties of unifiers.

The following propositions characterize the unifiers for different classes of t-expressions.

Proposition (application)

The sentences

$$\begin{matrix} (\forall\, fun\ f,\, g) \\ (\forall\, tuple\ s,\, t) \\ (\forall\, sub\ \theta) \end{matrix} \begin{bmatrix} (f \bullet s) \triangleleft \theta\ =\ (g \bullet t) \triangleleft \theta \\ \equiv \\ f = g\ \ and\ \ s \triangleleft \theta = t \triangleleft \theta \end{bmatrix} \qquad (application\ unifier)$$

$$\begin{matrix} (\forall\, fun\ f,\, g) \\ (\forall\, tuple\ s,\, t) \end{matrix} \begin{bmatrix} unifiable(f \bullet s,\, g \bullet t) \\ \equiv \\ f = g\ \ and\ \ unifiable(s,\, t) \end{bmatrix} \qquad (application\ unifiable)$$

are valid.

In other words, θ unifies expressions of form $f(s_1,\, \ldots,\, s_n)$ and $g(t_1,\, \ldots,\, t_n)$ precisely when $f = g$ and θ unifies the tuples $\langle s_1,\, \ldots,\, s_n \rangle$ and $\langle t_1,\, \ldots,\, t_n \rangle$. Hence

$f(s_1, \ldots, s_n)$ and $g(t_1, \ldots, t_n)$ are unifiable precisely when $f = g$ and the tuples $\langle s_1, \ldots, s_n \rangle$ and $\langle t_1, \ldots, t_n \rangle$ are unifiable. This implies that, if f and g are distinct, the expressions $f(s_1, \ldots, s_n)$ and $g(t_1, \ldots, t_n)$ are not unifiable.

Proof

We prove each part separately.

Application unifier

To show the *application-unifier* part, consider arbitrary function symbols f and g, arbitrary tuples s and t, and an arbitrary substitution θ. We would like to show that

$$(f \bullet s) \blacktriangleleft \theta \;=\; (g \bullet t) \blacktriangleleft \theta$$
$$\equiv$$
$$f = g \;\; and \;\; s \blacktriangleleft \theta = t \blacktriangleleft \theta.$$

But we have

$$(f \bullet s) \blacktriangleleft \theta \;=\; (g \bullet t) \blacktriangleleft \theta$$

precisely when (by the *application* axiom for ◄)

$$f \bullet (s \blacktriangleleft \theta) \;=\; g \bullet (t \blacktriangleleft \theta)$$

precisely when (by the *application* uniqueness axiom for expressions)

$$f = g \;\; and \;\; s \blacktriangleleft \theta = t \blacktriangleleft \theta,$$

as we wanted to show.

Application unifiable

We can show now the *application-unifiable* part of the proposition; that is, under the same suppositions, we show that

$$unifiable(f \bullet s, \; g \bullet t)$$
$$\equiv$$
$$f = g \;\; and \;\; unifiable(s, \, t).$$

We have

$$unifiable(f \bullet s, \; g \bullet t),$$

precisely when (by the definition of *unifiable*), for some substitution θ,

$$(f \bullet s) \blacktriangleleft \theta \;=\; (g \bullet t) \blacktriangleleft \theta$$

precisely when (by the first part of this proposition), for some substitution θ,

$$f = g \quad and \quad s \blacktriangleleft \theta = t \blacktriangleleft \theta$$

precisely when (by the definition of *unifiable*, again)

$$f = g \quad and \quad unifiable(s,\, t),$$

as we wanted to show. ⌙

Proposition (insertion)

The sentences

$$
\begin{array}{l}
(\forall \, exp \; d, \, e) \\
(\forall \, tuple \; s, \, t) \\
\quad (\forall \, sub \; \theta)
\end{array}
\left[
\begin{array}{l}
(d \diamond s) \blacktriangleleft \theta \; = \; (e \diamond t) \blacktriangleleft \theta \\
\quad \equiv \\
d \blacktriangleleft \theta = e \blacktriangleleft \theta \;\; and \;\; s \blacktriangleleft \theta = t \blacktriangleleft \theta
\end{array}
\right]
\qquad (\textit{insertion unifier})
$$

$$
\begin{array}{l}
(\forall \, exp \; d, \, e) \\
(\forall \, tuple \; s, \, t)
\end{array}
\left[
\begin{array}{l}
if \;\; unifiable(d \diamond s, \; e \diamond t) \\
then \;\; unifiable(d, \, e) \;\; and \;\; unifiable(s, \, t)
\end{array}
\right]
$$
$$(\textit{insertion unifiable})$$

are valid. ⌙

In other words, the unifiers of $d \diamond s$ and $e \diamond t$ are precisely the substitutions that are unifiers both of d and e and of s and t.

The proof is analogous to that of the previous proposition (**Problem 9.2**).

Remark (insertion unifiable)

Note that the *insertion-unifiable* property holds only in one direction. It is possible for two expressions d and e to be unifiable, and for two tuples s and t to be unifiable, but for the corresponding results of the insertions $d \diamond s$ and $e \diamond t$ not to be unifiable.

For example, the two expressions

$$d : \;\; \text{A} \qquad and \qquad e : \;\; \text{X}$$

are unifiable, with unifier

$$\theta : \;\; \{\text{X} \leftarrow \text{A}\}.$$

Also the tuples

$$s : \;\; \langle \text{B} \rangle \qquad and \qquad t : \;\; \langle \text{X} \rangle$$

are unifiable, with unifier

$$\phi: \quad \{X \leftarrow B\}.$$

On the other hand, the results of the insertions

$$d \diamond s: \quad \langle A, \; B \rangle \qquad \text{and} \qquad e \diamond t: \quad \langle X, \; X \rangle$$

are not unifiable at all. ◢

MORE PROPERTIES

If two expressions are identical, they are certainly unifiable:

$$(\forall\, t\text{-}exp\; \ell)\big[\mathit{unifiable}(\ell,\; \ell)\big] \qquad\qquad\qquad (same)$$

The following properties establish the nonunifiability of certain t-expressions:

$$(\forall\, t\text{-}exp\; \ell,\, m) \begin{bmatrix} if \;\; \ell \Subset m \\ then \;\; not \;\big(\mathit{unifiable}(\ell,\, m)\big) \end{bmatrix} \qquad (occurrence)$$

In other words, if one t-expression occurs properly in another, the two are not unifiable.

$$\begin{array}{l}(\forall\, exp\; e)\\ (\forall\, tuple\; t)\end{array}\Big[not\;\big(\mathit{unifiable}(e,\, t)\big)\Big] \qquad\qquad (expression\text{-}tuple)$$

In other words, expressions and tuples of expressions are not unifiable.

$$\begin{array}{l}(\forall\, exp\; e)\\ (\forall\, tuple\; t)\end{array}\Big[not\;\big(\mathit{unifiable}(\langle\,\rangle,\, e \diamond t)\big)\Big] \qquad (empty\text{-}insertion)$$

In other words, the empty tuple and an insertion are not unifiable.

The proofs of the three properties are straightforward and do not require induction. The proof of the *occurrence* property follows by the *monotonicity* property of the application function ◄ and the irreflexivity of the proper-occurrence relation $\Subset$; the proofs of the two other properties follow by the corresponding uniqueness axioms.

9.2 MOST-GENERAL UNIFIERS

Before we introduce the concept of a most-general unifier, we establish a relationship between the various unifiers of two t-expressions.

INSTANCES OF UNIFIERS

We have observed in the preview that there may be several distinct unifiers for a given pair of t-expressions. Indeed, any instance of a unifier is also a unifier.

Proposition (instance unifier)

The sentence

$$(\forall t\text{-}exp\ \ell,\ m)\ \begin{bmatrix} if & \begin{bmatrix} \ell \blacktriangleleft \theta = m \blacktriangleleft \theta \\ and \\ \theta \succeq_{gen} \phi \end{bmatrix} \\ then\ \ \ell \blacktriangleleft \phi = m \blacktriangleleft \phi \end{bmatrix} \qquad (instance\ unifier)$$
$$(\forall\ sub\ \theta,\ \phi)$$

is valid. ⌟

We first illustrate the proposition with an example.

Example

Consider the two expressions

$$\ell:\ \text{X} \qquad and \qquad m:\ \text{F(Y)}.$$

These t-expressions have the unifier

$$\theta:\ \ \{\text{X} \leftarrow \text{F(Y)}\}$$

because

$$\ell \blacktriangleleft \theta\ =\ \text{X} \blacktriangleleft \{\text{X} \leftarrow \text{F(Y)}\}\ =\ \text{F(Y)}$$
$$m \blacktriangleleft \theta\ =\ \text{F(Y)} \blacktriangleleft \{\text{X} \leftarrow \text{F(Y)}\}\ =\ \text{F(Y)}.$$

The substitution

$$\phi\ =\ \{\text{X} \leftarrow \text{F(B)},\ \text{Y} \leftarrow \text{B}\}$$

is an instance of θ, because

$$\theta \,\square\, \{\text{Y} \leftarrow \text{B}\} =\ \{\text{X} \leftarrow \text{F(Y)}\} \,\square\, \{\text{Y} \leftarrow \text{B}\}$$
$$=\ \{\text{X} \leftarrow \text{F(B)},\ \text{Y} \leftarrow \text{B}\}\ =\ \phi,$$

and hence

$$\theta \succeq_{gen} \phi.$$

Then, according to the proposition, ϕ is also a unifier of ℓ and m, that is,

$$\ell \triangleleft \phi \; = \; m \triangleleft \phi.$$

Indeed,

$$\ell \triangleleft \phi \; = \; \text{X} \triangleleft \{\text{X} \leftarrow \text{F(B)}, \; \text{Y} \leftarrow \text{B}\} \; = \; \text{F(B)}$$

$$m \triangleleft \phi \; = \; \text{F(Y)} \triangleleft \{\text{X} \leftarrow \text{F(B)}, \; \text{Y} \leftarrow \text{B}\} \; = \; \text{F(B).} \quad \blacksquare$$

The proof of the *instance-unifier* proposition is straightforward.

Proof

For arbitrary t-expressions ℓ and m and substitutions θ and ϕ, suppose that θ is a unifier of ℓ and m, that is,

$$\ell \triangleleft \theta \; = \; m \triangleleft \theta,$$

and that θ is more general than ϕ, that is,

$$\theta \succeq_{gen} \phi.$$

We would like to show that then ϕ is also a unifier of ℓ and m, that is,

$$\ell \triangleleft \phi \; = \; m \triangleleft \phi.$$

Because θ is more general than ϕ, we know (by the definition of the *generality* relation between substitutions) that there exists a substitution λ such that

$$\theta \,\square\, \lambda = \phi.$$

Now, because $\ell \triangleleft \theta = m \triangleleft \theta$, we have

$$(\ell \triangleleft \theta) \triangleleft \lambda = (m \triangleleft \theta) \triangleleft \lambda$$

or, equivalently (by the *composition* proposition),

$$\ell \triangleleft (\theta \,\square\, \lambda) = m \triangleleft (\theta \,\square\, \lambda).$$

Therefore, because $\theta \,\square\, \lambda = \phi$, we have

$$\ell \triangleleft \phi = m \triangleleft \phi,$$

that is, ϕ is a unifier of ℓ and m, as we wanted to show. $\quad \blacksquare$

MOST-GENERAL UNIFIERS

We shall see later that, if they exist at all, the unifiers of a pair of t-expressions ℓ and m are all instances of a *most-general unifier* of ℓ and m. We now define that notion.

Definition (most-general unifier)

A substitution θ is said to be a *most-general unifier* of two t-expressions ℓ and m, denoted by $mgu(\ell, m, \theta)$, if

θ is a unifier of ℓ and m and
θ is more general than any unifier of ℓ and m.

The *mgu* relation is defined by the following axiom:

$$(\forall\, t\text{-}exp\ \ell,\ m) \left[\begin{array}{l} mgu(\ell,\ m,\ \theta) \\[4pt] \equiv \\[4pt] \left[\begin{array}{l} sub(\theta) \\ and \\ \ell \blacktriangleleft \theta = m \blacktriangleleft \theta \\ and \\ (\forall\ sub\ \phi) \left[\begin{array}{l} if\ \ \ell \blacktriangleleft \phi = m \blacktriangleleft \phi \\ then\ \ \theta \succeq_{gen} \phi \end{array} \right] \end{array} \right] \end{array} \right] \qquad (mgu)$$
$(\forall\ \theta)$

The following two propositions provide examples of most-general unifiers for certain simple pairs of t-expressions.

Proposition (empty unifier)

The sentence

$$(\forall\, t\text{-}exp\ \ell)\big[mgu\big(\ell,\ \ell,\ \{\,\}\big)\big] \qquad\qquad (empty\ unifier)$$

is valid.

In other words, the empty substitution $\{\,\}$ is a most-general unifier of a t-expression and itself.

Proof

For an arbitrary t-expression ℓ, it suffices (by the definition of *mgu*) to show that $\{\,\}$ is a substitution, that is,

$$sub(\{\,\});$$

that $\{\,\}$ is a unifier of ℓ and ℓ, that is,

$$\ell \triangleleft \{\,\} \;=\; \ell \triangleleft \{\,\};$$

and that $\{\,\}$ is most-general, that is,

$$(\forall \, sub \; \phi) \left[\begin{array}{l} if \;\; \ell \triangleleft \phi = m \triangleleft \phi \\ then \;\; \{\,\} \succeq_{gen} \phi \end{array} \right].$$

But $sub(\{\,\})$ is the *empty* generation axiom for substitutions; $\ell \triangleleft \{\,\} = \ell \triangleleft \{\,\}$ follows from the reflexivity of equality; and we know (by the *empty* property of the generality relation $\succeq_{gen}$ for substitutions) that, for an arbitrary substitution ϕ,

$$\{\,\} \succeq_{gen} \phi. \quad \lrcorner$$

We established earlier that, if one t-expression occurs properly in another, the two are not unifiable. We can now show that, if a variable x does not occur properly in an expression e, the two are unifiable, with the most-general unifier $\{x \leftarrow e\}$.

Proposition (replacement unifier)

The sentence

$$(\forall \, var \; x) \; \left[\begin{array}{l} if \;\; not \; (x \Subset e) \\ then \;\; mgu(x, \; e, \; \{x \leftarrow e\}) \end{array} \right] \qquad (replacement \; unifier)$$
$$(\forall \, exp \; e)$$

is valid. $\quad \lrcorner$

Thus, by this proposition, $\theta = \{\mathrm{Y} \leftarrow \mathrm{F}(\mathrm{z})\}$ is a most-general unifier of Y and $\mathrm{F}(\mathrm{z})$.

Proof

Consider an arbitrary variable x and expression e, where x does not occur properly in e, that is,

$$not \; (x \Subset e).$$

We would like to show that $\{x \leftarrow e\}$ is a most-general unifier of x and e, that is,

$$mgu(x, \; e, \; \{x \leftarrow e\}).$$

It suffices (by the definition of mgu) to show that $\{x \leftarrow e\}$ is a substitution; that $\{x \leftarrow e\}$ is a unifier of x and e, that is,

(††) $x \blacktriangleleft \{x \leftarrow e\} = e \blacktriangleleft \{x \leftarrow e\};$

and that $\{x \leftarrow e\}$ is most-general, that is,

(‡‡) $(\forall\ sub\ \phi) \begin{bmatrix} if & x \blacktriangleleft \phi = e \blacktriangleleft \phi \\ then & \{x \leftarrow e\} \succeq_{gen} \phi \end{bmatrix}.$

That $\{x \leftarrow e\}$ is a substitution is the *sort* property of the replacement function.

To show (††), that $\{x \leftarrow e\}$ is a unifier, we have (by the *variable* property of the replacement function)

$$x \blacktriangleleft \{x \leftarrow e\} = e.$$

Therefore it suffices to show that

$$e \blacktriangleleft \{x \leftarrow e\} = e.$$

In the case in which x and e are distinct, that is, $not(x = e)$, because we have supposed $not(x \Subset e)$, we have $not(x \Subset e)$, and therefore (by the *replacement-invariance* property)

$$e \blacktriangleleft \{x \leftarrow e\} = e.$$

On the other hand, in the case in which $x = e$, we have (by the *variable* property of the replacement function)

$$e \blacktriangleleft \{x \leftarrow e\} = x \blacktriangleleft \{x \leftarrow e\} = e.$$

It remains to show (‡‡), that $\{x \leftarrow e\}$ is most-general, that is,

$$(\forall\ sub\ \phi) \begin{bmatrix} if & x \blacktriangleleft \phi = e \blacktriangleleft \phi \\ then & \{x \leftarrow e\} \succeq_{gen} \phi \end{bmatrix}.$$

For an arbitrary substitution ϕ, suppose that ϕ unifies x and e, that is,

$$x \blacktriangleleft \phi = e \blacktriangleleft \phi.$$

We would like to show that $\{x \leftarrow e\}$ is more general than ϕ,

$$\{x \leftarrow e\} \succeq_{gen} \phi,$$

that is (by the definition of the generality relation $\succeq_{gen}$ for substitutions), that

$$(\exists\ sub\ \lambda) \big[\{x \leftarrow e\} \square \lambda = \phi \big].$$

We have

$$\phi = (x \leftarrow x \blacktriangleleft \phi) \square \phi$$
$\quad$ (by the *representation* property of substitutions)

$$= (x \leftarrow e \blacktriangleleft \phi) \square \phi$$
$\quad$ (by our supposition that $x \blacktriangleleft \phi = e \blacktriangleleft \phi$)

$$= \{x \leftarrow e\} \square \phi$$
$\quad$ (by the *replacement* property of the composition function $\square$).

Therefore, taking λ to be ϕ itself, we have

$$\{x \leftarrow e\} \square \lambda = \phi,$$

as we wanted to show. ⌋

EQUALLY-GENERAL UNIFIERS

Most-general unifiers are not unique. All the most-general unifiers of a given pair of t-expressions, however, are equally general; furthermore, any unifier equally general to a most-general unifier is also a most-general unifier.

Proposition (equally-general unifier)

The sentence

$$(\forall \, t\text{-}exp \; \ell, \, m) \atop (\forall \, sub \; \theta) \left[if \; mgu(\ell, \, m, \, \theta) \atop then \; (\forall \, sub \; \phi) \left[mgu(\ell, \, m, \, \phi) \atop \equiv \atop \theta \approx_{gen} \phi \right] \right]$$

$\qquad\qquad\qquad\qquad\qquad\qquad$ (*equally-general unifier*)

is valid. ⌋

Proof

For arbitrary t-expressions ℓ and m, suppose that θ is a most-general unifier of ℓ and m, that is,

$$mgu(\ell, \, m, \, \theta).$$

We would like to show that then the most-general unifiers of ℓ and m are precisely the substitutions that are equally general to θ, that is,

$$(\forall\ sub\ \phi)\ \begin{bmatrix} mgu(\ell,\ m,\ \phi) \\ \equiv \\ \theta \approx_{gen} \phi \end{bmatrix}.$$

Consider an arbitrary substitution ϕ; we prove each direction separately.

$(\Rightarrow)$

Suppose that ϕ is also a most-general unifier of ℓ and m, that is,

$$mgu(\ell,\ m,\ \phi).$$

We would like to show that then θ and ϕ are equally general, that is,

$$\theta \approx_{gen} \phi.$$

Because θ and ϕ are both most-general unifiers of ℓ and m, we have (by the definition of mgu) that θ and ϕ are unifiers of ℓ and m, that is,

$$\ell \blacktriangleleft \theta = m \blacktriangleleft \theta \quad \text{and} \quad \ell \blacktriangleleft \phi = m \blacktriangleleft \phi,$$

and that θ and ϕ are most-general, that is,

$$(\forall\ sub\ \lambda)\ \begin{bmatrix} if\ \ \ell \blacktriangleleft \lambda = m \blacktriangleleft \lambda \\ then\ \ \theta \succeq_{gen} \lambda \end{bmatrix}$$

and

$$(\forall\ sub\ \rho)\ \begin{bmatrix} if\ \ \ell \blacktriangleleft \rho = m \blacktriangleleft \rho \\ then\ \ \phi \succeq_{gen} \rho \end{bmatrix}.$$

In particular, taking λ and ρ to be ϕ and θ, respectively, we have (because $\ell \blacktriangleleft \phi = m \blacktriangleleft \phi$ and $\ell \blacktriangleleft \theta = m \blacktriangleleft \theta$)

$$\theta \succeq_{gen} \phi \quad \text{and} \quad \phi \succeq_{gen} \theta.$$

Therefore (by the definition of the equally-general relation $\approx_{gen}$)

$$\theta \approx_{gen} \phi,$$

as we wanted to show.

$(\Leftarrow)$

Suppose that θ and ϕ are equally general, that is,

$$\theta \approx_{gen} \phi.$$

We would like to show that then ϕ is a most-general unifier of ℓ and m, that is,

$$mgu(\ell,\ m,\ \phi).$$

We know that ϕ is a substitution. Because θ and ϕ are equally general, we have (by the definition of the equally-general relation $\approx_{gen}$) that each is more general than the other, that is,

$$\theta \succeq_{gen} \phi \quad \text{and} \quad \phi \succeq_{gen} \theta.$$

Because θ is a unifier of ℓ and m (by our initial supposition and the definition of mgu) and ϕ is an instance of θ, we know (by the *instance-unifier* proposition) that ϕ is also a unifier of ℓ and m, that is,

$$\ell \blacktriangleleft \phi = m \blacktriangleleft \phi.$$

It remains to show (by the definition of mgu) that ϕ is most-general, that is,

$$(\forall\ sub\ \lambda) \begin{bmatrix} if\ \ \ell \blacktriangleleft \lambda = m \blacktriangleleft \lambda \\ then\ \ \phi \succeq_{gen} \lambda \end{bmatrix}.$$

Consider an arbitrary unifier λ of ℓ and m, that is,

$$\ell \blacktriangleleft \lambda = m \blacktriangleleft \lambda.$$

We would like to show that then ϕ is more general than λ, that is,

$$\phi \succeq_{gen} \lambda.$$

Because, by our initial supposition, θ is a most-general unifier of ℓ and m, we know (by the definition of mgu) that θ is more general than λ, that is,

$$\theta \succeq_{gen} \lambda.$$

But, because ϕ is more general than θ, that is, $\phi \succeq_{gen} \theta$, we have (by the transitivity of the generality relation $\succeq_{gen}$ for substitutions) that

$$\phi \succeq_{gen} \lambda,$$

as we wanted to show. ◢

Example (equally-general unifiers)

As noted in the preview,

$$\{x \leftarrow y\} \quad \text{and} \quad \{y \leftarrow x\}$$

are both most-general unifiers of the expressions x and y. The proposition predicts that they will be equally general; we have already seen that this is so.

If we compose the most-general unifier $\{x \leftarrow y\}$ with the permutation

$$\{y \leftarrow z, z \leftarrow y\},$$

we obtain the substitution

$$\theta : \{x \leftarrow z, y \leftarrow z, z \leftarrow y\}.$$

We know (by the *equally-general* property of permutations) that θ is equally general to $\{x \leftarrow y\}$, and hence (by the proposition) is another most-general unifier of x and y.

We could have found other substitutions equally general to $\{x \leftarrow y\}$ by composing it with any permutation π. Consequently, there are actually an infinite number of most-general unifiers of x and y, all of them equally general.

We have remarked that the unifier

$$\phi : \{x \leftarrow z, y \leftarrow z\}$$

of x and y is not most-general; roughly, it does unnecessary work in unifying x and y with z. In particular, it is not more general than the unifier $\{x \leftarrow y\}$. To see this, suppose, to the contrary, that

$$\phi \succeq_{gen} \{x \leftarrow y\}.$$

That is, for some substitution λ,

$$\phi \square \lambda = \{x \leftarrow y\}.$$

Then, in particular,

$$x \blacktriangleleft (\phi \square \lambda) = x \blacktriangleleft \{x \leftarrow y\} \qquad \text{and} \qquad z \blacktriangleleft (\phi \square \lambda) = z \blacktriangleleft \{x \leftarrow y\}.$$

Hence

$$(x \blacktriangleleft \phi) \blacktriangleleft \lambda = y \qquad \text{and} \qquad (z \blacktriangleleft \phi) \blacktriangleleft \lambda = z,$$

and hence

$$z \blacktriangleleft \lambda = y \qquad \text{and} \qquad z \blacktriangleleft \lambda = z.$$

But this is impossible. ⌙

The reader is asked to compare different unifiers for the same two expressions in **Problem 9.3**.

MORE PROPERTIES

We have also the following properties of most-general unifiers:

$$
\begin{array}{l}
(\forall\,fun\ f,\ g) \\
(\forall\,tuple\ s,\ t) \\
(\forall\,sub\ \theta)
\end{array}
\left[
\begin{array}{l}
mgu(f{\bullet}s,\ g{\bullet}t,\ \theta) \\
\equiv \\
f = g \ \ and \ \ mgu(s,\ t,\ \theta)
\end{array}
\right]
\qquad (application)
$$

In other words, θ is a most-general unifier of $f{\bullet}s$ and $g{\bullet}t$ precisely when $f = g$ and θ is a most-general unifier of s and t.

The reader is requested to prove this property in **Problem 9.4**.

9.3   UNIFY FUNCTION

For any two t-expressions ℓ and m, there are systematic methods (*algorithms*) for determining whether or not the two are unifiable, and, if so, for producing a most-general unifier. We shall call this process *unification*.

One method for unifying two t-expressions is provided by the definition of the binary function $unify(\ell,\ m)$ given in this section; the axioms for $unify(\ell,\ m)$ can be viewed as defining an algorithm for determining whether or not ℓ and m are unifiable. This is the same algorithm that was presented informally in the preview of unification.

The function $unify(\ell,\ m)$ produces a most-general unifier of ℓ and m if they are unifiable; otherwise, it produces a special domain element denoted by the constant symbol *nil*. The element *nil* is assumed to be distinct from any substitution, as expressed by the following axiom:

$$
not\ \big(sub(nil)\big) \qquad\qquad\qquad\qquad\qquad\qquad\qquad\qquad (nil)
$$

We first present the definition for the *unify* function; later, we establish that it has the desired properties.

The *unify* function is defined in terms of an auxiliary function $diff(\ell,\ m)$, called the *difference* of ℓ and m. Speaking loosely, this function attempts to find a single replacement pair $\{x \leftarrow e\}$ that "reduces the difference" between ℓ and m; applying this pair to ℓ and m makes them more similar. If ℓ and m are already identical, $diff(\ell,\ m)$ is to be the empty substitution $\{\ \}$. If, on the other hand, the differences between ℓ and m are found to be irreconcilable, $diff(\ell,\ m)$ will be the special element *nil*. The substitution produced by the *unify* function, if successful, is to be the composition of all the difference pairs found by successive applications of *diff*.

THE UNIFY AXIOM

We begin by giving the axiom for the *unify* function in terms of the difference function *diff*. In this discussion, we use the notation

$$let \ \theta = t \ in \ e[\theta],$$

for any expression $e[\theta]$ and term t, to stand for

$$e[t].$$

This turns out to be an abbreviation in the case in which t is large and there is more than one occurrence of θ in $e[\theta]$.

The *unify* axiom is then

$$
(\forall \ t\text{-}exp \ \ell, m) \quad
\left[
\begin{array}{l}
unify(\ell, m) \ = \\
\quad \left\{
\begin{array}{l}
let \ \sigma = diff(\ell, m) \\
in \ \ if \ \ \sigma = \{\ \} \\
\quad then \ \ \{\ \} \\
\quad else \ if \ \sigma = nil \\
\qquad then \ \ nil \\
\qquad else \ \ let \ \ \theta = unify(\ell \blacktriangleleft \sigma, m \blacktriangleleft \sigma) \\
\qquad\qquad in \ \ if \ \ \theta = nil \\
\qquad\qquad\quad then \ \ nil \\
\qquad\qquad\quad else \ \ \sigma \square \theta
\end{array}
\right.
\end{array}
\right]
$$

$$(unify)$$

In other words, the *unify* function first invokes the difference function. If the difference function can give a conclusive answer, that the two t-expressions are either identical or not unifiable, the *unify* function reports the same result. Otherwise, the difference function produces a single replacement pair $\sigma : \{x \leftarrow e\}$, which reduces the difference between ℓ and m. This substitution is applied to the arguments, and *unify* is applied recursively to the resulting t-expressions $\ell \blacktriangleleft \sigma$ and $m \blacktriangleleft \sigma$, producing θ. If it is found that these t-expressions are not unifiable (that is, $\theta = nil$), *unify* reports that ℓ and m are not unifiable either. Otherwise, θ is a substitution, and *unify* produces the composition $\sigma \square \theta$ as the unifier of ℓ and m.

Subsequently we give some examples of the application of *unify* and prove its correctness. First, however, let us give the axioms for the auxiliary difference pair function.

THE DIFF FUNCTION

The axioms for *diff* are divided into several groups.

The variable axioms

These axioms apply if one of the arguments is a variable x and the other is an expression e.

$$\begin{array}{l}(\forall\ var\ x)\\ (\forall\ exp\ e)\end{array}\left[\ diff(x,\ e)\ =\ \begin{cases} if\ \ x \in e \\ then\ \ nil \\ else\ \ \{x \leftarrow e\} \end{cases}\right] \qquad (left\ variable)$$

$$\begin{array}{l}(\forall\ var\ x)\\ (\forall\ appl\ e)\end{array}\left[\ diff(e,\ x)\ =\ \begin{cases} if\ \ x \in e \\ then\ \ nil \\ else\ \ \{x \leftarrow e\} \end{cases}\right] \qquad (right\ variable)$$

In other words, if the variable x occurs properly in the expression e, we report that these two arguments are not unifiable. Otherwise, *diff* produces the substitution $\{x \leftarrow e\}$. If x and e are identical, this is the empty substitution $\{\ \}$. Note that the *right-variable* axiom applies only if the expression e is an application, not a variable; this is to avoid an inconsistency between the two axioms that will be discussed later.

The tuple axioms

These axioms apply if both arguments are tuples.

$$diff(\langle\ \rangle,\ \langle\ \rangle)\ =\ \{\ \} \qquad (empty)$$

$$\begin{array}{l}(\forall\ exp\ e)\\ (\forall\ tuple\ t)\end{array}\left[\ diff(\langle\ \rangle,\ e \diamond t)\ =\ nil\ \right] \qquad (empty\text{-}insertion)$$

$$\begin{array}{l}(\forall\ exp\ e)\\ (\forall\ tuple\ t)\end{array}\left[\ diff(e \diamond t,\ \langle\ \rangle)\ =\ nil\ \right] \qquad (insertion\text{-}empty)$$

In other words, if one of the two tuples is empty but the other is not, we report that the two are not unifiable.

The following axiom applies if the arguments are both nonempty tuples

$$d \diamond s\ =\ \langle d, s_1,\ \ldots, s_m \rangle \qquad and \qquad e \diamond t\ =\ \langle e, t_1,\ \ldots, t_n \rangle.$$

$$
(\forall\ exp\ d, e)\ \left[diff(d \diamond s, e \diamond t) = \left\{ \begin{array}{l} let\ \tau = diff(d,\ e) \\ in\ \ if\ \ \tau = nil \\ \quad then\ \ nil \\ \quad else\ if\ \ \tau = \{\ \} \\ \qquad then\ \ diff(s,\ t) \\ \qquad else\ \ \tau \end{array} \right\} \right]
$$

$$(\forall\ tuple\ s, t)$$

(*insertion*)

In other words, we first find the difference pair τ for the first elements d and e; if these turn out not to be unifiable (that is, $\tau = nil$), we report that $d \diamond s$ and $e \diamond t$ are not unifiable either. If d and e are identical (that is, $\tau = \{\ \}$), we produce the difference pair of $s = \langle s_1, \ldots, s_m \rangle$ and $t = \langle t_1, \ldots, t_n \rangle$. Otherwise, we produce the difference pair τ itself.

The application axiom

This axiom applies if both arguments are applications

$$f \bullet s = f(s_1, \ldots, s_m) \qquad \text{and} \qquad g \bullet t = g(t_1, \ldots, t_n).$$

$$
(\forall\ fun\ f, g) \\
(\forall\ tuple\ s, t)
\ \left[diff(f \bullet s, g \bullet t) = \left\{ \begin{array}{l} if\ \ f = g \\ then\ \ diff(s,\ t) \\ else\ \ nil \end{array} \right\} \right]
$$

(*application*)

In other words, we distinguish between two cases, depending on whether the function symbols f and g are identical or distinct. In the former case, we find the difference pair for the argument tuples $s = \langle s_1, \ldots, s_m \rangle$ and $t = \langle t_1, \ldots, t_n \rangle$; otherwise, we report that $f \bullet s$ and $g \bullet t$ are not unifiable.

Recall that we regard constants as 0-ary functions; thus this axiom applies if both arguments are constants.

From these axioms we can establish the property

$$(\forall\ t\text{-}exp\ \ell) \big[diff(\ell, \ell) = \{\ \} \big]$$

(*equal*)

In computing difference pairs, we shall use this property as if it were one of the axioms.

THE MISMATCH AXIOMS

The following axioms apply if one argument is an expression and the other is a
tuple, so that there is no hope of unifying them.

$$\begin{array}{|l}
(\forall\ exp\ e) \\
(\forall\ tuple\ t)
\end{array}\left[diff\,(e,\ t) = nil\right] \qquad\qquad (expression\text{-}tuple)$$

$$\begin{array}{l}
(\forall\ exp\ e) \\
(\forall\ tuple\ t)
\end{array}\left[diff\,(t,\ e) = nil\right] \qquad\qquad (tuple\text{-}expression)$$

Remark (right-variable axiom)

We have mentioned that the condition that e be an application (rather than
an expression) was required in the *right-variable* axiom for *diff* to avoid an inconsistency. For instance, suppose the condition were omitted; then the axiom
would read

$$\begin{array}{l}
(\forall\ var\ x) \\
(\forall\ exp\ e)
\end{array}\left[diff\,(e,\ x) = \left\{\begin{array}{l} if\ \ x \in e \\ then\ \ nil \\ else\ \ \{x \leftarrow e\}\end{array}\right\}\right].$$

In this case, we could conclude (taking x and e to be the distinct variables U and
V, respectively) that

$$diff\,(\text{V},\ \text{U})\ =\ \{\text{U} \leftarrow \text{V}\},$$

since $not\ (\text{U} \in \text{V})$.

On the other hand, by the *left-variable* axiom, we can conclude that

$$diff\,(\text{V},\ \text{U})\ =\ \{\text{V} \leftarrow \text{U}\},$$

since $not\ (\text{V} \in \text{U})$, and hence

$$\{\text{U} \leftarrow \text{V}\}\ =\ \{\text{V} \leftarrow \text{U}\}.$$

This is an inconsistency because $\{\text{U} \leftarrow \text{V}\}$ and $\{\text{V} \leftarrow \text{U}\}$ are distinct substitutions.

As usual, we cannot be certain when we define a function by a set of axioms
whether, for a given interpretation, the axioms define a unique function or, indeed,
whether they define any function at all. If the axioms for *unify* or *diff* failed to
cover some possible case, many different functions could satisfy them. On the
other hand, if the axioms were inconsistent, no function could satisfy them all.
As it turns out, the axioms cover all possible cases and are consistent. ∎

EXAMPLES

The preceding axioms for the function *unify* suggest a systematic method for unification, a *unification algorithm*. Such an algorithm produces a most-general unifier if its arguments are unifiable, and the special element *nil* otherwise. Before we establish that the function does indeed behave as expected, let us illustrate the suggested *unification* algorithm with some examples. The presentation of examples is hierarchical: details omitted from some examples are spelled out in subsequent ones.

Example 1: *unify*(ℓ, m) where
$$\ell:\ \text{F}(\text{X, B}) \quad \text{and} \quad m:\ \text{F}\big(\text{G}(\text{Y}),\ \text{Y}\big).$$

We follow the *unify* axiom.

Let
$$\sigma = \textit{diff}\,(\ell,\ m)$$
$$= \{\text{X} \leftarrow \text{G}(\text{Y})\}$$
(by the results of Subexample 1.1, following).

Let
$$\theta = \textit{unify}(\ell \blacktriangleleft \sigma,\ m \blacktriangleleft \sigma)$$
$$= \textit{unify}\big(\text{F}\big(\text{G}(\text{Y}),\ \text{B}\big),\ \text{F}\big(\text{G}(\text{Y}),\ \text{Y}\big)\big)$$
$$= \{\text{Y} \leftarrow \text{B}\}$$
(by the results of Subexample 1.2).

Therefore
$$\textit{unify}(\ell,\ m)\ = \sigma \,\square\, \theta$$
$$= \{\text{X} \leftarrow \text{G}(\text{Y})\}\,\square\,\{\text{Y} \leftarrow \text{B}\}$$
$$= \{\text{X} \leftarrow \text{G}(\text{B}),\ \text{Y} \leftarrow \text{B}\}.$$

In other words,
$$\{\text{X} \leftarrow \text{G}(\text{B}),\,\text{Y} \leftarrow \text{B}\}$$

is a most-general unifier of ℓ and m.

Subexample 1.1:   *diff* (ℓ, m) where
$$\ell:\ \text{F}(\text{X, B}) \quad \text{and} \quad m:\ \text{F}\big(\text{G}(\text{Y}),\ \text{Y}\big).$$

We follow the axioms for *diff*.

$$diff\,(\ell,\ m)\ =\ diff\left(\text{F}\bullet\langle\text{X, B}\rangle,\ \text{F}\bullet\langle\text{G(Y), Y}\rangle\right)$$

$$=\ diff\left(\langle\text{X, B}\rangle,\ \langle\text{G(Y), Y}\rangle\right)$$
(by the *application* axiom for *diff*)

$$=\ diff\left(\text{X}\diamond\langle\text{B}\rangle,\ \text{G(Y)}\diamond\langle\text{Y}\rangle\right).$$

We now follow the *insertion* axiom for *diff*.

Let

$$\tau\ =\ diff\left(\text{X, G(Y)}\right)$$

$$=\ \{\text{X}\leftarrow\text{G(Y)}\}$$
(by the *left-variable* axiom for *diff*, because *not* $\left(\text{X}\in\text{G(Y)}\right)$).

Therefore

$$diff\,(\ell,\ m)\ =\ \{\text{X}\leftarrow\text{G(Y)}\}.$$

Subexample 1.2: $\quad unify(\ell,\ m)\quad$ where
$$\ell:\ \text{F}\big(\text{G(Y), B}\big)\quad\text{and}\quad m:\ \text{F}\big(\text{G(Y), Y}\big).$$

We follow the *unify* axiom.

Let

$$\sigma\ =\ diff\,(\ell,\ m)$$

$$=\ \{\text{Y}\leftarrow\text{B}\}$$
(by the results of Subexample 1.3).

Let

$$\theta\ =\ unify(\ell\blacktriangleleft\sigma,\ m\blacktriangleleft\sigma)$$

$$=\ unify\big(\text{F(G(B), B)},\ \text{F(G(B), B)}\big)$$

$$=\ \{\ \}$$
(by the *equal* property of *diff*).

Therefore

$$unify(\ell,\ m)\ =\ \sigma\,\square\,\theta$$

$$=\ \{\text{Y}\leftarrow\text{B}\}\,\square\,\{\ \}$$

$$=\ \{\text{Y}\leftarrow\text{B}\}.$$

Subexample 1.3: $\textit{diff}\,(\ell,\, m)$ where
$$\ell: \; \mathrm{F}\big(\mathrm{G}(\mathrm{Y}),\, \mathrm{B}\big) \quad \text{and} \quad m: \; \mathrm{F}\big(\mathrm{G}(\mathrm{Y}),\, \mathrm{Y}\big).$$

We follow the axioms for *diff*.

$$\textit{diff}\,(\ell,\, m) \; = \; \textit{diff}\,\big(\mathrm{F} \bullet \langle \mathrm{G}(\mathrm{Y}),\, \mathrm{B}\rangle, \; \mathrm{F} \bullet \langle \mathrm{G}(\mathrm{Y}),\, \mathrm{Y}\rangle\big)$$

$$= \; \textit{diff}\,\big(\langle \mathrm{G}(\mathrm{Y}),\, \mathrm{B}\rangle, \; \langle \mathrm{G}(\mathrm{Y}),\, \mathrm{Y}\rangle\big)$$

$$= \; \textit{diff}\,\big(\mathrm{G}(\mathrm{Y}) \diamond \langle \mathrm{B}\rangle, \; \mathrm{G}(\mathrm{Y}) \diamond \langle \mathrm{Y}\rangle\big).$$

We now follow the *insertion* axiom for *diff*.

Let

$$\tau \; = \; \textit{diff}\,\big(\mathrm{G}(\mathrm{Y}),\, \mathrm{G}(\mathrm{Y})\big)$$

$$= \; \{\,\}$$
(by the *equal* property of *diff*).

Therefore

$$\textit{diff}\,(\ell,\, m) \; = \; \textit{diff}\,\big(\langle \mathrm{B}\rangle,\, \langle \mathrm{Y}\rangle\big)$$

$$= \; \textit{diff}\,\big(\mathrm{B} \diamond \langle\;\rangle, \; \mathrm{Y} \diamond \langle\;\rangle\big)$$

$$= \; \{\mathrm{Y} \leftarrow \mathrm{B}\}$$
(by the *insertion* and *right-variable* axioms for *diff*). ⏌

We now give an example in which the expressions turn out not to be unifiable. We omit some of the details.

Example 2: $\textit{unify}(\ell,\, m)$ where
$$\ell: \; \mathrm{F}\big(\mathrm{X},\, \mathrm{G}(\mathrm{X})\big) \quad \text{and} \quad m: \; \mathrm{F}(\mathrm{Y},\, \mathrm{Y})$$

We follow the *unify* axiom.

Let

$$\sigma \; = \; \textit{diff}\,(\ell,\, m)$$

$$= \; \textit{diff}\,\big(\mathrm{F}\big(\mathrm{X},\, \mathrm{G}(\mathrm{X})\big), \; \mathrm{F}(\mathrm{Y},\, \mathrm{Y})\big)$$

$$= \; \{\mathrm{X} \leftarrow \mathrm{Y}\}$$
(by axioms for *diff*).

Let

$$\theta = \mathit{unify}\big(F(X, G(X)) \blacktriangleleft \sigma,\ F(Y, Y) \blacktriangleleft \sigma\big)$$

$$= \mathit{unify}\big(F(Y, G(Y)),\ F(Y, Y)\big)$$

$$= \mathit{nil}$$
(by the result of Subexample 2.1).

Therefore,

$$\mathit{unify}(\ell, m) = \mathit{nil}.$$

In other words, the two t-expressions are not unifiable.

Subexample 2.1: $\mathit{unify}(\ell, m)$ where
$$\ell:\ F(Y, G(Y)) \quad \text{and} \quad m:\ F(Y, Y)$$

We follow the *unify* axiom.

Let

$$\sigma = \mathit{diff}(\ell, m)$$

$$= \mathit{diff}\big(F \bullet \langle Y, G(Y)\rangle,\ F \bullet \langle Y, Y\rangle\big)$$

$$= \mathit{diff}\big(\langle Y, G(Y)\rangle,\ \langle Y, Y\rangle\big)$$
(by the *application* axiom for *diff*)

$$= \mathit{diff}\big(Y \diamond \langle G(Y)\rangle,\ Y \diamond \langle Y\rangle\big)$$

$$= \mathit{diff}\big(\langle G(Y)\rangle,\ \langle Y\rangle\big)$$
(by the *insertion* axiom for *diff*, because $\mathit{diff}(Y, Y) = \{\ \}$)

$$= \mathit{diff}\big(G(Y) \diamond \langle\ \rangle,\ Y \diamond \langle\ \rangle\big).$$

We follow the *insertion* axiom for *diff* again.

Let

$$\tau = \mathit{diff}\big(G(Y), Y\big)$$

$$= \mathit{nil}$$
(by the *right-variable* axiom for *diff*, because $Y \in G(Y)$).

Therefore

$$\sigma = \mathit{nil}.$$

Therefore

$$\mathit{unify}(\ell, m) = \mathit{unify}\big(F(Y, G(Y)),\ F(Y, Y)\big) = \mathit{nil}.\quad \lrcorner$$

In **Problem 9.5** the reader is requested to unify certain pairs of t-expressions.

9.4   UNIFICATION PROPOSITION

We establish that the function $unify(\ell, m)$ does indeed perform unification; that is, it produces a most-general unifier for ℓ and m if they are unifiable, and the special domain object nil otherwise.

Proposition (unification)

The sentence

$$(\forall\ t\text{-}exp\ \ell,\ m) \begin{bmatrix} if & unifiable(\ell, m) \\ then & mgu(\ell, m, unify(\ell, m)) \\ else & unify(\ell, m)\ =\ nil \end{bmatrix}$$

is valid.   ⌟

The proof of the proposition is rather substantial and illustrates many of the notions we have introduced so far. If we regard the axioms for *unify* and *diff* as a program, we may consider the proof as a *verification* of that program, in that we establish that the program behaves in the way we expect.

THE DIFFERENCE LEMMAS

The proof of the proposition depends on several lemmas about the auxiliary function $diff(\ell, m)$, the difference of ℓ and m. These properties reflect our informal description of how this function is to behave.

Lemma (empty)

The sentence

$$(\forall\ t\text{-}exp\ \ell,\ m) \begin{bmatrix} diff(\ell, m) = \{\ \} \\ \equiv \\ \ell = m \end{bmatrix} \qquad (empty)$$

is valid.   ⌟

In other words, the difference of two t-expressions is the empty substitution precisely when the two are identical.

Lemma (pair)

The sentence

$$(\forall\ t\text{-}exp\ \ell,\ m)\ \left[if\ \begin{bmatrix} not\ \big(diff(\ell,\ m) = \{\ \}\big)\ \ and \\ not\ \big(diff(\ell,\ m) = nil\big) \end{bmatrix} \\ then\ (\exists\ var\ x)(\exists\ exp\ e) \\ \begin{bmatrix} diff(\ell,\ m)\ =\ \{x \leftarrow e\}\ \ and \\ \begin{bmatrix} (x \in \ell\ \ and\ \ e \in m)\ \ or \\ (x \in m\ \ and\ \ e \in \ell) \end{bmatrix}\ and \\ not\ (x \in e) \end{bmatrix} \right] \qquad (pair)$$

is valid. ⏌

In other words, in the case in which $diff(\ell,\ m)$ is neither empty nor *nil*, it is actually a replacement pair $\{x \leftarrow e\}$, whose variable x occurs in one of the t-expressions and whose expression e occurs in the other, such that x does not occur in e.

Lemma (replacement)

The sentence

$$\begin{matrix} (\forall\ t\text{-}exp\ \ell,\ m) \\ (\forall\ sub\ \phi) \end{matrix}\ \left[\begin{matrix} if\ \ \ell \blacktriangleleft \phi = m \blacktriangleleft \phi \\ then\ \ not\ \big(diff(\ell,\ m) = nil\big)\ \ and \\ (\exists\ sub\ \lambda)\big[\phi\ =\ diff(\ell,\ m) \square \lambda\big] \end{matrix} \right]$$

$$(replacement)$$

is valid. ⏌

In other words, any unifier ϕ of ℓ and m is an instance of the difference $diff(\ell,\ m)$. As a consequence of this property, we have the following result.

Lemma (nil)

The sentence

$$(\forall\ t\text{-}exp\ \ell,\ m)\ \begin{bmatrix} if\ \ diff(\ell,\ m) = nil \\ then\ \ not\ unifiable(\ell,\ m) \end{bmatrix} \qquad (nil)$$

is valid. ⏌

Note that the converse of the *nil* property is not valid. For example,

$$diff\big(\mathrm{F}(\mathrm{X}, \mathrm{B}),\ \mathrm{F}(\mathrm{A}, \mathrm{C})\big) \ = \ \{\mathrm{X} \leftarrow \mathrm{A}\},$$

even though $\mathrm{F}(\mathrm{X}, \mathrm{B})$ and $\mathrm{F}(\mathrm{A}, \mathrm{C})$ are not unifiable.

PROOF: LEMMAS $\Rightarrow$ PROPOSITION

We first show that the *difference* lemmas imply the *unification* proposition. Later we shall establish the *difference* lemmas themselves.

The proof is by well-founded induction over the relation $\prec_{un}$, defined by the axiom

$$(\forall\ t\text{-}exp\ \ell, m, \ell', m') \left[\begin{array}{l} \langle \ell,\ m \rangle \prec_{un} \langle \ell',\ m' \rangle \\ \equiv \\ varset(\ell) \cup varset(m) \ \subset \ varset(\ell') \cup varset(m') \end{array} \right]$$

In other words, with respect to this relation, one pair is less than another if the variables that occur in one are a proper subset of the variables that occur in the other. For example,

$$\langle \mathrm{X},\ \mathrm{X} \rangle \prec_{un} \langle \mathrm{X},\ \mathrm{F}(\mathrm{Y}) \rangle$$

because $\{\mathrm{X}\} \cup \{\mathrm{X}\} \subset \{\mathrm{X}\} \cup \{\mathrm{Y}\}$, that is, $\{\mathrm{X}\} \subset \{\mathrm{X}, \mathrm{Y}\}$. The well-foundedness of this relation is induced by the well-foundedness of the proper-subset relation over sets of variables.

We take the inductive sentence to be

$$\mathcal{U}[\ell,\ m]: \quad \begin{array}{l} \textit{if}\ \ \textit{unifiable}(\ell,\ m) \\ \textit{then}\ \ \textit{mgu}\big(\ell,\ m,\ \textit{unify}(\ell,\ m)\big) \\ \textit{else}\ \ \textit{unify}(\ell,\ m)\ =\ \textit{nil}. \end{array}$$

According to the *well-founded induction* principle over pairs (Section 4.1), to show the *unification* proposition, that is,

$$(\forall\ t\text{-}exp\ \ell,\ m)\mathcal{U}[\ell,\ m],$$

it suffices to establish a single inductive step,

$$(\forall\ t\text{-}exp\ \ell,\ m) \left[if\ (\forall\ t\text{-}exp\ \ell', m') \left[\begin{array}{l} if\ \langle \ell',\ m' \rangle \prec_{un} \langle \ell,\ m \rangle \\ then\ \mathcal{U}[\ell',\ m'] \end{array} \right] \\ then\ \mathcal{U}[\ell,\ m] \right].$$

Consider arbitrary t-expressions ℓ and m and assume as our induction hypothesis that

$$(*) \qquad (\forall \ t\text{-}exp \ \ell', m') \left[\begin{array}{l} if \ \langle \ell', m' \rangle \prec_{un} \langle \ell, m \rangle \\ then \ \mathcal{U}[\ell', m'] \end{array} \right].$$

We would like to establish that then

$$\mathcal{U}[\ell, m].$$

The proof follows the *unify* axiom and relies on the *difference* lemmas. We let

$$\sigma = diff(\ell, m).$$

Case: $\sigma = \{ \}$

Then (by the *unify* axiom)

$$unify(\ell, m) = \{ \}$$

and also (by the *empty* property of *diff*, because $diff(\ell, m) = \{ \}$ in this case)

$$\ell = m.$$

Therefore (by the *same* property of *unifiable* and the *empty-unifier* property of *mgu*)

$$unifiable(\ell, m) \ and \ mgu\big(\ell, m, unify(\ell, m)\big),$$

which implies the desired conclusion $\mathcal{U}[\ell, m]$.

Case: $\sigma = nil$

Then (by the *unify* axiom)

$$unify(\ell, m) = nil$$

and also (by the *nil* property of *diff*, because $diff(\ell, m) = nil$ in this case)

$$not \ unifiable(\ell, m).$$

But this implies the desired conclusion $\mathcal{U}[\ell, m]$.

Inductive Cases

Henceforth, we may assume

$$not \ (\sigma = \{ \}) \quad and \quad not \ (\sigma = nil).$$

In preparation for applying the induction hypothesis, we seek to show that

$$\langle \ell \blacktriangleleft \sigma, \ m \blacktriangleleft \sigma \rangle \prec_{un} \langle \ell, \ m \rangle,$$

that is (by the definition of $\prec_{un}$), that

(††) $varset(\ell \blacktriangleleft \sigma) \cup varset(m \blacktriangleleft \sigma) \subset varset(\ell) \cup varset(m).$

Note that, in this case (by the *pair* property of *diff*),

$$\sigma \ = \ diff(\ell, \ m) \ = \ \{x \leftarrow e\}$$

for some variable x and expression e such that

(†) $\begin{bmatrix} (x \equiv \ell \ \ and \ \ e \equiv m) \ \ or \\ (x \equiv m \ \ and \ \ e \equiv \ell) \end{bmatrix} \ and \ \ not \ (x \equiv e).$

Therefore

$$e \equiv \ell \ \ or \ \ e \equiv m$$

and

$$varset(\ell \blacktriangleleft \sigma) \ \subseteq \ varset(\ell) \cup varset(e)$$
$$\text{(by the } \textit{variable-introduction} \text{ property}$$
$$\text{of the replacement function)}$$

$$\subseteq \ varset(\ell) \cup varset(m)$$
$$\text{(by the } \textit{monotonicity} \text{ property of } \textit{varset}).$$

Similarly,

$$varset(m \blacktriangleleft \sigma) \ \subseteq \ varset(\ell) \cup varset(m)$$

and hence

$$varset(\ell \blacktriangleleft \sigma) \cup varset(m \blacktriangleleft \sigma) \ \subseteq \ varset(\ell) \cup varset(m).$$

To show that this inclusion is proper, it suffices to find a single variable that belongs to the right-hand set but not the left-hand set.

We know (by (†)) that

$$x \equiv \ell \ \ or \ \ x \equiv m$$

and hence (by the *occur* property of *varset*),

$$x \ \in \ varset(\ell) \cup varset(m).$$

Also, we have (by (†)) that

$$not \ (x \equiv e)$$

and hence (by the *variable-elimination* property of the replacement function)

$$not\ \big(x \in varset(\ell \blacktriangleleft \sigma)\big) \quad \text{and} \quad not\ \big(x \in varset(m \blacktriangleleft \sigma)\big).$$

Therefore

$$not\ \Big(x \in varset(\ell \blacktriangleleft \sigma) \cup varset(m \blacktriangleleft \sigma)\Big).$$

Thus x belongs to the right-hand set but not the left-hand set. This establishes the desired result (††), that the inclusion is proper, and hence that

$$\langle \ell \blacktriangleleft \sigma,\ m \blacktriangleleft \sigma \rangle \prec_{un} \langle \ell,\ m \rangle.$$

Therefore we may apply our induction hypothesis (∗), taking ℓ' and m' to be $\ell \blacktriangleleft \sigma$ and $m \blacktriangleleft \sigma$, respectively, to conclude that

$$\mathcal{U}[\ell \blacktriangleleft \sigma,\ m \blacktriangleleft \sigma],$$

that is, letting

$$\theta\ =\ unify(\ell \blacktriangleleft \sigma,\ m \blacktriangleleft \sigma),$$

that

(‡) $\quad$ if $\ unifiable(\ell \blacktriangleleft \sigma,\ m \blacktriangleleft \sigma)$
$\quad\quad\quad$ then $\ mgu(\ell \blacktriangleleft \sigma,\ m \blacktriangleleft \sigma,\ \theta)$
$\quad\quad\quad$ else $\ \theta = nil.$

The proof of our desired conclusion $\mathcal{U}[\ell,\ m]$ continues to follow the definition of *unify*.

Case: $\ \theta = nil$

Then (by the *unify* axiom)

$$unify(\ell,\ m)\ =\ nil.$$

To prove $\mathcal{U}[\ell,\ m]$, it suffices to show that then

$$not\ unifiable(\ell,\ m).$$

Suppose, to the contrary, that ℓ and m are unifiable, and let ϕ be a unifier; that is,

$$\ell \blacktriangleleft \phi\ =\ m \blacktriangleleft \phi.$$

Then (by the *replacement* property of *diff*, recalling that $\sigma = diff(\ell, m)$), we have that, for some substitution λ,

$$\phi\ =\ \sigma \square \lambda.$$

Therefore

$$\ell \blacktriangleleft (\sigma \square \lambda) \;=\; m \blacktriangleleft (\sigma \square \lambda)$$

and hence (by the *composition* property of substitutions)

$$(\ell \blacktriangleleft \sigma) \blacktriangleleft \lambda \;=\; (m \blacktriangleleft \sigma) \blacktriangleleft \lambda.$$

In other words, $\ell \blacktriangleleft \sigma$ and $m \blacktriangleleft \sigma$ are unifiable, that is,

$$unifiable(\ell \blacktriangleleft \sigma,\, m \blacktriangleleft \sigma),$$

and hence (by (‡))

$$mgu(\ell \blacktriangleleft \sigma,\, m \blacktriangleleft \sigma,\, \theta).$$

Therefore, θ must be a substitution, contradicting our assumption that, in this case, $\theta = nil$.

Case: $not\ (\theta = nil)$

Then (by the *unify* axiom)

$$unify(\ell,\, m) \;=\; \sigma \square \theta.$$

To prove our desired conclusion $\mathcal{U}[\ell,\, m]$, it thus suffices to show that

$$mgu(\ell,\, m,\, \sigma \square \theta)$$

and (hence) $unifiable(\ell,\, m)$.

First we show that $\sigma \square \theta$ is a unifier of ℓ and m; then we show that it is most-general. In this case (by the consequence (‡) of our induction hypothesis, because $not\ (\theta = nil)$, in this case), we know that $unifiable(\ell \blacktriangleleft \sigma,\, m \blacktriangleleft \sigma)$ and

$$(\S) \qquad mgu(\ell \blacktriangleleft \sigma,\, m \blacktriangleleft \sigma,\, \theta).$$

Therefore

$$(\ell \blacktriangleleft \sigma) \blacktriangleleft \theta \;=\; (m \blacktriangleleft \sigma) \blacktriangleleft \theta$$

and hence (by the *composition* property)

$$\ell \blacktriangleleft (\sigma \square \theta) \;=\; m \blacktriangleleft (\sigma \square \theta).$$

Thus $\sigma \square \theta$ is indeed a unifier of ℓ and m.

To show that $\sigma \square \theta$ is most-general, suppose ϕ is a unifier of ℓ and m, that is, that

$$\ell \blacktriangleleft \phi \;=\; m \blacktriangleleft \phi.$$

We would like to find a substitution λ' such that

$$\phi \;=\; (\sigma \,\square\, \theta)\,\square\,\lambda'.$$

We have (by the *replacement* property of *diff*, recalling that $\sigma = diff(\ell,\, m)$) that, for some substitution λ,

$$\phi \;=\; \sigma \,\square\, \lambda.$$

Therefore

$$\ell \blacktriangleleft (\sigma \,\square\, \lambda) \;=\; m \blacktriangleleft (\sigma \,\square\, \lambda)$$

and hence (by the *composition* property)

$$(\ell \blacktriangleleft \sigma) \blacktriangleleft \lambda \;=\; (m \blacktriangleleft \sigma) \blacktriangleleft \lambda,$$

that is, λ is a unifier of $\ell \blacktriangleleft \sigma$ and $m \blacktriangleleft \sigma$. But we have found (§) that θ is a most-general unifier of $\ell \blacktriangleleft \sigma$ and $m \blacktriangleleft \sigma$; hence there is some substitution λ' such that

$$\lambda \;=\; \theta \,\square\, \lambda'.$$

Therefore

$$\phi \;=\; \sigma \,\square\, \lambda \;=\; \sigma \,\square\, (\theta \,\square\, \lambda')$$

and hence (by the associativity of composition)

$$\phi \;=\; (\sigma \,\square\, \theta)\,\square\,\lambda',$$

as we wanted to show. ⌟

PROOF OF LEMMAS

It remains to establish the *difference* lemmas. These proofs are routine; we shall give parts of some of them just to illustrate how they go.

Proof (replacement lemma)

Consider an arbitrary substitution ϕ. We would like to show

$$(\forall\, t\text{-}exp\;\ell, m) \left[\begin{array}{l} if\ \ \ell \blacktriangleleft \phi \;=\; m \blacktriangleleft \phi \\ then\ \ not\ \big(diff(\ell,\, m) \;=\; nil\big)\ \ and \\ \qquad (\exists\ sub\ \lambda)\big[\phi \;=\; diff(\ell,\, m)\,\square\,\lambda\big] \end{array} \right].$$

The proof is by well-founded induction with respect to the proper-suboccurrence relation $\in$, which is well-founded over the t-expressions. We take our inductive sentence to be

$$\mathcal{D}[\ell]: \quad (\forall \, t\text{-}exp \, m) \left[\begin{array}{l} if \;\; \ell \blacktriangleleft \phi = m \blacktriangleleft \phi \\ then \;\; not \, \big(diff\,(\ell, m) = nil\big) \;\; and \\ \quad (\exists \, sub \, \lambda)[\phi \; = \; diff\,(\ell, m)\,\square\,\lambda] \end{array} \right].$$

We consider an arbitrary t-expression ℓ and attempt to show $\mathcal{D}[\ell]$, assuming the induction hypothesis

$$(\dagger) \qquad (\forall \, t\text{-}exp \, \ell') \left[\begin{array}{l} if \;\; \ell' \in \ell \\ then \;\; \mathcal{D}[\ell'] \end{array} \right].$$

Consider an arbitrary t-expression m. We must show

$$(\dagger\dagger) \qquad \begin{array}{l} if \;\; \ell \blacktriangleleft \phi \; = \; m \blacktriangleleft \phi \\ then \;\; not \, \big(diff\,(\ell, m) \; = \; nil\big) \;\; and \\ \quad (\exists \, sub \, \lambda)[\phi \; = \; diff\,(\ell, m)\,\square\,\lambda]. \end{array}$$

The proof distinguishes among several cases, according to the structure of ℓ and m. We consider only a few representative cases.

Case: $var(\ell)$ and $exp(m)$ and $\ell \in m$

We must show ($\dagger\dagger$). But if $\ell \in m$, we know (by the *strict-monotonicity* property of $\blacktriangleleft$) that $\ell \blacktriangleleft \phi \in m \blacktriangleleft \phi$, and therefore the antecedent

$$\ell \blacktriangleleft \phi \; = \; m \blacktriangleleft \phi$$

must be false; hence ($\dagger\dagger$) is true.

Case: $var(\ell)$ and $exp(m)$ and $not \, (\ell \in m)$

Then (by the *left-variable* axiom for $diff$)

$$diff\,(\ell, m) \; = \; \{\ell \leftarrow m\}$$

and (hence)

$$not \, \big(diff\,(\ell, m) \; = \; nil\big).$$

Also, $\{\ell \leftarrow m\}$ is a most-general unifier of ℓ and m.

To show ($\dagger\dagger$), suppose

$$\ell \blacktriangleleft \phi \; = \; m \blacktriangleleft \phi,$$

that is, ϕ is a unifier of ℓ and m. Then, because $\{\ell \leftarrow m\}$ is a most-general unifier of ℓ and m, there is some substitution λ such that

$$\phi = \{\ell \leftarrow m\} \square \lambda.$$

This completes the proof of (††) in this case.

Case: ℓ and m are both nonempty tuples

Then

$$\ell = d \diamond s \qquad \text{and} \qquad m = e \diamond t$$

for some expressions d and e and tuples s and t. Hence

$$d \in \ell \qquad \text{and} \qquad s \in \ell.$$

We can thus conclude, by two applications of our induction hypothesis (†), that

$$\mathcal{D}[d]: \quad (\forall\ t\text{-}exp\ e') \begin{bmatrix} if\ \ d \triangleleft \phi = e' \triangleleft \phi \\ then\ \ not\ (diff(d,\ e') = nil)\ \ and \\ (\exists\ sub\ \lambda)[\phi = diff(d,\ e') \square \lambda] \end{bmatrix}$$

and

$$\mathcal{D}[s]: \quad (\forall\ t\text{-}exp\ t') \begin{bmatrix} if\ \ s \triangleleft \phi = t' \triangleleft \phi \\ then\ \ not\ (diff(d,\ t') = nil)\ \ and \\ (\exists\ sub\ \lambda)[\phi = diff(s,\ t') \square \lambda] \end{bmatrix}.$$

(For clarity, we have renamed m, first as e', then as t'.)

To show (††), we suppose the antecedent, that

$$\ell \triangleleft \phi = m \triangleleft \phi,$$

and attempt to show the consequent, that

$$not\ (diff(\ell,\ m) = nil)\ \ and$$
$$(\exists\ sub\ \lambda)[\phi = diff(\ell,\ m) \square \lambda].$$

Then (by our supposition and the *insertion-unifier* property)

$$d \triangleleft \phi = e \triangleleft \phi \qquad \text{and} \qquad s \triangleleft \phi = t \triangleleft \phi.$$

Therefore, by $\mathcal{D}[d]$ and $\mathcal{D}[s]$, taking e' and t' to be e and t, respectively, we have

$$\mathcal{D}_d: \quad \begin{aligned} &not\ (diff(d,\ e) = nil)\ \ and \\ &(\exists\ sub\ \lambda)[\phi = diff(d,\ e) \square \lambda] \end{aligned}$$

and

$$\mathcal{D}_s: \quad \begin{aligned} &not\,\bigl(diff(s,\,t)\,=\,nil\bigr) \ \ and \\ &(\exists\ sub\ \lambda)[\phi\,=\,diff(s,\,t)\,\square\,\lambda]. \end{aligned}$$

From this point the proof follows the *insertion* axiom for *diff*. Let

$$\tau\,=\,diff(d,\,e).$$

We distinguish among three subcases.

Subcase: $\tau = nil$

This case cannot arise, by $\mathcal{D}_d$.

Subcase: $\tau = \{\,\}$

Then (by the *insertion* axiom for *diff*)

$$diff(\ell,\,m)\,=\,diff(s,\,t)$$

and hence (by $\mathcal{D}_s$)

$$\begin{aligned} &not\,\bigl(diff(\ell,\,m)\,=\,nil\bigr) \ \ and \\ &(\exists\ sub\ \lambda)[\phi\,=\,diff(\ell,\,m)\,\square\,\lambda], \end{aligned}$$

which is the consequent of our desired (††).

Subcase: $not\,(\tau = nil)$ and $not\,(\tau = \{\,\})$

Then (by the *insertion* axiom for *diff*)

$$diff(\ell,\,m)\,=\,\tau\,=\,diff(d,\,e)$$

and hence (by $\mathcal{D}_d$)

$$\begin{aligned} &not\,\bigl(diff(\ell,\,m)\,=\,nil\bigr) \ \ and \\ &(\exists\ sub\ \lambda)[\phi\,=\,diff(\ell,\,m)\,\square\,\lambda], \end{aligned}$$

which is the consequent of our desired (††).

This concludes the proof of the replacement lemma for the case in which ℓ and m are both nonempty tuples. ⌟

The reader is requested (**Problems 9.6, 9.7**, and **9.8**) to provide the proofs of the *empty* and *pair* lemmas and the missing parts of the proof of the *replacement* lemma for the difference function.

The *unification* proposition establishes that, if two t-expressions ℓ and m are unifiable, they have a most-general unifier, namely, $unify(\ell, m)$. We also know (by the *equally-general unifier* proposition) that then the set of all most-general unifiers of ℓ and m is precisely the set of substitutions equally general to $unify(\ell, m)$. This set is (by the *equally-general* property of the permutations) precisely the set of substitutions of form

$$unify(\ell, m) \,\square\, \pi,$$

where π is a permutation substitution.

The *unification* algorithm actually produces an idempotent unifier in the case in which its arguments are unifiable, although this is not established by the proposition. A property of most-general, idempotent unifiers is given in **Problem 9.9**.

UNIFYING A TUPLE

The *unification* algorithm we have given applies to two t-expressions. Sometimes it is necessary to unify more than two expressions at once, that is, to test whether they have a common instance and, if so, to find a most-general substitution that makes them identical. We formulate this problem as one of unifying a tuple of expressions. (We need not consider tuples of general t-expressions.) We shall use the *unification* algorithm (for two expressions) we have already constructed to help solve the more general problem (for tuples of expressions).

Definition (unifier of a tuple)

A substitution θ is said to be a *unifier* of a tuple t (of expressions) if the elements of $t \triangleleft \theta$ are all identical.

A tuple is *unifiable*, denoted by $unifiable(t)$, if it has a unifier. ⌟

Example

The tuple

$$t: \quad \langle \text{F}(\text{X}, \text{Y}, \text{C}), \;\; \text{F}(\text{X}, \text{B}, \text{Z}), \;\; \text{F}(\text{A}, \text{Y}, \text{Z}) \rangle$$

is unifiable because, for

$$\theta: \quad \{\text{X} \leftarrow \text{A}, \; \text{Y} \leftarrow \text{B}, \; \text{Z} \leftarrow \text{C}\},$$

all the elements of

$$t \blacktriangleleft \theta : \quad \langle \text{F}(\text{A}, \text{B}, \text{C}), \ \text{F}(\text{A}, \text{B}, \text{C}), \ \text{F}(\text{A}, \text{B}, \text{C}) \rangle$$

are identical. ⏌

Definition (most-general unifier of a tuple)

A substitution θ is said to be a *most-general unifier* of a tuple t (of expressions) if

θ is a unifier of t and
θ is more general than any other unifier of t.

We shall use the abbreviation *mgutuple*(t, θ) to stand for "θ is a most-general unifier of t." ⏌

Example

The substitution

$$\theta : \quad \{\text{X} \leftarrow \text{Y}\}$$

is a most-general unifier for the tuple of expressions

$$t : \quad \langle \text{F}(\text{X}), \ \text{F}(\text{Y}) \rangle.$$

The substitution

$$\phi : \quad \{\text{X} \leftarrow \text{Z}, \ \text{Y} \leftarrow \text{Z}\}$$

is a unifier, but is not most-general. In fact, $\phi = \theta \square \{\text{Y} \leftarrow \text{Z}\}$. ⏌

We regard any substitution as a unifier for the empty tuple $\langle \ \rangle$. Of course, any substitution is also a unifier for a singleton tuple, that is, a tuple of one element.

The reader is asked to provide axioms defining the *unifiable* and *mgutuple* relations for tuples in **Problem 9.10**.

We now present an algorithm for unifying a tuple of expressions. This algorithm is presented as the definition of a function *unifytuple*(t), which produces a most-general unifier of a tuple t if t is unifiable, and the special element *nil* otherwise. The function is defined in terms of *unify*.

$$unifytuple(\langle\,\rangle) \;=\; \{\,\} \qquad\qquad (empty)$$

$$(\forall exp\ e)\Big[unifytuple(\langle e\rangle)\Big] \;=\; \{\,\} \qquad\qquad (singleton)$$

$$
(\forall\ exp\ d,\ e) \atop (\forall\ tuple\ t)
\left[
\begin{array}{l}
unifytuple(d \diamond (e \diamond t)) \;= \\
\quad let\ \ \theta = unify(d,\ e) \\
\quad in\ \ if\ \ \theta = nil \\
\qquad then\ \ nil \\
\qquad else\ \ let\ \ \phi = unifytuple((e \diamond t) \blacktriangleleft \theta) \\
\qquad\qquad in\ \ if\ \ \phi = nil \\
\qquad\qquad\quad then\ \ nil \\
\qquad\qquad\quad else\ \ \theta \,\square\, \phi
\end{array}
\right]
$$

$$(double\ insertion)$$

In other words, empty and singleton tuples are all unifiable, with the empty substitution as a most-general unifier. To unify a tuple with at least two elements, we first attempt to unify the first two elements, obtaining θ. If this attempt fails, our entire unification enterprise is doomed. Otherwise, we apply θ to the tail of our tuple, and attempt (recursively) to unify the resulting tuple, obtaining ϕ. If this attempt fails, our entire unification effort fails. Otherwise, we return the composition $\theta \,\square\, \phi$ as our most-general unifier.

That the algorithm behaves as we expect is expressed in the following result.

Proposition (tuple unification)

The sentence

$$
(\forall\ tuple\ t)
\left[
\begin{array}{l}
if\ \ unifiable(t) \\
then\ \ mgutuple\big(t,\ unifytuple(t)\big) \\
else\ \ unifytuple(t) = nil
\end{array}
\right]
$$

is valid. ⌟

The proof of the proposition is requested in **Problem 9.11**.

PROBLEMS

Problem 9.1 (unifiers)   page 334

Consider the two terms

$$\ell: \quad G(X, Z) \quad \text{and} \quad m: \quad G\big(Y, F(Y)\big).$$

Which of the following substitutions unify ℓ and m?

(a) $\{X \leftarrow Y, \; Z \leftarrow F(Y)\}$

(b) $\{X \leftarrow A, \; Y \leftarrow A, \; Z \leftarrow F(A)\}$

(c) $\{Y \leftarrow X, \; Z \leftarrow F(Y)\}$

(d) $\{X \leftarrow Z, \; Y \leftarrow Z, \; Z \leftarrow F(Z)\}.$

Problem 9.2 (insertion of unifiers)   page 336

Prove the two parts of the *insertion* proposition of unifiers:

(a) *Insertion unifier*

$$\begin{array}{l} (\forall \; exp \; d, \; e) \\ (\forall \; tuple \; s, \; t) \\ (\forall \; sub \; \theta) \end{array} \left[\begin{array}{l} (d \diamond s) \triangleleft \theta \; = \; (e \diamond t) \triangleleft \theta \\ \equiv \\ d \triangleleft \theta = e \triangleleft \theta \;\; and \;\; s \triangleleft \theta = t \triangleleft \theta \end{array} \right]$$

(b) *Insertion unifiable*

$$\begin{array}{l} (\forall \; exp \; d, \; e) \\ (\forall \; tuple \; s, \; t) \end{array} \left[\begin{array}{l} if \;\; unifiable(d \diamond s, \; e \diamond t) \\ then \;\; unifiable(d, \; e) \;\; and \;\; unifiable(s, \; t) \end{array} \right].$$

Problem 9.3 (comparing unifiers)   page 346

(a) Find three different unifiers θ_1, θ_2, and θ_3 of

$$F\big(G(X, \; Y), \; Z\big) \quad \text{and} \quad F\big(G(Z, \; A), \; X\big).$$

(b) For each pair of distinct unifiers θ_i and θ_j, state whether $\theta_i \succeq_{gen} \theta_j$ and, if so, find a substitution λ such that

$$\theta_i \; \square \; \lambda \; = \; \theta_j.$$

Problem 9.4 (most-general unifiers)   page 347

Prove the following *application* property of most-general unifiers:

$$\begin{array}{l} (\forall \; fun \; f, \; g) \\ (\forall \; tuple \; s, \; t) \\ (\forall \; sub \; \theta) \end{array} \left[\begin{array}{l} mgu(f \bullet s, \; g \bullet t, \; \theta) \\ \equiv \\ f = g \;\; and \;\; mgu(s, \; t, \; \theta) \end{array} \right].$$

Problem 9.5 (unification examples)   page 356

Apply the *unification* algorithm suggested by the axioms for the function *unify* to produce a most-general unifier of the following t-expressions if they are unifiable, and the special domain element *nil* otherwise:

(a) $F(X, B)$ and $F(F(Y, Y), Y)$

(b) $\langle X, G(X) \rangle$ and $\langle G(Y), Y \rangle$

(c) $H(X, F(Y, A), G(G(U)))$ and $H(Z, F(Z, U), Y)$

(d) $H(X, F(Y, A), G(G(X)))$ and $H(Z, F(Z, U), Y)$

(e) $H(X, F(Y, A), Y)$ and $H(F(F(B, Z), Z), X, F(Z, A))$.

Display the intermediate steps.

Problem 9.6 (empty lemma)   page 366

Prove the *empty* property for the difference function *diff*, that is, that the sentence

$$(\forall \, t\text{-}exp \, \ell, m) \left[\begin{array}{c} diff(\ell, m) = \{ \} \\ \equiv \\ \ell = m \end{array} \right]$$

is valid.

Problem 9.7 (pair lemma)   page 366

Prove the *pair* property of the difference function *diff*, that is, that the sentence

$$(\forall \, t\text{-}exp \, \ell, m) \left[if \begin{array}{l} \left[\begin{array}{l} not \, (diff(\ell, m) = \{ \}) \ and \\ not \, (diff(\ell, m) = nil) \end{array} \right] \\ then \, (\exists \, var \, x)(\exists \, exp \, e) \\ \quad \left[\begin{array}{l} diff(\ell, m) = \{x \leftarrow e\} \ and \\ \left[\begin{array}{l} (x \Subset \ell \ and \ e \Subset m) \ or \\ (x \Subset m \ and \ e \Subset \ell) \end{array} \right] and \\ not \, (x \Subset e) \end{array} \right] \end{array} \right]$$

is valid.

Problem 9.8 (replacement lemma)   page 366

In the text, we have given a partial proof of the *replacement* lemma, that is,
that the sentence

$$(\forall\ t\text{-}exp\ \ell,\ m) \atop (\forall\ sub\ \phi) \left[\begin{matrix} if\ \ \ell \blacktriangleleft \phi\ =\ m \blacktriangleleft \phi \\ then\ \ not\ \big(diff(\ell,\ m)\ =\ nil \big)\ and \\ (\exists\ sub\ \lambda)\big[\phi\ =\ diff(\ell,\ m)\square\lambda\big] \end{matrix} \right]$$

is valid. We have given the proof of the inductive step for the cases in which ℓ is a
variable and m is an expression and in which ℓ and m are both nonempty tuples.

Complete the proof for the remaining cases (m is a variable and ℓ is an
expression; ℓ and m are both applications; one argument is an expression and the
other is a tuple; both arguments are the empty tuple; and one argument is an
empty tuple and the other is nonempty).

Problem 9.9 (most-general, idempotent unifiers)   page 367

Show that a unifier θ of two tchap10ssions ℓ and m is most-general and
idempotent precisely when

$$(\forall\ sub\ \psi) \left[\begin{matrix} if\ \ \ell \blacktriangleleft \psi\ =\ m \blacktriangleleft \psi \\ then\ \ \theta\square\psi\ =\ \psi \end{matrix} \right].$$

Problem 9.10 (unifiers of tuples)   page 368

Give axioms defining the following relations.

(a)   *unifiable*(t), that is, tuple t is unifiable.

(b)   *mgutuple*$(t,\ \theta)$, that is, substitution θ is a most-general unifier of tuple t.

Problem 9.11 (tuple unification)   page 369

Apply the *tuple-unification* algorithm suggested by the *unifytuple* axioms to
attempt to unify the following tuples of expressions:

(a) $\langle F(X,\ U,\ A),\ F\big(G(Y),\ Y,\ V\big),\ F\big(W,\ H(Z),\ Z\big)\rangle$

(b) $\langle F(X),\ F\big(G(Y)\big),\ F(Y)\rangle.$

You should give intermediate steps in the computation of *unifytuple*, but you may
omit intermediate steps in the computation of *unify*.

(c) Find a tuple of three expressions that is not unifiable but all of whose proper subtuples are unifiable.

∗ (d) Prove the *tuple-unification* proposition, that is, that the sentence

$$(\forall\ tuple\ t)\ \left[\begin{array}{ll} if & unifiable(t) \\ then & mgutuple\,(t,\ unifytuple(t)) \\ else & unifytuple(t) = nil \end{array}\right]$$

is valid.

IV

Predicate

Logic

10

Logical
Apparatus

In Chapter 5, we presented the logical apparatus we need to develop a formal deductive system for propositional logic. In this chapter, we introduce the corresponding apparatus for predicate logic.

We extend the substitutions of Part III to apply to the expressions (i.e., terms and sentences) of predicate logic rather than to those of the theory of expressions. In this way, we can employ the *unification* algorithm from the previous chapter to unify predicate-logic terms and sentences.

A principal result of this chapter will be a method for removing quantifiers from a predicate-logic sentence without affecting its validity, allowing us to treat predicate logic using methods from propositional logic.

10.1   UNIFICATION IN PREDICATE LOGIC

We begin by showing how our results on unification are introduced into our formal deductive system.

THE UNIFICATION ALGORITHM

In the theory of expressions, the domain objects of our intended model included terms, not sentences. The quantifier-free expressions of predicate logic, however, which include sentences as well as terms, constitute the objects of another model for this theory. In this model, we include the predicate symbols, connectives, and term constructor among the function symbols of the domain. In other words, we treat a predicate symbol such as p, a connective such as *if-then*, or the term constructor *if-then-else* just as we would treat a function symbol such as F. A constant symbol such as a is treated as a term A( ), where A is a 0-ary function symbol. Therefore all the results of Part III, Unification, can be applied to quantifier-free predicate-logic expressions.

For example, we can apply the *unification* algorithm to the two sentences

$$\textit{if } p(x) \textit{ then } q(b) \qquad \text{and} \qquad \textit{if } p(a) \textit{ then } q(y),$$

to obtain the most-general unifier $\{x \leftarrow a,\ y \leftarrow b\}$. Here we have treated the *if-then* connective and the predicate symbols p and q just as we would treat function symbols.

Recall that the theory of expressions allowed the number of arguments of a function symbol to vary. We shall not require this flexibility in applying the *unification* algorithm to predicate-logic expressions, in which each function and predicate symbol has fixed arity.

SAFE SUBSTITUTION

We apply the *unification* algorithm only to quantifier-free expressions. We shall apply substitutions, however, to expressions with quantifiers. If $\mathcal{F}$ is an expression (which may contain quantifiers) and θ a substitution, we henceforth write $\mathcal{F}\theta$, instead of $\mathcal{F} \blacktriangleleft \theta$, to stand for the result of applying θ to $\mathcal{F}$. Similarly, if θ and ϕ are both substitutions, we henceforth write $\theta\phi$, instead of $\theta \square \phi$, to stand for the composition of θ and ϕ.

We always apply substitutions safely. For example, if $\mathcal{F}$ is the sentence

$$\mathcal{F}:\ (\forall y)p(x,\, y)$$

and θ is the substitution $\{x \leftarrow y\}$, then $\mathcal{F}\theta$ is the sentence $(\forall y')p(y,\, y')$; the variable y of the quantifier $(\forall y)$ has been renamed y' to avoid capturing. Also, if ϕ is the substitution $\{y \leftarrow x\}$, then $\mathcal{F}\phi$ is $\mathcal{F}$ itself, that is $(\forall y)p(x,\, y)$; the bound variable y is not replaced by a safe substitution.

We must combine our substitution notation with the concise notation of Section [I]3.3.

Definition (combined substitution notation)

> Suppose that $\mathcal{G}$ and $\mathcal{H}$ are expressions, either both sentences or both terms, that $\mathcal{F}[\mathcal{G}]$ is an expression, and that θ is a substitution. Then
>
> $$\mathcal{F}\theta[\mathcal{H}]$$
>
> denotes the result of
>
> - safely applying θ to $\mathcal{F}[\mathcal{G}]$, obtaining $(\mathcal{F}[\mathcal{G}])\theta$, and then
>
> - safely replacing all free occurrences of $\mathcal{G}\theta$ in $(\mathcal{F}[\mathcal{G}])\theta$ with $\mathcal{H}$. ◢

In other words, we first apply the substitution, then perform the indicated replacements.

Example

> Suppose
>
> $$\mathcal{F}\big[p(x)\big] \quad \text{is} \quad (\forall y)\big[p(x) \ \ and \ \ q(x,\, y)\big]$$
>
> $$\theta \qquad \text{is} \quad \{x \leftarrow a\}.$$
>
> Then (safely applying the substitution)
>
> $$(\mathcal{F}\big[p(x)\big])\theta \quad \text{is} \quad (\forall y)\big[p(a) \ \ and \ \ q(a,\, y)\big]$$
>
> and therefore (safely replacing $p(x)\theta$, that is, $p(a)$, with $p(y)$)
>
> $$\mathcal{F}\theta\big[p(y)\big] \qquad \text{is} \quad (\forall y')\big[p(y) \ \ and \ \ q(a,\, y')\big]. \quad ◢$$

Note that some of the free occurrences of $\mathcal{G}\theta$ in $(\mathcal{F}[\mathcal{G}])\theta$, which must be replaced, may not actually correspond to occurrences of $\mathcal{G}$ in $\mathcal{F}[\mathcal{G}]$.

Example

> Suppose
>
> $$\mathcal{F}\big[p(x)\big] \quad \text{is} \quad (p(x) \ \ and \ \ p(a))$$
>
> $$\theta \qquad \text{is} \quad \{x \leftarrow a\}.$$
>
> Then (safely applying the substitution)
>
> $$(\mathcal{F}\big[p(x)\big])\theta \quad \text{is} \quad (p(a) \ \ and \ \ p(a))$$

and therefore (safely replacing $p(x)\theta$, that is, $p(a)$, with $q(a)$)

$$\mathcal{F}\theta[q(a)] \quad\text{is}\quad (q(a) \ and \ q(a)).$$

Here the second occurrence of $p(x)\theta$, that is, $p(a)$, in $(\mathcal{F}[p(x)])\theta$ does not correspond to an occurrence of $p(x)$ in $\mathcal{F}[p(x)]$. ⌐

We may define a partial combined substitution notation analogous to the preceding total substitution notation. If $\mathcal{F}\langle\mathcal{G}\rangle$ is an expression, in forming

$$\mathcal{F}\theta\langle\mathcal{H}\rangle$$

we safely replace zero, one, or more free occurrences of $\mathcal{G}\theta$ in $(\mathcal{F}\langle\mathcal{G}\rangle)\theta$ with $\mathcal{H}$.

Both the total and partial combined substitution notations may be extended to allow multiple replacements.

Example

Suppose

$$\mathcal{F}\langle p(x), q(y)\rangle \quad\text{is}\quad p(x) \ and \ p(y) \ and \ q(y)$$

$$\theta \quad\text{is}\quad \{x \leftarrow a, \ y \leftarrow a\}.$$

Then (safely applying the substitution)

$$(\mathcal{F}\langle p(x), q(y)\rangle)\theta \quad\text{is}\quad p(a) \ and \ p(a) \ and \ q(a)$$

and therefore (safely replacing zero, one, or more occurrences of $p(a)$ and $q(a)$ with $q(b)$ and $p(b)$, respectively),

$$\mathcal{F}\theta\langle q(b), p(b)\rangle \quad\text{is}\quad q(b) \ and \ p(a) \ and \ p(b)$$

$$\text{or}\quad p(a) \ and \ q(b) \ and \ q(a)$$

$$\text{or any of several other sentences.} \quad⌐$$

Remark (**multiple replacements**)

Suppose that, in the expression $\mathcal{F}[\mathcal{G}_1, \ \mathcal{G}_2]$, the substitution θ unifies $\mathcal{G}_1$ and $\mathcal{G}_2$, that is, $\mathcal{G}_1\theta$ and $\mathcal{G}_2\theta$ are identical. Then, if we form the new expression $\mathcal{F}\theta[\mathcal{H}_1, \ \mathcal{H}_2]$, we require that $\mathcal{H}_1$ and $\mathcal{H}_2$ be identical too. Otherwise, the instruction to safely replace all occurrences of $\mathcal{G}_1\theta$ with $\mathcal{H}_1$ and $\mathcal{G}_2\theta$ with $\mathcal{H}_2$ may be inconsistent.

For example, if

$$\mathcal{F}[p(x),\ p(y)] \quad \text{is} \quad p(x)\ \text{and}\ p(y)$$

$$\theta \qquad\qquad\qquad \text{is} \quad \{x \leftarrow a,\ y \leftarrow a\}$$

then

$$(\mathcal{F}[p(x),\ p(y)])\theta \quad \text{is} \quad p(a)\ \text{and}\ p(a).$$

Therefore

$$\mathcal{F}\theta[q(b),\ q(b)] \quad \text{is} \quad q(b)\ \text{and}\ q(b),$$

but $\mathcal{F}\theta[q(b),\ q(c)]$ has no meaning.

A similar requirement is imposed if more than two separate replacements are indicated. ◢

10.2   POLARITY

We have already introduced the notion of the polarity of an occurrence of a subsentence of a propositional-logic sentence. We now extend this notion to the subsentences of a sentence in predicate logic.

POLARITY OF OCCURRENCES

We define the polarity of each individual occurrence of a subsentence of a given sentence using the same rules as the propositional-logic definition, plus some new rules for conditional terms and quantified subsentences.

Definition (polarity of occurrences)

If S is a sentence, we assign a *polarity*, positive $(+)$, negative $(-)$, or both $(\pm)$, to every occurrence of a subsentence of S according to the following *polarity-assignment rules*:

- *Top* rule

    The sentence S itself is positive in S; that is,

    $$S^{+}.$$

- Propositional-connective rules

  The rules for the propositional connectives are the same for predicate logic as for propositional logic.

- *Conditional-term* rule

  If a subterm of S is of form

$$\textit{if } \mathcal{F} \textit{ then } r \textit{ else } s,$$

  then its *if*-clause $\mathcal{F}$ has both positive and negative polarity in S; that is,

$$\left[\textit{if } \mathcal{F} \textit{ then } r \textit{ else } s\right]^{\pi} \Rightarrow \textit{if } \mathcal{F}^{\pm} \textit{ then } r \textit{ else } s.$$

- *Quantifier* rules

  If a subsentence $\mathcal{E}$ of S is of form

$$(\forall x)\mathcal{F} \qquad \text{or} \qquad (\exists x)\mathcal{F},$$

  then its component $\mathcal{F}$ has the same polarity as $\mathcal{E}$ in S; that is,

$$\left[(\forall x)\mathcal{F}\right]^{\pi} \Rightarrow (\forall x)\mathcal{F}^{\pi}$$

$$\left[(\exists x)\mathcal{F}\right]^{\pi} \Rightarrow (\exists x)\mathcal{F}^{\pi}. \quad \blacksquare$$

The definition of strict polarity is analogous to the corresponding propositional-logic definition.

Definition (strict polarity of occurrences)

An occurrence of a subsentence $\mathcal{E}$ in a sentence S has *strictly positive polarity* if $\mathcal{E}$ has positive but not negative polarity in S.

Similarly, $\mathcal{E}$ has *strictly negative polarity* in S if $\mathcal{E}$ has negative but not positive polarity in S. $\blacksquare$

Example

Let us gradually annotate the sentence

$$S: \quad \begin{array}{l} \textit{if } (\forall x)q(x) \\ \textit{then } (\exists y)p(y) \equiv r(a) \end{array}$$

with the polarities of each of its subsentences, using the preceding polarity-assignment rules to obtain each row from the previous row (as in propositional logic, the boxes indicate the subsentences being considered at each stage):

$$
\boxed{\begin{aligned} & if \ \ (\forall x)q(x) \\ & then \ \ (\exists y)p(y) \ \equiv \ r(a) \end{aligned}}^{+}
$$

$$
\begin{aligned} & if \ \ \boxed{(\forall x)q(x)}^{-} \\ & then \ \ \boxed{(\exists y)p(y) \ \equiv \ r(a)}^{+} \end{aligned}
$$

$$
\begin{aligned} & if \ \ (\forall x)\boxed{q(x)}^{-} \\ & then \ \ \boxed{(\exists y)p(y)}^{\pm} \ \equiv \ \boxed{r(a)}^{\pm} \end{aligned}
$$

$$
\begin{aligned} & if \ \ (\forall x)q(x) \\ & then \ \ (\exists y)\boxed{p(y)}^{\pm} \ = \ r(a). \end{aligned}
$$

Thus, as a result of this annotation process, we obtain the full polarity annotation

$$
\left[\begin{aligned} & if \ \ \left[(\forall x)\left[q(x)\right]^{-}\right]^{-} \\ & then \ \ \left[\left[(\exists y)\left[p(y)\right]^{\pm}\right]^{\pm} \ \equiv \ \left[r(a)\right]^{\pm}\right]^{+} \end{aligned}\right]^{+} .
$$

⌐

The reader is requested in **Problem 10.1** to annotate all the subsentences of several sentences according to their polarity.

THE POLARITY LEMMA

The polarity lemma for predicate logic is identical to that for propositional logic.

Lemma (polarity)

Suppose that S is a sentence, S' is an occurrence of a subsentence in S, and $\mathcal{E}$ is an occurrence of a subsentence in S'; that is,

$$\mathcal{E} \trianglelefteq S' \trianglelefteq S.$$

Then

$\mathcal{E}$ is positive in S

    precisely when

$$\left[\begin{array}{l} \mathcal{E} \text{ is positive in } S' \text{ and } S' \text{ is positive in } S \\ \text{or} \\ \mathcal{E} \text{ is negative in } S' \text{ and } S' \text{ is negative in } S \end{array} \right] \qquad (positive)$$

and

$\mathcal{E}$ is negative in S

    precisely when

$$\left[\begin{array}{l} \mathcal{E} \text{ is positive in } S' \text{ and } S' \text{ is negative in } S \\ \text{or} \\ \mathcal{E} \text{ is negative in } S' \text{ and } S' \text{ is positive in } S \end{array} \right] \qquad (negative)$$

Recall that in speaking of the polarity of a subsentence in the lemma, we are referring to the polarity of the particular occurrence of that subsentence under consideration, even though the same subsentence may have other occurrences.

From the lemma, we can conclude the following corollary.

Corollary (polarity)

Suppose that S is a sentence, S' is an occurrence of a subsentence in S, and $\mathcal{E}$ is an occurrence of a subsentence in S'; that is,

$$\mathcal{E} \trianglelefteq S' \trianglelefteq S.$$

Then

    if $\mathcal{E}$ is strictly positive in S
       and S' is negative [positive] in S,
       then $\mathcal{E}$ is strictly negative [strictly positive] in S' (*positive*)

Also

    if $\mathcal{E}$ is strictly negative in S
       and S' is negative [positive] in S,
       then $\mathcal{E}$ is strictly positive [strictly negative] in S' (*negative*)

The proof is omitted.

THE POLARITY PROPOSITION

The *polarity* proposition for predicate logic is similar to the corresponding proposition for propositional logic.

Proposition (polarity)

Suppose that $\mathcal{E}$, $\mathcal{F}$, and $S\langle\mathcal{E}^+\rangle$ are sentences. Then the universal closure of the sentence

$$
\begin{aligned}
&if\ (if\ \mathcal{E}\ then\ \mathcal{F}) \\
&\quad then\ \big(if\ S\langle\mathcal{E}^+\rangle\ then\ S\langle\mathcal{F}^+\rangle\big)
\end{aligned}
\qquad\qquad (positive)
$$

is valid.

Suppose that $\mathcal{E}$, $\mathcal{F}$, and $S\langle\mathcal{E}^-\rangle$ are sentences. Then the universal closure of the sentence

$$
\begin{aligned}
&if\ (if\ \mathcal{E}\ then\ \mathcal{F}) \\
&\quad then\ \big(if\ S\langle\mathcal{F}^-\rangle\ then\ S\langle\mathcal{E}^-\rangle\big)
\end{aligned}
\qquad\qquad (negative)
$$

is valid. ⌟

Here again, we write S as $S\langle\mathcal{E}^+\rangle$ so that later, when we refer to $S\langle\mathcal{F}^+\rangle$, it is clear we are safely replacing zero, one, or more strictly positive free occurrences of $\mathcal{E}$ with $\mathcal{F}$. Similarly, we write S as $S\langle\mathcal{E}^-\rangle$ so that later, when we refer to $S\langle\mathcal{F}^-\rangle$, it is clear we are safely replacing zero, one, or more strictly negative free occurrences of $\mathcal{E}$ with $\mathcal{F}$.

The proposition, like its propositional-logic counterpart, says that the truth of a sentence is directly related to the truth of its strictly positive subsentences, but inversely related to the truth of its strictly negative subsentences.

Example

Consider the sentence

$$
S:\quad [p(x)]^+\ and\ q(x).
$$

The subsentence $p(x)$ has a free strictly positive occurrence in S. Therefore, by the *positive* part of the proposition, the sentence

$$
(\forall x)\left[
\begin{aligned}
&if\ [if\ p(x)\ then\ r(x)] \\
&then\ \left[
\begin{aligned}
&if\ (p(x)\ and\ q(x)) \\
&then\ (r(x)\ and\ q(x))
\end{aligned}
\right]
\end{aligned}
\right]
$$

is valid. In other words, safely replacing the strictly positive free occurrence of $p(x)$ with the "truer" sentence $r(x)$ makes the entire sentence "truer." ⌐

Example

Consider the sentence

$$S: \quad (\forall y) \begin{bmatrix} if \ [p(x)]^{-} \\ then \ not \ ([p(x)]^{-} \ or \ q(y)) \end{bmatrix}$$

The subsentence $p(x)$ has two strictly negative free occurrences in S. Therefore, by the *negative* part of the proposition, the sentence

$$(\forall x, y) \begin{bmatrix} if \ [if \ p(x) \ then \ r(x, y)] \\ then \ \begin{bmatrix} if \ (\forall y') \begin{bmatrix} if \ r(x, y) \\ then \ not \ (r(x, y) \ or \ q(y')) \end{bmatrix} \\ then \ (\forall y') \begin{bmatrix} if \ p(x) \\ then \ not \ (p(x) \ or \ q(y')) \end{bmatrix} \end{bmatrix} \end{bmatrix}$$

is valid. In other words, safely replacing the strictly negative free occurrences of $p(x)$ with the "truer" sentence $r(x, y)$ makes the entire sentence "false." In making the safe replacement, we renamed the variable y of the quantifier $(\forall y)$ in S as y' to avoid capturing the free occurrence of y in $r(x, y)$. ⌐

Let us now prove the *polarity* proposition.

Proof (polarity)

We prove both the *positive* and the *negative* parts at once, but we include only part of the proof because it is similar to the propositional-logic version.

We shall assume that none of the bound variables of $S\langle \mathcal{E}^{+}\rangle$ occurs free in $\mathcal{F}$. This may be achieved by renaming the bound variables of $S\langle \mathcal{E}^{+}\rangle$ in advance as necessary, obtaining an equivalent sentence, guaranteeing that the subsequent replacement of $\mathcal{E}$ in $S\langle \mathcal{E}^{+}\rangle$ with $\mathcal{F}$ will never require any renaming of variables to avoid capturing.

The proof is by induction on the structure of $S\langle \mathcal{E}\rangle$. Thus we consider an arbitrary sentence $S\langle \mathcal{E}\rangle$, assume inductively that the proposition holds for each proper subsentence $S'\langle \mathcal{E}\rangle$ of $S\langle \mathcal{E}\rangle$, and prove that the proposition then holds for $S\langle \mathcal{E}\rangle$ as well.

In the case in which $\mathcal{E}$ does not occur freely in $S\langle\mathcal{E}\rangle$ at all, $S\langle\mathcal{F}\rangle$ is identical to $S\langle\mathcal{E}\rangle$ and the proposition is evident. We henceforth assume that $\mathcal{E}$ does occur freely in $S\langle\mathcal{E}\rangle$ at least once.

We distinguish among several cases.

Case: $S\langle\mathcal{E}\rangle$ is identical to $\mathcal{E}$

Then $\mathcal{E}$ is strictly positive in $S\langle\mathcal{E}\rangle$ and $S\langle\mathcal{F}\rangle$ is $\mathcal{E}$ or $\mathcal{F}$ itself. The sentence of the *positive* part,

$$\begin{aligned} &if\ (if\ \mathcal{E}\ then\ \mathcal{F}) \\ &then\ \big(if\ S\langle\mathcal{E}^{+}\rangle\ then\ S\langle\mathcal{F}^{+}\rangle\big), \end{aligned}$$

reduces to the sentences

$$\begin{array}{ccc} \begin{aligned} &if\ (if\ \mathcal{E}\ then\ \mathcal{F}) \\ &then\ (if\ \mathcal{E}\ then\ \mathcal{E}) \end{aligned} & or & \begin{aligned} &if\ (if\ \mathcal{E}\ then\ \mathcal{F}) \\ &then\ (if\ \mathcal{E}\ then\ \mathcal{F}), \end{aligned} \end{array}$$

respectively, whose universal closures must be valid, by propositional logic. The *negative* part holds vacuously because in this case there are no strictly negative free occurrences of $\mathcal{E}$ in $S\langle\mathcal{E}\rangle$, and therefore $S\langle\mathcal{F}\rangle$ is identical to $S\langle\mathcal{E}\rangle$.

Note that this includes the case in which $S\langle\mathcal{E}\rangle$ is a proposition; that is, $S\langle\mathcal{E}\rangle$ is *true*, *false*, or a propositional symbol.

Henceforth, we assume that $S\langle\mathcal{E}\rangle$ and $\mathcal{E}$ are not identical and that $S\langle\mathcal{E}\rangle$ is not a proposition.

Case: $S\langle\mathcal{E}\rangle$ is of form $(\forall x)S'\langle\mathcal{E}\rangle$

Then, by our assumption that $\mathcal{E}$ and $S\langle\mathcal{E}\rangle$ are distinct, $\mathcal{E}$ is a subsentence of $S'\langle\mathcal{E}\rangle$ and

$$S'\langle\mathcal{F}\rangle:\ (\forall x)S'\langle\mathcal{F}\rangle.$$

By our assumption, x does not occur free in $\mathcal{F}$ and therefore no renaming is necessary here.

The polarity of an occurrence of $\mathcal{E}$ in $S'\langle\mathcal{E}\rangle$ is the same as the polarity of the corresponding occurrence of $\mathcal{E}$ in $S\langle\mathcal{E}\rangle$, and $S'\langle\mathcal{E}\rangle$ is smaller than $S\langle\mathcal{E}\rangle$. Note that because, by our earlier assumption, $\mathcal{E}$ has at least one free occurrence in $(\forall x)S'\langle\mathcal{E}\rangle$, we know that x does not occur free in $\mathcal{E}$.

Positive part

Let us first prove the *positive* part, in which the replaced occurrences of $\mathcal{E}$ in $S\langle\mathcal{E}\rangle$ are strictly positive in $S\langle\mathcal{E}\rangle$; we therefore write $S\langle\mathcal{E}\rangle$ as $S\langle\mathcal{E}^{+}\rangle$. Then, because $S'\langle\mathcal{E}\rangle$ is positive in $S\langle\mathcal{E}^+\rangle$, we know (by the *positive* part of the *polarity corollary*) that the replaced occurrences of $\mathcal{E}$ are also strictly positive in $S'\langle\mathcal{E}\rangle$. We therefore write $S'\langle\mathcal{E}\rangle$ as $S'\langle\mathcal{E}^+\rangle$.

Because $S'\langle\mathcal{E}^+\rangle$ is a proper subsentence of $S\langle\mathcal{E}\rangle$, we can apply the *positive* part of our induction hypothesis to conclude that the universal closure of the sentence

$$(*) \qquad \begin{array}{l} \textit{if } (\textit{if } \mathcal{E} \textit{ then } \mathcal{F}) \\ \quad \textit{then } \big(\textit{if } S'\langle\mathcal{E}^+\rangle \textit{ then } S'\langle\mathcal{F}^+\rangle\big) \end{array}$$

is valid.

We would like to show that the universal closure of the sentence

$$\begin{array}{l} \textit{if } (\textit{if } \mathcal{E} \textit{ then } \mathcal{F}) \\ \quad \textit{then } \big(\textit{if } (\forall x)S'\langle\mathcal{E}^+\rangle \textit{ then } (\forall x)S'\langle\mathcal{F}^+\rangle\big) \end{array}$$

is valid; that is (by the *validity-of-closures* proposition in [I]2.6), that the sentence itself is true under any interpretation.

For an arbitrary interpretation I of the sentence, suppose that

$$(\dagger) \qquad \textit{if } \mathcal{E} \textit{ then } \mathcal{F}$$

and

$$(\ddagger) \qquad (\forall x)S'\langle\mathcal{E}^+\rangle$$

are true under I; hence it suffices to show that

$$(\forall x)S'\langle\mathcal{F}^+\rangle$$

is true under I. Equivalently (by the semantic rule for the universal quantifier), we would like to show that, for an arbitrary domain element d, the sentence

$$S'\langle\mathcal{F}^+\rangle$$

is true under the extended interpretation $\langle x \leftarrow d\rangle \circ I$.

We know that the replaced occurrences of $\mathcal{E}$ are strictly positive in $S'\langle\mathcal{E}^+\rangle$; by the preceding instance $(*)$ of our induction hypothesis, therefore, it suffices to show that

$$\textit{if } \mathcal{E} \textit{ then } \mathcal{F}$$

and

$$S'\langle\mathcal{E}^+\rangle$$

are both true under $\langle x \leftarrow d\rangle \circ I$.

Because, by our supposition (†), the sentence (*if* $\mathcal{E}$ *then* $\mathcal{F}$) is true under I, and because x does not occur free in $\mathcal{E}$ or in $\mathcal{F}$, we can conclude (by the *agreement* proposition in Section [I]2.5) that the sentence is also true under $\langle x \leftarrow d \rangle \circ I$. Also, because, by our supposition (‡), the sentence $(\forall x) S' \langle \mathcal{E}^+ \rangle$ is true under I, we can conclude (by the semantic rule for the universal quantifier) that $S' \langle \mathcal{E}^+ \rangle$ is true under the extended interpretation $\langle x \leftarrow d \rangle \circ I$, as we wanted to show.

This concludes the proof of the *positive* part for this case. The proof of the *negative* part, which is entirely analogous, is omitted.

Case: $S \langle \mathcal{E} \rangle$ is of the form $(\exists x) S' \langle \mathcal{E} \rangle$

The proof for this case is similar to the proof for the preceding case and is left as an exercise (**Problem 10.2**).

The proofs for the other cases are very similar to the proofs for the corresponding cases of the *polarity* proposition for propositional logic (Section [I]5.1). These proofs are omitted altogether. ⌟

10.3   FORCE OF QUANTIFIERS

The role a quantifier plays in a sentence depends upon the polarity of the subsentence in which it occurs. For example, the existential quantifier in the sentence

$$not \ (\exists x) \mathcal{F}$$

plays the same role as the universal quantifier in the equivalent sentence

$$(\forall x) \big[not \ \mathcal{F} \big]$$

because the surrounding *not* connective of the former sentence gives the existential quantifier a universal "force."

In our deductive system, we assign a force, universal or existential, to each occurrence of a quantifier in a given sentence S. Intuitively, an occurrence of a quantifier is of *universal force* in S if it is a universal [existential] quantifier in the scope of an even [odd] number of *not*'s. Similarly, an occurrence of a quantifier is of *existential force* in S if it is an existential [universal] quantifier in the scope of an even [odd] number of *not*'s. When we count *not*'s, we consider implicit as well as explicit negations. Thus the force gives a syntactic indication as to how the quantifier affects the sentence as a whole.

DEFINITIONS

Let us make this rough observation more precise by defining the force (universal, existential, or both) of an occurrence of a quantifier in a sentence.

Definition (force of quantifiers)

Consider an occurrence of a subsentence $(\dots x)\mathcal{F}$ in a sentence S, where $(\dots x)$ is a quantifier, either $(\forall x)$ or $(\exists x)$. We determine the force of this occurrence of the quantifier as follows:

- The occurrence of the quantifier has *universal force* in S, annotated by the superscript $(\dots x)^{\forall}$, if

    - it is a universal quantifier and $(\dots x)\mathcal{F}$ is of positive polarity in S, that is,

$$[(\forall x)\mathcal{F}]^{+} \;\Rightarrow\; (\forall x)^{\forall}\mathcal{F},$$

    or
    - it is an existential quantifier and $(\dots x)\mathcal{F}$ is of negative polarity in S, that is,

$$[(\exists x)\mathcal{F}]^{-} \;\Rightarrow\; (\exists x)^{\forall}\mathcal{F}.$$

- The occurrence of the quantifier has *existential force* in S, annotated by the superscript $(\dots x)^{\exists}$, if

    - it is an existential quantifier and $(\dots x)\mathcal{F}$ is of positive polarity in S, that is,

$$[(\exists x)\mathcal{F}]^{+} \;\Rightarrow\; (\exists x)^{\exists}\mathcal{F},$$

    or
    - it is a universal quantifier and $(\dots x)\mathcal{F}$ is of negative polarity in S, that is,

$$[(\forall x)\mathcal{F}]^{-} \;\Rightarrow\; (\forall x)^{\exists}\mathcal{F}.$$

- The occurrence of the quantifier has *both forces* in S, annotated by the superscript $(\dots x)^{\forall\exists}$, if

    - $(\dots x)\mathcal{F}$ is of both polarities in S, that is,

$$[(\dots x)\mathcal{F}]^{\pm} \;\Rightarrow\; (\dots x)^{\forall\exists}\mathcal{F}. \quad \lrcorner$$

Intuitively, a quantifier of universal force plays the role of a universal quantifier even though it may be literally of the existential form $(\exists x)$; similarly, a quantifier of existential force plays the role of an existential quantifier even though it may be literally of the universal form $(\forall x)$.

Let us illustrate how the force of each quantifier of a sentence is determined.

Example

Consider the following sentence, annotated with the polarity of the relevant subsentences and with the forces of all the quantifiers:

$$if \; \left[(\forall x)^{\exists}\Big(not \; [(\exists y)^{\exists}q(x,y)]^{+}\Big)\right]^{-}$$
$$then \; not \; \left[(\exists x)^{\forall}r(x)\right]^{-}.$$

- Because the subsentence

  $$(\exists y)q(x,y)$$

  has positive polarity, its quantifier $(\exists y)$ has existential force.

- Because the subsentence

  $$(\exists x)r(x)$$

  has negative polarity, its quantifier $(\exists x)$ has universal force.

- Because the subsentence

  $$(\forall x)\big(not \; (\exists y)q(x,y)\big)$$

  has negative polarity, its quantifier $(\forall x)$ has existential force. ⌐

In **Problem 10.3** the reader is requested to annotate several sentences with the forces of their quantifiers.

Definition (strict force of quantifiers)

We say that an occurrence of a quantifier has

- *strict universal force* if it has universal force but not existential force,

- *strict existential force* if it has existential force but not universal force. ⌐

Note that a quantifier of strict force cannot occur within the scope of a quantifier of both forces. This is because a quantifier of both forces must occur in a subsentence of both polarities, and any subsentence of a subsentence of both polarities also has both polarities.

Example

Consider the following sentence, annotated with the forces of its quantifiers:

$$(\exists x)^{\exists} q(x) \quad and \quad \left[\begin{array}{l} (\forall y)^{\forall \exists} \left(p(y) \quad or \quad (\exists z)^{\forall \exists} r(y, z) \right) \\ \equiv \\ r(z) \end{array} \right].$$

Note that all the quantifiers within the scope of the $\equiv$ connective have both forces. ⌐

THE FORCE-MANIPULATION PROPOSITION

Let us consider the following equivalent sentences, obtained by gradually pulling the quantifier $(\forall x)$ outside by equivalences of predicate logic:

$$not \left(\begin{array}{l} if \ \ not \ \left(\left[(\forall x)^{\exists} p(x) \right]^{-} \ \ or \ \ q(y) \right) \\ then \ \ r(y) \end{array} \right)$$

$$not \left(\begin{array}{l} if \ \ not \ \left[(\forall x)^{\exists} (p(x) \ \ or \ \ q(y)) \right]^{-} \\ then \ \ r(y) \end{array} \right)$$

$$not \left(\begin{array}{l} if \ \ \left[(\exists x)^{\exists} (not \ (p(x) \ \ or \ \ q(y))) \right]^{+} \\ then \ \ r(y) \end{array} \right)$$

$$not \left[(\forall x)^{\exists} \left(\begin{array}{l} if \ \ not \ (p(x) \ \ or \ \ q(y)) \\ then \ \ r(y) \end{array} \right) \right]^{-}$$

$$\left[(\exists x)^{\exists} \ not \ \left(\begin{array}{l} if \ \ not \ (p(x) \ \ or \ \ q(y)) \\ then \ \ r(y) \end{array} \right) \right]^{+}.$$

Note the interesting phenomenon that the quantifier of each of these sentences is of existential force, although it changes from universal to existential form and back again as it passes across an explicit or implicit negation.

The following proposition makes precise some of our observations about the force of quantifiers.

In the discussion in the rest of this chapter, we often use the abbreviated notation $(\dots x)$ to stand for either $(\forall x)$ or $(\exists x)$. Then $(\dots x)^{\forall}$ indicates a quantifier over x of universal force (not necessarily strict), where it is irrelevant if it is itself a universal or existential quantifier; similarly for $(\dots x)^{\exists}$ and $(\dots x)^{\forall\exists}$.

We use an informal pictorial notation to make the reading easier. In this notation we write only the part of the sentence in which we are interested; the rest is indicated by a line ___ .

Proposition (force manipulation)

Consider a particular occurrence of the subsentence $(\dots x)P$ in the sentence $\mathcal{F}$, denoted by

$$\mathcal{F}: \quad \text{\_\_\_} (\dots x)P\text{\_\_\_} \ .$$

We assume that the following restrictions are satisfied:

- The variable x has no free occurrences in $\mathcal{F}$.

- The occurrence of $(\dots x)P$ in $\mathcal{F}$ is not within the scope of any quantifier.

Then, if $(\dots x)^{\forall}$ is of strict universal force in $\mathcal{F}$,

$$\text{\_\_\_}(\dots x)^{\forall}P\text{\_\_\_}$$

     is equivalent to   (*universal*)

$$(\forall x)\big[\text{\_\_\_} P\text{\_\_\_}\big]$$

and, if $(\dots x)^{\exists}$ is of strict existential force in $\mathcal{F}$,

$$\text{\_\_\_}(\dots x)^{\exists}P\text{\_\_\_}$$

     is equivalent to   (*existential*)

$$(\exists x)\big[\text{\_\_\_} P\text{\_\_\_}\big],$$

where ___P___ is the result of removing the occurrence of the quantifier $(\dots x)$ under consideration from $\mathcal{F}$. ⌐

Example

As we remarked in a previous example, the sentence

$$not \left(\begin{array}{l} if \ \ not \ \left(\boxed{(\forall x)^{\exists}p(x)} \ \ or \ \ q(y) \right) \\ then \ \ r(y) \end{array} \right)$$

is equivalent to the sentence

$$(\exists x) \ not \ \left(\begin{array}{l} if \ not \ \left(\boxed{p(x)} \ or \ q(y) \right) \\ then \ r(y) \end{array} \right),$$

obtained by "pulling out" the quantifier. The boxes indicate the subsentence occurrences under consideration.

This illustrates the *existential* part of the *force-manipulation* proposition; the given sentence is of form

$$\underline{\qquad} (\forall x)^{\exists} p(x) \underline{\qquad}$$

and the equivalent resulting sentence is of form

$$(\exists x) \left[\underline{\qquad} p(x) \underline{\qquad} \right]. \quad \lrcorner$$

Proof (force manipulation)

We prove both parts together. The proof is by induction on the structure of sentences: we consider an arbitrary sentence $\mathcal{F}$, assume inductively that the theorem holds for all proper subsentences of $\mathcal{F}$, and prove that it must then hold for $\mathcal{F}$ as well.

The proof distinguishes among several cases, depending on the structure of $\mathcal{F}$. We present only a representative sample.

Case: $\mathcal{F}$ is a proposition

This case cannot occur because we have assumed that $\mathcal{F}$ contains a quantifier $(\ldots x)$.

Case: $\mathcal{F}$ is of form $(\mathcal{F}_1 \equiv \mathcal{F}_2)$

This case cannot occur because in each part we assume the quantifier $(\ldots x)$ is of strict universal or existential force. Any quantifier within $\mathcal{F}_1$ or $\mathcal{F}_2$ must have both forces.

Case: $\mathcal{F}$ is identical to $(\ldots x)\mathcal{P}$

To prove the *universal* part, we assume the quantifier $(\ldots x)$ to be of strict universal force in $\mathcal{F}$; then in this case the quantifier is literally $(\forall x)$, and the desired conclusion reduces to the true statement that

$$(\forall x)\mathcal{P}$$

is equivalent to

$$(\forall x)\,P.$$

The *existential* part can be proved similarly.

Case: $\mathcal{F}$ is of form $(\dots y)\big[\underline{\quad}(\dots x)\,P\underline{\quad}\big]$

This case cannot occur because we have assumed the quantifier $(\dots x)$ is not within the scope of any quantifier.

Case: $\mathcal{F}$ is of form $not\big(\underline{\quad}(\dots x)\,P\underline{\quad}\big)$

To prove the *universal* part, we assume the quantifier $(\dots x)$ to be of strict universal force in $\mathcal{F}$; then (by the *polarity* corollary) it must be of strict existential force in the proper subsentence $\underline{\quad}(\dots x)^{\exists}\,P\underline{\quad}$.

Thus, by the induction hypothesis,

$$\underline{\quad}(\dots x)^{\exists}\,P\underline{\quad}$$

is equivalent to

$$(\exists x)\big[\underline{\quad}P\underline{\quad}\big].$$

Therefore

$$not\Big(\underline{\quad}(\dots x)^{\forall}\,P\underline{\quad}\Big)$$

is equivalent to

$$not\,(\exists x)\big[\underline{\quad}P\underline{\quad}\big],$$

which is equivalent (by predicate logic) to

$$(\forall x)\,not\,\big[\underline{\quad}P\underline{\quad}\big].$$

This is what we wanted to show.

The proof of the *existential* part, in which the quantifier $(\dots x)$ is of strict existential force, is similar in this case.

Case: $\mathcal{F}$ is of form $\big(\underline{\quad}(\dots x)\,P\underline{\quad}\big)$ *and* $\mathcal{Q}$

Because we have assumed that x is not free in $\mathcal{F}$, it is not free in $\mathcal{Q}$. To prove the *universal* part, we assume the quantifier $(\dots x)$ to be of strict universal force in $\mathcal{F}$; then (by the *polarity* corollary) it must be of strict universal force in the proper subsentence $\underline{\quad}(\dots x)^{\forall}\,P\underline{\quad}$.

Thus, by the induction hypothesis,

$$\text{\textemdash}\,(\dots\,x)^{\forall}P\,\text{\textemdash}$$

is equivalent to

$$(\forall x)[\text{\textemdash}\,P\,\text{\textemdash}].$$

Therefore

$$(\text{\textemdash}\,(\dots\,x)^{\forall}P\,\text{\textemdash})\ \ and\ \ \mathcal{Q}$$

is equivalent to

$$(\forall x)[\text{\textemdash}\,P\,\text{\textemdash}]\ \ and\ \ \mathcal{Q},$$

which is equivalent (by predicate logic, because x is not free in $\mathcal{Q}$) to

$$(\forall x)\Big[(\text{\textemdash}\,P\,\text{\textemdash})\ \ and\ \ \mathcal{Q}\Big].$$

This is what we wanted to prove.

The proof of the *existential* part, in which the quantifier $(\dots\,x)$ is of existential force, is similar in this case.

The proofs for the cases we have omitted are also similar. ⌟

Note that, by repeated application of the *force-manipulation* proposition, we could pull all the quantifiers of strict force in a given sentence to the outermost level, obtaining an equivalent sentence. To ensure that the restrictions of the proposition are satisfied, we pull out quantifiers in a left-to-right order and rename their variables as required.

THE FORCE-INSTANTIATION PROPOSITION

Recall the *quantifier-instantiation* proposition that was presented in Section [I]3.5:

For any variable x, sentence $\mathcal{F}[x]$, and term t, the universal closures of the sentences

$$if\ \ (\forall x)\mathcal{F}[x]\ \ then\ \ \mathcal{F}[t] \hspace{3cm} (universal)$$

$$if\ \ \mathcal{F}[t]\ \ then\ \ (\exists x)\mathcal{F}[x] \hspace{3cm} (existential)$$

are valid.

The following *force-instantiation* proposition resembles this proposition, but applies to quantifiers that are not necessarily at the top level of the given sentence.

Proposition (force instantiation)

Consider a particular occurrence of the subsentence $(\ldots x)P[x]$ in the sentence $\mathcal{F}$, denoted by

$$\mathcal{F}: \quad \underline{\quad}(\ldots x)P[x]\underline{\quad}.$$

For any term t,

If the occurrence of the quantifier $(\ldots x)$ is of strict universal force in $\mathcal{F}$, then the universal closure of the sentence

$$if \quad \underline{\quad}(\ldots x)P[x]\underline{\quad} \qquad\qquad (universal)$$
$$then \quad \underline{\quad}P[t]\underline{\quad}$$

is valid.

If the occurrence of the quantifier $(\ldots x)$ is of strict existential force in $\mathcal{F}$, then the universal closure of the sentence

$$if \quad \underline{\quad}P[t]\underline{\quad} \qquad\qquad (existential)$$
$$then \quad \underline{\quad}(\ldots x)P[x]\underline{\quad}$$

is valid.

Here $P[t]$ is the result of dropping the quantifier $(\ldots x)$ in the occurrence of the subsentence $(\ldots x)P[x]$, and replacing the free occurrences of x in $P[x]$ with t. ∎

The proof is requested in **Problem 10.4**.

QUANTIFIER REMOVAL

In developing formal methods for predicate logic, it is of great help to eliminate quantifiers from sentences, allowing techniques for proving theorems of propositional logic to be readily extended to predicate logic. In the following sections, we introduce a way to remove quantifiers from closed predicate-logic sentences while preserving their validity. In other words, the sentence we obtain as a result of removing quantifiers will be valid precisely when the given sentence is valid. The process, known as *skolemization*, does not necessarily preserve equivalence; that is, the two sentences may not be equivalent.

We shall remove quantifiers when we are attempting to prove the validity of a given closed sentence. Thus we would be quite concerned if the given sentence were valid but the resulting sentence were not. We would be equally disturbed if the given sentence were not valid but the resulting sentence were. We do not worry, however, if the sentences are not equivalent, that is, if they happen to have different truth-values for some particular interpretation.

The term "quantifier removal" is a bit misleading. While quantifiers of strict universal force are actually eliminated, quantifiers of strict existential force are merely brought to the top level. If we "remove" all the quantifiers from a given closed sentence $\mathcal{F}$, we actually obtain a closed sentence $\mathcal{G}$ of form $(\exists y_1) \ldots (\exists y_n) \mathcal{G}'$, where $\mathcal{G}'$ has no quantifiers. Later we shall see that, in the deductive tableaux for proving the validity of predicate-logic sentences, we can also drop the outermost quantifiers $(\exists y_1) \ldots (\exists y_n)$.

Often we want to remove all the quantifiers from the given closed sentence, but the skolemization process is more general: it allows us to remove a single quantifier from the sentence. This will be of particular importance when we extend skolemization to theories with induction; there we must leave some quantifiers in place to employ the induction principle. On the other hand, repeated application of the process will allow us to remove all the quantifiers if necessary.

Because the skolemization process is somewhat mysterious, we give an intuitive preview here before presenting the full details.

10.4 QUANTIFIER REMOVAL: INTUITIVE PREVIEW

In the skolemization process, we eliminate a particular quantifier from a given sentence $\mathcal{F}$, obtaining a new, somewhat different sentence $\mathcal{G}$.

The way the quantifier is removed will depend on its force in $\mathcal{F}$. If the quantifier is of both forces, we repeatedly apply equivalence-preserving rewritings, until the quantifier is "split" into multiple occurrences of quantifiers of strict force, which may then be removed separately. This will be explained in the more general treatment of skolemization. Henceforth, in this preview, we may consider removing only quantifiers of strict force.

In removing a quantifier of strict force from a closed sentence $\mathcal{F}$, we do not always obtain an equivalent sentence $\mathcal{G}$, but we must be sure that $\mathcal{G}$ is valid precisely when $\mathcal{F}$ is valid. To show this, it is useful to associate with each closed sentence a *validity game*. This will be an infinite game we play against a malevolent universe. If we win, the sentence is valid; if the universe wins, the sentence is not valid. Thus, to show that skolemization preserves validity, we need show only that the winner of the game for $\mathcal{F}$ is the same as the winner of the game for $\mathcal{G}$.

THE VALIDITY GAME

The game for a closed sentence $\mathcal{F}$ may be regarded as a computation to determine whether or not $\mathcal{F}$ is valid. To establish its validity, we must show that $\mathcal{F}$ is true under all interpretations. In the game, we may expect that the malevolent universe will propose an interpretation under which $\mathcal{F}$ is false, if such an interpretation exists.

In choosing an interpretation, the universe initially selects a domain and assigns values to all the constant, function, and predicate symbols in $\mathcal{F}$, attempting to falsify $\mathcal{F}$ if possible; these values will be domain elements, functions, and relations, respectively.

In the balance of the game, one player or the other chooses values for the quantified variables in $\mathcal{F}$. The universe selects domain elements for variables whose quantifiers have strict universal force in $\mathcal{F}$, while we ourselves select domain elements for variables whose quantifiers have strict existential force in $\mathcal{F}$. In choosing its values, the universe makes things as difficult for us as possible; it selects domain elements that make $\mathcal{F}$ false, if such a selection exists. We, on the other hand, naturally select values making $\mathcal{F}$ true, if possible.

The order in which the values for the variables are selected depends on the order in which the quantifiers occur in the sentence. If one quantifier surrounds another, a value for its variable must be selected first. In making a choice, each player has knowledge of the previous choices of the opposing player, but is ignorant of the subsequent choices.

In this intuitive preview, we do not give all the details of the game, nor do we treat the general skolemization process. We do, however, consider several representative cases.

UNIVERSAL FORCE

For a quantifier of universal force, the universe chooses a value for its variable. In particular, suppose $\mathcal{F}$ is of the form

$$\mathcal{F}: \quad (\forall x)^{\forall} P[x].$$

In the validity game for $\mathcal{F}$, the universe first chooses an interpretation I, attempting to falsify $\mathcal{F}$ if possible. The outermost quantifier $(\forall x)$ of $\mathcal{F}$ is of universal force in $\mathcal{F}$; therefore the universe subsequently selects a domain element d to serve as a value for x. The universe will choose d so that the subsentence $P[x]$ will be false under the extended interpretation $\langle x \leftarrow d \rangle \circ I$, if such a domain element d exists; otherwise, the universe will choose an arbitrary element.

If we apply the skolemization process (to be described) to eliminate the quantifier $(\forall x)$ from the sentence $\mathcal{F}$, we obtain the sentence

$$\mathcal{G}: \quad P[a],$$

where a is a "new" constant, i.e., one that does not already occur in $\mathcal{F}$. In the validity game for $\mathcal{G}$, the universe first chooses an interpretation J, attempting to falsify $\mathcal{G}$ if possible.

Suppose the universe was able to win the validity game for $\mathcal{F}$ by choosing an interpretation I and assigning to x the domain element d, so that $P[x]$ was indeed false under the extended interpretation $\langle x \leftarrow d \rangle \circ I$. Then, in playing the game for $\mathcal{G}$, it can choose to assign d to the new constant a, leaving the assignments to the other symbols the same as under I. That is, in the validity game for $\mathcal{G}$, the universe may choose the interpretation J to be $\langle a \leftarrow d \rangle \circ I$. The value of the constant a in the game for $\mathcal{G}$, that is, d, will be the same as the value the universe chose for x in the game for $\mathcal{F}$. Thus the universe will be able to make $P[a]$ false by choosing J. In short, if the universe is able to win the game for $\mathcal{F}$, it will also be able to win the game for $\mathcal{G}$.

On the other hand, suppose the universe can win the validity game for $\mathcal{G}$. That is, it can choose an interpretation J under which $P[a]$ is false. Then J must assign some domain element, say d, to the constant a.

In the game for $\mathcal{F}: (\forall x)^\forall P[x]$, the universe can choose the same interpretation J. It can then assign the domain element d to the variable x. The value of x in the game for $\mathcal{F}$ will thus be the same as the value of a in the game for $\mathcal{G}$. If the universe was able to win the game for $\mathcal{G}$, it will also be able to win the game for $\mathcal{F}$.

To summarize, the winner of the validity game for $\mathcal{F}$ is the same as the winner of the validity game for $\mathcal{G}$. That is, $\mathcal{F}$ is valid precisely when $\mathcal{G}$ is valid.

Note that $\mathcal{F}$ and $\mathcal{G}$ are not necessarily equivalent; that is, for individual interpretations, they may have different truth-values. In particular, we may have an interpretation under which $\mathcal{G}: p(a)$ is true but $p(b)$, for instance, is false and hence $\mathcal{F}: (\forall x)p(x)$ is false. There must then be another interpretation, however, under which $\mathcal{G}: p(a)$ is false, and hence neither sentence is valid. In short, validity has been preserved even though equivalence has not.

EXISTENTIAL FORCE

For a quantifier of existential force, we ourselves choose a value for its variable. In particular, suppose $\mathcal{F}$ is of the form

$$\mathcal{F}: \quad (\exists y)^\exists P[y].$$

In the validity game for $\mathcal{F}$, the universe again chooses an interpretation $\mathcal{I}$, attempting to make $\mathcal{F}$ false if possible. This time, the outermost quantifier $(\exists y)$ is of existential force in $\mathcal{F}$; therefore we ourselves get to choose a value d for the variable y. We shall choose the domain element d so that the subsentence $P[y]$ will be true under the extended interpretation $\langle y \leftarrow d \rangle \circ \mathcal{I}$, if possible.

The quantifier $(\exists y)$ is already in the desired outermost position in $\mathcal{F}$, and therefore will not be changed by the skolemization process. The sentence we obtain,

$$\mathcal{G}: \quad (\exists y)P[y],$$

is the same as $\mathcal{F}$. Since $\mathcal{F}$ and $\mathcal{G}$ are the same, validity has clearly been preserved.

UNIVERSAL-EXISTENTIAL FORCE

The order in which values for variables are chosen depends on the relative position of their quantifiers in the sentence. In particular, suppose $\mathcal{F}$ is of the form

$$\mathcal{F}: \quad (\forall x)^\forall (\exists y)^\exists \mathcal{Q}[x, y].$$

This is an instance of the universal-force case in which $P[x]$ is taken to be $(\exists y)\mathcal{Q}[x, y]$.

In the validity game for $\mathcal{F}$, the universe first selects an interpretation $\mathcal{I}$. Since the outermost quantifier $(\forall x)^\forall$ is of universal force in $\mathcal{F}$, the universe gets to choose a value d for x. It will choose d so that the subsentence $(\exists y)\mathcal{Q}[x, y]$ will be false under the extended interpretation $\langle x \leftarrow d \rangle \circ \mathcal{I}$, if possible. Because the next quantifier $(\exists y)^\exists$ is of existential force, we then get to choose a value e for y. We attempt to remedy the situation by choosing e so that the subsentence $\mathcal{Q}[x, y]$ will be true under the extended interpretation $\langle y \leftarrow e \rangle \circ \langle x \leftarrow d \rangle \circ \mathcal{I}$, if possible. The universe must make its choice for x blindly, in ignorance of our subsequent choice for y; we, on the other hand, may take the universe's choice for x into account in making our choice for y.

The skolemization process to be described will not allow us to remove a quantifier of existential force, such as $(\exists y)^\exists$, if it is surrounded by a quantifier of universal force, such as $(\forall x)^\forall$. If we want to remove the quantifier $(\forall x)^\forall$ from $\mathcal{F}$, we can apply the process to obtain the sentence

$$\mathcal{G}: \quad (\exists y)^\exists \mathcal{Q}[a, y],$$

where a is a new constant. The existential quantifier $(\exists y)$ is already in the desired outermost position in $\mathcal{G}$; it need not be removed by any subsequent skolemization step.

We have seen that the winner of the validity game for $\mathcal{F}$ is the same as that for $\mathcal{G}$. In the validity game for $\mathcal{G}$, the universe must choose its value for a blindly, but our choice of a value for y may depend on previous choices the universe has made, including its choice of a value for a.

EXISTENTIAL-UNIVERSAL FORCE

We now consider the most confusing aspect of the skolemization process. We suppose the sentence is of form

$$\mathcal{F}: \quad (\exists y)^{\exists}(\forall z)^{\forall} \mathcal{Q}[y, z].$$

This is an instance of the existential-force case in which $P[y]$ is taken to be $(\forall z)\mathcal{Q}[y, z]$.

In the validity game for $\mathcal{F}$, the universe first selects an interpretation I, attempting to falsify $\mathcal{F}$ if possible. Since the outermost quantifier $(\exists y)$ is of existential force in $\mathcal{F}$, we ourselves get to choose a value d to assign to the variable y, so that the subsentence $(\forall z)\mathcal{Q}[y, z]$ is true under the extended interpretation $\langle y \leftarrow d \rangle \circ I$, if possible.

The next quantifier $(\forall z)$ is of universal force in $\mathcal{F}$; therefore the universe gets to choose a value e to assign to the variable z, so that the subsentence $\mathcal{Q}[y, z]$ is false under the extended interpretation $\langle z \leftarrow e \rangle \circ \langle y \leftarrow d \rangle \circ I$, if possible.

Although we must choose d blindly, the universe may take our choice of d into account in selecting e.

Thus, suppose the universe can win the validity game for $\mathcal{F}$. Then, whatever domain element d we choose, the universe can choose a domain element e such that $\mathcal{Q}[y, z]$ is false under the appropriate extended interpretation. Let $k(d)$ be the function that, for whatever domain element d we choose, yields the corresponding domain element e selected by the universe. We shall call k the *winning function* (for $\mathcal{Q}$).

The existential quantifier $(\exists y)$ is already in the desired outermost position in $\mathcal{F}$; there is no need to do anything to it. If we want to remove the quantifier $(\forall z)$, we may apply the skolemization process to be described to obtain the sentence

$$\mathcal{G}: \quad (\exists y)\mathcal{Q}[y, f(y)],$$

where f is a "new" function symbol, i.e., one that does not already occur in $\mathcal{F}$.

In the validity game for $\mathcal{G}$, the universe first chooses an interpretation J, attempting to falsify $\mathcal{G}$ if possible. This must include an assignment of a function to the function symbol f. This choice of a value for f must be made blindly, in ignorance of our subsequent choice of a value for y. Because y is an argument of f in the term $f(y)$, however, the value of $f(y)$ itself may certainly depend on our choice of a value for y.

We now show that the winner of the validity game for $\mathcal{F}$ is the same as that for $\mathcal{G}$. Suppose that the universe was able to win the validity game for $\mathcal{F}$ by choosing an interpretation I and using the winning function k for $\mathcal{Q}$. Then, in playing the game for $\mathcal{G}$, it can choose to assign k to f, leaving the assignments to the other symbols the same as under I. That is, in the game for $\mathcal{G}$ the universe may choose the interpretation J to be $\langle f \leftarrow k \rangle \circ I$.

Since the outermost quantifier $(\exists y)$ is of existential force in $\mathcal{G}$, we ourselves get to choose a value d for y. Whatever value we choose, however, the value of the term $f(y)$ in $\mathcal{G}$, that is, $k(d)$, will be the same as the domain element e the universe would have chosen for z in the game for $\mathcal{F}$. Thus, if the universe was able to win the game for $\mathcal{F}$, it will also be able to win the game for $\mathcal{G}$.

On the other hand, suppose that the universe can win the validity game for $\mathcal{G}$. That is, it can choose an interpretation J under which

$$\mathcal{G}: \quad (\exists y)^{\exists} \mathcal{Q}[y,\, f(y)]$$

is false. Then J must assign some function, say k, to the function symbol f. Whatever value d we choose subsequently for y, the value of $\mathcal{Q}[y,\, f(y)]$ will be false under the appropriate extended interpretation.

In the validity game for

$$\mathcal{F}: \quad (\exists y)^{\exists} (\forall z)^{\forall} \mathcal{Q}[y,\, z],$$

the universe can choose the same interpretation J. Whatever value d we choose for y, the universe may then assign the domain element $k(d)$ to z. The value of the variable z in the game for $\mathcal{F}$ will thus be the same as the value of $f(y)$ in the game for $\mathcal{G}$. If the universe was able to win the game for $\mathcal{G}$, it will also be able to win the game for $\mathcal{F}$.

To summarize, if the universe can win either game, it will be able to win the other; the winners of the two games will be the same. That is, $\mathcal{F}$ is valid precisely when $\mathcal{G}$ is valid.

In this case, it can be shown that $\mathcal{F}$ and $\mathcal{G}$ are not equivalent. In particular, it is possible to find an interpretation under which $\mathcal{F}$ is false but $\mathcal{G}$ is true.

NEGATED SENTENCES

Up to now, we have mentioned quantifiers only at the outermost level. In the
validity game, quantifiers are treated according to their forces, which are reversed
by surrounding negation connectives. For instance, suppose our sentence is of
form

$$\mathcal{F}: \quad not\ (\forall y)^{\exists}(\exists z)^{\forall}\mathcal{Q}[y, z].$$

The argument here will mirror the argument in the previous case.

In the validity game for $\mathcal{F}$, the universe first selects an interpretation I,
attempting to falsify $\mathcal{F}$, if possible. This means that the universe will attempt
to make the subsentence $(\forall y)(\exists z)\mathcal{Q}[y, z]$ true. Since the quantifier $(\forall y)^{\exists}$ is
of existential force in $\mathcal{F}$, we ourselves get to choose a value d to assign to the
variable y, attempting to force the subsentence $(\exists z)\mathcal{Q}[y, z]$ to be false (under the
appropriate extended interpretation), so that $\mathcal{F}$ will be true.

The next quantifier $(\exists z)^{\forall}$ is of universal force in $\mathcal{F}$; therefore the universe gets
to choose a domain element e to assign to z, attempting to force the subsentence
$\mathcal{Q}[y, z]$ to be true, so that $\mathcal{F}$ will be false.

Suppose that the universe can win the validity game for $\mathcal{F}$. Then, whatever
domain element d we choose, the universe can select a domain element e that
forces $\mathcal{Q}[y, z]$ to be true, so that $\mathcal{F}$ will be false. Let $k(d)$ be the function that, for
whatever domain element d we choose, yields the corresponding domain element
e selected by the universe. We again call k the *winning function*.

We may apply the skolemization process to either quantifier in $\mathcal{F}$. If we want
to remove the quantifier $(\exists z)^{\forall}$, we obtain the sentence

$$\mathcal{G}: \quad not\ (\forall y)^{\exists}\mathcal{Q}[y, f(y)],$$

where f is a new function symbol.

In the validity game for $\mathcal{G}$, the universe first chooses an interpretation J for
$\mathcal{G}$. If the universe was able to win the game for $\mathcal{F}$, it may take J to be $\langle f \leftarrow k\rangle \circ I$,
where k is the winning function.

Since the quantifier $(\forall y)^{\exists}$ is of existential force in $\mathcal{G}$, we ourselves get to
choose a value d for y. Whatever value we choose, however, the value of the term
$f(y)$ in $\mathcal{G}$, that is, $k(d)$, will be the same as the domain element e the universe
would have chosen for z in the game for $\mathcal{F}$. Thus, if the universe was able to win
the game for $\mathcal{F}$, it will also be able to win the game for $\mathcal{G}$.

By an argument similar to that for the previous case, we can also show that
if the universe can win the validity game for $\mathcal{G}$, it can win the validity game for
$\mathcal{F}$. This is, $\mathcal{F}$ is valid precisely when $\mathcal{G}$ is valid.

If we want to remove the remaining quantifier $(\forall y)^{\exists}$ from $\mathcal{G}$, we may apply the skolemization process once more, to obtain the sentence

$$\mathcal{G}': \quad (\exists y)\Big[\textit{not } \mathcal{Q}[y,\, f(y)]\Big].$$

Here the quantifier has not literally been removed, but rather moved to the desired outermost position. Note that (by the *force-manipulation* proposition) this stage of the process has actually preserved equivalence as well as validity.

Quantifiers (of strict force) at deeper levels are treated in the same way, in accordance with their force.

We are now ready to begin the more general treatment of the quantifier-elimination process.

10.5   REMOVING BOTH FORCES

A quantifier of both forces must be within the scope of a $\equiv$ connective or within the *if*-clause of an *if-then-else* conditional connective or conditional operator. (Recall that we distinguish between the two forms of the conditional construct: the *if-then-else* connective, which yields a sentence, and the *if-then-else* operator, which yields a term.) The offending constructs, however, can be paraphrased in terms of other constructs, by repeated application of the following equivalences:

- For $\equiv$,

$$
\begin{array}{ccc}
\mathcal{F} \equiv \mathcal{G} & & \mathcal{F} \equiv \mathcal{G} \\
\equiv & & \equiv \\
\begin{bmatrix} \textit{if } \mathcal{F} \textit{ then } \mathcal{G} \\ \textit{and} \\ \textit{if } \mathcal{G} \textit{ then } \mathcal{F} \end{bmatrix} & \text{or} & \begin{bmatrix} \mathcal{F} \textit{ and } \mathcal{G} \\ \textit{or} \\ (\textit{not } \mathcal{F}) \textit{ and } (\textit{not } \mathcal{G}) \end{bmatrix}.
\end{array}
$$

- For the *if-then-else* connective,

$$
\begin{array}{ccc}
\textit{if } \mathcal{F} \textit{ then } \mathcal{G} \textit{ else } \mathcal{H} & & \textit{if } \mathcal{F} \textit{ then } \mathcal{G} \textit{ else } \mathcal{H} \\
\equiv & & \equiv \\
\begin{bmatrix} \textit{if } \mathcal{F} \textit{ then } \mathcal{G} \\ \textit{and} \\ \textit{if } (\textit{not } \mathcal{F}) \textit{ then } \mathcal{H} \end{bmatrix} & \text{or} & \begin{bmatrix} \mathcal{F} \textit{ and } \mathcal{G} \\ \textit{or} \\ (\textit{not } \mathcal{F}) \textit{ and } \mathcal{H} \end{bmatrix}.
\end{array}
$$

- For the *if-then-else* operator,

$$q(..., \text{if } \mathcal{F} \text{ then } s \text{ else } t, ...)$$

$$\equiv$$

$$\begin{bmatrix} \textit{if } \mathcal{F} \\ \textit{then } q(...,s,...) \\ \textit{else } q(...,t,...) \end{bmatrix}$$

and

$$f(..., \text{if } \mathcal{F} \text{ then } s \text{ else } t, ...)$$

$$\equiv$$

$$\begin{bmatrix} \textit{if } \mathcal{F} \\ \textit{then } f(...,s,...) \\ \textit{else } f(...,t,...) \end{bmatrix}.$$

Each of these equivalences produces a sentence equivalent to the given sentence. We have provided two equivalences for each connective; one may apply whichever equivalence is found more convenient. The repeated application of these equivalences can make the resulting sentence more complex, but once all the $\equiv$ connectives and *if-then-else* connectives and operators have been removed, we can be certain that no quantifiers of both forces remain.

Example

Consider the sentence

$$(\forall y)(\exists z) \begin{bmatrix} (\exists x_1)^{\forall\exists} p(x_1) \\ \equiv \\ q\left(\begin{array}{l} \textit{if } (\forall x_2)^{\forall\exists} p(x_2) \\ \textit{then } f(y) \\ \textit{else } z \end{array} \right) \end{bmatrix}.$$

Note that the sentence has two quantifier occurrences of both forces. These occurrences are within the scope of the $\equiv$ connective; one of them is also within the *if*-clause of the *if-then-else* operator.

Applying the equivalence

$$q(\,...,\text{if } \mathcal{F} \text{ then } s \text{ else } t, \,...\,)$$

$$\equiv$$

$$\text{if } \mathcal{F} \text{ then } q(\,...,s,\,...\,) \text{ else } q(\,...,t,\,...\,),$$

we obtain the sentence

$$(\forall y)(\exists z) \begin{bmatrix} (\exists x_1)^{\forall\exists} p(x_1) \\ \equiv \\ \begin{bmatrix} \textit{if } (\forall x_2)^{\forall\exists} p(x_2) \\ \textit{then } q\big(f(y)\big) \\ \textit{else } q(z) \end{bmatrix} \end{bmatrix}.$$

Applying the equivalence

$$\mathcal{F} \equiv \mathcal{G}$$
$$\equiv$$
$$(if\ \mathcal{F}\ then\ \mathcal{G})\ and\ (if\ \mathcal{G}\ then\ \mathcal{F}),$$

we obtain the sentence

$$(\forall y)(\exists z)\begin{bmatrix} if\ (\exists x_1)^\forall p(x_1) & & if\ if\ (\forall x_2)^{\forall\exists}p(x_2) \\ then\ if\ (\forall x_2)^{\forall\exists}p(x_2) & and & then\ q(f(y)) \\ then\ q(f(y)) & & else\ q(z) \\ else\ q(z) & & then\ (\exists x_1)^\exists p(x_1) \end{bmatrix}.$$

Applying the equivalence

$$if\ \mathcal{F}\ then\ \mathcal{G}\ else\ \mathcal{H}$$
$$\equiv$$
$$(if\ \mathcal{F}\ then\ \mathcal{G})\ and\ \big(if\ (not\ \mathcal{F})\ then\ \mathcal{H}\big),$$

we obtain the sentence

$$(\forall y)(\exists z)\begin{bmatrix} \begin{bmatrix} if\ (\exists x_1)^\forall p(x_1) \\ then\ \begin{bmatrix} if\ (\forall x_2)^\exists p(x_2)\ then\ q(f(y)) \\ and \\ if\ not\ (\forall x_2)^\forall p(x_2)\ then\ q(z) \end{bmatrix} \end{bmatrix} \\ and \\ \begin{bmatrix} if\ \begin{bmatrix} if\ (\forall x_2)^\forall p(x_2)\ then\ q(f(y)) \\ and \\ if\ not\ (\forall x_2)^\exists p(x_2)\ then\ q(z) \end{bmatrix} \\ then\ (\exists x_1)^\exists p(x_1) \end{bmatrix} \end{bmatrix}.$$

Thus, by repeatedly applying the preceding equivalences, we can remove quantifiers of both forces from a sentence. The resulting sentence may have many "copies" of the original quantifiers, but all will have strict force. In the next two sections, we describe techniques for removing quantifiers of strict universal and existential force.

10.6   REMOVING STRICT UNIVERSAL FORCE

Removing quantifiers of strict universal force is more complicated than the other stages of quantifier removal. Also, it is the only stage of the process that does not necessarily preserve equivalence.

In the procedure for eliminating quantifiers from a given closed sentence $\mathcal{F}$, a quantifier $(...z)^\forall$ of strict universal force is dropped; every occurrence of the variable z bound by this quantifier is replaced by a term $f(y_1, \ldots, y_n)$. Here, f is a "new" function symbol, in the sense that it does not already occur in $\mathcal{F}$. We shall refer to f as a "skolem" function symbol and $f(y_1, \ldots, y_n)$ as a "skolem" term. Also, $y_1, \ldots, y_n$ are the variables of all the quantifiers $(...y_1)^\exists, \ldots, (...y_n)^\exists$ of existential force that surround the eliminated quantifier $(...z)^\forall$, that is, that contain $(...z)^\forall$ within their scopes. (These quantifiers all have strict force since the force of $(...z)^\forall$ is strict.)

Henceforth we abbreviate $y_1, \ldots, y_n$ as $\overline{y}$ and $(...y_1)^\exists, \ldots, (...y_n)^\exists$ as $(...\overline{y})^\exists$. In the special case in which there are no quantifiers $(...\overline{y})^\exists$ surrounding the elimi- nated quantifier $(...z)^\forall$, the occurrences of z are replaced by a new skolem constant a.

Let us now describe our general procedure for removing quantifiers of strictly universal force and prove that it preserves the validity of the transformed sentence.

Proposition (universal elimination)

Let $\mathcal{F}$ be a closed sentence that satisfies the following restrictions:

- $\mathcal{F}$ contains an occurrence of a subsentence $(...z)^\forall P[z]$, where $(...z)^\forall$ is a quantifier of strict universal force in $\mathcal{F}$.

- The quantifiers of existential force that surround the occurrence $(...z)^\forall P[z]$ are $(...\overline{y})^\exists$, that is, $(...y_1)^\exists, (...y_2)^\exists, \ldots, (...y_n)^\exists$.

- The variables $\overline{y}$ and z are all distinct.

In our pictorial notation, we can write $\mathcal{F}$ as

$$\mathcal{F}: \underline{} (...y_1)^\exists \Big[\cdots \underline{} (...y_n)^\exists \Big[\underline{} (...z)^\forall P[z] \underline{} \Big] \underline{} \cdots \Big] \underline{}$$

Let $\mathcal{G}$ be the sentence obtained by replacing the subsentence occurrence $(...z)^\forall P[z]$ with the sentence $P\big[f(\overline{y})\big]$, where f is a new function symbol, i.e., one that does not occur in $\mathcal{F}$. That is, the resulting sentence is

$$\mathcal{G}: \underline{} (...y_1)^\exists \Big[\cdots \underline{} (...y_n)^\exists \Big[\underline{} P[f(\overline{y})] \underline{} \Big] \underline{} \cdots \Big] \underline{} .$$

In the special case in which $n = 0$, that is, there are no surrounding quantifiers $(...y_i)^\exists$, we take $f(\overline{y})$ to stand for a new constant a. Thus $\mathcal{G}$ is obtained from $\mathcal{F}$ by replacing the subsentence occurrence $(...z)^\forall P[z]$ with the sentence $P[a]$, where a is a new constant, i.e., one that does not occur in $\mathcal{F}$. That is, in this case, the resulting sentence is

$$\mathcal{G}: \underline{} (...y_1)^\exists \Big[\cdots \underline{} (...y_n)^\exists \Big[\underline{} P[a] \underline{} \Big] \underline{} \cdots \Big] \underline{} .$$

Then

    (a)   For every interpretation I,
        if $\mathcal{F}$ is false under I,
        then there is an interpretation I' such that
            $\mathcal{G}$ is false under I',
            and I and I' agree except perhaps on new symbols.

    (b)   For every interpretation J,
        if $\mathcal{G}$ is false under J,
        then $\mathcal{F}$ is also false under J.

Therefore

    (c) $\mathcal{F}$ is valid
        precisely when
        $\mathcal{G}$ is valid.   ∎

We sometimes refer to $f(\bar{y})$ (or a) as a *skolem term*.

Proof

First note that, because each of the constant, function, and predicate symbols of $\mathcal{F}$ also occurs in $\mathcal{G}$, every interpretation for $\mathcal{G}$ is also an interpretation for $\mathcal{F}$. The converse does not hold, however, because the new function symbol f (or constant a) occurs in $\mathcal{G}$ but not in $\mathcal{F}$.

Proof of (c)

It is clear that conclusion (c) is implied by the first two conclusions. For, by the definition of validity, (c) is equivalent to

      $\mathcal{F}$ is false under some interpretation I
        precisely when
      $\mathcal{G}$ is false under some interpretation I',

which follows directly from (a) and (b). We now prove Part (b), which is used in proving Part (a).

Proof of (b)

We suppose that $\mathcal{F}$ is true under some interpretation J and show that $\mathcal{G}$ is also true under J.

In our pictorial notation, it will be convenient for us to write $\mathcal{F}$ as

$$\mathcal{F}: \quad \underline{\quad} (\dots z)^{\forall} P[z] \, \underline{\quad}$$

and $\mathcal{G}$ as

$$\mathcal{G}: \underline{\quad} P[f(\overline{y})] \underline{\quad} .$$

Note that $\mathcal{G}$ is closed; the newly introduced variables $\overline{y}$ are within the scope of the quantifiers $(\overline{...y})^{\exists}$. (In the case in which $n = 0$, we would have a rather than $f(\overline{y})$, but we shall often avoid mentioning this case.)

The proof relies on the earlier *force-instantiation* proposition, which tells us that the (closed) sentence

$$if \underline{\quad} (...z)^{\forall} P[z] \underline{\quad}$$
$$then \underline{\quad} P[f(\overline{y})] \underline{\quad}$$

is valid. The antecedent of this sentence is $\mathcal{F}$, and the consequent is $\mathcal{G}$. Therefore, if $\mathcal{F}$ is true under J, so is $\mathcal{G}$, as we wanted to show.

Proof of (a)

The proposition allows us to remove any quantifier of strict universal force, regardless of its position in the sentence. As a first step, however, we prove the proposition for the case in which the quantifier is at the top level.

- *Very Special Case:* $\mathcal{F}$ is of form $(\exists \overline{y})(\forall z)^{\forall} P[\overline{y}, z]$.

Since

$$\mathcal{F}: \quad (\exists \overline{y})(\forall z)^{\forall} P[\overline{y}, z]$$

is closed, $\overline{y}$ and z are the only free variables in $P[\overline{y}, z]$. In this case,

$$\mathcal{G}: \quad (\exists \overline{y}) P[\overline{y}, f(\overline{y})].$$

The proof depends on the *function-introduction* proposition (in Section [I]3.6), which tells us that, if f is a new symbol,

if $(\forall \overline{y})(\exists z)[not\ P[\overline{y}, z]]$ is true under an interpretation I,

then $(\forall \overline{y})[not\ P[\overline{y}, f(\overline{y})]]$ is true under some interpretation I',

where I and I' agree on all symbols except perhaps on f. The original property applies only to a single quantifier $(\forall y)$, but we extend it to n quantifiers $(\forall \overline{y})$.

Consider an interpretation I for $\mathcal{F}$. We suppose that

$\mathcal{F}$, that is, $(\exists \overline{y})(\forall z) P[\overline{y}, z]$, is false under I.

Then, by the semantic rules for quantifiers and negation,

$(\forall \overline{y})(\exists z)[not\ P[\overline{y}, z]]$ is true under I.

Hence, by the *function-introduction* proposition,

$$(\forall \overline{y})[not\ P[\overline{y},\ f(\overline{y})]]\ \text{is true under some interpretation}\ I',$$

where I and I' agree on all symbols except perhaps the new symbol f. In other words, by the semantic rules for quantifiers and negation, again,

$$(\exists \overline{y})P[\overline{y},\ f(\overline{y})],\ \text{that is},\ \mathcal{G},\ \text{is false under}\ I',$$

as we wanted to show.

We next establish Part (a) in a *somewhat special* case, not quite as restricted as the *very special* case, but still not fully general.

- *Somewhat Special Case:* The quantifier $(...z)^\forall$ is an outermost quantifier of universal force.

The proof relies on the *very special* case. Here we no longer require that $(...z)^\forall$ be at the top level, but we do insist that it be within the scope of no other quantifiers of universal force. That is, the only quantifiers surrounding $(...z)$ are the quantifiers $(...\overline{y})^\exists$ of existential force. Let us write $\mathcal{F}$ in our special notation as

$$\mathcal{F}:\quad \underline{\hspace{1em}}(...y_1)^\exists\Big[\cdots \underline{\hspace{1em}}(...y_n)^\exists\Big[\underline{\hspace{1em}}(...z)^\forall P[z]\underline{\hspace{1em}}\Big]\underline{\hspace{1em}}\cdots\Big]\underline{\hspace{1em}}.$$

By repeated application of the earlier *force-manipulation* proposition, $\mathcal{F}$ is equivalent to the sentence obtained by pulling out the quantifiers,

$$\mathcal{F}':\quad (\exists \overline{y})(\forall z)\Big[\underline{\hspace{1em}}\Big[\cdots \underline{\hspace{1em}}\Big[\underline{\hspace{1em}}P[z]\underline{\hspace{1em}}\Big]\underline{\hspace{1em}}\cdots\Big]\underline{\hspace{1em}}\Big].$$

Similarly, $\mathcal{G}$, that is,

$$\mathcal{G}:\quad \underline{\hspace{1em}}(...y_1)^\exists\Big[\cdots \underline{\hspace{1em}}(...y_n)^\exists\Big[\underline{\hspace{1em}}P[f(\overline{y})]\underline{\hspace{1em}}\Big]\underline{\hspace{1em}}\cdots\Big]\underline{\hspace{1em}}$$

is equivalent to

$$\mathcal{G}':\quad (\exists \overline{y})\Big[\underline{\hspace{1em}}\Big[\cdots \underline{\hspace{1em}}\Big[\underline{\hspace{1em}}P[f(\overline{y})]\underline{\hspace{1em}}\Big]\underline{\hspace{1em}}\cdots\Big]\underline{\hspace{1em}}\Big].$$

Here $\mathcal{F}'$ is of the form covered by the *very special* case, and $\mathcal{G}'$ is obtained from $\mathcal{F}'$ by removing the quantifier $(\forall z)$. Thus conclusion (a) holds for $\mathcal{F}'$ and $\mathcal{G}'$, and hence for $\mathcal{F}$ and $\mathcal{G}$.

We are finally ready to consider the general case.

- *General Case*

The proof relies on the *somewhat special* case. Here we no longer require that $(...z)^\forall$ be an outermost quantifier of universal force. It may be within the scope of k quantifiers $(...z_1)^\forall$, $\ldots$, $(...z_k)^\forall$ of universal force. Because $(...z)^\forall$ is of strict force, so are the surrounding quantifiers.

The proof is by induction on k. We assume inductively that conclusion (a) holds when the number of quantifiers of universal force surrounding $(...z)^\forall$ is fewer than k.

In the case in which $k = 0$, we know that $(...z)^\forall$ is actually an outermost quantifier of universal force. We have already considered this possibility under the *somewhat special* case.

In the case in which $k > 0$, let us write $\mathcal{F}$ in our pictorial notation as

$$
\begin{array}{c}
—\,(...z_1)^\forall\Big[—\,(...z_2)^\forall\Big[\,\cdots\;—\,(...z_k)^\forall\Big[— \\[4pt]
\mathcal{F}: \qquad (...z)^\forall\,P\big[z_1,\;z_2,\;\ldots,\;z_k,\;z\big] \\[4pt]
—\Big]—\,\cdots\Big]—\Big]—.
\end{array}
$$

Consider an interpretation $\mathcal{I}$ for $\mathcal{F}$. Suppose that $\mathcal{F}$ is false under $\mathcal{I}$.

Because $(...z_1)^\forall$ is an outermost quantifier of universal force, we can use the *somewhat special* case to drop it, obtaining the sentence

$$
\begin{array}{c}
—\Big[—\,(...z_2)^\forall\Big[\,\cdots\;—\,(...z_k)^\forall\Big[— \\[4pt]
\mathcal{F}_1: \qquad (...z)^\forall\,P\big[f_1(...),\;z_2,\;\ldots,\;z_k,\;z\big] \\[4pt]
—\Big]—\,\cdots\Big]—\Big]—.
\end{array}
$$

Here occurrences of the variable z_1 in the scope of the quantifier have been (safely) replaced by skolem terms $f_1(...)$, where f_1 is a new function symbol. (We do not write down its arguments.)

The sentence $\mathcal{F}_1$ is false under some interpretation $\mathcal{I}_1$ that agrees with $\mathcal{I}$ except perhaps on the new function symbol f_1.

In the sentence $\mathcal{F}_1$, the quantifier $(...z)^\forall$ is within the scope of $k-1$ quantifiers of universal force. Therefore we may use our induction hypothesis to remove the quantifier $(...z)^\forall$ itself, obtaining the sentence

$$
\begin{array}{c}
—\Big[—\,(...z_2)^\forall\Big[\,\cdots\;—\,(...z_k)^\forall\Big[— \\[4pt]
\mathcal{G}_1: \qquad P\big[f_1(...),\;z_2,\;\ldots,\;z_k,\;f(\overline{y})\big] \\[4pt]
—\Big]—\,\cdots\Big]—\Big]—.
\end{array}
$$

Here occurrences of the variable z have been replaced by skolem terms $f(\overline{y})$, where f is the new function symbol.

The sentence $\mathcal{G}_1$ is false under some interpretation I_1' that agrees with I_1 except perhaps on new symbols. Therefore I_1' also agrees with I except perhaps on new symbols.

Finally, we use Part (b) of this proposition to restore the outermost quantifier $(\ldots z_1)^\forall$ of universal force, obtaining the desired sentence

$$
\mathcal{G}: \quad
\begin{array}{l}
\underline{\hphantom{xx}} (\ldots z_1)^\forall \Big[\underline{\hphantom{xx}} (\ldots z_2)^\forall \Big[\cdots \underline{\hphantom{xx}} (\ldots z_k)^\forall \Big[\underline{\hphantom{xx}} \\[4pt]
\quad P\big[z_1,\, z_2,\, \ldots,\, z_k,\, f(\bar{y})\big] \\[4pt]
\underline{\hphantom{xx}} \Big] \underline{\hphantom{xx}} \cdots \Big] \underline{\hphantom{xx}} \Big] \underline{\hphantom{xx}}.
\end{array}
$$

This sentence is also false under I_1'. The proof of the *general* case is thus complete. ◢

Let us give a more complex illustration of the *universal-elimination* proposition.

Example

Suppose that $\mathcal{A}$ is the closed sentence

$$
\mathcal{A}: \quad
\begin{array}{l}
\text{if } \ (\forall y_1)^\exists (\exists z_1)^\forall p(y_1,\, z_1) \\[4pt]
\text{then } \ (\forall z_2)^\forall (\exists y_2)^\exists p(y_2,\, z_2),
\end{array}
$$

where we have indicated the force of each of the quantifiers. (This sentence is not in fact valid.) There are two quantifiers of (strict) universal force in this sentence: $(\exists z_1)^\forall$ and $(\forall z_2)^\forall$.

First let us eliminate the quantifier $(\exists z_1)$. This quantifier is within the scope of the quantifier $(\forall y_1)^\exists$ of (strict) existential force. Therefore the quantifier $(\exists z_1)$ can be dropped and the occurrence of z_1 replaced by the term $f_1(y_1)$, where f_1 is a skolem function. The resulting sentence is

$$
\mathcal{B}: \quad
\begin{array}{l}
\text{if } \ (\forall y_1)^\exists p(y_1,\, f_1(y_1)) \\[4pt]
\text{then } \ (\forall z_2)^\forall (\exists y_2)^\exists p(y_2,\, z_2).
\end{array}
$$

By the proposition, $\mathcal{B}$ is valid precisely when $\mathcal{A}$ is valid.

This sentence still contains a quantifier $(\forall z_2)^\forall$ of universal force. This quantifier is not within the scope of any quantifier of existential force. Therefore we may drop the quantifier $(\forall z_2)^\forall$ and replace the occurrence of z_2 with a skolem constant a. The resulting sentence is

$$
\mathcal{C}: \quad
\begin{array}{l}
\text{if } \ (\forall y_1)^\exists p(y_1,\, f_1(y_1)) \\[4pt]
\text{then } \ (\exists y_2)^\exists p(y_2,\, a).
\end{array}
$$

By the proposition, C is valid precisely when B is valid, and hence when A is valid.

In fact, by two applications of the proposition, we can show that, for every interpretation I, if A is false under I, then C is false under some interpretation I'', where I and I'' agree on all symbols except perhaps new symbols. Furthermore, for every interpretation J, if C is false under J, A is also false under J.

In **Problem 10.5**, the reader is asked to show that we have not preserved equivalence in passing from sentence A to sentence C. ⌐

The quantifiers of the sentence C obtained in the preceding example all have strict existential force. This brings us to the next phase of the skolemization process.

10.7   REMOVING STRICT EXISTENTIAL FORCE

So far, we have discussed only two stages of the quantifier-removal process: the elimination of quantifiers of both forces and of strict universal force. We now consider the final stage: the elimination of quantifiers of strict existential force. As the reader will recall, such quantifiers are not actually removed, but merely moved to the outermost level. We first illustrate the basis for the technique with an example.

Example

Consider the sentence C that we obtained in the previous example (by removing both quantifiers of strict universal force from the given sentence A):

$$C : \quad \begin{aligned} &\textit{if } \; (\forall y_1)^{\exists} p(y_1, f_1(y_1)) \\ &\textit{then } \; (\exists y_2)^{\exists} p(y_2, a). \end{aligned}$$

Both quantifiers in this sentence have strict existential force. We first remove the quantifier $(\forall y_1)^{\exists}$.

The sentence is equivalent (by the *force-manipulation* proposition) to the sentence

$$D : \quad (\exists y_1) \left[\begin{aligned} &\textit{if } \; p(y_1, f_1(y_1)) \\ &\textit{then } \; (\exists y_2)^{\exists} p(y_2, a) \end{aligned} \right].$$

Now let us consider a subsentence of $\mathcal{D}$,

$$\mathcal{D}_0 : \quad \begin{array}{l} \textit{if } \; p(y_1, f_1(y_1)) \\ \textit{then } \; (\exists y_2)^{\exists} p(y_2, a). \end{array}$$

This subsentence is equivalent (by the *force-manipulation* proposition, again) to the sentence

$$\mathcal{E}_0 : \quad (\exists y_2) \left[\begin{array}{l} \textit{if } \; p(y_1, f_1(y_1)) \\ \textit{then } \; p(y_2, a) \end{array} \right],$$

obtained by pulling out the quantifier $(\exists y_2)^{\exists}$.

Therefore the entire sentence $\mathcal{D}$ is equivalent to the sentence

$$\mathcal{E} : \quad (\exists y_1)(\exists y_2) \left[\begin{array}{l} \textit{if } \; p(y_1, f_1(y_1)) \\ \textit{then } \; p(y_2, a) \end{array} \right].$$

From our sentence $\mathcal{C}$ we have obtained an equivalent sentence $\mathcal{E}$ by pulling out its quantifiers of (strict) existential force to the outermost level. (Note that the order of these quantifiers is not significant.) In the context of deductive tableaux in which we attempt to prove validity, we shall be able to drop outermost existential quantifiers; therefore we regard this as a quantifier-removal step. The resulting sentence $\mathcal{E}$ is not equivalent to the original sentence $\mathcal{A}$ we had at the end of the previous section; we lost equivalence when we dropped the quantifiers of strict universal force. Nevertheless, we know that we have preserved validity; that is, $\mathcal{A}$ is valid precisely when $\mathcal{E}$ is valid. ◢

Now let us state the general proposition that justifies removing quantifiers of strict existential force.

Proposition (existential elimination)

Let $\mathcal{F}$ be a closed sentence satisfying the following conditions:

- $\mathcal{F}$ contains an occurrence of a subsentence $(\ldots y)^{\exists} \mathcal{P}$, where $(\ldots y)^{\exists}$ is of strict existential force in $\mathcal{F}$. In our pictorial notation,

  $$\mathcal{F} : \quad \underline{\quad} (\ldots y)^{\exists} \mathcal{P} \underline{\quad} .$$

- The occurrence of $(\ldots y)^{\exists} \mathcal{P}$ is within the scope of no quantifier of universal force.

- The occurrence of $(\ldots y)^{\exists} \mathcal{P}$ is within the scope of no other quantifier $(\forall y)$ or $(\exists y)$ with the same variable y.

Let $\mathcal{G}$ be the sentence $(\exists y)\mathcal{G}_0$, where $\mathcal{G}_0$ is obtained from $\mathcal{F}$ by dropping the quantifier $(\ldots y)^{\exists}$ from the occurrence of $(\ldots y)^{\exists}P$, leaving only P. That is,

$$\mathcal{G}: \quad (\exists y)\Big[\!-\!-\, P\, -\!-\Big].$$

Then

$$\mathcal{F} \text{ is equivalent to } \mathcal{G}. \quad \lrcorner$$

Proof

We can write $\mathcal{F}$ in more detail as

$$\mathcal{F}: \quad -\!-\,(\ldots y_1)^{\exists}\Big[\!-\!- \cdots -\!-\,(\ldots y_n)^{\exists}\big[\!-\!-\,(\ldots y)^{\exists}P\,-\!-\big]-\!- \cdots -\!-\Big]-\!-\,.$$

Here $(\ldots y_1)^{\exists}, \ldots, (\ldots y_n)^{\exists}$ are the only quantifiers that surround our occurrence $(\ldots y)^{\exists}P$; by the restrictions on the proposition, we know that these quantifiers are of existential force and that (renaming if necessary) all the variables y_i are distinct from each other and from y.

By repeated application of the *force-manipulation* proposition, $\mathcal{F}$ is equivalent to the sentence obtained by pulling out all these quantifiers,

$$(\exists \overline{y})(\exists y)\Big[\!-\!-\big[\!-\!- \cdots -\!-\,[\!-\!-\,P\,-\!-\,]\,-\!- \cdots -\!-\big]-\!-\Big].$$

Here again, $\overline{y}$ is an abbreviation for $y_1, \ldots, y_n$. (The requirement that the quantified variables be distinct is necessary to ensure that we do not pull out a quantifier $(\exists y_j)$, say, over a free occurrence of y_j, violating the conditions of the *force-manipulation* proposition.)

We may freely rearrange the outermost existential quantifiers, obtaining the equivalent sentence

$$(\exists y)(\exists \overline{y})\Big[\!-\!-\big[\!-\!- \cdots -\!-\,[\!-\!-\,P\,-\!-\,]\,-\!- \cdots -\!-\big]-\!-\Big].$$

Finally, by repeated application of the *force-manipulation* proposition again, we may restore the quantifiers $(\ldots y_j)^{\exists}$ to their original places in the sentence, obtaining the equivalent sentence

$$\mathcal{G}: \quad (\exists y)\Big[\!-\!-\,(\ldots y_1)^{\exists}\big[\!-\!- \cdots -\!-\,(\ldots y_n)^{\exists}[\!-\!-\,P\,-\!-\,]\,-\!- \cdots -\!-\big]-\!-\Big].$$

But this is our desired sentence $\mathcal{G}$.

This concludes the proof of the *existential-elimination* proposition. $\quad \lrcorner$

In the following we shall refer to the *universal-elimination* and the *existential-elimination* propositions collectively as the *quantifier-elimination* proposition.

10.8   SUMMARY OF THE SKOLEMIZATION PROCESS

In some circumstances we may wish to remove only a particular occurrence of a single quantifier, while, in other cases, we may wish to remove all the quantifiers in a given sentence. Let us describe each process separately.

REMOVAL OF A PARTICULAR OCCURRENCE

Suppose we would like to remove an occurrence of a quantifier from a given closed sentence. Then

- If the occurrence is of both forces, it must be within the scope of one or more $\equiv$ connectives or within the *if*-clause of one or more *if-then-else* connectives or operators. The offending constructs are paraphrased by repeated application of rewritings. This will cause multiple occurrences of the quantifier to appear. Each of these occurrences, however, will be of strict force and can be removed separately by the succeeding stages of the process.

- Rename the bound variables of the sentence, if necessary, to ensure they are distinct from one another.

- If the quantifier to be removed is of strict universal force, it is removed by the *universal-elimination* proposition, introducing a skolem constant or skolem function.

- If the quantifier to be removed is of strict existential force, ensure that it is not within the scope of any quantifier of universal force, removing any offending quantifiers by application of the preceding stage of the process. Then, by the *existential-elimination* proposition, pull out the quantifier of strict existential force.

We say that the quantifier we have removed has been *skolemized*; the process is called *skolemization*.

Each of the stages just described preserves the equivalence (and hence validity) of the sentence, except for the removal of a quantifier of strict universal force, which preserves validity but not necessarily equivalence. As a whole, therefore, the entire process preserves the validity of the sentence. In other words, the sentence $\mathcal{G}$ we obtain is valid precisely when the given sentence $\mathcal{F}$ is valid. In fact, if $\mathcal{G}$ is false under some interpretation $\mathcal{I}$, then $\mathcal{F}$ is false under the same interpretation $\mathcal{I}$. And, if $\mathcal{F}$ is false under some interpretation $\mathcal{I}$, then $\mathcal{G}$ is false under an interpretation I' such that I and I' agree on all symbols except perhaps on skolem constant and function symbols.

REMOVAL OF ALL QUANTIFIERS

Suppose we would like to remove all the quantifiers from a given closed sentence. Then

- Remove all occurrences of $\equiv$ connectives that contain quantifiers in their scopes, and all occurrences of *if-then-else* connectives and operators that contain quantifiers in their *if*-clauses, by application of the appropriate rewritings. This ensures that no quantifiers have both forces.

- Rename the bound variables of the sentence to ensure that they are distinct from one another.

- Remove all quantifiers of strict universal force, by repeated application of the *universal-elimination* proposition.

- Remove (pull out) all quantifiers of strict existential force, by repeated application of the *existential-elimination* proposition.

As before, each of these stages preserves the validity of the sentence. Only the removal of the quantifiers of universal force sometimes fails to preserve equivalence. As a result of applying this process to a given closed sentence $\mathcal{F}$, we obtain a sentence $\mathcal{G}$ of form $(\exists *)\mathcal{G}_0$, where $\mathcal{G}_0$ is quantifier-free, such that $\mathcal{F}$ is valid precisely when $\mathcal{G}$ is valid. Again, interpretations that falsify the two sentences, if any, agree on all symbols other than, perhaps, skolem constant and function symbols. We will say that $\mathcal{G}$ is obtained from $\mathcal{F}$ by (*full*) *skolemization*.

The reader is requested in **Problem 10.6** to eliminate the quantifiers of several sentences.

10.9 REMOVING QUANTIFIERS IN SPECIAL THEORIES

The skolemization process has been described and justified for pure predicate logic. We shall also be interested in removing quantifiers in special theories. Removing quantifiers of both forces and quantifiers of strict existential force presents no problem because these phases of the process preserve equivalence; if two sentences are equivalent in predicate logic, they are equivalent in any special theory.

The trouble arises when we attempt to remove quantifiers of strict universal force, because this phase does not preserve equivalence, but only validity; a process that preserves validity in predicate logic may not preserve validity in a special theory. In predicate logic, to be valid a sentence must be true under all interpretations; in a theory, to be valid a sentence must be true only under the models of the theory.

We shall first exhibit an unusual theory in which skolemization does not preserve validity. We then present a condition that a theory must satisfy to guarantee that validity is preserved by skolemization.

This is a theoretical section, which may be skipped on first reading.

EXAMPLE: THE NO-SKOLEMIZATION THEORY

Consider a theory with a predicate symbol p and constants a_1, a_2, ..., defined by the following axiom schema:

> For every constant a in the vocabulary,
>
> $p(a)$
>
> is an axiom.

The axiom schema ensures that any model for this theory assigns to each constant a_i a domain element for which p is true. In the following, we refer to this as the *no-skolemization theory*.

Note that the sentence

$$\mathcal{F} : (\forall z)p(z)$$

is not valid in this theory. For instance, the interpretation whose domain is all the integers, under which $p(x)$ means "x is nonnegative" and each constant a_i is assigned a nonnegative integer, is a model for the no-skolemization theory. The sentence $\mathcal{F}$ is false under this model, because p is false for any negative integer.

Now suppose we remove the quantifier $(\forall z)$ from $\mathcal{F}$, introducing instead the new skolem constant a_1, to obtain the closed sentence

$$\mathcal{G} : p(a_1).$$

According to the schema, the sentence $p(a_1)$ is one of the axioms, and naturally is valid in the theory. Thus we have exhibited a sentence $(\forall z)p(z)$ that is not valid in the theory but that becomes valid after skolemization. In other words, in this theory, skolemization does not preserve validity.

The difficulty with the no-skolemization theory is that the meaning of every constant in the vocabulary has already been restricted by the axiom schema. In a sense, there are no new constants. These considerations motivate the following subsection, in which we characterize theories in which skolemization does preserve validity.

THEORIES WITH NEW SYMBOLS

We begin with a definition.

Definition (new symbols)

For a given theory and sentence $\mathcal{H}[\overline{y}, z]$, where $\overline{y}$ and z are the only free variables, we shall say that

f is a *new function symbol corresponding to* $\mathcal{H}[\overline{y}, z]$ if
f does not occur in $\mathcal{H}[\overline{y}, z]$ and the following condition holds:

if $(\forall \overline{y})(\exists z)\mathcal{H}[\overline{y}, z]$ is true under some model I,
then $(\forall \overline{y})\mathcal{H}[\overline{y}, f(\overline{y})]$ is true under some model I',

where I and I' agree on all sentences not containing f.

In the special case in which there are no free variables $\overline{y}$ in $\mathcal{H}$, we shall say that

a is a *new constant corresponding to* $\mathcal{H}[z]$ if
a does not occur in $\mathcal{H}[z]$ and the following condition holds:

if $(\exists z)\mathcal{H}[z]$ is true under some model I,
then $\mathcal{H}[a]$ is true under some model I',

where I and I' agree on all sentences not containing a.

A theory *has new symbols* if every such sentence $\mathcal{H}$ has a corresponding ·
new function (or constant) symbol. ⌐

Note that in the preceding definition we do not require that the two models I and I' agree on all symbols other than f, but only on all sentences not containing f. This is to admit the possibility that the models may differ on symbols other than f and may actually have different domains.

Example (the no-skolemization theory)

We first remark that the no-skolemization theory does not have new symbols. To see this, take $\mathcal{H}[z]$ in the definition to be the sentence

$$\mathcal{H}[z]: \quad not \; p(z).$$

Then, in the theory, there is no new constant corresponding to $\mathcal{H}[z]$. That is, there is no constant a such that

> if $(\exists z)[not \; p(z)]$ is true under some model I
> then $not \; p(a)$ is true under some model I',

where I and I' agree on all sentences not containing a. For, as we have seen, $(\exists z)[not \; p(z)]$, that is, $not \; (\forall z)p(z)$, is true under some models for the theory, but, by the axiom schema, $(not \; p(a))$ is not true under any model I'. ⌐

Example (finite theory)

Any *finite* theory, i.e., one defined by a finite set of axioms $\mathcal{A}_1, \ldots, \mathcal{A}_n$, has new symbols, provided its vocabulary includes an infinite set of constants and, for each positive integer m, an infinite set of function symbols of arity m.

To see this, consider a sentence $\mathcal{H}[\overline{y}, z]$ whose free variables are $\overline{y} = y_1, \ldots, y_m$ (where m could be 0) and z, and suppose

$$(\forall \overline{y})(\exists z)\mathcal{H}[\overline{y}, z]$$

is true under some model I for the theory. Then (by the semantic rules for quantifiers)

> for any domain elements $\overline{d}$,
> (∗)   there exists a domain element e such that
> $\mathcal{H}[\overline{y}, z]$ is true under the extended model $\langle z \leftarrow e \rangle \circ \langle \overline{y} \leftarrow \overline{d} \rangle \circ I$.

For any domain elements $\overline{d}$, let $k(\overline{d})$ be a domain element e such that (∗) holds. Let f be any function symbol of arity m that does not occur in $\mathcal{H}$ or in any of the axioms of the theory; we know such a symbol exists because there are infinitely many function symbols of arity m but only finitely many axioms. (In the special case in which $m = 0$, we choose a constant a instead of a function symbol f.)

Let I' be $(f \leftarrow k) \circ I$. Then I' and I agree on all sentences not containing f. Also, I' is a model for the theory because f does not occur in any of the axioms. Finally, $(\forall \overline{y})\mathcal{H}[\overline{y}, f(\overline{y})]$ is true under I'. Hence f is a new function symbol corresponding to $\mathcal{H}[\overline{y}, z]$. ⌐

Example (the theory of the nonnegative integers)

The theory of the nonnegative integers does have new symbols, provided that the vocabulary is extended to include an infinite set of constants and function symbols of each arity.

To see this, consider a sentence $\mathcal{H}[\overline{y}, z]$ whose free variables are $\overline{y}$ and z, and suppose

$$(\forall \overline{y})(\exists z)\mathcal{H}[\overline{y}, z]$$

is true under some model $\mathcal{I}$ for the theory. Then (by the semantic rules for quantifiers)

(†) for any nonnegative integers $\overline{d}$,
     there exists a nonnegative integer e such that
     $\mathcal{H}[\overline{y}, z]$ is true under the extended model $\langle z \leftarrow e \rangle \circ \langle \overline{y} \leftarrow \overline{d} \rangle \circ \mathcal{I}$.

For any nonnegative integers $\overline{d}$, let $k(\overline{d})$ be the least nonnegative integer e such that (†) holds. Let f be any function (or constant) symbol that does not occur in $\mathcal{H}$ or explicitly in any of the axioms for the theory. (Of course, any function symbol f occurs implicitly in some instance of the *induction* schema, because that schema applies to all sentences.) Let $\mathcal{I}'$ be $(f \leftarrow k) \circ \mathcal{I}$. Then $\mathcal{I}'$ and $\mathcal{I}$ agree on all sentences not containing f, $\mathcal{I}'$ is also a model for the theory, and $(\forall \overline{y})\mathcal{H}[\overline{y}, f(\overline{y})]$ is true under $\mathcal{I}'$. Hence f is a new function symbol corresponding to $\mathcal{H}[\overline{y}, z]$. ⌟

A similar argument shows that the other theories with which we deal, such as the trees and tuples, also have new symbols, provided their vocabularies are suitably extended.

QUANTIFIER-ELIMINATION PROPOSITION

As we have remarked, the only stage of skolemization that requires special justification in a theory is the removal of quantifiers of strict universal force; the other stages preserve equivalence and hence apply directly. The following proposition allows the removal of quantifiers of strict universal force in a special theory.

Proposition (universal-quantifier elimination in a special theory)

In a theory with new symbols, let $\mathcal{F}$ be a closed sentence satisfying the restrictions of the *universal-elimination* proposition for predicate logic, and let $\mathcal{G}$ be the sentence obtained by removing a quantifier $(...z)^{\forall}$ of strict universal force in $\mathcal{F}$.

Then

(a) For every model I (for the theory),
       if $\mathcal{F}$ is false under I,
          then there is a model I' (for the theory) such that
                $\mathcal{G}$ is false under I',
                and I and I' agree on all sentences not containing new symbols.

(b) For every model J (for the theory),
       if $\mathcal{G}$ is false under J,
          then $\mathcal{F}$ is also false under J.

Therefore
(c) $\mathcal{F}$ is valid (in the theory)
          precisely when
       $\mathcal{G}$ is valid (in the theory). ◢

The proof is the same as the proof of the proposition for predicate logic, except that where that proof refers to interpretations, this proof refers to models for the theory. Where that proof invokes the *function-introduction* property, this proof depends on the definition of a theory with new symbols.

We can thus remove quantifiers in a theory with new symbols just as in predicate logic. We must ensure, however, that the theories with which we deal do indeed have new symbols.

PROBLEMS

Problem 10.1 (polarity annotation)   page 383

Annotate all the subsentences of the following sentences according to their polarity:

(a)
$$\begin{array}{l} if\ \ not\ p(x) \\ then\ \ (\exists y)q(y) \end{array}$$

(b)
$$\begin{array}{l} not\ \big(q(x)\ \ or\ \ r(x,y)\big) \\ \quad and \\ (\forall x)q(x) \end{array}$$

(c)   if $\begin{bmatrix} if & (p(x) \ and \ p(y)) \\ then & q(y,z) \\ else & q(y,w) \end{bmatrix}$ then $(\exists u)q(y,u).$

Problem 10.2 (polarity proposition)   page 389

Complete the proof of the *polarity* proposition in the case in which the sentence $S\langle\mathcal{E}\rangle$ is of form $(\exists x)S'\langle\mathcal{E}\rangle$. Show both the *positive* and *negative* parts.

Problem 10.3 (force of quantifiers)   page 391

Annotate the following sentences with the forces of their quantifiers:

(a) $(\forall x)\big[not \ (\exists y)q(x, \ y)\big]$

(b)   *if* $(\forall x)p(x)$ *then* $(\forall y)r(y)$

(c) $(\forall x)p(x) \ \equiv \ r(y).$

* Problem 10.4 (force instantiation)   page 397

Prove the *force-instantiation* proposition.

Hint: The proof is by induction on the structure of $\mathcal{F}$. It resembles the proof of the *universal-elimination* proposition (in Section 10.6).

Problem 10.5 (universal-quantifier elimination)   page 414

(a)   Show that the sentence of our extended example,

$$\mathcal{A}: \quad \begin{array}{l} if \ (\forall y_1)^\exists(\exists z_1)^\forall p(y_1, z_1) \\ then \ (\forall z_2)^\forall(\exists y_2)^\exists p(y_2, z_2), \end{array}$$

is not equivalent to the sentence obtained by dropping its quantifiers of universal force,

$$\mathcal{C}: \quad \begin{array}{l} if \ (\forall y_1)^\exists p\big(y_1, f_1(y_1)\big) \\ then \ (\exists y_2)^\exists p(y_2, a). \end{array}$$

To do this, construct an interpretation under which one of the sentences is true and the other false.

(b)   Construct interpretations $\mathcal{I}$ and $\mathcal{I}''$ such that $\mathcal{A}$ is false under $\mathcal{I}$, $\mathcal{C}$ is false under $\mathcal{I}''$, and $\mathcal{I}$ and $\mathcal{I}''$ agree on all symbols except f_1 and a.

Problem 10.6 (skolemization)   page 418

- Remove the quantifier (... z) in each of the following sentences, preserving validity in each case. Remove other quantifiers only if necessary.

- In each case, decide whether the resulting sentence is equivalent to the given sentence. If not, give an interpretation under which they have different truth-values.

- Then remove any remaining quantifiers from each sentence, still preserving validity.

(a) $(\forall z)q(a, z)$

(b) $(\exists y)[r(y) \ \ or \ \ (\exists z)q(y, z)]$

(c) $if \ \ (\forall x)p(x)$
     $then \ \ (\forall z)p(z)$

(d) $(\forall y)(\exists z)q(y, z)$

(e) $(\exists y)[(\forall z)q(y, z) \ \ and \ \ (\forall x)r(x, y)]$

(f) $(\forall x) \begin{bmatrix} if \ \ p(x) \\ then \ \ (\forall x)(\forall z)q(x, z) \end{bmatrix}$

(g) $(\exists z)r(z) \ \equiv \ p(a).$

11

Deductive
Tableaux

We have already seen, in Chapter 6, the deductive-tableau system for propositional logic; in this chapter we extend the same system to prove the validity of sentences in predicate logic. We first apply the notion of a deductive tableau to predicate logic.

11.1   TABLEAUX: NOTATION AND MEANING

As was the case for propositional logic, our basic structure is a tableau of assertions and goals. In this system, however, each assertion and goal is a sentence in predicate logic, not in propositional logic. For example, the tableau $\mathcal{T}_1$ is a predicate-logic deductive tableau.

assertions	goals
A1. $p(a)$	
	G2. $(\forall z)q(y, z)$ *and* $p(x)$

A3. $(\exists y)q(x,\,y)$	
	G4. $q(z,\,a)$

Tableau $\mathcal{T}_1$

Note that sentences may contain quantifiers, such as $(\forall z)$ in goal G2 and $(\exists y)$ in assertion A3, and may contain free variables, such as x and y in goal G2, x in assertion A3, and z in goal G4.

MEANING OF A TABLEAU

As in propositional logic, an interpretation for a tableau is an interpretation for its constant, function, and predicate symbols. Under a given interpretation, a tableau will be either true or false according to the following semantic rule for tableaux.

Definition (semantic rule for tableaux)

A tableau with the assertions $\mathcal{A}_1, \mathcal{A}_2, \ldots, \mathcal{A}_m$ and the goals $\mathcal{G}_1, \mathcal{G}_2, \ldots, \mathcal{G}_n$ is *true under* an interpretation I if the following condition holds:

if the universal closures $(\forall *)\mathcal{A}_i$ of all the assertions $\mathcal{A}_i$
are true under I,
then the existential closure $(\exists *)\mathcal{G}_j$ of at least one of the goals $\mathcal{G}_j$
is true under I.

On the other hand, the tableau is *false under* I if the following condition holds:

the universal closures $(\forall *)\mathcal{A}_i$ of all the assertions $\mathcal{A}_i$
are true under I and
the existential closures $(\exists *)\mathcal{G}_j$ of all the goals $\mathcal{G}_j$
are false under I. ◢

Example

In the preceding tableau $\mathcal{T}_1$, the universal closures of the assertions A1 and A3 are

$$p(a) \qquad \text{and} \qquad (\forall x)(\exists y)q(x,\,y),$$

and the existential closures of the goals G2 and G4 are

$$(\exists y)(\exists x)\Big[(\forall z)q(y,\ z)\ and\ p(x)\Big]\qquad and\qquad (\exists z)q(z,\ a).$$

The tableau $\mathcal{T}_1$ is false under the interpretation $\mathcal{I}$ defined as follows:

- The domain of $\mathcal{I}$ is the nonnegative integers.

- The predicate p is assigned the "equals zero" relation, that is, $p_{\mathcal{I}}(d)$ is true precisely when $d = 0$.

- The predicate q is assigned the "less than" relation, that is, $q_{\mathcal{I}}(d, e)$ is true precisely when $d < e$.

- The constant a is assigned 0.

For then, the intuitive meanings of the universal closures of the two assertions are

$$0 = 0$$

and

> for every nonnegative integer d_x
> there exists a nonnegative integer d_y such that
> $d_x < d_y,$

respectively, which are both true for the nonnegative integers. On the other hand, the intuitive meanings of the existential closures of the two goals are

> there exist nonnegative integers d_y and d_x such that
> for every nonnegative integer d_z, $d_y < d_z$ and $d_x = 0,$

and

> there exists a nonnegative integer d_z such that
> $d_z < 0,$

which are both false for the nonnegative integers. ⌟

Remark (semantic rule)

By the semantic rule for tableaux, we may conclude that a tableau $\mathcal{T}$ is true under an interpretation $\mathcal{I}$ precisely when

> the universal closure $(\forall *)\mathcal{A}_i$ of at least one of the assertions $\mathcal{A}_i$
> is false under $\mathcal{I}$
>> or
>
> the existential closure $(\exists *)\mathcal{G}_j$ of at least one of the goals $\mathcal{G}_j$
> is true under $\mathcal{I}$.

We shall regard this as an alternative form of the semantic rule. ⌐

THE ASSOCIATED SENTENCE

As in propositional logic, the meaning of a tableau can be characterized in terms of a single predicate-logic sentence.

Definition (associated sentence)

If a tableau contains the assertions

$$\mathcal{A}_1, \ \mathcal{A}_2, \ \ldots, \ \mathcal{A}_m$$

and the goals

$$\mathcal{G}_1, \ \mathcal{G}_2, \ \ldots, \ \mathcal{G}_n,$$

its *associated sentence* is

$$if \ \Big[(\forall *)\mathcal{A}_1 \ and \ (\forall *)\mathcal{A}_2 \ and \ \ldots \ and \ (\forall *)\mathcal{A}_m\Big]$$

$$then \ \Big[(\exists *)\mathcal{G}_1 \ or \ (\exists *)\mathcal{G}_2 \ or \ \ldots \ or \ (\exists *)\mathcal{G}_n\Big]. \ ⌐$$

Example

The associated sentence of the preceding tableau $\mathcal{T}_1$ is

$$if \ \begin{bmatrix} p(a) \\ and \\ (\forall x)(\exists y)q(x,\,y) \end{bmatrix} \ then \ \begin{bmatrix} (\exists y)(\exists x)\big[(\forall z)q(y,\,z) \ and \ p(x)\big] \\ or \\ (\exists z)q(z,\,a) \end{bmatrix}. \ ⌐$$

In **Problem 11.1**, the reader is asked to show that the associated sentence of a tableau is equivalent to the sentence

$$(\exists *) \ \begin{bmatrix} if \ (\mathcal{A}_1 \ and \ \mathcal{A}_2 \ and \ \ldots \ and \ \mathcal{A}_m) \\ then \ (\mathcal{G}_1 \ or \ \mathcal{G}_2 \ or \ \ldots \ or \ \mathcal{G}_n) \end{bmatrix}.$$

The importance of the associated sentence follows from the following proposition.

Proposition (truth of a tableau)

A tableau is true under an interpretation I
     precisely when
its associated sentence is true under I. ⌟

Proof

We have

a tableau is true under an interpretation I

precisely when (by the semantic rule for tableaux)

if the universal closures $(\forall *)\mathcal{A}_i$ of all the assertions $\mathcal{A}_i$
     are true under I,
then the existential closure $(\exists *)\mathcal{G}_j$ of at least one of the goals $\mathcal{G}_j$
     is true under I

precisely when (by the semantic rules for *and* and *or*)

if $\left[(\forall *)\mathcal{A}_1 \ \ and \ \ (\forall *)\mathcal{A}_2 \ \ and \ \ \ldots \ \ and \ \ (\forall *)\mathcal{A}_m\right]$ is true under I,

then $\left[(\exists *)\mathcal{G}_1 \ \ or \ \ (\exists *)\mathcal{G}_2 \ \ or \ \ \ldots \ \ or \ \ (\exists *)\mathcal{G}_n\right]$ is true under I

precisely when (by the semantic rule for *if-then*)

the associated sentence is true under I. ⌟

VALIDITY AND EQUIVALENCE

The notions of validity and equivalence for tableaux are analogous to the same
notions for sentences.

Definition (validity of a tableau)

A tableau $\mathcal{T}$ is *valid* if, for every interpretation I,

$\mathcal{T}$ is true under I.

Equivalently, a tableau is valid precisely when its associated sentence is
valid. ⌟

Definition (equivalence of tableaux)

Two tableaux $\mathcal{T}$ and $\mathcal{T}'$ are *equivalent* if, for every interpretation $\mathcal{I}$,

> $\mathcal{T}$ is true under $\mathcal{I}$
>   precisely when
> $\mathcal{T}'$ is true under $\mathcal{I}$.

Equivalently, two tableaux are equivalent precisely when their associated sentences are equivalent. ⌟

Example

The preceding tableau $\mathcal{T}_1$ is not valid; we have already exhibited an interpretation under which it is false.

As we see later in this section, tableau $\mathcal{T}_1$ and the following tableau $\mathcal{T}_2$ are equivalent.

assertions	goals
	G1. *not* $p(a)$
	G2. $(\forall z')q(y,\ z')$ *and* $p(x)$
A3. $(\exists y)q(z,\ y)$	
	G4. $q(z,\ a)$
	G5. $q(b,\ a)$

Tableau $\mathcal{T}_2$

⌟

For predicate-logic tableaux, the notion of equivalence is sometimes too strong for our purposes. We introduce a weaker notion, that of two tableaux having the "same meaning."

Definition (same meaning of tableaux)

Two tableaux $\mathcal{T}$ and $\mathcal{T}'$ are said to have the *same meaning* if

> $\mathcal{T}$ is valid
>   precisely when
> $\mathcal{T}'$ is valid. ⌟

It is clear that if two tableaux are equivalent, they have the same meaning. It is possible, however, for two tableaux to have the same meaning even though they are not equivalent. For instance, if the two are both not valid, they automatically have the same meaning. They are not equivalent if there is some interpretation under which one is true and the other false.

SUBTABLEAUX

We may introduce notions of a subtableau and of the union of two tableaux for predicate logic just as we did for propositional logic. The corresponding properties are the same.

Definition (subtableau)

A tableau $\mathcal{T}'$ is a *subtableau* of a tableau $\mathcal{T}$, written $\mathcal{T}' \subseteq \mathcal{T}$, if every row of $\mathcal{T}'$ is also a row of $\mathcal{T}$. ⏌

Proposition (subtableau)

For any tableaux $\mathcal{T}$ and $\mathcal{T}'$,

if $\mathcal{T}' \subseteq \mathcal{T}$
then, for any interpretation $\mathcal{I}$,
    if $\mathcal{T}'$ is true under $\mathcal{I}$
    then $\mathcal{T}$ is true under $\mathcal{I}$. ⏌

Definition (union of tableaux)

The *union* $\mathcal{T}_1 \cup \mathcal{T}_2$ of two tableaux $\mathcal{T}_1$ and $\mathcal{T}_2$ is the tableau whose rows are all the rows of $\mathcal{T}_1$ and all the rows of $\mathcal{T}_2$. ⏌

Proposition (union tableau)

For any tableaux $\mathcal{T}_1$ and $\mathcal{T}_2$ and any interpretation $\mathcal{I}$,

$\mathcal{T}_1 \cup \mathcal{T}_2$ is true under $\mathcal{I}$
    precisely when
$\mathcal{T}_1$ is true under $\mathcal{I}$ or
$\mathcal{T}_2$ is true under $\mathcal{I}$. ⏌

Proposition (intermediate tableau)

For any tableaux T_1, T_2, and T_3,

> if $T_1 \subseteq T_2 \subseteq T_3$
> then, if T_1 is equivalent to T_3,
> > then T_1 is equivalent to T_2 and T_2 is equivalent to T_3. ◣

We omit the proofs, which are similar to their propositional-logic counterparts.

As a consequence of the *intermediate-tableau* property, we observe that if we can add a certain number of rows to a tableau while preserving its equivalence, we can add only a portion of those rows and still preserve its equivalence.

We extend the notion of agreement from sentences to tableaux.

Definition (agreement)

We say that two interpretations I and I' *agree* on a tableau T if

> T is true under I
>   precisely when
> T is true under I'.

In other words, T has the same truth-value under I and under I'. ◣

Note that we do not require that I and I' assign the same meanings to any particular symbols of the two tableaux.

11.2   BASIC PROPERTIES

The properties we have established for propositional-logic tableaux carry over to predicate-logic tableaux. In particular, the *implied-row* and *duality* properties of propositional-logic tableaux have their counterparts in predicate logic. In addition, we have special properties for predicate logic such as the *renaming* and *instantiation* properties. We do not include the properties as deduction rules in our deductive system, but rather use them to justify deduction rules.

IMPLIED-ROW PROPERTY

The *implied-row* property for predicate logic reflects the corresponding property of propositional-logic tableaux.

Proposition (implied row)

Assertion part

Suppose the universal closure of a sentence $\mathcal{A}$ is implied by the universal closures of all the assertions $\mathcal{A}_1, \ldots, \mathcal{A}_m$ of a tableau $\mathcal{T}$; that is,

$$(\dagger) \qquad \begin{array}{l} \textit{if } (\forall *)\mathcal{A}_1 \text{ and } \ldots \text{ and } (\forall *)\mathcal{A}_m \\ \textit{then } (\forall *)\mathcal{A} \end{array}$$

is valid. Then $\mathcal{T}$ is equivalent to the tableau $\mathcal{T}_{\mathcal{A}}$ obtained from $\mathcal{T}$ by introducing the new assertion

$\mathcal{A}$	

Goal part

Similarly, suppose the existential closure of a sentence $\mathcal{G}$ implies the existential closures of some of the goals $\mathcal{G}_1, \ldots, \mathcal{G}_n$ of the tableau $\mathcal{T}$; that is,

$$(\ddagger) \qquad \begin{array}{l} \textit{if } (\exists *)\mathcal{G} \\ \textit{then } (\exists *)\mathcal{G}_1 \text{ or } \ldots \text{ or } (\exists *)\mathcal{G}_n \end{array}$$

is valid. Then $\mathcal{T}$ is equivalent to the tableau $\mathcal{T}_{\mathcal{G}}$ obtained from $\mathcal{T}$ by introducing the new goal

	$\mathcal{G}$	

Remark (valid assertions and contradictory goals)

As in propositional logic, the *implied-row* property tells us that we may add to the tableau as an assertion any sentence whose universal closure is valid; similarly, we may add to the tableau as a goal any sentence whose existential closure is contradictory (i.e., never true). In particular, we may add (or remove) the *trivial* assertion

true	

or the trivial goal

	false	

Equivalence of the tableau is preserved in each case.

Proof (implied row)

We prove only the *assertion* part. Under a given interpretation,

the tableau $\mathcal{T}$ is false

precisely when (by the semantic rule for tableaux)

the universal closures $(\forall *)\mathcal{A}_1, \ldots, (\forall *)\mathcal{A}_m$ of the
assertions of $\mathcal{T}$ are true
  and
the existential closures $(\exists *)\mathcal{G}_1, \ldots, (\exists *)\mathcal{G}_n$ of the
goals of $\mathcal{T}$ are false

precisely when (by (†))

the universal closures $(\forall *)\mathcal{A}_1, \ldots, (\forall *)\mathcal{A}_m$, and $(\forall *)\mathcal{A}$ of the
assertions of $\mathcal{T}_{\mathcal{A}}$ are true
  and
the existential closures $(\exists *)\mathcal{G}_1, \ldots, (\exists *)\mathcal{G}_n$ of the
goals of $\mathcal{T}_{\mathcal{A}}$ are false

precisely when (by the semantic rule for tableaux, again)

the tableau $\mathcal{T}_{\mathcal{A}}$ is false.

In short, under any interpretation, $\mathcal{T}$ is false precisely when $\mathcal{T}_{\mathcal{A}}$ is false. Hence the two tableaux are equivalent.

The *goal* part is proved similarly. ⏌

DUALITY PROPERTY

Predicate-logic tableaux exhibit the same *duality* property as propositional-logic tableaux.

Proposition (duality)

A tableau containing an assertion $\mathcal{A}$
  is equivalent to
the tableau containing instead the goal (*not* $\mathcal{A}$).
                                         (*assertion-to-goal*)

A tableau containing a goal $\mathcal{G}$
  is equivalent to
the tableau containing instead the assertion (*not* $\mathcal{G}$).
                                         (*goal-to-assertion*) ⏌

Proof

We prove only the *assertion-to-goal* part. Observe that, under a given interpretation,

> the original tableau (containing $\mathcal{A}$ as an assertion) is false

precisely when (by the semantic rule for tableaux)

> $(\forall *)\mathcal{A}$ is true,
> the universal closures of all the other assertions are true,
> and the existential closures of all the goals are false

precisely when (by the semantic rules for *not* and quantifiers)

> the universal closures of all the other assertions are true,
> $(\exists *)(not\ \mathcal{A})$ is false,
> and the existential closures of all the goals are false

precisely when (by the semantic rule for tableaux)

> the new tableau (containing $(not\ \mathcal{A})$ as a goal) is false.

Thus the original tableau (containing $\mathcal{A}$ as an assertion) is false under a given interpretation $\mathcal{I}$ precisely when the new tableau (containing $(not\ \mathcal{A})$ as a goal) is false under $\mathcal{I}$; that is, the two tableaux are equivalent.

The *goal-to-assertion* part is proved similarly. ⌟

Remark (replacing versus adding rows)

Note that the *duality* property allows us to replace one row with another, preserving the equivalence of the tableau. In fact, as in propositional logic, the property also allows us to add the new row without replacing the original one. To see this, we observe that, by the semantic rule for tableaux, we may make an additional copy of the original row, preserving equivalence. We may then (by the *duality* property) replace only one of the two copies. A similar remark applies to any other property that allows us to replace rows. ⌟

RENAMING PROPERTY

The free variables of an assertion or goal of a tableau are "dummies." The *renaming* property states that we may systematically rename the free variables of any row, obtaining an equivalent tableau.

Recall that a *permutation* substitution (Section 8.5) is one that always replaces the set of (distinct) variables in its domain with the same set of variables, but in a different order. For example,

$$\pi \;=\; \{x \leftarrow y,\; y \leftarrow z,\; z \leftarrow x\}$$

is a permutation because the domain elements x, y, z are replaced by y, z, x, respectively. Also, the substitution $\{x \leftarrow y,\; y \leftarrow z\}$ is not a permutation, but $\{x \leftarrow y,\; y \leftarrow x\}$ is a permutation. A permutation substitution can never replace two distinct variables with the same variable.

Every permutation substitution π has *inverse* π^{-1}; for example, for the preceding permutation π, we have the inverse

$$\pi^{-1} \;=\; \{y \leftarrow x,\; z \leftarrow y,\; x \leftarrow z\}.$$

In fact, π is a permutation substitution precisely when there is a permutation substitution π^{-1} such that

$$\pi \,\square\, \pi^{-1} \;=\; \{\;\}.$$

Proposition (renaming)

For any permutation substitution π,

> a tableau containing an assertion $\mathcal{A}$ [or goal $\mathcal{G}$]
>   is equivalent to
> the tableau containing instead the assertion $\mathcal{A}\pi$ [or goal $\mathcal{G}\pi$]. ⌟

Here $\mathcal{A}\pi$ and $\mathcal{G}\pi$ stand for the result of total safe substitution; in other words, we may have to change variables in $\mathcal{A}$ and $\mathcal{G}$ to avoid capturing during the substitution process.

Example

Suppose a tableau contains the goal

assertions	goals
	$\mathcal{G}:\quad p(x,\,z)\;\; and \;\;(\forall z)q(x,\,y,\,z)$

and suppose we would like to interchange the free variables y and z in $\mathcal{G}$. We thus take π to be

$$\{y \leftarrow z,\; z \leftarrow y\}.$$

The given tableau is equivalent to the altered tableau that contains the goal

	$\mathcal{G}\pi:\quad p(x,\,y)\ \ and\ \ (\forall z')q(x,\,z,\,z')$

instead of $\mathcal{G}$. Here the variable z of the quantifier $(\forall z)$ has been changed to z' to avoid capturing the occurrence of z introduced by the renaming when y was replaced by z. ◢

Remark (why permutations?)

A renaming of x to x' can be achieved by applying a permutation

$$\{x \leftarrow x',\ x' \leftarrow x\}.$$

If x' does not actually occur in the renamed row, the replacement pair $x' \leftarrow x$ will not have any effect on the row.

By requiring that the substitution π in the *renaming* property be a permutation, we have eliminated the possibility that two distinct variables are replaced by the same variable. ◢

Now let us justify the property.

Proof (renaming)

Let π be any permutation substitution. The proof depends on showing that the sentences associated with the two tableaux are equivalent; hence the two tableaux are equivalent. We consider only the assertion case.

The sentence associated with the altered tableau is obtained from the sentence associated with the original tableau by replacing the subsentence

$$(\forall *)\mathcal{A},$$

the universal closure of $\mathcal{A}$, with the sentence

$$(\forall *)(\mathcal{A}\pi),$$

the universal closure of $\mathcal{A}\pi$. We show that these two corresponding subsentences are equivalent.

Let $\mathcal{A}'$ be the sentence obtained from $\mathcal{A}$ by changing the variables of the quantifiers of $\mathcal{A}$, as required, to avoid capturing free variables introduced by the renaming substitution π; then (by predicate logic),

$$(\forall *)\mathcal{A} \quad \text{is equivalent to} \quad (\forall *)\mathcal{A}'$$

and (because changing variables is part of the safe application of π to A)

$$A\pi \quad \text{is identical to} \quad A'\pi.$$

It remains to show that

$$(\forall *)A' \quad \text{is equivalent to} \quad (\forall *)(A'\pi).$$

Let π^{-1} be the inverse permutation. Then

$$(A'\pi)\pi^{-1} \quad \equiv \quad A'(\pi \,\square\, \pi^{-1}) \quad \equiv \quad A'(\{\ \}) \quad \equiv \quad A'.$$

Thus $(A'\pi)\pi^{-1}$ is A' itself.

By the *universal closure-instantiation* proposition (Section [I]3.5),

$$(\forall *)A' \quad \text{implies} \quad (\forall *)(A'\pi).$$

By the same proposition,

$$(\forall *)(A'\pi) \quad \text{implies} \quad (\forall *)\big((A'\pi)\pi^{-1}\big), \quad \text{that is,} \quad (\forall *)A'.$$

Hence

$$(\forall *)A' \quad \text{is equivalent to} \quad (\forall *)(A'\pi),$$

as we wanted to show.

The proof of the goal case is similar. ⌟

INSTANTIATION PROPERTY

The *instantiation* property states that we may add to the tableau any instance of any of its rows, obtaining an equivalent tableau. That is, we may replace all free occurrences of a variable in any row with an arbitrary term and add the new row to the tableau.

Proposition (instantiation)

For a substitution

$$\theta \;=\; \{x_1 \leftarrow t_1,\ x_2 \leftarrow t_2,\ \ldots,\ x_k \leftarrow t_k\}$$

that replaces distinct variables with terms,

　　　a tableau containing an assertion A [or goal G]
　　　　　is equivalent to
　　　the tableau containing in addition the assertion $A\theta$ [or goal $G\theta$]. ⌟

Recall that $\mathcal{A}\theta$ and $\mathcal{G}\theta$ stand for the result of total safe substitution. In other words, all occurrences of x_i are replaced by t_i in $\mathcal{A}$ [or in $\mathcal{G}$], and we may have to rename variables in $\mathcal{A}$ [or in $\mathcal{G}$] to avoid capturing during the substitution process.

Note that this property, in contrast to the *duality* and *renaming* properties, allows us to add a new row but not to replace an old one.

First let us illustrate the property with some examples; afterwards we justify the property.

Example

If a tableau contains an assertion

assertions	goals
$\mathcal{A}:\quad \Big(p(x)\ \ and\ \ q(x,\,y,\,a)\Big)\ \ or\ \ r(u)$	

and θ is the substitution

$$\{x \leftarrow f(z),\ y \leftarrow b\},$$

then we may add the new assertion

$\mathcal{A}\theta:\quad \Big(p(f(z))\ \ and\ \ q(f(z),\,b,\,a)\Big)\ \ or\ \ r(u)$	

to the tableau; the new tableau is equivalent to the given tableau. Note that the substitution θ was applied to all occurrences of x and y in the assertion $\mathcal{A}$. ⌟

Example

If a tableau contains a goal

assertions	goals
	$\mathcal{G}:\quad (\exists z)\big[q(x,\,z)\ \ and\ \ r(z,\,y)\big]$

and θ is the substitution

$$\{x \leftarrow f(x,\,y,\,z)\},$$

then we may add the new goal

	$\mathcal{G}\theta:\quad (\exists z')[q(f(x,\,y,\,z),\,z')\ \ and\ \ r(z',\,y)]$

to the tableau; the new tableau is equivalent to the given tableau. Note that we have renamed the variable z of the quantifier $(\exists z)$ as z' to avoid capturing the variable z in the substitution. ⌟

Now let us justify the property.

Proof (instantiation)

We first justify the assertion case. The *universal closure-instantiation* proposition (Section [I]3.5) states that for any distinct variables $x_1, x_2, \ldots, x_k$, sentence $\mathcal{A}[x_1, x_2, \ldots, x_k]$, and terms $t_1, t_2, \ldots, t_k$, the sentence

$$if\ \ (\forall *)\mathcal{A}[x_1,\,x_2,\,\ldots,\,x_k]$$
$$then\ \ (\forall *)\mathcal{A}[t_1,\,t_2,\,\ldots,\,t_k]$$

is valid. That is, for the substitution

$$\theta\ =\ \{x_1 \leftarrow t_1,\,x_2 \leftarrow t_2,\,\ldots,\,x_k \leftarrow t_k\},$$

the sentence

$$if\ \ (\forall *)\mathcal{A}$$
$$then\ \ (\forall *)(\mathcal{A}\theta)$$

is valid. Therefore (by the *implied-row* property), the assertion $\mathcal{A}\theta$ may be added to the tableau, preserving equivalence.

The goal case may be proved in a similar way. We use the *existential closure-instantiation* proposition to show that

$$if\ \ (\exists *)(\mathcal{G}\theta)$$
$$then\ \ (\exists *)\mathcal{G}$$

is a valid sentence. We then use the *implied-row* property to justify introducing the new goal $\mathcal{G}\theta$.

Alternatively, we may use the assertion case and the *duality* property to justify the goal case. ⌟

Remark (adding versus replacing rows)

We have remarked that the *instantiation* property does not allow us to replace any row, but only to add a new one. In fact, if we were to delete the assertion $\mathcal{A}$ [or goal $\mathcal{G}$], we might not preserve equivalence.

For example, suppose a tableau $\mathcal{T}_1$ consists of the single goal

assertions	goals
	$p(x)$

The sentence associated with this tableau is

$$S_1 : \quad (\exists x)p(x).$$

Now suppose we applied the *instantiation* property incorrectly and deleted the goal $p(x)$, introducing in its place the instance $p(a)$. The tableau $\mathcal{T}_2$ we obtain consists of the single goal

assertions	goals
	$p(a)$

The sentence associated with this tableau is

$$S_2 : \quad p(a).$$

Because the sentences associated with these tableaux are not equivalent, the two tableaux are not equivalent either. ⌐

JUSTIFICATION CONDITION

In the following sections, we introduce deduction rules for predicate-logic tableaux analogous to the propositional-logic deduction rules. In propositional logic, we required that our rules preserve the equivalence of the tableau. In predicate logic, on the other hand, we say that a rule is *sound* if it merely preserves the validity of the tableau to which it is applied. Of course, if a rule preserves equivalence it also preserves validity, but in predicate logic we shall require a rule to preserve validity but not necessarily equivalence.

In this section, we develop the justification condition for determining whether a predicate-logic deduction rule is sound.

Recall that the *required rows* (assertions and goals) are those rows that must be present in the *old tableau* for a deduction rule to be applied, and the *generated rows* (assertions and goals) are those that are added to the tableau by the rule, to form the *new tableau*. In applying a deduction rule, we always add rows, never delete them.

In the tableau notation, we write a rule in the form

	assertions	goals
$\mathcal{T}_r$:		
$\mathcal{T}_g$:		

where the required rows are those that appear above the double line, and the generated rows are those that appear below the double line. The required rows form the *required subtableau*, denoted by $\mathcal{T}_r$, and the generated rows form the *generated subtableau*, denoted by $\mathcal{T}_g$.

The deduction rule is applied only if the required subtableau $\mathcal{T}_r$ occurs as part of the old tableau $\mathcal{T}_0$, that is, $\mathcal{T}_r \subseteq \mathcal{T}_o$. The new tableau $\mathcal{T}_n$ is obtained by adding the generated subtableau to the old tableau, that is, $\mathcal{T}_n = \mathcal{T}_o \cup \mathcal{T}_g$.

The following *justification* proposition will be used to establish the *soundness* of a deduction rule. In other words, it allows us to prove that, by applying a deduction rule, validity is preserved, i.e., the new tableau is valid precisely when the old tableau is valid.

Proposition (general justification)

A deduction rule is sound (i.e., preserves validity) if the following (*general*) *justification condition* holds:

For every interpretation $\mathcal{I}$ and tableau $\mathcal{T}_o$,

> if the required subtableau $\mathcal{T}_r$ is false under $\mathcal{I}$,
> then the generated subtableau $\mathcal{T}_g$ is false under some interpretation $\mathcal{I}'$,
> where $\mathcal{I}$ and $\mathcal{I}'$ agree on the tableau $\mathcal{T}_o$. ⌟

In other words, if the *justification* condition holds, the rule preserves the validity of the tableau to which it is applied.

Proof

We want to show that the new tableau T_n formed by adding the generated rows is valid precisely when the old tableau T_o is valid. We actually show that T_n is false under some interpretation precisely when T_o is false under some (perhaps different) interpretation. We prove each direction separately.

One direction is true whether or not the *justification* condition is satisfied. We suppose that $T_n = T_o \cup T_g$ is false under some interpretation I and show that then T_o is false under the same interpretation I. Since T_o is a subtableau of T_n, that follows from the *subtableau* property.

The other direction makes use of the *justification* condition. We suppose that T_o is false under some interpretation I and show that then T_n is false under some interpretation I'. Since T_o is false, its required subtableau T_r is false under I (by the *subtableau* property). Therefore, by the *justification* condition, there exists some interpretation I' such that the generated subtableau T_g is false under I', where I and I' agree on T_o.

Because, by our supposition, T_o is false under I, it follows that T_o is false under I'.

Therefore (by the *union* property of tableaux), the new tableau T_n, that is, $T_o \cup T_g$, is false under I'. ◢

In order to justify a deduction rule, it suffices to take I' to be I itself and show the following special case.

Corollary (special justification)

A deduction rule preserves the equivalence of any tableau to which it is applied if the following *special justification condition* holds:

For every interpretation I,

> if the required subtableau T_r is false under I,
> then the generated subtableau T_g is false under I. ◢

Note that the *general justification* condition guarantees only the weak property of preserving validity, i.e., the new tableau is valid precisely when the old tableau is valid. On the other hand, the *special justification* condition guarantees the stronger property of preserving equivalence, i.e., the new tableau is equivalent to the old tableau.

In predicate logic, all the deduction rules, with one exception (the ∀-*elimi-nation* rule) have the property of preserving equivalence. This will be shown in the following sections, using the preceding *special justification* condition. The ∀-*elimination* rule does not necessarily preserve equivalence, but it has the weaker property of preserving validity. To justify this rule, we will use the *general justi-fication* condition.

11.3   THE DEDUCTIVE PROCESS

We now give an overview of the deductive-tableau system for predicate logic.

OUTLINE OF THE DEDUCTIVE SYSTEM

The deductive system for predicate logic is modeled on the propositional-logic system. As before, to *prove* the validity of a given (closed) sentence S,

- We form the *initial tableau* whose sole goal is the (simplified) sentence S. We may include as assertions any sentences that have previously been proven valid.

- The tableau is developed by applying *deduction rules* succes-sively; each rule adds one or more rows to the tableau, in such a way that validity is preserved.

- The process continues until the final assertion *false* or the final goal *true* appears in the tableau.

Because the final tableau is valid and the deduction rules preserve validity, we have thus established the validity of the initial tableau and, therefore, of the given sentence S. We shall say that the final tableau is a *proof* of the sentence S. Any sentence that has a proof will be called a *theorem* of predicate logic.

We may add S as an assertion in all initial tableaux of subsequent predicate-logic proofs.

THE DEDUCTION RULES

The deduction rules for predicate logic we will apply are divided into five groups:

- The *rewriting* rule, which replaces a subsentence with an equiv-alent sentence.

- The *splitting* rules, which break a row down into its logical components.

- The *resolution* rule, which performs a case analysis on the truth of a subsentence.

- The *equivalence* rule, which facilitates our handling of the equivalence connective $\equiv$.

- The *quantifier-elimination (skolemization)* rules, which remove quantifiers from the assertions or goals. There are two such rules, $\forall$-*elimination* and $\exists$-*elimination*, for removing quantifiers of universal force and existential force, respectively.

The *splitting* rules are identical to the propositional-logic *splitting* rules. The *rewriting, resolution,* and *equivalence* rules are adapted from their propositional counterparts. The *skolemization* rules are entirely new.

Note that, unlike our propositional-logic deductive system, in predicate logic the new generated tableau is not necessarily equivalent to the old tableau. As we have remarked, the *rewriting, splitting, resolution, equivalence,* and $\exists$-*elimination* rules do preserve equivalence. The $\forall$-*elimination* rule, however, does not preserve equivalence in general, but does preserve validity. Thus the deduction rules all preserve validity, which suffices to establish the correctness of our deductive process.

As in propositional logic, recall that duality is a property and not a rule. Therefore we may use duality to justify a rule but may not apply it as a rule. Similarly, the *implied row, renaming,* and *instantiation* properties are not rules. We could have introduced these properties as rules without compromising the soundness of the system. For any proof that uses one of these properties as a rule, however, there is a shorter proof that does not.

SIMPLIFICATION

Any assertion or goal introduced into a tableau is subject to an automatic simplification process, in which certain subsentences are replaced by equivalent but simpler subsentences. As in propositional logic, simplification is not regarded as a separate rule. Whenever we add a new row to a tableau, it is simplified as much as possible.

Examples of simplifications we had in propositional logic are the *not-not* simplification

$$not\ (not\ \mathcal{F}) \quad \Rightarrow \quad \mathcal{F}$$

and the *and-false* simplification

$$\mathcal{F} \ \ and \ \ false \ \ \Rightarrow \ \ false.$$

We shall carry all the simplifications of propositional logic over into predicate logic. Also, we add the following simplifications for quantifiers and conditional terms:

- Redundant quantifier

$$(\forall x)\mathcal{F} \ \ \Rightarrow \ \ \mathcal{F} \qquad \text{if } x \text{ is not free in } \mathcal{F} \hspace{3em} (all)$$

$$(\exists x)\mathcal{F} \ \ \Rightarrow \ \ \mathcal{F} \qquad \text{if } x \text{ is not free in } \mathcal{F} \hspace{3em} (some)$$

- Conditional term

$$if \ \ true \ \ then \ \ s \ \ else \ \ t \ \ \Rightarrow \ \ s \hspace{3em} (\textit{cond-term true})$$

$$if \ \ false \ \ then \ \ s \ \ else \ \ t \ \ \Rightarrow \ \ t \hspace{3em} (\textit{cond-term false})$$

$$if \ \ \mathcal{F} \ \ then \ \ s \ \ else \ \ s \ \ \Rightarrow \ \ s \hspace{3em} (\textit{cond-term two})$$

Note that, in the redundant-quantifier simplifications, x is intended to stand for any variable. Thus we can simplify $(\exists y)p(a)$ to $p(a)$. Also, in the conditional-term simplifications, both sides of each simplification are terms. In applying these simplifications, we are replacing a subterm with an equal term, not a subsentence with an equivalent sentence.

Example

Suppose we are about to introduce into a tableau an assertion

$$\boxed{(\forall z)\, q(a,\, y)} \ \ and \ \ q(a, y).$$

We must first apply the *all* redundant-quantifier simplification to obtain the new sentence

$$\boxed{q(a,\, y) \ \ and \ \ q(a,\, y)}$$

We must then apply the *and-two* propositional simplification to obtain the new sentence

$$q(a,\, y),$$

which is added to the tableau as the assertion

$q(a, y)$	

Note that, according to the redundant-quantifier simplifications, we can perform such operations as replacing $(\forall x)true$ with *true* and $(\exists x)false$ with *false*. Also, any sentence of form $(\forall x)(\forall x)\mathcal{F}$ or $(\exists x)(\forall x)\mathcal{F}$ can be replaced by $(\forall x)\mathcal{F}$.

We now describe each of the deduction rules in turn.

11.4 REWRITING RULE

As in propositional logic, we introduce a *rewriting* rule that allows us to replace certain subexpressions of a tableau with equivalent or equal expressions. Each application of the rule replaces only a single subexpression occurrence. In contrast to simplification, rewriting does not always give us a simpler and easier to prove sentence. It is not applied automatically, but is considered to be a deduction rule, and is used only at our discretion. Also, we add the rewritten row to the tableau without deleting the original row.

Justification of the *rewriting* rule is straightforward because the new row is always equivalent to one of the existing rows. All the propositional-logic rewritings are permitted in predicate-logic tableaux. In addition, we include the following rewritings, which apply only to predicate-logic tableaux:

- Quantifier reversal

$$(\forall x)(\forall y)\mathcal{F} \quad \Leftrightarrow \quad (\forall y)(\forall x)\mathcal{F} \qquad\qquad (all)$$

$$(\exists x)(\exists y)\mathcal{F} \quad \Leftrightarrow \quad (\exists y)(\exists x)\mathcal{F} \qquad\qquad (some)$$

- Quantifier duality

$$not\ (\forall x)\mathcal{F} \quad \Leftrightarrow \quad (\exists x)(not\ \mathcal{F}) \qquad\qquad (not\ all)$$

$$not\ (\exists x)\mathcal{F} \quad \Leftrightarrow \quad (\forall x)(not\ \mathcal{F}) \qquad\qquad (not\ some)$$

- Quantifier manipulation

$$(\forall x)\big[\mathcal{F}\ \ and\ \ \mathcal{G}\big] \quad \Leftrightarrow \quad (\forall x)\mathcal{F}\ \ and\ \ (\forall x)\mathcal{G} \qquad\qquad (all\ and)$$

$$(\exists x)\big[\mathcal{F}\ \ or\ \ \mathcal{G}\big] \quad \Leftrightarrow \quad (\exists x)\mathcal{F}\ \ or\ \ (\exists x)\mathcal{G} \qquad\qquad (some\ or)$$

$$(\exists x)\big[if\ \ \mathcal{F}\ \ then\ \ \mathcal{G}\big] \quad \Leftrightarrow \quad if\ \ (\forall x)\mathcal{F}\ \ then\ \ (\exists x)\mathcal{G} \qquad\qquad (some\ if)$$

- Conditional manipulation

$$p(\overline{x},\ if\ \mathcal{F}\ then\ s\ else\ t,\ \overline{y}) \quad \Leftrightarrow \quad if\ \mathcal{F}\ then\ p(\overline{x},\ s,\ \overline{y})\ else\ p(\overline{x},\ t,\ \overline{y})$$

$$(predicate)$$

$$f(\overline{x}, \ if \ \mathcal{F} \ then \ s \ else \ t, \ \overline{y}) \quad \Leftrightarrow \quad if \ \mathcal{F} \ then \ f(\overline{x}, \ s, \ \overline{y}) \ else \ f(\overline{x}, \ t, \ \overline{y})$$

$$(function)$$

In the conditional-manipulation rewritings, p is a predicate symbol and f is a function symbol, and $\overline{x}$ and $\overline{y}$ stand for $x_1, \ldots, x_m$ and $y_1, \ldots, y_n$, respectively. Note that both sides of the *function* rewriting are terms. In applying this rewriting, we are replacing a subterm with an equal term. Also note that in the *predicate* rewriting, the left-hand *if-then-else* is the conditional (term) operator, while the right-hand *if-then-else* is the conditional (sentence) connective.

11.5   SPLITTING RULES

Although the predicate-logic and propositional-logic *splitting* rules are identical, the predicate-logic rules require special justification because of the possible occurrence of free variables in the assertions and goals to which they are applied.

AND-SPLIT RULE

assertions	goals
$\mathcal{A}_1 \ and \ \mathcal{A}_2$	
$\mathcal{A}_1$	
$\mathcal{A}_2$	

OR-SPLIT RULE

assertions	goals
	$\mathcal{G}_1 \ or \ \mathcal{G}_2$
	$\mathcal{G}_1$
	$\mathcal{G}_2$

IF-SPLIT RULE

assertions	goals
	if $\mathcal{A}$ *then* $\mathcal{G}$
$\mathcal{A}$	
	$\mathcal{G}$

Let us justify that the *if-split* rule indeed preserves equivalence, that is, that the new tableau is equivalent to the old tableau. The justification of the other *splitting* rules are similar.

Justification (*if-split*)

By the *special justification* corollary, the special case of the *general justification* proposition, it suffices to show that, for any interpretation $\mathcal{I}$ under which the required tableau is false, that is, its associated sentence

$$(\exists *)[\textit{if } \mathcal{A} \textit{ then } \mathcal{G}]$$

is false, the generated tableau is false, that is, its associated sentence

$$\textit{if } (\forall *)\mathcal{A} \textit{ then } (\exists *)\mathcal{G}$$

is false, under $\mathcal{I}$.

The proof depends on manipulating quantifiers according to the predicate-logic equivalence, that any sentence of form

$$(\exists x)[\textit{if } \mathcal{F}_1 \textit{ then } \mathcal{F}_2]$$

is equivalent to the corresponding sentence of form

$$\textit{if } (\forall x)\mathcal{F}_1 \textit{ then } (\exists x)\mathcal{F}_2.$$

Because some variables may occur free in $\mathcal{A}$ but not in $\mathcal{G}$, or vice versa, we must then eliminate any redundant quantifiers to conclude that the two associated sentences are equivalent. ⌙

11.6   RESOLUTION RULE

For propositional logic, the *resolution* rule allows us to derive from two assertions

$$\mathcal{A}_1[P] \quad \text{and} \quad \mathcal{A}_2[P],$$

with identical subsentences, a new assertion

$$\mathcal{A}_1[true] \quad or \quad \mathcal{A}_2[false].$$

Intuitively, a case analysis is performed on the truth of the common subsentence P of the two assertions. The extension of this rule to predicate logic allows us to draw a similar conclusion from two assertions with subsentences that are not necessarily identical but that are unifiable.

THE BASIC FORM

We first illustrate the rule.

Example

Suppose our tableau contains the two assertions

assertions	goals
$\mathcal{A}_1$: $\boxed{p(a,\ y)}^{\ -}$ or $r(y)$	
$\mathcal{A}_2$: if $\boxed{p(x,\ b)}^{\ +}$ $then$ $q(x)$	

The propositional-logic *resolution* rule could not be applied directly to these two assertions because they have no identical subsentences in common. If, however, we apply the substitution

$$\theta : \ \{x \leftarrow a, \ y \leftarrow b\}$$

to the tableau, we obtain the two intermediate assertions

$$\mathcal{A}_1\theta : \quad \boxed{p(a,\ b)}^{\ -} \quad or \quad r(b)$$

and

$$\mathcal{A}_2\theta : \quad if \quad \boxed{p(a,\ b)}^{\ +} \quad then \quad q(a).$$

These assertions can be added to the tableau, by the *instantiation* property, without altering its validity. They have the common subsentence $p(a, b)$; therefore, now we can apply the propositional version of the *resolution* rule directly, obtaining the intermediate sentence

$$false \quad or \quad r(b)$$
$$or$$
$$if \quad true \quad then \quad q(a),$$

which reduces (under *true-false* simplification) to the new assertion

$r(b)$ or $q(a)$	

The predicate-logic *resolution* rule allows us to apply the substitution θ and the propositional version of the rule in a single step, without adding the intermediate assertions. The rule also allows us to replace several distinct subsentences $P_1, \ldots, P_k$, $k \geq 1$, of the given rows A_1 and A_2, if these subsentences become identical on application of θ.

The basic form of the *resolution* rule is expressed as follows.

Rule (AA-resolution)

assertions	goals
$A_1[\overline{P}]$	
$A_2[\overline{P'}]$	
$A_1\theta[\overline{false}]$ *or* $A_2\theta[\overline{true}]$	

where

- $\overline{P}$ stands for the free, quantifier-free subsentences $P_1, \ldots, P_k$ $(k \geq 1)$ that occur in A_1.

- $\overline{P'}$ stands for the free, quantifier-free subsentences $P'_1, \ldots, P'_\ell$ $(\ell \geq 1)$ that occur in A_2.

- θ is a most-general unifier for all the subsentences in $\overline{P}$ and $\overline{P'}$; that is, $\overline{P}\theta$ and $\overline{P'}\theta$ are all identical sentences.

- $\overline{false}$ stands for *false*, $\ldots$, *false* (k times).

- $\overline{true}$ stands for *true*, $\ldots$, *true* (ℓ times).

More precisely, to apply the *AA-resolution* rule to two assertions A_1 and A_2 of a tableau:

- Rename the variables of $\mathcal{A}_1$ and $\mathcal{A}_2$ if necessary to ensure that they have no free variables in common.

- Choose some free, quantifier-free subsentences $\overline{P} = P_1, \ldots, P_k$ ($k \geq 1$), of $\mathcal{A}_1$ and free, quantifier-free subsentences $\overline{P'} = P'_1 \ldots, P'_\ell$ ($\ell \geq 1$), of $\mathcal{A}_2$, such that they are all unifiable by a most-general unifier θ; that is,

$$P_1\theta, \ \ldots, \ P_k\theta \quad \text{and} \quad P'_1\theta, \ \ldots, \ P'_\ell\theta$$

are all the same sentence, which we shall call $P\theta$.

- Apply θ to the two assertions $\mathcal{A}_1$ and $\mathcal{A}_2$, replacing all free occurrences of $P\theta$ in $\mathcal{A}_1\theta$ with the truth symbol *false* and all free occurrences of $P\theta$ in $\mathcal{A}_2\theta$ with the truth symbol *true*, obtaining the disjuncts $\mathcal{A}_1\theta[\overline{false}]$ and $\mathcal{A}_2\theta[\overline{true}]$, respectively.

- Simplify the disjunction

$$\mathcal{A}_1\theta[\overline{false}] \quad or \quad \mathcal{A}_2\theta[\overline{true}].$$

- Add the simplified disjunction to the tableau as a new assertion.

We will say that the new assertion is a *resolvent*, obtained by *applying the resolution rule to* the assertions $\mathcal{A}_1[\overline{P}]$ and $\mathcal{A}_2[\overline{P'}]$, *matching* $\overline{P}$ *and* $\overline{P'}$, *with* θ.

Although the total substitution notation does not require that the subsentences $\overline{P}$ occur in $\mathcal{A}_1[\overline{P}]$ or that the subsentences $\overline{P'}$ occur in $\mathcal{A}_2[\overline{P'}]$, we intend here that each subsentence occur at least once.

DUAL FORMS

The dual forms of the rule are as follows.

Rule (GG-resolution)

assertions	goals
	$\mathcal{G}_1[\overline{P}]$
	$\mathcal{G}_2[\overline{P'}]$
	$\mathcal{G}_1\theta[\overline{false}]$ *and* $\mathcal{G}_2\theta[\overline{true}]$

where $\mathcal{G}_1$ and $\mathcal{G}_2$ satisfy the same conditions as $\mathcal{A}_1$ and $\mathcal{A}_2$, respectively, in the *AA-resolution* rule. ⌐

Rule (AG-resolution)

assertions	goals
$\mathcal{A}[\,\overline{\mathcal{P}}\,]$	
	$\mathcal{G}[\,\overline{\mathcal{P}'}\,]$
	$not\ (\mathcal{A}\theta[\,\overline{false}\,])$ *and* $\mathcal{G}\theta[\,\overline{true}\,]$

where $\mathcal{A}$ and $\mathcal{G}$ satisfy the same conditions as $\mathcal{A}_1$ and $\mathcal{A}_2$, respectively, in the *AA-resolution* rule. ⌐

Rule (GA-resolution)

assertions	goals
	$\mathcal{G}[\,\overline{\mathcal{P}}\,]$
$\mathcal{A}[\,\overline{\mathcal{P}'}\,]$	
	$\mathcal{G}\theta[\,\overline{false}\,]$ *and* $not\ (\mathcal{A}\theta[\,\overline{true}\,])$

where $\mathcal{G}$ and $\mathcal{A}$ satisfy the same conditions as $\mathcal{A}_1$ and $\mathcal{A}_2$, respectively, in the *AA-resolution* rule. ⌐

POLARITY STRATEGY

The *polarity* strategy we introduced for the propositional-logic *resolution* rule can be applied also to the predicate-logic rule.

Strategy (polarity)

Suppose that $\mathcal{F}_1[\overline{P}]$ and $\mathcal{F}_2[\overline{P'}]$ are two assertions or goals in a tableau with free, quantifier-free subsentences, respectively,

$$\overline{P} = P_1, \ldots, P_k \quad \text{and} \quad \overline{P'} = P'_1, \ldots, P'_\ell.$$

Assume that the *resolution* rule has been applied to $\mathcal{F}_1[\overline{P}]$ and $\mathcal{F}_2[\overline{P'}]$, replacing every occurrence of $P\theta$ in $\mathcal{F}_1\theta$ with *false* and replacing every occurrence of $P\theta$ in $\mathcal{F}_2\theta$ with *true*.

Then we will say that the rule has been applied in accordance with the *polarity strategy* if

> at least one of the subsentences $P_1, \ldots, P_k$ of $\mathcal{F}_1$ (whose instances are replaced by *false* in applying the rule) is of negative polarity in the tableau

and

> at least one of the subsentences $P'_1, \ldots, P'_\ell$ of $\mathcal{F}_2$ (whose instances are replaced by *true* in applying the rule) is of positive polarity in the tableau.

These polarities need not be strict. ⌟

EXAMPLES

Before we justify the *resolution* rule, let us illustrate it with some more examples. We start with a simple example applying *AA-resolution* to two assertions $\mathcal{A}_1[\overline{P}]$ and $\mathcal{A}_2[\overline{P'}]$, where $\overline{P}$ and $\overline{P'}$ each are a single subsentence.

Example

Suppose that our tableau contains the two assertions

assertions	goals
$\mathcal{A}_1[P]:$ *if* $q(x, z)$ *then* $\boxed{p(a) \ \ and \ \ q(y, x)}$ $^-$	
$\mathcal{A}_2[P']:$ $\Big(not \ \boxed{p(x) \ \ and \ \ q(x, f(x))} ^+\Big) \ \ or \ \ r(x)$	

Here we annotate with boxes and polarities the subsentences P and P' to be matched when the *resolution* rule is applied.

These assertions have the free variable x in common. We can escape this coincidence, however, by renaming the variable x as $\widehat{x}$ in the first assertion $\mathcal{A}[\mathcal{P}]$, obtaining

$$\widehat{\mathcal{A}_1}[\widehat{\mathcal{P}}]: \quad \textit{if } q(\widehat{x}, z) \textit{ then } \boxed{p(a) \textit{ and } q(y, \widehat{x})}^{\;-}$$

Consider the boxed subsentences

$$\widehat{\mathcal{P}}: \quad p(a) \textit{ and } q(y, \widehat{x})$$

of $\widehat{\mathcal{A}_1}$ and

$$\mathcal{P}': \quad p(x) \textit{ and } q\big(x, f(x)\big)$$

of $\mathcal{A}_2$; these quantifier-free subsentences are free in $\widehat{\mathcal{A}_1}$ and $\mathcal{A}_2$, respectively. Also, they are unifiable, with most-general unifier

$$\theta: \quad \{x \leftarrow a, \; y \leftarrow a, \; \widehat{x} \leftarrow f(a)\}.$$

(Note that, had we not renamed the free variable x as $\widehat{x}$ in $\mathcal{A}_1$, the two subsentences would not have been unifiable.) The resulting common instance is

$$\mathcal{P}\theta: \quad p(a) \textit{ and } q\big(a, f(a)\big).$$

To apply the *AA-resolution* rule, we first obtain the intermediate sentences

$$\widehat{\mathcal{A}_1}\theta: \quad \textit{if } q\big(f(a), z\big) \textit{ then } \boxed{p(a) \textit{ and } q(a, f(a))}^{\;-}$$

$$\mathcal{A}_2\theta: \quad \Big(\textit{not } \boxed{p(a) \textit{ and } q(a, f(a))}^{\;+}\Big) \textit{ or } r(a).$$

We then apply the propositional version of the rule, matching

$$p(a) \textit{ and } q(a, f(a)),$$

to obtain the new assertion

$$\textit{if } q(f(a), z) \textit{ then false}$$
$$\textit{or}$$
$$(\textit{not true}) \textit{ or } r(a),$$

which reduces (by *true-false* simplification) to

$\textit{not } q\big(f(a), z\big)$	
$\textit{or}$	
$r(a)$	

Note that we do not add the renamed assertion $\widehat{\mathcal{A}_1}$, the intermediate assertions $\widehat{\mathcal{A}_1}\theta$ and $\mathcal{A}_2\theta$, and the unsimplified resolvent to the tableau; we regard the (simplified) resolvent

$$not\ q\big(f(a), z\big)$$
$$or$$
$$r(a)$$

as having been obtained directly by an application of the predicate-logic *resolution* rule to the assertions $\mathcal{A}_1$ and $\mathcal{A}_2$.

Note also that the preceding application of the *resolution* rule has been in accordance with the *polarity* strategy. ⌟

In the following example, we apply *GG-resolution* to two goals $\mathcal{G}_1$ and $\mathcal{G}_2$, emphasizing the possible need to rename variables to avoid capturing in applying the substitution θ to $\mathcal{G}_1$ and $\mathcal{G}_2$.

Example

Suppose our tableau contains the two goals

assertions	goals
	$\mathcal{G}_1:\quad not\ \boxed{p(y)}\ ^-$
	$\mathcal{G}_2:\quad \boxed{p(x)}\ ^+\ and\ (\forall y)q(x,\, y)$

These goals have no free variables in common. The boxed quantifier-free subsentences

$$\mathcal{P}:\ p(y) \qquad and \qquad \mathcal{P}':\ p(x)$$

are free in $\mathcal{G}_1$ and $\mathcal{G}_2$, respectively. They are unifiable with most-general unifier

$$\theta:\ \{x \leftarrow y\}.$$

To apply the *GG-resolution* rule to $\mathcal{G}_1$ and $\mathcal{G}_2$, we first obtain the intermediate sentences

$$\mathcal{G}_1\theta:\quad not\ \boxed{p(y)}\ ^-$$

$$\mathcal{G}_2\theta:\quad \boxed{p(y)}\ ^+\ and\ (\forall y')q(y,\, y').$$

(Note that, in applying safe substitution θ to $\mathcal{G}_2$, we have renamed the variable of the quantifier $(\forall y)$ as y', to avoid capturing.) Then we form the goal

> *not false*
> *and*
> *true and* $(\forall y')q(y,\, y')$,

which reduces (by *true-false* simplification) to the resolvent

	$(\forall y')q(y,\, y')$

Note that this application of the *resolution* rule is in accordance with the *polarity* strategy. ⌐

In the following example, we apply *AG-resolution* to an assertion $\mathcal{A}[\,\overline{P}\,]$ and a goal $\mathcal{G}[\,\overline{P'}\,]$, where $\overline{P} = P_1,\, P_2$ in $\mathcal{A}$ and $\overline{P'} = P'_1,\, P'_2$ in $\mathcal{G}$. This will illustrate the need to unify more than one subsentence of each row.

Example

Suppose our tableau contains the assertion and the goal

assertions	goals
$\mathcal{A}[\,\overline{P}\,]:$ $\quad$ $\boxed{p(f(a))}$ $^-$ $\quad$ *and* $\quad$ *if* $\boxed{p(y)}$ $^+$ *then* $r(y)$	
	$\mathcal{G}[\,\overline{P'}\,]:$ $\quad$ $\boxed{p(z)}$ $^+$ $\quad$ *and* $\quad$ $\boxed{p(f(x))}$ $^+$ *or* $q(x)$

These rows have no free variables in common.

Consider the boxed quantifier-free subsentences

$$P_1:\ p(f(a)) \quad \text{and} \quad P_2:\ p(y),$$

which are free in $\mathcal{A}[\,\overline{P}\,]$, and the boxed quantifier-free subsentences

$$P'_1:\ p(z) \quad \text{and} \quad P'_2:\ p(f(x)),$$

which are free in $\mathcal{G}[\overline{\mathcal{P}'}]$.

These four subsentences are unifiable, with most-general unifier

$$\theta: \ \{x \leftarrow a, \ y \leftarrow f(a), \ z \leftarrow f(a)\}.$$

Then, to apply *AG-resolution* to $\mathcal{A}$ and $\mathcal{G}$, we first obtain the intermediate assertion

$$\mathcal{A}\theta: \quad \begin{array}{c} \boxed{p(f(a))} \\ and \\ if \ \boxed{p(f(a))} \ then \ r(f(a)) \end{array}$$

and goal

$$\mathcal{G}\theta: \quad \begin{array}{c} \boxed{p(f(a))} \\ and \\ \boxed{p(f(a))} \ or \ q(a). \end{array}$$

The conjunction

$$\begin{array}{c} not \ \mathcal{A}\theta[\,\overline{false}\,] \\ and \\ \mathcal{G}\theta[\,\overline{true}\,] \end{array}$$

is the goal

$$\begin{array}{c} not \ \Big(false \ and \ \big(if \ false \ then \ r(f(a))\big)\Big) \\ and \\ true \ and \ \big(true \ or \ q(a)\big), \end{array}$$

which reduces (by *true-false* simplification) to the final goal

	true

Note that this application of the rule has been in accordance with the *polarity* strategy. Even though the occurrence of $p(y)$ in $\mathcal{A}$, whose instance is replaced by *false* in forming the resolvent, is positive in the tableau, the occurrence of $p(f(a))$ in $\mathcal{A}$, which is also replaced by *false*, is negative in the tableau. ⌐

The following example illustrates that the choice of subsentences to be unified makes a difference.

Example

In the previous example, suppose we had not selected the subsentence $p(f(x))$ to be unified. The annotated rows would then appear as follows:

assertions	goals
$\mathcal{A}:$ $\boxed{p(f(a))}^{-}$ and $if\ \boxed{p(y)}^{+}\ then\ r(y)$	
	$\mathcal{G}[\overline{P'}]:$ $\boxed{p(z)}^{+}$ and $p(f(x))\ or\ q(x)$

The most-general unifier for the three remaining annotated subsentences is

$$\theta:\ \{y \leftarrow f(a),\ z \leftarrow f(a)\}.$$

No replacement is made for x. Then, by application of the *AG-resolution* rule to $\mathcal{A}$ and $\mathcal{G}$, we obtain the intermediate sentence

$$not\ \begin{bmatrix} false \\ and \\ if\ false\ then\ r(f(a)) \end{bmatrix}\ and\ \begin{bmatrix} true \\ and \\ p(f(x))\ or\ q(x) \end{bmatrix},$$

which reduces (under *true-false* simplification) to the goal

	$p(f(x))\ or\ q(x)$

Thus, by neglecting to choose the subsentence $p(f(x))$, we failed to obtain the final goal *true* as before. ◢

Remark (replace all occurrences)

Suppose our tableau contains the assertions

assertions	goals
$\mathcal{A}_1:$ $\boxed{p(a)}^{-}$	
$\mathcal{A}_2:$ *if* $\boxed{p(x)}^{+}$ *then* $p(a)$	

The boxed subsentences are unifiable under the most-general unifier

$$\theta:\ \{x \leftarrow a\}.$$

The unified subsentence is $p(a)$. In applying the rule, we must therefore replace all occurrences of $p(a)$ in $\mathcal{A}_1\theta$ and $\mathcal{A}_2\theta$ with a truth symbol.

As it turns out, $\mathcal{A}_2\theta$ contains an occurrence of $p(a)$ that does not correspond to a boxed subsentence in $\mathcal{A}_2$. This occurrence must be replaced with *true* in applying the rule, even though it was not selected initially to be replaced. ◢

JUSTIFICATION

The *AA-resolution* rule actually preserves equivalence, not just validity. To justify it, we show that the new tableau (which includes the resolvent of $\mathcal{A}_1$ and $\mathcal{A}_2$) is equivalent to the old tableau (before the application of the rule). For this purpose, we may use the *special justification* corollary, rather than the *general justification* proposition. The justification of the other forms follows from the *duality* property.

Justification (*AA-resolution*)

Suppose that $\mathcal{A}_1$ and $\mathcal{A}_2$ are two assertions that satisfy the restrictions for applying the *AA-resolution* rule. Consider an interpretation $\mathcal{I}$ for $\mathcal{A}_1$ and $\mathcal{A}_2$ under which the required tableau $\mathcal{T}_r$ is false, i.e., the universal closures of the required assertions $\mathcal{A}_1$ and $\mathcal{A}_2$ are both true under $\mathcal{I}$.

By the *special justification* corollary, it suffices to show that the generated tableau $\mathcal{T}_g$ is false under $\mathcal{I}$; that is, the universal closure of the generated resolvent, the simplified disjunction

$$\mathcal{A}_1\theta[\,\overline{false}\,]$$
$$or$$
$$\mathcal{A}_2\theta[\,\overline{true}\,],$$

is true under $\mathcal{I}$.

Because the universal closures of $\mathcal{A}_1$ and $\mathcal{A}_2$ are assumed to be true, the universal closures of $\mathcal{A}_1\theta$ and $\mathcal{A}_2\theta$ are also true under I, by the *universal closure-instantiation* proposition (Section [I]3.5). Therefore, by the *semantic rule for universal closure* proposition (Section [I]2.6), $\mathcal{A}_1\theta$ and $\mathcal{A}_2\theta$ are themselves true under any extension of I to the free variables of $\mathcal{A}_1\theta$ and $\mathcal{A}_2\theta$; let I' be any such extension.

The proof now distinguishes between two cases, depending on the truth-value of the unified subsentence $\mathcal{P}\theta$ under I'.

Case: $\mathcal{P}\theta$ is true under I'

Then, because $\mathcal{A}_2\theta$ is true under I' and because $\mathcal{P}\theta$ and the truth symbol *true* have the same truth-value under I',

$$\mathcal{A}_2\theta[\,\overline{true}\,]$$

is also true under I'. It follows (by the semantic rule for the *or* connective) that the (simplified) disjunction

$$\mathcal{A}_1\theta[\,\overline{false}\,]$$
$$or$$
$$\mathcal{A}_2\theta[\,\overline{true}\,]$$

is true under I'.

Case: $\mathcal{P}\theta$ is false under I'

Then, because $\mathcal{A}_1\theta$ is true and because $\mathcal{P}\theta$ and the truth symbol *false* have the same truth-value under I',

$$\mathcal{A}_1\theta[\,\overline{false}\,]$$

is also true under I'. It follows (by the semantic rule for the *or* connective) that the (simplified) disjunction

$$\mathcal{A}_1\theta[\,\overline{false}\,]$$
$$or$$
$$\mathcal{A}_2\theta[\,\overline{true}\,]$$

is true under I'.

In each case, we have concluded that the generated resolvent, i.e., the simplified disjunction

$$\mathcal{A}_1\theta[\,\overline{false}\,]$$
$$or$$
$$\mathcal{A}_2\theta[\,\overline{true}\,],$$

is true under I', for any extension I' of I to the free variables of $\mathcal{A}_1\theta$ and $\mathcal{A}_2\theta$, and hence to the free variables of the resolvent.

Therefore (by the *semantic rule for universal closure* proposition) the universal closure of the resolvent is true under I, as we wanted to show.

This concludes the justification of the *AA-resolution* rule. ⌟

WHY DO WE NEED THE CONDITIONS?

The side conditions required by the *resolution* rule, that the rows have no free variables in common, that the subsentences are free and quantifier-free, and that the unifier is most general, are necessary. Let us consider the consequences if not all of these conditions are satisfied.

Suppose that the assertions $\mathcal{A}_1$ and $\mathcal{A}_2$ have free variables in common. In this case, a failure to rename the common free variables will never allow us to draw an unjustifiable conclusion. It may prevent us, however, from finding sets of unifiable subsentences $\mathcal{P}$ and $\mathcal{P}'$ and deriving useful resolvents. A simple example is as follows.

Example (common free variables)

Suppose that our tableau contains the assertion and the goal

assertions	goals
$\mathcal{A}:$ $\boxed{p(f(x))}$ $^-$	
	$\mathcal{G}:$ $\boxed{p(x)}$ $^+$

We cannot apply the *resolution* rule at once because $p(f(x))$ and $p(x)$ are not unifiable. It is only an unfortunate accident, however, that the free variable x is used in both of these rows. If we rename the free variable of $\mathcal{A}$ as $\widehat{x}$, we obtain the new assertion

$\widehat{\mathcal{A}}:$ $\boxed{p(f(\widehat{x}))}$ $^-$

We can then unify the subexpressions $p(f(\widehat{x}))$ and $p(x)$, taking the most-general unifier θ to be $\{x \leftarrow f(\widehat{x})\}$. Therefore we can apply *AG-resolution* to $\mathcal{A}$ and $\mathcal{G}$, obtaining the new goal

not false
   and
true,

which reduces (by *true-false* simplification) to the final goal

	true

⌐

Even if common free variables do not block the *resolution* rule altogether, they may cause us to obtain a resolvent that is less general than we could have reached otherwise. We illustrate this with another example.

Example (common free variables)

Suppose that our tableau contains the assertions

assertions	goals
$\mathcal{A}_1:$ $\boxed{p(a)}^{\,-}$ *or* $q(x)$	
$\mathcal{A}_2:$ $\left(not\ \boxed{p(a)}^{\,+}\right)$ *or* $r(x)$	

Note that the assertions have the free variable x in common. The boxed subsentences $p(a)$ of $\mathcal{A}_1$ and of $\mathcal{A}_2$ are unifiable, taking the most-general unifier θ to be the empty substitution $\{\ \}$.

If we fail to rename x in these assertions, we obtain (by *AA-resolution* and *true-false* simplification) the assertion

false or $q(x)$
   or
(*not true*) *or* $r(x)$,

which reduces (by *true-false* simplification) to the assertion

$\boxed{q(x)\ \ or\ \ r(x)}^{\,-}$	

which is certainly a valid conclusion to draw.

If we rename the free variable x as $\widehat{x}$ in $\mathcal{A}_1$, however, yielding the assertion

$\widehat{\mathcal{A}_1}:$ $\boxed{p(a)}^{\,-}$ *or* $q(\widehat{x})$

then we can obtain the more general (and hence more useful) resolvent

$\boxed{q(\widehat{x}) \; \; or \; \; r(x)}$ −	

Such a failure to draw the most general possible conclusion can lead to a failure to complete a proof. For instance, if our tableau also happens to contain the goal

	$\boxed{q(a) \; \; or \; \; r(b)}$ +

then we can apply *AG-resolution* to the more general resolvent

$$q(\widehat{x}) \; \; or \; \; r(x),$$

and the goal

$$q(a) \; \; or \; \; r(b),$$

taking the most-general unifier θ to be $\{\widehat{x} \leftarrow a, \; x \leftarrow b\}$, to obtain the final goal

	true

If, however, we have obtained only the less general resolvent

$$q(x) \; \; or \; \; r(x),$$

we cannot unify this assertion with the goal.   ⌐

Suppose one or more of the unifiable subsentences $\overline{P} = P_1, \ldots, P_k$ and $\overline{P'} = P'_1, \ldots, P'_\ell$ is not free. If we applied the rule in this case, the rule would not be sound; i.e., it might alter the validity of the tableau.

Example (free subsentences)

Suppose that our tableau is simply

assertions	goals
$\mathcal{A}:$ $(\exists x)\boxed{p(x)}$ −	
	$\mathcal{G}:$ $(\forall x)\boxed{p(x)}$ +

Then the identical subsentences $p(x)$ and $p(x)$ are clearly unifiable with the empty substitution { }. However, both subsentences $p(x)$ of $\mathcal{A}$ and $\mathcal{G}$ are not free; they are within the scope of the quantifiers $(\exists x)$ and $(\forall x)$, respectively.

If we disregard the restriction and apply the *AG-resolution* rule, we obtain the new goal

 not $(\exists x)$ *false*
  and
 $(\forall x)$ *true*

which reduces (by *true-false* simplification) to the final goal

	true

This is not a justifiable conclusion; the original tableau is not valid. For consider the interpretation whose domain is the nonnegative integers and that assigns $p(x)$ the relation "$x = 0$." Then the assertion $\mathcal{A}$ is assigned the intuitive meaning "there exists an integer 0," which is true, but the goal $\mathcal{G}$ is assigned the intuitive meaning "every integer is 0," which is false. Thus the tableau is false under this interpretation and hence is not valid.

The final tableau, on the other hand, is valid because it contains the final goal *true*. Thus, by applying the rule incorrectly, we have altered the validity of the tableau. We have taken a tableau that is not valid and produced one that is. ⌐

Suppose the unifier θ of $\overline{P}$ and $\overline{P'}$ is not most-general. In this case, the resolvent we obtain is indeed a justifiable conclusion of the required sentences, but it is less general, and hence less useful, than if we had used a most-general unifier.

Example (most-general unifier)

Suppose that our entire tableau is

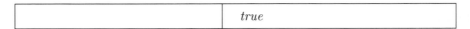

assertions	goals
$\mathcal{A}_1$: $\boxed{p(y)}$ $^-$	
$\mathcal{A}_2$: *if* $\boxed{p(x)}$ $^+$ *then* $r(x)$	
	$\mathcal{G}$: $\boxed{r(b)}$ $^+$

Then the subsentence $p(y)$ of $\mathcal{A}_1$ and the subsentence $p(x)$ of $\mathcal{A}_2$ are unifiable under the most-general unifier

$$\theta : \quad \{x \leftarrow y\}.$$

By applying the *AA-resolution* rule, we obtain the new assertion

> *false*
>
> *or*
>
> *if   true   then $r(y)$,*

which reduces (by *true-false* simplification) to

$\mathcal{A}_3$: $\boxed{r(y)}$ –	

The proof may then be concluded by applying *AG-resolution* to assertion $\mathcal{A}_3$ and goal $\mathcal{G}$, taking θ to be $\{y \leftarrow b\}$, to obtain the final goal

	true

Suppose, however, that in applying the *resolution* rule to assertions $\mathcal{A}_1$ and $\mathcal{A}_2$ we use the substitution

$$\theta' : \quad \{x \leftarrow a, \ y \leftarrow a\};$$

this is a unifier of $p(y)$ and $p(x)$ but is not most-general. The resolvent we obtain is then

$\mathcal{A}_3'$: $r(a)$	

Assertion $\mathcal{A}_3'$ is not unifiable with the goal $\mathcal{G}$. Thus we cannot conclude the proof by applying *AG-resolution* to the new assertion $\mathcal{A}_3'$ and goal $\mathcal{G}$, as we did before to $\mathcal{A}_3$ and $\mathcal{G}$. ⌟

11.7   EQUIVALENCE RULE

The *equivalence* rule enables us to replace subsentences of the tableau with equivalent sentences, treating the $\equiv$ connective in an especially efficient way.

The predicate-logic version of the *equivalence* rule is an adaptation of the propositional-logic version that allows us to apply a most-general unifier θ to two sentences if that will enable us to match subsentences.

THE BASIC FORM

We first illustrate the rule.

Example

Suppose our tableau contains the two assertions

$\mathcal{A}_1:$ *if* $q(c)$ *then* $\left[\boxed{\boxed{p(a,\,y)}} \;\equiv\; q(a)\right]^-$	
$\mathcal{A}_2:$ $\boxed{p(x,\,b)}$ *or* $q(b)$	

If we were to transport the propositional *equivalence* rule directly into predicate logic, we could not apply it here because the boxed subsentences are not
identical. If, however, we apply the unifying substitution

$$\theta: \quad \{x \leftarrow a,\; y \leftarrow b\},$$

we obtain the two instances

$$\mathcal{A}_1\theta: \quad \begin{array}{l} \textit{if } q(c) \\ \textit{then } \left[\boxed{\boxed{p(a,\,b)}} \;\equiv\; q(a)\right] \end{array}$$

and

$$\mathcal{A}_2\theta: \quad \boxed{p(a,\,b)} \;\; \textit{or} \;\; q(b).$$

The boxed subsentences are now identical; we can apply the propositional version
of the *equivalence* rule to obtain the intermediate sentence

$$\begin{array}{l} \left[\begin{array}{l}\textit{if } q(c) \\ \textit{then } \textit{false}\end{array}\right] \\ \quad \textit{or} \\ q(a) \;\; \textit{or} \;\; q(b), \end{array}$$

which reduces (by *true-false* simplification) to

$\big(\textit{not } q(c)\big)$ *or* $q(a)$ *or* $q(b)$	

The predicate-logic *equivalence* rule enables us to obtain this row in a single
step from the two given assertions, without introducing their instances into the
tableau. ⌐

Now let us state the rule precisely.

Rule (AA-equivalence, left-to-right)

assertions	goals
$\mathcal{A}_1\left[\,\overline{P \equiv Q}\,\right]$	
$\mathcal{A}_2\langle\,\overline{P'}\,\rangle$	
$\mathcal{A}_1\theta\left[\,\overline{false}\,\right]$ *or* $\mathcal{A}_2\theta\langle\,\overline{Q\theta}\,\rangle$	

where

- $\overline{P \equiv Q}$ stands for the free, quantifier-free equivalences $P_1 \equiv Q_1$, $\ldots, P_k \equiv Q_k$ $(k \geq 1)$, which occur in $\mathcal{A}_1$.

- $\overline{P'}$ stands for the free, quantifier-free subsentences $P'_1, \ldots, P'_\ell$ $(\ell \geq 1)$, which occur in $\mathcal{A}_2$.

- $\overline{P\theta}$ stands for $P_1\theta, \ldots, P_k\theta$; also, $\overline{P'\theta}$ stands for $P'_1\theta, \ldots, P'_\ell\theta$, and $\overline{Q\theta}$ stands for $Q_1\theta, \ldots, Q_k\theta$.

- θ is a most-general unifier for the subsentences in $\overline{P}$, $\overline{P'}$, and for the subsentences in $\overline{Q}$; that is, $\overline{P\theta}$ and $\overline{P'\theta}$ are all identical sentences and $\overline{Q\theta}$ are all identical sentences. (The sentences $\overline{P\theta}$ must be distinct from the sentences $\overline{Q\theta}$.)

- $\overline{false}$ stand for *false*, $\ldots$, *false* (k times). ◢

More precisely, to apply the AA-*equivalence* rule to two assertions $\mathcal{A}_1$ and $\mathcal{A}_2$ of a tableau,

- Rename the variables of $\mathcal{A}_1$ and $\mathcal{A}_2$ if necessary to ensure that they have no free variables in common.

- Select free, quantifier-free subsentence occurrences of $\mathcal{A}_1$,

$$\overline{P \equiv Q}: \quad P_1 \equiv Q_1, \quad \ldots, \quad P_k \equiv Q_k \quad (k \geq 1),$$

and free, quantifier-free subsentence occurrences of $\mathcal{A}_2$,

$$\overline{P'}: \quad P'_1, \ldots, P'_\ell \quad (\ell \geq 1),$$

such that there exists a most-general unifier θ that unifies $P_1, \ldots, P_k, P'_1, \ldots, P'_\ell$ and also unifies $Q_1, \ldots, Q_k$; that is,

- $P_1\theta, \ldots, P_k\theta$ and $P'_1\theta, \ldots, P'_\ell\theta$ are all the same sentence, which we shall call $P\theta$.

- $Q_1\theta, \ldots, Q_k\theta$ are all the same sentence, which we shall call $Q\theta$.

- Apply θ to the assertion A_1 and replace all free occurrences of $P\theta \equiv Q\theta$ in $A_1\theta$ with the truth symbol *false*, obtaining the disjunct

$$A_1\theta[\,\overline{false}\,].$$

- Apply θ to the assertion A_2 and replace one or more occurrences of $P\theta$ in $A_2\theta$ with $Q\theta$, obtaining the disjunct

$$A_2\theta\langle\,\overline{Q\theta}\,\rangle.$$

- Simplify the disjunction

$$A_1\theta[\,\overline{false}\,] \quad or \quad A_2\theta\langle\,\overline{Q\theta}\,\rangle.$$

- Add the simplified disjunction to the tableau as a new assertion.

In the preceding *left-to-right* version of the rule, we replace instances of the left-hand side P_i of the equivalence with corresponding instances of the right-hand side Q_i. By the symmetry of the $\equiv$ connective, we can apply the rule *right-to-left* to replace instances of the right-hand side Q_i with instances of the left-hand side P_i.

Rule (AA-equivalence, right-to-left)

assertions	goals
$A_1[\,P \equiv Q\,]$	
$A_2\langle\,\overline{Q'}\,\rangle$	
$A_1\theta[\,\overline{false}\,]$ *or* $A_2\theta\langle\,\overline{P\theta}\,\rangle$	

where $\mathcal{A}_1$ and $\mathcal{A}_2$ satisfy the conditions analogous to those of the left-to-right version of the rule. ⌟

POLARITY

The *polarity* strategy we applied in the propositional-logic rule can also be applied to the predicate-logic *equivalence* rule.

Strategy (polarity)

An application of the *AA-equivalence* rule is in accordance with the *polarity strategy* if

at least one of the occurrences of

$$P_1 \equiv \mathcal{Q}_1, \quad \ldots, \quad P_k \equiv \mathcal{Q}_k,$$

in $\mathcal{A}_1$, whose instances are replaced by *false* in applying the rule, is of negative polarity in the tableau. ⌟

Note that the *polarity* strategy places no restriction on the polarity of the subsentences $P'_1, \ldots, P'_\ell$ [or, in the right-to-left version, $\mathcal{Q}'_1, \ldots, \mathcal{Q}'_\ell$] of $\mathcal{A}_2$. The negative polarity required by the strategy need not be strict; the equivalence may have both polarities.

Example

Suppose our tableau contains the two assertions

assertions	goals
$\mathcal{A}_1:\quad \left[\boxed{p(x,\,a)} \equiv q(x)\right]^{-}$	
$\mathcal{A}_2:\quad \boxed{p(b,\,y)}\ \ and\ \ r(y,\,x)$	

Let us apply the *AA-equivalence* rule left-to-right to these assertions. The subsentences P and P' to be matched are indicated by boxes. Noting that $\mathcal{A}_1$ and $\mathcal{A}_2$ have the free variable x in common, we rename this variable in $\mathcal{A}_2$ to $\widehat{x}$, obtaining

$$\widehat{\mathcal{A}_2}:\quad \boxed{p(b,\,y)}\ \ and\ \ r(y,\,\widehat{x}).$$

Here $\mathcal{A}_1$ contains the free subsentence

$$\mathcal{P}: \quad p(x, a)$$

and $\widehat{\mathcal{A}_2}$ contains the free subsentence

$$\mathcal{P}': \quad p(b, y).$$

These subsentences are unifiable under the most-general unifier

$$\theta: \quad \{x \leftarrow b, \, y \leftarrow a\}.$$

The unified sentence is

$$\mathcal{P}\theta: \quad p(b, a).$$

Applying θ to $\mathcal{A}_1$, we obtain

$$\mathcal{A}_1\theta: \quad \boxed{p(b, a)} \; \equiv \; q(b);$$

applying θ to $\widehat{\mathcal{A}_2}$, we obtain

$$\widehat{\mathcal{A}_2}\theta: \quad \boxed{p(b, a)} \; and \; r(a, \widehat{x}).$$

Replacing $(\mathcal{P} \equiv \mathcal{Q})\theta: \; p(b, a) \equiv q(b)$ with *false* in $\mathcal{A}_1\theta$, we obtain simply

false;

replacing $\mathcal{P}\theta: p(b, a)$ with $\mathcal{Q}\theta: q(b)$ in $\widehat{\mathcal{A}_2}\theta$, we obtain

$$q(b) \; and \; r(a, \widehat{x}).$$

Taking the disjunction, we obtain the new assertion

false
or
$q(b)$ and $r(a, \widehat{x})$,

which reduces (by *true-false* simplification) to

$q(b)$ and $r(a, \widehat{x})$	

This assertion may be added to our tableau.

Note again that the intermediate sentences $\widehat{\mathcal{A}_2}$, $\mathcal{A}_1\theta$, $\widehat{\mathcal{A}_2}\theta$, and the unsimplified disjunction are not added to the tableau; these are only aids in finding the simplified disjunction, which is added to the tableau as a new assertion. ⌐

JUSTIFICATION

Let us justify the *AA-equivalence* rule, showing that the old (given) tableau is equivalent to the new tableau. We justify the left-to-right version of the rule. (The justification of the right-to-left version depends on the symmetry of the $\equiv$ connective.) The rule actually preserves equivalence; therefore we may use the *special justification* corollary in proving its soundness. The justification resembles that of the *AA-resolution* rule.

Justification (*AA-equivalence*)

Suppose that A_1 and A_2 are two assertions that satisfy the restrictions for applying the *AA-equivalence* rule. Let I be an interpretation for A_1 and A_2 under which the required tableau T_r is false, i.e., the universal closures of the required assertions A_1 and A_2 are both true under I. By the *special justification* corollary, it suffices to establish that the generated tableau T_g is false under I, i.e., that the universal closure of the generated assertion, the simplified disjunction

$$A_1\theta\left[\,\overline{false}\,\right]$$
$$or$$
$$A_2\theta\langle\,\overline{Q\theta}\,\rangle,$$

is also true under I.

Because the universal closures of A_1 and A_2 are assumed to be true, the universal closures of $A_1\theta$ and $A_2\theta$ are also true under I, by the *universal closure-instantiation* proposition. Therefore, by the *semantic rule for universal closure* proposition, $A_1\theta$ and $A_2\theta$ are themselves true under any extension of I to the free variables of $A_1\theta$ and $A_2\theta$. Let I' be any such extension.

The proof now distinguishes between two cases.

Case: $(P \equiv Q)\theta$ is false under I'

Then, because $A_1\theta$ is true under I' and because $(P{\equiv}Q)\theta$ and the propositional constant *false* have the same truth-value under I',

$$A_1\theta\left[\,\overline{false}\,\right]$$

is also true under I'. It follows (by the semantic rule for the *or* connective) that the (simplified) disjunction

$$A_1\theta\left[\,\overline{false}\,\right]$$
$$or$$
$$A_2\theta\langle\,\overline{Q\theta}\,\rangle$$

is also true under I'.

Case: $(P \equiv Q)\theta$ is true under I'

That is, $P\theta \equiv Q\theta$ is true under I'. Then (by the semantic rule for the $\equiv$ connective) $P\theta$ and $Q\theta$ have the same truth-value under I'. Hence, because $A_2\theta$ is true under I',

$$A_2\theta\langle \overline{Q\theta} \rangle$$

is also true under I'. It follows (by the semantic rule for the *or* connective) that the (simplified) disjunction

$$A_1\theta\lbrack \overline{false} \rbrack$$
$$or$$
$$A_2\theta\langle \overline{Q\theta} \rangle$$

is true under I'.

In each case, we have concluded that the generated assertion, the simplified disjunction

$$A_1\theta\lbrack \overline{false} \rbrack$$
$$or$$
$$A_2\theta\langle \overline{Q\theta} \rangle,$$

is true under I', for any extension I' of I to the free variables of $A_1\theta$ and $A_2\theta$, and hence to the free variables of the new assertion.

Therefore (by the *semantic rule for universal closure* proposition), the universal closure of the generated assertion is true under I, as we wanted to prove. ◢

DUAL FORMS

We have given the *AA-equivalence* rule. The corresponding dual forms of the rule are as follows.

Rule (GG-equivalence, left-to-right)

assertions	goals
	$G_1\lbrack \overline{P \equiv Q} \rbrack$
	$G_2\langle \overline{P'} \rangle$
	$G_1\theta\lbrack \overline{false} \rbrack$ *and* $G_2\theta\langle \overline{Q\theta} \rangle$

where $\mathcal{G}_1$ and $\mathcal{G}_2$ satisfy the same conditions as $\mathcal{A}_1$ and $\mathcal{A}_2$, respectively, in the *AA-equivalence* rule. ⌐

Rule (AG-equivalence, left-to-right)

assertions	goals
$\mathcal{A}\left[\overline{\mathcal{P} \equiv \mathcal{Q}}\right]$	
	$\mathcal{G}\langle \overline{\mathcal{P}'} \rangle$
	$not\ \left(\mathcal{A}\theta\left[\overline{false}\right]\right)$ and $\mathcal{G}\theta\langle \overline{\mathcal{Q}\theta} \rangle$

where $\mathcal{A}$ and $\mathcal{G}$ satisfy the same conditions as $\mathcal{A}_1$ and $\mathcal{A}_2$, respectively, in the *AA-equivalence* rule. ⌐

Rule (GA-equivalence, left-to-right)

assertions	goals
	$\mathcal{G}\left[\mathcal{P} \equiv \mathcal{Q}\right]$
$\mathcal{A}\langle \overline{\mathcal{P}'} \rangle$	
	$\mathcal{G}\theta\left[\overline{false}\right]$ and $not\ \left(\mathcal{A}\theta\langle \overline{\mathcal{Q}\theta} \rangle\right)$

where $\mathcal{G}$ and $\mathcal{A}$ satisfy the same conditions as $\mathcal{A}_1$ and $\mathcal{A}_2$, respectively, in the *AA-equivalence* rule. ⌐

There are analogous right-to-left forms. The justification of the dual forms follows by duality.

The *polarity* strategy for the dual forms of the rule is analogous to the one for the *AA-equivalence* rule: at least one of the occurrences of $\mathcal{P}_1 \equiv \mathcal{Q}_1, \ldots, \mathcal{P}_k \equiv \mathcal{Q}_k$, whose instances are replaced by *false* in applying the rules, is of negative polarity in the tableau.

Example

Suppose our tableau contains the assertion and the goal

assertions	goals
$\mathcal{A}:$ $\begin{bmatrix} p(x) \equiv \boxed{q(a)} \end{bmatrix}^{-}$ or $\begin{bmatrix} p(a) \equiv \boxed{q(x)} \end{bmatrix}^{-}$	
	$\mathcal{G}:$ $\boxed{q(y)}$ or $q(a)$

Let us apply the *AG-equivalence* rule right-to-left to $\mathcal{A}$ and $\mathcal{G}$.

We consider the subsentences

$$\mathcal{P}_1 \equiv \mathcal{Q}_1: \quad p(x) \equiv q(a)$$

and

$$\mathcal{P}_2 \equiv \mathcal{Q}_2: \quad p(a) \equiv q(x)$$

of $\mathcal{A}$ and the subsentence

$$\mathcal{Q}': \quad q(y)$$

of $\mathcal{G}$.

The substitution

$$\theta: \quad \{x \leftarrow a, \, y \leftarrow a\}$$

is a most-general substitution that unifies

$$p(x) \quad \text{and} \quad p(a)$$

and also unifies

$$q(a), \quad q(x), \quad \text{and} \quad q(y).$$

The unified subsentences are

$$\mathcal{P}\theta: \, p(a) \quad \text{and} \quad \mathcal{Q}\theta: \, q(a).$$

Applying θ to $\mathcal{A}$, we obtain

$$\mathcal{A}\theta: \quad \begin{array}{c} p(a) \equiv \boxed{q(a)} \\ or \\ p(a) \equiv \boxed{q(a)} \end{array}.$$

Applying θ to $\mathcal{G}$, we obtain

$$\mathcal{G}\theta : \quad \boxed{q(a)} \quad or \quad q(a).$$

Replacing every occurrence of the equivalence $(p(a) \equiv q(a))$ with *false* in $\mathcal{A}\theta$, we obtain

$$false \quad or \quad false;$$

replacing the selected occurrence of the right-hand side $q(a)$ of the equivalence with the left-hand side $p(a)$ in $\mathcal{G}\theta$, we obtain

$$p(a) \quad or \quad q(a).$$

Therefore the new goal is

$$not \; (false \;\; or \;\; false)$$
$$and$$
$$p(a) \;\; or \;\; q(a),$$

which reduces (by *true-false* simplification) to the goal

	$p(a) \;\; or \;\; q(a)$

Note that two equivalence occurrences in $\mathcal{A}\theta$ were replaced by *false*, that only the selected occurrence of $q(a)$ in $\mathcal{G}\theta$ was replaced by $p(a)$, and that the rule was applied in the right-to-left direction. ◢

11.8   QUANTIFIER-ELIMINATION RULES

The *quantifier-elimination* (*skolemization*) rules allow us to remove certain quantifiers from the assertions and goals of our tableau. These rules are valuable because they pave the way for other rules, such as *resolution* and *equivalence* rules, that apply only to free, quantifier-free subsentences.

For example, suppose that we have a tableau with the assertion and the goal

assertions	goals
$\mathcal{A} : \quad (\forall x)p(x)$	
	$\mathcal{G} : \quad (\exists y)p(y)$

Intuitively, this tableau is valid, because we can take y in the goal to be any domain element at all. We might expect to be able to apply the *AG-resolution* rule in this case, matching the subsentence $p(y)$ of the goal against the subsentence $p(x)$ of the assertion; this application, however, is forbidden because these subsentences are not free. By applying the *skolemization* rules of this section, we will be able to drop these quantifiers and then apply the *resolution* rule.

FORCE OF A QUANTIFIER

Before we describe the *skolemization* rules, let us extend the notion of the force of a quantifier, which we have defined for predicate logic, to apply to the quantifiers in a tableau.

Definition (force of quantifiers)

In a tableau $\mathcal{T}$,

- An occurrence of a quantifier $(\ldots\, x)$ of a subsentence of the form $\mathcal{E} : (\ldots\, x)\mathcal{F}$ has *universal force* in $\mathcal{T}$, annotated by the superscript $(\ldots\, x)^{\forall}$, if

  - it is a universal quantifier and $\mathcal{E}$ is of positive polarity in $\mathcal{T}$, that is,

  $$[(\forall x)\mathcal{F}]^{+} \;\Rightarrow\; (\forall x)^{\forall}\mathcal{F},$$

    or

  - it is an existential quantifier and $\mathcal{E}$ is of negative polarity in $\mathcal{T}$, that is,

  $$[(\exists x)\mathcal{F}]^{-} \;\Rightarrow\; (\exists x)^{\forall}\mathcal{F}.$$

- An occurrence of a quantifier $(\ldots\, x)$ of a subsentence of the form $\mathcal{E} : (\ldots\, x)\mathcal{F}$ has *existential force* in $\mathcal{T}$, annotated by the superscript $(\ldots\, x)^{\exists}$, if

  - it is an existential quantifier and $\mathcal{E}$ is of positive polarity in $\mathcal{T}$, that is,

  $$[(\exists x)\mathcal{F}]^{+} \;\Rightarrow\; (\exists x)^{\exists}\mathcal{F},$$

    or

> ■ it is a universal quantifier and $\mathcal{E}$ is of negative polarity
> in $\mathcal{T}$, that is,

$$[(\forall x)\mathcal{F}]^- \;\Rightarrow\; (\forall x)^{\exists}\mathcal{F}.$$

- An occurrence of a quantifier $(\ldots x)$ is of *strict* (*universal* or *existential*) *force* in $\mathcal{T}$ if it does not have both universal and existential force. ⌐

As before, if we wish to indicate that an occurrence of a quantifier has universal or existential force in a tableau, we annotate it with the superscript $(\ldots x)^{\forall}$ or $(\ldots x)^{\exists}$, respectively. If an occurrence of a quantifier $(\ldots x)$ has both forces, we annotate it with the combined superscript $(\ldots x)^{\forall\exists}$. Thus, in the assertion

$if \;\; \left[(\exists x)^{\exists}(\forall y)^{\forall}q(x,\,y)\right]^+$	
$then \;\; \left[(\forall x)^{\exists}(\exists y)^{\forall}q(x,\,y)\right]^-$	

the quantifiers have been annotated according to their forces in the tableau.

Recall that assertions always have negative polarity in a tableau. Therefore outermost universal quantifiers in an assertion always have existential force, and outermost existential quantifiers always have universal force.

BOTH FORCES

There is no rule for directly eliminating quantifiers of both forces, $(\ldots x)^{\forall\exists}$. Such quantifiers must always occur within the scope of an equivalence connective $\equiv$, or within the *if*-clause of a conditional connective or conditional operator. Without these symbols, we can have no quantifiers of both forces.

In fact, we can eliminate any equivalence or conditional construct by repeated application (left-to-right) of the following rewritings:

- Equivalence elimination

$$\mathcal{F} \equiv \mathcal{G} \quad \Leftrightarrow \quad (if \;\; \mathcal{F} \;\; then \;\; \mathcal{G}) \;\; and \;\; (if \;\; \mathcal{G} \;\; then \;\; \mathcal{F})$$

$$\mathcal{F} \equiv \mathcal{G} \quad \Leftrightarrow \quad (\mathcal{F} \;\; and \;\; \mathcal{G}) \;\; or \;\; ((not \;\; \mathcal{F}) \;\; and \;\; (not \;\; \mathcal{G}))$$

- Conditional (connective) elimination

$$if \;\; \mathcal{F} \;\; then \;\; \mathcal{G} \;\; else \;\; \mathcal{H} \quad \Leftrightarrow \quad \begin{array}{l} (if \;\; \mathcal{F} \;\; then \;\; \mathcal{G}) \;\; and \\ (if \;\; (not \;\; \mathcal{F}) \;\; then \;\; \mathcal{H}) \end{array}$$

$$if \;\; \mathcal{F} \;\; then \;\; \mathcal{G} \;\; else \;\; \mathcal{H} \quad \Leftrightarrow \quad (\mathcal{F} \;\; and \;\; \mathcal{G}) \;\; or \;\; ((not \;\; \mathcal{F}) \;\; and \;\; \mathcal{H})$$

- Conditional (operator) manipulation

$$p(\overline{x}, \textit{if } \mathcal{F} \textit{ then } s \textit{ else } t, \overline{y}) \quad \Leftrightarrow \quad \textit{if } \mathcal{F} \textit{ then } p(\overline{x}, s, \overline{y}) \textit{ else } p(\overline{x}, t, \overline{y})$$

$$f(\overline{x}, \textit{if } \mathcal{F} \textit{ then } s \textit{ else } t, \overline{y}) \quad \Leftrightarrow \quad \textit{if } \mathcal{F} \textit{ then } f(\overline{x}, s, \overline{y}) \textit{ else } f(\overline{x}, t, \overline{y})$$

(Note that we have a choice of two rules each for eliminating the conditional and equivalence connectives.)

Thus, to eliminate a quantifier of both forces, we can repeatedly apply the preceding rewritings, as appropriate, to all of the surrounding equivalence and conditional constructs. The quantifier of both forces in the original sentence is replaced by many quantifiers of strict force in the resulting sentence. These quantifiers can subsequently be removed by the *skolemization* rules.

Example

Suppose a tableau contains the following goal:

assertions	goals
	$(\exists y) \left[p \left(f \left(\begin{array}{l} \textit{if } (\forall x)^{\forall \exists} q(x) \equiv r(a) \\ \textit{then } g(y) \\ \textit{else } h(y) \end{array} \right) \right) \right]$

The annotated quantifier $(\forall x)^{\forall \exists}$ has both forces in the tableau: it is surrounded by both a conditional operator and an equivalence connective. If we wish to eliminate this quantifier, we must first remove these constructs.

We first remove the conditional operator. By the *conditional-manipulation* rewriting for functions, we may obtain

	$(\exists y) \left[p \left(\begin{array}{l} \textit{if } (\forall x)^{\forall \exists} q(x) \equiv r(a) \\ \textit{then } f(g(y)) \\ \textit{else } f(h(y)) \end{array} \right) \right]$

By the *conditional-manipulation* rewriting for predicates, we may obtain

	$(\exists y) \left[\begin{array}{l} \textit{if } (\forall x)^{\forall \exists} q(x) \equiv r(a) \\ \textit{then } p(f(g(y))) \\ \textit{else } p(f(h(y))) \end{array} \right]$

By one of the *conditional-elimination* rewritings, we may obtain

$$(\exists y) \begin{bmatrix} if & ((\forall x)^{\forall \exists} q(x) \equiv r(a)) & then & p(f(g(y))) \\ & and & \\ if & not \ ((\forall x)^{\forall \exists} q(x) \equiv r(a)) & then & p(f(h(y))) \end{bmatrix}$$

We have succeeded in removing the conditional construct. Each of the resulting $(\forall x)$ quantifiers, however, is still surrounded by an equivalence connective, and still has both forces. To remove these quantifiers, we (twice) apply an *equivalence-elimination* rewriting, to obtain

$$(\exists y) \begin{bmatrix} \begin{bmatrix} if & \begin{bmatrix} (\forall x)^{\exists} q(x) \ and \ r(a) \\ or \\ (not \ (\forall x)^{\forall} q(x)) \ and \ (not \ r(a)) \end{bmatrix} \\ then \ p(f(q(y))) \end{bmatrix} \\ and \\ \begin{bmatrix} if \ not & \begin{bmatrix} (\forall x)^{\forall} q(x) \ and \ r(a) \\ or \\ (not \ (\forall x)^{\exists} q(x)) \ and \ (not \ (r(a))) \end{bmatrix} \\ then \ p(f(h(y))) \end{bmatrix} \end{bmatrix}$$

In the resulting goal, we have four occurrences of the quantifier $(\forall x)$, two of strict universal force and two of strict existential force. These quantifiers may be removed by application of the *skolemization* rules. ◢

There are two *skolemization* rules: one for eliminating quantifiers of strict universal force, the other for eliminating quantifiers of strict existential force.

∀-ELIMINATION RULE

The following ∀-*elimination* rule, expressed in tableau notation, allows us to remove a quantifier of strict universal force. We first give the rule for removing a quantifier from an assertion.

Rule (∀-elimination, A-form)

assertions	goals
$\mathcal{A}$	
$\mathcal{A}'$	

where the following restrictions are satisfied:

- The required assertion $\mathcal{A}$ contains at least one occurrence of a subsentence

$$(\ldots z)^{\forall} P[z],$$

  where $(\ldots z)^{\forall}$ is of strict universal force in the tableau; we consider a particular occurrence of this subsentence.

- The only free variables in $\mathcal{A}$ are $\overline{x}$, that is, $x_1, \ldots, x_m$, where $m \geq 0$.

- The only quantifiers of existential force that surround the occurrence $(\ldots z)^{\forall} P[z]$ are $(\overline{\ldots y})^{\exists}$, that is, $(\ldots y_1)^{\exists}, \ldots, (\ldots y_n)^{\exists}$, where $n \geq 0$.

- The variables $\overline{x}, \overline{y}$, and z are all distinct; this should be achieved by renaming if necessary.

- The generated assertion $\mathcal{A}'$ is obtained from $\mathcal{A}$ by replacing the occurrence $(\ldots z)^{\forall} P[z]$ with

$$P\big[f(\overline{x}, \overline{y})\big],$$

  where f is a new skolem function symbol, i.e., one that has not occurred in the tableau so far.

In the special case in which there are no such free variables $\overline{x}$ and no surrounding quantifiers $(\overline{\ldots y})^{\exists}$, that is, $m = n = 0$, $\mathcal{A}'$ is obtained from $\mathcal{A}$ by replacing the occurrence $(\ldots z)^{\forall} P[z]$ with

$$P[a],$$

where a is a new skolem constant symbol, i.e., one that has not occurred in the tableau so far. ⌐

The dual form of the rule, for removing a quantifier of universal force from a goal, is as follows.

Rule ($\forall$-elimination, G-form)

assertions	goals
	$\mathcal{G}$
	$\mathcal{G}'$

Here $\mathcal{G}'$ is obtained from $\mathcal{G}$ in the same way that $\mathcal{A}'$ is obtained from $\mathcal{A}$. The restrictions for applying the G-form are the same as those for the A-form of the $\forall$-*elimination* rule. ⌐

Example

Suppose that our tableau contains the assertion

assertions	goals
$\mathcal{A}:$ $r(x)$ *or* $(\forall\,y)^{\exists}\Big[q(x,\,y) \ \ and \ \ \boxed{(\exists\,z)^{\forall}p(x,\,y,\,z)}\Big]$	

We would like to remove the quantifier $(\exists\,z)^{\forall}$, annotated with a box. Note that

- The occurrence of the quantifier $(\exists\,z)^{\forall}$ to be removed is of strict universal force in the tableau.

- The only free variable in $\mathcal{A}$ is x.

- The only quantifier of existential force that contains the occurrence of the subsentence $(\exists\,z)^{\forall}p(x,y,z)$ within its scope is $(\forall\,y)^{\exists}$.

Let f be a new skolem function symbol. Then we may add to our tableau the new assertion

$\mathcal{A}':$ $r(x)$ *or* $(\forall\,y)^{\exists}\big[q(x,y) \ \ and \ \ p(x,\,y,\,f(x,y))\big]$	

obtained from $\mathcal{A}$ by dropping the quantifier $(\exists\,z)^{\forall}$ and replacing the occurrence of z in $p(x,y,z)$ with the skolem term $f(x,y)$. ⌐

Example

Suppose our tableau contains the goal

assertions	goals
	$\mathcal{G}:$ $(\forall\,y)^{\forall}\Big[q(y) \ \ or \ \ \boxed{(\forall\,z)^{\forall}p(y,\,z)}\Big]$

We would like to remove the quantifier $(\forall\,z)^{\forall}$, annotated with a box. Note that

- The occurrence of $(\forall z)^\forall$ to be removed is of strict universal force in the tableau.

- There are no free variables in $\mathcal{G}$.

- There are no quantifiers of existential force that contain the occurrence of $(\forall z)^\forall p(y, z)$ within their scope.

Let a be a new skolem constant. Then we may add to our tableau the new goal

	$\mathcal{G}' : \quad (\forall y)^\forall [q(y) \ \text{ or } \ p(y, a)]$

obtained from $\mathcal{G}$ by dropping the quantifier $(\forall z)^\forall$ and replacing the occurrence of z in $p(y, z)$ with the skolem constant a. ⌐

Let us justify the G-form of the $\forall$-*elimination* rule, showing that the old (given) tableau is valid precisely when the new tableau, after adding the generated goal, is valid. The justification of the dual A-form of the rule follows by duality. This is an exceptional rule in the sense that the stronger equivalence result does not hold: the old tableau is not necessarily equivalent to the new tableau. Therefore we cannot use the *special justification* corollary to prove the soundness of the rule, and must instead use the *general justification* proposition.

Justification ($\forall$-*elimination*, G-form)

The justification depends on the *universal-elimination* proposition from Section 10.6.

By the *general justification* proposition, it suffices to show that, if the required row $\mathcal{T}_r$, that is, the existential closure of the sentence $\mathcal{G}$, is false under some interpretation $\mathcal{I}$, then there exists some interpretation $\mathcal{I}'$ such that the generated row $\mathcal{T}_g$, that is, the existential closure of the sentence $\mathcal{G}'$, is false under $\mathcal{I}'$, where $\mathcal{I}$ and $\mathcal{I}'$ agree on the old tableau. If the existential closure of $\mathcal{G}$ is false under $\mathcal{I}$, then, by the *universal-elimination* proposition, there exists an interpretation $\mathcal{I}'$ that agrees with $\mathcal{I}$ except perhaps on new symbols, such that the existential closure of $\mathcal{G}'$ is false under $\mathcal{I}'$. Since we know that no new symbols occur in any of the given assertions and goals, $\mathcal{I}$ and $\mathcal{I}'$ agree on the old tableau.

The justification of the special case, where $m = n = 0$, is similar. ⌐

The following example illustrates the fact that the $\forall$-*elimination* rule may not preserve equivalence.

Example (equivalence not preserved)

Suppose our tableau consists of the single goal

assertions	goals
	$(\forall y)^{\forall} p(y)$

The quantifier has strict universal force in the tableau. By the $\forall$-*elimination* rule, we may drop this quantifier from the goal, replacing the variable y with the skolem constant a. We introduce the new goal

	$p(a)$

Equivalence has not been preserved: there are interpretations under which the old tableau is false but the new tableau is true, that is, the two do not have the same truth-value. In particular, for any interpretation under which $p(a)$ is true but $(\forall y)p(y)$ is false, the old tableau is false but the new tableau is true.

On the other hand, validity has been preserved, as the preceding justification guarantees. In fact, neither the old tableau nor the new tableau is valid. ⌐

∃-ELIMINATION RULE

The $\forall$-*elimination* rule allows us to remove quantifiers of strict universal force; the following $\exists$-*elimination* rule allows us to remove quantifiers of strict existential force. We first give the rule for removing quantifiers from an assertion.

Rule (∃-elimination, A-form)

assertions	goals
$\mathcal{A}$	
$\mathcal{A}'$	

where the following restrictions are satisfied:

- The required assertion $\mathcal{A}$ contains at least one occurrence of a subsentence

  $(... \, y)^{\exists} \mathcal{P}[y],$

where $(\ldots y)^{\exists}$ is of strict existential force in the tableau; we consider a particular occurrence of this subsentence.

- The occurrence of $(\ldots y)^{\exists} P[y]$ is not within the scope of any quantifier of universal force; this can be achieved by prior application of the $\forall$-*elimination* rule if necessary.

- The occurrence of $(\ldots y)^{\exists} P[y]$ is not within the scope of any other quantifier $(\forall y)$ or $(\exists y)$ with the same variable; this can be achieved by renaming if necessary.

- The variable y is distinct from any of the free variables of $\mathcal{A}$; this can be achieved by renaming if necessary.

The generated assertion $\mathcal{A}'$ is obtained from $\mathcal{A}$ by dropping the occurrence of the quantifier $(\ldots y)^{\exists}$, that is, by replacing the occurrence of $(\ldots y)^{\exists} P[y]$ with $P[y]$. ◢

The dual form of the rule, for removing the quantifier from a goal, is as follows.

Rule ($\exists$-elimination, G-form)

assertions	goals
	$\mathcal{G}$
	$\mathcal{G}'$

Here $\mathcal{G}'$ is obtained from $\mathcal{G}$ in the same way that $\mathcal{A}'$ is obtained from $\mathcal{A}$ in the A-form of the rule. The restrictions for applying the G-form are the same as those for applying the A-form. ◢

Example

Suppose our tableau contains the goal

assertions	goals
	$\mathcal{G}: \quad (\exists y_1)^{\exists}\Big[p(y_1) \quad and \quad \boxed{(\exists y_2)^{\exists} q(y_1, y_2)}\Big]$

We would like to remove the inner quantifier $(\exists y_2)^{\exists}$. Note that

- The occurrence of $(\exists\, y_2)^\exists$ to be removed is of strict existential force in the tableau.

- No quantifier of universal force contains the quantifier $(\exists\, y_2)^\exists$ within its scope.

- The occurrence of $(\exists\, y_2)^\exists$ is not within the scope of any other occurrence of a quantifier $(\ldots\, y_2)$.

- The variable y_2 is distinct from any of the free variables of the goal.

Then we may add to our tableau the new goal

	$\mathcal{G}'$: $(\exists\, y_1)^\exists\big[p(y_1)\ \ and\ \ q(y_1, y_2)\big]$

obtained from $\mathcal{G}$ by dropping the quantifier $(\exists\, y_2)^\exists$.   ⌙

The justification depends on the *existential-elimination* proposition from Section 10.7. We justify the G-form of the rule. The justification of the A-form follows by appeal to the *duality* property.

Justification ($\exists$-*elimination*, G-form)

By the *special justification* corollary, it suffices to show that, if the existential closure of the required goal $\mathcal{G} : \mathcal{F}\langle(\ldots\ y)^\exists P[y]\rangle$ is false under some interpretation $\mathcal{I}$, then the existential closure of the generated goal $\mathcal{G}' : \mathcal{F}\langle P[y]\rangle$ is also false under $\mathcal{I}$. But this holds by the *existential-elimination* proposition.   ⌙

Although the $\exists$-*elimination* rule, like all deduction rules, retains the required row, in this case equivalence would have been preserved even if the required row were dropped.

11.9   EXAMPLES OF COMPLETE PROOFS

In this section we examine proofs of the validity of predicate-logic sentences. These proofs use many deduction rules together.

Example

Suppose we would like to prove the validity of the sentence

> *if* $(\exists x)(\forall y)q(x,\, y)$
> *then* $(\forall y)(\exists x)q(x,\, y)$.

We begin with the initial goal

assertions	goals
	G1. *if* $(\exists x)(\forall y)q(x, y)$ *then* $(\forall y)(\exists x)q(x, y)$

By the *if-split* rule, we obtain the new assertion and goal

A2. $(\exists x)^{\forall}(\forall y)q(x, y)$	
	G3. $(\forall y)^{\forall}(\exists x)q(x, y)$

By the $\forall$-*elimination* rule applied to the outermost quantifier $(\exists x)^{\forall}$ of assertion A2, we obtain

A4. $(\forall y)^{\exists}q(a, y)$	

Here we have replaced the variable x with the new skolem constant a.

By the same rule applied to the outermost quantifier $(\forall y)^{\forall}$ of goal G3, we obtain

	G5. $(\exists x)^{\exists}q(x, b)$

Here we have replaced the variable y with the new skolem constant b.

Now that the quantifier $(\forall y)^{\exists}$ of assertion A4 is no longer within the scope of any quantifier of universal force, we can apply the $\exists$-*elimination* rule to drop the quantifier, obtaining

A6. $\boxed{q(a, y)}$ $^{-}$	

Applying the same rule to goal G5 to drop the quantifier $(\exists x)^{\exists}$, we obtain

	G7. $\boxed{q(x, b)}$ $^{+}$

We can then apply the *AG-resolution* rule to assertion A6 and goal G7, taking the most-general unifier to be

$$\{x \leftarrow a, y \leftarrow b\},$$

to obtain the final goal

	G8. *true*

⌐

Example (attempting to prove a nonvalid sentence)

The converse

$$if \ (\forall y)(\exists x)q(x, y)$$
$$then \ (\exists x)(\forall y)q(x, y)$$

of the sentence from the previous example is not valid. Let us attempt to imitate the proof of that example, to show where it breaks down.

We begin with the initial goal

assertions	goals
	G1. *if* $(\forall y)(\exists x)q(x, y)$ *then* $(\exists x)(\forall y)q(x, y)$

By the *if-split* rule, we obtain the new assertion and goal

A2. $(\forall y)^{\exists}(\exists x)q(x, y)$	
	G3. $(\exists x)^{\exists}(\forall y)q(x, y)$

Applying the ∃-*elimination* rule to drop the outermost quantifiers of assertion A2 and goal G3, we obtain the new assertion and goal

A4. $(\exists x)^{\forall}q(x, y)$	
	G5. $(\forall y)^{\forall}q(x, y)$

respectively.

Applying the ∀-*elimination* rule to the outermost quantifiers of assertion A4 and goal G5, we obtain the new assertion and goal

A6. $\boxed{q(f(y), y)}^{\,-}$	

	G7. $\boxed{q\big(x,\,g(x)\big)}^{\,+}$

respectively. Here we have replaced the variable x of assertion A4 with the skolem term $f(y)$, where f is a new skolem function; the variable y is free in assertion A4. Similarly, we have replaced the variable y of goal G5 with the skolem term $g(x)$, where g is a new skolem function; the variable x is free in goal G5.

At the analogous point in the previous example, we applied the *AG-resolution* rule to assertion A6 and goal G7; we cannot do this here, however, because these sentences are not unifiable.

We cannot conclude from the failure of a single proof attempt that a sentence is not valid. We already know (Section [I]2.5), however, that this sentence is not valid. Thus, by the soundness of our deductive rules, no proof of this sentence is possible. ⌐

Example

Suppose we would like to prove the validity of the sentence

$$if \quad \begin{bmatrix} (\forall x)\big[p(x) \; \equiv \; q(x)\big] \\ and \\ (\exists x)\big[q(x) \; \equiv \; r(x)\big] \end{bmatrix}$$
$$then \;\; (\exists x)\big[p(x) \;\; \equiv \;\; r(x)\big].$$

We begin with the initial goal

assertions	goals
	G1. *if* $\begin{bmatrix} (\forall x)\big[p(x) \; \equiv \; q(x)\big] \\ and \\ (\exists x)\big[q(x) \; \equiv \; r(x)\big] \end{bmatrix}$ *then* $(\exists x)[p(x) \; \equiv \; r(x)]$

By the *if-split* and *and-split* rules, we obtain

A2. $(\forall x)^{\exists}\big[p(x) \; \equiv \; q(x)\big]$	
A3. $(\exists x)^{\forall}\big[q(x) \; \equiv \; r(x)\big]$	
	G4. $(\exists x)^{\exists}\big[p(x) \; \equiv \; r(x)\big]$

By the ∃-*elimination* rule, we can drop the quantifier $(\forall x)^{\exists}$ from assertion A2 and the quantifier $(\exists x)^{\exists}$ from goal G4; the dropped quantifiers both have strict existential force in the tableau. By the ∀-*elimination* rule, we can drop the quantifier $(\exists x)^{\forall}$ from assertion A3, replacing the variable x with a new skolem constant a; the removed quantifier has strict universal force in the tableau. We obtain

A5. $\left[p(x) \equiv \boxed{q(x)} \right]^{-}$	
A6. $\boxed{q(a)} \equiv r(a)$	
	G7. $\boxed{p(x) \equiv r(x)}^{+}$

Applying the *AA-equivalence* rule (right-to-left) to assertions A5 and A6, with unifier $\{x \leftarrow a\}$, we can replace $q(a)$ with $p(a)$ in assertion A6, obtaining

A8. $\boxed{p(a) \equiv r(a)}^{-}$	

Finally, by the *AG-resolution* rule, applied to assertion A8 and goal G7, with unifier $\{x \leftarrow a\}$, we obtain the goal

	G9. *true*

⌐

We conclude the chapter with two remarks about skolemization.

Remark (why new skolem function?)

Let us see why it is important to choose new skolem constant and function symbols.

We "prove" the sentence

$$\text{if } (\exists x)p(x) \text{ then } p(a).$$

This sentence is actually not valid; it is false under any interpretation for which $p(a)$ is false but $p(x)$ is true for some other domain element.

The initial tableau is

assertions	goals
	G1. *if* $(\exists x)^{\forall} p(x)$ *then* $p(a)$

Then, by the ∀-*elimination* rule (erroneously applied), we obtain the goal

> *if p(a) then p(a),*

which is simplified to the final goal

	G2. *true*

In other words, we proved a nonvalid sentence.

The problem is that, in applying the rule, x was replaced by the constant symbol a, which is not a new constant, since it already occurs in the sentence.

A correct application of the ∀-*elimination* rule will yield the goal

	G2'. *if p(b) then p(a)*

Here x has been replaced by the new constant symbol b. This goal cannot be simplified to the final goal *true*. ⌟

Remark (automatic outermost skolemization)

If an assertion is universally quantified, i.e., if it is of form

$(\forall\ x_1,\ \ldots,x_m)^{\exists}\mathcal{A}$	

then the outermost universal quantifiers are of strict existential force. Therefore we can drop them by repeatedly applying the ∃-*elimination* rule, obtaining the assertion

$\mathcal{A}$	

Similarly, we can drop the outermost existential quantifiers of an existentially quantified goal

	$(\exists\ x_1,\ \ldots,x_m)^{\exists}\mathcal{G}$

to obtain

	$\mathcal{G}$

To simplify the exposition, we shall often drop such quantifiers automatically, without mentioning the application of the rule or the intermediate steps. For example, instead of writing the assertion

$(\forall\, x)(\exists\, y)p(x,\, y)$	

we shall immediately write

$(\exists\, y)p(x,\, y)$	

The reader is requested (in **Problem 11.2**) to prove the validity of several sentences.

PROBLEMS

Problem 11.1 (associated sentence)   page 430

Show that the associated sentence of assertions $\mathcal{A}_1, \mathcal{A}_2, \ldots, \mathcal{A}_m$ and goals $\mathcal{G}_1, \mathcal{G}_2, \ldots, \mathcal{G}_n$ is equivalent to the sentence

$$(\exists *) \begin{bmatrix} \textit{if } (\mathcal{A}_1 \ \textit{and} \ \mathcal{A}_2 \ \textit{and} \ \ldots \ \textit{and} \ \mathcal{A}_m) \\ \textit{then } (\mathcal{G}_1 \ \textit{or} \ \mathcal{G}_2 \ \textit{or} \ \ldots \ \textit{or} \ \mathcal{G}_n) \end{bmatrix} .$$

Problem 11.2 (tableau proofs of valid sentences)   page 494

Use the deductive-tableau system to prove the validity of the following sentences:

(a) $\begin{array}{l} \textit{if } (\forall x)p(x) \ \textit{or} \ (\forall x)r(x) \\ \textit{then } (\forall x)\big[p(x) \ \textit{or} \ r(x)\big] \end{array}$

(b) $\begin{array}{l} \textit{if } (\forall x)\,p(x) \\ \textit{then } p(a) \end{array}$

(c) $\begin{array}{l} \textit{if } (\forall x)\big[p(x) \ \equiv \ \neg q(x)\big] \\ \textit{then } \big((\exists x)\,p(x)\big) \ \equiv \ \big(\neg(\forall x)\,q(x)\big) \end{array}$

(d)   if $\begin{bmatrix} (\forall x,\, y,\, z) \begin{bmatrix} if\ p(x,\, y)\ and\ p(y,\, z) \\ then\ p(x,\, z) \end{bmatrix} \\ and \\ (\forall x)\,[not\ p(x,\, x)] \end{bmatrix}$ then $(\forall x,\, y) \begin{bmatrix} if\ p(x,\, y) \\ then\ not\ p(y,\, x) \end{bmatrix}$

(e)   if $\begin{bmatrix} (\exists x)\, p(f(x)) \\ and \\ (\forall x)\,[if\ p(x)\ then\ p(f(x))] \end{bmatrix}$ then $(\exists x)\, p(f(f(f(x))))$.

(f)   if $\begin{bmatrix} (\forall x)\,[p(x,\, f(x))\ \ or\ \ p(f(x),\, x)] \\ and \\ (\forall x,\, y)\,[if\ p(x,\, y)\ then\ p(f(x),\, f(y))] \end{bmatrix}$

then $(\forall x)(\exists y)p(f(x),\, y)$

(g)   if $\begin{bmatrix} (\forall x)(\exists y)\,[if\ p(x,\, f(y))\ then\ q(x)] \\ and \\ (\exists x)\,[not\ q(x)]\ \equiv\ (\forall x,\, y)p(x,\, y) \end{bmatrix}$

then $(\forall z)q(z)$.

12

Special
Theories

We have introduced a deductive-tableau system to prove the validity of sentences in predicate logic. In this chapter, we adapt the system to prove validity in special theories, including theories with induction.

12.1 FINITE THEORIES

In our discussion of special theories in predicate logic (Section [I]4.1), we showed how to describe a particular theory by presenting a (possibly infinite) set of closed sentences,

$$\mathcal{A}_1, \ \mathcal{A}_2, \ \mathcal{A}_3, \ \ldots,$$

which are the axioms of the theory. We defined an interpretation to be a *model* of the theory if each axiom $\mathcal{A}_i$ of the theory is true under the interpretation. A closed sentence $\mathcal{S}$ of the theory is *valid* in the theory if $\mathcal{S}$ is true under every model for the theory. Similarly, two sentences are *equivalent* in the theory if they have the same truth-value under every model for the theory.

For instance, we defined the theory of strict partial orderings by the two axioms

$$\mathcal{A}_1: \quad (\forall x,\, y,\, z) \begin{bmatrix} if\ \ x \prec y\ \ and\ \ y \prec z \\ then\ \ x \prec z \end{bmatrix} \qquad (transitivity)$$

$$\mathcal{A}_2: \quad (\forall x)[not\ (x \prec x)] \qquad\qquad\qquad (irreflexivity)$$

Here we take $\prec$ to stand for any binary predicate symbol. This theory has many models, including the less-than ordering $<$ over the nonnegative integers and the proper-subset relation $\subset$ over the sets. To determine that a closed sentence S is valid in the strict partial-ordering theory, we must establish that S is true under all these models.

A *tableau of a theory* is a tableau whose constant, function, and predicate symbols all belong to the vocabulary of the theory. A tableau is said to be *valid in a theory* if its associated sentence is valid in the theory, and two tableaux are said to be *equivalent in a theory* if their associated sentences are equivalent in the theory.

Suppose we wish to prove that a closed sentence S is valid in a *finite theory*, that is, one defined by a finite set of axioms. In the deductive-tableau framework, we can do this by proving the initial tableau

assertions	goals
$\mathcal{A}_1$	
$\mathcal{A}_2$	
$\vdots$	
$\mathcal{A}_n$	
	S

where each assertion $\mathcal{A}_i$ is a sentence known to be valid in the theory, either because it is an axiom or because it has been previously proved valid in the theory. A sentence that has been proved valid in a theory is called a *theorem of the theory*.

For example, to establish that a closed sentence S is valid in the theory of strict partial orderings, defined by the *transitivity* and *irreflexivity* axioms, we prove the initial tableau

assertions		goals
$\mathcal{A}_1$:	$\begin{array}{l} \textit{if } x \prec y \textit{ and } y \prec z \\ \textit{then } x \prec z \end{array}$ (*transitivity*)	
$\mathcal{A}_2$: $\textit{not } (x \prec x)$	(*irreflexivity*)	
		$\mathcal{S}$

Here, by automatic outermost skolemization, we have dropped the outermost universal quantifiers from the two assertions. (Because any finite theory has new symbols, we can also use the $\forall$-*elimination* rule in proving the validity of the tableau.)

Once we have proved the validity of a sentence in the theory of strict partial orderings, we may add $\mathcal{S}$ as an assertion in any future tableaux over the theory.

Example (theory of strict partial orderings)

Suppose we would like to show that the *asymmetry* property is valid in the theory of strict partial orderings, that is,

$$(\forall x, y) \begin{bmatrix} \textit{if } x \prec y \\ \textit{then } \textit{not } (y \prec x) \end{bmatrix} \qquad (\textit{asymmetry})$$

For this purpose it suffices to prove the tableau

assertions	goals
$\begin{array}{l} \textit{if } x \prec y \textit{ and } y \prec z \\ \textit{then } x \prec z \end{array}$ (*transitivity*)	
$\textit{not } (x \prec x)$ (*irreflexivity*)	
	G1. $(\forall x, y)^{\forall} \begin{bmatrix} \textit{if } x \prec y \\ \textit{then } \textit{not } (y \prec x) \end{bmatrix}$

Note that we did not number the two axioms (as A1 and A2). We shall usually refer to such assertions (axioms or theorems) by name.

Applying the $\forall$-*elimination* rule twice in succession to goal G1, replacing the bound variables x and y with the skolem constants a and b, respectively, we obtain the goal

	G2. *if $a \prec b$* *then not $(b \prec a)$*

By the *if-split* rule, this decomposes into

A3. $\boxed{a \prec b}$ $^-$	

	G4. *not* $\boxed{b \prec a}$ $^-$

By the *resolution* rule, applied to assertion A3 and the *transitivity* axiom

if $\boxed{x \prec y}$ $^+$ *and* $y \prec z$ *then* $x \prec z$	

with $\{x \leftarrow a,\ y \leftarrow b\}$, we obtain

A5. *if* $\boxed{b \prec z}$ $^+$ *then* $a \prec z$	

By the *resolution* rule, applied to goal G4 and assertion A5, with $\{z \leftarrow a\}$, we obtain

	G6. $\boxed{not\ (a \prec a)}$ $^+$

By the *resolution* rule, applied to the *irreflexivity* axiom

$\boxed{not\ (x \prec x)}$ $^-$	

and goal G6, we obtain the final goal

	G7. *true*

Note that henceforth we do not indicate which of the dual forms (AA, AG, and so on) of the *resolution* or *equivalence* rule is being applied; this should be evident.

Because we have proved the validity of the *asymmetry* property, we may add it as an assertion in future proofs within the theory of strict partial orderings.

Example (family theory)

In Section [I]4.1, we defined a theory of family relationships. In the "family" interpretation I we have in mind, the domain is the set of people, and, intuitively, for the function symbols f and m,

$f(x)$ is the father of x

$m(x)$ is the mother of x,

and, for the predicate symbols p, gf, and gm,

$p(x, y)$ means y is a parent of x

$gf(x, y)$ means y is a grandfather of x

$gm(x, y)$ means y is a grandmother of x.

(We have changed the notation slightly to give it mnemonic associations.) We define the theory by the following set of axioms:

$(\forall x)p(x, f(x))$	(*father*)
$(\forall x)p(x, m(x))$	(*mother*)
$(\forall x, y)[if\ p(x, y)\ then\ gf(x, f(y))]$	(*grandfather*)
$(\forall x, y)[if\ p(x, y)\ then\ gm(x, m(y))]$	(*grandmother*)

That is, everyone's father or mother is his or her parent, and the father [mother] of one's parent is his or her grandfather [grandmother].

In this *family theory* we gave an informal argument to show the validity of the sentence

$$(\forall x)(\exists z)gm(x, z),$$

that is, everyone has a grandmother. We can now prove it as a theorem in the theory using the deductive-tableau system.

We begin with the tableau

assertions		goals
$p(x, f(x))$	(*father*)	

$p(x, m(x))$	*(mother)*	
if $p(x, y)$ *then* $gf(x, f(y))$	*(grandfather)*	
if $p(x, y)$ *then* $gm(x, m(y))$	*(grandmother)*	
		G1.　$(\forall x)^{\vee}(\exists z)^{\exists} gm(x, z)$

By the ∀-*elimination* and ∃-*elimination* rules, we may drop the quantifiers of goal G1, to obtain

	G2.　$\boxed{gm(a, z)}^{+}$

The bound variable x, whose quantifier is of universal force in goal G1, is replaced by the skolem constant a in forming goal G2.

Applying the *resolution* rule to the *grandmother* axiom

if $p(x, y)$ *then* $\boxed{gm(x, m(y))}^{-}$	

and goal G2, with $\{x \leftarrow a,\ z \leftarrow m(y)\}$, we derive the goal

	G3.　$\boxed{p(a, y)}^{+}$

By the *resolution* rule, applied to the *father* axiom

$\boxed{p(x, f(x))}^{-}$	

and goal G3, with $\{x \leftarrow a,\ y \leftarrow f(a)\}$, we obtain the final goal

	G4.　*true*

The reader may observe that the deductive-tableau proof reflects the informal reasoning of Volume I. In **Problem 12.1**, the reader is requested to carry out a deductive-tableau proof in a simple theory.

If a theory is defined by an infinite set of axioms, we cannot include all the axioms as assertions, because each tableau can have only a finite number of assertions. Instead, we extend the system by introducing a new deduction rule that takes the place of infinitely many axioms. In the next section, we illustrate this for the theory of equality.

12.2   EQUALITY RULE

If we want to prove the validity of a sentence S in a theory with equality, the most straightforward approach is to add the equality axioms as assertions of our initial tableau. We have three simple axioms and two axiom schemata. The three axioms are

$$
(\forall\, x,\, y,\, z) \begin{bmatrix} if \;\; x = y \;\; and \;\; y = z \\ then \;\; x = z \end{bmatrix} \qquad\qquad (transitivity)
$$

$$
(\forall\, x,\, y) \begin{bmatrix} if \;\; x = y \\ then \;\; y = x \end{bmatrix} \qquad\qquad (symmetry)
$$

$$
(\forall\, x)[x = x] \qquad\qquad (reflexivity)
$$

The two axiom schemata are

For every function symbol f, we have the axiom

$$
(\forall\, x, y, \bar z) \begin{bmatrix} if \;\; x = y \\ then \begin{bmatrix} f(z_1,\, \ldots,\, z_{i-1},\, x,\, z_{i+1},\, \ldots,\, z_k) \\ = \\ f(z_1,\, \ldots,\, z_{i-1},\, y,\, z_{i+1},\, \ldots,\, z_k) \end{bmatrix} \end{bmatrix} \begin{pmatrix} functional \\ substitutivity \end{pmatrix}
$$

For every predicate symbol p, we have the axiom

$$
(\forall\, x, y, \bar z) \begin{bmatrix} if \;\; x = y \\ then \begin{bmatrix} p(z_1,\, \ldots,\, z_{j-1},\, x,\, z_{j+1},\, \ldots,\, z_\ell) \\ \equiv \\ p(z_1,\, \ldots,\, z_{j-1},\, y,\, z_{j+1},\, \ldots,\, z_\ell) \end{bmatrix} \end{bmatrix} \begin{pmatrix} predicate \\ substitutivity \end{pmatrix}
$$

The *functional-substitutivity* axiom schema actually represents a set of axioms: one for every k-ary function symbol f in the vocabulary of the theory and for each i from 1 through k. Similarly, the *predicate-substitutivity* axiom schema represents a set of axioms: one for every ℓ-ary predicate symbol p (other than $=$) in the vocabulary of the theory and for each j from 1 through ℓ.

This approach fails if there are infinitely many function symbols in the vocabulary because we can only have finitely many assertions in a tableau. Even if there are only finitely many function symbols, the number of assertions required may be too large. A more practical approach is to drop the *symmetry, transitivity, functional-substitutivity,* and *predicate-substitutivity* assertions altogether (leaving only the *reflexivity* assertion) and introduce instead a special *equality* rule, which resembles the *equivalence* rule for predicate logic and enables us to treat equality in an efficient way.

THE BASIC FORM

The basic form of the equality rule is expressed as follows.

Rule (AA-equality, left-to-right)

assertions	goals
$\mathcal{A}_1\left[\,\overline{s=t}\,\right]$	
$\mathcal{A}_2\left\langle\,\overline{s'}\,\right\rangle$	
$\mathcal{A}_1\theta\left[\,\overline{false}\,\right]$ *or* $\mathcal{A}_2\theta\left\langle\,\overline{t\theta}\,\right\rangle$	

where

- $\overline{s = t}$ stands for the free, quantifier-free equalities $s_1 = t_1, \ldots,$ $s_k = t_k$ $(k \geq 1)$, which occur in $\mathcal{A}_1$.

- $\overline{s'}$ stands for the free, quantifier-free subterms $s'_1, \ldots, s'_\ell (\ell \geq 1)$, which occur in $\mathcal{A}_2$.

- θ is a most-general unifier for the subterms $\overline{s}$, $\overline{s'}$ and for the subterms $\overline{t}$; that is, $\overline{s}\theta$ and $\overline{s'}\theta$ are all identical terms and $\overline{t}\theta$ are all identical terms.

- $\overline{false}$ stands for *false*, $\ldots$, *false* $(k$ times$)$.

- $\overline{t\theta}$ stands for $t_1\theta, \ldots, t_\ell\theta$. ⌟

More precisely, to apply the *AA-equality* rule to two assertions $\mathcal{A}_1$ and $\mathcal{A}_2$ of a tableau,

- Rename the variables of $\mathcal{A}_1$ and $\mathcal{A}_2$ if necessary to ensure that they have no free variables in common.

- Select free, quantifier-free subsentences of $\mathcal{A}_1$,

$$\overline{s = t}: \quad s_1 = t_1, \quad \ldots, \quad s_k = t_k \qquad (k \geq 1),$$

and select free, quantifier-free subterms of $\mathcal{A}_2$,

$$\overline{s'}: \quad s'_1, \quad \ldots, \quad s'_\ell \qquad (\ell \geq 1),$$

such that there exists a most-general unifier θ that unifies $s_1, \ldots, s_k, s'_1, \ldots, s'_\ell$ and also unifies $t_1, \ldots, t_k$; that is,

  - $s_1\theta, \quad \ldots, \quad s_k\theta$ and $s'_1\theta, \quad \ldots, \quad s'_\ell\theta$ are all the same term, which we shall call $s\theta$.

  - $t_1\theta, \quad \ldots, \quad t_k\theta$ are all the same term, which we shall call $t\theta$. We require that $s\theta$ and $t\theta$ be distinct.

- Apply θ to the assertion $\mathcal{A}_1$ and replace all free occurrences of $s\theta = t\theta$ in $\mathcal{A}_1\theta$ with *false*, obtaining the disjunct

$$\mathcal{A}_1\theta\left[\,\overline{false}\,\right].$$

- Apply θ to the assertion $\mathcal{A}_2$ and replace one or more occurrences of $s\theta$ in $\mathcal{A}_2\theta$ with $t\theta$, obtaining the disjunct

$$\mathcal{A}_2\theta\langle\,\overline{t\theta}\,\rangle.$$

- Take the disjunction

$$\mathcal{A}_1\theta\left[\,\overline{false}\,\right] \quad \text{or} \quad \mathcal{A}_2\theta\langle\,\overline{t\theta}\,\rangle$$

and apply to it all possible simplifications.

- Add the simplified disjunction to the tableau as a new assertion.

Remark (at least one replacement)

Although the substitution notation admits the possibility that no equality $\overline{s = t}$ actually occurs in $\mathcal{A}_1$, the wording of the rule requires that some equalities actually do occur. Similarly, we require that at least one subterm of $\mathcal{A}_2\theta$ actually be replaced, even though the notation does not imply this. Otherwise, there would be no point in applying the rule. For the same reason, we do not apply the rule if $s\theta$ and $t\theta$ are identical. ◢

The *equality* rule allows us to drop the *symmetry, transitivity, functional-substitutivity,* and *predicate-substitutivity* axioms from our tableau; we must still retain as an assertion the simple *reflexivity* axiom

$$(\forall x)[x = x].$$

We also have the following *right-to-left version* of the *equality* rule.

Rule (AA-equality, right-to-left)

assertions	goals
$\mathcal{A}_1\big[\,\overline{s = t}\,\big]$	
$\mathcal{A}_2\big\langle\,\overline{t'}\,\big\rangle$	
$\mathcal{A}_1\theta\big[\,\overline{false}\,\big]$ or $\mathcal{A}_2\theta\big\langle\,\overline{s\theta}\,\big\rangle$	

where $\mathcal{A}_1$ and $\mathcal{A}_2$ satisfy the same restrictions as in the left-to-right version of the rule. ◢

This rule allows us to replace occurrences of $t\theta$ in $\mathcal{A}_2\theta$ with $s\theta$, rather than the other way around.

POLARITY

The *polarity* strategy for the *AA-equivalence* rule can also be applied to both versions of the *equality* rule.

Strategy (polarity)

An application of the *AA-equality* rule is in accordance with the *polarity strategy* if at least one of the occurrences of

$$s_1 = t_1, \quad \ldots, \quad s_k = t_k$$

in $\mathcal{A}_1$, whose instances are replaced by *false* in applying the rule, is of negative polarity in the tableau. ⌙

In the *polarity* strategy, the negative polarity need not be strict; the occurrence in question may actually have both polarities. Note that the *polarity* strategy places no restriction on the polarity of the subterms $s'_1, \ldots, s'_\ell$ of $\mathcal{A}_2$.

Example

Suppose our tableau contains the assertions

assertions	goals
$\mathcal{A}_1$: $\quad$ if $r(x)$ $\quad$ then $\left[\boxed{f(x,\, a)} = g(x,\, y)\right]^{-}$	
$\mathcal{A}_2$: $\quad q\left(\boxed{f(b,\, z)},\, y,\, z\right)$	

Let us apply the *AA-equality* rule, left-to-right, to $\mathcal{A}_1$ and $\mathcal{A}_2$. The subterms to be matched are indicated by boxes.

Note that $\mathcal{A}_1$ and $\mathcal{A}_2$ have the free variable y in common. We therefore rename y as $\widehat{y}$ in $\mathcal{A}_2$, to obtain the assertion

$$\widehat{\mathcal{A}_2} : \quad q\left(\boxed{f(b,\, z)},\, \widehat{y},\, z\right).$$

Consider the free subsentence

$$s = t : \quad f(x,\, a) = g(x,\, y)$$

in $\mathcal{A}_1$ and the free subterm

$$s' : \quad f(b, z)$$

in $\widehat{\mathcal{A}_2}$. The terms

$$s : \quad f(x,\, a) \quad \text{and} \quad s' : \quad f(b,\, z)$$

are unifiable under the most-general unifier

$$\theta : \quad \{x \leftarrow b,\, z \leftarrow a\};$$

the unified terms $s\theta$ and $s'\theta$ are identical to $f(b, a)$.

Applying θ to $\mathcal{A}_1$, we obtain

$$\mathcal{A}_1\theta : \quad \textit{if } r(b) \textit{ then } f(b, a) = g(b, y),$$

where the unified equality is

$$(s = t)\theta : \quad f(b, a) = g(b, y).$$

Replacing the equality $f(b, a) = g(b, y)$ with the truth symbol *false* in $\mathcal{A}_1\theta$, we obtain

$$\mathcal{A}_1^* : \quad \textit{if } r(b) \textit{ then false.}$$

Applying θ to $\widehat{\mathcal{A}_2}$, we obtain

$$\widehat{\mathcal{A}_2}\theta : \quad q\big(f(b, a), \, \widehat{y}, \, a\big).$$

Replacing the subterm $s\theta : f(b, a)$ with $t\theta : g(b, y)$ in $\widehat{\mathcal{A}_2}\theta$, we obtain

$$\mathcal{A}_2^* : \quad q\big(g(b, y), \, \widehat{y}, \, a\big).$$

Forming the disjunction $(\mathcal{A}_1^* \textit{ or } \mathcal{A}_2^*)$, we obtain

$$\textit{if } r(b) \quad \textit{then } \textit{false}$$
$$\textit{or}$$
$$q\big(g(b, y), \, \widehat{y}, \, a\big).$$

This reduces (under *true-false* simplification) to the new assertion

not $r(b)$ *or* $q\big(g(b, y), \, \widehat{y}, \, a\big)$	

which is added to the tableau.

As usual, we do not add the intermediate sentences $\widehat{\mathcal{A}_2}$, $\mathcal{A}_1\theta$, $\widehat{\mathcal{A}_2}\theta$, $\mathcal{A}_1^*$, $\mathcal{A}_2^*$, or the simplified disjunction to the tableau.

This application of the rule is in accordance with the *polarity* strategy because the occurrence of the equality

$$f(x, a) = g(x, y)$$

in $\mathcal{A}_1$ is negative in the tableau.   ⌟

JUSTIFICATION

To justify the *AA-equality* rule, we must show that the old (given) tableau is equivalent to the new tableau. The justification of the *AA-equality* rule is analogous to that of the *AA-equivalence* rule. We justify the left-to-right version of the rule. Because the rule preserves equivalence, we can use the *special justification* corollary, rather than the *general justification* proposition, in the proof.

Justification (*AA-equality*)

   Suppose that A_1 and A_2 are two assertions that satisfy the restrictions for applying the *AA-equality* rule. Let I be an interpretation for A_1 and A_2 under which the required tableau T_r is false; that is, the universal closures of the required assertions A_1 and A_2 are both true under I.

   By the *special justification* corollary, it suffices to establish that the generated tableau T_g is false under I, that is, that the universal closure of the generated assertion, the simplified disjunction

$$A_1\theta\left[\,\overline{false}\,\right]$$
$$or$$
$$A_2\theta\langle\,\overline{t\theta}\,\rangle,$$

is also true under I.

   Because the universal closures of A_1 and A_2 are true, the universal closures of $A_1\theta$ and $A_2\theta$ are also true under I, by the *universal closure-instantiation* proposition. Therefore, by the *semantic rule for universal closure* proposition, $A_1\theta$ and $A_2\theta$ are themselves true under any extension of I to the free variables of $A_1\theta$ and $A_2\theta$. Let I' be any such extension.

   The proof now distinguishes between two cases.

Case: $(s = t)\theta$ is false under I'

   Then, because $A_1\theta$ is true, and because $(s = t)\theta$ and the propositional constant *false* have the same truth-value under I',

$$A_1\theta\left[\,\overline{false}\,\right]$$

is also true under I'. It follows (by the semantic rule for the *or* connective) that the (simplified) disjunction

$$A_1\theta\left[\,\overline{false}\,\right]$$
$$or$$
$$A_2\theta\langle\,\overline{t\theta}\,\rangle$$

is also true under I'.

Case: $(s = t)\theta$ is true under I'

That is, $s\theta = t\theta$ is true under I'. Then, by the *substitutivity of equality* proposition (Section [I]5.1), we have that

$$\mathcal{A}_2\theta\langle\,\overline{s\theta}\,\rangle \;\equiv\; \mathcal{A}_2\theta\langle\,\overline{t\theta}\,\rangle$$

is true under I'. Hence, because $\mathcal{A}_2\theta$ is true under I',

$$\mathcal{A}_2\theta\langle\,\overline{t\theta}\,\rangle$$

is also true under I'. It follows (by the semantic rule for the *or* connective) that the (simplified) disjunction

$$\mathcal{A}_1\theta\big[\,\overline{false}\,\big]$$
$$or$$
$$\mathcal{A}_2\theta\langle\,\overline{t\theta}\,\rangle$$

is true under I'.

In each case, we have concluded that the generated assertion, the simplified disjunction

$$\mathcal{A}_1\theta\big[\,\overline{false}\,\big]$$
$$or$$
$$\mathcal{A}_2\theta\langle\,\overline{t\theta}\,\rangle,$$

is true under I', for any extension I' of I to the free variables of $\mathcal{A}_1\theta$ and $\mathcal{A}_2\theta$, and hence to the free variables of the new assertion. Therefore (by the *semantic rule for universal closure* proposition), the universal closure of the generated assertion is true under I, as we wanted to prove. ⌟

The justification of the right-to-left version of the rule depends on the symmetry of equality.

DUAL FORMS

We have given the AA-form of the rule, which applies to two assertions. By duality, we can apply the rule to an assertion and a goal, or to two goals. We present only the AG-form (left-to-right version), which applies to an assertion and a goal. This is the most commonly used form.

Rule (AG-equality, left-to-right)

assertions	goals
$\mathcal{A}\big[\,\boxed{s=t}\,\big]$	
	$\mathcal{G}\langle\,\overline{s'}\,\rangle$
	$not\ \big(\mathcal{A}\theta\big[\,\overline{false}\,\big]\big)$
	and
	$\mathcal{G}\theta\langle\overline{t\theta}\rangle$

where $\mathcal{A}$ and $\mathcal{G}$ satisfy the same conditions as $\mathcal{A}_1$ and $\mathcal{A}_2$, respectively, in the AA-*equality* rule. ⌋

There are analogous right-to-left forms. The justification of the dual forms of the *equality* rule follows by duality.

The *polarity* strategy for each dual form of the rule is analogous to that for the AA-*equality* rule: at least one of the free occurrences of $s_1 = t_1,\ \ldots,\ s_k = t_k$, which are replaced by *false* in applying the rule, should be negative in the tableau.

Example

Suppose our tableau contains the assertion and goal

assertions	goals
$\mathcal{A}:\ \big[f(x,\,y)\ =\ \boxed{g(x,\,a)}\,\big]^{-}$	
	$\mathcal{G}:\ (\forall y)\ q\Big(\,\boxed{g(b,\,z)}\,,\,y,\,z\Big)$

Let us apply the AG-*equality* rule, right-to-left, to assertion $\mathcal{A}$ and goal $\mathcal{G}$. The subterms to be matched are indicated with boxes. Note that $\mathcal{A}$ and $\mathcal{G}$ have no free variables in common.

Consider the free subsentence

$$s = t:\quad f(x,\,y)\ =\ g(x,\,a)$$

in $\mathcal{A}$, which has a negative polarity in the tableau, and consider the free subterm

$$t':\quad g(b,\,z)$$

in $\mathcal{G}$.

The terms

$$t: \ g(x, a) \qquad \text{and} \qquad t': \ g(b, z)$$

are unifiable under the most-general unifier

$$\theta: \ \{x \leftarrow b, \ z \leftarrow a\};$$

the unified term is $g(b, a)$.

We apply θ to the assertion $\mathcal{A}$ and the goal $\mathcal{G}$, obtaining

$$\mathcal{A}\theta: \ f(b, y) \ = \ g(b, a)$$

and

$$\mathcal{G}\theta: \ (\forall y)q(g(b, a), y, a),$$

respectively. Replacing the equality

$$(s = t)\theta: \ \ f(b, y) = g(b, a)$$

in $\mathcal{A}\theta$ with *false*, and (safely) replacing the subterm

$$t\theta: \ \ g(b, a)$$

in $\mathcal{G}\theta$ with

$$s\theta: \ \ f(b, y),$$

we obtain the new goal

> *not false*
>   *and*
> $(\forall y') \, q\big(f(b, y), \, y', \, a\big).$

Note that we have renamed the variable y of the quantifier $(\forall y)$ as y' to avoid capturing the free occurrence of y in $f(b, y)$.

The new goal reduces (by *true-false* simplification) to

	$(\forall y') \, q\big(f(b, y), \, y', \, a\big)$

In **Problem 12.2**, the reader is requested to show that the *transitivity* and *symmetry* of equality can actually be proved in a tableau with the *equality* rule.

12.3 FINITE THEORIES WITH EQUALITY

A tableau that includes among its initial assertions the *reflexivity* axiom and to which we may apply the *equality* rule, as well as any of the predicate-logic rules, will be called a *tableau with equality*.

We have seen that we can prove a sentence S within a particular finite theory by adding the axioms for the theory as the initial assertions in a predicate-logic tableau, and adding S as the initial goal. In the same way, if we want to prove a sentence S in a finite theory with equality (that is, one defined by the equality axioms plus a finite set of special axioms), we may add the special axioms as the initial assertions of a tableau with equality that has S as its initial goal.

In the following sections, we apply the deductive-tableau framework to prove the validity of sentences in several finite theories with equality. We start with the theory of weak partial orderings.

THEORY OF WEAK PARTIAL ORDERINGS

We have earlier defined (Section [I]5.2) the theory of weak partial orderings as the theory with equality whose special axioms are

$$(\forall x, y, z) \begin{bmatrix} if \ \ x \preceq y \ \ and \ \ y \preceq z \\ then \ \ x \preceq z \end{bmatrix} \qquad (transitivity)$$

$$(\forall x, y) \begin{bmatrix} if \ \ x \preceq y \ \ and \ \ y \preceq x \\ then \ \ x = y \end{bmatrix} \qquad (antisymmetry)$$

$$(\forall x)[x \preceq x] \qquad (reflexivity)$$

To prove the validity of a sentence S in the theory of weak partial orderings within the tableau framework, we need only prove the following tableau with equality:

assertions		goals
if $x \preceq y$ and $y \preceq z$ then $x \preceq z$	(*transitivity*)	
if $x \preceq y$ and $y \preceq x$ then $x = y$	(*antisymmetry*)	

$x \preceq x$ (*reflexivity*)	
	S

Here again, by automatic outermost skolemization, we have dropped the outermost universal quantifiers from the initial assertions.

Recall that, because this is a tableau with equality, we also include the *reflexivity* axiom $(x = x)$ among our initial assertions, and during the proof we may apply the *equality* rule (both the left-to-right and right-to-left versions) as well as the other predicate-logic rules. We need not include the axioms for equality (other than *reflexivity*) as assertions in the tableau.

Example (irreflexive restriction)

Consider the augmented theory formed by adding to the theory of weak partial orderings the following axiom, which defines the *irreflexive restriction* $\prec$ associated with the given weak partial ordering $\preceq$:

$(\forall x, y) \begin{bmatrix} x \prec y \\ \equiv \\ x \preceq y \ \ and \ \ not\,(x = y) \end{bmatrix}$	(*irreflexive restriction*)

It can then be shown that $\prec$ is indeed a strict partial ordering, i.e., that $\prec$ is transitive and irreflexive. We show the irreflexivity of $\prec$ here; its transitivity is left as an exercise (**Problem 12.3**).

Suppose we would like to show the validity of the *irreflexivity* property

$$(\forall x)\big[not\,(x \prec x)\big] \qquad\qquad (\textit{irreflexivity})$$

in this theory.

We begin with a tableau over the weak partial orderings that contains, in addition to the *reflexivity* axiom for equality and the axioms for a weak partial ordering, the definition of the irreflexive-restriction relation

assertions	goals
$\begin{bmatrix} \boxed{x \prec y} \\ \equiv \\ x \preceq y \ \ and \ \ not\,(x = y) \end{bmatrix}^{-}$ (*irreflexive restriction*)	

as an initial assertion and the desired *irreflexivity* property,

	G1. $(\forall x)^{\vee}[not\ (x \prec x)]$

as its initial goal.

By the $\forall$-*elimination* rule, we may drop the quantifier $(\forall x)^{\vee}$ from the initial goal G1, replacing the bound variable x with the skolem constant a, to obtain

	G2. $not\ \boxed{a \prec a}$

Applying the *equivalence* rule to the *irreflexive restriction* axiom and goal G2, with $\{x \leftarrow a,\ y \leftarrow a\}$, we obtain the goal

	G3. $not\ \left(a \preceq a\ and\ not\ \boxed{a = a}^{+}\right)$

Applying the *resolution* rule to the *reflexivity* axiom for equality,

and goal G3, we obtain the final goal

	G4. $true$

In **Problem 12.4** the reader is requested to prove the corresponding results about the reflexive closure $\preceq$ associated with a given strict partial ordering $\prec$ in the theory of strict partial orderings.

Remark (reflexivity of equality)

In the final step of the previous example, we applied the *resolution* rule to goal G3 and the *reflexivity* axiom $x = x$, to obtain the goal G4. Resolution with the *reflexivity* axiom is a frequent step in proofs in theories with equality. It will be convenient for us to apply this step automatically whenever a (positive) subsentence of form $t = t$ appears. We may then say that goal G4 is obtained from goal G3 "by the reflexivity of equality," without giving the assertion or mentioning the resolution step. We shall still annotate the subsentence $(a = a)$ in G3 with a box indicating its positive polarity.

THEORY OF GROUPS

We have defined the theory of groups (Section [I]5.4) as the theory with equality whose special axioms are

$(\forall x)\big[x \circ e \ = \ x\big]$	(*right identity*)
$(\forall x)\big[x \circ x^{-1} \ = \ e\big]$	(*right inverse*)
$(\forall x,\, y,\, z)\big[(x \circ y) \circ z \ = \ x \circ (y \circ z)\big]$	(*associativity*)

To prove the validity of a sentence $\mathcal{S}$ in this theory, we must prove the following tableau with equality:

assertions		goals
$x \circ e \ = \ x$	(*right identity*)	
$x \circ x^{-1} = e$	(*right inverse*)	
$(x \circ y) \circ z = x \circ (y \circ z)$	(*associativity*)	
		$\mathcal{S}$

Again, because this is a tableau with equality, it includes implicitly the *reflexivity* axiom $(x = x)$ among its assertions, and during the proof we may apply the *equality* rule, as well as the other predicate-logic deduction rules.

Example (**right cancellation**)

Suppose we would like to prove the validity of the property

$$(\forall x,\, y,\, z) \begin{bmatrix} if & x \circ z = y \circ z \\ then & x = y \end{bmatrix} \qquad (\textit{right cancellation})$$

in the theory of groups. Our deductive-tableau proof resembles the informal proof of the same proposition in Section [I]5.4.

We consider the initial goal

assertions	goals
	G1. $(\forall x,\, y,\, z)^{\forall} \begin{bmatrix} if & x \circ z = y \circ z \\ then & x = y \end{bmatrix}$

By the ∀-*elimination* rule, we may drop the quantifiers from goal G1, replacing the bound variables x, y, and z with skolem constants a, b, and c, respectively, to obtain

	G2. *if* $a \circ c = b \circ c$ *then* $a = b$

By the *if-split* rule, we decompose goal G2 into the assertion and goal

A3. $\left[\,\boxed{a \circ c}\, = b \circ c\,\right]^{-}$	
	G4. $\boxed{a} = b$

Applying the *equality* rule (right-to-left) to the *right-identity* axiom,

$\left[x \circ e\, = \boxed{x}\,\right]^{-}$	

and goal G4, with $\{x \leftarrow a\}$, we replace a with $a \circ e$ in the goal, to obtain

	G5. $a \circ e = \boxed{b}$

Applying the *equality* rule (right-to-left) once more to the *right-identity* axiom and goal G5, with $\{x \leftarrow b\}$, we replace b with $b \circ e$ in the goal, to obtain

	G6. $a \circ \boxed{e} = b \circ e$

By the *equality* rule (right-to-left) with the *right-inverse* axiom,

$\left[x \circ x^{-1} = \boxed{e}\,\right]^{-}$	

we replace the annotated occurrence of e in goal G6 with $x \circ x^{-1}$, to obtain

	G7. $a \circ (x \circ x^{-1}) = b \circ \boxed{e}$

We would like to apply the *equality* rule again to the *right-inverse* axiom and goal G7; these rows, however, have the free variable x in common. We rename the variables in these rows to avoid this coincidence, to obtain

$\left[x_1 \circ x_1^{-1} = \boxed{e} \right]^{-}$	
	G7'. $a \circ (x_2 \circ x_2^{-1}) = b \circ \boxed{e}$

(To avoid future renaming, we have actually renamed x in both rows.)

Now we may apply the *equality* rule (right-to-left) to replace e with $x_1 \circ x_1^{-1}$ in goal G7', obtaining

	G8. $\boxed{a \circ (x_2 \circ x_2^{-1})} = \boxed{b \circ (x_1 \circ x_1^{-1})}$

By two applications of the *equality* rule (right-to-left) to the *associativity* axiom,

$\left[(x \circ y) \circ z = \boxed{x \circ (y \circ z)} \right]^{-}$	

and goal G8, with $\{x \leftarrow a,\ y \leftarrow x_2,\ z \leftarrow x_2^{-1}\}$ and then with $\{x \leftarrow b,\ y \leftarrow x_1,\ z \leftarrow x_1^{-1}\}$, we may rewrite the goal as

	G9. $\left(\boxed{a \circ x_2} \right) \circ x_2^{-1} = (b \circ x_1) \circ x_1^{-1}$

By the *equality* rule, applied to assertion A3 and goal G9, with $\{x_2 \leftarrow c\}$, we replace $a \circ x_2$ with $b \circ c$ in the goal, to obtain

	G10. $\boxed{(b \circ c) \circ c^{-1} = (b \circ x_1) \circ x_1^{-1}}^{+}$

At last, applying the *resolution* rule to the *reflexivity* axiom for equality and goal G10, with $\{x_1 \leftarrow c\}$, we obtain the final goal

	G11. *true*

Now that we have proved the *right-cancellation* property, we can add it as an assertion to the tableau of any subsequent group-theory proof. ⌐

In **Problem 12.5** the reader is requested to use the deductive-tableau technique to prove the following properties of the theory of groups:

$$(\forall x)\big[e \circ x = x\big] \qquad\qquad (\textit{left identity})$$

$$(\forall x)\big[x^{-1} \circ x = e\big] \qquad\qquad (\textit{left inverse})$$

$$(\forall x, y, z)\begin{bmatrix} \textit{if } z \circ x = z \circ y \\ \textit{then } x = y \end{bmatrix} \qquad\qquad (\textit{left cancellation})$$

$$(\forall x)\begin{bmatrix} \textit{if } x \circ x = x \\ \textit{then } x = e \end{bmatrix} \qquad\qquad (\textit{nonidempotence})$$

The following example illustrates how, within a special theory, we may define new functions by providing additional special axioms.

Example (**quotient**)

Suppose we define the quotient x/y of two elements x and y of a group by the following axiom:

$$(\forall x, y)\big[x/y = x \circ y^{-1}\big] \qquad\qquad (\textit{quotient})$$

We would like to prove that the *cancellation* property holds, that is,

$$(\forall\ x,\ y)\big[(x/y) \circ y = x\big] \qquad\qquad (\textit{cancellation})$$

We attempt to prove the initial tableau over the groups,

assertions	goals
$\Big[\boxed{x/y} = x \circ y^{-1}\Big]^{-}$ (*quotient*)	
	G1. $(\forall\ x,\ y)^{\forall}\big[(x/y) \circ y = x\big]$

The *quotient* axiom for the quotient function is included among the assertions; because the tableau is over the groups, the group axioms and previously proved group theorems are also present.

By the $\forall$-*elimination* rule, we may drop the quantifiers of goal G1, to obtain

	G2. $\boxed{a/b} \circ b \ = \ a$

By the *equality* rule, applied to the *quotient* axiom and the goal G2, with $\{x \leftarrow a, \ y \leftarrow b\}$, we obtain

	G3. $\boxed{(a \circ b^{-1}) \circ b} \ = \ a$

By the *equality* rule (left-to-right), applied to the *associativity* axiom

$\left\lceil \boxed{(x \circ y) \circ z} \ = \ x \circ (y \circ z) \right\rceil^{-}$	

and goal G3, with $\{x \leftarrow a, \ y \leftarrow b^{-1}, \ z \leftarrow b\}$, we obtain

	G4. $a \circ \left(\boxed{b^{-1} \circ b} \right) \ = \ a$

By the *equality* rule (left-to-right), applied to the *left-inverse* property

$\left\lceil \boxed{x^{-1} \circ x} \ = \ e \right\rceil^{-}$	

and goal G4, with $\{x \leftarrow b\}$, we obtain

	G5. $\boxed{a \circ e \ = \ a}^{+}$

Applying the *resolution* rule to the *right-identity* axiom

$\boxed{x \circ e \ = \ x}^{-}$	

and goal G5, with $\{x \leftarrow a\}$, we obtain the final goal

	G6. *true*

Note that the proof of the *cancellation* property depends on the proof of the

left-inverse property, which was requested as an exercise. Had we attempted to prove the *cancellation* theorem without having proved the other theorem first, the proof, of course, would have been more cumbersome.

In **Problem 12.6** we interchange the roles of the *quotient* axiom and *cancellation* property. We assume that the quotient function x/y is defined alternatively by the axiom

$$(\forall\ x,\ y)\big[(x/y) \circ y\ =\ x\big] \qquad\qquad (cancellation)$$

and ask the reader to prove that the quotient x/y is then the same as $x \circ y^{-1}$, that is,

$$(\forall\ x,\ y)\big[x/y\ =\ x \circ y^{-1}\big] \qquad\qquad (quotient)$$

12.4 THEORIES WITH INDUCTION

We have seen how we can add axioms as assertions into tableaux in predicate logic (with or without equality) to establish the validity of sentences in particular finite theories. The various forms of the principle of mathematical induction, however, are all axiom schemata, each corresponding to an infinite set of axioms. We have devised no method for dealing with axiom schemata within the tableau framework. We cannot introduce an infinite set of assertions into a tableau. Instead, for each theory, we represent the induction principle as a new deduction rule. We begin by reviewing a typical theory with stepwise induction, that of the nonnegative integers.

THE NONNEGATIVE INTEGERS: AXIOMS

The nonnegative integers have been defined by a set of generation and uniqueness axioms and by the induction principle (Section [I]6.1). Let us consider first the axioms.

In the theory of nonnegative integers we have the generation axioms

$integer(0)$	(*zero*)
$(\forall\ integer\ x)\big[integer(x+1)\big]$	(*successor*)

and the uniqueness axioms

$$(\forall \, integer \; x)\big[not \; (x + 1 \; = \; 0)\big] \hspace{4cm} (zero)$$

$$(\forall \, integer \; x, \; y) \begin{bmatrix} if & x + 1 \; = \; y + 1 \\ then & x \; = \; y \end{bmatrix} \hspace{2cm} (successor)$$

A tableau over the nonnegative integers is a tableau with equality with the *zero* and *successor* generation axioms and the *zero* and *successor* uniqueness axioms as initial assertions.

The relativized-quantifiers notation ($\forall \, integer$ ...) requires special attention here. Without using this notation, the *successor* generation axiom, for example, is actually

$$(\forall \, x) \begin{bmatrix} if & integer(x) \\ then & integer(x + 1) \end{bmatrix}.$$

Thus the corresponding assertion should be

assertions	goals
$(\forall x)^{\exists} \begin{bmatrix} if & integer(x) \\ then & integer(x + 1) \end{bmatrix}$	

Applying the $\exists$-*elimination* rule, we obtain

$\begin{aligned} &if \;\; integer(x) \\ &then \;\; integer(x + 1) \end{aligned}$	$(successor)$	

Similarly for the uniqueness axioms:

$\begin{aligned} &if \;\; integer(x) \\ &then \;\; not \; (x + 1 = 0) \end{aligned}$	$(zero)$	
$\begin{aligned} &if \;\; integer(x) \;\; and \;\; integer(y) \\ &then \;\; if \;\; x + 1 = y + 1 \\ &\hspace{1.5cm} then \;\; x = y \end{aligned}$	$(successor)$	

Remark (pure theory)

In case the assertions are used in the pure theory of the nonnegative integers, rather than a combined theory, every element must be an integer, and therefore there is no need for the generation axioms. In this case, we may also add to our simplification catalog the *integer* simplification

$$integer(u) \ \Rightarrow \ true.$$

When the *integer* simplification is applied to the *zero* and *successor* uniqueness assertions, we obtain (after *true-false* simplification) the axioms

$not\ (x + 1 = 0)$	*(zero)*	
$if\ \ x + 1\ =\ y + 1$ $then\ \ x = y$	*(successor)*	

The axioms that define new functions (e.g., multiplication) or new relations (e.g., less than) are included as assertions, as before. Once we have proved a property over the nonnegative integers, we may add it as an assertion to all subsequent tableaux over the nonnegative integers.

Because the theory of nonnegative integers has new symbols, in conducting any proof we may use the ∀-*elimination* rule, as well as the ∃-*elimination* rule and the other predicate-logic deduction rules. Because the tableau is with equality, we also include the *reflexivity* axiom $(x = x)$ among our assertions, and we may also use the *equality* rule.

THE NONNEGATIVE INTEGERS: INDUCTION RULE

In addition to the generation and uniqueness axioms, the nonnegative integers were defined also in terms of the (stepwise) induction principle:

For each sentence $\mathcal{F}[x]$ in the theory,
the universal closure of the sentence

$$if \ \begin{bmatrix} \mathcal{F}[0] \\ and \\ (\forall \ integer \ x) \begin{bmatrix} if \ \ \mathcal{F}[x] \\ then \ \ \mathcal{F}[x + 1] \end{bmatrix} \end{bmatrix} \qquad (stepwise \ induction)$$

then $(\forall \ integer \ x)\mathcal{F}[x]$

is an axiom.

We would like to incorporate this axiom schema, which was used for informal proofs, into our deductive-tableau framework as a deduction rule. We therefore include in a tableau over the nonnegative integers a new deduction rule for mathematical induction. This induction rule allows us to establish a goal of form

$$(\forall\ integer\ x)\mathcal{F}[x]$$

by proving the conjunction of a base case and an inductive step.

Rule (stepwise induction)

For a closed sentence

$$(\forall\ integer\ x)\mathcal{F}[x],$$

we have

assertions	goals
	$(\forall\ integer\ x)\mathcal{F}[x]$
	$\mathcal{F}[0]$ *and* $\begin{bmatrix} if\ \ integer(m) \\ then\ \ if\ \ \mathcal{F}[m] \\ \qquad\qquad then\ \ \mathcal{F}[m+1] \end{bmatrix}$

where m is a new constant.　⌐

Here the conjunct

$$\mathcal{F}[0]$$

corresponds to the base case, and the conjunct

$$if\ \ integer(m)$$
$$then\ \ if\ \ \mathcal{F}[m]$$
$$then\ \ \mathcal{F}[m+1]$$

corresponds to the inductive step of an informal stepwise-induction proof.

Remark (pure theory)

If the derivation is conducted in the pure theory of the nonnegative integers, we apply the *integer* simplification,

$$integer(u)\ \ \Rightarrow\ \ true,$$

to obtain (after *true-false* simplification) the simplified goal

	$\mathcal{F}[0]$
	and
	$\begin{bmatrix} if & \mathcal{F}[m] \\ then & \mathcal{F}[m+1] \end{bmatrix}$

Remark (beware of hasty skolemization)

In a pure predicate-logic tableau proof, there is little harm in applying the skolemization rules to eliminate all quantifiers, at least those of strict force. On the other hand, in a proof in a tableau over the nonnegative integers, we must exercise some discretion in removing quantifiers. If we remove the outermost universal quantifier ($\forall$ *integer x*) of a goal, we cannot apply the induction rule on x to the resulting goal.

Remark (closed sentence)

We are permitted to apply the *stepwise-induction* rule only if the goal is a closed sentence. Otherwise, if the goal ($\forall$ *integer x*)$\mathcal{F}[x]$ contains a free variable y, it actually stands for the existentially quantified goal

$$(\exists\ y)(\forall\ integer\ x)\mathcal{F}[x].$$

We cannot apply the *induction* principle to prove an existentially quantified sentence.

We give an informal justification of the rule.

Justification (*stepwise induction*)

The induction rule preserves validity, not equivalence. Let us show that, if the required goal

assertions	goals
	($\forall$ *integer x*)$\mathcal{F}[x]$

appears in the tableau, then we may derive the generated rows without affecting the validity of the tableau.

By the *stepwise-induction* principle, we know that, to prove the truth of a closed sentence

$$(\forall \ integer \ x)\mathcal{F}[x],$$

it suffices to establish the conjunction

$$\begin{array}{l} \mathcal{F}[0] \\ \quad and \\ (\forall \ integer \ x) \begin{bmatrix} if \ \ \mathcal{F}[x] \\ then \ \ \mathcal{F}[x+1] \end{bmatrix}. \end{array}$$

(We need not consider the universal closure of the sentence since by our assumption it contains no free variables.)

Thus (by the *implied-row* property) we may add to our tableau the new goal

	$\begin{array}{l} \mathcal{F}[0] \\ \quad and \\ (\forall \ integer \ x) \begin{bmatrix} if \ \ \mathcal{F}[x] \\ then \ \ \mathcal{F}[x+1] \end{bmatrix} \end{array}$

that is,

	$\begin{array}{l} \mathcal{F}[0] \\ \quad and \\ (\forall x)^{\forall} \begin{bmatrix} if \ \ integer(x) \\ then \ \ if \ \ \mathcal{F}[x] \\ \qquad then \ \ \mathcal{F}[x+1] \end{bmatrix} \end{array}$

Because the quantifier $(\forall x)$ of this goal is of universal force, we may drop the quantifier (by the $\forall$-*elimination* rule), replacing the variable x with the new skolem constant m (because the goal has no free variables), to obtain

	$\begin{array}{l} \mathcal{F}[0] \\ \quad and \\ \begin{bmatrix} if \ \ integer(m) \\ then \ \ if \ \ \mathcal{F}[m] \\ \qquad then \ \ \mathcal{F}[m+1] \end{bmatrix} \end{array}$

This is precisely the goal derived by the rule. By the *intermediate-tableau* property, we do not need to include the intermediate goal. ⌐

THE NONNEGATIVE INTEGERS: EXAMPLES

We illustrate the proof of some properties in the pure theory of nonnegative integers. The reader may observe that there is a close correspondence between these deductive-tableau proofs and informal proofs of the same properties in Section [I]6.2.

Example (left-zero)

The addition function + is defined by the two axioms

$$(\forall \, integer \; x)\big[x + 0 \; = \; x\big] \hspace{3cm} (right \; zero)$$

$$(\forall \, integer \; x, \, y)\big[x + (y + 1) \; = \; (x + y) + 1\big] \hspace{1cm} (right \; successor)$$

We would like to show that 0 is a left identity for addition, that is,

$$(\forall \, integer \; x)\big[0 + x \; = \; x\big] \hspace{3cm} (left \; zero)$$

We begin with the goal

assertions	goals
	G1. $(\forall \, integer \; x)\big[0 + x \; = \; x\big]$

in a tableau over the nonnegative integers.

The tableau contains among its assertions the uniqueness axioms for the nonnegative integers, the *reflexivity* axiom for equality, and the two axioms for addition,

$x + 0 \; = \; x$	*(right zero)*	
$x + (y + 1) \; = \; (x + y) + 1$	*(right successor)*	

Since we consider the pure theory of the nonnegative integers, there is no need for the generation axioms and we may apply freely the *integer* simplification

$$integer(u) \; \Rightarrow \; true.$$

We actually applied the *integer* simplification to eliminate *integer*(x) and *integer*(y) from the preceding assertions.

Applying the *stepwise-induction* rule to goal G1, we obtain the goal (after *integer* simplification to eliminate *integer*(m))

	G2. $\boxed{0 + 0 = 0}^{+}$
	and
	$\begin{bmatrix} if \ \ 0 + m \ = \ m \\ then \ \ 0 + (m+1) \ = \ m+1 \end{bmatrix}$

The first conjunct corresponds to the base case and the second to the inductive step of an informal stepwise-induction proof.

Recall the *right-zero* axiom for addition,

$\boxed{x + 0 \ = \ x}^{-}$	

By the *resolution* rule, applied to the axiom and goal G2, with $\{x \leftarrow 0\}$, the first conjunct of goal G2 may be dropped, leaving

	G3. $\quad if \ \ 0 + m \ = \ m$
	$\qquad then \ \ 0 + (m+1) \ = \ m+1$

We thus proved the base case of the induction; it remains to show the inductive step, i.e., goal G3.

By the *if-split* rule, we may break down goal G3 into

A4. $\quad 0 + m = m$	
	G5. $\boxed{0 + (m+1)} \ = \ m+1$

Assertion A4 corresponds to the induction hypothesis, and goal G5 to the desired conclusion of the inductive step of an informal induction proof.

Recall the *right-successor* axiom for addition,

$\left[\boxed{x + (y+1)} \ = \ (x+y) + 1 \right]^{-}$	

By the *equality* rule, with $\{x \leftarrow 0,\ y \leftarrow m\}$, we may rewrite goal G5 as

	G6. $\boxed{0 + m} + 1\ =\ m + 1$

By the *equality* rule again, using the induction hypothesis (assertion A4),

$\left[\boxed{0 + m}\ =\ m\right]^{-}$	

we may reduce goal G6 to

	G7. $\boxed{m + 1\ =\ m + 1}^{+}$

Finally, by the reflexivity of equality, we obtain the goal

	G8. *true*

This completes the proof of the *left-zero* property

$$(\forall\ integer\ x)\big[0 + x\ =\ x\big].$$

We may now include this property as an assertion in future tableaux over the nonnegative integers. ⌙

Note that the base case and the inductive step of an informal proof by induction correspond to a single proof in the deductive-tableau system.

Example (left successor)

Suppose we would like to show the *left-successor* property of addition, that is,

$$(\forall\ integer\ x, y)\ \big[(x + 1) + y\ =\ (x + y) + 1\big] \qquad (left\ successor)$$

We begin with the goal

assertions	goals
	G1. $(\forall\ integer\ x, y)\big[(x + 1) + y\ =\ (x + y) + 1\big]$

We have several options in applying skolemization and induction on x and y. For this proof, we prefer to skolemize x first and then to apply induction on y.

Abandoning the relativized quantifier notation in ($\forall$ *integer* x), we can express goal G1 as

$$\text{G1.}\quad (\forall x)^\forall \begin{bmatrix} if & integer(x) \\ then & (\forall\ integer\ y) \begin{bmatrix} (x+1)+y\ = \\ (x+y)+1 \end{bmatrix} \end{bmatrix}$$

By application of the $\forall$-*elimination* rule (followed by *integer* simplification), we may drop the outermost quantifier of goal G1, replacing the variable x with the skolem constant k, to obtain

$$\text{G2.}\quad (\forall\ integer\ y)\big[(k+1)+y\ =\ (k+y)+1\big]$$

By the *stepwise-induction* rule applied to goal G2, we obtain

$$\text{G3.}\quad \boxed{(k+1)+0}\ =\ (k+0)+1$$

and

$$\begin{bmatrix} if & (k+1)+m\ =\ (k+m)+1 \\ then & (k+1)+(m+1)\ =\ \big(k+(m+1)\big)+1 \end{bmatrix}$$

We first establish the base case, the first conjunct $(k+1)+0\ =\ (k+0)+1$.

Base Case

Recall the *right-zero* axiom for addition,

$$\Big[\boxed{x+0}\ =\ x\Big]^-$$

By the *equality* rule, applied to the axiom and goal G3, with $\{x \leftarrow k+1\}$, the goal is reduced to

$$\text{G4.}\quad k+1\ =\ \boxed{k+0}+1$$

and

$$\begin{bmatrix} if & (k+1)+m\ =\ (k+m)+1 \\ then & (k+1)+(m+1)\ =\ \big(k+(m+1)\big)+1 \end{bmatrix}$$

By the *equality* rule, applied once more to the same axiom and goal G4, with $\{x \leftarrow k\}$, the goal is reduced further to

$$G5. \quad \boxed{k+1 \ = \ k+1}^{+}$$

and

$$\left[\begin{array}{l} if \ (k+1)+m \ = \ (k+m)+1 \\ then \ (k+1)+(m+1) \ = \ \big(k+(m+1)\big)+1 \end{array} \right]$$

By the reflexivity of equality, the first conjunct of goal G5 may now be dropped altogether, leaving the goal

$$G6. \quad if \ (k+1)+m \ = \ (k+m)+1 \\ then \ (k+1)+(m+1) \ = \ \big(k+(m+1)\big)+1$$

The remaining goal corresponds to the inductive step of an informal stepwise-induction proof.

Inductive Step

By the *if-split* rule, we may break down goal G6 into

$$A7. \quad \left[\begin{array}{c} \boxed{(k+1)+m} \\ = \\ (k+m)+1 \end{array} \right]^{-}$$

$$G8. \quad \boxed{(k+1)+(m+1)} \\ = \\ \boxed{k+(m+1)} \ +1$$

Assertion A7 corresponds to the induction hypothesis and goal G8 to the desired conclusion of the inductive step.

Recall the *right-successor* axiom for addition,

$$\left[\boxed{x+(y+1)} \ = \ (x+y)+1 \right]^{-}$$

By the *equality* rule, applied twice to the axiom and the goal G8, first with $\{x \leftarrow k+1, \ y \leftarrow m\}$ and then with $\{x \leftarrow k, \ y \leftarrow m\}$, we may rewrite the goal as

	G9. $\boxed{(k+1)+m}\ +1$
	$=$
	$\big((k+m)+1\big)+1$

Applying the *equality* rule to the induction hypothesis (assertion A7) and goal G9, we may rewrite the goal as

	G10. $\boxed{\begin{array}{c}\big((k+m)+1\big)+1\\ =\\ \big((k+m)+1\big)+1\end{array}}^{\ +}$

Finally, by the reflexivity of equality, we obtain the final goal

	G11. *true*

⌐

The proof in the following example uses each of the previous two properties as assertions.

Example (commutativity)

Suppose we would like to show that addition is commutative, i.e., that

$$(\forall \; integer \; x, \; y)\big[x + y \; = \; y + x\big] \qquad\qquad (commutativity)$$

Our initial goal is

assertions	goals
	G1. $(\forall \; integer \; x, y)\big[x + y \; = \; y + x\big]$

Again, we have some freedom in applying skolemization and induction on x and y. In this proof, we prefer to skolemize y first and to apply induction on x later.

Abandoning the relativized quantifier notation in $(\forall \; integer \; y)$, we can express goal G1 as

	G1. $(\forall \; integer \; x)(\forall \; y)^{\forall}\begin{bmatrix}if \;\; integer(y)\\ then \;\; x + y \; = \; y + x\end{bmatrix}$

By application of the ∀-*elimination* rule (followed by *integer* simplification), we may drop the quantifier $(\forall y)$ of goal G1, replacing the variable y with the skolem constant ℓ, to obtain

	G2. $(\forall \ integer \ x)\big[x + \ell \ = \ \ell + x\big]$

Applying the *stepwise-induction* rule on x to goal G2, we obtain

	G3. $0 + \ell \ = \ \boxed{\ell + 0}$ *and* $\begin{bmatrix} if \ \ m + \ell = \ell + m \\ then \ \ (m+1) + \ell = \ell + (m+1) \end{bmatrix}$

The first conjunct corresponds to the base case and the second to the inductive step of an informal stepwise-induction proof.

Base Case

Recall the *right-zero* axiom for addition,

$\Big[\boxed{x + 0} \ = \ x\Big]^{-}$.	

By the *equality* rule, applied to the axiom and goal G3, with $\{x \leftarrow \ell\}$, the goal is reduced to

	G4. $\boxed{0 + \ell = \ell}^{\ +}$ *and* $\begin{bmatrix} if \ \ m + \ell = \ell + m \\ then \ \ (m+1) + \ell = \ell + (m+1) \end{bmatrix}$

In an earlier example, we proved the *left-zero* property for addition, which we may therefore include in our tableau as an assertion:

$\boxed{0 + x \ = \ x}^{\ -}$	

By the *resolution* rule, applied to the property and goal G4, with $\{x \leftarrow \ell\}$, the first conjunct of the goal may now be dropped, leaving

$$\text{G5.} \quad \textit{if } \ m + \ell \ = \ \ell + m$$
$$\textit{then } \ (m+1) + \ell \ = \ \ell + (m+1)$$

We have thus disposed of the base case; it remains to complete the inductive step.

Inductive Step

By application of the *if-split* rule, we may break down goal G5 into the assertion

$$\text{A6.} \quad \left[m + \ell \ = \ \boxed{\ell + m} \right]^{-}$$

and the goal

$$\text{G7.} \quad (m+1) + \ell \ = \ \boxed{\ell + (m+1)}$$

Assertion A6 corresponds to the induction hypothesis, and goal G7 to the desired conclusion of the inductive step.

Recall the *right-successor* axiom for addition,

$$\left[\boxed{x + (y+1)} \ = \ (x+y)+1 \right]^{-}$$

By the *equality* rule, applied to the axiom and goal G7, with $\{x \leftarrow \ell, \ y \leftarrow m\}$, we may rewrite the goal as

$$\text{G8.} \quad (m+1) + \ell \ = \ \boxed{\ell + m} \ + 1$$

By the *equality* rule (right-to-left), applied to the induction hypothesis (assertion A6) and goal G8, we may rewrite the goal as

$$\text{G9.} \quad \boxed{(m+1) + \ell \ = \ (m+\ell)+1}^{+}$$

Recall the *left-successor* property for addition (which we proved in the preceding example),

| $\boxed{(x+1)+y \;=\; (x+y)+1}$ ⁻ | |

By the *resolution* rule, applied to the property and goal G9, with $\{x \leftarrow m, y \leftarrow \ell\}$, we obtain the final goal

| | G10.   *true* |

We have remarked that the preceding proof of the *commutativity* property used both the *left-zero* and *left-successor* properties as assertions. Had we attempted to prove the *commutativity* property without having proved the other two properties first, it would have been difficult to complete the proof. In practice, if in the course of a proof we discover we need an instance of some other property, we may interrupt the main proof and attempt to prove the required property as a subsidiary proposition, or *lemma*, in a separate tableau. Once we have completed the proof of the lemma, we can add it as an assertion in the tableau of the interrupted main proof, and continue the main proof.

The proofs of some properties of the multiplication, exponentiation, and factorial functions are requested in **Problems 12.7**, **12.8**, and **12.9**, respectively. The *fibonacci* function is introduced in **Problem 12.10**.

The *stepwise-induction* rule applies to goals. There is a dual assertion version that applies to assertions.

Rule (stepwise induction, A-form)

For a closed sentence

$$(\exists \; integer \; x)\,\mathcal{F}[x],$$

we have

assertions	goals
$(\exists \; integer \; x)\,\mathcal{F}[x]$	
$\mathcal{F}[0]$ *or* $\begin{bmatrix} integer(m) & and \\ \big(not \; \mathcal{F}[m]\big) & and \\ \mathcal{F}[m+1] & \end{bmatrix}$	

where m is a new constant. ⌐

We seldom use this version. Roughly, it says that if $\mathcal{F}[x]$ is true for some integer x, either it is true for 0 or there is some point at which it becomes true. Its justification is requested in an exercise (**Problem 12.11(a)**).

THE STRINGS: AXIOMS AND INDUCTION RULE

In the same way that we introduced the *stepwise-induction* rule over the non-negative integers in the deductive-tableau framework as a new deduction rule, we can incorporate the *stepwise-induction* rules for other theories with induction, including strings, lists, trees, sets, bags, tuples, expressions, and substitutions. We consider the theory of strings as an example.

A tableau over the strings is a tableau with equality with the following axioms expressed as assertions:

The generation axioms

assertions		goals
$string(\Lambda)$	(*empty*)	
if $char(u)$ *then* $string(u)$	(*character*)	
if $char(u)$ *and* $string(x)$ *then* $string(u \bullet x)$	(*prefix*)	

The uniqueness axioms

if $char(u)$ *and* $string(x)$ *then* $not\ (u \bullet x = \Lambda)$	(*empty*)	
if $char(u)$ *and* $char(v)$ *and* $\quad string(x)$ *and* $string(y)$ *then* *if* $u \bullet x = v \bullet y$ $\quad\quad$ *then* $u = v$ *and* $x = y$	(*prefix*)	

The special equality axiom

if $char(u)$ then $u \bullet \Lambda = u$ (*character*)	

Remark (pure theory)

If the assertions are used in the pure theory of the strings, we apply the *string* simplification,

$$string(u) \Rightarrow true,$$

automatically. In this case, every element must be a string and therefore there is no need for the generation axioms. The uniqueness assertions can be simplified to obtain

if $char(u)$ then $not\ (u \bullet x = \Lambda)$ (*empty*)	
if $char(u)$ and $char(v)$ then if $u \bullet x = v \bullet y$ then $u = v$ and $x = y$ (*prefix*)	

The *character* equality axiom remains unchanged. ⌙

The axioms that define any new constructs (e.g., concatenation of strings) are also represented as assertions. As usual, any previously proved properties may be incorporated as assertions.

Because the tableau is with equality, we also include the *reflexivity* axiom ($x = x$) among our assertions, and we may use the *equality* rule in conducting any proof. Because the theory of strings has new symbols, we can use the ∀-*elimination* rule, as well as the ∃-*elimination* rule and the other predicate-logic deduction rules.

In addition, we include in a tableau over the strings a new deduction rule for stepwise induction. The *stepwise-induction* rule for strings allows us to establish a goal of form $(\forall\ string\ x)\mathcal{F}[x]$ by proving the conjunction of a base case and an inductive step.

Rule (stepwise induction)

For a closed sentence

$$(\forall\ string\ x)\mathcal{F}[x],$$

we have

assertions	goals
	$(\forall\ string\ x)\mathcal{F}[x]$
	$\mathcal{F}[\Lambda]$ and $\begin{bmatrix} if\ \ string(r)\ \ and\ \ char(\sigma) \\ then\ \ if\ \ \mathcal{F}[r] \\ \qquad then\ \ \mathcal{F}[\sigma \bullet r] \end{bmatrix}$

where σ and r are new constants. ⌟

Here the conjunct

$$\mathcal{F}[\Lambda]$$

corresponds to the base case, and the conjunct

$$if\ \ string(r)\ \ and\ \ char(\sigma)$$
$$then\ \ if\ \ \mathcal{F}[r]$$
$$then\ \ \mathcal{F}[\sigma \bullet r]$$

corresponds to the inductive step of an informal induction proof. Note that, as in the theory of the nonnegative integers, we are permitted to apply the *stepwise-induction* rule only if the goal is a closed sentence.

The justification for the rule is analogous to that for the *stepwise-induction* rule over the nonnegative integers (**Problem 12.12**). The reader is requested to formulate and justify an A-form of this rule, which applies to assertions (**Problem 12.11(b)**).

If the derivation is conducted in the pure theory of the strings, we may apply the *string* simplification to the generated goal to obtain

$$\begin{array}{l} \mathcal{F}[\Lambda] \\ \quad and \\ \left[\begin{array}{l} if \ \ char(\sigma) \\ then \ \ if \ \ \mathcal{F}[r] \\ \qquad\qquad then \ \ \mathcal{F}[\sigma \bullet r] \end{array}\right] \end{array}$$

THE STRINGS: EXAMPLE

In the following example, we illustrate the proof of a property in the pure theory of strings. Again, the reader can observe the close similarity between this proof and the corresponding informal proof in Section [I]7.4.

The example illustrates some of the strategic aspects of the use of the induction principle: the treatment of generalization in a tableau setting and the importance of the order in which skolemization and induction are applied.

Example (alternative reverse)

The *reverse* function, which reverses the characters in a string, is defined by the following two axioms:

$$reverse(\Lambda) \ = \ \Lambda \qquad\qquad\qquad (empty)$$

$$\begin{array}{l}(\forall \ char \ u) \\ (\forall \ string \ x)\end{array}\left[reverse(u \bullet x) \ = \ reverse(x) * u\right] \qquad (prefix)$$

The concatenation function $*$, used in the *prefix* axiom for *reverse*, is defined by the following two axioms:

$$(\forall \ string \ y)\left[\Lambda * y \ = \ y\right] \qquad\qquad\qquad (left \ empty)$$

$$\begin{array}{l}(\forall \ char \ u) \\ (\forall \ string \ x, \ y)\end{array}\left[(u \bullet x) * y \ = \ u \bullet (x * y)\right] \qquad (left \ prefix)$$

From these axioms, we can prove within the deductive-tableau system the following properties of concatenation:

$$(\forall\ char\ u) \atop (\forall\ string\ y) \Big[u * y\ =\ u \bullet y\Big] \qquad\qquad (character)$$

$$(\forall\ string\ x)\Big[x * \Lambda\ =\ x\Big] \qquad\qquad (right\ empty)$$

$$(\forall\ string\ x,\ y,\ z)\Big[(x * y) * z\ =\ x * (y * z)\Big] \qquad (associativity)$$

Suppose we define a function $rev2(x,\ y)$, which reverses the string x and concatenates the result with the string y, by the following two axioms:

$$(\forall\ string\ y)[rev2(\Lambda,\ y)\ =\ y] \qquad\qquad (left\ empty)$$

$$(\forall\ char\ u) \atop (\forall\ string\ x,\ y) \Big[rev2(u \bullet x,\ y)\ =\ rev2(x,\ u \bullet y)\Big] \qquad (left\ prefix)$$

The property we would like to show in this example is that the function $rev2$ gives us an alternative definition of the *reverse* function, that is,

$$(\forall\ string\ x)\Big[reverse(x)\ =\ rev2(x,\ \Lambda)\Big] \qquad\qquad (special)$$

We must first prove the more general property

$$(\forall\ string\ x,\ y)\Big[rev2(x,\ y)\ =\ reverse(x) * y\Big] \qquad\qquad (general)$$

Then we will be able to use the *general* property as an assertion in the proof of the desired *special* property.

Proof of the General Property

To prove the *general* property, we begin with the goal

assertions	goals
	G1. $(\forall\ string\ x)(\forall\ string\ y) \begin{bmatrix} rev2(x,\ y)\ = \\ reverse(x) * y \end{bmatrix}$

Here again we have a choice in applying skolemization and induction on x and y. In this case we prefer to apply induction on x first, eliminating the quantifier for y only later. This order is essential, as we shall explain.

By the *stepwise-induction* rule applied to goal G1, it suffices to prove the conjunction of a base case and an inductive step,

$$G2. \quad (\forall \ string \ y)^{\forall} \left[rev2(\Lambda, \ y) \ = \ reverse(\Lambda) * y \right]$$
$$and$$
$$\left[\begin{array}{l} if \ \ char(\sigma) \\ then \ \ if \ \ (\forall \ string \ y')^{\exists} \left[\begin{array}{l} rev2(r, \ y') \ = \\ reverse(r) * y' \end{array} \right] \\ \qquad then \ \ (\forall \ string \ y'')^{\forall} \left[\begin{array}{l} rev2(\sigma \bullet r, \ y'') \ = \\ reverse(\sigma \bullet r) * y'' \end{array} \right] \end{array} \right]$$

The quantified variable y was renamed in anticipation of the following steps.

By the $\forall$- and $\exists$-*elimination* rules (and *string* simplification), we may drop the remaining quantifiers of goal G2, leaving

$$G3. \quad \boxed{rev2(\Lambda, \ t)} \ = \ \boxed{reverse(\Lambda)} * t$$
$$and$$
$$\left[\begin{array}{l} if \ \ char(\sigma) \\ then \ \ if \ \left[\begin{array}{l} rev2(r, \ y') \ = \\ reverse(r) * y' \end{array} \right] \\ \qquad then \ \left[\begin{array}{l} rev2(\sigma \bullet r, \ s) \ = \\ reverse(\sigma \bullet r) * s \end{array} \right] \end{array} \right]$$

Note that the bound variables y and y'' of goal G2 have been replaced in goal G3 by the skolem constants t and s, respectively.

- *Base Case*

Recall the *left-empty* axiom for *rev2* and the *empty* axiom for *reverse*,

$\left[\boxed{rev2(\Lambda, \ y)} \ = \ y \right]^{-}$	
$\left[\boxed{reverse(\Lambda)} \ = \ \Lambda \right]^{-}$	

By the *equality* rule, applied twice in succession to the two axioms and goal G3, we may reduce the goal to

	G4. $t = \boxed{\Lambda * t}$ *and* $[\dots]$

Recall the *left-empty* axiom for concatenation,

$\left[\boxed{\Lambda * y} = y\right]^{-}$	

By the *equality* rule, applied to the axiom and goal G4, with $\{y \leftarrow t\}$, we may
reduce the base case G4 further, to

	G5. $\boxed{t = t}^{+}$ *and* $[\dots]$

By the reflexivity of equality, we may now drop the base case of goal G5
altogether, leaving the inductive step

	G6. *if* $char(\sigma)$ *then if* $\begin{bmatrix} rev2(r, y') & = \\ reverse(r) * y' \end{bmatrix}$ *then* $\begin{bmatrix} rev2(\sigma \bullet r, s) & = \\ reverse(\sigma \bullet r) * s \end{bmatrix}$

■ *Inductive Step*

By two applications of the *if-split* rule, we have

A7. $char(\sigma)$	
A8. $rev2(r, y') =$ $\quad reverse(r) * y'$	
	G9. $\boxed{rev2(\sigma \bullet r, s)} =$ $\quad reverse(\sigma \bullet r) * s$

Here assertion A8 corresponds to the induction hypothesis, and goal G9 to the desired conclusion of the inductive step.

Recall the *left-prefix* axiom for *rev2*,

if $char(u)$ *then* $\left[\dfrac{\boxed{rev2(u \bullet x,\ y)}}{rev2(x,\ u \bullet y)} = \right]^{-}$	

By the *equality* rule, applied to the axiom and goal G9, with $\{u \leftarrow \sigma,\ x \leftarrow r,\ y \leftarrow s\}$, we obtain

	G10. $char(\sigma)$ *and* $\left[\dfrac{rev2(r,\ \sigma \bullet s)\ =}{\boxed{reverse(\sigma \bullet r)}\ * s}\right]$

Recall the *prefix* axiom for *reverse*,

if $char(u)$ *then* $\left[\dfrac{\boxed{reverse(u \bullet x)}}{reverse(x) * u} = \right]^{-}$	

By the *equality* rule, applied to the axiom and goal G10, with $\{u \leftarrow \sigma,\ x \leftarrow r\}$, and simplifying $\big(char(\sigma)\ and\ char(\sigma)\big)$ to $char(\sigma)$, we obtain

	G11. $char(\sigma)$ *and* $\left[\dfrac{rev2(r,\ \sigma \bullet s)\ =}{\big(reverse(r) * \sigma\big) * s}\right]$

Recall the *associativity* property of concatenation,

$\left[\boxed{(x * y) * z}\ =\ x * (y * z)\right]^{-}$	

By the *equality* rule, applied to the property and goal G11, with $\{x \leftarrow reverse(r),\ y \leftarrow \sigma,\ z \leftarrow s\}$, we obtain

$$\boxed{\begin{array}{l} \text{G12.} \quad char(\sigma) \ \ and \\[4pt] \left[\begin{array}{l} rev2(r,\ \sigma \bullet s) \ = \\[4pt] reverse(r) \ * \ \boxed{\sigma * s} \end{array}\right]^{-} \end{array}}$$

Recall the *character* property of concatenation,

$$\boxed{\begin{array}{l} if \ \ char(u) \\[4pt] then \ \ \left[\ \boxed{u * y}\ = u \bullet y\ \right]^{-} \end{array}}$$

By the *equality* rule, applied to the axiom and goal G12, with $\{u \leftarrow \sigma,\ y \leftarrow s\}$, we obtain

$$\boxed{\begin{array}{l} \text{G13.} \quad char(\sigma) \ \ and \\[4pt] \boxed{\begin{array}{l} rev2(r,\ \sigma \bullet s) \ = \\[4pt] reverse(r) \ * \ (\sigma \bullet s) \end{array}}^{+} \end{array}}$$

Recall our induction hypothesis (assertion A8),

$$\boxed{\text{A8.} \quad \boxed{\begin{array}{l} rev2(r,\ y') \ = \\[4pt] reverse(r) * y' \end{array}}^{-}}$$

By the *resolution* rule, applied to the induction hypothesis and goal G13, with $\{y' \leftarrow \sigma \bullet s\}$, the second conjunct of the goal may now be dropped, to obtain

$$\boxed{\text{G14.} \quad \boxed{char(\sigma)}^{+}}$$

Finally, recall the earlier assumption (assertion A7)

$$\boxed{\text{A7.} \quad \boxed{char(\sigma)}^{-}}$$

By the *resolution* rule, applied to the assumption and goal G14, we obtain the final goal

$$\boxed{\text{G15.} \quad true}$$

Now that we have completed the proof of the *general* property of *rev2*,

$$(\forall\ string\ x,\ y)\big[rev2(x,\ y)\ =\ reverse(x) * y\big],$$

we may use it as an assertion in the proof of *special* property of *rev2*,

$$(\forall\ string\ x)\big[reverse(x)\ =\ rev2(x,\ \Lambda)\big].$$

Proof of the Special Property

We begin with the tableau in which the *general* property is given as an assertion

assertions	goals
$rev2(x,\ y)\ =\ reverse(x) * y$	

and the initial goal is the *special* property

	G1. $(\forall\ string\ x)^{\forall}\ \begin{bmatrix} reverse(x)\ = \\ rev2(x,\ \Lambda) \end{bmatrix}$

By the $\forall$-*elimination* rule (and *string* simplification), we may drop the quantifier of goal G1, leaving

	G2. $reverse(s)\ =\ \boxed{rev2(s,\ \Lambda)}$

Here the bound variable x of goal G1 has been replaced by the skolem constant s.

Recall the *general* property of *rev2*,

$\Big[\boxed{rev2(x,\ y)}\ =\ reverse(x) * y\Big]^{-}$	

By the *equality* rule, applied to the property and goal G2, with $\{x \leftarrow s,\ y \leftarrow \Lambda\}$, we obtain

	G3. $reverse(s)\ =\ \boxed{reverse(s) * \Lambda}$

Recall the *right-empty* property of concatenation,

$$\left[\boxed{x * \Lambda} \;=\; x\right]^{-}$$

By the *equality* rule, applied to the assertion and goal G3, with $\{x \leftarrow reverse(s)\}$, we obtain

	G4. $\boxed{reverse(s) \;=\; reverse(s)}^{\,+}$

By the reflexivity of equality, we obtain the final goal

	G5. *true*

This concludes the proof of the desired *special* property

$$(\forall\, string\; x)\big[reverse(x) \;=\; rev2(x, \Lambda)\big]. \quad \lrcorner$$

In the preceding example, we proved the *general* property by induction, and then used it in the proof of the *special* property. Had we attempted to prove the *special* property itself by induction, the proof would have failed because the induction hypothesis would not have been strong enough to allow us to establish the conclusion. Part of the difficulty of proving a property such as the *special* property for *rev2* is discovering the appropriate *general* property.

Note that, in the proof of the *general* property, we did not apply the $\forall$-*elimination* rule to remove the second quantifier ($\forall\, string\; y$) in goal G1 until after we had applied the induction principle. This is crucial: had we removed this quantifier too early, the proof would not have succeeded. As it is, the induction hypothesis, assertion A8, contains the variable y'. The variable y' was then replaced by the term $\sigma \bullet s$ in resolution with goal G13. Had we removed the quantifier first, the induction hypothesis would have contained a skolem constant instead of the variable y', and this step would have been impossible.

In this example, we have mentioned all the properties we used in the proof at the beginning. Henceforth, we shall usually not mention such properties until they are used. We shall assume, nevertheless, that they are present in the initial tableau.

This concludes our discussion of how to introduce the *stepwise-induction* principle in the deductive-tableau framework. In the same way that we have formulated tableau theories of the nonnegative integers and the strings, we can also formulate analogous tableau versions of other theories with stepwise induction, including lists, trees, sets, and expressions.

Proofs of some properties of the concatenation function are requested in **Problem 12.13**. Another property of strings, that the *reverse* function "distributes" over the concatenation function $*$, is proposed in **Problem 12.14**. A property of a relation over strings is set forth in **Problem 12.15**.

12.5 WELL-FOUNDED INDUCTION RULE

We have seen how to introduce theories with various forms of stepwise induction into a deductive-tableau framework. In this section, we introduce a tableau form of the *well-founded induction* principle described in Section 1.2.

For a given well-founded relation $\prec$, the *well-founded induction* principle was defined as follows:

For each sentence $\mathcal{F}[x]$, with no free occurrences of u,
the universal closure of the sentence

$$
\textit{if}\ \ (\forall\, obj\ x)\ \begin{bmatrix} \textit{if}\ \ (\forall\, obj\ u)\ \begin{bmatrix} \textit{if}\ \ u \prec x \\ \textit{then}\ \ \mathcal{F}[u] \end{bmatrix} \\ \textit{then}\ \ \mathcal{F}[x] \end{bmatrix}
$$
$$
\textit{then}\ \ (\forall\, obj\ x)\,\mathcal{F}[x]
$$

(well-founded induction principle)

is valid in the given theory.

This principle is represented in the tableau system as a deduction rule.

THE RULE

We include among the deduction rules of our tableau the following general induction rule.

Rule (well-founded induction)

In a theory, for a closed sentence

$$(\forall\, obj\ x)\,\mathcal{F}[x]$$

and an arbitrary relation $\prec$ that is known to be well-founded over *obj*,

assertions	goals
	$(\forall \; obj \; x) \mathcal{F}[x]$
$obj(a)$	
if $obj(u)$ *then if* $u \prec a$ *then* $\mathcal{F}[u]$	
	$\mathcal{F}[a]$

where a is a new constant. ⌐

There is a clear correspondence between the generated assertions and goal and an informal proof by well-founded induction. Here, the first generated assertion corresponds to the assumption that a is an object, the second generated assertion to the induction hypothesis, and the generated goal to the desired conclusion of the inductive step.

Let us justify the new rule.

Justification

Let us show that, if the required goal

assertions	goals
	$(\forall \; obj \; x) \mathcal{F}[x]$

appears in the tableau, then we may derive the generated rows without affecting the validity of the tableau.

If the relation $\prec$ is well-founded, we know that the corresponding instance of the *well-founded induction* principle is valid, that is,

$$if \; (\forall \, obj \; y) \begin{bmatrix} if \; (\forall \, obj \; u) \begin{bmatrix} if \; u \prec y \\ then \; \mathcal{F}[u] \end{bmatrix} \\ then \; \mathcal{F}[y] \end{bmatrix}$$
$$then \; (\forall \, obj \; x) \mathcal{F}[x].$$

It therefore suffices (by the *implied-row* property) to show as a new goal the antecedent of this instance, that is,

$$(\forall \ obj \ y) \left[\begin{array}{l} if \ (\forall \ obj \ u) \left[\begin{array}{l} if \ u \prec y \\ then \ \mathcal{F}[u] \end{array}\right] \\ then \ \mathcal{F}[y] \end{array}\right]$$

which we can rewrite without the relative quantifier notation as

$$(\forall y)^{\forall} \left[\begin{array}{l} if \ \ obj(y) \\ then \ \ if \ (\forall u)^{\exists} \left[\begin{array}{l} if \ \ obj(u) \\ then \ \ if \ \ u \prec y \\ \qquad\quad then \ \ \mathcal{F}[u] \end{array}\right] \\ \qquad\quad then \ \ \mathcal{F}[y] \end{array}\right]$$

By the $\forall$- and $\exists$-*elimination* rules, we could drop the quantifiers from the goal, obtaining

$$\begin{array}{l} if \ \ obj(a) \\ then \ \ if \ \ if \ \ obj(u) \\ \qquad\quad then \ \ if \ \ u \prec a \\ \qquad\qquad\quad then \ \ \mathcal{F}[u] \\ \qquad then \ \ \mathcal{F}[a] \end{array}$$

Recall that by our assumption, $\mathcal{F}[u]$ and $\mathcal{F}[y]$ have no free variables other than u and y, respectively. Here the variable y, whose quantifier has strict universal force, has been replaced by the skolem constant a.

By two applications of the *if-split* rule, we can break down the goal to obtain

$obj(a)$	
$if \ \ obj(u)$ $then \ \ if \ \ u \prec a$ $\qquad then \ \ \mathcal{F}[u]$	
	$\mathcal{F}[a]$

These are precisely the three rows we obtain by application of the *well-founded induction* rule. By the *intermediate-tableau* property, we do not need to include the intermediate rows. This concludes the justification of the rule. ⏌

EXAMPLES

We illustrate several applications of the *well-founded induction* rule. In the first example we apply the rule to any well-founded relation. That is, we consider a theory defined by a single axiom schema, the *well-founded induction* principle over $\prec$.

Example (asymmetry of a well-founded relation)

Now let us show that any well-founded relation $\prec$ is asymmetric, i.e., that

$$(\forall\, obj\ x,\ y)\ \begin{bmatrix} if\ \ x \prec y \\ then\ \ not\ (y \prec x) \end{bmatrix} \qquad\qquad (asymmetry)$$

Let $\prec$ be an arbitrary well-founded relation.

Our initial tableau (writing the quantifiers separately) is

assertions	goals
	G1. $(\forall\, obj\ x)\ \begin{bmatrix}(\forall\, obj\ y)\ \begin{bmatrix} if\ x \prec y \\ then\ \ not\ (y \prec x) \end{bmatrix}\end{bmatrix}$

Applying the *well-founded induction* rule to goal G1, we may assume the assertion

A2. $obj(a)$	

and the induction hypothesis

A3. $if\ \ obj(u)$ $\quad then\ \ if\ \ u \prec a$ $\qquad then\ \ (\forall\, obj\ y)\ \begin{bmatrix} if\ \ u \prec y \\ then\ \ not\ (y \prec u) \end{bmatrix}$	

and attempt to establish the conclusion

	G4. $(\forall\, obj\ y)\ \begin{bmatrix} if\ \ a \prec y \\ then\ \ not\ (y \prec a) \end{bmatrix}$

Let us rewrite assertion A3 and goal G4 without the relative-quantifier notation:

A3'. *if obj(u)*
    then if u ≺ a
        then $(\forall y)^{\exists}$ $\begin{bmatrix} if \ obj(y) \\ then \ if \ u \prec y \\ then \ not \ (y \prec u) \end{bmatrix}$

and

G4'. $(\forall y)^{\forall}$ $\begin{bmatrix} if \ obj(y) \\ then \ if \ a \prec y \\ then \ not \ (y \prec a) \end{bmatrix}$

Applying now the ∃-*elimination* rule to assertion A3' and the ∀-*elimination* rule to goal G4', we may drop the quantifiers from these rows, to obtain

A5. *if obj(u)*
    then if u ≺ a
        then if obj(y)
            then if $\boxed{u \prec y}^{+}$
                then not (y ≺ u)

and

G6. *if obj(s)*
    then if a ≺ s
        then not (s ≺ a)

Note that the variable y of goal G4' is replaced by the skolem constant s in goal G6, while the skolemized induction hypothesis, assertion A5, retains the variable y.

By two applications of the *if-split* rule, we may decompose goal G6 into

A7. *obj(s)*

A8. *a ≺ s*

G9. *not* $\boxed{s \prec a}^{-}$

By the *resolution* rule applied to our goal G9 and the skolemized induction hypothesis (assertion A5), with $\{u \leftarrow s, \; y \leftarrow a\}$, we obtain

$$
\begin{array}{l}
\textit{not false} \\[4pt]
\quad \textit{and} \\[4pt]
\qquad not \;
\left[
\begin{array}{l}
\textit{if} \;\; obj(s) \\
\textit{then} \;\; \textit{if} \;\; \textit{true} \\
\qquad\quad \textit{then} \;\; \textit{if} \;\; obj(a) \\
\qquad\qquad\quad \textit{then} \;\; \textit{if} \;\; \textit{true} \\
\qquad\qquad\qquad\quad \textit{then} \;\; not \; (a \prec s)
\end{array}
\right] ,
\end{array}
$$

which simplifies to the goal

	G10. $not \; \left[\begin{array}{l} \textit{if} \;\; \boxed{obj(s)}^{\,+} \\ \textit{then} \;\; \textit{if} \;\; \boxed{obj(a)}^{\,+} \\ \qquad\quad \textit{then} \;\; not \; a \prec s \end{array}\right]$

By the *resolution* rule applied twice in succession, to assertions A7 and A2

A7. $\boxed{obj(s)}^{\,-}$	
A2. $\boxed{obj(a)}^{\,-}$	

and goal G10, we obtain

	G11. $\boxed{a \prec s}^{\,+}$

Finally, by the *resolution* rule applied to assertion A8

A8. $\boxed{a \prec s}^{\,-}$	

and goal G11, we obtain the final goal

	G12. *true*

Note that in this example, again, we did not apply the $\forall$-*elimination* rule to remove the second quantifier $(\forall \; obj \; y)$ in the goal until after we had applied the induction principle. As it is, the induction hypothesis, assertion A5, contains the variable y, which was then replaced by the constant a in resolution with goal G9. Had we removed the quantifier first, the induction hypothesis would have contained a skolem constant, say b, instead of the variable y, and this step would have been impossible. ⌐

In **Problem 12.16** the reader is requested to prove in the same way that any well-founded relation is irreflexive.

The next example illustrates a proof in a combination of three theories.

Example (tips)

We consider a theory that combines the nonnegative integers with the tuples of trees. In this theory, the elements of the tuples are themselves trees, rather than atoms. We construct it by replacing the symbol *atom* with *tree* in all the axioms and properties of the theory of tuples. We also include, of course, the usual axioms and properties of the theories of trees and nonnegative integers. In the theory of trees, the symbol *atom* is permitted to remain because our trees will be built from atoms.

Recall that, in the theory of trees, we defined the function $tips(t)$, the number of atoms ("leaves") in the tree t, by the axioms (Problem [I]8.4)

$$(\forall\ atom\ u)\big[tips(u)\ =\ 1\big] \qquad\qquad\qquad (atom)$$

$$(\forall\ tree\ x,\ y)\big[tips(x \bullet y)\ =\ tips(x) + tips(y)\big] \qquad (construction)$$

Here $\bullet$ is the construction function for trees.

The *tips* function can be shown to satisfy the *sort* property

$$(\forall\ tree\ x)\big[integer\big(tips(x)\big)\big] \qquad\qquad\qquad (sort)$$

In this theory, we would like to formulate an alternative definition for the *tips* function. We introduce a function *tipstuple*; if t is a tuple of trees, $tipstuple(t)$ is the sum of the number of atoms in all the trees in t. We define *tipstuple* by the following axioms:

$$tipstuple(\langle\ \rangle)\ =\ 0 \qquad\qquad\qquad\qquad (empty)$$

$$(\forall\ atom\ u)\ \begin{bmatrix}tipstuple(u \diamond w)\ =\ \\ 1 + tipstuple(w)\end{bmatrix} \qquad (atom\ insertion)$$
$$(\forall\ tuple\ w)$$

$$(\forall\ tree\ x,\ y)\ \begin{bmatrix}tipstuple\big((x \bullet y) \diamond w\big)\ = \\ tipstuple\big(x \diamond (y \diamond w)\big)\end{bmatrix} \qquad (construction\ insertion)$$
$$(\forall\ tuple\ w)$$

Here $\diamond$ is the insertion function for tuples.

The argument of the *tipstuple* function is viewed computationally as a stack of trees. If an atom is at the head of the stack, it is counted and removed from the stack. If a nonatom is at the head, it is decomposed into its left and right components, which are replaced on the stack. The computation continues until the stack is empty.

We would like to show that the preceding axioms actually provide an alternative definition for the *tips* function, in the sense that

$$(\forall\ tree\ x)\big[tips(x)\ =\ tipstuple(\langle x\rangle)\big] \qquad\qquad (special\ tips)$$

where $\langle x\rangle$ denotes the tuple ("singleton") whose sole element is the tree x.

We first prove the more general property,

$$\begin{matrix}(\forall\ tree\ x)\\(\forall\ tuple\ w)\end{matrix}\Big[tipstuple(x\diamond w)\ =\ tips(x) + tipstuple(w)\Big]$$
$$(general\ tips)$$

This *general-tips* property establishes that the *tipstuple* function indeed behaves as we expect. Once we have proved it, we may use it as an assertion in the proof of the desired *special-tips* property.

In our presentation, we shall reverse this order. We shall assume we have already proved the *general-tips* property, and use it in proving the *special-tips* property. Only then do we actually prove the *general-tips* property.

Proof of the special-tips property

The proof is straightforward and does not require induction; it does show us something about the treatment of relative quantifiers and sort conditions in a combined theory.

We begin with the initial tableau. The initial goal G1 is the desired *special-tips* property.

assertions	goals
	G1. $(\forall\ tree\ x)\big[tips(x) = tipstuple(\langle x\rangle)\big]$

We include the *general-tips* property as an assertion in our initial tableau because we are assuming that this sentence has already been proved to be valid.

A2. $\begin{matrix}(\forall\ tree\ x)\\(\forall\ tuple\ w)\end{matrix}\begin{bmatrix}tipstuple(x\diamond w) =\\ tips(x) + tipstuple(w)\end{bmatrix}$	

We would like to remove the quantifiers in our initial tableau. For this purpose, let us rewrite it without using the relative-quantifier notation:

	G1. $(\forall x)^\forall$ $\begin{bmatrix} if & tree\,(x) \\ then & tips(x) = tipstuple\,(\langle x \rangle) \end{bmatrix}$

and

A2. $(\forall x,\ w)^\exists$ $\begin{bmatrix} if & tree\,(x)\ and\ tuple(w) \\ then & \begin{bmatrix} tipstuple(x \diamond w) = \\ tips(x) + tipstuple(w) \end{bmatrix} \end{bmatrix}$	

By the $\forall$- and $\exists$-*elimination* rules, replacing x with the new constant r in G1, we obtain

	G3. $if\ \ tree\,(r)$ $then\ \ tips(r) = tipstuple\,(\langle r \rangle)$

and

A4. $if\ \ tree\,(x)\ and\ \ tuple(w)$ $then\ \ \begin{bmatrix} tipstuple(x \diamond w) = \\ tips(x) + tipstuple(w) \end{bmatrix}$	

Applying the *if-split* rule to goal G3, we obtain

A5. $tree\,(r)$	
	G6. $tips(r) = tipstuple\left(\boxed{\langle r \rangle}\right)$

In future steps, we shall often perform these steps automatically: abandoning the relative-quantifier notation, applying the quantifier-elimination rules, and applying the splitting rules as appropriate.

Recall the *singleton* axiom for tuples (Section [I]12.1), after eliminating the relative quantifier as before:

$if\ \ tree\,(x)$ $then\ \ \left[\boxed{\langle x \rangle} = x \diamond \langle \, \rangle\right]^-$	

Note that, in our combined theory, the elements of tuples are trees, not atoms.

By the *equality* rule, applied to the axiom and goal G6, with $\{x \leftarrow r\}$, we obtain

	G7. $\boxed{tree\,(r)}^{+}$ *and*
	$tips(r) \;=\; tipstuple\,(r \diamond \langle\,\rangle)$

Recall assertion A5:

A5. $\boxed{tree\,(r)}^{-}$	

By the *resolution* rule:

	G8. $tips(r) \;=\; \boxed{tipstuple\,(r \diamond \langle\,\rangle)}$

Note that we have disposed of the sort condition $tree\,(r)$ by resolution with an assertion. Removal of sort conditions is often a routine and monotonous part of a proof; in such cases, we will do the steps automatically, with the annotation "removal of sort conditions."

Recall the *general-tips* property (after quantifier elimination):

A4. *if* $tree\,(x)$ *and* $tuple(w)$	
then $\begin{bmatrix} \boxed{tipstuple(x \diamond w)} \;= \\[4pt] tips(x) + tipstuple(w) \end{bmatrix}^{-}$	

By the *equality* rule, applied to goal G8, with $\{x \leftarrow r,\; w \leftarrow \langle\,\rangle\}$, and removal of sort conditions:

	G9. $tips(r) \;=\; tips(r) + \boxed{tipstuple(\langle\,\rangle)}$

Here we have removed the sort conditions $tree\,(r)$ and $tuple(\langle\,\rangle)$ automatically, by resolution with two assertions.

Recall the *empty* axiom for *tipstuple*:

$\left[\boxed{tipstuple\,(\langle\,\rangle)} \;=\; 0\right]^{-}$	

By the *equality* rule:

	G10. $tips(r) = \boxed{tips(r) + 0}$

Recall the *right-zero* axiom for addition:

$if\ integer(v)$ $then\ \left[\boxed{v + 0} = v\right]^{-}$	

By the *equality* rule, with $\{v \leftarrow tips(r)\}$:

	G11. $\boxed{integer(tips(r))}^{+}$ *and* $tips(r) = tips(r)$

We have not yet removed the sort condition $integer(tips(r))$. Because this requires an extra step, we shall show how it is done this time.

Recall the *sort* property of the *tips* function:

$if\ tree(x)$ $then\ \boxed{integer(tips(x))}^{-}$	

By the *resolution* rule, with $\{x \leftarrow r\}$, applied to goal G11, and removal of a sort condition:

	G12. $\boxed{tips(r) = tips(r)}^{+}$

By the reflexivity of equality, we obtain the final goal

	G13. *true*

This concludes the proof of the *special-tips* property.

Proof of the general-tips property

We have shown that, once we have proved the *general-tips* property, we can prove the desired *special-tips* property. Now let us prove the *general-tips* property.

We begin with the initial tableau:

$$\text{G1.} \quad (\forall\ tree\ x)\left[(\forall\ tuple\ w)\begin{bmatrix}tipstuple(x \diamond w) \; = \\ tips(x) + tipstuple(w)\end{bmatrix}\right]$$

We shall use the *well-founded induction* rule with respect to the proper-subtree relation $\prec_{tree}$, which is well-founded over *tree*. The only property of the subtree relation we shall use in the proof is the following *left-right* property:

$$(\forall\ tree\ x)\begin{bmatrix}if\ \ not\,(atom(x)) \\ then\ \ left(x) \prec_{tree} x\ \ and\ \ right(x) \prec_{tree} x\end{bmatrix} \qquad (\textit{left-right})$$

By the *well-founded induction* rule, we obtain the assertions

A2. $tree\,(a)$	

A3.   *if* $tree\,(y)$
    then if $y \prec_{tree} a$
      then $(\forall\ tuple\ w)^{\exists}\begin{bmatrix}tipstuple(y \diamond w)\ = \\ tips(y) + tipstuple(w)\end{bmatrix}$	

and the goal

	$\text{G4.} \quad (\forall\ tuple\ w)^{\forall}\begin{bmatrix}tipstuple(a \diamond w)\ = \\ tips(a) + tipstuple(w)\end{bmatrix}$

Applying the ∃-*elimination* rule to assertion A3 (abandoning the relative-quantifier notation), we obtain

A5.   *if* $tree\,(y)$
    then if $y \prec_{tree} a$
      then if $tuple(w)$
        then $\begin{bmatrix}tipstuple(y \diamond w)\ = \\ tips(y) + tipstuple(w)\end{bmatrix}$	

Applying the ∀-*elimination* rule to goal G4 (abandoning the relative-quantifier notation), replacing w with the new constant t, followed by the *if-split* rule:

A6. $tuple(t)$	

	G7. $tipstuple(a \diamond t) =$ $tips(a) + tipstuple(t)$

Intuitively, we now treat separately the case in which r is atomic.

■ *Atomic Case*

Recall the *atom-insertion* axiom for *tipstuple* and goal G7 :

if $atom(u)$ *and* $tuple(w)$ *then* $\left[\dfrac{\boxed{tipstuple(u \diamond w)}}{1 + tipstuple(w)} = \right]^{-}$	
	G7. $\boxed{tipstuple(a \diamond t)} =$ $tips(a) + tipstuple(t)$

By the *equality* rule, with $\{u \leftarrow a,\ w \leftarrow t\}$, and removing a sort condition:

	G8. $atom(a)$ *and* $\left[1 + tipstuple(t) = \atop \boxed{tips(a)} + tipstuple(t) \right]$

The sort condition we have removed is $tuple(t)$ (using assertion A6). The condition $atom(a)$ that the rule introduces into the goal column corresponds to the case assumption that a is atomic.

Recall the *atom* axiom for *tips*:

if $atom(u)$ *then* $\left[\boxed{tips(u)} = 1 \right]^{-}$	

By the *equality* rule, applied to the axiom and goal G8, with $\{u \leftarrow a\}$:

	G9. $atom(a)$ *and* $\left[1 + tipstuple(t) = \atop 1 + tipstuple(t) \right]^{+}$

By the reflexivity of equality, we obtain from goal G9:

	G10. $\boxed{atom(a)}^{+}$

Intuitively, in developing goal G10, we have completed the proof for the case in which a is atomic. By duality, the goal can be regarded as an assertion $not\,(atom(a))$. In other words, we may henceforth assume that a is nonatomic.

■ *Nonatomic Case: The Decomposition of the Tree*

Recall the *decomposition* property of trees and goal G7:

if $tree\,(x)$ *and* $not\,(atom(x))$ *then* $\left[\boxed{x} = left(x) \bullet right(x)\right]^{-}$	
	G7. $tipstuple\left(\boxed{a}\diamond t\right) =$ $tips(a) + tipstuple(t)$

By the *equality* rule, with $\{x \leftarrow a\}$, and removal of a sort condition:

	G11. $not\,(atom(a))$ *and* $\left[\boxed{tipstuple\left((left(a) \bullet right(a)) \diamond t\right)} = tips(a) + tipstuple(t)\right]$

Recall the *construction-insertion* axiom for *tipstuple*:

if $tree\,(x)$ *and* $tree\,(y)$ *and* $tuple(w)$ *then* $\left[\boxed{tipstuple\,((x \bullet y) \diamond w)} = tipstuple\,(x \diamond (y \diamond w))\right]^{-}$	

By the *equality* rule, with $\{x \leftarrow left(a), y \leftarrow right(a), w \leftarrow t\}$, and removal of sort conditions:

G12.   *not* $(atom(a))$ *and*

$$\left[\boxed{tipstuple\left(left(a) \diamond \left(right(a) \diamond t\right)\right)} = tips(a) + tipstuple(t) \right]$$

The sort conditions that were removed, by resolution with sort properties and assertions, were $tree(left(a))$, $tree(right(a))$, and $tuple(t)$.

At this stage we invoke the induction hypothesis twice in succession.

- *Use of the Induction Hypothesis*

Recall assertion A5 (the skolemized induction hypothesis):

A5.   *if* $tree\,(y)$
        then *if* $y \prec_{tree} a$
            then *if* $tuple(w)$
                then $\left[\boxed{tipstuple(y \diamond w)} = tips(y) + tipstuple(w) \right]^{-}$

By the *equality* rule, with $\{y \leftarrow left(a),\ w \leftarrow right(a) \diamond t\}$, applied to goal G12, and removal of sort conditions:

G13. $left(a) \prec_{tree} a$ *and*
        not $(atom(a))$ *and*

$$\left[tips(left(a)) + \boxed{tipstuple(right(a) \diamond t)} = tips(a) + tipstuple(t) \right]^{-}$$

By the *equality* rule, applied to assertion A5 (again) and goal G13, with $\{y \leftarrow right(a),\ w \leftarrow t\}$:

G14. $left(a) \prec_{tree} a$ *and* $right(a) \prec_{tree} a$ *and*
        not $(atom(a))$ *and*

$$\left[\boxed{tips(left(a)) + tips(right(a))} + tipstuple(t) = tips(a) + tipstuple(t) \right]$$

We have reordered the conjuncts in goal G14 for pedagogical reasons.

Recall the *construction* axiom for the *tips* function:

$$\text{if} \ \ tree\,(x) \ \ and \ \ tree\,(y)$$
$$\text{then} \ \ \left[tips(x \bullet y) = \boxed{tips(x) + tips(y)} \right]^{-}$$

By the *equality* rule, right-to-left, with $\{x \leftarrow left(a),\ y \leftarrow right(a)\}$, and removing sort conditions:

> **G15.** $left(a) \prec_{tree} a$ *and* $right(a) \prec_{tree} a$ *and*
> $not \ (atom(a))$ *and*
> $$\left[tips\left(\boxed{left(a) \bullet right(a)} \right) + tipstuple(t) \right.$$
> $$\left. = \ tips(a) + tipstuple(t) \right]$$

Recall the *decomposition* property of trees:

$$\text{if} \ \ tree\,(x) \ \ and \ \ not \ (atom(x))$$
$$\text{then} \ \ \left[x = \boxed{left(x) \bullet right(x)} \right]^{-}$$

By the *equality* rule, right-to-left, with $\{x \leftarrow a\}$, and removing a sort condition:

> **G16.** $left(a) \prec_{tree} a$ *and* $right(a) \prec_{tree} a$ *and*
> $not \ (atom(a))$ *and*
> $$\boxed{\begin{array}{l} tips(a) + tipstuple(t) \ = \\ tips(a) + tipstuple(t) \end{array}}^{+}$$

By the reflexivity of equality:

> **G17.** $\boxed{left(a) \prec_{tree} a \ \ and \ \ right(a) \prec_{tree} a}^{+}$
> $and \ not \ (atom(a))$

At this stage we turn our attention to the conditions associated with the well-founded relation.

- *Establishing the Well-founded Relation*

Recall the *left-right* property of the subtree relation:

if $tree\,(x)$ *and* $not\,(atom(x))$ *then* $\boxed{left(x) \prec_{tree} x \ \ and \ \ right(x) \prec_{tree} x}$ $^-$	

By the *resolution* rule, with $\{x \leftarrow a\}$, and removing a sort condition:

	G18. $\quad not \ \boxed{atom(a)}$ $^-$

By the *resolution* rule, applied to goals G18 and G10:

	G19. $\quad true$

This completes the proof of the *general-tips* property. ◣

In **Problems 12.17–12.21**, the reader is requested to use the *well-founded induction* rule in the deductive-tableau framework to prove the validity of various properties.

The *well-founded induction* rule applies to goals; there is a dual version that applies to assertions.

Rule (well-founded induction, A-form)

In a theory, for a closed sentence

$$(\exists \ obj \ x)\mathcal{F}[x]$$

and an arbitrary relation $\prec$ that is known to be well-founded over *obj*,

assertions	goals
$(\exists \ obj \ x)\mathcal{F}[x]$	
$obj(a)$	
if $obj(u)$ *then if* $u \prec a$ $\quad\quad$ *then* $(not \ \mathcal{F}[u])$	
$\mathcal{F}[a]$	

where a is a new constant. ⌟

This version is actually a statement of the *minimal-element* condition (Section 1.5). Roughly, it says that if there is an object x for which $\mathcal{F}[x]$ is true, there is a minimal object a for which $\mathcal{F}[a]$ is true. The justification is left as an exercise (**Problem 12.11(c)**).

WELL-FOUNDED INDUCTION OVER PAIRS

As discussed and illustrated in Chapter 4, sometimes it is convenient to use well-founded induction over pairs of objects, rather than over the objects themselves.

In Section 4.1 we stated and proved the following *well-founded induction over pairs* proposition:

> In the theory of pairs over obj_1 and obj_2, suppose the binary relation $\prec$ is well-founded over *pair*.
>
> Then, for each sentence $\mathcal{F}[x_1, x_2]$, with no free occurrences of x'_1 and x'_2, the universal closure of
>
> $$if \; \begin{matrix} (\forall \, obj_1 \; x_1) \\ (\forall \, obj_2 \; x_2) \end{matrix} \left[if \; \begin{matrix} (\forall \, obj_1 \; x'_1) \\ (\forall \, obj_2 \; x'_2) \end{matrix} \begin{bmatrix} if \; \langle x'_1, x'_2 \rangle \prec \langle x_1, x_2 \rangle \\ then \; \; \mathcal{F}[x'_1, x'_2] \end{bmatrix} \right]$$
> $$then \; \begin{matrix} (\forall \, obj_1 \; x_1) \\ (\forall \, obj_2 \; x_2) \end{matrix} \mathcal{F}[x_1, x_2]$$
>
> is valid (in the theory).

We therefore include among the deduction rules of our tableau the following derived rule, which is a tableau form of this proposition.

Rule (well-founded induction over pairs)

In the theory of pairs over obj_1 and obj_2, for a closed sentence

$$(\forall \, obj_1 \; x_1)(\forall \, obj_2 \; x_2)\mathcal{F}[x_1, x_2]$$

and an arbitrary relation $\prec$ that is known to be well-founded over pairs,

assertions	goals
	$(\forall\ obj_1\ x_1)\atop(\forall\ obj_2\ x_2)$ $\mathcal{F}[x_1,\ x_2]$
$obj_1(a_1)\ \ and\ \ obj_2(a_2)$	
$if\ \ obj_1(u_1)\ \ and\ \ obj_2(u_2)$ $then\ \ if\ \ \langle u_1,\ u_2\rangle \prec \langle a_1,\ a_2\rangle$ $then\ \ \mathcal{F}[u_1,\ u_2]$	
	$\mathcal{F}[a_1,\ a_2]$

where a_1, a_2 are new constants.

As before, the second generated assertion corresponds to the induction hypothesis, and the generated goal to the desired conclusion of an informal proof.

In particular, we can take $\prec$ to be $\prec_{lex}$, the lexicographic relation corresponding to binary relations $\prec_1$ and $\prec_2$ (Section 4.2), provided that $\prec_1$ and $\prec_2$ are well-founded over obj_1 and obj_2, respectively. In that case, we know (by the *lexicographic-relation* proposition) that $\prec_{lex}$ is well-founded over the pairs. We call this instance of the rule the *lexicographic well-founded induction* rule.

The justification for this rule, which we omit, resembles the justification for the ordinary *well-founded induction* rule for tableaux.

The *well-founded induction* rule over pairs allows us to do induction on two variables at once. The rule can clearly be extended to allow us to do induction on three, four, and more variables at once in an appropriate theory of triples, quadruples, and so forth, respectively.

The following example illustrates not only the application of the *well-founded induction* rule over pairs, but also the proof that the *mergesort* "program," expressed as a collection of axioms, does satisfy certain properties we expect of it. An informal proof of this was given in Section 4.5.

Example (mergesort)

Recall that, in the theory of tuples of nonnegative integers, we defined the function $mergesort(z)$, which sorts the nonnegative integers in a tuple z. To sort a given tuple $x \diamond y$, where the division into a "left half" x and a "right half" y

is arbitrary, we simply sort the two "halves" x and y separately, and merge the results. The *mergesort* function is defined by the following axioms:

$$mergesort(\langle\,\rangle) \;=\; \langle\,\rangle \qquad\qquad (empty)$$

$$(\forall\, atom\; u)\big[mergesort(\langle u\rangle) \;=\; \langle u\rangle\big] \qquad\qquad (singleton)$$

$$(\forall\, tuple\; x,\; y)\left[\begin{array}{l} mergesort(x \diamond y) \;=\; \\ merge(mergesort(x),\; mergesort(y)) \end{array}\right] \qquad (append)$$

Here $\diamond$ is the tuple append function.

The auxiliary function $merge(x,\, y)$, which intermixes, in (weakly) increasing order, the integers in two ordered tuples x and y, is defined by the following additional axioms:

$$(\forall\, tuple\; y)\big[merge(\langle\,\rangle,\; y) \;=\; y\big] \qquad\qquad (left\; empty)$$

$$(\forall\, tuple\; x)\big[merge(x,\; \langle\,\rangle) \;=\; x\big] \qquad\qquad (right\; empty)$$

$$\begin{array}{l} (\forall\, atom\; u,\; v) \\ (\forall\, tuple\; x,\; y) \end{array} \left[\begin{array}{l} merge(u \diamond x,\; v \diamond y) \\ = \left\{\begin{array}{l} if\;\; u \leq v \\ then\;\; u \diamond merge(x,\; v \diamond y) \\ else\;\; v \diamond merge(u \diamond x,\; y) \end{array}\right\} \end{array}\right] \qquad (insertion)$$

Here $\diamond$ is the tuple insertion function.

To show that the *mergesort* function does indeed yield a sorted version of the tuple x, one must prove

$$(\forall\, tuple\; x)\big[perm(x,\; mergesort(x))\big] \qquad\qquad (permutation)$$

that is, the elements of $mergesort(x)$ are the same as those of x, in some order, and

$$(\forall\, tuple\; x)\big[ordered(mergesort(x))\big] \qquad\qquad (ordered)$$

that is, the elements of $mergesort(x)$ are in (weakly) increasing order.

The proofs of these properties of the function *mergesort* depend on the following properties of the auxiliary function *merge*:

$$(\forall\, tuple\; x,\; y)\big[perm(x \diamond y,\; merge(x,\; y))\big] \qquad\qquad (permutation)$$

that is, the elements of $merge(x, y)$ are the same as those of x and y together, in some order, and

$$(\forall \; tuple \; x, y) \begin{bmatrix} if & ordered(x) \;\; and \;\; ordered(y) \\ then & ordered\,(merge\,(x, y)) \end{bmatrix} \qquad (ordered)$$

that is, the elements of $merge(x, y)$ are in increasing order, provided the elements of x and y are in increasing order.

The reader has already been requested (in Problem 4.7) to provide an informal proof of the *permutation* property of *merge*; we present a tableau proof later in the section. In this proof we use the *well-founded induction* principle over pairs.

An informal proof of the *ordered* property of *merge* appears in Section 4.6. The reader is requested (in **Problem 12.22**) to provide a tableau proof. Tableau proofs of the *permutation, ordered,* and *sorting* properties of *mergesort* itself are also requested in this problem.

The proof of the *permutation* property of *merge* refers to the *head* and *tail* functions for tuples, which are defined by the axioms

$$\begin{array}{ll} (\forall \; atom \; u) \\ (\forall \; tuple \; x) \end{array} \Big[head(u \diamond x) = u \Big] \qquad\qquad (head)$$

$$\begin{array}{ll} (\forall \; atom \; u) \\ (\forall \; tuple \; x) \end{array} \Big[tail(u \diamond x) = x \Big] \qquad\qquad (tail)$$

These axioms imply the *decomposition* property

$$(\forall \; tuple \; x) \begin{bmatrix} if & not \; (x = \langle \; \rangle) \\ then & x = head(x) \diamond tail(x) \end{bmatrix} \qquad (decomposition)$$

We shall also rely on the following *append-insertion* property of the *perm* relation:

$$\begin{array}{l} (\forall \; tuple \; x_1, \; x_2, \; y) \\ (\forall \; atom \; u) \end{array} \begin{bmatrix} perm\big(x_1 \diamond (u \diamond x_2), \; u \diamond y\big) \\ \equiv \\ perm(x_1 \diamond x_2, \; y) \end{bmatrix} \qquad (append\text{-}insertion)$$

Applying the Induction Rule

To prove the *permutation* property of the *merge* function,

$$(\forall \; tuple \; x, y) \big[perm(x \diamond y, \; merge(x, \; y)) \big],$$

we begin with the initial tableau

assertions	goals
	G1. $(\forall \, tuple \, x_1, \, x_2)\big[perm\big(x_1 \diamond x_2, \, merge(x_1, \, x_2)\big)\big]$

The proof is by lexicographic well-founded induction. In other words, we are applying the rule over pairs, taking obj_1 and obj_2 each to be *tuple*. The well-founded relation will be $\prec_{lex}$, where $\prec_1$ and $\prec_2$ are each taken to be the proper-subtuple relation $\subset$.

Rather than use the definition of $\prec_{lex}$ directly, it will be convenient to invoke the *first* and *second* properties of $\prec_{lex}$,

$$(\forall \, tuple \, x_1, \, x_2, \, y_1, \, y_2) \begin{bmatrix} if \;\; x_1 \subset y_1 \\ then \;\; \langle x_1, \, x_2 \rangle \prec_{lex} \langle y_1, \, y_2 \rangle \end{bmatrix} \qquad (first)$$

$$(\forall \, tuple \, x_1, \, x_2, \, y_1, \, y_2) \begin{bmatrix} if \;\; x_1 = y_1 \;\; and \;\; x_2 \subset y_2 \\ then \;\; \langle x_1, \, x_2 \rangle \prec_{lex} \langle y_1, \, y_2 \rangle \end{bmatrix} \qquad (second)$$

These follow from the definition of the $\prec_{lex}$ relation by propositional logic.

We shall also invoke the *tail* property of the proper-subtuple relation,

$$(\forall \, tuple \, x) \begin{bmatrix} if \;\; not \; (x = \langle \, \rangle) \\ then \;\; tail(x) \subset x \end{bmatrix} \qquad (tail)$$

By the *lexicographic well-founded induction* rule:

A2. $tuple(r_1) \;\; and \;\; tuple(r_2)$	
A3. $if \;\; tuple(y_1) \;\; and \;\; tuple(y_2)$ $\quad then \;\; if \;\; \langle y_1, \, y_2 \rangle \prec_{lex} \langle r_1, \, r_2 \rangle$ $\qquad then \;\; perm\big(y_1 \diamond y_2, \, merge(y_1, y_2)\big)$	

and

	G4. $perm\big(r_1 \diamond r_2, \, merge(r_1, \, r_2)\big)$

Here assertion A3 corresponds to our induction hypothesis, and goal G4 to our desired conclusion.

Intuitively, we now treat separately the case in which the constants r_1 and r_2 are nonatomic.

Nonatomic Case: *Decomposing the Arguments*

We decompose the arguments r_1 and r_2 into their heads and tails.

Recall the *decomposition* property of *head* and *tail*:

$$
\begin{aligned}
&if \;\; tuple(x) \\
&then \;\; if \;\; not \, \big(x = \langle\,\rangle\big) \\
&\qquad\qquad then \;\; \left[\boxed{\;x\;} \;=\; head(x) \diamond tail(x)\right]^{-}
\end{aligned}
$$

Also recall goal G4:

$$
\text{G4.} \quad perm\!\left(\boxed{r_1}\diamond\boxed{r_2},\; merge\!\left(\boxed{r_1},\,\boxed{r_2}\right)\right)
$$

Applying the *equality* rule twice, once with $\{x \leftarrow r_1\}$ and once with $\{x \leftarrow r_2\}$, removing a sort condition:

$$
\begin{aligned}
\text{G5.} \quad & not\,\big(r_1 = \langle\,\rangle\big) \;\; and \;\; not\,\big(r_2 = \langle\,\rangle\big) \;\; and \\
& perm\!\left(
\begin{array}{l}
\big(head(r_1) \diamond tail(r_1)\big) \diamond \big(head(r_2) \diamond tail(r_2)\big), \\
merge\!\big(head(r_1) \diamond tail(r_1),\; head(r_2) \diamond tail(r_2)\big)
\end{array}
\right)
\end{aligned}
$$

Let us henceforth abbreviate $head(r_1)$ and $tail(r_1)$ as h_1 and t_1, respectively, and $head(r_2)$ and $tail(r_2)$ as h_2 and t_2, respectively. Thus, goal G5 may be written

$$
\begin{aligned}
\text{G5.} \quad & not\,\big(r_1 = \langle\,\rangle\big) \;\; and \;\; not\,\big(r_2 = \langle\,\rangle\big) \;\; and \\
& perm\!\left((h_1 \diamond t_1) \diamond (h_2 \diamond t_2),\; \boxed{merge(h_1 \diamond t_1,\, h_2 \diamond t_2)}\right)
\end{aligned}
$$

The Case Split

In the next few steps, we distinguish between two subcases, according to whether or not $h_1 \le h_2$.

Recall the *insertion* axiom for *merge*:

$$
\begin{array}{l}
\textit{if}\ \ atom(u)\ \ and\ \ atom(v)\ \ and \\
\quad tuple(x)\ \ and\ \ tuple(y) \\[4pt]
\textit{then}\quad
\left[\ \boxed{merge(u \diamond x,\ v \diamond y)}\ =\
\left\{
\begin{array}{l}
if\ \ u \leq v \\
then\ \ u \diamond merge(x,\ v \diamond y) \\
else\ \ v \diamond merge(u \diamond x,\ y)
\end{array}
\right\}
\ \right]^{-}
\end{array}
$$

By the *equality* rule, with $\{u \leftarrow h_1,\ x \leftarrow t_1,\ v \leftarrow h_2,\ y \leftarrow t_2\}$, applied to goal G5, removing sort conditions and simplifying:

$$
\begin{array}{ll}
\text{G6.} & not\ (r_1 = \langle\,\rangle)\ \ and\ \ not\ (r_2 = \langle\,\rangle)\ \ and \\[4pt]
& perm\left(
\begin{array}{l}
(h_1 \diamond t_1) \diamond (h_2 \diamond t_2), \\[4pt]
\left(
\begin{array}{l}
if\ \ h_1 \leq h_2 \\
then\ \ h_1 \diamond merge(t_1,\ h_2 \diamond t_2) \\
else\ \ h_2 \diamond merge(h_1 \diamond t_1,\ t_2)
\end{array}
\right)
\end{array}
\right)
\end{array}
$$

Applying the rewriting rule, with the *predicate* conditional manipulation

$$p(\overline{x},\ \textit{if}\ \mathcal{F}\ then\ s\ else\ t,\ \overline{y}) \quad \Leftrightarrow \quad \textit{if}\ \mathcal{F}\ then\ p(\overline{x}, s, \overline{y})\ else\ p(\overline{x}, t, \overline{y}),$$

the *cond-or* elimination

$$\textit{if}\ \mathcal{F}\ then\ \mathcal{G}\ else\ \mathcal{H} \quad \Leftrightarrow \quad (\mathcal{F}\ and\ \mathcal{G})\ or\ ((not\ \mathcal{F})\ and\ \mathcal{H}),$$

and the *and-or* distributivity

$$\mathcal{F}\ and\ (\mathcal{G}\ or\ \mathcal{H}) \quad \Leftrightarrow \quad (\mathcal{F}\ and\ \mathcal{G})\ or\ (\mathcal{F}\ and\ \mathcal{H}),$$

followed by the *or-split* rule, we obtain

$$
\begin{array}{ll}
\text{G7.} & not\ (r_1 = \langle\,\rangle)\ \ and\ \ not\ (r_2 = \langle\,\rangle)\ \ and \\[4pt]
& h_1 \leq h_2\ \ and \\[4pt]
& perm\left(\ \boxed{(h_1 \diamond t_1) \diamond (h_2 \diamond t_2)}\ ,\ h_1 \diamond merge(t_1,\ h_2 \diamond t_2)\right)
\end{array}
$$

$$
\begin{array}{ll}
\text{G8.} & not\ (r_1 = \langle\,\rangle)\ \ and\ \ not\ (r_2 = \langle\,\rangle)\ \ and \\[4pt]
& not\ (h_1 \leq h_2)\ \ and \\[4pt]
& perm\left((h_1 \diamond t_1) \diamond (h_2 \diamond t_2),\ h_2 \diamond merge(h_1 \diamond t_1,\ t_2)\right)
\end{array}
$$

These two goals correspond to two distinct subcases, according to whether or not $h_1 \leq h_2$. We treat each subcase separately.

The First Subcase

Recall the *left-insertion* axiom for append:

$$\begin{array}{l} if \ \ atom(u) \ \ and \ \ tuple(x) \ \ and \ \ tuple(y) \\ then \ \ \left[\boxed{(u \diamond x) \diamond y} \ = \ u \diamond (x \diamond y)\right]^{-} \end{array}$$

By the *equality* rule, with $\{u \leftarrow h_1, \ x \leftarrow t_1, \ y \leftarrow h_2 \diamond t_2\}$, applied to goal G7, removing sort conditions:

$$\begin{array}{l} \text{G9.} \quad not \ (r_1 = \langle \ \rangle) \ \ and \ \ not \ (r_2 = \langle \ \rangle) \ \ and \\ \qquad h_1 \leq h_2 \ \ and \\ \qquad \boxed{perm\Big(h_1 \diamond (t_1 \diamond (h_2 \diamond t_2)), \ h_1 \diamond merge(t_1, h_2 \diamond t_2)\Big)} \end{array}$$

Recall the *equal-insertion* property of *perm*:

$$\begin{array}{l} if \ \ atom(u) \ \ and \ \ tuple(x) \ \ and \ \ tuple(y) \\ then \ \ \left[\boxed{perm(u \diamond x, \ u \diamond y)} \ \equiv \ perm(x, \ y)\right]^{-} \end{array}$$

By the *equivalence* rule, with $\{u \leftarrow h_1, \ x \leftarrow t_1 \diamond (h_2 \diamond t_2), \ y \leftarrow merge(t_1, h_2 \diamond t_2)\}$, removing sort conditions:

$$\begin{array}{l} \text{G10.} \quad not \ (r_1 = \langle \ \rangle) \ \ and \ \ not \ (r_2 = \langle \ \rangle) \ \ and \\ \qquad h_1 \leq h_2 \ \ and \\ \qquad \boxed{perm\big(t_1 \diamond (h_2 \diamond l_2), \ merge(t_1, h_2 \diamond t_2)\big)}^{+} \end{array}$$

We are now ready to use the induction hypothesis. The induction hypothesis is actually used twice in this proof, once in each subcase.

First Use of the Induction Hypothesis

Recall our induction hypothesis, assertion A3:

$$\begin{array}{l} \text{A3.} \quad if \ \ tuple(y_1) \ \ and \ \ tuple(y_2) \\ \qquad then \ \ if \ \ \langle y_1, \ y_2 \rangle \prec_{lex} \langle r_1, \ r_2 \rangle \\ \qquad\qquad then \ \ \boxed{perm\big(y_1 \diamond y_2, \ merge(y_1, y_2)\big)}^{-} \end{array}$$

By the *resolution* rule, with $\{y_1 \leftarrow t_1, y_2 \leftarrow (h_2 \diamond t_2)\}$, applied to goal G10, removing sort conditions:

G11. $\boxed{\langle t_1, h_2 \diamond t_2 \rangle \prec_{lex} \langle r_1, r_2 \rangle}^{+}$ *and*

$not\ (r_1 = \langle\ \rangle)\ \ and\ \ not\ (r_2 = \langle\ \rangle)$

$and\ \ h_1 \leq h_2$

Recall the *first* property of the lexicographic relation $\prec_{lex}$:

$if\ \ tuple(x_1)\ \ and\ \ tuple(x_2)\ \ and$

$\quad tuple(y_1)\ \ and\ \ tuple(y_2)$

$then\ \ if\ \ x_1 \subset y_1$

$\qquad then\ \ \boxed{\langle x_1, x_2 \rangle \prec_{lex} \langle y_1, y_2 \rangle}^{-}$

By the *resolution* rule, with $\{x_1 \leftarrow t_1, x_2 \leftarrow (h_2 \diamond t_2), y_1 \leftarrow r_1, y_2 \leftarrow r_2\}$, removing sort conditions:

G12. $t_1 \subset r_1\ \ and$

$not\ (r_1 = \langle\ \rangle)\ \ and\ \ not\ (r_2 = \langle\ \rangle)$

$and\ \ h_1 \leq h_2$

At this point it is convenient to abandon our abbreviation for t_1:

G12. $\boxed{tail(r_1) \subset r_1}^{+}$ *and*

$not\ (r_1 = \langle\ \rangle)\ \ and\ \ not\ (r_2 = \langle\ \rangle)$

$and\ \ h_1 \leq h_2$

Recall the *tail* property of the proper-subtuple relation:

$if\ \ tuple(x)$

$then\ \ if\ \ not\ (x = \langle\ \rangle)$

$\qquad then\ \ \boxed{tail(x) \subset x}^{-}$

By the *resolution* rule, with $\{x \leftarrow r_1\}$, removing sort conditions:

G13. $not\ (r_1 = \langle\ \rangle)\ \ and\ \ not\ (r_2 = \langle\ \rangle)$

$and\ \ h_1 \leq h_2$

Let us set this subcase aside for a while.

The Second Subcase

The second subcase deals with the case in which $not\ (h_1 \leq h_2)$. To deal with this possibility, we return our attention to the earlier goal G8, which we have neglected until now:

> G8. $not\ (r_1 = \langle\,\rangle)$ and $not\ (r_2 = \langle\,\rangle)$ and
>
> $not\ (h_1 \leq h_2)$ and
>
> $\boxed{perm\Big((h_1 \diamond t_1) \diamond (h_2 \diamond t_2),\ h_2 \diamond merge(h_1 \diamond t_1,\ t_2)\Big)}$

Recall the *append-insertion* property of *perm*:

> if $tuple(x_1)$ and $tuple(x_2)$ and
>
> $tuple(y)$ and $atom(u)$
>
> then $\left[\ \boxed{\begin{array}{c} perm\big(x_1 \diamond (u \diamond x_2),\ u \diamond y\big) \\ \equiv\ perm\big(x_1 \diamond x_2,\ y\big) \end{array}}^{-}\ \right]$

By the *equivalence* rule applied to the goal G8, with $\{x_1 \leftarrow (h_1 \diamond t_1),\ u \leftarrow h_2,$ $x_2 \leftarrow t_2,\ y \leftarrow merge(h_1 \diamond t_1, t_2)\}$, removing sort conditions:

> G14. $not\ (r_1 = \langle\,\rangle)$ and $not\ (r_2 = \langle\,\rangle)$ and
>
> $not\ (h_1 \leq h_2)$ and
>
> $\boxed{perm\big((h_1 \diamond t_1) \diamond t_2,\ merge(h_1 \diamond t_1,\ t_2)\big)}^{+}$

Second Use of the Induction Hypothesis

Recall our induction hypothesis, assertion A3:

> A3. if $tuple(y_1)$ and $tuple(y_2)$
>
> then if $\langle y_1,\ y_2 \rangle \prec_{lex} \langle r_1,\ r_2 \rangle$
>
> then $\boxed{perm\big(y_1 \diamond y_2,\ merge(y_1,\ y_2)\big)}^{-}$

By the *resolution* rule, with $\{y_1 \leftarrow (h_1 \diamond t_1),\ y_2 \leftarrow t_2\}$, removing sort conditions:

G15.　$\boxed{\langle h_1 \diamond t_1,\, t_2\rangle \prec_{lex} \langle r_1,\, r_2\rangle}^{+}$

$$and\ not\ (r_1 = \langle\,\rangle)\ \ and\ \ not\ (r_2 = \langle\,\rangle)$$
$$and\ \ not\ (h_1 \le h_2)$$

Recall the *second* property of the lexicographic relation $\prec_{lex}$:

$$if\ \ tuple(x_1)\ \ and\ \ tuple(x_2)\ \ and$$
$$tuple(y_1)\ \ and\ \ tuple(y_2)$$
$$then\ \ if\ \ x_1 = y_1\ \ and\ \ x_2 \subset y_2$$
$$then\ \ \boxed{\langle x_1,\, x_2\rangle \prec_{lex} \langle y_1,\, y_2\rangle}^{-}$$

By the *resolution* rule, with $\{x_1 \leftarrow (h_1 \diamond t_1),\, x_2 \leftarrow t_2,\, y_1 \leftarrow r_1,\, y_2 \leftarrow r_2\}$, removing sort conditions:

G16.　$(h_1 \diamond t_1) = r_1\ \ and\ \ t_2 \subset r_2\ \ and$
$$not\ (r_1 = \langle\,\rangle)\ \ and\ \ not\ (r_2 = \langle\,\rangle)$$
$$and\ \ not\ (h_1 \le h_2)$$

In anticipation of the next step, it is again convenient to abandon some occurrences of our abbreviation:

G16.　$\boxed{head(r_1) \diamond tail(r_1)} = r_1\ \ and$
$$tail(r_2) \subset r_2\ \ and$$
$$not\ (r_1 = \langle\,\rangle)\ \ and\ \ not\ (r_2 = \langle\,\rangle)$$
$$and\ \ not\ (h_1 \le h_2)$$

Recall again the *decomposition* property of *head* and *tail*:

$$if\ \ tuple(x)$$
$$then\ \ if\ \ not\ (x = \langle\,\rangle)$$
$$then\ \ \left[x = \boxed{head(x) \diamond tail(x)}\right]^{-}$$

By the *equality* rule (right-to-left), with $\{x \leftarrow r_1\}$, removing a sort condition, and the reflexivity of equality:

G17. $\boxed{tail(r_2) \subset r_2}^+$ and

not $(r_1 = \langle\,\rangle)$ and not $(r_2 = \langle\,\rangle)$
and not $(h_1 \leq h_2)$

Recall the *tail* property of the subtuple relation:

if $tuple(x)$
  then if not $(x = \langle\,\rangle)$
    then $\boxed{tail(x) \subset x}^-$

By the *resolution* rule, with $\{x \leftarrow r_2\}$, removing a sort condition:

G18.   not $(r_1 = \langle\,\rangle)$ and not $(r_2 = \langle\,\rangle)$
and not $\left(\boxed{h_1 \leq h_2}^- \right)$

We can now combine the results of the two cases.

Recall goal G13, at the end of the first subcase:

G13.   not $(r_1 = \langle\,\rangle)$ and not $(r_2 = \langle\,\rangle)$
and $\boxed{h_1 \leq h_2}^+$

By the *resolution* rule:

G19.   not $\left[\boxed{r_1} = \langle\,\rangle \right]^-$ and not $(r_2 = \langle\,\rangle)$

This concludes our treatment of the case in which r_1 and r_2 are both nonempty. By duality, goal G19 may be regarded as an assertion

$$(r_1 = \langle\,\rangle) \ or \ (r_2 = \langle\,\rangle),$$

that r_1 is empty or r_2 is empty. These are the cases that remain to be treated.

Atomic Case: r_1 *is empty*

Recall our desired conclusion, goal G4:

$$\text{G4.} \quad perm\left(\boxed{r_1}\,\diamond\, r_2,\; merge\left(\boxed{r_1},\, r_2\right)\right)$$

By the *equality* rule, applied to goal G19:

$$\text{G20.} \quad not\,(r_2 = \langle\,\rangle)\;\; and$$
$$perm\left(\boxed{\langle\,\rangle \diamond r_2}\,,\; \boxed{merge(\langle\,\rangle,\, r_2)}\right)$$

Recall the *left-empty* axioms for append and merge:

if $tuple(y)$ *then* $\left[\boxed{\langle\,\rangle \diamond y} = y\right]^{-}$	
if $tuple(y)$ *then* $\left[\boxed{merge(\langle\,\rangle,\, y)} = y\right]^{-}$	

By two successive applications of the *equality* rule, applied to the axioms and goal G20, with $\{y \leftarrow r_2\}$, removing sort conditions:

$$\text{G21.} \quad not\,(r_2 = \langle\,\rangle)\;\; and$$
$$\boxed{perm(r_2,\, r_2)}^{+}$$

Recall the *reflexivity* property of *perm*:

if $tuple(x)$ *then* $\boxed{perm(x,\, x)}^{-}$	

By the *resolution* rule, with $\{x \leftarrow r_2\}$, removing a sort condition:

$$\text{G22.} \quad not\left[\boxed{r_2} = \langle\,\rangle\right]^{-}$$

We have thus disposed of the case in which r_1 is empty. By duality, goal G22 corresponds to an assertion

$$r_2 = \langle\,\rangle,$$

that r_2 is empty. This is the remaining case we must consider.

Atomic Case: r_2 *is empty*

Recall again the desired conclusion, goal G4:

	G4. $\quad perm\left(r_1 \diamond \boxed{r_2}, \; merge\left(r_1, \boxed{r_2}\right)\right)$

By the *equality* rule, applied to goals G22 and G4:

	G23. $\quad perm\left(\boxed{r_1 \diamond \langle\,\rangle}, \boxed{merge\left(r_1, \langle\,\rangle\right)}\right)^{+}$

The balance of the proof resembles the proof for the previous case, so we will treat it briskly.

Recall the *right-empty* property of append, the *right-empty* axiom for merge, and the *reflexivity* property of *perm*:

if $tuple(x)$ *then* $\left[\boxed{x \diamond \langle\,\rangle} = x\right]^{-}$	
if $tuple(x)$ *then* $\left[\boxed{merge\left(x, \langle\,\rangle\right)} = x\right]^{-}$	
if $tuple(x)$ *then* $\boxed{perm\left(x, x\right)}^{-}$	

By two successive applications of the *equality* rule and one application of the *resolution* rule, removing sort conditions, we derive the final goal

	G24. $\quad true$

The reader is given an opportunity to use the *lexicographic well-founded induction* rule in **Problem 12.23**.

PROBLEMS

Use the deductive-tableau technique to carry out the following proofs.

Problem 12.1 (redhead)   page 503

Suppose the *grandparent theory* is defined by the single axiom

$$(\forall\ x,\ z)\Big[gp(x,\ z)\ \equiv\ (\exists y)\big[par(x,\ y)\ and\ par(y,\ z)\big]\Big] \quad (grandparent)$$

Intuitively, this means that x is a grandparent of z precisely when, for some person y, x is a parent of y and y is a parent of z. Within this theory, give a proof of the following sentence:

$$if\ (\exists\ x,\ z)\begin{bmatrix}gp(x,\ z)\ and\\ red(x)\ and\ not\ red(z)\end{bmatrix} \quad (redhead)$$

$$then\ (\exists\ x,\ z)\begin{bmatrix}par(x,\ z)\ and\\ red(x)\ and\ not\ red(z)\end{bmatrix}.$$

Intuitively, if $red(x)$ stands for "x is a redheaded person," this means that if someone is redheaded but that person's grandchild is not, then someone is redheaded but that person's child is not.

Problem 12.2 (transitivity and symmetry of equality)   page 512

In a tableau with the *equality* rule, show the *transitivity* and *symmetry* of equality.

(a) *Transitivity*

$$(\forall\ x,\ y,\ z)\begin{bmatrix}if\ x=y\ and\ y=z\\ then\ x=z\end{bmatrix} \quad (transitivity)$$

(b) *Symmetry*

$$(\forall\ x,\ y)[if\ x=y\ then\ y=x] \quad (symmetry)$$

Problem 12.3 (irreflexive restriction)   page 514

In the theory of weak partial orderings, prove that the irreflexive restriction $\prec$ associated with a given weak partial ordering $\preceq$ is transitive, that is,

$$(\forall x,\ y,\ z)\begin{bmatrix}if\ x \prec y\ and\ y \prec z\\ then\ x \prec z\end{bmatrix} \quad (transitivity)$$

Problem 12.4 (reflexive closure)   page 515

The theory of strict partial orderings (Section [I]4.4) was defined by the axioms

$$(\forall x, y, z) \begin{bmatrix} if & x \prec y & and & y \prec z \\ then & x \prec z \end{bmatrix} \qquad (transitivity)$$

$$(\forall x)\big[not\ (x \prec x)\big] \qquad (irreflexivity)$$

We can prove within the deductive-tableau system the *asymmetry* property

$$(\forall x, y) \begin{bmatrix} if & x \prec y \\ then & not\ (y \prec x) \end{bmatrix} \qquad (asymmetry)$$

Prove that the corresponding reflexive-closure relation, defined by

$$(\forall x, y) \begin{bmatrix} x \preceq y \\ \equiv \\ x \prec y\ \ or\ \ x = y \end{bmatrix} \qquad (reflexive\ closure)$$

is a weak partial ordering, i.e., that the following properties hold:

(a) *Transitivity*

$$(\forall x, y, z) \begin{bmatrix} if & x \preceq y & and & y \preceq z \\ then & x \preceq z \end{bmatrix}$$

(b) *Antisymmetry*

$$(\forall x, y) \begin{bmatrix} if & x \preceq y & and & y \preceq x \\ then & x = y \end{bmatrix}$$

(c) *Reflexivity*

$$(\forall x)[x \preceq x].$$

Problem 12.5 (theory of groups)   page 519

Prove the following properties of the theory of groups:

(a) *Left identity*

$$(\forall x)\big[e \circ x = x\big]$$

(b) *Left inverse*

$$(\forall x)\big[x^{-1} \circ x = e\big]$$

(c) *Left cancellation*

$$(\forall x, y, z) \begin{bmatrix} if & z \circ x = z \circ y \\ then & x = y \end{bmatrix}$$

(d) *Nonidempotence*

$$(\forall x) \begin{bmatrix} if & x \circ x \ = \ x \\ then & x \ = \ e \end{bmatrix}.$$

Problem 12.6 (quotient versus inverse)   page 521

Suppose we define the quotient x/y of two elements x and y of a group by the following axiom:

$$(\forall \ x, \ y) \big[(x/y) \circ y \ = \ x \big] \hspace{3cm} (cancellation)$$

Prove that the quotient x/y is then the same as $x \circ y^{-1}$, that is,

$$(\forall \ x, \ y) \big[x/y \ = \ x \circ y^{-1} \big] \hspace{3cm} (quotient)$$

Problem 12.7 (multiplication)   page 535

In the theory of nonnegative integers, the multiplication function $x \cdot y$ was defined by the following two axioms:

$$(\forall \ integer \ x)[x \cdot 0 \ = \ 0] \hspace{3cm} (right \ zero)$$

$$(\forall \ integer \ x, \ y) \big[x \cdot (y+1) \ = \ x \cdot y + x \big] \hspace{2cm} (right \ successor)$$

Prove the following properties of multiplication in the pure theory of the nonnegative integers:

(a) *Right one*

$$(\forall \ integer \ x)[x \cdot 1 \ = \ x]$$

Hint: Recall that 1 is a notation for $(0+1)$.

(b) *Left zero*

$$(\forall \ integer \ x)[0 \cdot x \ = \ 0]$$

(c) *Left successor*

$$(\forall \ integer \ x, \ y) \big[(x+1) \cdot y \ = \ x \cdot y + y \big]$$

(d) *Right distributivity*

$$(\forall \ integer \ x, \ y, \ z) \big[x \cdot (y+z) \ = \ x \cdot y + x \cdot z \big].$$

Problem 12.8 (exponentiation)   page 535

The exponentiation function x^y was defined by the axioms

$$(\forall \, integer \; x)[x^0 \;=\; 1] \qquad\qquad\qquad (exp \; zero)$$

$$(\forall \, integer \; x, \, y)[x^{y+1} \;=\; x^y \cdot x] \qquad\qquad (successor)$$

and the $exp3(x, y, z)$ function was defined by the axioms

$$(\forall \, integer \; x, \, z)\big[exp3(x, \, 0, \, z) \;=\; z\big] \qquad\qquad (zero)$$

$$(\forall \, integer \; x, \, y, \, z)\big[exp3(x, \, y+1, \, z) \;=\; exp3(x, \, y, \, x \cdot z)\big]$$
$$(successor)$$

Prove, in the pure theory of the nonnegative integers, that $exp3$ provides an alternative definition for x^y, in the sense that

$$(\forall \, integer \; x, \, y)\big[x^y \;=\; exp3(x, \, y, \, 1)\big] \qquad (alternative \; definition)$$

Hint: In a separate tableau, first prove a more general property. See the informal proof in Section [I]6.3.

Problem 12.9 (factorial)   page 535

The factorial function $x!$ was defined (in Problem [I]6.4) by the following axioms:

$$0! \;=\; 1 \qquad\qquad\qquad\qquad (zero)$$

$$(\forall \, integer \; x)\big[(x+1)! \;=\; (x+1) \cdot (x!)\big] \qquad\qquad (successor)$$

An alternative definition for the factorial function was introduced by defining a function $fact2(x, y)$ as follows:

$$(\forall \, integer \; y)\big[fact2(0, \, y) \;=\; y\big] \qquad\qquad (zero)$$

$$(\forall \, integer \; x, \, y)\big[fact2(x+1, \, y) \;=\; fact2\big(x, \, (x+1) \cdot y\big)\big] \quad (successor)$$

Prove, in the pure theory of the nonnegative integers, that $fact2$ does indeed provide an alternative definition for the factorial function, in the sense that

$$(\forall \, integer \; x)\big[x! \;=\; fact2(x, \, 1)\big] \qquad\qquad (alternative \; definition)$$

Hint: Prove a more general property.

Problem 12.10 (fibonacci function)   page 535

Suppose the *fibonacci function* $fib(x)$ is defined by the following axioms:

$$fib(0) \ = \ 0 \hspace{6cm} (zero)$$

$$fib(1) \ = \ 1 \hspace{6cm} (one)$$

$$(\forall \ integer \ x)\big[fib\big((x+1)+1\big) \ = \ fib(x+1) + fib(x)\big] \hspace{0.8cm} (plus \ two)$$

The sequence of successive values $fib(0)$, $fib(1)$, $fib(2)$, ..., that is, 0, 1, 1, 2, 3, 5, 8, ... is known as the *fibonacci sequence*.

Suppose the function $fib3(x, y, z)$ is defined by the following axioms:

$$(\forall \ integer \ y, \ z)\big[fib3(0, \ y, \ z) \ = \ y\big] \hspace{4cm} (zero)$$

$$(\forall \ integer \ x, \ y, \ z)\big[fib3(x+1, \ y, \ z) \ = \ fib3(x, \ z, \ y+z)\big]$$
$$(successor)$$

(a) Prove, in the pure theory of the nonnegative integers, that

$$(\forall \ integer \ x, \ y, \ z)\big[fib3(x+1, \ y, \ z) \ = \ \big(y \cdot fib(x)\big) \ + \ \big(z \cdot fib(x+1)\big)\big]$$
$$(fib3)$$

(b) Prove, in the pure theory of the nonnegative integers, that the function $fib3$ provides an alternative definition for the fibonacci function, in the sense that

$$(\forall \ integer \ x)\big[fib(x) \ = \ fib3(x, \ 0, \ 1)\big] \hspace{1.2cm} (alternative \ definition)$$

Problem 12.11 (dual versions of induction rules)   pages 536, 538, 564

(a) Justify the A-form of the *stepwise-induction* rule for the nonnegative integers.

(b) Formulate an analogous dual version of the *stepwise-induction* rule for strings.

(c) Justify the A-form of the *well-founded induction* rule.

Problem 12.12 (stepwise induction for strings)   page 538

Justify the *stepwise-induction* rule for strings.

Problem 12.13 (concatenation)   page 547

In the theory of strings, prove the following properties of the concatenation function:

(a) *Right empty*

$$(\forall\ string\ x)[x * \Lambda\ =\ x]$$

(b) *Associativity*

$$(\forall\ string\ x,\ y,\ z)\big[(x * y) * z\ =\ x * (y * z)\big].$$

Conduct your proof in the pure theory of strings; i.e., apply the *string* simplification automatically.

Problem 12.14 (reverse) page 547

Prove that the *reverse* function distributes over the concatenation function *, that is,

$$(\forall\ string\ x,\ y)\big[reverse(x * y)\ =\ reverse(y) * reverse(x)\big]$$
$$(concatenation)$$

In your proof you may assume that the following properties of concatenation have already been proved:

$$(\forall\ string\ x)[x * \Lambda\ =\ x] \qquad\qquad\qquad (right\ empty)$$

$$(\forall\ string\ x,\ y,\ z)\big[(x * y) * z\ =\ x * (y * z)\big] \qquad (associativity)$$

Conduct your proof in the pure theory of the strings, i.e., apply the *string* simplification automatically.

Problem 12.15 (initial substring) page 547

Suppose we define the *initial-substring relation* $\preceq_{init}$ by the following axioms:

$$(\forall\ string\ y)[\Lambda \preceq_{init} y] \qquad\qquad\qquad (left\ empty)$$

$$\begin{array}{l}(\forall\ char\ u)\\(\forall\ string\ x)\end{array}\Big[not\ (u \bullet x \preceq_{init} \Lambda)\Big] \qquad\qquad (right\ empty)$$

$$\begin{array}{l}(\forall\ char\ u,\ v)\\(\forall\ string\ x,\ y)\end{array}\left[\begin{array}{c}u \bullet x \preceq_{init} v \bullet y\\\equiv\\u = v\ \ and\ \ x \preceq_{init} y\end{array}\right] \qquad (prefix)$$

In the pure theory of strings, show that the relation $x \preceq_{init} y$ does indeed hold precisely when x is an initial substring of y, that is, the sentence

$$(\forall\ string\ x,\ y)\left[\begin{array}{c}x \preceq_{init} y\\\equiv\\(\exists\ string\ z)[x * z\ =\ y]\end{array}\right] \qquad (concatenation)$$

is valid. *Hint*: Prove each direction separately.

Problem 12.16 (irreflexivity of a well-founded relation)   page 553

Use the *well-founded induction* rule of deductive tableaux to prove that any well-founded relation $\prec$ is irreflexive, that is,

$$(\forall\, obj\ x)\big[not\ (x \prec x)\big].$$

Problem 12.17 (flattree)   page 563

Consider a theory that combines the theories of the strings and the trees. In the combined theory we identify the characters of the strings with the atoms of the trees; this is expressed by the axiom

$$(\forall x)\big[char(x)\ \equiv\ atom(x)\big] \qquad\qquad (character\ atom)$$

Recall that, in Section [I]8.4, we defined a function $flattree(x)$, which, for any tree x, yields the string whose characters are the atoms of x, in left-to-right order. The function *flattree* was defined by the following axioms:

$$(\forall\, atom\ x)\big[flattree(x)\ =\ x\big] \qquad\qquad (atom)$$

$$(\forall\, tree\ x,\ y)\begin{bmatrix}flattree(x \bullet y) = \\ flattree(x) * flattree(y)\end{bmatrix} \qquad (construction)$$

Here $\bullet$ is the construction function for trees, and $*$ is the concatenation function for strings.

Suppose we define another function $flattree2(x,\ z)$, which, for any tree x and string z, flattens x and concatenates the resulting string with the string z. The function is defined by the following axioms:

$$\begin{matrix}(\forall\, atom\ u)\\ (\forall\, string\ z)\end{matrix}\big[flattree2(u,\ z)\ =\ u \bullet z\big] \qquad\qquad (atom)$$

$$\begin{matrix}(\forall\, tree\ x,\ y)\\ (\forall\, string\ z)\end{matrix}\begin{bmatrix}flattree2(x \bullet y,\ z) = \\ flattree2\big(x,\ flattree2(y,\ z)\big)\end{bmatrix} \qquad (construction)$$

Here $u \bullet z$ is the insertion function for strings applied to the character u and the string z.

Use the deductive-tableau method to prove that

$$(\forall\, tree\ x)\big[flattree(x)\ =\ flattree2(x,\ \Lambda)\big] \qquad (special\ tree)$$

Hint: First prove the more general property that

$$\begin{matrix}(\forall\, tree\ x)\\ (\forall\, string\ z)\end{matrix}\big[flattree2(x,\ z)\ =\ flattree(x) * z\big] \qquad (general\ tree)$$

Problem 12.18 (evolution)   page 563

Consider a theory of animals. In the "evolution" interpretation we have in mind, the domain is the set of all animals, and, intuitively,

$mon(u)$ means u is a monkey

$u \prec_{par} v$ means u is a parent of v

$anc(u, v)$ means u is an ancestor of v.

The only axiom you may use is

$$(\forall\ animal\ u,\ v)\Big[anc(u,\ v)\ \equiv\ \big[u \prec_{par} v\ \ or\ \ (\exists w)\big[anc(u,\ w)\ \ and\ \ w \prec_{par} v\big]\big]\Big].$$

Assuming that the *parent* relation $\prec_{par}$ is well-founded over *animal*, use the deductive-tableau method to prove

$$(\forall\ animal\ x,\ y)\ \begin{bmatrix} if\ \ anc(x,\ y)\ \ and \\ \qquad mon(x)\ \ and\ \ not\ mon(y) \\ \\ then\ \ (\exists\ animal\ x',\ y')\begin{bmatrix} x' \prec_{par} y'\ \ and \\ mon(x')\ \ and\ \ not\ \big(mon(y')\big) \end{bmatrix} \end{bmatrix}.$$

In other words, if someone who is not a monkey has an ancestor who is, then someone who is not a monkey has a parent who is.

Problem 12.19 (quotient-remainder)   page 563

In the theory of the nonnegative integers, the quotient function $quot(x, y)$ was defined by the axioms

$$(\forall\ integer\ x)\begin{bmatrix} if\ \ x < y \\ then\ \ quot(x,\ y)\ =\ 0 \end{bmatrix} \qquad (less\text{-}than)$$
$$(\forall\ positive\ y)$$

$$(\forall\ integer\ x)\Big[quot(x + y,\ y)\ =\ quot(x,\ y) + 1\Big] \qquad (addition)$$
$$(\forall\ positive\ y)$$

The remainder function $rem(x, y)$ was defined by the axioms

$$(\forall\ integer\ x)\begin{bmatrix} if\ \ x < y \\ then\ \ rem(x,\ y)\ =\ x \end{bmatrix} \qquad (less\text{-}than)$$
$$(\forall\ positive\ y)$$

$$(\forall\ integer\ x)\Big[rem(x + y,\ y)\ =\ rem(x,\ y)\Big] \qquad (addition)$$
$$(\forall\ positive\ y)$$

Use the deductive-tableau method to prove the *quotient-remainder* property

$$(\forall \ integer \ x) \atop (\forall \ positive \ y) \left[{x \ = \ y \cdot quot(x, \ y) + rem(x,y) \atop {and \atop rem(x, \ y) < y}} \right].$$

Hint: Follow the informal proof in Section [I]6.9. You may use any of the properties invoked in that proof.

Problem 12.20 (greatest common divisor)   page 563

The function $gcd(x, \ y)$ has been defined in the theory of nonnegative integers by the following axioms:

$$(\forall \ integer \ x)\left[gcd(x, \ 0) \ = \ x\right] \qquad\qquad (zero)$$

$$(\forall \ integer \ x) \atop (\forall \ positive \ y) \left[gcd(x, \ y) \ = \ gcd\bigl(y, \ rem(x, \ y)\bigr)\right] \qquad (remainder)$$

Prove that $gcd(x, \ y)$ is indeed a common divisor of x and y, that is,

$$(\forall \ integer \ x, \ y) \left[{gcd(x, \ y) \ \preceq_{div} \ x \atop {and \atop gcd(x, \ y) \ \preceq_{div} \ y}} \right] \qquad (common \ divisor)$$

Hint: Follow the proof in Section [I]6.11. You may use any of the properties invoked in that proof.

Problem 12.21 (sum)   page 563

In the theory of tuples of nonnegative integers, we define (Problem 2.1) the function $sum(x)$ to compute the sum of the elements of a tuple x, by the axioms

$$sum(\langle \ \rangle) \ = \ 0 \qquad\qquad (empty)$$

$$(\forall \ integer \ u) \atop (\forall \ tuple \ x) \left[sum(u \diamond x) \ = \ u + sum(x)\right] \qquad\qquad (insertion)$$

We also define the function $sumc(x)$ for the same purpose by the axioms

$$sumc(\langle \ \rangle) \ = \ 0 \qquad\qquad (empty)$$

$$(\forall \ integer \ u) \left[sumc(\langle u \rangle) \ = \ u\right] \qquad\qquad (singleton)$$

$$(\forall \ integer \ u, \ v) \atop (\forall \ tuple \ x) \left[sumc\bigl(u \diamond (v \diamond x)\bigr) \ = \ sumc\bigl((u + v) \diamond x\bigr)\right]$$

$$(double \ insertion)$$

Show that these axioms do indeed define the same function, that is,

$$(\forall \ tuple \ x)\big[sumc(x) \ = \ sum(x)\big] \qquad\qquad (alternative \ definition)$$

Problem 12.22 (mergesort)   page 567

Use the deductive-tableau method to prove the following properties of the *merge* and *mergesort* functions:

* (a) *Ordered* property of *merge*

$$(\forall \ tuple \ x, \ y) \begin{bmatrix} if \ \ ordered(x) \ \ and \ \ ordered(y) \\ then \ \ ordered\big(merge(x, \ y)\big) \end{bmatrix}$$

(b) *Permutation* property of *mergesort*

$$(\forall \ tuple \ x)\big[perm(x, \ mergesort(x))\big]$$

(c) *Ordered* property of *mergesort*

$$(\forall \ tuple \ x)\big[ordered(mergesort(x))\big]$$

(d) *Sorting* property of *mergesort*

$$(\forall \ tuple \ x)\big[mergesort(x) \ = \ sort(x)\big].$$

Hint: See the informal proof in Section 4.5.

Problem 12.23 (gcdplus)   page 577

Suppose we define the function $gcdplus(x, \ y)$ over the nonnegative integers by the following axioms (Section 4.4):

$$(\forall \ integer \ x)\big[gcdplus(0, \ x) \ = \ x\big] \qquad\qquad (left \ zero)$$

$$(\forall \ integer \ x, \ y)\big[gcdplus(x, \ x + y) \ = \ gcdplus(x, \ y)\big] \qquad (addition)$$

$$(\forall \ integer \ x, \ y)\big[gcdplus(x, \ y) \ = \ gcdplus(y, \ x)\big] \qquad (symmetry)$$

Prove that $gcdplus(x, \ y)$ is a common divisor of x and y, that is,

$$(\forall \ integer \ x, \ y) \begin{bmatrix} gcdplus(x, \ y) \preceq_{div} x \\ and \\ gcdplus(x, \ y) \preceq_{div} y \end{bmatrix} \qquad (common \ divisor)$$

13

Decidability and Completeness Issues

Until now, we have avoided certain natural questions concerning the power of a deductive system. We mean such questions as, Can we prove any valid sentence, or Can we detect when a sentence is not valid? We do not have the space to give detailed treatment to such questions in this book. In this section, we survey the results. For proofs, the reader should consult the list of references.

13.1   DEDUCTION PROCEDURES

A *deduction procedure* is a computational method that attempts to test the validity of sentences in a particular theory, such as propositional logic, predicate logic, predicate logic with equality, or the nonnegative integers. Given a (closed) sentence S of the theory, a deduction procedure may respond in one of three ways:

- It may terminate and return *true*, to indicate that S is valid.

- It may terminate and return *false*, to indicate that S is not valid.

- It may fail to terminate (i.e., continue to run forever) without deciding whether or not S is valid.

It is desirable that a deduction procedure have certain properties, which we introduce here. For a given theory,

- A deduction procedure is *sound* if

   if the procedure returns *true*,
   then the sentence S is indeed valid
        and
   if the procedure returns *false*,
   then S is indeed not valid.

- A deduction procedure is *complete (for validity)* if

   if the sentence S is valid,
   then the procedure returns *true*.

- A deduction procedure is *complete for nonvalidity* if

   if the sentence S is nonvalid,
   then the procedure returns *false*.

- A deduction procedure is a *decision procedure* if

   it is complete both for validity and nonvalidity.

Note that a sound procedure may not be a decision procedure because it may run forever on some sentences. In fact, even a sound, complete procedure may not be a decision procedure because it may run forever on some nonvalid sentences.

A decision procedure clearly must terminate. It must also be sound. For if the procedure returns *true*, it does not return *false*, and hence S cannot be nonvalid, that is, S must be valid. Similarly, if the procedure returns *false*, it does not return *true*, and hence S cannot be valid, that is, S must be nonvalid.

Conversely, any procedure that is sound and that terminates must be a decision procedure. It is complete because if the given sentence is valid, a sound procedure cannot return *false*, and hence it must return *true*. Similarly, it is complete for nonvalidity, because if the given sentence is nonvalid, a sound procedure cannot return *true*, and hence it must return *false*.

The theories we deal with impose limitations on what kinds of deduction procedures we can hope to build. For propositional logic, we can construct a decision procedure. For predicate logic, and for predicate logic with equality, we can construct a sound, complete procedure but not a decision procedure: any sound procedure will run forever on some nonvalid sentences. For the theory of nonnegative integers and the other inductive theories, we can construct a sound procedure but, in a certain sense, there do not exist sound, complete procedures. These limitations can be established with great generality; they do not apply only to deductive-tableau deduction procedures, but to deduction procedures based on any methods.

13.2 PROPOSITIONAL LOGIC

Let us design a decision procedure for propositional logic based on the deductive-tableau framework.

A DECISION PROCEDURE

Procedure *prove(S):*

   To determine whether a given sentence S of propositional logic is valid, form the following tableau T_0:

assertions	goals
	S_0

The goal S_0 is the result of simplifying S. Execute the procedure *provetab(T_0)*. ⌙

Procedure *provetab(T)*

   To determine whether the tableau T consisting entirely of a (simplified) goal G is valid,

- If G is the truth symbol *true*, return *true*.

- If G is the truth symbol *false*, return *false*.

- Otherwise, G contains some propositional symbol P.

  - Apply the *resolution* rule to G and itself, matching P.

  - Simplify the resulting sentence, obtaining G'.

  - Form the tableau T' consisting entirely of the goal G'.

  - Execute the procedure *provetab(T')*. ⌙

Note that, in executing the procedure *provetab*, we are always dealing with a tableau containing a single goal (and no assertions). Contrary to our usual practice, after applying the *resolution* rule, we discard the original goal and form a new tableau for the new goal. We also disregard the *polarity* strategy in applying this procedure. This is only for simplicity of exposition; we can formulate a similar decision procedure in which no goals are discarded and the *polarity* strategy is observed.

Before we establish that *prove(S)* is a decision procedure, let us illustrate its application with two examples.

Example (valid sentence)

Let us apply the decision procedure to the valid sentence

$$S: \quad \begin{array}{l} (P \ and \ Q) \ or \ false \\ \quad or \\ (not \ P) \ or \ (not \ Q). \end{array}$$

We form a tableau $\mathcal{T}_0$ consisting entirely of the simplified goal S_0:

assertions	goals
	$S_0: \quad \begin{array}{c} \boxed{P} \ and \ Q \\ or \\ \left(not \ \boxed{P}\right) \ or \ (not \ Q) \end{array}$

We execute the procedure *provetab*($\mathcal{T}_0$).

The goal is neither *true* nor *false*, but it contains the propositional symbol P. Applying the *resolution* rule to S_0 and itself, matching P, we obtain the sentence

$$\begin{bmatrix} false \ and \ Q \\ or \\ (not \ false) \ or \ (not \ Q) \end{bmatrix} \ and \ \begin{bmatrix} true \ and \ Q \\ or \\ (not \ true) \ or \ (not \ Q) \end{bmatrix}.$$

We simplify this sentence and introduce the result as the goal of the new tableau $\mathcal{T}_1$:

assertions	goals
	$S_1: \quad \boxed{Q} \ or \ \left(not \ \boxed{Q}\right)$

We execute the procedure *provetab*($\mathcal{T}_1$).

The goal is again neither *true* nor *false*, but it contains the propositional symbol Q. Applying the *resolution* rule to S_1 and itself, matching Q, we obtain the sentence

> *false or (not false)*
>   *and*
> *true or (not true).*

We simplify the sentence and enter the result S_2 as the goal of a new tableau $\mathcal{T}_2$:

	$S_2 :$ *true*

We execute the procedure *provetab*($\mathcal{T}_2$).

The goal S_2 is the truth symbol *true*. Therefore we return *true*, indicating that the original sentence S is valid. ⌙

Example (nonvalid sentence)

Let us apply the decision procedure to the nonvalid sentence

> $S :$ *P.*

We form the tableau $\mathcal{T}_0$ whose sole goal is the simplified sentence

	$S_0 :$ P

We execute the procedure *provetab*($\mathcal{T}_0$).

The goal is neither *true* nor *false*, but it contains the propositional symbol P. Applying the *resolution* rule to P and itself, matching P, we obtain the sentence

> *false and true.*

We simplify this sentence and introduce the result as the goal of the new tableau $\mathcal{T}_1$:

	$S_1 :$ *false*

We execute the procedure *provetab*($\mathcal{T}_1$).

The goal is the truth symbol *false*. Therefore we return *false*, indicating that the original sentence S is not valid. ⌙

JUSTIFICATION OF THE DECISION PROCEDURE

It is not immediately obvious that the procedure we have outlined is indeed a decision procedure for propositional logic. To show this, we show separately that the procedure terminates and is sound; this will imply that it is a decision procedure. The proof is informal.

Termination

We first observe that, whenever we execute $provetab(T)$, if the goal G in the tableau T is neither *true* nor *false*, it cannot (since it is simplified) contain any occurrence of *true* or *false*, and hence must contain some propositional symbol, P. (If we had not provided a full set of *true-false* simplification rules, this would not be the case.)

We next observe that, each time we apply the *resolution* rule to goal G and itself, matching P, we remove the propositional symbol P from the goal and do not introduce any new propositional symbols. In the subsequent simplification, we do not introduce any new propositional symbols either. Consequently, the new tableau T' has strictly fewer distinct propositional symbols than the given tableau T. Since the original tableau has only finitely many distinct propositional symbols, we cannot continue to do this forever. That is, every execution of $provetab(T)$ terminates.

An execution of $prove(S)$ consists of only a single execution of $provetab(T_0)$. Hence each execution of $prove(S)$ also terminates.

Soundness

To show soundness, we show that if the procedure $prove(S)$ returns *true*, then the original sentence S is valid, and that if the procedure $prove(S)$ returns *false*, then the original sentence S is not valid. To show this, we must show a *soundness* lemma concerning the procedure $provetab(T)$.

Lemma (soundness)

With each execution of the procedure $provetab(T)$,

> the tableau T is valid
>   precisely when
> the original sentence S is valid. ◢

Let us see why this is enough to establish soundness.

Soundness Lemma ⇒ *Soundness*

We must show that if the procedure *prove*(S) returns *true* (or *false*, respectively), then S is indeed valid (or not, respectively).

Suppose that *prove*(S) returns *true*. This means that, at some point, we have executed *provetab*(T), where the tableau T consists of the goal *true*. That is, T is valid, and hence (by the lemma) S is also valid.

Similarly, suppose that *prove*(S) returns *false*. This means that, at some point, we have executed *provetab*(T), where T consists of the goal *false*. Therefore T is not valid, and hence (by the lemma) S is not valid either.

It remains to prove the soundness lemma.

Proof (soundness)

We actually show an equivalent condition, that, at every execution of the procedure *provetab*(T),

> the original sentence S is false under some interpretation I
>   precisely when
> the tableau T is false under some interpretation J.

This implies the desired lemma because if either S or T is valid, there is no interpretation under which it is false, hence (by the preceding condition) there is no interpretation under which the other is false, and hence the other must be valid, too.

The condition holds at the first execution of *provetab*(T_0) because then the sole goal of T_0 is S_0, the simplification of S, which is equivalent to S.

If the condition holds at some execution of *provetab*(T), it also holds for the subsequent execution of *provetab*(T'). To show this, it suffices to show that

> the tableau T is false under some interpretation J
>   precisely when
> the subsequent tableau T' is false under some interpretation J'.

In the forward direction, this follows from the justification of the *resolution* rule itself. After all, the goal G' of T' is obtained from the goal G of T by applying the *resolution* rule and simplifying. Suppose, to the contrary, that T is false under some interpretation J, that is, the goal G of T is not valid, but that T' is not false under any interpretation J', that is, T' is valid and therefore the goal G' of T' is valid. Thus we have obtained a valid sentence G' by applying the *resolution* rule to a sentence G that is not valid and simplifying, contradicting the soundness of the *resolution* rule .

To show the reverse direction, let us write the goal $\mathcal{G}$ of $\mathcal{T}$ as $\mathcal{G}[P]$. We suppose that the goal $\mathcal{G}'$ of $\mathcal{T}'$ is false under some interpretation $\mathcal{J}'$, and show that then $\mathcal{G}[P]$ is false under some interpretation $\mathcal{J}$. We know that $\mathcal{G}'$ is the result of simplifying the sentence

$$\mathcal{G}[\mathit{false}] \;\; \mathit{and} \;\; \mathcal{G}[\mathit{true}].$$

Hence one of the two conjuncts is false under $\mathcal{J}'$. We treat each possibility separately.

Case: $\mathcal{G}[\mathit{false}]$ is false under $\mathcal{J}'$

We take $\mathcal{J}$ to be the extended interpretation $\langle P \leftarrow \mathit{false} \rangle \circ \mathcal{J}'$. Because P does not occur in $\mathcal{G}[\mathit{false}]$, we know $\mathcal{G}[\mathit{false}]$ has the same truth-value under $\mathcal{J}$ and $\mathcal{J}'$, that is, $\mathcal{G}[\mathit{false}]$ is false under $\mathcal{J}$. Because P and false have the same truth-value under $\mathcal{J}$, we know $\mathcal{G}[P]$ and $\mathcal{G}[\mathit{false}]$ have the same truth-value under $\mathcal{J}$, that is, $\mathcal{G}[P]$ is false under $\mathcal{J}$, as we wanted to show.

Case: $\mathcal{G}[\mathit{true}]$ is false under $\mathcal{J}'$

This case is treated similarly. We take $\mathcal{J}$ to be the extended interpretation $\langle P \leftarrow \mathit{true} \rangle \circ \mathcal{J}'$ and show that $\mathcal{G}[P]$ is false under $\mathcal{J}$, as before.

This concludes the proof of the soundness lemma and the justification of the decision procedure for propositional logic. ⌐

Propositional logic is an ideal theory, in that we can test its sentences for validity. We do not have this luxury for the other theories in our repertoire.

13.3   PREDICATE LOGIC

According to Church's theorem, there is no decision procedure for predicate logic (see our references). We can nevertheless develop a sound, complete procedure. Such a procedure will return *true* precisely when given a valid sentence of predicate logic. On the other hand, if the sentence is not valid, the procedure will sometimes return *false*, but at other times will run on forever. The difficulty in using such a procedure is that if after several hours it continues to run, we do not know whether the sentence is valid and the procedure will ultimately return *true*, or whether the sentence is not valid and the procedure will run on forever.

A SOUND, COMPLETE PROCEDURE

The procedure we present is not efficient enough to be used in practice for any but the simplest examples, but it does have the desired properties of soundness and completeness.

Procedure *prove(S)*

To attempt to determine whether a sentence S of predicate logic is valid, form the following initial tableau T_0:

assertions	goals
	S_0

Here S_0 is the result of simplifying S. Then execute the procedure *provetab(T_0).* ⌙

Procedure *provetab(T)*

To attempt to determine whether the tableau T is valid,

- If T contains a final row, either the final goal *true* or the final assertion *false*, return *true*.

- Otherwise, let T' be the tableau obtained by adding to T every possible row derived from T by the application of a single predicate-logic deduction rule (after simplification).

  - If no new rows can be derived, that is, T' has the same rows as T, return *false*. This situation is known as a *stalemate*.

  - Otherwise, execute the procedure *provetab(T').* ⌙

This procedure will systematically apply all possible deduction rules to the initial tableau and will ultimately discover a proof of S if one exists.

JUSTIFICATION OF THE PROCEDURE

The soundness of this procedure follows from the soundness of the deduction rules for predicate logic. If the procedure returns *true*, we must have derived a final row. That is, we have discovered a proof of the given sentence S, indicating that S is valid.

We shall not show the completeness of the procedure. It can be shown that if S is a valid sentence of predicate logic, it has a deductive-tableau proof. In this case, the procedure will ultimately derive a final row and return *true*.

If S is not valid, the procedure may discover a stalemate and return *false*, but it may continue to derive more and more new rows, without ever obtaining a final row. We illustrate each of these possibilities with an example.

Example (stalemate)

Let us apply the procedure *prove*(S) to the nonvalid sentence

$$S : \; p(a).$$

We form the initial tableau $\mathcal{T}_0$:

assertions	goals
	$p(a)$

We then execute the procedure *provetab*($\mathcal{T}_0$).

No deduction rules apply to the tableau. Therefore a stalemate has occurred, and we return *false*.   ◢

In this example, a stalemate has occurred immediately. Often a stalemate will occur after several rows have been derived but no new rows can be obtained.

Now let us consider an example in which the procedure fails to terminate.

Example (runs forever)

Let us apply the procedure *prove*(S) to the nonvalid sentence

$$S : \;\; (\exists x)\big[p(x) \;\; and \;\; not \; p\big(f(x)\big)\big].$$

We form the initial tableau $\mathcal{T}_0$:

assertions	goals
	$(\exists x)^{\exists}\big[p(x) \;\; and \;\; not \; p\big(f(x)\big)\big]$

We then execute the procedure $provetab(\mathcal{T}_0)$.

By the $\exists$-*elimination* rule, we may drop the quantifier from the goal, obtaining the new row

	$p(x)$ *and* *not* $\boxed{p(f(x))}^{-}$

This row is added to the tableau $\mathcal{T}_0$ to form the tableau $\mathcal{T}_1$. We execute the procedure $provetab(\mathcal{T}_1)$.

In preparation for applying the *resolution* rule to the preceding goal, let us make another copy of the row, renaming the variable:

	$\boxed{p(x')}^{+}$ *and* *not* $p(f(x'))$

By application of the *resolution* rule, taking $\{x' \leftarrow f(x)\}$, we obtain (after simplification) the row

	$p(x)$ *and* *not* $p(f(f(x)))$

It is possible to obtain other new rows as well. All of these rows are added to the tableau $\mathcal{T}_1$ to form the tableau $\mathcal{T}_2$. We execute the procedure $provetab(\mathcal{T}_2)$.

Applying the *resolution* rule to the new row and itself, taking $\{x' \leftarrow f(f(x))\}$, we may obtain the row

	$p(x)$ *and* *not* $p(f(f(f(f(x)))))$

This row is included (among others) in the tableau $\mathcal{T}_3$. We execute the procedure $provetab(\mathcal{T}_3)$.

The reader can see that stalemate is impossible; we can continue the process indefinitely, always obtaining a new row. Also, since the sentence S is not valid and the procedure is sound, we can never obtain a final row and can never return *true*. Therefore the procedure will run forever in this case. ⌐

PROOF STRATEGIES

The preceding procedure is far too expensive to be of practical value. Typically, in executing the procedure $provetab(\mathcal{T})$ for a tableau $\mathcal{T}$ of any size, there are many ways to apply deduction rules, yielding many new rows, so that the tableau T' is considerably larger than the tableau T. We quickly exhaust the available space and time before we discover a proof. It is necessary to apply strategies that restrict the application of deduction rules, so that fewer new rows are added. The *polarity* strategy is one such restriction, but it is far from sufficient to make the procedure useful.

It is desirable that strategies retain completeness, that is, that the procedure with the strategy is still complete for predicate logic. This is the case for the *polarity* strategy. The efficiency problem is sufficiently severe, however, that strategies that destroy completeness are still worthy of consideration. A procedure employing such a strategy will fail to prove some valid sentences, but perhaps it can still prove an important class of theorems.

13.4   SPECIAL THEORIES

The completeness problem for a special theory is simplified if there are only finitely many axioms.

FINITE THEORIES

If a special theory is defined by giving a finite set of axioms $A_1, \ldots, A_m$, we can easily adapt the procedure *prove*(S) for predicate logic to provide a sound, complete procedure for the special theory.

Procedure *prove*(S)

To attempt to determine whether a sentence S is valid in a finite theory whose axioms are (after simplification) $A_1, \ldots, A_m$, form the initial tableau T_0:

assertions	goals
A_1	
$\vdots$	
A_m	
	S_0

Here S_0 is the result of simplifying S. Then execute the procedure *provetab*(T_0). ⌟

Procedure *provetab*($\mathcal{T}$)

The procedure *provetab*($\mathcal{T}$) is the same as for predicate logic. ⌐

Many of our theories, including the theory of equality and the inductive theories, are defined with the help of an axiom schema, which stands for an infinite set of axioms. We cannot treat such theories as before, because we can only include a finite number of assertions in any tableau. What we have done in such cases is to provide additional deduction rules (e.g., the *equality* rule or the *induction* rule) to take the place of these axioms.

THEORY OF EQUALITY

In the case of the theory of equality, we can obtain a sound, complete procedure.

Procedure *prove*($\mathcal{S}$)

To attempt to determine whether a sentence $\mathcal{S}$ is valid in the theory of equality, form the initial tableau $\mathcal{T}_0$:

$x = x$	
	$\mathcal{S}_0$

Here $\mathcal{S}_0$ is the result of simplifying $\mathcal{S}$. Then execute the procedure *provetab*($\mathcal{T}_0$). ⌐

Procedure *provetab*($\mathcal{T}$)

This is the same as the procedure *provetab*($\mathcal{T}$) for predicate logic, except that here we apply the *equality* rule, as well as the predicate-logic deduction rules, to $\mathcal{T}$ in forming the rows of the new tableau $\mathcal{T}'$. ⌐

The procedure *prove*($\mathcal{S}$) may be shown to be sound and complete, but it may run forever if given a nonvalid sentence of the theory. Again, even for valid sentences it is grossly inefficient.

This procedure can be extended to any theory with equality defined by a finite number of axioms $\mathcal{A}_1, \ldots, \mathcal{A}_m$ simply by taking the initial tableau to be $\mathcal{T}_0$:

assertions	goals
$\mathcal{A}_1$	
$\vdots$	
$\mathcal{A}_m$	
$x = x$	
	S_0

The resulting procedure, although again sound and complete, will not be a decision procedure.

THEORY OF NONNEGATIVE INTEGERS

The situation is more complex in formulating deduction procedures for our theories with induction. We will talk about the basic theory of the nonnegative integers here, but similar remarks apply to the theories of strings, lists, and tuples, and the other theories with induction.

The axioms for the theory of nonnegative integers fail to describe only the intended models; there are other, *nonstandard* models, under which the axioms are true even though these models do not correspond to our intuitive notion of the nonnegative integers.

The domain of our intended models looks like this:

$$0 \rightarrow 1 \rightarrow 2 \rightarrow \ \ldots \ .$$

Here, 0, 1, 2, ... are the ordinary nonnegative integers, and the arrow $\rightarrow$ indicates the action of the successor function. Every domain element is a finite nonnegative integer.

In contrast, the domain of one of the nonstandard models looks like this:

$$0 \ \rightarrow \ \ 1 \ \ \rightarrow \ \ 2 \ \ \rightarrow \ \ \ldots$$

$$\ldots \ \rightarrow \ d{-}2 \ \rightarrow \ d{-}1 \ \rightarrow \ d \ \rightarrow \ d{+}1 \ \rightarrow \ d{+}2 \ \rightarrow \ \ \ldots \ .$$

The "infinite" elements d, $d \pm 1$, $d \pm 2$, ... are distinct from any of the finite nonnegative integers 0, 1, 2, ... (Certain restrictions are imposed by the axioms on what relations and functions over this domain our predicate and function symbols may denote.) The axioms for the nonnegative integers all hold under these models.

According to the *Gödel incompleteness* theorem, which we shall not prove, there are some sentences in the theory of nonnegative integers that are true under all the intended models but that do not follow from the axioms. These sentences are false under some of the nonstandard models.

The flaw is not with our particular set of axioms. Any (finitely many) axioms or axiom schemata that hold under the intended models also hold under some nonstandard models. In the corresponding theory, there will be some sentences that are true under the intended models but false under some of the nonstandard models; naturally, we will be unable to prove such sentences.

Let us say that a (closed) sentence is *i-valid* if it is true under all the intended models for the theory. For the theory of the nonnegative integers, we are more interested in i-validity than in ordinary validity. As a further consequence of *Gödel's incompleteness* theorem, we cannot develop a deduction procedure for the nonnegative integers that is *i-sound* and *i-complete*, in the sense that it can prove precisely the i-valid sentences. The best we can do is to develop a procedure that is simply i-sound. Given an i-valid sentence, an i-sound procedure may return *true* but may run on forever. Given a non-i-valid sentence, an i-sound procedure may return *false* but may run on forever.

For the theory of the nonnegative integers, here is a simple procedure with these properties.

Procedure *prove(S)*

To attempt to determine whether a sentence S of the theory of nonnegative integers is i-valid, form the initial tableau T_0:

A_1	
A_2	
A_3	
A_4	
$x = x$	
	S_0

where A_1, A_2, A_3, and A_4 are the generation and uniqueness axioms for the nonnegative integers, and S_0 is the result of simplifying S. Execute the procedure *provetab(T_0)*. ⌟

Procedure *provetab*($\mathcal{T}$)

This is the same as the procedure for predicate logic, except that we apply to $\mathcal{T}$ the *stepwise induction* rule and the *equality* rule, as well as the deduction rules of predicate logic, in forming the rows of the new tableau $\mathcal{T}'$. ⌐

This procedure is i-sound but is neither i-complete nor a decision procedure. In fact, as it stands, the procedure will never be able to establish that a given sentence is non-i-valid; that is, it will never return *false*. The only way for *provetab*($\mathcal{T}$) to return *false* is to produce a stalemate, in which no new rows are generated. In the preceding tableau, however, unless a strategy is imposed, it is always possible to derive the endless sequence of assertions

$integer(0^+)$	
$integer\big((0^+)^+\big)$	
$integer\big(((0^+)^+)^+\big)$	
$\vdots$	

That is, stalemate cannot occur.

A similar i-sound deduction procedure can be constructed for the augmented theories of the nonnegative integers and for the other theories with induction.

References: A Selection

We make no attempt to give a complete survey of the literature. Rather, we include only a selection of reference books and a few technical papers, which will provide further information on the topics included in this volume.

Introductions to mathematical logic that are oriented toward automated deduction or associated topics:

P. B. ANDREWS, *An Introduction to Mathematical Logic and Type Theory: To Truth through Proof.* Orlando, Florida: Academic Press, 1986. Includes higher-order logic, in which one can quantify over relations and functions as well as over domain elements.

C. L. CHANG and R. C. T. LEE, *Symbolic Logic and Mechanical Theorem Proving.* New York: Academic Press, 1973. A clear, classical treatment of resolution theorem proving and its extensions.

H. B. ENDERTON, *Elements of Set Theory.* New York: Academic Press, 1977. Includes a discussion of well-founded relations and well-founded induction.

J. H. GALLIER, *Logic for Computer Science: Foundations of Automatic Theorem Proving.* New York: Harper and Row, 1986. Especially good on the relation between theorem proving and conventional deduction systems.

D. W. LOVELAND, *Automated Theorem Proving: A Logical Basis.* New York: North-Holland, 1978. A thorough treatment of (primarily) resolution theorem proving.

J. A. ROBINSON, *Logic: Form and Function. The Mechanization of Deductive Reasoning.* New York: North-Holland, 1979. An introduction to automated deduction emphasizing resolution and its extensions.

L. WOS, R. OVERBEEK, E. LUSK, and J. Boyle, *Automated Reasoning: Introduction and Applications*, Englewood Cliffs, New Jersey: Prentice-Hall, 1984. Special emphasis on the implementation and strategic aspects of resolution theorem proving.

Introductions to automated reasoning emphasizing nonresolution approaches:

R. S. BOYER and J S. MOORE, *A Computational Logic.* New York: Academic Press, 1979. A complete description of a well-known theorem-proving system, which can do proofs using mathematical induction.

A. BUNDY, *The Computer Modelling of Mathematical Reasoning.* London: Academic Press, 1983. Includes methods based on rewriting.

Decidability, computability, and completeness issues:

H. B. ENDERTON, *A Mathematical Introduction to Logic.* New York: Academic Press, 1972. Includes a good discussion of nonstandard models.

E. MENDELSON, *Introduction to Mathematical Logic.* Monterey, California: Wadsworth and Brooks, 1987. Includes a full treatment of undecidability.

H. ROGERS, JR., *Theory of Recursive Functions and Effective Computability.* New York: McGraw-Hill, 1967. A thorough treatment of which functions can and cannot be computed mechanically.

Application of automated deduction to artificial intelligence and program synthesis:

M. R. GENESERETH and N. J. NILSSON, *Logical Foundations of Artificial Intelligence.* Los Altos, California: Morgan Kaufmann, 1987. Includes reasoning about knowledge and belief and probabilistic reasoning.

R. KOWALSKI, *Logic for Problem Solving.* New York: North Holland, 1979. Includes relationship with logic programming.

Z. MANNA and R. WALDINGER, The Origin of a Binary-Search Paradigm. *Science of Computer Programming* 9 (1987) 37–83. Extension of the deductive-tableau system to the derivation of programs.

Historical references:

T. SKOLEM, Logisch-kombinatorische Untersuchungen über die Erfüllbarkeit oder Beweisbarkeit Mathematischer Sätze nebst einem Theorem über Dichte Mengen. *Videnskopsselskapits skifter,* I. *Matematik-Naturvidenskabelig Klasse* 4 (1920). English translation, Logico-Combinatorial Investigations in the Satisfiability or Provability of Mathematical Propositions: A Simplified Proof of a Theorem by

L. Löwenheim and Generalizations of the Theorem. In van Heijenoort [1967]. Introduces the notion of skolemization.

J. HERBRAND, *Recherches sur la Théorie de la Démonstration*. Ph.D. dissertation, University of Paris, Paris, 1930. Introduces the notion of unification and several other ideas influential in theorem proving.

K. GÖDEL, Über Formal Unentscheidbare Sätze der Principia Mathematica und Verwandter Systeme I, *Monatschefte für Mathematik und Physik* 38 (1931), 173–198. English translation, On Formally Undecidable Propositions of Principia Mathematica and Related Systems. In van Heijenoort [1967]. Establishes the incompleteness of the theory of nonnegative integers.

E. ZERMELO, Grundlagen einer Allgemeinen Theorie der Mathematischen Satzsysteme. *Fundamenta Mathematicae* 25 (1935) 136–146. Introduces the notion of a well-founded relation.

A. CHURCH, A Note on the Entscheidungsproblem, *Journal of Symbolic Logic* 1 (1936) 40–41. Correction 101–102. Establishes the undecidability of predicate logic.

J. VAN HEIJENOORT (editor), *From Frege to Gödel*. Cambridge, Massachusetts: Harvard Univesity Press, 1967. A collection of classical papers in mathematical logic.

J. SIEKMANN and G. WRIGHTSON, *Automation of Reasoning 1: Classical Papers on Computational Logic 1957–1966*. Berlin: Springer-Verlag, 1983. A collection of early theorem-proving papers.

J. A. ROBINSON, A Machine-oriented Logic Based on the Resolution Principle, *Journal of the ACM* 12 (1965) 23–41. Introduces the resolution rule.

Papers that provide theoretical background for this book:

Z. MANNA and R. WALDINGER, A Deductive Approach to Program Synthesis, *ACM Transactions on Programming Languages and Systems* 2 (1980) 90–121. Introduces nonclausal resolution and applies it to program synthesis.

N. MURRAY, Completely Nonclausal Theorem Proving, *Artificial Intelligence* 18 (1) 1982, 67–85. Introduces nonclausal resolution independently from Manna and Waldinger [1980] and establishes its completeness for predicate logic.

J. HSIANG and M. RUSINOWITCH, A New Method for Establishing Refutational Completeness in Theorem Proving, *Eighth International Conference on Automated Deduction*. Berlin: Springer-Verlag, 1986, 141–152. Establishes the completeness of the resolution and equality rules for the theory of equality.

Index of Symbols

General Index